Edward VII
Prince and King

Edward VII

Prince and King

GILES ST. AUBYN

COLLINS
St James's Place, London
1979

William Collins Sons & Co Ltd
London · Glasgow · Sydney · Auckland
Toronto · Johannesburg

First published 1979
© Giles St. Aubyn 1979

ISBN 0 00 216203 2

Set in Monotype Baskerville
Made and printed in Great Britain by
William Collins Sons & Co Ltd, Glasgow

This Book
is dedicated to Eton College
whose sons figure so prominently in its pages
and to the Members of my House
who for eighteen years prevented me from writing it.
1959–1976

Contents

Illustrations

Acknowledgements

I am deeply grateful to Her Majesty the Queen for graciously permitting me to publish letters of which she owns the copyright, and to reproduce certain pictures and photographs from the Royal Collection.

This book would never have been begun were it not for the kindness and generosity of Margaret Viscountess Knollys in permitting me to work on her father-in-law's papers. I was greatly assisted in the course of my research by Miss Deirdre Janson-Smith, Peregrine Horden, David Brock and Matthew Dobbs. Patrick Savage and Richard Ollard read the book in proof. Not only did they save me from blunders, but helped me with fruitful suggestions.

The system of Source References employed in the present work is modelled on that pioneered by Kenneth Rose in *The Later Cecils*. I trust he will regard imitation as the sincerest form of flattery.

I have been greatly assisted in selecting illustrations by Sir Oliver Millar, Sir Robin Mackworth-Young and Miss Dimond.

I would like to thank the following authors and publishers for permission to quote from their books:

THÉOPHILE DELCASSÉ AND THE MAKING OF THE ENTENTE CORDIALE by C. Andrew (Macmillan).
DIARY OF SIR E. WALTER HAMILTON by Dudley W. R. Bahlman (Oxford University Press).
QUEEN ALEXANDRA by Georgina Battiscombe (Constable and Houghton Mifflin, Boston).
MY DEAR DUCHESS by A. Kennedy (John Murray).
EDWARD VII by Philip Magnus (John Murray and E. P. Dutton, N.Y.).
THE QUEEN THANKS SIR HOWARD by M. H. McClintock (John Murray).
LORD CARNOCK by Harold Nicolson (Constable).

THE TURNING POINT by M. Paléologue (Hutchinson).
RECOLLECTIONS OF THREE REIGNS by Sir Frederick Ponsonby (Macmillan).
QUEEN MARY by James Pope-Hennessy (Allen & Unwin and Alfred A. Knopf, N.Y.).
C.B. by J. Wilson (Constable and St Martin's Press, N.Y.).
QUEEN VICTORIA: HER LIFE AND TIMES by Cecil Woodham-Smith (Hamish Hamilton and Alfred A. Knopf, N.Y.).
LETTERS OF QUEEN VICTORIA (John Murray).

I am also deeply indebted to Lord Esher for permission to quote from his grandfather's JOURNALS AND LETTERS and to Roger Fulford for most generous permission to quote extensively from the books he has written and edited.

Finally, I would like to express my gratitude to Mrs Valerie Day whose flawless typing and unfailing efficiency have relieved authorship of many of its burdens.

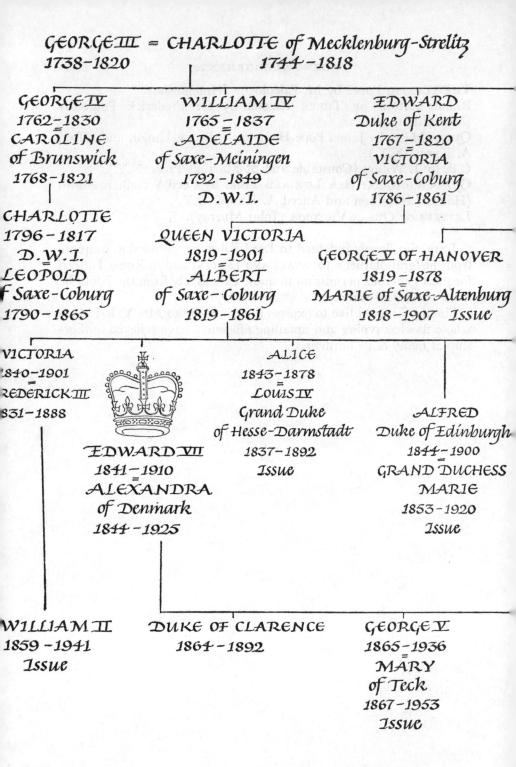

GEORGE III = CHARLOTTE of Mecklenburg-Strelitz
1738-1820   1744-1818

GEORGE IV
1762-1830
CAROLINE
of Brunswick
1768-1821

CHARLOTTE
1796-1817
D.W.1.
LEOPOLD
F Saxe-Coburg
1790-1865

WILLIAM IV
1765-1837
ADELAIDE
of Saxe-Meiningen
1792-1849
D.W.1.

QUEEN VICTORIA
1819-1901
ALBERT
of Saxe-Coburg
1819-1861

EDWARD
Duke of Kent
1767-1820
VICTORIA
of Saxe-Coburg
1786-1861

GEORGE V OF HANOVER
1819-1878
MARIE of Saxe-Altenburg
1818-1907   Issue

VICTORIA
1840-1901
FREDERICK III
1831-1888

ALICE
1843-1878
LOUIS IV
Grand Duke
of Hesse-Darmstadt
1837-1892
Issue

EDWARD VII
1841-1910
ALEXANDRA
of Denmark
1844-1925

ALFRED
Duke of Edinburgh
1844-1900
GRAND DUCHESS
MARIE
1853-1920
Issue

WILLIAM II
1859-1941
Issue

DUKE OF CLARENCE
1864-1892

GEORGE V
1865-1936
MARY
of Teck
1867-1953
Issue

ERNEST
Duke of Cumberland
King of Hanover
1771 – 1851
FREDERICA
of Mecklenburg – Strelitz
1778 – 1841

ADOLPHUS
Duke of Cambridge
1774 – 1850
AUGUSTA
of Hesse – Cassel
1797 – 1889

GEORGE Duke of Cambridge
1819 – 1904
LOUISA FAIRBROTHER
1816 – 1890 Issue

AUGUSTA
1822 – 1916
DUKE OF
MECKLENBURG STRELITZ
1819 – 1904 Issue

MARY ADELAIDE
1833 – 1897
FRANCIS
of Teck
1837 – 1900

HELENA
1846 – 1923
CHRISTIAN
of Schleswig – Holstein
1831 – 1917
Issue

LOUISE
1848 – 1939
DUKE OF ARGYLL
1845 – 1914
D.W.I.

ARTHUR
Duke of Connaught
1850 – 1942
LOUISE OF PRUSSIA
1860 – 1917
Issue

LEOPOLD
Duke of Albany
1853 – 1884
HELEN
of Waldeck
1861 – 1922
Issue

BEATRICE
1857 – 1944
HENRY
of Battenberg
1858 – 1896
Issue

LOUISE
1867 – 1931
DUKE OF FIFE
1840 – 1912
Issue

VICTORIA
1868 – 1935

MAUD
1869 – 1938
HAAKON VII
of Norway
1872 – 1957
Issue

QUEEN MARY
1867 – 1953
GEORGE V
1865 – 1936
Issue

Preface

Edward VII has been fortunate in his biographers. My principal excuse for writing another Life of the King is that I have been privileged to study letters about him which were thought not to exist. For approaching half a century, from 1863 until 1910, Francis Knollys, the Prince of Wales's Private Secretary, preserved thousands of documents amassed in the course of his duties. When King Edward left him instructions to sort through the Royal Archives and burn anything compromising, that most prudent of men dutifully destroyed some of the most fascinating records of the nineteenth century. But, contrary to general belief, he spared his own correspondence. I have used this unique material as the principal source for this portrait of the King, while drawing gratefully on the labours of my predecessors.

Hartland's Quay,   Giles St. Aubyn
Eton.

Albert Junior

It is melancholy to reflect that mankind has suffered more from ill-judged philanthropy than calculated malice. The road to hell is no less harrowing for being paved with good intentions. Prince Albert's plans for bringing up his eldest son could scarcely have been better meant or worse contrived. If they had a redeeming feature it was their failure to achieve the purposes inspiring them.

The Prince of Wales was born at Buckingham Palace on 9 November 1841: five years before James Simpson began using chloroform in childbirth. In retrospect, the Queen considered that of her nine children she 'suffered far the most severely' with Bertie. The Prince Consort, the Duchess of Kent, Sir Robert Peel, who had recently become Prime Minister, and the Duke of Wellington, were in attendance. Never before in English history had a Queen Regnant given birth to an heir. On leaving the Palace, Wellington met Lord Hill, who had served under him in the Peninsula. 'All over,' said the Duke, 'fine boy – very fine boy, almost as red as you are, Hill!' Later that morning, an official bulletin was issued. 'The Queen was safely delivered of a Prince this morning at 48 minutes past 10 o'clock. Her Majesty and the infant Prince are going on well.' The word 'infant' was inserted on the Queen's instructions. Without it, she said, the reference could apply equally to her husband. The announcement was signed by Sir James Clark, her personal physician, who had made his name by attending Keats.

After Edward III made his son Prince of Wales in 1337, his successors bestowed that honour on their heirs-apparent soon after birth. Accordingly, on 4 December 1841, the month-old Prince was granted the title he bore for the next sixty years. The Queen, furthermore, ordered that the Royal Arms of Saxony should be quartered with those of England on the child's insignia, which led Whigs like Lord Palmerston to mutter about German prejudice at Court. But the boy's paternal inheritance was of far greater consequence to his mother than insular criticism from disaffected persons.

The Queen and Prince Consort's choice of godparents did little to allay the suspicion that the Royal Family was too foreign and too fond of foreigners. Nobody could pretend that the infant to be baptised was not of German descent, although he soon showed that by disposition he was English to the backbone. The Queen's father, Edward Duke of Kent, was Hanoverian, and her mother came from Saxe-Coburg. The Duchess of Kent's brother, Ernest Ist, married Princess Louise of Saxe-Gotha-Altenburg, so their son, Prince Albert, was as German as his cousin Victoria. Every one of the sponsors at the christening was German, the so-called 'English' contingent consisting of two of George the Third's surviving children: Adolphus, Duke of Cambridge, his favourite son; and a spinster daughter, Princess Sophia. Neither the Duke nor his sister possessed any more English blood than their godson. The most distinguished of the Prince of Wales's godparents was Frederick William the Fourth, King of Prussia, whom Albert had chosen to further his life's ambition: Anglo-German friendship. The king's aggressive Protestantism was an added bonus. Lord Melbourne told the Queen that the choice had given the country 'great satisfaction,' apart from 'Puseyites and Newmanites.' In so saying, he knew how little Her Majesty would mind ruffling Tractarian susceptibilities.

Before he was three weeks old, the Queen decided to christen her son Albert after her husband and Edward after her father. She solved the problem of having two Alberts in the family by calling the boy 'Bertie'. Lord Melbourne ventured to remonstrate. While conceding that Albert was 'an old Anglo-Saxon name,' he observed it had not been 'much in use since the Conquest.' On the other hand, Edward was 'a good English appellation and had a certain degree of popularity attached to it by ancient associations.' The Queen remained unconvinced, for she longed for her son to share his father's beloved name and follow in his footsteps. 'I wonder very much,' she wrote to her Uncle Leopold, 'who our little boy will be like. You will understand *how* fervent my prayers and I am sure everybody's must be, to see him resemble his angelic dearest

Father in *every, every* respect, both in body and mind.' Lord Melbourne, in answering a letter expressing similar sentiments, assured Her Majesty that she could not 'offer up for the young Prince a more judicious prayer than that he may resemble his father.' Nor was the Prince Consort himself averse to suggestions that his son might be fashioned in his image, for he did not suffer from those feelings of unworthiness which beset lesser mortals. If the Queen proposed to turn the Prince of Wales into 'Albert junior,' it was not for him to challenge the wisdom of so doing.

The christening took place in St George's Chapel, Windsor, on 25 January 1842. Archbishop Howley officiated, with the assistance of the Archbishop of York and four other bishops. Prince Albert supervised all the arrangements, the Duchess of Buccleuch, the Mistress of the Robes, held the infant, and the Duke of Wellington carried the Sword of State. Albert Edward was baptised with Jordan Water from the font used for the christening of Charles I. According to *The Times* 'the little Gentleman behaved with a truly princely decorum.' As the congregation drifted out into the winter sunshine, the choir ended the service with the 'Hallelujah Chorus'.

The Queen and Prince Consort were only too conscious they were nurturing a future king. Believing that 'L'Enfant d'Angleterre' belonged to the country, they half suffocated him with solicitude. Baron Stockmar, the *éminence grise* of the Coburgs, complained 'the nursery gives me more trouble than the government of a kingdom.' With effortless ineptitude he infected the anxious parents with his own morbid misgivings. But, as the Queen grew older, she became more inclined to proffer advice than accept it. 'I often think,' she told her eldest daughter, 'too great care, too much constant watching leads to those very dangers hereafter, which one wishes to avoid.' Had she practised what she preached, she might have spared herself much wasted agony.

Prince Albert, a child of the German Enlightenment, innocently believed that there was virtually nothing which education could not achieve. It was the finest legacy, he once said, a father could leave his children. Lord Melbourne, preferring experience to theory, hinted that such notions were moonshine. 'Be not over solicitous about education,' he warned the Queen. 'It may be able to do much, but it does not do so much as is expected from it. It may mould and direct the character, but it rarely alters it.' Once, when the Prince Consort caught his second son Alfred smoking, even he permitted himself a moment of scepticism. 'Really,' he protested, 'education can do nothing for children.'

Behind Prince Albert's liberal façade lurked the autocrat itching to interfere. He possessed in generous measure that rigidity of mind to which the Teutonic temperament is reputedly inclined, and which is perhaps the most dangerous defect of ideological thinkers. His instinct was to tackle problems by reference to first principles. Rather than formulate plans to suit his son's disposition, he expected the boy to conform to his own preconceptions.

Unfortunately, these imperfections in the Prince's character were encouraged by Baron Stockmar, a fellow countryman and a fellow spirit. Like some short-sighted gardener he cherished the weeds while destroying the choicest plants. Stockmar began his career as a doctor, during the Napoleonic wars. After peace was restored, he attended Princess Charlotte, whose last coherent words were, 'Stocky, they have made me drunk.' Next, her husband, Prince Leopold, employed him as his physician and adviser. Not only did the Baron play a foremost part in helping Leopold become King of the Belgians, but he also negotiated the marriage treaty between Prince Albert and Queen Victoria. Nobody contributed more to making Coburg 'the stud farm of Europe.'

Writing of Baron Stockmar in later years, the Queen remarked 'no-one gave us better and wiser advice on the education of our children.' It is difficult to understand why she and the Prince reposed such trust in a man whom Gladstone described, with unwonted astringency, as 'a mischievous old prig.' Stockmar's theoretical knowledge was as prodigious as his practical experience was slight. King Edward, who was noted for his generosity, never forgave the Baron for making his childhood wretched. Conceivably Stockmar's reputation for sagacity may be traced to the fact that his opinions almost always coincided with those of Prince Albert, whose mind he had helped to form, whose prejudices he sustained, and whose faults he took for virtues.

Stockmar committed his educational plans to a series of massive memoranda. In the nature of things, no summary can do justice to the prolixity of their style. They provided a daunting mixture of self-evident truths, hardly justifying restatement, with that species of pretentious rubbish their subject often inspires. Anticipating Freud, Stockmar claimed, 'A man's education begins the first day of his life.' As by his own precept there was no time to be lost, he set to work, in the Royal Pavilion at Brighton, on a memorandum completed on 6 March 1842. It dealt principally with the early education of the infant Prince of Wales, and contained 'some of the worst advice ever given to young parents.' They were warned 'that their position was a more difficult one than that of any other parents in the kingdom.' The welfare of England was at stake. Seeing that they were far too young to bring up the heir to the throne, it became 'their sacred duty' to consult more experienced persons and 'follow their advice.'

Stockmar went on to attribute most of the failings of the age to the profligacy of the Queen's uncles. 'The errors of these princes,' he wrote, seated as he was amidst the oriental splendours of the chief of them, 'were of the most glaring kind, and we can find their explanation only in the supposition that their tutors were either incapable of engrafting on their minds during youth the principles of truth or morality, or that they most culpably neglected their duties . . . There can be no doubt that the conduct of these princes contributed more than any other circumstance to weaken the respect and influence of Royalty in this country . . . That George IV by his iniquities did not accomplish his own exclusion was owing to the strength of the English Constitution.'

Stockmar concluded that it was essential for the survival of the monarchy that Albert Edward should be brought up according to the strictest moral principles. As children are 'prone to imitate,' they should be surrounded by 'those who are good and pure, who will teach not only by precept but by living example.' Samuel Wilberforce, Bishop of Oxford, echoed Stockmar's sentiments. 'The great object in view,' he said, was to make the infant prince 'the most perfect man.' When Lord Melbourne became acquainted with the current wisdom, he prophesied 'this damned morality will ruin everything.'

Prince Albert needed no persuading either that the Prince Regent had nearly destroyed the monarchy, or that tainted Hanoverian blood coursed through his son's veins. He told a Canon of Windsor that his great object was to make the Prince of Wales 'as unlike as possible to any of his great uncles.' Greville, the Clerk to the Privy Council, described the Prince's remarks as 'imprudent and ungracious.' He had learned enough of the lurid history of the Dukes of Saxe-Coburg to find such hypocrisy distasteful. Albert's father, to look no further, was notoriously licentious, and there were few deviations from morality or convention he had not pioneered. Compared with the Prince Consort's family, the Hanoverians might have come out of a monastery. Be that as it may, the Prince of Wales's hereditary

endowment provided cause for concern. But the Queen and Prince
Consort, encouraged by Stockmar, over-reacted. Their obsession with
education partly proceeded from the delusion that the dreaded con-
tamination might be withstood by keeping their son in moral
quarantine.

As may be imagined, 'morally good, intelligent, well informed
and experienced people', are sparingly distributed this side of
Purgatory. Only after numberless consultations and endless enquiries
did Queen Victoria invite Sarah Lady Lyttelton to become governess to the Prince of Wales and his elder sister, the Princess Royal,
'the most remarkable English princess of modern history.' Lady
Lyttelton, or 'Laddle' as she soon became known in the nursery,
was a daughter of the second Lord Spencer, whose wife was a Lucan.
When her father was First Lord of the Admiralty she and her mother
heard rumours of a naval battle. They rushed to Lord Spencer to
discover what had happened, only to find him sprawled on the floor
in a dead faint, clutching Nelson's Despatch from the Nile. As a
girl at Althorp, Gibbon taught her to multiply, but she remembered
nothing of the great historian except his majestic girth. Her husband,
the third Lord Lyttelton, died after a long illness in 1837.

Lady Sarah, although a loyal Whig, was old-fashioned in appearance, conservative in many opinions, and inclined towards High
Church ways. The Queen's attitude towards religion was barely
distinguishable from that of her dissenting subjects, for she had
been brought up on Lutheran principles and had married a Lutheran
husband. Consequently her suspicions of what she called 'Pusey'
views, were easily aroused. 'It quite grieved Her Majesty that Lady
Lyttelton should have so many opinions (good perhaps in themselves
but very peculiar at some points) from which she entirely differed.'
The Queen had visions of Vicky and Bertie prostrated at the feet
of the Pope.

Long before Lady Lyttelton took up her duties in February 1842,
she told her family she was 'born to be a schoolmistress.' In the
event she proved an admirable one, although her disciplinary
powers were sometimes overtaxed. According to the Queen, when
she left her service in 1850, 'all the nurses and maids were in tears –
she was so beloved.'

Lady Lyttelton adored Prince Albert and rejoiced to see him in
the nursery. During one such visit, he ignorantly sat in her chair.
The Princess Royal was almost beside herself with indignation.
'Papa!' she protested, 'don't sit there, get up! Go away! It is Laddle's

chair! Give Laddle her chair.' The Prince was at his best playing
with his children. In their company he momentarily recaptured his
own carefree youth and cast off the shyness which shrouded his
affection. Most Englishmen would have been amazed to see this
distant and forbidding prince playing 'hide and seek' with Vicky
and Bertie, flying kites, turning somersaults in a haystack,
catching butterflies. 'He is so kind to them,' wrote the Queen, 'and
romps with them so delightfully, and manages them so beautifully
and firmly.' But often in the midst of the fun, lessons would be
remembered and the revels ended. The Prince Consort, knowing
that drudgery was wholesome, if not divine, looked upon pleasure
with distrust, and shared the Queen's morbid fear of spoiling
children. Louis Philippe was only permitted to present the Prince of
Wales with a toy gun by representing it as a special favour.

The Queen took rather less interest in the children than her
husband, candidly confessing that in his absence she derived 'no
especial pleasure or compensation' from their company. She attributed this to the fact that she had been brought up exclusively in
adult society. In some quarters it was rumoured that she regarded
the Prince of Wales with feelings bordering on hostility. Certainly
she made no secret of her indignation at having a second child
so soon, and the 'very severe pains' associated with his birth could
easily have bred resentment. Greville notes in his Diary: 'The
hereditary and unfailing antipathy of our Sovereigns to their Heirs
Apparent seems thus early to be taking root.'

The Prince of Wales was pre-eminently his mother's child. Lady
Lyttelton believed, for example, that he had inherited her uncompromising regard for truth. The Queen was only too aware of the
resemblance, and saw in him what she least liked in herself. 'He is
my caricature,' she wrote, 'that is the misfortune.'

But however hard she and Albert struggled to make the Court
respectable, however conscientiously they strove to bring up their
family 'to fear God and honour the Queen,' the spectre of the Prince
Regent mocked their efforts. And every time she looked at Bertie,
with his blue Hanoverian eyes and his receding Hanoverian chin,
she was reminded of her eccentric Uncle William, and her wicked
Uncle George, and her detestable Uncle Ernest, who was reported
to have murdered his valet, who had almost come to blows with
Albert in an effort to deny him his proper precedence, and who
was now King of Hanover because the Salic law debarred her from
the throne. It was really too provoking to be so constantly reminded

of things which were much better forgotten.

Between 1842 and 1850, when Lady Lyttelton presided over the royal nursery, its population increased threefold. Princess Alice was born in 1843, Prince Alfred in 1844, Princess Helena in 1846 and Princess Louise in 1848. Probably the Prince of Wales got on best with Alice. Once, when she had been sent to her room in the hope that she might repent the error of her ways, Bertie was caught paying her a surreptitious visit. His excuse for so doing was disarming. He only intended, he claimed, to bring her a 'morsel of news.'

The Prince of Wales was Lady Lyttelton's favourite. Certainly he was an 'easier proposition' than Vicky, who was an exceptionally advanced young lady. When he was barely a year old, 'Laddle' spoke of him as looking at her 'through his large clear blue eyes with a frequent very sweet smile.' But at times she was forced to admit he was 'passionate and determined enough for an autocrat.' By the time he was four it had become evident that he had not inherited his father's scholarly habits. Indeed, Lady Lyttelton was obliged to report to the Queen that her pupil was 'uncommonly averse to learning and requires much patience, from wilful inattention and constant interruptions, getting under the table, upsetting the books and sundry other anti-studious practices.'

When pressure was exerted to make him work, he was prone to outbursts of fury and defiance. Sometimes he screamed and stamped and hurled things around, as if demented. Later in life, for all his charm and geniality, he remained given to sudden gusts of fury.

Possibly because he showed himself resistant to learning, or perhaps because of comparisons with the Princess Royal, his parents concluded that Bertie was the fool of the family. It is true Bertie sometimes stuttered, but that hardly proved him half-witted. The fact that he spoke three languages before he was six was no mean achievement. Lady Lyttelton neither inspired nor shared these low opinions of her pupil, whom she often described as 'very intelligent,' or as continuing 'most promising for kindness and nobleness of mind.' Had his parents shown rather more of these qualities, they must have reached a better understanding of their son.

Prince Albert believed that 'the welfare of the world' depended upon 'the good education of Princes.' It was in this conviction that he supervised his son's studies. Every moment of his life was mapped out for him. Lord Esher found it 'almost painful to look back upon the days and nights of worry and anxiety spent by the Queen and

Prince over the minutest details of the physical, intellectual and moral training of their children, and especially of their eldest son ... No thing – not the smallest thing – was left to chance . . . Not a week, not a day, not an hour of the time of this precious youth could safely or properly be wasted . . . For this boy even the pages of Sir Walter Scott were closed, and he must concentrate, ever concentrate upon "Modern Languages", upon "History", upon "the sciences", in short, upon laying solidly the intellectual and moral foundations which, in the eyes of his conscientious and high-minded father, alone could safely bear the mighty superstructure of the Throne.'

Bertie's parents, encouraged by Stockmar, thought that provided they took sufficient care over 'tending their rare plant in the early stages of its growth . . . they could train every shoot of a young mind.' Had they succeeded, they would either have produced an insufferable prig, or, conceivably, a saint. In fact, 'they fashioned a very human Prince,' far better qualified to inherit the Crown 'than the stunted ideal of which they had dreamed.'

By an inexorable dialectical process, the sheer perversity of which stunned his father, Bertie instinctively preferred the antithesis of every proposition commended to him. Extensive as was Prince Albert's command of the Queen's English, he never wholly mastered Burns's daunting dialect. Consequently, he was obliged to learn from experience what the poet could otherwise have taught him, that 'The best laid schemes o' mice an' men gang aft a-gley.'

Prince Hohenlohe, who was related to the Queen through her half-sister, Princess Feodore of Leiningen, knew Albert well, and deplored his doctrinaire nature. After meeting him at Buckingham Palace in 1859, he noted how 'unfortunate it was for the Prince that he should come straight from a German University to his present position, after a course of superficial study,' without 'having the corners rubbed off' by encountering all sorts and conditions of men. It was doubtless splendid that Prince Albert should denounce the world, like some latter-day St Augustine, but Prince Hohenlohe was right: he might have learned more from it had he been better acquainted with it. But instead, with his head stuck in the heavens, he stubbornly refused to modify the 'fallacious formula,' whereby his son was to be made his replica. 'His father did not smoke, so he must learn by abstinence to abhor it; his father had no taste for ordinary social intercourse, so he must learn to despise it; his father from his earliest years was a natural student, devoted to books,' so he must travel in those 'realms of gold' and relish every minute of it.

Prince Albert's educational plans excited indignation and ridicule. Everybody perceived the errors of the system except its perpetrators. At least in one respect, it was not only misguided but cruel. The Queen was obsessed by 'a great fear of young and carefully brought up boys mixing with older boys and indeed with any boys in general, for the mischief done by bad boys and the things they may hear and learn from them cannot be overrated.' Having herself been deprived of companions of her own age, under what was termed the 'Kensington System,' she should have known better. In her efforts to shield her son from temptation, she rendered him helplessly vulnerable to it.

The Prince Consort had an added reason for wanting the boy to be brought up at home: his distrust of Public Schools, which he regarded as barbarous, degrading and seminaries of vice. When it was decided to found a Public School in honour of the Duke of Wellington, Prince Albert's first concern was that it 'should in *no way* become an Eton or Harrow.' He never could forget a cricket match he saw on Upper Club, during which his attention was absorbed by a nonchalant Etonian in the out-field. For almost three hours this gilded youth did nothing whatever, apart from throwing the ball back if it came in his direction, or languidly sucking a blade of grass. It was incomprehensible to the Prince that such aimless pursuits should be encouraged by the School authorities. Little wonder the poet Gray had written, 'No sense have they of ills to come, nor care beyond to-day.' And so the idea of letting the Prince of Wales 'mix freely with his contemporaries and make friends of his own, with whom he would speedily become unpopular unless he behaved himself', was unthinkable.

Unthinkable, that is, to the boy's parents, for it was usually the first suggestion which commended itself to others. When Lord Granville was consulted about the Prince's education, he 'strongly recommended his being mixed up with others of his own age away from home.' Working by himself, he was deprived of every incentive which rivalry inspires, and being by nature gregarious he tired of his own company. In later life King Edward often regretted having seen so little of his contemporaries when he was young. The Queen once complained to General Bruce, then the Prince's 'Governor', of her son's ill-bred behaviour. He replied that 'occasional solecisms' must be attributed to the fact that His Royal Highness had 'never experienced to their full extent those checks and restraints, and those

practical lessons in what is due to others, and ourselves, which belong
to the ordinary social intercourse of equals.' He further argued that
a tendency 'to form hasty and mistaken judgements,' not to mention
a disposition to 'intolerance,' were to be traced to the same source.

The Prince of Wales was permitted occasional visitors to mitigate
the rigours of his solitary confinement. A small number of carefully
selected Etonians were invited to tea at Windsor. Amongst the
chosen few were Charles Carrington, Frederick Stanley, Charles
Wood, George Cadogan and young William Gladstone, whose aunt
had married Lady Lyttelton's son. Prince Albert hardly ever left
them alone 'lest they should throw bread-pellets at each other or talk
lewdly,' as boys sometimes will. So conversation was 'frosted by his
restraining presence,' until the visitors 'made their bows and
scuttled down the hill again.' If ever the Prince was left alone with
his conscripted companions, he so ill-treated them, that, according
to the Queen, 'the parents, at least of some of them, *refused* to send
their children.' Even the Head Master of Eton, Doctor Hawtrey,
felt obliged to complain about the behaviour of the Prince, regretting
that he appeared to show 'pleasure in giving pain to others.'

In 1849 the Prince of Wales was handed over to a tutor. As may
be imagined, almost as much care was taken to find the right man
as is ordinarily employed in selecting a Prime Minister or Archbishop. In the summer of 1846, Stockmar presented the Queen with
yet another memorandum. It had been provoked by a pamphlet
published earlier that year: 'Who should educate the Prince of
Wales.' It was really too impertinent of an anonymous author to
venture to advise the Royal parents on such matters. But although,
for once, the Baron was not first in the field, he won the battle of
words by weight and numbers.

In times of change, he argued, the leading question is: 'Whether
the education of the Prince should be one which will prepare him for
approaching events, or one which will stamp, perhaps indelibly, an
impression of the sacred character of all existing institutions on his
youthful mind.' Stockmar finally reached the conclusion that the
Prince should be brought up a judicious mixture of liberal Anglican
and progressive conservative, with the stress on progressive. In
matters of religion he should be 'imbued with a deep conviction of
the indispensable necessity of practical morality,' and taught not to
regard 'the supernatural portions of Christianity as its most valuable
elements.' Stockmar appears to have assumed that the Prince of
Wales should play no part whatever in forming his own opinions.

Greville believed that Samuel Wilberforce, who had won high favour at Court, sought 'to be Preceptor to the Prince of Wales, an office to which I would prefer digging at a canal, or breaking stones on the road, so intolerable would be the slavery of it.' Lady Lyttelton, who held the Archdeacon in the highest esteem, heard similar rumours. 'The *report* (it is nothing more yet, alas! and may be a dream) of his going to be tutor to Princey gains ground. To be sure I should be thankful for it as a real mercy to myself.' But it was not to be. The Archdeacon became Bishop of Oxford and it was thought wrong to entice him from his flock.

Henry Liddell, co-author with Robert Scott of a celebrated Greek lexicon, was discreetly sounded, but having just been appointed Head Master of Westminster, declined the honour. Bunsen pressed the claims of Arthur Stanley, the disciple and biographer of Dr Arnold, who possessed in a pre-eminent degree the very broad Church sympathies which Stockmar thought so necessary. But the Baron insisted that the post was unsuited to a clergyman. The person eventually chosen, Henry Birch, was presumably a sufficiently promising young man to overcome the double handicap of intending to take Holy Orders and possessing so daunting a name.

In the summer of 1848 Prince Albert had a long conversation with Birch and was favourably impressed. 'I can imagine,' he told Lord Morpeth, 'that children would easily attach themselves to him.' Birch had been a Scholar of Eton, had won the Newcastle, and become Captain of the School. From Eton he went to King's, where he distinguished himself by gaining four University prizes. After leaving Cambridge, he returned as an assistant Master to his old school. In April 1849, when Birch joined the Royal Family at Windsor, Prince Albert wrote to his step-mother, the Dowager Duchess of Gotha, to tell her the news. 'Bertie will be given over in a few weeks into the hands of a tutor, whom we have found in a Mr Birch, a young, good-looking, amiable man, who was a tutor at Eton, and who not only himself took the highest honours at Cambridge, but whose pupils have also won especial distinction.' Lady Lyttelton warmly approved the choice. 'I do hope and wish,' she said, 'the man may but stay on! He does seem so perfect for his place.'

The Prince of Wales enjoyed shorter holidays, and worked under greater pressure than any other schoolboy in the kingdom. Birch taught him English, Geography and Calculating; while assistant tutors were responsible for Handwriting, Drawing, Religion, Music,

German, French, Archaeology, Science and History.

The repressive nature of Prince Albert's schemes was singularly ill-adapted to develop his son's talents, although well-calculated to make him impatient of restraint and resentful of dictation. Whenever the boy showed signs of repugnance to learning, his parents redoubled their efforts, extended his curriculum, lengthened his timetables, increased the number of his instructors and exchanged memoranda, in the belief that such feverish activity must reconcile him to his educational ordeal. Birch was in such despair that he felt tempted to resign after the first few months of his labours, believing himself incapable of teaching one so easily distracted, so given to tantrums, and so 'anti-studious'. But gradually, as he became increasingly attached to his wayward pupil, he found he was making progress.

It soon became clear that Birch was expected to devote every moment of the day to the Prince of Wales, despite what he called 'the morbid feelings' which were liable 'to result from being morning, noon and night in the company of a child.' When permitted a brief and rare holiday, he is said to have been 'like a colt let out of a dark stable into a green field, bubbling over with irrepressible spirits.' If the tutor felt like a 'discharged prisoner' after only a few months of Prince Albert's unblinking vigilance, how much more must the pupil have suffered, for his was a life sentence.

The Queen, with her horror of Tractarians, scented the taint of Puseyism in the purest Protestant air. Some ill-judged comment led her to suspect that her son's tutor, despite his Cambridge credentials, had contrived to catch the dreaded Oxford malady. Even after Birch protested he was 'plain straightforward Church of England,' she was not completely reassured. It was suggested that it would be best to avoid all reference to the Catechism in his teaching. If the Thirty-Nine Articles could be understood in a Catholic sense, as Dr Newman had claimed before defecting to Rome, what sinister significance might not popish casuistry discover elsewhere in the Prayer Book? The prohibition was only grudgingly withdrawn when Birch threatened to resign. The strained relations created during this dispute were not forgotten. 'I never felt at my ease with Birch,' the Queen subsequently told Stockmar. 'There always seemed to be something between us. Whenever I was with him, I always felt as if either he was in my way, or I in his.' Possibly the fact that he accepted St Paul's teaching on charity too literally may have contributed to his fall from grace. Had he been more of a courtier, he would have learned to echo parental complaints. Instead, he had the temerity to take his pupil's part and look indulgently on faults it was his duty to rebuke.

The Prince of Wales became passionately attached to his tutor, the only adult he had come across who tried to understand him rather than alter him. 'I seem,' Birch told Stockmar, 'to have found the key to his heart.' Because this was so evidently true, it was decided to appoint someone else. Prince Albert must have forgotten his own youthful devotion to Herr Florshütz, or he could not have been so callous. Lady Canning, one of Queen Victoria's Ladies-in-Waiting, wrote of Birch's impending departure: 'It has been a trouble and sorrow to the Prince of Wales, who has done no end of touching things since he heard that he was to lose him. He is such an affectionate dear little fellow; his notes and presents which Mr Birch used to find on his pillow were really too moving.' After Birch had gone, his pupil was so downcast that he felt he owed his successor some sort of apology. 'You cannot wonder,' he said, 'if we are somewhat dull today. We are sorry Mr Birch is gone. It is very natural is it not?' Prince Albert's parting comment was less agreeable. 'Mr Birch takes up a living at Lord Wilton's of £3000 a year with four curates, and no one can blame him.' The Prince of Wales never forgot his friends and his old tutor ended his days a Canon of Worcester.

Before leaving to take charge of his four curates, Birch wrote a final report on his pupil in which he condemned the policy of keeping the Prince from school and listed the damage attributable to it. He was beyond caring how offensive Prince Albert found his comments. It sufficed that they were true. At first, he admitted, he had found his pupil insolent, bad-tempered and defiant. Although he hated chaff, 'I thought it better, notwithstanding his sensitiveness, to laugh at him . . . and to treat him as I know that boys would have treated him at an English public school.' The boy, moreover, was inclined to be moody, had little capacity for concentration, and at times verged on mental collapse. On the other hand, he possessed a most 'amiable and affectionate disposition,' was forgiving by nature, singularly observant, and endowed with a 'keen perception of right and wrong.'

It was Birch's 'deliberate opinion' that many of the Prince of Wales's 'peculiarities arise from want of contact with boys of his own age, and from his being continually in the society of older persons, and from his finding himself the centre round which everything seems to move . . . He has no standard by which to measure his own powers . . . Nothing that a tutor can say, or even a parent, has such influence as intercourse with sensible boys of the same age . . . I always found that boys' characters at Eton were formed as much by contact with others as by the precepts of their tutors.' Nevertheless, Birch concluded, he saw every reason to hope 'that the Prince of Wales will eventually turn out a *good* and, in my humble opinion, a *great* man.'

Birch was succeeded by Frederick Waymouth Gibbs, a Fellow of Trinity and a barrister on the Northern Circuit. Prince Albert, as Chancellor of Cambridge, consulted Sir James Stephen, Professor of Modern History, about possible tutors for the Prince of Wales and Prince Alfred. He warmly recommended Gibbs, whom he had brought up from early childhood with his own family after the boy's father had lost his money and his mother her wits. Sir James, who had earlier drafted the bill abolishing slavery in the British Empire, now unwittingly promoted the practice within the Queen's four walls, for his protégé soon proved as tyrannical as any sugar planter in the Indies.

Gibbs had been brought up as a member of the professional Middle Class and his father belonged to a dissenting sect. These two facts sufficed to disqualify him in the eyes of most of the Court, but they commended him to his royal employers. Prince Albert preferred bourgeois to patrician virtues, and the Queen saw in his non-conformist parentage a defence against Pusey and Pius IX. Stephen wrote a confidential report which might have been extracted from Newman's *Lives of the Saints*. The young man, said Sir James, was 'exempt from reproach' in whatever related to 'Truth, to Honour, to sobriety and to Chastity . . . He fears nothing . . . is exceedingly free from all anxious forebodings, and never quailed before the face of any human being. The faults of his character are akin to his temperament . . . He is self-confident and has a strength of will which occasionally degenerates into obstinacy.'

Gibbs might not 'quail' before the Prince Consort, but his compliance verged on the obsequious, and it soon became evident that he proposed to ingratiate himself with the father, not the son. In response to royal commands, Gibbs increased Bertie's lessons to seven hours a day, six days a week, occupying such intervals as remained with gymnastics, riding and drill. There would be no idle hands for Satan to employ under his auspices. When their son showed signs of dropping with fatigue, his parents were utterly mystified, until it dawned on them that the boy was naturally lazy and needed to be driven harder.

Victor Emmanuel II, having heard so much from the Queen of the admirable way in which she and Albert were bringing up their children, thought it proper to ask Gibbs to let him have further details. Nothing provides more cogent testimony to the defects of the system than Gibbs's exposition of it. In his own words, he and it stand condemned. As requested, he told the King of Sardinia how the Princes were taught Latin, German and French, how they studied the literature of their own and other languages, how they were instructed in mathematics so as to understand the scientific principles underlying Arts and Manufactures, how they constantly wrote essays on historical and moral themes, how they prepared maps, studied social economy, and yet somehow found time for drawing and music. Splendid as it was made to sound, what it amounted to was this: the Prince of Wales was being treated like a goose destined for *pâté de foie gras* and heartlessly over-stuffed.

Gibbs's Journal provides a less elevating but more convincing glimpse of the realities of his job. 'The Q. and P. sent to ask me if the P. of W. was unwell. He had behaved rudely to his sister in their presence. I told them he had been so to me, and had struck me with a stick in a passion. The Prince told me not to allow this – that if he did so, I must box his ears, or take the same stick and rap his knuckles "sharply".' 'A very bad day. The P. of W. has been like a person half silly. I could not gain his attention. He was very rude, particularly in the afternoon, throwing stones in my face. During his lesson in the morning, he was running first in one place, then in another. He made faces, and spat. Dr Becker complained also of his great naughtiness. There was a great deal of bad words.'

Gibbs spared no effort to interest his pupil. Once, while staying at Windsor, he persuaded Prince Albert's Private Secretary, Charles Phipps, to write to his friend Colonel Knollys to see if he knew of a book which made mathematics attractive. 'The Prince of Wales's tutor,' wrote Phipps, 'has asked me to consult you confidentially with respect to some practical and elementary book of fortification . . . by which the boy's attention might be directed to mathematical questions, through the medium of his paramount taste, which is certainly military.'

A year before he died, King Edward sent for Lord Esher 'and went through two volumes of old letters and memoranda covering his early education. He spoke about his tutors and his boyhood . . . He liked old Tarver . . . but *not* Gibbs. They never "got on".' Nevertheless, when the moment for his departure came, in the autumn of 1858, there were moving farewells. 'I took leave of poor Mr Gibbs,' the Queen told Vicky, 'he was affected and low – and it upset me a good deal. We always got on extremely well together. Bertie was much affected too, at parting from him.'

Gibbs's retirement was partly prompted by a letter which Phipps received earlier that year. It came from Colonel Lindsay, who two years after winning a VC in the Crimea was appointed a Gentleman-in-Waiting to the Prince of Wales. From this vantage point, he felt bound to tell Phipps that in his view 'a continuance of the present system will not be beneficial to the Prince . . . Mr Gibbs has *no* influence. He and the Prince are so much out of sympathy with one another that a wish expressed by Mr Gibbs is sure to meet with opposition on the part of the Prince . . . Mr Gibbs has devoted himself to the boy, but no affection is given him in return, nor do I wonder at it, for they are by nature thoroughly unsuited to one another. I confess I quite understand the Prince's feeling towards Mr Gibbs, for tho' I respect his uprightness and devotion, I could not give him sympathy, confidence or friendship.'

The Queen, despite her regard for Gibbs, remarked when he left that he had 'failed completely' and, in particular, 'during the last two years entirely, incredibly.' Bertie bore little resemblance to his father, the measure of human perfection. The most plausible explanation for this lamentable shortcoming was that the boy was perverse and his tutor inadequate. It was axiomatic that no blame could attach to the parents.

Charles Carrington, one of the select Etonians invited to Windsor as a companion for the Prince of Wales, liked him far better than his brother, 'Affie.' 'He had such an open, generous disposition and the kindest heart imaginable. He was a very plucky boy and always ready for fun which often got him into scrapes. He was afraid of his father who seemed a proud, shy, stand-offish man, not calculated to make friends easily with children. I was frightened to death of him.'

That Bertie should have precedence over her husband provoked the Queen's furious indignation, and it is not inconceivable that the injured party shared his wife's resentment. When she contemplated the possibility of an early death, most probably in childbirth, the prospect appeared the more disagreeable because beloved Albert, so good, so wise and so utterly dedicated to affairs of state, would be pushed aside to make way for her backward and frivolous son. And what made matters worse was that the Prince of Wales seemed incapable of learning from his father. When the Prince of Orange vainly endeavoured to win Princess Alice's hand, and before her parents discovered how disreputable he was, the Queen wrote Vicky a letter contrasting the 'Orange boy' with Bertie. Although very shy, 'he pays great attention to what is said. (I mean when Papa talks at breakfast, etc. about politics and military matters, etc.) which a nameless youth never does.'

Criticism of the 'nameless youth' was not confined to remarks made behind his back, for his parents seldom disguised their disappointment in him. Considering he was brought up under a bombardment of abuse and disparagement, his own subsequent comment to Lady Augusta Stanley erred on the side of restraint. 'We were perhaps a little too much spoken to and at – at least we thought we could never do anything right.'

The Prince Consort could be cruelly contemptuous of those who opposed him, and nobody suffered more than his eldest son. Indeed, such a pitch of disagreeableness was reached that the fearless Gibbs told Prince Albert to explore other means of reproof; and Lord Clarendon was so distressed at the way the royal children were treated that he too ventured a reproof. The Prince defended himself by blaming the Queen for what he was pleased to call her 'aggressive' system, and complained that the 'office of punishment had always devolved upon him.' Clarendon, however, told Greville that he was disposed to blame both parents, and 'that the Prince himself, in spite of his natural good sense, had been very injudicious in his way of treating his children.' He also alleged that 'the Prince of Wales resented very much the severity he had experienced.' In so saying, he was almost certainly mistaken. Birch, in his final report, stressed his pupil's 'most forgiving disposition,' which he particularly noticed when he was obliged 'to complain of him to his parents or to punish him.'

Somehow the Prince of Wales resisted the temptation to transgress the Fifth Commandment, though it is not easy to honour those who bully and abuse one. Nevertheless, there is reason to suppose that he succeeded in so doing. Christopher Teesdale, who became his Equerry and constant companion after Gibbs retired, maintained that the Prince 'simply adored his father.' Roger Fulford, in his life of the Prince Consort, asserts that 'there is no evidence either in the Royal Archives or in the printed authorities to justify the belief that the relations between the Prince and his eldest son were other than deeply affectionate.' Some years after his father's death, the Prince of Wales began referring to him at a Royal Academy Banquet, but was so overcome by the recollection of his loss that he could not continue speaking.

Prince Albert never abandoned his hope that it might prove possible to alter Bertie's nature, as if it were commonplace for leopards to change their spots. In a number of letters he urged the Princess Royal to persuade her brother to take life more seriously. 'Perhaps you could let him share in some of your lectures,' he suggested, during Bertie's first visit to Berlin in 1858. 'An elder sister's influence can often be effective.'

Some parents would not have been astounded to discover that their seventeen-year-old sons were more concerned about the cut of a hacking-jacket than the intricacies of political economy. But the Prince Consort was not numbered amongst them. He was stunned to find that Bertie 'takes no interest in anything but clothes and again clothes. Even when out shooting he is more occupied with his trousers than with the game!' Admittedly, the boy showed 'remarkable social talent,' and could be 'lively, quick and sharp when his mind is set on anything, which is seldom . . . But usually his intellect is of no more use than a pistol packed at the bottom of a trunk if one were attacked in the robber-infested Apennines.'

It would be idle to pretend that Bertie showed signs of becoming a student prince. In this respect, as in most others, he was the reverse image, not the duplicate of his father. The contrast between the two seems more remarkable when one remembers the effort devoted to turning the Prince of Wales into Albert Junior. Prince Albert regarded tobacco with disgust. Bertie smoked twelve cigars and twenty cigarettes a day. Prince Albert took wine like medicine. Bertie delighted in it. Prince Albert was scared of women. Bertie was never happier than in their company. Prince Albert loved reading, his student lamp was a prized possession. Bertie greatly preferred conversation. The Prince Consort shunned society, his son led it. The father was so weary of the world he died without a fight, his son exulted in living. They approached problems from opposite directions. Prince Albert formed his judgements from books and theories. The Prince of Wales based his on observation and experience. Little wonder these two individuals found each other incomprehensible, or that the father regarded his son's tastes with repugnance and dismay.

Prince Albert conceived it to be his mission to promote friendship between the German states and Britain. Vicky's marriage to Fritz, the Crown Prince of Prussia, seemed a triumph for his policy: nobody foreseeing that the child of that union would one day involve the two nations in war. The Queen, who shared her husband's aspirations, was anxious that Bertie should be brought up speaking German, appreciating Germany, working for Anglo-German unity.

Just as Prussians complained that the Crown Princess remained far too English, so Lord Aberdeen grumbled about Prince Albert's 'excessive Germanism.' If loyalty to one's country is a crime, Prince Albert was guilty. Before leaving Coburg for England in 1839, he expressed his resolve to 'be untiring in my efforts and labours for the country to which I shall in future belong.' Nevertheless, 'I shall never cease to be a true *German*, a true *Coburg* and *Gotha* man.' He can hardly be blamed if he encouraged his son to share his loyalties and ambitions, and it would be wrong to exaggerate his failure.

As a young man, the Prince of Wales was far more favourably disposed to Prussia than he subsequently became, after Bismarck and his nephew, William II, had done their worst. Baron Eckardstein, who was ten years at the Court of St James between 1895 and 1905, writing after the First World War, says that 'nothing could be further from the truth than the conviction current in Germany that King Edward was from the first a sworn enemy of Germany.' On the contrary, he 'received from his Coburg father an education that was largely German; he was a complete master of the German language, and he had grown up in the old tradition of the Anglo-German comradeship-in-arms. For during the Victorian age the Waterloo tradition was dominant.' Moreover, the Queen, particularly after the Prince Consort's death, insisted that 'the German element' should be 'cherished and kept up in our beloved home.' Of course, she had no illusions about her son, and wrote to Vicky saying, 'I hope you have Germanized Bertie as much as possible, for it is most necessary.' But even he looked forward to the closest friendship with Prussia, once his brother-in-law and sister succeeded to the throne. It was not until 1888, when the Emperor Frederick died, after reigning for ninety-nine days, and his son, William II, became Kaiser, that serious differences arose between Uncle and nephew and the countries they represented.

Prince Albert was repeatedly warned that his son was being overtaxed by a system at which even the infant John Stuart Mill might have quailed. Dr Voisin, Bertie's French Master, thought that too much was expected of the child, and told Gibbs: 'You will wear him out early . . . Make him climb trees! Run! Leap! Row! Ride!' Dr

Becker, Prince Albert's librarian, who taught the Prince of Wales German, wrote HRH a long memorandum claiming that his pupil's passionate outbursts of rage were symptoms of the excessive strains imposed upon him.

Becker's descriptions of the Prince's fits of fury make alarming reading, although they left little impression upon the person ultimately responsible for them. 'He takes everything that is at hand and throws it with the greatest violence against the wall or window, without thinking the least of the consequences of what he is doing; or he stands in the corner stamping with his legs and screaming in the most dreadful manner.' Dr Becker discussed these storms with the Prince's other instructors and it was generally agreed that they were nervous reactions to pressures exerted upon a body and mind too exhausted to respond. Becker was at pains to stress that 'these outbreaks of passion . . . must be *destructive* to the child.' The memorandum concluded by begging the royal parents to recognize that '*encouragement* of every kind' was what the boy needed. 'The expression of too high expectations which he finds himself not able to meet discourages him instantly and makes him unhappy.'

Not only was Bertie taught too much, but much of what he was taught was altogether 'unsuited for one destined by the gods to wear a crown rather than a mortar-board.' The Prince of Wales had a singularly independent mind and his character was formed by opposing most of the opinions thrust upon him. It is difficult to recognize in Bertie's portrait as painted by his parents the heroic small boy who succeeded in defying a regiment of tutors, not to mention his Sovereign and her Consort.

In August 1855, during the Crimean War, the Queen and Prince Consort paid an official visit to Napoleon III, taking Vicky and Bertie with them. Half a century later, the King still vividly remembered the nine days he spent as the Emperor's guest, for they were the happiest of his childhood and kindled in him that enduring love for France which shaped the destiny of Europe. Earlier in the year, Napoleon and the Empress Eugénie had stayed at Windsor, so this was a return visit. It was also intended as a demonstration of goodwill between allied sovereigns.

It was the Queen's first visit to Paris; indeed no British monarch had set foot in the city since Henry VI. From the Gare du Chemin de Fer de Strasbourg, they drove in open carriages down the Bois de Boulogne to the Palace of St Cloud. In the fading light they could see the whole route lined with troops. They were welcomed by

vast crowds shouting, 'Vive la Reine d'Angleterre!' 'Vive l'
Empereur!' 'Vive le Prince Albert!' The Queen was especially
gratified to be told by a veteran Marshal of France, who had
served as a young officer under the first Napoleon, that he remembered the Emperor, parading through the streets of his capital
having conquered half Europe being greeted with less acclaim.

The royal party were thrilled by the beauty of St Cloud, its
noble rooms, its magnificent Gobelin tapestries, its splendid avenues
of beech trees, its orange blossoms and its fountains. From the
balcony of her room the Queen could see the distant outline of the
Arc de Triomphe looming over the twinkling lights of Paris. Vicky
and Bertie were given 'charming rooms,' on the floor below their
parents', 'hung with beautiful little pictures' and 'opening on a
lovely little flower-garden.' The Queen's accounts of her visit are
breathless with excitement. No wonder she was enchanted and
overwhelmed, for the Emperor spared nothing to make her stay
magical. Whatever faults the Second Empire possessed, it was
neither dull nor sombre, and Napoleon's gift for entertainment and
ceremonial amounted to genius. Even Prince Albert, the least
flamboyant of men, was stirred by the most brilliant spectacle of
the age.

Writing to King Leopold from St Cloud, his niece described
herself as *'delighted, enchanted, amused,* and *interested,* and I never saw
anything more *beautiful* and gay than Paris – or more splendid than
all the Palaces.' From Osborne, she wrote once more to her 'Dearest
Uncle,' telling him, 'Here we are again, after the *pleasantest* and
most interesting and triumphant ten days that I think I ever passed.'
She also sent Stockmar a glowing account of 'our triumphant, most
interesting, and most enjoyable visit to Paris!' She confessed she
could think of nothing else. 'I am deeply *touched* by the extraordinary warm heartedness and enthusiasm with which we have
been received by *all* ranks and the kindness shown to everyone . . .
beginning with ourselves and ending with the lowest of our servants.'

One reason why the Queen enjoyed herself so much, was that
she had fallen under the Emperor's spell. His approach was sedately
flirtatious, and she was 'mightily tickled by it,' never 'having con-
versed with a man of the world on a footing of equality.' Napoleon,
like Disraeli, was an engaging romantic, who did not hesitate to
flatter the Queen outrageously. There was also a hint of mystery
about him which intrigued her. She told Stockmar that she had
'conceived a *real* affection and friendship' for him. 'We have now

seen him for full *ten days*, from twelve to fourteen hours every day –
often alone; and I cannot say *how* pleasant and easy it is to live
with him, or how attached one becomes to him. I know *no* one who
puts me more at my ease, or to whom I felt more inclined to talk
unreservedly, or in whom involuntarily I should be more inclined
to confide . . . He is so simple, so *naif*, never making *des phrases*, or
paying compliments – so full of tact, good taste, high breeding . . .
Wonderful it is that this *man* – whom certainly we were not over well-
disposed to – should by *force* of *circumstances* be drawn into such
close connection with us, and become *personally* our friend, and *this*
entirely by his *own personal* qualities, in spite of so much that *was
and could* be said against him! . . . I shall always look back on the time
passed not only in France, but with *him* personally, as most agreeable.'

It was not only the Queen who was captivated by her imperial
hosts. Vicky never tired of praising the kindness and beauty of the
Empress, and even Prince Albert, the Queen remarked, took some
notice of her. The Prince of Wales became deeply attached to the
Emperor, who went out of his way to entertain the children. In her
journal the Queen records: 'The Emperor kindly took Bertie out
in his curricle, which he drove himself – one with two servants
behind – not the least interesting incident in this most eventful and
delightful visit – and drove him about Paris.' Napoleon treated
Bertie, who was not quite fifteen, as if the difference in their ages
signified nothing. Instead of preaching about work or duty, he
unashamedly enjoyed himself. For the first time in his life the
Prince of Wales glimpsed a promised land. 'The beauty of the French
capital, the liveliness of the French people, the bonhomie of the
French Emperor, the elegance of the French Empress, made an
indelible impression on his young pleasure-hungry nature.'

The most dramatic moment of their stay in Paris was the
Queen's visit to the Hôtel des Invalides to see Napoleon's tomb.
She arrived unexpectedly and the Governor was much put out.
Nevertheless, the Invalides, many of them veterans of Wagram,
Borodino and Waterloo, reinforced by survivors from Inkerman
and Balaclava, were hastily drawn up to form a Guard of Honour.
Napoleon's remains had been brought back from St Helena fifteen
years before, but, as the crypt designed to receive them was still being
constructed, the coffin stood in the side chapel of St Jérome. 'Into
this the Emperor led me,' wrote the Queen in her journal, 'and
there I stood, at the arm of Napoleon III, his nephew, before the
coffin of England's bitterest foe; I, the grand-daughter of that

King who hated him most, and who most vigorously opposed him, and this very nephew, who bears his name, being my nearest and dearest ally!'

As they stood gazing at the coffin, draped in a black pall decorated with golden bees, a violent thunderstorm raged outside. 'Strange and wonderful indeed,' wrote the Queen. 'It seems, as if in this tribute of respect to a departed and dead foe, old enmities and rivalries were wiped out, and the seal of Heaven placed upon that bond of unity, which is now happily established between two great and powerful nations!' The Queen was so moved that she told the Prince of Wales, still wearing the kilt which fascinated Parisians, to pay homage to the man whom Englishmen had long regarded as their foremost enemy. At the sight of the young Prince kneeling before the coffin of their great Emperor, battle-scarred warriors were seen wiping tears from their eyes.

The Royal Family's 'delightful and never-to-be-forgotten' visit ended with a ball at Versailles. They drove over by moonlight from St Cloud, and were greeted by the Empress at the top of the staircase. When Napoleon saw her in her white dress trimmed with diamonds, he whispered, 'comme tu es belle.' They went through the Galerie des Glaces, wreathed in flowers and blazing with light, to watch a superb display of fireworks the like of which the Queen had never seen. 'The finale was the representation in fireworks of Windsor Castle, a very pretty attention.' A number of presentations followed: amongst those thus honoured was the Prussian Minister at Frankfurt, Count Bismarck. Next, they had supper in the theatre. 'The sight was truly magnificent. The whole stage was covered in, and four hundred people sat down to supper at forty small tables of ten each . . . It was quite one of the finest and most magnificent sights we have ever witnessed. There had not been a ball at Versailles since the time of Louis XVI.' It was nearly two when they left, 'much delighted' and 'the children in ecstasies.'

The Queen, in thanking the Emperor for all his kindness during their visit, particularly mentioned that shown to her children. 'Leur séjour en France a été la plus heureuse époque de leur vie et ils ne cessent pas d'en parler.' The Prince of Wales had indeed returned to England with his head full of the glittering imperial court, which made the entertainments at Buckingham Palace appear so drab by comparison. Not for him the killjoy austerities of the lesser German principalities, with their stiff and forbidding formalities, for he had seen Paris under the Second Empire, had drunk its wine, admired its women, heard its songs. The grass at St Cloud looked greener than any he saw from the schoolroom window at Windsor.

When the Prince of Wales was sixteen it was decided he should be confirmed. The Queen contributed to his preparation by reading him Dr Arnold's sermons. The day before the ceremony, the Dean of Windsor, Gerald Wellesley, rigorously cross-examined him before Archbishop Summer, and his answers showed a thorough understanding of the Sacraments and Catechism. That evening, in an effort to create a sacred atmosphere, Affie was kept out of the way. The ceremony took place on 1 April, 1858, in St George's Chapel, Windsor. Bertie stood throughout the service and seemed impressed by the Archbishop's sermon on the duties of a Christian. Although he did not always live up to his faith, he never lost it. 'I do not mind what religion a man professes,' he once remarked, 'but I distrust him who has none.'

Shortly after his Confirmation, the Prince of Wales was sent to live at White Lodge, Richmond Park, the house in which Nelson had dipped his finger in a glass of port and sketched his plan for the Battle of Trafalgar on a table in the study. The reason for giving the Prince a separate establishment was not to permit him greater independence, but to intern him under conditions of strict security so that he might 'be away from the world and devote himself exclusively to study.' Prince Albert wrote Stockmar a letter explaining his plan, which was partly designed in accordance with the Baron's principle that the young should only associate with 'those who are good and pure,' and that nothing should be left to the lottery of chance encounters. 'As companions for him we have appointed three very distinguished young men . . . who are to occupy in monthly rotation a kind of equerry's place about him, and from whose more intimate intercourse I anticipate no small benefit to Bertie. They are Lord Valletort, the eldest son of Lord Mount Edgecumbe, who is a thoroughly good, moral and accomplished man.' Amongst other recommendations, he was 'never at a public school.' Next, there was Major Teesdale, of the Artillery, who as a young aide-de-camp had won a VC in the Crimea; and finally, there was Major Lindsay of the Scots Fusilier Guards, 'who received the Victoria Cross for Alma and Inkerman, where he carried the colours of the regiment, and by his courage drew upon himself the attention of the whole army.'

When Gibbs departed on 10 November 1858, he was replaced

by Colonel Robert Bruce, who was officially described as the Prince's 'Governor.' Bruce's father, the seventh Lord Elgin, won fame by transporting the Parthenon Marbles back to England, and his sister, who later married Dean Stanley, was one of the Queen's closest friends. The Colonel was a martinet, combining the dourness of his Presbyterian upbringing with the severity of one accustomed to command a battalion of Grenadier Guards. Much of his time he spent frowning, or clearing his throat, preparatory to some rebuke. Bertie was told by his parents that he must never leave White Lodge without reporting himself to his Governor, who would settle 'who is to accompany you, and will give general directions as to the disposition of the day.'

The Queen told Vicky that her brother was 'very fond' of Colonel Bruce, 'looks up to him and seems proud of him, which is a great blessing!' Certainly, she and Prince Albert agreed that they could not have found 'a better man as his companion.' Their confidence in the Colonel was based on his critical reports. The more he complained of Bertie's shortcomings, the more reassured they felt that he understood their son.

The Gentlemen 'appointed to attend on the Prince of Wales' were presented with a confidential memorandum, written by the Prince Consort, listing their duties and the various ways in which they were expected to set an example. Lord Redesdale thought it might have been composed 'for the use and guidance of a seminary for young ladies.' It began with one of those resplendent truisms of which Stockmar was such a master. The Prince of Wales had arrived at the transitional state between boy and man, which was 'the most important, the most critical and the most difficult period of a life-time.' In other words, he was adolescent. As his exalted position made it impossible for him to mix on equal terms with those of his own age, his father had carefully chosen equerries, representative of 'a good set,' to supply the want of ordinary friendships and to be appropriate companions for 'the first gentleman of England.' The equerries were warned to be particularly careful of what they wore. 'There are many habits and practices which might be quite natural and unobjectionable for these gentlemen at their own homes and in their ordinary life, which would form dangerous examples for the Prince of Wales to copy, and Her Majesty and His Royal Highness would wish them, without any formality, or stiffness of manner, to remember both in deportment and in dress that they are in attendance on the eldest son of the Queen.'

Under the heading, 'Manners and Conduct towards others' it was laid down that 'A prince should never say a harsh or a rude word to anybody, nor indulge in satirical or bantering expressions.' If it became known that 'the Prince of Wales had laughed at this or that person,' it could give great offence. 'These remarks apply, of course, in a still stronger degree to anything approaching to a *practical joke*, which should never be permitted.' The conversation at White Lodge must be such as to help the Prince cultivate his mind. 'Mere games of cards and billiards, and idle gossiping talk, will never teach this.' Presumably, Lord Valletort was supposed to discuss the state of the rupee with Major Teesdale to encourage the boy to take an interest in monetary trends.

King Edward once told Lord Esher 'that he hated the memory of White Lodge,' where he had been 'bored to death in his youth,' surrounded by middle-aged men, and 'cut off from young companionship.' In bringing up his own sons he was at pains to ensure that they were never 'coddled' and experienced 'the rough as well as the smooth.' There were few respects in which the Prince's regime differed from that of a prison. Sir James Clark, one of the worst doctors in England, decreed that the Prince's breakfast was to consist of bread and butter and an egg; luncheon and dinner of meat and vegetables but no pudding. Seltzer water was recommended at midday, while a diluted glass of claret was permitted with the evening meal. Any republican who wished to preserve his illusions would have been ill-advised to have shared the Prince's supper.

On his seventeenth birthday, Bertie was handed a letter from his parents. According to Greville, it made a 'profound impression' upon him, and 'touched his feelings to the quick. He brought it to Gerald Wellesley in floods of tears.' Greville believed that it emancipated the Prince from parental authority, and he described it as 'one of the most admirable letters' ever penned. In reality, it overflowed with what Delane once called, 'that most cruel of all afflictions – good advice.' Greville had been totally misinformed about its purport. The boy was told – as if he did not know it already – that 'life is composed of duties, and in the due, punctual and cheerful performance of them the true Christian, true soldier and true gentleman is recognized.' It went on to point out that Colonel Bruce was Mr Gibbs writ large, and it concluded with a homily about being courteous to servants. It was enough to make anyone weep.

As early as March 1854, Gibbs recognized that the Prince of Wales learned more from conversations and expeditions than he did from reading. Knowing that the best way to persuade the Prince Consort that this was so would be to compose a memorandum, he prepared a formidable analysis of the advantage of travel. Two years later his arguments bore fruit, and in September 1856, instead of paying his annual visit to Balmoral, Bertie, accompanied by Gibbs and Colonel Cavendish, one of the Queen's Grooms-in-Waiting, set out on a walking tour of Dorset. They had hoped that no one would recognize them but the secret oozed out. After the vigilant Editor of *The Bridport News* informed his fellow townsmen that the Heir Apparent to the Crown had recently stayed at the Bull Hotel, and that 'His Royal Highness is making a tour of the provinces incognito,' the party was so pestered that they abandoned their expedition at Honiton and returned to Osborne.

Refusing to be discouraged by this setback, a more ambitious journey was planned for the following summer, involving a walking tour of the Lake District and a visit to Bonn. As a great concession, the Prince was permitted four companions of his own age, if not his own choice. In fact, their selection was left to the Head Master of Eton, who seems to have preferred hereditary expectations to less predictable accomplishments. The only commoner amongst them was William Gladstone, son of the future Prime Minister. After General Grey and Colonel Ponsonby had been added to the party, the young gentlemen were heavily outnumbered, but Prince Albert nevertheless remained apprehensive that somehow these hand-picked youths would contrive to corrupt his son. So he got Tarver, Bertie's Chaplain and classical tutor, to set him an essay on 'Friends and Flatterers.'

The tour proved outstandingly successful, Ponsonby particularly contributing to the laughter and high spirits. The Prince, normally starved of companionship, was very lively, and even Mr Gibbs, that ever-present reminder of life's sterner aspect, could not altogether spoil the fun. It is true there was one unfortunate episode on the first evening in Germany. The Prince of Wales, having dined not wisely but too well, and having drunk something rather more stimulating than claret diluted with seltzer, so far forgot himself as to embrace a young lady after a somewhat slender acquaintance. When Mr Gladstone, then Chancellor of the Exchequer, heard of the incident from his son Willy, it made him feel 'what we should, I think, have suspected, viz: that the Prince of Wales has not been educated up to his position. This sort of unworthy little indulgence is the compensation. Kept in childhood beyond his time, he is allowed to make that childhood what it should never be in a Prince, or anyone else, namely wanton.'

Apart from what the Chancellor termed, 'this little squalid debauch,' the most memorable moment of the tour was dining with the aged Prince Metternich in his castle at Johannisberg. Prince Albert yearned for a detailed account of all the great statesman said, particularly as he had discussed the diplomatic secrets of more than half a century. But all he could discover of this momentous encounter was that Metternich was 'a very nice old gentleman and very like the late Duke of Wellington.' Metternich himself remarked of his young guest: 'Il avait l'air embarrassé et très triste.'

In January 1858, Vicky married Prince Frederick William of Prussia, and in November, Bertie, accompanied by Colonel Bruce and Major Teesdale, visited her at Potsdam. Although she was expecting a child, she saw to it that he was entertained everywhere. She even ignored her father's proposal that he might accompany her to lectures. It was during this visit that Bertie formed a deep friendship with his brother-in-law, Fritz. On his return to Windsor for Christmas, the Queen complained that he talked 'constantly of Berlin,' particularly about people, parties, balls and theatres, but said nothing 'of the fine works of art, etc.,' unless particularly asked.

The most ambitious of these early journeys was that undertaken in 1859, after a series of consultations with Ministers of the Crown, the President of the Royal Academy, the Director of the British Museum and John Ruskin. The Prince was to reside in Rome and study Art, Archaeology and Ancient History, despite his own preference for going to Aldershot. His programme, as ever, was strictly supervised: poetry before breakfast, languages in the morning, sightseeing after luncheon, and then private reading and study until dinner time. Bruce, more vigilant than ever, felt singularly ill at ease in the Eternal City, where God and the Devil seemed on suspiciously equable terms. But he did his duty manfully and turned down enticing invitations by the score. It was dead Rome, not living Rome, to which the Prince Consort wanted his son introduced. So day after day, distinguished experts dragged the youth from Picture Galleries to Museums, from Museums to Churches, and from Churches to Ancient Ruins. 'You look at two mouldering stones and are told it's the temple of something,' said the Prince dejectedly.

Despite Bruce's vociferous misgivings, it was decided that the Prince should visit the Pope. As a special concession Pius IX permitted the Colonel to be present during the audience. Initially the conversation touched on nothing more alarming than the Queen's recent speech in Parliament and Fritz's visit to Italy five years before. But suddenly Pio Nono turned to a highly controversial theme: his restoration of the Catholic hierarchy in England, which had provoked bitter protests against 'papal aggression.' No sooner had he begun explaining that his motives had been primarily spiritual, than Bruce began shuffling his feet and clearing his throat. Despite the tradition that the initiative for concluding Audiences belonged to His Holiness, the Colonel hurriedly ended the interview and strode out of the Vatican with Bertie at his heels.

It required months of patient negotiations to repair the havoc of this goodwill visit. The Queen seemed unaware of the damage done, although sensitively alert to other dangers, for she told King Leopold: 'Bertie's interview with the Pope went off extremely well. He was extremely kind and gracious, and Colonel Bruce was present; it would never have done to let Bertie go alone, as they might hereafter have pretended, God knows! what Bertie had said.' Unhappily, the royal tour came to as sudden a halt as the visit to the Pontiff, for Austria declared war on Sardinia and Napoleon III crossed the Alps, promising to free Northern Italy. As neither Lord Palmerston, nor the Prince's parents, wished him to be swept into the fighting, he was ordered to board HMS *Scourge* at Civita Vecchia and sail home by way of Gibraltar.

No sooner had the Prince of Wales returned from Italy, than he was despatched to Edinburgh for further study. One of the principal reasons for sending him north was that he might sit at the feet of Dr Lyon Playfair, who had helped Prince Albert plan the Great Exhibition in 1851. After spending the morning in the Professor's Laboratory, the Prince would visit a factory, mine or shipyard, to see for himself the practical way in which scientific knowledge was applied in industry. During his three months in Edinburgh, his social life was confined to presiding over dinners given to the City Fathers or senior members of the University. When Bruce remarked in a letter to the Queen on the 'poignant contrast between the portly grey-haired guests and the faintly epicene beauty of their adolescent host,' she promptly ordered her son to part his hair in a less 'girlish and effeminate way.'

In October 1859 the Prince of Wales went up to Oxford, which the Queen described as 'wet and muggy' and 'very odious.' In theory, he was an undergraduate of Christ Church, but, in fact, resided at Frewin Hall, a house off the Cornmarket, with his Governor, now promoted to General, and Major Teesdale. The Dean of Christ Church, Henry Liddell, argued that it would be better for the Prince to live in the College with friends of his own age. But Prince Albert, carefully sheltering his son from the advantages Oxford offered, insisted on keeping him apart so that Bruce could choose his associates. This was no capricious decree but a matter of principle, reached 'after anxious reflection and much communication with the different Ministers of the day, who look, as we do, upon the Prince's life as a *public matter* not unconnected with the present and prospective welfare of the nation and the state.'

The Prince of Wales hated being forced to live at Frewin. In later years he often said it had been a mistake to oblige him to do so. 'The real choice lay between a regular Collegiate life and not going to the University at all.' Within a month, the Prince Consort paid a visit to Oxford to see how things were going. What he found made him 'terribly anxious for the future.' Bertie was spending most of his time enjoying himself. Bruce was instantly instructed to refuse invitations. 'We cannot afford,' he was told, 'to lose whole days out of the week for amusements, or to trench upon the hours of study by social calls . . . The only use of Oxford is that it is a place for *study*, a refuge from the world and its claims.'

Despite everything that was done to ensure that the Prince was surrounded by earnest and scholarly persons, he sought the acquaintance of precisely that 'slang' set his parents most deplored. So far from regarding Oxford as 'a refuge from the world,' his new friends devoted their time to riotous living, breaking everything in sight including the Ten Commandments. Amongst such choice spirits were Harry Hastings, the 'Wicked Marquis,' Sir Frederick Johnstone, and Lord Chaplin, 'the Magnifico.' Their style of living was utterly reprehensible. Hastings, for example, breakfasted on mackerel fried in gin, caviare on toast and a bottle of claret. Chaplin kept four hunters, his own pack of hounds, and often appeared in the Cathedral with hunting boots visible beneath his surplice.

Because he had been protected so assiduously from just such people, the Prince found them irresistibly attractive. Oxford, to the Queen, was 'that old monkish place, which I have a horror of,' but it was the saintly Dr Pusey, rather than the 'Wicked Marquis,' who inspired her repugnance. Prince Albert soon enough sensed that Bertie's mind was not on his books, and wrote to Vicky from Windsor complaining that he had never in his life 'met such a thorough and cunning lazybones. Since he has been here he has not read a single line . . . it does grieve me when it is my own son and when one considers he might be called upon at any moment to take over the reins of government.' But Dean Liddell, whose daughter Alice was soon to be portrayed in Wonderland by his colleague Charles Dodgson, formed a more favourable impression of his pupil, describing him as the 'nicest fellow possible, so simple, naïve, ingenuous, and modest, and moreover with extremely good wits; possessing also the Royal faculty of never forgetting a face.'

In the Long Vacation of 1860 the Prince of Wales undertook a royal tour of his own. During the war in the Crimea, the Canadians, who had levied a regiment to fight under Lord Raglan, invited the Queen to visit their country. Although they were told it would be undesirable to expose Her Majesty to the risks of the voyage and the fatigue of travelling across Canada, they were consoled by a promise that, when the Prince of Wales was old enough to do so, he would be happy to accept such an invitation. In fulfilment of this undertaking, it was arranged that the Prince would open the railway bridge spanning the St Lawrence at Montreal, lay the foundation stone of the Federal Parliament Building at Ottawa, and see as many places in the country as time would permit. When news of this visit reached Washington, the President, James Buchanan, suggested that the Prince might extend his tour to the United States. The Queen agreed that he should do so, provided it was understood that the moment he left British soil he would travel incognito. It was therefore as Lord Renfrew, the humblest of his subsidiary titles, that the illustrious visitor was welcomed in America.

The royal party, which set sail from Plymouth on 10 July in HMS *Hero*, consisted, amongst others, of General Bruce, Major Teesdale, and the Colonial Secretary, the Duke of Newcastle. This austere and melancholy figure, whose wife abandoned him to run off with a Belgian courier, had been bitterly attacked when he was Secretary of State for War for the deficiencies of the Army in the Crimea. While His Grace contributed little to the exuberance of the occasion, the mere fact of his presence lent it political weight.

The Prince's tour was triumphantly successful. Wherever he went there was a fever of excitement and he won all hearts. His charm, his youth, his gaiety, his unaffected ways, were irresistible. Even the rough fishermen of Newfoundland, temperamentally unused to the melting mood, went 'wild about him.' The Duke of Newcastle sent the Queen glowing reports of their progress. Future years, he claimed, would 'demonstrate the good that had been done. The attachment to the Crown of England has been greatly cemented, and other nations have learned how useless it will be in case of war to tamper with the allegiance of the North American provinces.'

Prince Albert could hardly believe that his backward boy could inspire such loyalty and enthusiasm, for he regarded Bertie's social gifts more as an obstacle to study than a way to win hearts. At first, he was incredulous and told Stockmar sardonically: 'From Canada we have the best possible accounts. Bertie is generally pronounced "the most perfect production of nature".' But then, as reports from all quarters confirmed the astonishing tidings, he seized on a sentence in one of Bruce's letters. 'HRH acquitted himself admirably and seems pleased with everything, himself included.' Success was evidently going to the boy's head. So the Prince Consort wrote his son a disagreeable letter warning him not to interpret the warmth of his welcome as a tribute to himself, but rather to see in it a demonstration of loyalty to the Queen. When Bertie succeeded, his parents claimed the credit, but when he failed, the fault was his alone.

The Prince's reception in the United States was even more tumultuous. As they owed their existence to their Declaration of Independence from British rule, Lord Renfrew's triumph could hardly be explained in terms of loyalty to the Crown. Indeed, he became so popular in the Republic that it was said he would be fortunate to escape nomination for President. When the 'Royal Youth' reached New York, according to one reporter, he received 'an ovation such as has seldom been offered to any monarch in ancient or modern times. It was not a reception. It was the grand impressive welcome of a mighty people.' The Duke of Newcastle was hardly less enthusiastic in describing 'the most wonderful and gratifying success of the visit to the United States.' The Duke had 'certainly never ventured to hope for anything approaching the scene which occurred here three days ago – such a scene as probably was never witnessed before – the enthusiasm of much more than half a million people, worked up almost to madness.'

On 12 October, the citizens of New York held a great Ball in the Academy of Music on East Fourteenth Street, to show their 'regard and affection' for the Prince. They intended it to be the most splendid entertainment in the history of their City. As it turned out, it was not quite the success they had wished.

The Prince told the Queen: 'Three thousand people were invited and five thousand came, which of course was not an improvement.' Newcastle confirmed that things were not 'well managed,' and noted that HRH 'was somewhat persecuted by attentions not in strict accordance with good breeding.' Two people who failed to get tickets committed suicide: presumably they were too punctilious to join the other two thousand gate-crashers. The Chairman of the Committee organizing the Ball was besieged in his office, and one young lady flung herself on the floor at his feet begging to be invited.

After most of the guests had arrived, a procession was formed, like the animals going into the Ark, to be presented to the Prince by Mr Hamilton Fish. Some fifty couples had filed past when there was a sound of cracking and part of the floor gave way. Despite the sudden disappearance of several guests, the Prince remained calm. During supper, an army of workmen hastily repaired the damage. Just as they finished, it was discovered that a carpenter had been nailed under the boards.

The Prince's return journey took twenty-six days owing to mountainous seas and storms. While the Queen had visions of *Hero* sinking with all hands, Prince Albert counted the days Bertie was missing at Oxford. When the traveller finally reached Windsor, he was well received, if not quite so deliriously as in the New World. The Queen noted that he had a great deal to say for himself, as well he might, having just made history. But, for once, she felt proud of him, and told Vicky 'He was immensely popular everywhere and really deserved the highest praise, which should be given him all the more as he was never spared any reproof.' She was particularly delighted with a letter from President Buchanan, which spoke of Bertie's 'noble and manly bearing,' and assured her that 'his conduct throughout had been such as became his age and station.'

Bertie's exhilarating journey in the New World encouraged his self-confidence. Unsparing criticism and disparagement had naturally taken their toll, but now, for the first time in his life, he discovered that the world held him in esteem, and that he possessed in generous measure precisely those qualities which royal duties demand. Having been fêted from Newfoundland to Mount Vernon, the restraints of Frewin Hall seemed intolerable. Even his Governor felt compelled to tell Prince Albert that 'the light of publicity in which the Prince had lately lived could not be suddenly extinguished and that the continuance of schoolboy discipline was out of keeping with the growth of circumstance.'

In January 1861 the Prince was sent to Cambridge, where his father decreed he was to live at Madingley Hall, four miles outside the city. Three times a week the Prince listened to Charles Kingsley

Albert Edward, Prince
of Wales, 1843. *Sir
William Ross*

Queen Victoria with
Victoria, Princess
Royal, and Albert
Edward, Prince of
Wales, 1842. *Sir
Edwin Landseer*

The Prince of Wales, 1846. *Sir William Ross*

The Prince of Wales and Prince Alfred, 1849. *Winterhalter*

The reception of Louis Philippe at Windsor
Castle, October 1844. *Winterhalter*.

The Royal Family, 1846. *Winterhalter*.

The Prince of Wales,
1852. *Winterhalter.*

F. W. Gibbs, the
Prince's tutor.

The Royal Family at Osborne, May, 1857.
Left to right : Princess Alice, Prince Arthur, Prince Albert,
Prince of Wales, Prince Leopold, Princess Louise, Queen
Victoria holding Princess Beatrice, Prince Alfred, Princess
Royal, Princess Helena.

Visit to the Invalides, August 1855. *E. M. Ward*.

A hospital visit to soldiers wounded in the Crimea, 1856.

Salmon leistering, 1854. *Haag*. John Macdonald with the Prince of Wales and Prince Alfred.

holding forth in his Drawing Room to a privileged audience of some dozen undergraduates. His lectures began with the reign of William III and ended with George IV. They ranged over a variety of themes: Divine Right, the National Debt, the Growth of the Empire, and the French Revolution. In common with all who heard them, the Prince was fascinated, by both what was said and the lecturer himself, for Kingsley was a man of many parts: Novelist, Controversialist, Christian Socialist. He loved a fight, and his robust and combative Protestantism, in which the emphasis was on protesting, earned him royal approval. The Queen told Vicky that Bertie was 'reading with Kingsley' and had 'taken to him very much.' Kingsley was equally fond of his royal pupil. His daughter once told the Prince that 'next to his own children I can truly say there was no human being my father loved as he did you.'

The Prince made more friends at Cambridge than at Oxford, partly because Bruce allowed him more freedom, and partly because of his growing self-assurance. Chief amongst them were Charles Carrington, whom he had first encountered amongst those reluctant Etonians ordered up to Windsor, and Nathaniel Rothschild, whose vast fortune was not the least attractive thing about him.

The Queen never really accustomed herself to the idea that her son was no longer a child. Even when he was nearly twenty, she reprimanded him as if he were half that age. For example, she wrote him a letter to Madingley in which she complained of his 'manner of sitting.' Apparently he had 'got into a habit of sitting quite bent, on one side, or lolling on the table,' and leaning back as if he was eating in his 'own room after a great fatigue. This dear child will NOT do for any person in your position. When I look round at dear Uncle, Papa, Philip, Louis and indeed any of your relations or of our visitors, I never recall seeing anything of the sort, and I feel quite pained at what has the effect of ill breeding or nonchalance.' The Prince dutifully replied that he was 'always very thankful' to receive any advice from his dear Mama, that 'when one is not thinking, habits grow upon one unintentionally,' and that now he had been made aware of his bad manners, he would endeavour to improve them.

Only on rare occasions did he show a trace of resentment. Once, it was reported to the General at Madingley that the Prince was nowhere to be found. Fearing he might surreptitiously have taken a train for London, warning telegrams were sent to Buckingham Palace announcing the prisoner's escape. When HRH stepped on to the platform, he was greeted by the stationmaster and a royal carriage. He is reputed to have told the coachman to drive him to Exeter Hall: a meeting-place for teetotallers, Sabbatarians and suchlike righteous persons.

For forty years, until he succeeded to the throne, the Prince of Wales sought useful employment, but despite his 'great wish to serve in the Army,' his mother 'said he could not.' Her refusal owed much to General Bruce having warned her of 'the temptations and unprofitable companionship' that beset young officers. In 1861, she so far relented as to permit him to spend ten weeks in the Curragh Camp, near Dublin, during his Long Vacation. Bertie was to be attached to a Battalion of the Grenadier Guards, in which he was to 'learn the duties of every grade from ensign upwards.' It was hoped that by the end of his visit he would be competent 'to command a battalion' and 'manoeuvre a Brigade in the field.' Naturally, it would never do for him to live in the Mess with his young brother officers, 'having regard to his position both as a Prince of the Blood and Heir to the Throne.' Twice a week he was to give dinner parties for senior officers and twice dine in his own Regimental Mess. Once, he might accept invitations to be guest of honour of other regiments, and on Sunday and one other evening, he was 'to read and dine quietly in his own rooms.'

Hard as he tried, the Prince of Wales proved unable to master in a couple of months what most officers took twenty years to learn. When, at the end of August, the Queen visited the Curragh, she hoped to see her son marching at the head of a battalion. But General Bruce regretfully had to report that HRH would only be able to perform the duties of a subaltern. Colonel Percy, the Prince's Commanding officer, told him: 'You are too imperfect in your drill, Sir. Your word of command is indistinct. I will *not* try to make the Duke of Cambridge think you are more advanced than you are.' Colonel Percy's conduct won him the Queen's commendation, for she 'thanked him for treating Bertie as he did, just as any other officer.'

Prince Albert was exceedingly grieved, and confessed to the Viceroy, Lord Carlisle, that he doubted whether the boy took soldiering seriously. Indeed, he went further, and spoke at some length about 'the idle tendencies of English youth,' and the lamentable way in which 'officers of the Army avoided professional topics on the ground they were "shop".'

General Bruce's misgivings about the corrupting influence of military life were fully justified when the Prince formed a most disreputable liaison with a vivacious young actress named Nellie Clifden. She was already a favourite at the Curragh and knew her way round the camp in the dark. Some of the Prince's fellow officers were intrigued by his sheltered life and saw the precautions designed to protect him as a challenge. Most of them thought nothing of keeping a mistress or two in their baggage, so it was not very surprising that after a wild evening in the mess, when General Bruce had retired for the night, Miss Clifden was shown into HRH's quarters. Admittedly, the Prince took the opportunity offered, but there is nothing to suggest it was a serious affair. The thing had been intended as a practical joke and he accepted it as such. But, when rumours of these happenings reached Windsor, Her Majesty was not amused, and what started in fun ended in tragedy.

The story, which caused such dreadful consternation at Court, was brought to the Prince Consort's notice when Lord Torrington came into waiting, three days after Bertie's twentieth birthday. His lordship, a descendant of Admiral Byng and a notorious gossip, could hardly contain himself with excitement. When it came to purveying news, he was virtually a professional. Indeed, he facetiously signed his letters to the editor of The Times: 'Your Windsor Special.'

At first, the Prince Consort refused to credit the rumour, but searching enquiry soon confirmed its truth. His disgust was such that one can only suppose the balance of his mind was disturbed, for the first symptoms of his fatal illness were just beginning to show. Had Bertie butchered his brothers and sisters and scattered their remains in the lake at Buckingham Palace he could hardly have reacted more vehemently.

The Queen, some years later, suggested to Vicky that Papa 'was too perfect for this world; it was impossible for him ever to have been really happy here. I saw how dreadfully the wickedness of this world grieved his pure, noble, heavenly spirit.' On the first anniversary of his hearing the news of Bertie's 'fall', his widow recalled 'the agony and misery of this day last year when beloved Papa first heard of poor Bertie's misfortune! Oh! that face, that heavenly face of woe and sorrow which was so dreadful to witness! Let Bertie not forget it! He was forgiven thank God! or I could never have looked at him again.' The following 12 November, the Queen reminded Uncle Leopold that she was writing on the day when the news arrived 'which broke my Angel's heart.'

Even in the nineteenth century, morally the most sensitive age

in our history, a good many English fathers could have heard of the
Curragh scrape without being greatly disturbed. But to the Prince
Consort it represented a disastrous defeat. For most of his married
life he had toiled unceasingly to bring up his son to live as he had:

> 'Wearing the white flower of a blameless life,
> Before a thousand peering littlenesses,
> In that fierce light that beats upon a throne,
> and blackens every blot.'

There was nothing he had left undone to shelter Bertie from temptation, to resist his dissolute Hanoverian heritage, to make him Bishop
Wilberforce's 'most perfect man.' And now, after endless discussions,
consultations, correspondence, memoranda, conferences and reports,
after his own unremitting efforts, not to mention those of Stockmar,
Birch, Gibbs and Bruce, he had met his match in a common harlot.

There are several possible explanations for the Prince Consort's
excessive display of grief and pain. Many a noble family had seen
its ancestral acres ravaged by the dissipations of an heir. Prudence
combined with morality to frown on attachments which could spell
ruin. Moreover, the Prince Consort was especially revolted by sins
of the flesh. During his youth in Coburg, he acquired a lasting distaste for debauchery from seeing the havoc it wrought in his own
family. Finally, he was terrified that the monarchy might suffer.
If royalty was to survive in a revolutionary age it must be seen to be
irreproachable. He and the Queen had established a Court of
conspicuous propriety, and now their son threatened to fritter away
the respect they had earned by twenty years' hard labour.

On 16 November, Prince Albert wrote his son a frenzied letter
about his misconduct at the Curragh. Had his 'own suffering not
been apparent in every line,' it would have constituted a 'piece of
gross and deliberate cruelty.' He began by saying that he wrote
with a heavy heart upon a subject which had caused him 'the greatest
pain I have yet felt in this life.' Bertie, he said, had become the talk
of the town. As for Nellie Clifden she was already being nicknamed
'the Princess of Wales.' In all probability she would have a child,
and, whoever the father might actually be, she would naturally
claim it was conceived at the Curragh. 'If you were to try to deny
it, she can drag you into a Court of Law to force you to own it and
there, with you in the witness box, she will be able to give before a
greedy multitude digusting details of your profligacy . . . Oh horrible
prospect, which this person has in her power, any day to realize!

and to break your poor parents' hearts.' Unlike Charles II, the Prince Consort would willingly have let poor Nellie starve.

The Prince of Wales was dismayed by his father's distress, and wrote him a contrite letter. Everybody felt wretched: Bertie because he had given his parents further reason to be disappointed in him, Prince Albert because he had signally failed to keep his son out of scrapes, and the Queen because her husband seemed worried to death. The Prince Consort spent sleepless nights, distracted by sorrow. He had lost faith in his eldest son and his interest in life. 'Albert has such nights since that great worry,' wrote the Queen, that 'it makes him weak and tired.'

On 25 November, Prince Albert decided to see the Prince of Wales and ordered a special train to Cambridge. He was 'greatly out of sorts,' having caught a chill three days before when he inspected the new Staff College buildings at Sandhurst in drenching rain. Father and son took a walk together down the country lanes near Madingley, during which the boy was forgiven with the proviso that the Almighty would probably prove less accommodating. When Prince Albert pulled into Windsor station an hour and a half after midnight, he felt weak and weary and ached all over. The Queen, in retrospect, saw this expedition as further proof that Bertie had broken Papa's heart. It was one of her less amiable idiosyncrasies that she preferred to blame her husband's death on her son than find fault with the plumbing at Windsor. Nobody seems to have told her that typhoid is caused by germs, not grief.

The Prince Consort was last seen in public on 20 November when he watched the Queen inspecting two hundred Eton volunteers. She thought they 'looked so nice' eating an 'ample' luncheon in the Orangery. But poor Albert looked terrible and felt as if cold water was being poured down his back. Although it was quite a warm day for November, he wore a fur coat turned up at the collar as if he were reviewing Cossacks in Siberia. The last entry in his diary referred to the Review. It ran: 'Ought not to go, but must.' The flame of duty burned to the end.

It was not until 7 December that Sir James Clark and his colleagues saw the rash which confirmed their suspicion that they were treating typhoid. They appeared to feel no apprehension. One of the doctors told the Queen the day her husband died: 'I never despair with fever, my own son was left for dead and recovered.' It is difficult to decide how far this misplaced optimism proceeded from policy or fecklessness. Certainly there were cogent reasons for disguising the gravity of the Prince's illness. He had persuaded himself he would never survive typhoid should he catch it, and kept saying 'it was very well *he* had *no* fever as he should not recover!' It was equally necessary to reassure the Queen. When her mother had died earlier in the year, she had broken down with grief. Had she suspected the Prince was going to die, she could not have concealed her distress, and he would have seen his danger in her eyes. So 'good kind old Sir James' blandly assured her there was no cause for alarm, and even after the patient's mind began wandering, the bulletins spoke of 'a feverish cold.'

When it became known that the Prince, who was only forty-two, had succumbed to fever, the doctors were thought to be largely to blame. Sir James Clark was over seventy and was best known for his mistakes. His colleague, Sir Henry Holland, was about the same age, and his fashionable practice owed at least as much to his charm as to his skill. Possibly recognizing that they were ill-equipped to deal with their illustrious patient, they called in William Jenner to assist them. Jenner was Holme Professor of Clinical Medicine at University College, and having established the distinct identities of typhus and typhoid fever was the most experienced man available. But he was not in charge of the case, and it is difficult to believe that he could have approved of the Prince being permitted to indulge his feverish restlessness by wandering about from room to room in a dressing gown. Lord Clarendon expressed his misgivings by saying that the eminent physicians at Windsor were 'not fit to attend a sick cat,' and he told the Duchess of Manchester that 'Holland and Clark are not even average old women, and nobody who is really ill would think of sending for either of them.'

Although Jenner blamed the drains at Windsor for the Prince's death, Sir James left the Queen with the impression that 'great worry and far too hard work ' had caused her husband's illness. In particular, he specified 'excessive mental excitement on one very recent occasion.' A further piece of evidence which confirmed her belief that the Prince had been killed by worrying about the dreadful business at the Curragh was that when his mind began to wander he kept on calling for General Bruce.

The Prince of Wales was taking his final exams at Cambridge when on Friday, 13 December, he received a telegram from Princess Alice summoning him to Windsor. In so doing, she acted on her own initiative, as the Queen showed no sign of sending for him; partly because she blamed him for what had happened and partly because his appearance might worry Albert. When Bertie appeared at three the following morning, he still did not know that his father was mortally ill. Lord Granville heard that the Prince Consort never recognized his son as he stood by his bed in the Blue Room, in which George IV and William IV had died, and where now a more precious life was drawing to its close.

On the morning of 14 December, Sir James spoke of a 'decided rally,' and Dr Brown, who looked after the Royal Family at Windsor, went so far as to claim 'there is ground to hope the crisis is over.' But as the day wore on it became clear that life was ebbing. At ten forty-five that evening, surrounded by most of his family, the Prince of Wales kneeling at the foot of his bed, the end came. 'Oh yes, this is death,' said the Queen. 'I know it. I have seen this before.' Lady Augusta Bruce, and her brother, the General, who had come at the Prince's desire, watched 'in agonized silence, the passing of that lofty and noble soul. Gentler than an infant slumber it was at the last.'

For years the Queen could not bring herself to record the scene in her Journal, but, when eventually she found the courage to do so, she recalled how Albert took 'Two or three long but perfectly gentle breaths . . . the hand clasping mine and . . . *all, all,* was over . . . I stood up, kissed his dear heavenly forehead and called out in a bitter and agonizing cry "Oh! my dear Darling!" and then dropped on my knees in mute, distracted despair, unable to utter a word or shed a tear!' Her half-nephew, Ernest Leiningen, and Sir Charles Phipps, supported her from the room. The Prince of Wales, throwing himself into her arms, promised he would do everything in his power to help and comfort her. 'I am sure, my dear boy, you will,' she murmured, kissing him again and again.

With Alice supporting her, she consoled the doctors for what Lady Augusta termed their 'unsuccess', and then the household filed past vainly seeking words of comfort. 'You will not desert me?' she asked pathetically, clutching them each by the hand. 'You will all help me?'

Acting on Uncle Leopold's advice, the Queen withdrew to Osborne. Four days later, on 23 December, the Prince of Wales represented her as chief mourner at his father's funeral, held in St George's Chapel, Windsor. His distress was evident to the whole congregation as his eyes were red with weeping. When the coffin was lowered into the vault he buried his face in his hands and was so overcome with grief that the Lord Chamberlain gently led him away. But not everyone felt so wretched. Lord Orford, an eccentric Norfolk nobleman, who distrusted all foreigners, celebrated the occasion by dressing like a bookmaker.

Prince Albert was never acceptable to most English gentlemen, who regarded him as excessively formal and possessed of the strangest ideas about sport: particularly shooting and stalking. The Duke of Beaufort, who boasted descent from Edward III, thought it beneath the dignity of the Somersets for a son of his to become Lord-in-waiting to a mere Prince of Saxe-Coburg. When Prince Albert ruined his gloves while laying a foundation stone at Eton, the young gentlemen so far forgot themselves as to show signs of delight. 'Truth to say,' wrote Lord Henry Lennox, 'the "swells" as a class, did not much like the Prince.'

During the autumn of 1861, Prince Albert had decided that the Prince of Wales should tour the Near East after leaving Cambridge. Amongst others, he consulted Arthur Stanley, who had written a book about his travels in Palestine. Within three weeks of his death, the Queen told General Bruce 'that she alone would decide, in conformity with her husband's counsels, to which none but herself had been admitted, the future of the Prince of Wales.' She had, so she told him, 'had many conversations with her beloved angel and she feels that *she* knows exactly what he wished. This being the case the Queen must decide what she thinks the best.' Later the same year, she told the general: 'The great object we must all have in view, and it was *the* only one our beloved Prince and Master, our Guide and Counsellor, had in view, is the *real* good of the Royal Princes.' In deciding precisely where their best interests lay, she felt 'that a higher power and a purer spirit than her own guides and strengthens her when most she needs it.' It was a very dangerous thing for her to feel, as it made it possible for her to claim that she was dutifully carrying out her Angel's wishes, when, in reality, she was merely indulging her selfish whims.

The Queen vowed over the 'sacred remains' that her every thought and action would henceforth be dedicated to, and directed by, her 'adored Angelic Husband.' She told Vicky's mother-in-law, Queen Augusta, that she now had nothing to look forward to, except 'future reunion with Him; my only comfort is in the constant spiritual communion with Him and in the endeavour to fulfil His wishes. To work for Him, to honour His memory more and more, to have memorials raised in His name – here is my only consolation.'

The day after the Prince Consort's funeral, the Queen informed Uncle Leopold, with a note of menace, of her '*firm* resolve, my *irre*-

vocable decision, viz. that *his* wishes – *his* plans – about everything, *his* views about *every*thing, are to be *my law*! And *no human power* will make me swerve from *what he* decided and wished . . . I apply this particularly as regards our children – Bertie, etc. – for whose future he had traced everything *so* carefully.' When Vicky suggested that Bertie might pay her a short visit on his return from the Holy Land she was told it would be '*impossible*', because 'in dear Papa's original plan, it was intended he should come home through Paris, stopping only a day.'

Because the Queen repeatedly insisted upon her determination to carry out Albert's wishes in meticulous detail, some writers have taken her protestations at face value. Certainly she never ceased to pay lip-service to the notion, particularly when the Prince Consort's wishes coincided with her own: and she was not without ingenuity in ensuring that they did. But increasingly often, without admitting it to herself and probably without realizing what she was doing, she discarded principles which no longer served her purpose. Albert had always insisted she should develop outside interests. In fact, she withdrew into monastic seclusion. Albert told her to look to the future, but after his death she lived in the past, substituting anniversaries for engagements. Albert considered Disraeli an impostor, but the Queen trusted him implicitly. Albert never tired of insisting that the Sovereign must be impartial, but in her hatred of Gladstone the Queen became vehemently partisan. Soon Albert's wishes became barely distinguishable from those of Her Majesty, but the distinction was, nevertheless, preserved, for to dispute His judgements was sacrilege.

The Prince of Wales was over twenty when his father died, and consequently expected to be given some responsibilities of his own, or, at least, to be permitted a greater freedom to live his own life. Neither expectation was fulfilled. The Queen's loyalty to Albert's memory convinced her that it was her duty, without any assistance, to complete his work: a decision made easier by the fact that she never fully acknowledged that her eldest son had grown up. In assessing him in his maturity, her judgement was hopelessly prejudiced by recollections of the indiscretions of his youth.

The Queen's matriarchal authority was enhanced by the deference owed to her as Sovereign, an advantage she exploited to the utmost. She never hesitated to remind her children of the triple allegiance they owed her as monarch, mother and head of the Family.

Lord Clarendon, after discussions with King Leopold and

Palmerston, and having visited the Queen at Osborne early in 1862, concluded that it would be best for the Prince of Wales to travel, 'for things would only go from bad to worse if he remained at home.' Like Palmerston, he found the Queen's 'unconquerable aversion' to her eldest son distressing. King Leopold told Clarendon 'that the relations between the Queen and the Prince of Wales are as bad as ever, if not worse, and that all his efforts to improve them had been fruitless – it seems to be an antipathy that is incurable but quite unjustifiable – it is entirely her fault as the poor boy asks nothing better than to devote himself to comforting his Mother and with that object would be delighted to give up his foreign expedition but she would not hear of it and seems only to wish to get rid of him.'

A month after the Prince Consort died, the Queen told Vicky to make sure that Fritz put Stockmar 'in possession of the sad truth' that the affair at the Curragh was what made 'beloved Papa so ill – for there must be no illusion about that – it was so; he was struck down – and I never can see B. – without a shudder! Oh! that bitterness – oh! that cross!' Vicky wrote back defending her brother as best she could, and begged the Queen to 'be kind, pitying, forgiving and loving to the poor boy for Papa's sake . . . He has no father now – oh! let him feel how great, generous and forgiving a mother's heart can be! . . .'

The Queen admitted that all Vicky said was 'right and affectionate.' But nonetheless she returned to the theme that Bertie's 'fall' had killed Papa. 'If you had seen what I saw, if you had seen Fritz struck down, day by day get worse and finally die, I doubt if you could bear the sight of the one who was the cause . . . '

As the Queen came to terms with her affliction – and the process was slow and bitter – her first anguished reactions gave place to more rational judgements. At the end of January 1862, she told Palmerston that Bertie 'was a very good and dutiful son,' although she also described him as 'the difficulty of the moment.' Just how admirable a son he was is shown by the generous way in which he accepted his mother's harshest strictures. Regardless of ill-treatment, he remained constant, loyal and magnanimous. Gradually the Queen forgot the unjustified things she had said when half out of her mind with despair. Soon after Bertie's forty-second birthday, she wrote in the secret pages of her Journal, 'he is always a very good son to me.' In 1887, after describing a 'most pleasant visit' to Balmoral, she added: 'He had not stayed alone with me, excepting for a couple of days in May in '68, at Balmoral, since he married! He is so kind and affectionate that it is a pleasure to be a little quietly together.'

In January 1862, the Queen drew up her final plans for the Prince of Wales's Eastern journey. He was to preserve the 'very strictest incognito,' and avoid all society, save that of royalty, or persons 'whose superior character and attainments' rendered their company 'interesting and improving.' Between visits to ancient monuments, he was to devote his time to serious reading. The Queen persuaded Dr Arthur Stanley to take charge of the expedition, despite his evident misgivings. She thought him 'quite charming and the most unclerical, and yet religious clergyman I ever talked to.' During their conversation she told him that the Prince Consort had said he was the only man in Oxford he could trust with the task. Stanley's association with the royal family was not without reward, for it led to his marriage to Lady Augusta Bruce, the General's sister, and the Deanery of Westminster. His reluctance to accept the Queen's offer derived from the unfavourable portrait she drew of her son.

On 6 February 1862, the Prince set out on his journey. Both he and the Queen were deeply moved when they parted. During the next five months, besides the Holy Land itself, the Prince visited Vienna, where he was entertained by the Emperor, Francis Joseph, Venice, Trieste, Cairo, sailed up the Nile to the First Cataract, landed at Jaffa, rode to Jerusalem, spent Good Friday at Nazareth, and returned home by way of Constantinople, Athens and Paris.

Much as he enjoyed shooting crocodiles, quails and vultures, examining antiquities was less to his taste, and Stanley found it almost impossible to produce 'any impression on a mind with no previous knowledge or interest to be awakened.' But again and again he reminded himself 'how vexed and tired I should be at being dragged about to see manufactories – in which, nevertheless, many people take as profound and rational interest as I do in historical scenes.' After climbing the Great Pyramid, the travellers went on to explore the tombs, but the Prince preferred to remain sitting in front of his tent, smoking, and reading *East Lynne*.

On one occasion the Prince came near to revolt when General Bruce said something about visiting the ruins at Thebes. 'Why should we go and see the tumbledown old Temple?' he asked. 'There will be nothing to see when we get there.' After a momentary silence, the General replied: 'Well sir, you need not go – but some of us wish to go and shall go.' In the event, HRH joined the others, and as Stanley put it, 'treated the pillars, and the sculptures, I will not say with interest or admiration, but with the most well-bred courtesy, as if he were paying a visit to a high personage.' On reaching Athens, Stanley noted with resignation that his pupil showed more interest in HMS *Marlborough* than in the Parthenon.

On first acquaintance, Stanley regarded the Prince as frivolous and pleasure-loving, but later admitted, 'There is more in him than I thought.' He admired, even envied, the boy's astounding memory for people and places, and found him a good-natured and considerate companion. However bored he might be, he never showed it openly. 'Even in seeing antiquities, he will, from strangers, bear the longest expositions without appearance of fatigue . . . I almost doubt whether I should have borne this trial as patiently.'

General Bruce, having contracted a fever in the Holy Land, collapsed at Athens and had to be left there to recover. When 'Lord Renfrew' arrived at Fontainebleau, as the guest of the Emperor, he never enjoyed himself more, partly because he had no Governor to restrain him, and partly because he was now of an age to savour the more sophisticated attractions of the imperial Court.

The Queen had only consented to this last visit because it had been part of 'dear Papa's original plan,' but she ensured that his stay in 'Sodom and Gomorrah' was as brief as possible. Although she herself had been intoxicated by Paris in 1855, her disillusion came four years later, 'when in '59, in spite of all our endeavours and warnings,' the Emperor 'made war in Italy against Austria, and deceived us.' Writing to Vicky after Prussia's victories in 1870, with that superior wisdom hindsight lends, the Queen regretted that the Prince of Wales had been 'carried away by that horrid Paris (beautiful though you may think it) and that frivolous and immoral Court,' which, she claimed, had done frightful harm to English society, and was very bad for Bertie, as 'Papa knew and saw.' Moreover, 'the fearful extravagance and luxury,' not to mention 'the utter want of seriousness and principle in everything,' all showed a 'rottenness which was sure to crumble and fall.'

Whatever the Prince learned from his journey, and Stanley doubted whether it was much, his absence made the Queen's heart grow fonder. Towards the end of May, she wrote him such an affectionate letter that he beamed with pleasure as he read it. On 14 June 1862 they were reunited at Windsor. 'Bertie arrived at half past five, looking extremely well. I was much upset at seeing him, and feeling his beloved father was not there to welcome him back. He would have been so pleased to see him so improved, and looking so bright and healthy. Dear Bertie was most affectionate, and the tears came into his eyes when he saw me.' Even after a fortnight together, she still thought him 'greatly improved.' Not only was he 'most affectionate, dutiful and amiable,' but resolved 'to do whatever his Mother and Father wished.' She told Vicky she was getting on 'very well' with her prodigal son, whom she began calling 'her dear darling boy.'

Within less than a fortnight of his return from Athens, General Bruce died. Such was the generosity of the Prince's nature that it appeared to the Queen that he felt 'the loss of his dear General very deeply.' Certainly, he was quick to forgive injuries. Moreover, his Governor had become such a part of his life that he could not but feel his loss, if only in the sense that one misses an aching tooth. But even death has its consolations, and the Prince ventured to suggest that, as the 'beloved and valued General' was irreplaceable, no attempt should be made to find a successor.

The Queen, however, had no intention of dispensing with a watchdog, and told Bertie that both she and the Prime Minister, Lord Palmerston, were agreed that it would '*not* do to leave you without a gentleman in *that* position.' Although he was 'now too near twentyone to have a Governor freshly appointed,' he, nevertheless, required 'a species of mentor, for no young Prince can be without a person of experience, and of a certain age, who would keep him from doing what was hurtful to him, or unfit for his position, and who would be responsible to me to a great extent for what took place.' The person chosen to fulfil this exacting role was General Sir William Knollys, who for fifteen years served the Prince as 'Comptroller and Treasurer.' In recommending him to her son, the Queen said she knew 'of *no* other person so well fitted as General Knollys, for *he* possessed beloved Papa's great esteem and confidence; he is very amiable . . . has great experience of the world and singular tact and temper . . . He is, besides, very fond of *young people.*'

Despite his initial reservations, the Prince of Wales got on famously with General Knollys, who proved much more accommodating than his predecessor, and who, unlike General Bruce, regarded his first loyalty as belonging to the Prince, not the Queen. Sir William had been educated at Harrow, commissioned in the Scots Guards, and had fought in the Peninsular War when he was sixteen. In 1830 he married Elizabeth St. Aubyn. Her father, Sir John, postponed his own wedding until he had fifteen children to support him at the ceremony. In 1850 Sir William became Colonel of his Regiment, and was appointed to command the recently formed camp at Aldershot in the middle of the Crimean War. It was a post which involved him in constant and confidential correspondence with Prince Albert, who took almost too lively an interest in Army training. The Prince, impatient of military obstruction, which of all the martial arts had been brought nearest to perfection, urged the General, even if it sounded 'like flat mutiny,' to act on his own responsibility. 'I would not care a – – – for Commander-in-Chief or Secretary for War – but I would do, and *make* them do, what was right.'

The Prince celebrated his twenty-first birthday on board the Royal Yacht *Osborne*, anchored in the Bay of Naples. After dinner that evening, General Knollys made a happy speech proposing his health. Vicky, who was sitting next to her brother, kissed him affectionately, and rockets sent up by the *Osborne* announced to British ships in the Bay that the toast had been proposed. Immediately, the sailors on the men-of-war began to cheer, and such a blaze of fireworks lit the sky that it seemed as if Vesuvius was erupting. Next year, the Prince was to marry and set up on his own. But the mere fact of achieving his majority did not suffice to liberate him. His widowed mother, from the seclusion of Windsor or Balmoral, continued to order his life as if he were still a schoolboy. Not until he was proclaimed King of England did he become his own master.

The Prince's Marriage

When the Prince of Wales was only sixteen, the Queen was already wondering whom he could marry. She told Vicky, 'We must look out for princesses for Bertie . . . Oh! if you would find us one!' She was not alone in contemplating the problem. King Leopold and Baron Stockmar were also giving their minds to it, and in July 1858 *The Times* printed a list of possible brides. It was not very long, because in all Europe there were only seven young ladies of the blood royal, the Protestant faith and his own age. By the following autumn the Queen and Prince Consort were seriously seeking a wife for their son in the hope that 'it would keep him out of mischief.' When Stockmar later told Prince Albert he had no right to negotiate an 'arranged' marriage – his real objection being that he had not arranged it himself – the Prince replied that nearly everybody told him: 'You must marry the Prince of Wales soon, unless you do so he is lost.'

During the summer of 1860, Vicky sat under the shade of a chestnut tree, studying the *Almanach de Gotha*, in the hope of finding the right bride for her brother. But 'princesses do not spring up like mushrooms out of the earth or grow upon trees.' There seemed an insuperable objection to every one of them, particularly as the Queen would settle for nothing less than perfection. Where was a daughter-in-law to be found who was beautiful, clever, resolute, quiet, dutiful and virtuous, besides being Lutheran, German and royal?

There was Marie of Altenburg, but she dressed shockingly and had a most disagreeable mother. There was Augusta of Meiningen, who was 'a very nice, clever good girl,' but she was still 'quite a child.' There were the Weimars, pleasant girls but delicate and not pretty. There was the Princess of Sweden, but she was decidedly too young, just as Princess Hilda of Dessau was too old. Princess Marie of the Netherlands was 'clever and ladylike, but too plain and not strong,' whereas poor Princess Alexandrine of Prussia was '*not* clever or pretty.' Anna of Hesse, Vicky thought, was probably the most promising, possessing the 'fewest disadvantages,' but, nevertheless, she had 'an incipient twitching in her eyes,' her teeth were 'nearly all spoilt,' she dressed terribly, had a gruff, abrupt way of speaking, and was given to frowning. Marie of Hohenzollern-Sigmaringen was '*quite lovely*' but regrettably a Roman Catholic. And then there was Elizabeth of Wied, who later became Queen of Rumania and wrote under the name 'Carmen Silva.' Stockmar alleged she was rather dowdy, but Vicky's accounts were more favourable. Admittedly, the Princess was neither 'distinguée' nor 'graceful,' but she possessed a 'fresh complexion and nice white teeth . . . She is what you would call a strong healthy looking girl.' But she was altogether too boisterous and uninhibited. 'She says such things sometimes that I do not know which way to look.'

There was one other possible bride for Bertie: Prince Christian of Denmark's daughter, Alexandra. In December 1860, Vicky told her mother, 'I have seen several people who have seen her of late – and who give such accounts of her beauty, her charms, her amiability, her frank natural manner and many excellent qualities. I thought it right to tell you all this in Bertie's interest, though I as a Prussian cannot wish Bertie should ever marry her.' But the Queen would not hear of it. 'The beauty of Denmark,' she wrote back, 'is much against our wishes,' but added regretfully, 'What a pity she is who she is.'

There were three serious drawbacks to a Danish match. First, the Queen wanted her son to marry a German princess. Second, she was anxious not to offend the King of Prussia who was pressing his claim to Schleswig-Holstein. Third, she disapproved of the Court at Copenhagen. In particular, she objected to King Frederick VII, who lived openly in sin and was seldom sober. In 1852, the Great Powers decided by the Protocol of London that if King Frederick should die without issue Prince Christian should succeed him. The two men were more distantly connected than was the Queen to the King of Hanover, or the Dukes of Saxe-Coburg. Nevertheless, she did not hesitate to blame Prince Christian for possessing such relations.

It was, however, Princess Alexandra's mother to whom the Queen objected most strongly. When Vicky met her she thought her clever and amiable and so sharp that nothing escaped her. But the Queen thought her false, odious, mischievous and intriguing. The root of the trouble was that Princess Christian belonged to the House of Hesse-Cassel, which was notorious for being high-spirited, pleasure-loving and frivolous, and upon whom Albert frowned. Had Her Majesty not been blinded by prejudice she would have seen much to admire in the Princess, who was artistic yet practical, loved music, was a strong believer in family life, and devoutly religious. Moreover, she brought up her children without pomp or fuss to be honest and self-reliant.

The Queen's Uncle, Adolphus, Duke of Cambridge, was married to Princess Augusta of Hesse, whose brother, Prince William, was Princess Christian's father. Besides their son, Prince George, the Cambridges had two daughters, Augusta and Mary, who represented, as the Queen saw it, all that was deplorable in the family. Princess Mary, in particular, roused her indignation. She was altogether immense: so large that she needed two chairs to sit on, so extravagant as to cause a flutter at Coutts, so jovial as to captivate a crowd. Indeed, the Queen once actually called Princess Christian 'a very superior woman' because she told Vicky that if Alexandra visited England she would see she avoided her Cambridge relations. 'She did not wish her,' she said, 'to have anything to do with the Duchess of Cambridge or Mary or Augusta as they cultivated acquaintances and frequented society which she would never allow her daughter to go near.' Mary's conversation 'was not fit for young girls,' and she had seen her 'flirt to that degree that she had said to Alix "If you ever become such a coquette as Mary you would get a box on the ears." '

Princess Christian's grandfather, Prince Frederick, left his descendants Rumpenheim, a castle on the banks of the Main, near Frankfurt, making it a condition that it became a gathering place for the Danish, Hessian and Cambridge families. This eighteenth-century building, destroyed by incendiary bombs in the Second World War, was unpretentious and old-fashioned. When ultimately central heating was installed, the Duke of Cambridge complained of desecration. Rumpenheim reunions became something of a cult. The life was not to everyone's taste. The food was bad, the house overcrowded and the practical jokes tiresome. There was plenty of gossip, some flirtation, little culture. Despite a reputation for political conspiracy the family seldom ventured beyond matrimonial intrigue. Naturally, as Prussia began extending her frontiers, trampling on one Hesse after another, the first toast after dinner at Rumpenheim was not Prince Bismarck's health.

Even before Rumpenheim became associated with hostility to Germany, the Queen regarded its family parties as 'the *very* worst society for Bertie possible . . . The Cambridges have got hold of him more than they ought.' It was precisely such gatherings that 'my Angel said he must be kept out of.' For political, moral and social reasons, the Hesse family 'would never do.'

Apart from Vicky, Mrs Paget was the first person to press Princess Alexandra's claims on the Queen and Prince Albert. She was a grand-daughter of Field-Marshal Gneisenau, and was born Walburga, Countess of Hohenthal. She went to Berlin with Vicky in 1858 as her lady-in-waiting, and two years later married Augustus Paget, the British Minister at Copenhagen. There, she 'felt more and more certain that it would be impossible to find anywhere a Princess better suited than Princess Alix to be the wife of the Prince of Wales.' In December, 1860, she was invited to Windsor, and sitting next to the Prince Consort during dinner boldly introduced the subject of the Prince of Wales's marriage. 'I told him that Mr Paget had often seen Princess Alix and thought her the most charming, pretty and delightful young Princess it was possible to imagine. The Prince repeated all this to the Queen, who was sitting on his other side, and after dinner Her Majesty asked me to send her the photograph of the young Princess . . . and to get all the information I could.' When Alix's photograph arrived, Prince Albert looked at it and said, 'From that photograph I would marry her at once.'

In February, 1861, the Queen asked Vicky whether she had heard 'anything more about the Danish beauty.' 'I hear almost every week,' came the reply, 'but never mentioned it as I thought you did not wish to hear anything more about her.' But the Queen was beginning to change her mind, partly because of what Mrs Paget had told her, and partly from fear of the Tsar. 'It would be dreadful,' said the Crown Princess, 'if this pearl went to the horrid Russians.' Her mother agreed, and besides, whatever the drawbacks, nobody else could be found.

Vicky renewed her enquiries and reported back that a nurse, who had been ten years with Princess Christian, thought Alix 'the sweetest girl who ever lived – and full of life and spirits. She says she has always been as strong and healthy as possible and has a very good constitution. That she has never ailed anything in her life except having the measles.' But all this was merely hearsay, and Vicky resolved to see Alix for herself. So in June, 1861, she and the Crown Prince invited themselves to stay with the Grand Duke of Mecklenburg-Strelitz to meet Princess Alexandra. Unfortunately, the Grand Duchess was none other than Princess Augusta of Cambridge, the Queen's first cousin, of whom she so strongly disapproved and to whom she had no wish to be indebted.

When they finally met, Vicky was bewitched. 'I never set eyes on a sweeter creature,' she wrote from Strelitz. 'She is lovely!' But Alix was more than strikingly beautiful. 'Her voice, her walk, carriage and manner are perfect, she is one of the most ladylike and aristocratic looking people I ever saw! She is as simple and natural and unaffected as possible – and seems exceedingly well brought up . . . She does not seem the least aware of her beauty and is very unassuming . . . You may go far before you find another princess like Princess Alix – I know you and Papa would be charmed with her . . . Oh, if only she was not a Dane and not related to the Hesses I should say yes – she is the one a thousand times over . . . The more I see of her the more charming and attractive I think her.' Although the Queen knew that her daughter was 'a little inclined to be carried away,' Vicky's views were confirmed in a letter from Fritz, who described the match as 'the very worst that could happen to us,' yet joined his wife in furthering it. What with these glowing reports from Strelitz and fear of the Russians, the Queen and the Prince Consort were won over to Alix.

The time had now come for the Prince of Wales to be permitted a small part in shaping his own destiny. His parents and sister arranged that on leaving the Camp at the Curragh he would visit the Prussian Army at Coblenz, and then join Vicky at Baden, by which time the Christians and their daughter would be staying at Rumpenheim not many miles away. On 24 September 1861, a carefully-contrived meeting took place in the Cathedral of Speyer. Somehow, Bertie and Alix became detached from the rest of the party, who were being shown the frescoes by the bishop. Next day, the Prince of Wales wrote home describing his encounter with 'the young lady of whom I had heard so much; and I can now candidly say that I thought her charming and very pretty.'

Vicky provided her parents with a fuller account of all that took place. She felt sure 'that Alix has made an impression on Bertie, though in his own funny, undemonstrative way. He said to me that he had never seen a young lady who pleased him so much.' She was not in the least shy, and talked to him in 'her pretty, simple unaffected' manner. 'I never saw a girl of sixteen so forward for her age . . . I think General Bruce must have been struck with her.'

The Queen seems to have thought it remiss of her son that he failed to fall instantly in love. When she saw him at Balmoral, he was 'certainly much pleased' with what he had seen of Alix. 'But as for being in love I don't think he can be.' His mother simply could not understand it. Confronted with a girl of 'outrageous' beauty, he looked the other way. 'I own it gives me a feeling of great sadness,' wrote Vicky, 'when I think of that sweet lovely flower – young and beautiful – that even makes my heart beat when I look at her – which would make most men fire and flames – not even producing an impression enough to last from Baden to England . . . If she fails to kindle a flame – none ever will succeed in doing so.'

Prince Albert's attitude was that expressed in the Book of Common Prayer 'that such persons as have not the gift of continency' should look to Holy Matrimony for 'a remedy against sin' and 'to avoid fornication.' Admittedly, after Bertie's 'fall', it was too late to reap the full benefit of the Prayer Book's advice. Nevertheless, as Vicky wrote in January 1862: 'Marry early Bertie must; I am more convinced of that every day; he has not resisted small temptations, only launch him alone in the London society and you will see what becomes of him . . . The chances are, if he married a nice wife that he likes, she will keep him straight; and, as he is too weak to keep from sin for virtue's sake, he will only keep out of it from other motives, and surely a wife will be the strongest?'

For some unfathomable reason, Bertie was seized with a sudden 'fear of marrying and above all of having children.' So Prince Albert resorted to a favourite device. Rather than talk things over, he wrote a memorandum. The document implied that Bertie's behaviour was ungrateful and unreasonable. After so much trouble had been taken to find him a wife, the least he could do was fall in love. The best thing now would be to invite Princess Alexandra and her parents to stay at Windsor, 'in order that you may propose to the young lady, if she pleases you on further acquaintance.' The only alternative would be to indicate that the affair was at an end. To act otherwise, 'would be most ungentlemanlike and insulting to the lady and her parents and would bring public disgrace upon you and us.'

It was a stark choice. After meeting Alix for a few hours, he must marry her or abandon her. There are two probable explanations for his hesitation. First, he was waiting for the Curragh affair to blow over, or, if the worst befell, for the storm to break. Secondly, he needed time to get to know Alix better. It was one thing to admit her charm and beauty, and another to marry her. Indeed, his parents should have been the first to discourage him after so brief an encounter from committing himself to the most irrevocable tie which can bind two mortals together: 'for better for worse, for richer for poorer, till death us do part.' Instead of rushing him into matrimony, against his better judgement, he should have been left to decide for himself the tempo of events. But that, of course, would have been to concede the alien principle that he was entitled to choose his own friends and marry whom he pleased.

After the Prince Consort's death, his widow was more determined than ever that Bertie should marry Alix. It was 'a sacred duty he, our darling Angel, left us to perform.' Meanwhile, Princess Christian, whose second daughter, Dagmar, was also approaching marriageable age, was once more in touch with Russia. No longer sure whether the Prince of Wales was in earnest, she decided to keep 'the Cesarewitch in reserve.'

A little over a month after Prince Albert's death, the Queen told Vicky that Princess Christian must not be left in ignorance of the character of Bertie. 'Were the poor girl to be very unhappy, I could not answer for it before God had she been entrapped into it.' But the Queen had second thoughts about the wisdom of creating further difficulties, and it was left to the Duke of Cambridge to tell Alix's mother about Bertie's escapade.

The Queen first learned of this wanton act of treachery when Vicky told her that she had 'heard from Wally Paget – what annoyed me very much – namely that Uncle George wrote to Princess Christian all about Bertie's unfortunate story, and told her besides that you were very angry with Bertie and that there was complete discord between you and him. Wally found Princess Christian one day in floods of tears with this letter from Uncle George in her hands and in great distress about it, saying she feared her daughter would be unhappy and that you would dislike her too if she became Bertie's wife . . . She had not heard a word of all this before. Of course Uncle George did not do this out of ill nature, but it was foolish and indiscreet, and springs from that insatiable love of gossip which makes the members of that family so dangerous.' When she heard that the secret was out, the Queen asked Mrs Paget to tell Princess Christian 'that wicked wretches had led our poor, innocent boy into a scrape which had caused his beloved father and myself the deepest pain, but that both of us had forgiven him this (one) sad mistake, that we had never disagreed and that I was very confident he would make a steady husband.'

The Queen, having never set eyes on her intended daughter-in-law, or, for that matter, Princess Christian, decided 'to see the girl,' not, as might be supposed to discover what sort of a wife she promised to make Bertie, but to judge, as she candidly put it, if 'she will suit me.' The meeting eventually took place on 3 September 1862, at Laeken, Uncle Leopold's Palace near Brussels. As the Queen was beginning a pilgrimage to Coburg, this brief diversion caused her the least inconvenience. When the 'Countess of Balmoral' disembarked at Ostend, nobody appears to have penetrated her somewhat flimsy disguise.

In preparation for the meeting, the Crown Princess warned Mrs Paget to impress Princess Christian and her family that they must address Her Majesty in subdued tones and on no account must they laugh in her presence. If her mother resolved to be miserable, her wishes must be respected.

A few minutes before the encounter took place, the Queen suddenly stood up and resting her head on Wally's shoulder burst into tears. 'You, dear Wally,' she sobbed, 'will understand what I feel at this moment, you have a husband you love and you know what I have lost.' She then dried her eyes, collected herself, and asked Mrs Paget to introduce her to Princess Christian, who, in her turn, presented Alix, Dagmar and her husband. After some desultory conversation, during which Her Majesty recalled Prince Christian's visit to her coronation, the Queen withdrew.

'After luncheon,' she wrote in her Journal, 'came the terribly trying moment for me. I had *alone* to say and do what, under other, former happy circumstances, had devolved on us both together.' Later that day, Alix appeared, in a plain black dress, without jewels, and with her hair hanging in curls over her shoulders. Nobody could have resisted her charm, simplicity and loveliness. 'How He would have doted on her and loved her,' wrote the Queen, which was the highest praise she could bestow.

So far the Queen had taken all initiatives, but now it was up to Bertie to complete what she had begun. Before leaving England, he visited the Prince Consort's tomb at Windsor, 'and prayed for dear Papa's blessing for the step which I am about to take.' Next day, he and Sir William travelled to Brussels. On 8 September, Bertie told Prince Christian that he loved his daughter and wished to make her his wife. The Prince could hardly have looked surprised after two years of negotiation, but, at least, seemed pleased.

The following evening, Bertie sat down in a daze and wrote his mother 'a touching and happy letter.' He described how Uncle Leopold had suggested taking a stroll in the garden, and how he and Alix walked 'some distance behind.' She told him that the Queen had given her some white heather from Balmoral, and he said he hoped it would bring her luck. 'I asked her how she liked our country, and if she would some day come to England, and how long she would remain. She said she hoped some time. I said that I hoped she would remain always there, and then offered her my hand and my heart. She immediately said *Yes*. I then kissed her hand and she kissed me . . . I told her how *very* sorry I was that she could never know dear Papa. She said she regretted it deeply and hoped he would have approved of my choice. I told her that it had always been his greatest wish; I only feared that I was not worthy of her . . . I cannot tell you how happy I feel . . . Love and cherish her you may be sure I will to the end of my life. May God grant that *our* happiness may throw a ray of light on your once so happy and now so desolate home. You may be sure that we shall both strive to be a comfort to you.'

Sir Charles Phipps, who accompanied the Prince of Wales to Brussels, wrote to the Queen by the same post as her son. As a man of business he did not permit sentiment to influence his judgement, so he told her bluntly: 'It would be absurd to suppose that a real feeling of *love* could as yet exist for a person whom His Royal Highness has only seen in all for a few hours.'

Two days after becoming engaged, Bertie wrote again to the Queen, in itself evidence that he was deeply stirred, assuring her that he did not think it possible to love a person as he did Alix. 'She is so kind and good, and I feel sure will make my life a happy one. I only trust that God will give me strength to do the same for her.' Lady Augusta Bruce, who was in waiting on the Queen in Coburg, declared that the Prince of Wales was 'desperately in love, and his Mother *much* pleased with him.' Although Stockmar had complained that this was an 'arranged' marriage, as it was in the sense that neither partner initiated it, their willing consent soon turned into something deeper. Indeed, Alix told one of her future sisters-in-law: 'You perhaps think that I like marrying your Brother for his position, but if he was a cowboy I should love him just the same and would marry no-one else.'

Bertie and Alix spent four happy days together. They went out riding and he admired her skill and courage. They inspected the battlefield of Waterloo, and perhaps he told her how when he was a boy the Duke of Wellington had admitted to him he had never seen Napoleon. In the evening, she played the piano and sang most sweetly. And for a few moments they were sometimes allowed to see each other alone: provided Princess Christian sat in an adjoining room with the door open. The Queen had drawn up precise rules for the preservation of propriety and this was the utmost licence she was prepared to permit. On 14 September, Bertie set out for Coburg and the Christians returned to Denmark. It would have been more tactful not to have told the Queen that their 'first parting' was 'a very trying time,' for compared with the agony of her own life-long separation his hardship was bound to seem trifling.

It was only natural that Alix's parents should want their prospective son-in-law to visit them at Copenhagen, and he was as anxious to go as they to have him. But the Queen would not hear of it, claiming that such a visit would be regarded in Europe as unmistakable proof that England supported Denmark in its dispute with Prussia over Schleswig-Holstein. The last thing she proposed to do was further antagonize her German relations. General Grey, her Private Secretary, 'told General Oxholme, the confidential adviser of the Danish royalties, that the visit of the Prince of Wales, or anything that could possibly give appearance of this marriage being a political one, must not be thought of . . . Whatever precautions were taken, it was impossible to prevent people putting a political construction upon the visit to Copenhagen and it would raise a great deal of disagreeable discussion, which the Queen was particularly anxious to avoid.'

Already, Vicky and Fritz had been bitterly criticized for their part in furthering the marriage, which they were the first to acknowledge was contrary to Prussia's interests. Indeed, their opposition to Bismarck's appointment as Minister-President, and their advocacy of the Danish match, created such strained relations with the King and made them so unpopular in Berlin, that when the Queen offered them the *Osborne* for a Mediterranean cruise they seized the chance of escape.

But General Grey told Augustus Paget, 'It was not so much the political question, the storm that would be raised among her German connections,' that had persuaded the Queen to forbid her son to set foot on Danish soil, as the fear 'I might almost say horror,' she has of Princess Christian's kin. As she herself expressed it, 'The Prince of Wales is so weak that he would be sure to get entangled with Princess Louise's relations, and it would be *too* horrid if he should become one of *that* family.'

Not only did the Queen forbid the Prince of Wales to visit Denmark, but she sent him instead to join Vicky and Fritz. Meanwhile, she summoned Alix to Osborne, intending to have her all to herself. Princess Christian was not even asked, and Alix's father, who escorted her to England, was invited for two nights. When he returned some weeks later to collect his daughter the Court had moved to Windsor, but he had to stay in a London hotel as there was no room in the Castle. The Queen's discourtesy to the Christians verged on the insulting, and she certainly made clear that she intended 'to exercise to the full the authority which has provided a stock joke against the most canvassed of human relationships.'

Princess Alexandra and her father crossed to England on board the *Black Eagle*. They were delayed by fog, but, by the time they arrived on the evening of 5 November, the moon was shining, there were lights burning along the pier, and the sky was ablaze with rockets. As they landed, a band struck up the Danish National Anthem. The Queen had sent Prince Leopold and Princess Helena, or 'Lenchen' as she was known to the family, to greet her royal guests. Princess Helena had a cold, so had to sit waiting in the carriage, while Leopold, who was only nine years old, kept asking Lady Augusta how he should make himself known, what he should say, and when he should give the Princess the bouquet of flowers he was clasping. They decided that Lady Augusta would 'solemnly pronounce his name, but before this could be achieved the pretty graceful Princess stepped lightly on shore, took the great representative of the House of England in her arms and kissed Him.' They then drove to Osborne, where the Queen received them in the hall. 'At last at 9,' wrote the Queen in her Journal, 'dear Alexandra arrived with her father, looking very lovely and well. A gleam of satisfaction for a moment shone in my heart as I led "*our*" future daughter upstairs to her room.'

In 1888, Archbishop Randall Davidson, then Dean of Windsor, after preaching one Sunday at Sandringham, sat next to Princess Alexandra at dinner. 'She described her first coming to England 25 years ago, and the (most reasonably) alarming character of her visit to Osborne "to be inspected" a few months before the marriage, when the Queen was in deepest mourning and the poor girl had to visit her for several days without anybody to break the gloom. She had not even a lady-in-waiting, and was terribly frightened at the whole process.' Moreover, she was not at all happy to be separated from her mother, she resented the treatment of her father, and she felt as if she was 'on approval.' But she kept these feelings to herself, and soon her sunny and affectionate nature thawed the Queen's chilled heart. One of the first times she laughed after 14 December was when Affie, presuming on Alix's innocence of English ways, persuaded her to ask his mother whether she had enjoyed her forty winks.

According to Princess Mary of Cambridge, 'Her bright joyous presence' did much 'to rouse the poor dear Queen who seems doatingly [sic] fond of her.' Such was the change, that the Queen was 'able to smile and even laugh cheerfully at times.' Vicky and Bertie on board the Osborne received constant letters about darling Alix, the list of whose virtues may partly have been intended as oblique rebukes. She regularly went to bed at ten o'clock as her parents wished, and was kind and loving to the younger members of the family. The Queen was particularly impressed by the pious books which Alix kept by her beside, 'all most well read, underlined old copies!!' In telling Vicky how much 'we all love her,' the Queen almost ran out of superlatives. 'She is so good, so simple, unaffected, frank, bright and cheerful, yet so quiet and gentle, that her presence soothes me.' Vicky's part in finding 'this jewel' was not forgotten. 'Dearest Child, we cannot thank you enough for all you have both done . . . She is one of those sweet creatures who seem to come from the skies to help and bless poor mortals and brighten for a time their path! . . . She lives in complete intimacy with us and she is so dear, so gentle, good, simple, unspoilt – so thoroughly honest and straightforward – so affectionate.'

One evening, they sat for an hour together and the Queen 'told her all about former happy times, our life, a great deal about dearest Papa, whom she seems to love quite dearly and to long to see; all about his illness; she showed such feeling, laid her dear head on my shoulder and cried, said how she prayed God to help her do all she could to help me and comfort me . . . She is so affectionately attached to me! It is a great blessing and I do thank God for it – that in our misery He has permitted this.'

Despite her fondness for Alix, the Queen continued to deplore the political aspect of the marriage. One reason she had wanted to see her future daughter-in-law alone was to take the opportunity to teach her a novel version of her duty. While not denying her right to love the country of her birth, she must, nevertheless, put patriotism second, and on no account try to persuade the Prince of Wales to support Denmark against Prussia. One of the troubles with the Danish Royal Family was their inability to value the 'German element,' which the Queen was so anxious should be 'cherished and kept up in our beloved home.' Much as she loved Alix as a person, she regretted her nationality. 'Oh! if Bertie's wife was only a good German and not a Dane!' she exclaimed in 1864, when family harmony had been disrupted by feuds over Schleswig-Holstein; and later that same year, thinking Affie might marry Princess Marie of Saxe-Altenburg, she said it would 'be such a blessing to have a real German daughter-in-law.'

It did not need a European crisis to impose severe stresses on Anglo-Danish relations. The Queen's capricious plans for the wedding sufficed to create dissension. She insisted, for example, that the ceremony should be held in St George's Chapel, Windsor, which severely restricted the number of guests it was possible to invite, and prevented most of the public watching the procession. *Punch* suggested that, as the marriage was to be held in an obscure Berkshire village, noted only for an old Castle with bad drains, *The Times* announcement should read as follows: 'On the 10th inst. by Dr Longley, Albert Edward England KG to Alexandra Denmark. No cards.'

Amongst those not invited were King Frederick VII of Denmark, virtually all Princess Christian's relations, the Grand Duchess Augusta of Mecklenburg-Strelitz, the Duchess of Manchester, and a formidable array of friends and connections, all of whom resented not being asked. In particular, the Danish Royal Family thought they had been treated with contemptuous discourtesy. The disputes which arose over the wedding arrangements increased the Queen's dislike of Alix's relations. While being thoroughly selfish, unreasonable and obstinate, she condemned the most tentative opposition to her whims as characterized by precisely these defects. But she did not allow her irritation with the Christians to diminish her affection for their daughter.

The Queen decided that the service should take place on 10 March 1863, which deeply affronted the clergy who opposed weddings in Lent. The Queen was superstitious about marriages in

May, February was too early, and June too late. Princess Alice expected a child in April, so that left March: Lent or no Lent. The Archbishop of Canterbury, supported by the Dean of Windsor, the Queen's trusted friend Gerald Wellesley, complained, but to no avail. Their protest was brushed aside. 'In my young days,' the Queen informed them, 'there was no Lent.' Presumably she regarded Easter as a Tractarian invention. Dr Longley's objection she told him was 'very Catholic,' and it was high time he took a more 'elevated view of one of God's holiest ordinances.' Marriage was 'a solemn holy act *not* to be classed with amusements.'

On the morning of 5 March 1863, Princess Alexandra, and such members of her family as were invited to the wedding, embarked on the *Victoria and Albert*, which had been sent to Antwerp to fetch them. The yacht was escorted across the Channel by a squadron of Ironclads, and anchored unexpectedly in Margate Roads as a storm threatened. Despite the rough weather, the Mayor rowed out next morning and presented the 'Sea-King's daughter,' as Tennyson called her in a welcoming Ode, with her first civic address. Next day she used it in the train to London as a weapon with which to pound her brother William on the head. From Margate they sailed to Sheerness, and on the morning of 7 March steamed up the Thames, escorted by Captain Tryon in HMS *Warrior*. Thirty years later this officer gave the fatal order in consequence of which his flagship HMS *Victoria* sank with all hands. At noon, the Royal Yacht anchored off Gravesend, where it was instantly surrounded by hundreds of small craft. Amidst a tremendous din of salutes and cheers, the Prince of Wales clambered aboard. The moment he saw his bride emerging from the stateroom, he took her in his arms and gave her a hug, much to the delight of thousands of onlookers.

From Gravesend they proceeded by the South Eastern Railway to London, the terminus then being the Bricklayer's Arms on the south side of the river. Lord Caithness, who was on the footplate, drove the train as slowly as he could so that those lining the track might catch a glimpse of his royal passengers. The procession through the streets of London was started soon after two by the Duke of Cambridge. It crossed London Bridge, went past the Mansion House and St Paul's, down Ludgate Hill, under Temple Bar, along Pall Mall and Piccadilly, to Paddington, by way of Park Lane and the Edgware Road.

The route was lavishly decorated with triumphal arches, flags, heraldic devices, and even a statue of Queen Victoria supported by two figures representing Wisdom and Strength. It was generally agreed that such a huge crowd had never before been seen in the history of the world. Augustus Paget said it was 'almost beyond the powers of imagination' to conceive, and he was told 'that lots of people were squashed to death.'

There was a great deal of criticism of the royal carriages which 'looked old and shabby, and the horses very poor, with no trappings, not even rosettes, and no outriders. In short, the shabbiness of the whole cortège was beyond anything one could imagine, everybody asking: Who is the Master of the Horse?' *The Times* wrote most disparagingly 'of that singularly ill-appointed establishment known as the Royal Mews of Pimlico' and declared that 'the servants, carriages, and cattle selected to convey the Danish Princess through joyful London' came from its 'very dregs.'

Despite these shortcomings, and despite a bitterly cold east wind, the crowd was determined to enjoy itself. Shops and houses were crammed to the chimneys with spectators, who consumed rivers of gin and champagne as they waited. If a stray dog ran down the road, or a pick-pocket was arrested, there were shouts of delight. When, at last, the first carriages appeared, they were discovered to be full of rather drab aldermen. Sir William Hardman, who watched the procession from a stand outside St Paul's, feared that these civic worthies 'would never cease dribbling along,' and he 'began to think we were doomed to see Common Councilmen for the rest of our days as a punishment for our folly in being among the spectators. It seemed as if an endless ring of those distinguished tradesmen were going round and round St Paul's to jeer and mock our misery.'

There was one sight, however, which delighted all who saw it: Princess Alexandra, sitting beside her mother in the back of an open carriage, opposite her father and the Prince of Wales. It was love at first sight. Her grace and beauty won all hearts. Housman said she achieved in a day a second Danish Conquest more lasting than the first. She did not have to wait until she became Queen 'to do no wrong.' From the instant she landed at Gravesend, she had England at her feet. Tennyson caught the mood:

> 'O joy to the people and joy to the throne,
> Come to us, love us and make us your own.'

Near the Mansion House the procession was brought to a halt by the crowd surging across the street. An officer of the Blues rode forward to try to clear a way. By some inexplicable accident, his horse's foreleg caught in the rear wheel of Alix's carriage. Without a moment's hesitation, she leant over and extricated the animal's hoof.

The royal party reached Paddington an hour late, and when their train drew into Slough it was almost dark and raining hard. Under these circumstances, it was decided not to stop at Eton, where the Provost was waiting to present an address, but to drive straight to Windsor. The Queen described in her Journal how 'at length, in pouring rain and when it was getting dark, the carriages and escort were seen coming . . . I went down nearly to the bottom of the staircase, and Bertie appeared, leading dear Alix, looking like a rose. I embraced her warmly.' She then took the Danish royal family, which included Alix's sisters, Dagmar and Thyra, and her brothers, William and Waldemar, to their rooms upstairs. 'It seemed so dreadful that all this must take place, strangers arrive, and *he*, my beloved one, not be there.' While the Queen waited to have dinner with General Bruce's widow, for she would not join the happy family gathering, 'dear gentle Alix knocked at the door, peeped in, and came and knelt before me, with that sweet loving expression which spoke volumes. I was much moved and kissed her again and again.'

The following day was Sunday, so they all attended Morning Prayer at St George's. The Bishop of Oxford, 'obeying the Pauline injunction to be all things to all men,' preached a sermon on the text: 'Rejoice with them that do rejoice and weep with them that weep.' Only Samuel Wilberforce had the dexterity to harmonize the funeral dirge so consoling to the Queen, with the happier refrain demanded by circumstances.

Next morning, the Queen took Bertie and Alix to the recently completed Mausoleum at Frogmore. 'I opened the shrine and took them in. Alix was much moved and so was I. I said, "*He* gives you his blessing!" and joined Alix's and Bertie's hands, taking them both in my arms. It was a very touching moment and we all felt it.' For the Queen that ceremony was almost as sacred as the Service held next day.

In the afternoon, the Prince and Princess drove down to Eton, which they had been obliged to pass by on Saturday evening. One young gentleman who saw the fun, described the scene in a letter home. 'There is great excitement here; triumphal arches all over the shop, stars, Chinese lamps and Prince of Wales' feathers. Last Monday the Prince and Princess drove out, so we were let off three schools. She came through Eton about four, and I and about half a dozen other chaps ran with her for nearly a mile by the side of her carriage, so I had a stunning view of her. She grinned away like beans.'

Twelve years later the Princess had a less happy reception when the train in which she was travelling was stoned as it passed the College and she was struck by a splinter of glass from the window of her carriage. The Queen was so furious that she complained to the Prime Minister, Disraeli, who promised a full enquiry, from which it transpired that this was by no means the first time that hooligans had bombarded trains on this stretch of line. Dr Hornby felt sure that the miscreants would be discovered amongst his juvenile neighbours at Eton Wick, but made it clear that 'if the culprits should be found to be boys of the College they will be flogged with the utmost severity and then expelled.'

During the evening of 9 March there were fireworks in the Home Park beneath the windows of the State Apartments. It was dreadfully cold and according to Lord Randolph Churchill, then a boy at Carter's, they 'were very pretty, only there were such an awful lot of rockets and too few catherine-wheels and all that sort of fun.'

The year before, when Alice married Prince Louis, Grand Duke of Hesse-Darmstadt, the Queen managed to make everyone feel miserable. 'This poor, unhappy marriage,' she wrote 'is more like a funeral than a wedding.' It never occurred to her how much she was to blame. When Vicky innocently betrayed pleasure at the prospect of her brother's marriage, she was told that her 'ecstasy' was 'incomprehensible'. 'Will you be able to rejoice,' her mother asked her, 'when at every step you will miss that blessed guardian angel, that one calm great being that led all?' The Queen warned her daughter that during the festivities she would take her meals alone, for she 'must keep very, very quiet,' and she begged Vicky to use her influence 'in checking noise and joyousness' in her presence.

After Albert's death, the Queen increasingly exploited imaginary ill-health to get her own way. Although well enough to do whatever she wanted, unwelcome demands were resisted with numberless afflictions. The pliant Dr Jenner won her unqualified confidence by endorsing her self-diagnosis and supporting her threats that worry and overwork would drive her mad. Even without his help she contrived to prescribe suspiciously convenient remedies for imaginary ills, which were then represented as forced upon her. General Grey and Henry Ponsonby, successively Private Secretaries, agreed with her daughter, Princess Louise, in condemning Jenner's pernicious encouragement of her fancies. Grey once bluntly declared that Her Majesty's moans had 'simply no effect whatever on me,' and he told Gladstone that 'neither health nor strength are wanting, were inclination what it should be. It is simply the long unchecked habit of self-indulgence that now makes it impossible for her, without some degree of nervous agitation to give up, even for ten minutes, the gratification of a single inclination, or even *whim*.'

The last Royal Wedding at Windsor had taken place in 1121, when Henry I married Adela of Louvain. But, despite the rarity of such events, Prince Waldemar begged to be left with his donkey rather than go to church. The Service began with a number of processions. It was generally agreed that the Knights of the Garter were under-rehearsed, and that nobody looked as majestic as Princess Mary of Cambridge as she sailed up the nave. Lord Granville said, 'I never saw a finer piece of acting than Princess Mary heading the English Royal Procession. Morally as well as physically, the place was not big enough to hold her.' The Crown Princess was the last to enter the Chapel before the Bridegroom. When she caught sight of the Queen, 'she made a very low courtsey, with an inexpressible look of love and respect, which had a most touching effect.'

All the while Frith sat busily sketching the scene for his painting. Apart from the Bride, whose exquisite radiance none could outshine, many thought Lady Spencer the loveliest person present. The dark blue gown she wore had once belonged to Marie Antoinette. Prince William of Prussia was very restive, and sought to make himself the centre of attention. At one moment his mother, who spent most of the time weeping, put out her hand to rebuke him. Later, his uncles complained he had bitten them during the service.

The Queen looked down on the congregation from Catherine of Aragon's Closet, which gave her a view like that from the Royal Box at Covent Garden. She was dressed in black, alleviated by the ribbon, star and badge of the Order of the Garter. At first she was agitated and restless, but soon grew inquisitive, and put countless questions to Mrs Bruce and the Duchess of Sutherland. There were several agonizing moments. A flourish of trumpets brought back to her mind 'my whole life of twenty years at *his* dear side, safe, proud, secure, and happy, I felt as if I should faint. Only by a violent effort could I succeed in mastering my emotion!' Even more trying was a performance of a chorale composed by Albert in which Vicky persuaded Jenny Lind to sing. As her magnificent voice soared above the choir and organ, the Queen raised her eyes to heaven and 'seemed to be with him alone before the throne of God.'

Whatever gloom might envelop the Queen, St George's Chapel was lit by sunshine. Clarendon thought the Prince of Wales, dressed in the uniform of a General with the Robe of the Garter, 'looked very like a gentleman and more *considerable* than he is wont to do.' The Prince was supported by his Uncle Ernest, who could not resist so conspicuous a part, despite his bitter opposition to the match, and by the Crown Prince, who had helped bring it about. The Bride was ten minutes late but was seldom ever again to be so punctual. Even if no room could be found for the King of Denmark, the Prince's former tutors were all invited, Birch and Tarver acting as honorary chaplains for the occasion. After the ceremony, the Prince presented them both with handsomely-bound Bibles, inscribed: 'From Albert Edward in remembrance of the 10th of March.' Kingsley was deeply impressed by the 'serious reverent dignity' of his 'dear young master, whose manner was perfect,' and Stanley, as he watched the bridegroom waiting 'in his long velvet mantle like a statue, so stately and so grand,' could not help asking himself, 'Can this be the boy of last year on the Nile?'

When Princess Alexandra failed to appear, some people 'began to wonder if the Bride was coy and to hope she had not changed her mind.' At last, the orchestra struck up Handel's *Processional March* as the Princess appeared, accompanied by the Duke of Cambridge and her father. 'I never saw in anyone,' wrote Clarendon, 'more grace and dignity and aplomb.' Lord Granville, anticipating W. S. Gilbert, said that, although the bridesmaids were 'hideous in full view,' they looked well 'when their backs were turned.' Bishop Wilberforce regarded the wedding as the most moving sight he ever saw. He was particularly impressed by the Crown Prince telling him that his own marriage to Vicky had been 'one long honeymoon.' Not every detail was flawless. For example, the orchestra began to tune their instruments when they thought that the Archbishop had preached long enough. But, for all that, the ceremony was, as Disraeli said, 'a fine affair, a thing to remember.'

The Bridal pair left the Chapel to the strains of the 'Hallelujah Chorus.' The Queen greeted them on their return to the Castle, hastening down the Grand Staircase, lined by Yeomen of the Guard, to the very door of their carriage, where she embraced them both in her outspread arms again and again. 'My *only* thought was that of welcoming *our children*.'

The Prince and Princess of Wales left Windsor for their honeymoon at Osborne soon after three-thirty. Lord Randolph Churchill, with some of his Eton friends, rushed after the carriage, in what he called 'a second Balaclava.' The police attempted to intervene, but were knocked down. 'Several old *genteel* ladies tried to stop me, but I snapped my fingers in their faces and cried "Hurrah!" and "What larks!" I frightened some of them horribly. There was a wooden palisade put up at the station but we broke it down; and there, to my unspeakable grief, I was bereaved of a portion of my clothing, viz my hat. I shrieked out a convulsive "Oh, my hat!" and was then borne on. I got right down to the door of the carriage where the Prince of Wales was, wildly shouting "Hurrah!" He bowed to me, I am perfectly certain.'

At last, the train moved off, the band played *God Save the Queen*, and young Randolph vainly sought to retrieve his top hat. Meanwhile, the 'special' ordered to convey Her Majesty's guests to Paddington was taken over by the rabble. The Duchess of Westminster, covered in diamonds worth half a million pounds, was lost in a crowd of roughs. The most eminent men in the kingdom were thankful to find a seat in a third-class compartment, and Disraeli was forced to sit on his wife's lap. The Archbishop only reached the station by hanging on to the back of a carriage, and Bishop Tait was not best pleased when he was hailed by the crowd as Colenso. While these unedifying scenes took place, the Queen drove to Frogmore with Princess Helena, in search of peace. In the silence of the Mausoleum she knelt and prayed by the 'beloved resting place,' where one day she herself would lie.

Phipps was probably wise to challenge the romantic notion that the Prince of Wales was devoted to Alix the moment he set eyes on her, but even he would have conceded that the young couple on board the *Fairy* crossing the Solent to Osborne, were truly in love. Before returning to Prussia Vicky paid her brother a brief visit and it did her good, she said, to see him so happy. She found him 'radiant,' 'beaming' and 'blissful,' and 'Darling Alix' charming and attractive as ever. 'Love has certainly shed its sunshine on these two dear young hearts and lends its unmistakable brightness to both their countenances.' The idyll proved short-lived, for the Prince preferred excitement and variety to a settled passion, and Alix was soon to discover that she was not the only woman in his life. But at least she could claim with good reason that 'he always loved me the best.'

The Prince and Princess of Wales had two establishments of their own: Marlborough House, opposite St James's Park, and Sandringham in Norfolk. Their London residence was built for the Great Duke by Wren on land which the Duchess persuaded Queen Anne to lease them. When in 1817 it reverted to the Crown, it was successively assigned to Princess Charlotte, the Dowager Queen Adelaide and the Prince of Wales. It was pleasantly secluded, being surrounded by high walls, and the best rooms were on the far side of a courtyard. Its ballroom was large enough to entertain the whole of London Society, and its lawns, running down to the Mall, provided a splendid setting for garden parties. Soon after the Prince moved in he invited his mother to come and look at the house now that it was finished. Before she had got far with her inspection, he suddenly remembered how shocked she would be when she came to the smoking room. But Lord Charles Beresford, who lacked neither ingenuity nor resource, came to the rescue. When the Queen reached the fatal door she sailed past, for on it was written in letters of chalk: 'Lavatory. Under Repair.'

Sandringham, a shooting estate of some seven thousand acres, was purchased in 1863 out of the revenue accumulated by the Duchy of Cornwall during the Prince of Wales's minority. Prince Albert skilfully invested the income to provide funds with which a property could be bought when his son came of age. It belonged to Charles Spencer Cowper, an absentee landlord, who spent most of his time in Paris, neglecting his duties, philandering and losing money at cards.

The property was basically unsuited for a royal residence, consequently attempts to make it one achieved limited success at enormous cost. Phipps once wrote Sir William Knollys a despairing letter from Osborne complaining of the increasing expense of Sandringham, the mischievous behaviour of Prince Alfred in giving the Queen exaggerated accounts of his brother's grandiose schemes, the Prince of Wales's instinct for accepting bad advice, and the unhappy lot of courtiers. Not only did Sandringham run away with money, but the Prince displayed a 'royal impetuosity in expecting improvements to be all carried out at once.' Prince Alfred's conduct was unforgivable, 'knowing, as he must, the effect that these reports create – and the worst of it is that you cannot always rely upon his facts. All this I would not breathe to anyone but you. I cannot think it kind or amiable to sow such seeds in a soil which he must know will give them such rapid growth . . . It is, however, a very grand misfortune in the character of your young master that – ready enough to take advice from those who will advise him wrongly – he flies in every way from good counsel.' This, said Sir Charles, was only a 'natural result of the radical defect in his character which renders it impossible for him to deny himself anything that he desires.'

Evidently Phipps was writing at the end of a dispiriting day for he concluded by saying, 'How little, my dear Knollys, people who only see courts from a distance, and who think you and me the most fortunate fellows in the world, guess all the anxieties, the difficulties, the unappreciated labours, with their unsatisfactory results – all the doubts and disappointments to which we, and all employed like us, are constantly exposed.'

The Prince of Wales had an annual income of a little over £100,000. This he derived from the revenue of the Duchy of Corn-wall, his Sandringham rents, interest from his investments, and a Parliamentary grant of £40,000. Many of the Queen's subjects possessed far greater fortunes. The Duke of Sutherland owned over a million and a quarter acres. The Duke of Buccleuch had at least three times as large an income and lived in a regal splendour which made Sandringham look like a villa. The Duke of Westminster, the richest man in England, owned great tracts of London. Even a relatively humble Cornish baronet like Sir William Knollys's father-in-law received £90,000 a year from his property in Devonport. And none of these people were expected to head the list of a hundred charities or to supply the want of a Court in the world's greatest capital. It might almost be represented as good management that HRH's annual deficit was little more than £20,000.

While it would be absurd to portray the Prince as a pauper, most Governments tended to treat him shabbily, and it was at least arguable – as he did argue – that when he performed the Queen's duties she should foot the bill. Alix was no help whatever in managing money. She had been brought up exceptionally frugally, even making her own dresses, serving at table and sharing a room with her sister: an experience which seems to have deprived her of all financial sense. Her trouble was not so much that she was personally extravagant as recklessly generous. She believed, for example, that relief must be instantaneous and precede enquiry. Her benefactions rained with haphazard bounty on deserving and undeserving alike, and she tended to double donations if their wisdom was disputed. In relieving poverty or suffering she was resolutely guided by her heart.

In 1874 newspapers at home and abroad announced that the Prince of Wales was £600,000 in debt. Possibly they believed the report to be accurate, but, whether true or false, critics of royalty seized the opportunity to denounce the Prince's extravagance, or the Queen's avarice in not rushing to his rescue. It was even rumoured that only the brothers Rothschild stood between him and bankruptcy. Although Sir William Knollys hastened to assure the Queen that this was not so, he felt bound to concede that attacks on HRH's gambling could not be dismissed so lightly, and he regretfully endorsed what Her Majesty 'was once pleased to observe to him, the Country could never bear to have George IV as Prince of Wales over again.'

In September, Henry Ponsonby, the Queen's Private Secretary, wrote to Sir Arthur Helps, who had assisted Her Majesty in publishing her *Highland Journal* and whose literary style was praised by Ruskin, saying that there was not one word of truth in accounts of the Prince of Wales's financial difficulties, but that, nevertheless, 'the Queen thinks that the repetition of this scandalous assertion may lead to its being believed.' She consequently wished 'some friendly hint given to the *Daily Telegraph*, whose editor I believe you know, as he might expose the falsehood of the whole story.' The editor of *The Times*, Delane, was also approached, and on 1 October his newspaper printed an article entitled: 'The Prince of Wales's Affairs.' This attributed most of his problems to his being 'saddled' with the cost of performing ceremonial duties for the Queen during her 'persistent seclusion': a drain on his resources which had not been anticipated in assessing his allowance.

Both the Prince and his advisers, who in all probability inspired *The Times* article, believed that the costs of representing the Sovereign should be met by the Queen, on whose behalf they were incurred and who received public money to defray such expenses. Like Gibbon's tutor at Oxford, she well remembered she had a salary to receive and only forgot that there was a duty to perform. As *The Times* declared: 'From his first entrance into public life the expenses of his position were larger than had been anticipated. Immediately upon his marriage he was called upon to assume a relation to English society and to foreign royalties which does not necessarily, or even usually, fall to subjects, however near the Throne. We all bear in mind that the Prince of Wales has represented the royal house of England for ten years in visits to the Chief Courts of Europe, and has been burdened with the expenditure required to discharge these duties. In Paris and Vienna, on the banks of the Suez Canal, or amid the splendours of the Russian capital, the heir to the British throne has been more than an ordinary prince, and could not, without what would seem unworthy parsimony, avoid incurring great expense. A large retinue, long journeys, and a hundred minor but necessary outlays, would strain a far larger income than the Prince has ever received.'

Francis Knollys, who became the Prince of Wales's Private Secretary in 1870, was firmly convinced that it was the Queen's duty to give HRH an allowance 'in consideration of the extra expenses which fall upon him by reason of her seclusion.' He was consequently delighted with Delane's article and the implications to be read between its lines. Writing to Ponsonby from Copenhagen he asked him: 'What do you think of the article in *The Times* on the Prince's debts? I receive letters every day applauding it, all saying how necessary it was that something should have been done owing to the belief generally entertained that HRH was heavily involved. It was also believed abroad and so much so that the Crown Princess of Germany and Princess Alice spoke to the Prince on the subject and asked if it were true. They were both strongly of opinion that a contradiction should appear and though, as you are aware, HRH is extremely averse to any newspaper denial on matters referring to his affairs, he thought that on this occasion an exception should be made to the rule.'

Ponsonby admitted that the Prince required more money but saw no reason for asking the Queen to provide it. 'I may as well tell you,' he wrote of *The Times* article that 'we (I speak collectively) do not applaud it here.' He went on to speak of Delane as 'firing a broadside at us. In short it is said that the Prince has spent £20,000 a year beyond his income on behalf of the Queen – that is for doing her duty. We strongly demur to this. It has brought down a host of comments that as this is the reason of the Prince's deficiencies it becomes the duty of the Queen to make it up to him.' It was argued that the Prince's foreign travels were undertaken on her behalf, which was at best a questionable half-truth. 'I quite agree that the Prince may fairly ask for an increase of income if he finds he has not enough on his own account. But why try to obtain this by an attack on us?'

Not without a measure of justification, the Radical press accused the Queen of hoarding public money. In 1871 George Otto Trevelyan, Lord Macaulay's nephew, published a pamphlet purporting to be written by 'Solomon Temple, Builder,' entitled: 'What Does She Do With It?' The answer he gave was that she salted away about two hundred thousand a year. In 1874, a satirical poem, 'The Siliad,' represented the Prince of Wales, thinly disguised as 'Guelpho,' indignantly repudiating strictures of extravagance. Although the author failed to capture the Prince's conversational style, the sentiment was authentic.

> 'Upon my honour, Ma (Guelpho broke in);
> That is not fair to talk about the tin;
> Remember, if you please, I have to do
> A heap of things that should be done by you.
> You choose to live an almost hermit life,
> Shut up from Royal State, and show and strife;
> Which means that I must, to a like degree,
> Come out and quite a proxy Monarch be.'

In 1889, when Lord Salisbury was Prime Minister, the Prince of Wales urged him to consider his financial problems, and consequently a Select Committee was set up, with W. H. Smith as its chairman, to enquire into the provision the State should make for HRH's family. After endless negotiation, it finally granted him £36,000 a year. Labouchere argued that the Queen's savings from the Civil List, and her revenue from Balmoral, Osborne and Windsor, 'would afford ample means' for providing for all her grandchildren. But, as Ponsonby told Francis Knollys, it was absurd for Radicals like Labouchere to image that the Queen's estates were a source of income for the Crown. 'Osborne costs us about £8000 a year instead of being a gain and Balmoral almost £6000 a year. The Windsor farms, which he says give us vast accumulations, cost us about £5000 or £6000 a year.'

Sometimes Labouchere was more courtly behind the scenes than before the public. While attacking royalty from the hustings, he privately assured the Prince he was loyal at heart. On the eve of Gladstone's defeat in 1886, he wrote to Francis Knollys from Northampton: 'I am sitting in an Inn calmly smoking and awaiting the result. When I go out, I am so handshaken by ardent but dirty radicals that I hide away . . . You may be certain of this: there is not the slightest anti-monarchical feeling amongst the Rads. They complain of excessive expense, and have their backs put up by little demands such as packets to Calais etc. I have always held that – as in other countries – there should be a lump sum for members of the Royal Family, exclusive of the Sovereign and the immediate heir.'

The Prince of Wales's Household was chosen for him by the Queen in consultation with her Ministers. General Knollys ruled the establishment as 'Comptroller and Treasurer.' Herbert Fisher, who instructed the Prince in law and history at Oxford, became his Private Secretary. Major Teesdale and Captain Charles Grey, father of the future Foreign Secretary, Sir Edward Grey, were appointed equerries. The political disposition of the Marlborough House staff was notably liberal, and the whole company formed a happy family party. In 1870 Fisher resigned and was succeeded by Francis Knollys, who since 1862 had been acting as his father's Secretary. For forty-eight years, Francis worked away with unfailing fidelity, wisdom and tact; while his sister, Charlotte, devoted herself to the Princess with equal loyalty and affection for over half a century. Between them the Knollys family rendered Edward and Alexandra services without precedent in history.

Francis, who was born on 16 July 1837, was named after Queen Elizabeth's devoted Treasurer from whom he was descended. As his father was Governor of Guernsey he was sent to school on the Island. After three years in the army, he transferred to the Civil Service. The General was so worried that Francis might 'lose caste' by joining the Audit Office that he asked Phipps whether the other Clerks were of 'gentlemen's families.' He was at pains to explain the nature of his concern. 'I trust, my dear Phipps, you will not misunderstand me, but as a poor man *position* is the only stock in trade I have for my children, and I therefore regard *salary* as a secondary consideration provided the situation now offered is generally filled by gentlemen of Francis's own class in society.' As the remuneration offered was ninety pounds a year, it was fortunate Sir William cared so little about money. The post, however, was looked upon as 'a beginning.' 'It was precisely in the same office and upon the same terms,' said Phipps, 'that my predecessor, George Anson, [Prince Albert's former Secretary] was first employed by the Government.' When Francis succeeded Fisher in 1870, the Queen strongly disapproved. Her objections were moral and political. She thought Francis was a great deal too fond of the ladies and not over-discriminating in his choice of them. She feared that he shared and would encourage her son's depraved tastes for late nights, cigars, the stage, frivolity and vice. Politically she distrusted his liberal sympathies and her suspicions were not unfounded. In his youth, Francis was no stranger to the pleasures of the town. In 1873 he approached Lord Rosebery asking him whether he would be willing to make his house in Berkeley Square 'a rendezvous for the Prince of Wales and the Duke of Edinburgh to meet their "actress friends"?' Rosebery declined the honour by saying that the place was too small. As for young Knollys's liberalism once more he could only plead guilty. Sir Lionel Cust went so far as to describe him as 'an advanced Radical.' Lady Warwick, one of the first Socialist aristocrats, spoke of the King enjoying 'the advantage of association with that honest man, good fellow, and model private secretary, Sir Francis Knollys, who was a liberal in politics, and also in everything else. Whatever feeling there was in King Edward for democracy was implanted there in the first instance by Knollys.'

Francis was far too discreet to make a habit of mentioning politics in his letters. But sometimes when writing to Ponsonby, who shared his views, he came out in the open. When Gladstone won the election of 1880, he admitted: 'I am just as surprised as you are at the liberal majority and quite as pleased as I hope you are. The Prince takes it very calmly and sensibly and looks upon it all as a matter of course, though he is sorry for the Queen, who I suppose hates the change like poison.'

Francis Knollys possessed almost all the qualities required of the perfect Private Secretary: he was wise, discreet, self-effacing, courteous, kind, imperturbable and loyal. His industry never faltered and his judgement seldom failed. Admiral Fisher writing to Francis, his 'beloved friend,' told him how right he was to describe Esher's judgement as unerring. 'Curiously enough,' he added, 'he was saying precisely the same thing of you yesterday.'

Knollys always kept a sense of perspective under the most trying circumstances, and his sly humour was never doused by the heaviest storms. Whilst the Queen's misgivings were understandable, they were proved mistaken. As Margot Asquith observed, 'the private secretaries of Queen Victoria, King Edward, and our present Sovereign [George V] have all been men of incalculable value, and had the Tsar or the Kaiser been fortunate enough to have men near them of the same goodness, wisdom and capacity, it is possible that we should not have lived to see the disruption of such great empires.' Beaconsfield, to whom admittedly flattery was second nature, told Francis in 1871 that 'it must be a great consolation to the Prince to be served by one so intelligent and devoted.'

Naturally Knollys possessed some shortcomings. He was an erratic shot, a hesitant linguist, and, what never ceased to grieve and astonish his master, incapable of appreciating the importance of decorations and honours. But, nevertheless, he won the Prince's unbounded confidence and trust. Francis 'saw everything, heard everything and was consulted about everything.' His ability to put matters right was unrivalled, and, 'above all, he knew how to be silent.'

In November 1863, Frederick VII of Denmark died, and in accordance with the Protocol of London Alix's father succeeded to the throne as Christian IX. Within a couple of months of his accession he found himself at war with Prussia over Schleswig-Holstein, provinces which had been part of Denmark since 1533. The complexities of the succession laws of the Duchies were legion, but Bismarck, Prussia's new Chancellor, was only interested in them in so far as they might prove useful in justifying his seizure of the territories. His campaign against Denmark in the winter of 1864 was the first of a series of aggressive wars undertaken to make Prussia dominant in Germany and Europe. England regarded Denmark as the victim of unprovoked aggression and admired her gallantry in resisting attack, despite the odds against her.

Largely inspired by chivalrous affection for the Princess of Wales, meetings were held up and down the country urging Palmerston to come to Denmark's rescue. There was every reason to expect the Prime Minister to respond to such appeals, because in July of 1863 he had warned Bismarck in a speech in the Commons, 'that if any violent attempt' were made against the integrity and independence of Denmark, 'those who made the attempt would find in the result, that it would not be Denmark alone with which they would have to contend.' But Bismarck called his bluff, recognizing that, unless he found allies, his army was too small to save Christian. Looking back on these events, Gladstone declared: 'When the troubles were arising between Prussia and Denmark, Palmerston said that, if the Danes were attacked, they would not stand alone. They were attacked; they did stand alone; and Palmerston did not resign.'

The Prince of Wales ardently supported Denmark. 'This horrible war,' he told General Bruce's widow in February 1864, 'will be a stain for ever on Prussian history, and I think it is *very* wrong of our Government not to have interfered before now. As to Lord Russell's everlasting Notes nobody cares twopence about them on the Continent.' In his opinion, rapid and decisive action could have preserved peace. 'If we had sent our fleet to the Baltic at the beginning, all this bloodshed might possibly have been avoided, and we should cut a much better figure in Europe than we do at present.'

The Queen supported Prussia throughout the war. Not only was she naturally inclined to such a policy, but having turned for guidance to the Prince Consort's papers, she felt sure he would have sympathized with Germany. In May 1864, she told Vicky, 'I am grieved and distressed to say that the feeling against Prussia has become *most violent* in England, and quite ungovernable. The people are carried away by imaginary fancies, and by the belief that Prussia wants to have the duchies for *herself.*' Of course, the Queen did not share this assessment, and invariably declared that she knew it 'to be false; but the feeling is there, and at present no reason is listened to.'

It is only too easy for a present-day writer to be wise after the event and to censure historical characters for failing to anticipate what for them was a shadowy future but for us is a well-defined past. Nevertheless, it must be said that the Queen was proved wrong, that the 'falsehoods' she refuted were the truth, that she was too slow to recognize the German threat, and that she allowed affection for her husband's homeland to blind her to its faults.

Alix was deeply distressed by events in Denmark. She spent Christmas at Osborne with the Queen, who told Vicky that her daughter-in-law was 'very unhappy about her poor father and cries much.' The Prince and Princess saw in the New Year, 1864, at Frogmore House, where the Duchess of Kent had lived in old age. It was a bitterly cold winter and hence a splendid time for skating. On 8 January, Alix drove to Virginia Water to see the fun. Soon after she returned home for tea, it became clear that she was going to give birth to a baby, two months before expected. Nothing, of course, was ready, but Lady Macclesfield, herself the mother of thirteen children, took charge. At ten minutes to nine that evening the Princess gave birth to a boy weighing three and three-quarter pounds. Dr Brown, who galloped across the Park from Windsor, arrived just in time to wrap the infant in cotton wool, for which he was given a knighthood. The premature delivery of Prince Albert Victor Christian Edward, known as 'Eddy' to his family, was naturally attributed to his mother's concern over Denmark.

The Prince of Wales was deeply moved by his wife's grief. His was too feeling a nature to watch her weeping over the misfortunes of her native land without sharing her distress. 'My heart bleeds,' Alix told the Queen, 'when I think of my poor beloved country which is being attacked in a most scandalous manner . . . God will not let Germany go unpunished for this unjust avarice.' Both the Prince and Princess agreed that it was England's bounden duty to support Denmark, and that, as Alix expressed it, 'the Duchies

belong to Papa.' For the first and last time in his life, the Prince was
so critical of Government policy that he resorted to conversations
with its conservative enemies in his efforts to resist it.

The Queen, who had long feared that Bertie would follow
Hanoverian precedents and confuse the duties of the Prince of Wales
with those of the Leader of the Opposition, was greatly alarmed by
all she heard, the more so as the Prussian Ambassador in London,
Count Bernstorff, also complained that the Prince flagrantly supported Denmark, accused the Foreign Office of pusillanimity, and
slandered Germany. Normally, she would have ignored Bernstorff's
grievances, for she regarded him as a 'shocking mischief maker,'
whose morbid sensitivity to imagined slights was only exceeded by
his disregard for the susceptibilities of others. But on this occasion
she could not but agree that Bertie was guilty of reckless freedom of
speech. So not only did she write reproaching him herself, but
begged Lord Clarendon to warn him against abusing Prussia, 'for
it is fearfully dangerous for the Heir to the throne to take up one side
violently . . . The Queen knows it is not *easy* where one's feelings are
strongly moved; but if one is determined . . . one can keep clear of
violent partisanship.'

As requested, Clarendon saw the Prince and was able to tell the
Queen that he had 'found his Royal Highness very reasonable and
right-minded on the subject of Denmark. He said that it would have
been unfeeling and unnatural on his part if he had not heartily
sympathized with the Princess, who passed sleepless nights and was
miserable about the trials that her parents were undergoing, but that
it was far from his Royal Highness's wish or intention to give expression to the feeling which he must be known to entertain.'

The Queen was almost as unhappy about the war as Alix,
claiming that she could hardly find words to describe 'what I suffer
now, alone without adored Papa, without help, or support, or love
and protection.' Her rest, it appeared, was 'disturbed, torn to pieces
with anxiety and sorrow,' and her 'worst fears about B's marriage
realized – so that there is division in the family!!' It was 'terrible to
have the poor boy on the wrong side,' which could have been avoided
had his wife been 'a good German and not a Dane!' She told Vicky
that 'Alix's parentage' had added to her 'sorrows and troubles and
put a great bar between our intimacy.'

Phipps was so concerned about the Queen's bouts of depression
that he told Sir William Knollys, 'I think she is in lower spirits than
I have seen her for a long time, and she has occasional outbursts of

grief which are very painful to witness. The fact is that the circumstances attending the present state of foreign politics weigh heavily upon her, and naturally make her feel more and more deeply the want of that support and counsel upon which she has for so many years implicitly relied.' Phipps told Sir William that he had written the Prince a letter telling him that the Queen 'requires to be treated with great gentleness and consideration,' and that an ill-chosen expression 'might give much more pain than it would at a time when the nerves were in better tone. He has a really good heart and I was sure would be careful not to give his mother pain.'

It so happened that when Frederick VII of Denmark died, the Queen had a family party at Windsor. Such was the conflict of loyalties that the peace of the Castle was threatened. Her Majesty's half-sister, Princess Feodore, was 'very anxious and violent,' particularly as her daughter Adelaide had married Prince Frederick of Augustenburg, one of the claimants to Schleswig-Holstein. For their part, Vicky and Fritz pressed Prussia's demands as vehemently as Bertie and Alix rejected them. 'No respect is paid to my opinion now,' the Queen told King Leopold. In the end she restored a semblance of peace by forbidding any discussion of Danish affairs. Sympathizing with her difficulties, Leopold wrote 'You will recollect when first Albert spoke to me about Alix that he said we take the Princess, but *not* her relations.' But the Queen was in no mood for fine distinctions and insisted that her daughter-in-law 'comes completely from the enemy's camp in every way – Stockmar was right.'

Long after the war of 1864 was over, the distrust it provoked lingered on. The Queen, ignoring the fact that her son was only twenty-two at the time, chose to regard his impetuous intervention as proof of innate indiscretion, and with feminine inconsistency accused him of openly supporting Denmark, regardless of the blatant way in which she herself defended the interests of Prussia: to such a degree that she was attacked in Parliament for so doing. Nor was she prepared to make any allowance for his feelings of chivalry towards Alix's compatriots in their courageous defiance of the mightiest army in Europe. In July 1862, she had written to General Grey stressing the importance of encouraging HRH to read despatches for an hour or so every day. But after the Danish War she persuaded herself that it would be wrong to share her sovereign power with an irresponsible youth. Until the last years of her reign she neither revised this opinion nor appeared to notice that her son grew wiser as he grew older.

Alix never forgave Prussia for conquering Denmark and depriving her of the Duchies. Long before she became Queen, she referred to 'bestial Germans,' and during the First World War spoke to Sir George Arthur of 'those hateful Huns.' When her son, Prince George, was made an honorary Colonel of a Prussian regiment, she was predictably indignant. 'My Georgie boy has become a real, live, filthy, blue-coated, Pickelhaube German soldier!!!' 'It was your misfortune,' she added magnanimously, 'not your fault.' So little attempt did she make to disguise her feelings either in word or deed, that Vicky, writing to her daughter Sophie in 1894, felt bound to acknowledge that 'dear Aunt Alix dislikes us Germans so.'

All King Christian's children shared Alix's sentiments, which they disseminated by means of influential marriages. Descendants of Christian IX sat on the thrones of Belgium, Britain, Denmark, Greece, Norway, Rumania, Spain and Yugoslavia. In 1866 Dagmar married the future Tsar, Alexander III. When war broke out in 1914, she granted the President of the Duma an audience at the Anichkoff Palace. 'You cannot imagine,' she told him, 'what a satisfaction it is to me, after being compelled to disguise my true feelings for fifty years, to be free at last to tell everybody how I hate the Germans!'

In 1878, Princess Thyra, Alix's youngest sister, married the Duke of Cumberland, whose father, George V, 'The blind King of Hanover,' had twelve years before been deprived of his kingdom by Prussia. The Duke hated the Hohenzollerns with obsessive intensity and never ceased to claim the possessions of which they had robbed him. Alix's brother, the Crown Prince Frederick, married Princess Louise of Sweden, Marshal Bernadotte's grand-daughter; and Prince Waldemar, despite his Protestantism, made Princess Marie of Orleans his bride. Finally, William, who was chosen King of the Hellenes in 1863, married the Grand Duchess Olga of Russia, who, like Dagmar's husband, was a grandchild of Nicholas I. Germany was consequently encircled by Danish royalty longing to avenge the loss of Schleswig-Holstein and inspired by intense hatred of the Second Reich. That Britain and Russia were allies in 1914 owed much to the influence of two sisters: the Dowager Queen Alexandra and the Dowager Empress of Russia.

After Denmark's capitulation in July 1864, Alix was eager to see her parents and show them their grandson. Moreover, Bertie had never visited Copenhagen and she longed to show him her home. The Queen, however, only consented to the journey with great reluctance and on strict conditions. Palmerston's support of the project merely increased her objections to it. On 28 August, the Prime Minister wrote to the Prince of Wales describing an audience he had had with the Queen the day before at Windsor. 'I found Her Majesty under some anxiety lest the natural feelings of Your Royal Highness upon recent events might during your Royal Highness's approaching tour be expressed in some manner so as to be reported, perhaps with exaggerations, with the result of embittering feelings which it would be desirable to allay. I ventured to assure Her Majesty that, however strong your Royal Highness's feelings on recent events must necessarily be, I was sure that the expression of them would be tempered by due discretion. I trust your Royal Highness will not think I am taking an undue liberty in mentioning to you that which I observed in my audience of yesterday.'

Mrs Paget shared Her Majesty's misgivings, for different reasons. She feared that the Prince and Princess might be ill received, 'as the irritation in Denmark against England was very great. The Danes considered themselves ill-used and even entrapped by the fallacious words of Lord Palmerston.'

The Queen's conditions for the visit were that the royal travellers should remain incognito, that they should forbid political discussions in their presence, that Prince Albert Victor should be sent to Balmoral when they left Denmark, and that Germany should be included in the itinerary, to show that the Prince of Wales was 'not only the son-in-law of the King of Denmark, but the Child of his Parents.'

The Prince and Princess, the infant Eddy, Sir William Knollys, and Lord and Lady Spencer sailed on the *Osborne* from Dundee to Elsinore. King Christian observed when he met them that it was the happiest day he had known since his country was invaded, and Alix was overjoyed to be reunited with her parents. But even the Prince's affection for his wife could not reconcile him to life at Fredensborg. The rooms were uncomfortable, the food monotonous, and the evenings excruciatingly tedious. To one who took the Second Empire as his model, Fredensborg seemed as dreary as a provincial vicarage. If only his mother had been right in supposing it to be a second Babylon! Mrs Paget's fears proved equally unfounded, for the Prince and his wife were rapturously received wherever they went. Presumably his unconcealed sympathy for Denmark, which the Queen so deplored, convinced the citizens of Copenhagen that he was as grieved as they were that the British Government had left them to fight alone.

Part of the political influence exercised by Christian IX's children may be traced to their family reunions held in Denmark every summer. Uncles and aunts, cousins and nephews, emperors and kings, 'Greek Nicky,' 'Alicky,' 'Minny,' 'Uncle Sasha' and the rest, gathered at Bernsdorff or Fredensborg as guests of 'Apapa' and 'Amama,' where, for a few carefree weeks, they escaped the restraints of royal existence and satisfied their yearning for Petit Trianons and Gelder Sheils. Tsars, who in Russia sheltered behind armed guards, roamed freely around the woods and foothills of Lake Esron, heedless of anarchist bombs. Members of these happy family parties shared rooms and cottages, helped themselves to breakfast and luncheon, went on picnics and bicycle rides and joined in hilarious games of croquet. In the evening, there were boisterous romps with pillows and soda-water siphons: childish, innocent fun, very unlike the home life of the Queen.

Nobody enjoyed this rough-and-tumble more than Princess Alexandra who never grew up and hardly grew old. As for Bertie, he did his best to conceal his boredom and to appear enchanted. A member of his household once complained: 'There is nowhere on earth, Sir, more boring than Fredensborg!' 'How dare you say that?' demanded the Prince, pretending to be furious, and then, after a stunned silence, added, 'I remember, of course, you have not been to Bernsdorff yet.'

When Prince William of Denmark became George I of the Hellenes, Athens became an Eastern Copenhagen to which the family flocked. E. F. Benson records how he was once lazing in the Palace Garden when he 'heard the sound of tripping feet and male laughter and female cries of dismay, and round the corner of the rose-pergola where he sat came King George, kicking in front of him what had once been a hat. Behind tripped the Princess of Wales, shrilly protesting "I beg you not to, George. It is my hat: so rude of you!" '

From Copenhagen, the Prince and Princess travelled to Stockholm, where they stayed at the Palace with Charles XV of Sweden. The Queen was furious at this change of plan, having intended them to remain privately at an hotel: a requirement inspired by the fear 'that the acceptance of hospitality or receptions from any foreign sovereigns' might encourage 'claims for a return of similar civilities.' On 1 October she wrote Bertie a reproachful letter from Balmoral, a copy of which Phipps was instructed to forward to Sir William. 'The Queen has directed me,' wrote Sir Charles, 'in the *strictest confidence*,' to send you 'the enclosed copy of a letter which she has written to the Prince of Wales. The fact is that both she and the Govt. have been rather alarmed at his apparently thinking that his visits to Courts abroad, are, like those of any private individual, to be decided upon by Himself without any consultation of the authorities at home.'

The enclosure read as follows. 'My dear Bertie, I cannot conceal from you that I was much surprised and annoyed at your accepting an invitation at Stockholm in the Palace, after it had been agreed upon and settled, with the concurrence of the Ministers, that your visit should be a perfectly private one, and that you should live at the Legation or in an Hotel, the King being no relation of yours or Alix's. As it is impossible, as well as not being the custom, for me or you to receive all foreign Princes who come over to England, it will not do for you to accept what cannot be returned. It is *absolutely* necessary when I allow you to go abroad that the plan arranged should be *strictly* adhered to, and not departed from except *by reference to me again*. It will I think be better that you should not prolong your stay at Copenhagen which is already now over three weeks . . . After such a prolonged stay in the North, it is absolutely necessary that you should also remain some little time in Germany . . . I am rather doubtful about your visit to Paris. If it does take place it must be on the *complete understanding* that it is *in real incognito*, which your other visits have not been, and that you stop at an Hotel, and do not lodge with the Emperor and Empress and do not accept an invitation to Compiègne and Fontainebleau, which *all* the Ministers strongly object to, as much as I do. The style of going on there being quite unfit for a young respectable Prince and Princess, like yourselves. Of course, you might accept a day's shooting at Compiègne and visit and drive with the Emperor and Empress, but nothing more.'

The Queen here made use of a favourite and characteristic device: the representation of her opinions as supported, even thrust upon her, by her Ministers. In truth, she was happy to claim their support without reference to their views. On the rare occasions when they were bold enough to oppose her, she found no problem in rejecting their advice. Her assertion that '*all* the ministers' objected to the plan of the Prince staying with the Emperor Napoleon, was disingenuous, for Lord Russell, the Foreign Secretary, was in favour of the visit.

In replying to the Queen's letter, the Prince of Wales defended himself for deviating from her plans. The hotels in the Swedish capital were mostly squalid and the Legation was far too cramped. 'I have not the intention of letting Alix be uncomfortably lodged if I can help it. Besides, as I said before, the King was immensely gratified by our visit, and what would have been the good of annoying him by not going to the Palace? . . . You may be sure that I shall try to meet your wishes as much as possible, but . . . if I am not allowed to use my own discretion we had better give up travelling altogether.' As for their delay in sending Eddy home, a subject to which the Queen repeatedly referred in her letters, they had postponed doing so on medical advice. Bertie reminded the Queen that whenever Vicky or Alice visited England, she expected them to remain for two or three months. But when he and Alix stayed in Denmark they were only permitted a fortnight's leave of absence. The Queen was furious at this exposure of her double standard and ordered the Prince to cancel his visit to France. When she sought Lord Russell's approval of her action he did not disguise from her that he thought it peremptory and imprudent.

The Queen's insistence that her son should visit Germany aggravated rather than resolved family differences. He and Alix met Vicky and Fritz at Cologne. The Crown Princess was torn between conflicting emotions: loyalty to Prussia, pride in Fritz, sympathy for King Christian and Alix, suspicion of Bismarck and admiration for the courage of the Danes. Fritz, equally unhappy and confused, felt ashamed at being awarded the Order of the Red Eagle for his part in defeating a defenceless enemy. Everyone felt ill at ease, the Crown Prince and Princess being the more tongue-tied because their patriotism was tempered by bewilderment and guilt. Fritz, who always wore uniform, displayed on his tunic the medal he had won at the Battle of Duppel. 'I can assure you,' the Prince of Wales told Lord Spencer, 'it was not pleasant to see him and his ADC always in Prussian uniform flaunting before our eyes a most objectionable ribbon which he received for his *deeds of valour*??? against the unhappy Danes.'

Princess Helena's engagement in 1865 rekindled family animosities. When Princess Alice married the Grand Duke of Hesse, the Queen resolved to find Helena a husband prepared to accept that his wife's first duty was not to him but her mother. In May, 1863, Queen Victoria wrote King Leopold a letter explaining her proposal for Lenchen. 'A married daughter I MUST have living with me, and must *not* be left constantly to look about for help, and to have to make shift for the day, which is too dreadful! I intend (and she wishes it herself) to look out in a year or two (for till nineteen or twenty I don't intend *she* should marry) for a young, sensible Prince, for Lenchen to marry, who can during *my lifetime* make my house his *principal* home. Lenchen is so useful, and her whole character so well adapted to live in the house, that . . . I could *not* give her up, without *sinking* under the *weight* of my desolation.'

One difficulty in finding Helena a husband was that she possessed neither charm nor looks: a problem eventually solved by finding her as unbecoming a Consort. 'Poor dear Lenchen,' the Queen admitted with her customary candour, 'though most useful and active and clever and amiable, does not improve in looks and has great difficulties with her figure and her want of calm, quiet, graceful manners.'

Alix's brother, the Crown Prince Frederick, saw a good deal of Helena during his time at Oxford. It became clear that he might well propose marriage. Dismayed at the prospect of Lenchen being carried off to Copenhagen, the Queen commanded General Grey to write to the British Minister to Denmark, Sir Augustus Paget, telling him to let it be known 'so clearly as to permit of no misunderstanding,' that she 'would never consent to a marriage of any of her daughters with the Crown Prince of Denmark. Quite probably there had been no such thought in the mind of King Christian, but she would be sorry if Prince Frederick should continue his studies in Oxford without being aware of her resolution in the matter.' It is hardly surprising that King Christian was deeply mortified to learn that Queen Victoria, having spurned his son, proposed to bestow Lenchen upon the younger brother of the Prince of Augustenburg: the 'rebel' whose claims to Schleswig-Holstein had led to war with Prussia.

At first sight, Prince Christian appeared to have little to commend him as a suitor. He was unattractive, dreary, and penniless. The last defect was the easiest to remedy. The Queen, dismissing the possibility of defeat, consulted Dr Jenner to see what might be done to improve HRH's appearance. 'If only he looked a little younger!' she complained. 'His manners and movements are so old. It is such a pity.' In 1865, Prince Christian was thirty-four while Helena was only nineteen. Much, however, could be forgiven or overlooked, even his detestable smoking habits, because, being an exile, he was prepared to live wherever the Queen wished and to leave Lenchen to look after her

Lady Geraldine Somerset, the Duchess of Cambridge's lady-in-waiting, reflected the view of the family she served with such devoted loyalty when she wrote of 'this *abominable, disgraceful* marriage' with 'a miserable starveling German Princeling.' On the other hand, General Grey took Her Majesty's part in declaring 'I cannot praise Prince Christian too highly. His tact and good feeling about everything, and above all his good sense and sound judgement cannot be compared.'

At first, Princess Alice opposed the engagement, fearing that it sacrificed Helena's happiness to the Queen's selfish wishes. She even went so far as to warn Prince Christian not 'to be put upon.' When her mother came to hear of it, she sharply reminded Alice that she was both her Parent and her Sovereign, and forbade her to interfere. Indeed, the Queen felt so bitter about her daughter's opposition that she ignored the genuine concern from which it sprang. She even accused her of 'wanting to have everything her own way.' 'In strict confidence,' she wrote to King Leopold, 'I grieve to tell you that Alice cannot conceal her extreme dislike to her sister's settlement in England which is mere jealousy and pains me.' Later, she told her Uncle that 'Alice (to my great sorrow for she used to be such a comfort to me) is very unamiable and altogether not changed to her advantage.' Considering the manner in which Alice, on this, as on other occasions, acted as the peacemaker of the family, it was less than just to accuse her of 'mischief and intrigue.'

Bertie and Alix, encouraged by the Cambridges, protested against the engagement even more vigorously than the Grand Duchess of Hesse. Alix saw the match as an insult and affront, and nothing would persuade her that Prince Christian was not an enemy. When Alice learned that her brother was threatening to boycott the wedding she began to have second thoughts. Not only was she distressed by the growing rift in the family, but she now realized that Helena was perfectly prepared to marry Christian and might never find another husband. She therefore decided to write to her brother to beg him to relent. 'Oh, darling Bertie,' she pleaded, 'don't let you be the one who cannot sacrifice his *own feelings* for the welfare of Mother and Sister. Mamma knows and deeply regrets what you feel, but, nowhere would she find another, and as she almost broke with Papa's only brother and all her other relations and friends for you and Alix, saying that never should political feelings stand between her and her son's happiness, do you both dear ones repress your feelings for a Mother's sake and let not political feelings towards

Alix's relations stand between you and your own sister's happiness.'

The Crown Princess and Prince Alfred joined Alice in her efforts to persuade Bertie not to oppose the match. Vicky insisted that it would be wrong to regard it as a sign of the Queen's diminishing affection for his wife. 'You know Mama loves Alix much; she must not take this marriage as a proof of the reverse, which it is not.' Affie argued that as nothing could change the decision 'we must put a good face on it,' however painful the relationship might be.

In the end, the Prince of Wales was persuaded to accept Helena's marriage. 'Bertie came to luncheon,' wrote the Queen to Vicky from Windsor, 'and, after it, I saw him and he was very nice and affectionate and amiable (and what I know will give you the greatest pleasure) all is quite satisfactory as regards Lenchen. He spoke most kindly and affectionately to her – sent Christian a kind message – and all is right. This happening yesterday on that solemn day [14 December, the fourth anniversary of the Prince Consort's death] gave me great satisfaction. Bertie has a loving, affectionate heart and never could bear to be long in disagreement with his family. Towards me also he was very dear and nice.'

Although Bertie, who hated dissension, accepted the inevitable, Alix was less easily reconciled to her new brother-in-law. As late as 1883, after 'Old Christian' had stayed a few days at Sandringham, she described him as doing 'nothing but *eat* and shoot other people's pheasants.' Her dislike of Helena's husband gravely compromised her relations with the Queen, who told Vicky: 'Bertie is most affectionate and kind but Alix is by no means what she ought to be. It will be long, if ever, before she regains my confidence.'

Shortly before the Wedding, it was alleged that Prince Christian was a lunatic, that he had fifteen children, 'one of whom was going to live with Lenchen,' that the King of Prussia had written to Her Majesty to warn her against her future son-in-law, and that the engagement was about to be broken off. Princess Helena was understandably 'vexed and annoyed,' General Grey said such rumours were 'utterly contemptible,' and the Queen was at a loss to discover why the world was so wicked.

On 5 July 1866, the marriage took place in St George's Chapel, Windsor, the Queen giving the Bride away. If 'dear Papa' was not there, 'I was the only one to do it,' she explained for the benefit of Fritz. The Duchess of Cambridge grudgingly attended the service, radiating disapproval. 'Lenchen looked extremely well,' wrote the Queen two days after the ceremony, 'and so did Christian, but certain relations (an old Aunt especially) made one uncomfortable. Bertie was very amiable and kind. There were great crowds and great enthusiasm.'

Another matter about which the Queen and Alix disagreed was bringing up children. The Queen felt resentful that her daughter-in-law was so little inclined to consult her: after all she had brought up a family of nine. But Alix had strong views on the subject, and avoided seeking advice she would probably ignore. Both got caught in the barbed wire along the treacherous frontier separating loving guidance from capricious meddling.

Alix was determined to bring up her family as simply as possible, as she herself had been. 'One thing she does insist on,' wrote the Queen, 'and that is great simplicity and an absence of all pride, and in that respect she has my fullest support.' The notion that children should be seen but not heard did not prevail at Marlborough House or Sandringham, where the young were very much in evidence. The Prince of Wales's standard of discipline was notably undemanding and his son's quarterdeck manner was learned from the Navy, not his father. 'If children are too strictly or perhaps too severely treated,' he once told his mother, 'they only fear those whom they ought to love.'

The Queen, contemplating the fruits of this philosophy, believed it stood self-condemned, for she regarded her grandchildren as so 'ill bred' and 'ill trained,' that she could not 'fancy them at all.' Lady Geraldine Somerset described the Prince's daughters as 'rampaging' little girls, and the boys as being 'past all management' and as 'wild as hawks.' But Edward Hamilton was more favourably impressed. Describing a visit to Sandringham in 1884, he noted: 'At Luncheon our numbers were increased by the presence of the three young Princesses – nice looking and so simple and unaffected – evidently brought up in the best of ways.'

The Princess might have provided Barrie's inspiration for Peter Pan for she had a horror of growing up. Her passionate devotion to her family tempted her to be dangerously possessive. When Prince George became engaged she told him, 'there is a bond of love between us, that of mother and child, which nothing can ever diminish or render less binding – and nobody can, or shall ever, come between me and my darling Georgie boy.' The Princess wanted time, like the clock at Grantchester, to stop at ten to three, if not rather earlier. She celebrated her eldest daughter's nineteenth birthday with a children's party, and ended a letter to Prince George, when he was in command of a gunboat, 'with a great big kiss for your lovely little face.'

Her daughters caught her trick of talking about 'the dear little thing,' or the 'poor little man': almost everybody was 'poor' unless they were royal. Queen Marie of Rumania described the Wales girls as being 'very mute' and invariably expressing themselves 'in a minor key.' From talking to them one derived 'a strange impression that life would have been very wonderful and everything very beautiful if it had not been so bad.'

Their whimsical if disturbing charm was very much in evidence in a letter Princess Louise, who was eighteen at the time, sent Francis Knollys in 1885. It was signed by her younger sisters, and brimmed over with affectionate private jokes. 'Dear old Thingy,' it read, 'At last we are sending you our photos [in fact, drawings of themselves represented as animals] which we have painted ourselves. *These* won't fade, but we suppose they will soon be *put aside*. We hope that the pictures will put you in mind of your little friends Toots, Gawks and Snipey. You must notice that Toots is practising her steps for the tiresome Court ball, that Gawks is going to bed instead like Cinderella, and that Snipey is trying to console herself with a song instead of singing her hymns in Church as she ought to do. You little *humbug!* We believe you are enjoying yourself very much in Ireland, in spite of oranges and onions thrown at your head as we see by the papers. We are afraid you won't be at all glad to see us *country bumpkins* again, as we shall have nothing to talk about but cows and cowslips. Now goodbye, old thingy and hoping you will appreciate the *works of art* we send you. Your affectionate little friends: Toots, Gawks and Snipey.' (Princesses Louise, Victoria, Maud.)

The Wales family was such a happy one they could not endure separation. When King Edward and Queen Alexandra attended a farewell luncheon on board the *Ophir* for Prince George and his wife, before they set off in 1901 on a tour of the British Empire, the Queen sobbed throughout the meal, the King was too overcome with emotion to propose a toast, and the Prince and Princess were so upset that they were obliged to hurry down to their cabin for a good cry. Whatever her shortcomings as a mother might be, Alix's family were exceptionally fond of one another.

Queen Victoria's conviction that Bertie's children would be retarded, although derived from a fanciful premiss, was strikingly endorsed by the youth she chose to call 'Albert Victor', and everyone else called 'Eddy'. Within a month of his birth she was already deploring his backwardness. Even Alix was forced to admit 'he is a little slow and dawdly,' but this, she said, was because he had 'grown so fast,' and besides he was 'a very good boy at heart.' His problems may have arisen from deafness, inherited from his mother and grandmother, or conceivably 'petit mal.' Alix's second son, George, born on 3 June 1865, grew up to be much more lively and intelligent than his brother.

The Queen wanted the boys to be sent to Wellington, in which the Prince Consort had taken so much interest. But the Prince of Wales, apparently agreeing with William IV that there is 'no place for making an English gentleman like the Quarterdeck of an English Man-of-War,' sent them to HMS *Britannia* at Dartmouth. It was his policy that they should mix with other boys and not be segregated as he had been. During their time as naval cadets they were looked after by a tutor, the Reverend John Dalton: Curate to Canon Prothero of Whippingham, the Parish Church of Osborne, and father to Hugh Dalton, the Labour Chancellor of the Exchequer. Lady Geraldine Somerset, sublimely underestimating the immensity of his task, wrote contemptuously of Dalton's efforts. Eddy, she heard, was '*charming*, as nice a youth as could be, simple, unaffected, unspoiled, affectionate, but! his *ignorance*! Lamentable. What on earth stupid Dalton has been about all these years! He has taught him *nothing*.' Eddy, she noted, suffered from 'sleepy apathetic laziness and total want of initiative,' and was 'so dull and heavy and hopelessly soft' that he did 'not care even for any field sports.'

Dalton's failure to arouse what he himself described as an abnormally dormant condition of mind was hardly his fault. When the Prince was sent to Cambridge one of his instructors doubted whether he could 'possibly derive much benefit from attending lectures,' as he 'hardly knows the meaning of the word *to read*.' At least he was left to live the life of an ordinary undergraduate, and was given rooms in Trinity, instead of being exiled to some secluded outpost.

After leaving Cambridge, Eddy joined the Tenth Hussars, but showed little more promise as a soldier than he had as a student. On one occasion, the Duke of Cambridge 'wanted to try him in some most elementary movement,' but 'the Colonel begged him not to attempt it as the Prince had not an *idea* of how to do it! The Duke of course not wishing to expose him let it alone.' The Prince hardly showed any interest in the Army, detested field days, and thought his General 'a lunatic.'

For reasons not easy to discern, he proved attractive to women.

Possibly he aroused their maternal instinct by his helplessness, or maybe they found his prospects irresistible. So recklessly did he fall in and out of love, that his father contemplated sending him on a colonial tour. The Queen, despite her secluded life, knew all about his affairs. 'I ask again,' wrote Knollys to Ponsonby, in 1891, '*who* is it tells the Queen these things?'

Rumours credited Eddy with every vice and folly. Sarah Bernhardt claimed that he was her son Maurice's father. It was even whispered that the Prince was Jack the Ripper, regardless of unanswerable alibis provided by the Court Circular. He was also reputed to have been compromised with Lord Arthur Somerset, his father's Superintendent of the Stables, in a homosexual bordello in Cleveland Street: the only evidence for which appears to have been Lord Salisbury's anxiety to keep the matter quiet.

That the Prime Minister was not attempting to shield Prince Eddy may be seen from a letter the Prince of Wales sent Knollys when the scandal broke in 1889. 'Your interview with Somerset must have been a very painful one. I had a very kind but sad letter from the poor Duke – and cannot say *how* deeply I feel for him and the Duchess. His having to break the news to her will be terrible. Since this dreadful affair – names of other people who we know will have been mentioned . . . It is really *too* shocking! One a married man whose hospitality I have frequently accepted! If these people are in the same boat as poor Podge [Lord Arthur Somerset] – are they to be allowed to go about as before – whilst he has fled the country?' That rhetorical question would hardly have been posed had the Prince being trying to hush matters up to save his son.

In May 1890, the Queen made Eddy Duke of Clarence and Avondale, thus adding to the absurdity of his double Christian name and making him the butt of endless puns and jokes. Labouchere launched a pungent attack on the infelicity of the chosen title. 'The only Duke of Clarence who is known in history is the numskull who was deservedly drowned in a butt of malmsey, and during the present century the title was associated with the aberrations and extravagances for which William IV was unenviably notorious.'

Before the Duke finally became engaged, three princesses were considered. The first was Princess Alexandra of Hesse, Alice's youngest daughter, who was fancied by the Kaiser and married the last of the Tsars. Queen Victoria greatly admired her 'strength of character' in refusing 'the greatest position there is,' although 'all her family and all of us wish it.'

Believing that matrimony alone could save Eddy – which is precisely what had been said of his father – it was suggested that he should consider 'Mossy', Vicky's youngest daughter. But she was far too German for Alix's liking. Francis Knollys told Ponsonby that he personally thought her an admirable choice. However, 'it would not I am afraid be agreeable to the Princess of Wales on account of her being a Prussian and a sister of the German Emperor. The Prince of Wales would not object to it at all . . . As you know from our conversation the other day I am a strong advocate for Pss Margaret and I wish the Princess would see these things differently, but she likes the girl herself and if it were not for the objection I have mentioned, would I think rather like her for a daughter-in-law.'

The third possible bride for Prince Eddy was one of his own choice, Hélène d'Orleans. Her father, the Comte de Paris, was Head of the House of Orleans and claimed the French throne. Probably in all Europe he could not have found a more impossible girl with whom to fall in love. The Third Republic was hardly likely to welcome the prospect of Princess Hélène becoming Queen of England. Moreover, under the terms of the Act of Settlement of 1701, Eddy would forfeit his right to the throne by taking a Popish wife. Because of these problems, the Queen told her grandson the marriage was out of the question. In May 1890 she wrote from Windsor: 'I have heard it rumoured that you had been thinking and talking of Princess Hélène d'Orleans! I can't believe this for you know that I told you (as I did your parents who agreed with me) that such a marriage is utterly *impossible*. None of our family can marry a Catholic without losing all their rights . . . Besides which *you* could not marry the daughter of the Pretender to the French Throne . . . That being the case you should avoid meeting her as much as possible as it would only lead to make you unhappy if you formed an attachment for her.'

Alix, however, rashly encouraged the match: romantically believing her son was passionately in love, and relieved that Hélène was not German. Eddy's sister, Princess Louise, Duchess of Fife, conspired with her mother to encourage the romance. As she lived at East Sheen Lodge, Richmond, a few hundred yards from the Comte de Paris, she proved most useful. In August 1890 the Fifes asked the Comte and Comtesse and their daughter to stay with them at Mar Lodge, which was situated on a hill above the Dee some twelve miles from Balmoral. Alix and Eddy were also invited. On 20 August, Eddy and Hélène became secretly engaged, and the momentous complications of what Lord Salisbury called the 'Royal Idyll' began to unfold.

Alix, appreciating her mother-in-law's romantic disposition, decided that the most effective way of overcoming her opposition would be for Eddy and Hélène to seek her blessing. Ignoring her son's reluctance to confront the Queen, – and it must be said that braver men than he, such as Prince Bismarck, had trembled at the prospect, – she hustled the pair into a carriage, complete with a picnic luncheon to sustain their flagging spirits, and ordered the coachman to drive to Balmoral. Her stratagem succeeded triumphantly, as Eddy told Prince George. 'I naturally expected Grandmama would be furious and say it was quite impossible etc. But instead of that she was very nice about it and promised to help us as much as possible, which she is now doing . . . I believe what pleased her most was my taking Hélène into her, and saying we had arranged it entirely between ourselves without consulting our parents first. This as you know was not quite true but she believed it all.'

Before her conversion to the marriage, the Queen not only wrote to Eddy saying it was unthinkable, but attempted to discourage Princess Hélène's parents. 'I am not sure whether you know the preface to our love story,' wrote Ponsonby to Knollys. 'The Queen suspected that Marlborough House was encouraging Hélène, so she wrote to an Orleans friend – I think the Princess of Coburg – to say that if these two met much they would inevitably fall in love, and as from religious reasons a union was impossible it was cruel to encourage it and that she ought to warn Hélène's parents against it. HM got the reply from her Orleans friend agreeing, and promising to warn the Comtesse de Paris, on the very morning of the day when the loving couple implored the Royal Blessing. The readiness to change religion of course destroyed the Queen's objection.' Lord Salisbury, the Prime Minister, was on holiday in France at the time, so his nephew, Arthur Balfour, was summoned to Balmoral to discuss the implications of the match. 'Will it be believed,' he wrote to his Uncle, 'that neither the Queen, nor the young Prince, nor Princess Hélène see anything which is not romantic, interesting, touching and praiseworthy in the young lady giving up her religion *to which she still professes devoted attachment*, in order to marry the man upon whom she has set her heart! . . . The Queen is much touched by the personal appeal to *herself*. With admirable dexterity (this surely cannot be the young man's idea) they came hand in hand straight to her, and implored her to smooth out not merely the political difficulties, but the family difficulties also. In making her their confidante, they have made her their ally. She would have been in a much less melting mood if the approaches had been conducted in due form through the parents.'

Balfour suspected that 'sentimental considerations' had been 'much strengthened' by the Queen's desire 'to see the young man married,' and that the Comtesse de Paris was 'more certain that it is good to be Queen of England than she is that it is bad to marry a Protestant. The Comte de Paris, on the other hand, is said to be a strict Roman Catholic – "but not bigoted" says the Queen. I shall be surprised, however, if he is not bigoted enough to object to his daughter changing her creed for a crown.'

Lord Salisbury, apparently untouched by romance, sent the Queen a formidable memorandum listing the problems as he saw them. He made no attempt to disguise his opinion that the marriage would be injudicious and that objections to it far outweighed its possible advantages. He began by saying that the Queen had instructed him not to consult the Cabinet upon the Duke of Clarence's proposed marriage, 'but only three colleagues – presumably Mr Smith, Mr Goschen and Mr Balfour . . . But the more I reflect upon the matter, the more convinced I am that this restriction cannot prudently be maintained: and that as soon as the Cabinet meets it ought to be consulted . . . I gather from Mr Balfour's letters that it is thought by those who know him best that the Comte de Paris will consent. On that point I will offer no opinion. But I will only submit that *unless* he consents, the marriage cannot take place. The Princess, I believe, is nineteen. Until she is twenty-one no English clergyman could marry her without her father's consent: any one who did so would be liable to imprisonment . . . When the consent of the Comte de Paris has been obtained, the Cabinet ought to be consulted. Of course, as the Duke of Clarence observes, the Queen is not bound by the opinion of her ministers. But they ought to have the opportunity of submitting it to her. For her consent to this marriage is a State Act of the greatest gravity. It may profoundly affect the feelings of the people towards the throne, and of foreign countries toward England: and therefore the opinions of her constitutional advisers ought to be before the Queen before her mind is made up.'

Lord Salisbury pointed out that national feeling for centuries had 'been hostile to France. Since the Wars of the Roses, we have had no French Queen except Henrietta Maria. Has the feeling of the people so changed that the French origin of their Queen will not affect their feelings towards the throne? It is a matter to be deeply weighed.' Moreover, it seemed 'at least possible' that Englishmen might 'not look upon the Princess' conversion as durable and thorough: but will anticipate that later in life, when the impulses at present acting upon her have passed away, she will fall back under the spiritual influences under which she has been brought up, and which are supposed to guide her parents.'

Then, said Lord Salisbury, there was the effect which the marriage would have abroad. It could not fail to make bad blood in France if the Comte de Paris became 'the father-in-law of the future King of England. It is needless to add that if the birth of the Princess makes her an object of apprehension to the dominant Republicans, her change of religion will secure the intense hostility of the Catholic and Royalist party.' He concluded by stressing the need to seek 'the best legal advice at the disposal of the Crown,' concerning 'the manner in which this marriage is affected by the Act of Settlement . . . The question whether the future Sovereign of this realm, will or will not disqualify himself by his marriage from reigning, is one on which no sort of doubt ought to exist.'

Much to Salisbury's relief, the Comte refused to permit his daughter to change her faith, but Knollys remained anxious. 'I don't quite understand the line which is now adopted by the Comte de Paris,' he told Ponsonby in January 1891. 'He has given his daughter permission to correspond with Prince Eddy and he makes no objection to their seeing each other. This is not the course which is usually observed by a Father when an engagement has been recently broken off. Is it that they, primed by Manning, whom they have consulted on the subject, think they may be able to get hold of Prince Eddy and induce him to turn a Roman Catholic? I think very strongly that if no arrangement is come to, the Prince and Princess of Wales should insist on everything coming to an end, correspondence and all. Otherwise the youth is being made a fool of. In the meanwhile he declares he will never marry anyone else, which I believe People have said before in similar cases.'

Before the end of the year Ponsonby was relieved to learn that the Duke of Clarence had become officially engaged to a Protestant princess, and that it would no longer be necessary 'to declare in Parliament how the Succession should go,' which he feared 'would raise a debate as to whether there should be any Succession at all.'

The girl to whom Eddy became engaged was Princess Mary of

Teck, whose mother was none other than the Queen's first cousin, Princess Mary Adelaide, the Duke of Cambridge's sister. When Princess 'May' was summoned to Balmoral in October 1891, her excited parents guessed she was 'on approval.' And approved she was. 'We have seen a great deal of May,' the Queen told Vicky, 'and I cannot say enough good about her. May is a particularly nice girl, so quiet and yet cheerful.' Soon afterwards, the Queen wrote to say that she hoped Eddy would marry her, 'for I think she is a superior girl – quiet and reserved *till* you know her well . . . She has no frivolous tastes, has been very carefully brought up and is very well informed and always occupied.' This was a rare tribute, as Her Majesty was ordinarily disposed to regard members of the Cambridge family as mischievous, misguided and light-hearted. On 3 December, Prince Eddy, while staying at Luton Hoo, proposed and was accepted. Four days later, the news of his engagement was made public. The Prince and Princess of Wales were delighted, their son was radiantly happy, for his enthusiasms were intense if transitory: being in love was the one thing which brought him fully to life. His fiancée however, hardly knew him, and accepted him from a sense of duty. Later, the Queen bluntly asserted: 'May never was in love with poor Eddy.'

The Wedding was fixed for 27 February 1892, and on 4 January Princess May and her parents joined the family party at Sandringham to celebrate Eddy's twenty-eighth birthday. A serious epidemic of influenza was raging at the time. In London alone there were five hundred deaths that January: Cardinal Manning being the most notable victim. Several people at Sandringham, including Princess Victoria and Francis Knollys, were struck down by the disease, and both Alix and Princess May had severe colds. The day before his birthday Eddy felt so wretched that he retired to bed. On the eighth, he managed to come downstairs to look at his presents, but, as his mother telegraphed to the Queen, 'Poor Eddy got influenza, cannot dine, so tiresome.' The following day, Dr Laking diagnosed pneumonia. By the thirteenth, the patient was delirious and fighting for life. In his frenzy, he shouted about his regiment and his love for the Queen, who in truth had shown him a forbearance she normally only extended to drunken gillies. Above all, his wandering mind dwelt on his romances. Again and again he cried out: 'Hélène! Hélène!'

In the early hours of 14 January, that fatal day of the month on which the Prince Consort died, Prince Eddy's condition became hopeless. Alix sat by her son's side, holding his hand and smiling bravely, while prayers for the dying were read. Murmuring the question, 'Who is that?' many times over, he sank into a sleep from which there was no awaking. Princess May described the final moments for the Queen. 'Never shall I forget that dreadful night of agony and suspense as we sat round His bed watching Him getting weaker and weaker. Darling Aunt Alix never left Him a moment and when a few minutes before the end she turned to Dr Laking and said "Can you do nothing more to save Him?" and he shook his head, the despairing look on her face was the most heart-rending thing I have ever seen.'

The Princess of Wales lavished so much affection on her backward son that it took her many years to get over his loss. Nevertheless, being deeply religious she found consolation in her faith. On the day he died she told Princess May 'it makes one more link with heaven.' Alix, with her daughters and future daughter-in-law, saw the funeral from Catherine of Aragon's closet, looking down on the coffin from the very place where the Queen had watched her wedding to Bertie. The Prince was so overcome that he sobbed throughout the ceremony.

Alix had requested that the service should be private, so was gravely displeased to find that three of Bertie's sisters had come from Osborne to witness the last rites. When they tried to leave the chapel, nobody for a time could open the door to their pew, and later Ponsonby was instructed to take up the matter with Marlborough House. He got a very dusty answer. 'The Prince of Wales,' wrote an Equerry, 'desires me to say that the harem of Princesses was *not* locked into the further Zenana pew closet but the door got jammed, and adds that they were none of them wanted at all. No ladies were to attend, and the Princess of Wales especially requested privacy – and to avoid meeting her Osborne relations. So they all came. If Princess Beatrice was annoyed it cannot be helped and she must get over it as she likes!' The Prince's resentment may partly be traced to grief, but it probably owed something to the fact that the Queen so often appeared to repose greater confidence in her daughters and their husbands than she did in her eldest son.

Like the room at Windsor in which the Prince Consort died, Eddy's bedroom at Sandringham was preserved untouched. A Union Jack was draped over his bed, and his dressing table was left just as it was on 14 January, complete with his watch, brushes, comb and soap. For many years a fire burned in the grate as if he was still alive.

Broken down as Bertie was by Eddy's death, he had not been the most judicious of parents. The young man had been left in little doubt that he was something of a disappointment. When Eddy was an undergraduate at Trinity he confessed to Lionel Cust that he was 'rather afraid of his father, and aware that he was not quite up to what his father expected of him.' Margot Asquith thought that he had been made a more 'backward, timid boy' because of 'his father's perpetual teasing – a form of ill-judged chaff' which Alix could not endure.

The Duke of Clarence's sudden death a month before his wedding, was less tragic than it appeared at the time, for Prince George made a far better King than Eddy could ever have done. 'It really is the saddest event,' wrote Ponsonby to Knollys. 'In any class of life it would have been a serious tragedy but happening to those who one knows and loves it strikes one with inexpressible sorrow . . . It will create a most profound sensation everywhere . . . I feel very much for you yourself who I know liked the poor fellow well . . . I think the change from joy to grief one of the most tragic events one has ever heard of.'

Gladstone's letter of condolence recalled the death of George IV's daughter, Princess Charlotte. 'Both my wife and I belong to the extremely small number of those still living who remember the only case which comes in essence somewhat near that of the Duke of Clarence. I mean the death of Princess Charlotte. We clearly recollect the wide prevalence and real poignancy of the public sorrow at that time: I all the more because as a very small boy of about six I could not fully comprehend it.'

The Duke of Cambridge, who was one of Eddy's more vigorous critics during his lifetime, evidently subscribed to the principle *De mortuis nil nisi bonum*. 'He was a very dear boy,' he wrote, 'and a very warm and kind hearted man . . . He was a thorough Gentleman and I never heard him say an unkind word of or to anyone. Personally I had the *greatest affection* for him.' The Duke, who was wintering in Cannes for his health's sake, was deeply touched by the Prince of Wales's thoughtfulness in telling him not to contemplate returning to England. 'The dear Prince of Wales has been so very good and considerate to me I never can sufficiently thank him for it. To have thought of me at all at such a terrible moment and to have so strongly urged me *not* to return was *perfect affection* on his part.'

The Prince playing whist at Abergeldie, October 1871. *Zichy*
Left to right: Prince Alfred, M. Brasseur, HRH's French tutor
(back view), Colonel Haig and the Prince of Wales.

The Prince of Wales and Crown
Prince Frederick of Denmark,
January 1869.

Francis Knollys in Paris,
December 1860.

The family of the Crown Prince Frederick of Prussia and the
Crown Princess, 1862. *Winterhalter*.

Wedding portrait of the Prince, 1863. *Winterhalter*.

Wedding portrait of the Princess, 1863. *Winterhalter.*

The marriage in St George's Chapel (detail), 10 March, 1863. *Frith*.

Queen Alexandra when Princess of Wales, 1885. *Lacretelle.*

Honeymoon photograph at Old Sandringham House, April 1863.

Prince George for some time was overwhelmed by Eddy's death. Not only had he lost the one person in the world with whom he had lived on terms of absolute equality, but he now stood in the direct line of the Succession. Hitherto, his ambitions had centred on his naval career, for which he was admirably suited, apart from the fact that like Nelson he suffered from seasickness. But now he was obliged to come ashore and take up royal duties. In May 1892, he was created Duke of York and took his seat in the House of Lords. Although she had bestowed it upon him, the Queen disliked the title. 'A Prince *no-one* else can be, whereas a Duke any nobleman can be.' Prince George was completely different from his brother, as Wally Paget noted. She described him as 'Short, dark, round-faced and full of fun and "go", a real sailor prince, he has a joyous laugh and great charm.'

Many people, including the Queen, his parents, and the Duke and Duchess of Teck, favoured the idea that George should marry May. There was, moreover, a family precedent for such a union. In 1865, Alix's sister, Dagmar, became engaged to the Grand Duke Nicholas of Russia who died soon after the match was announced. The following year she married his younger brother 'Sasha'. Prince George proposed to May at Sheen Lodge, where Eddy had per- suaded Hélène to be his wife. Princess Louise provided her brother with his opportunity by suggesting he should take May into the garden to look at the frogs in the pond. Despite such unromantic auspices it proved a supremely happy marriage. The Queen received the announcement with the greatest satisfaction and May and George were convinced that Eddy gave them his blessing.

The Wedding took place in overpowering heat, on 6 July 1893, in the Chapel Royal, St James's Palace. The Kaiser was represented by his brother Prince Henry, and the Tsar by Prince Nicholas, the last of the Romanovs to reign. Nicholas looked so like the bride- groom that constant confusion ensued. The Prince and Princess of Wales gave a gigantic Garden Party for five thousand people the day before the marriage, at which one of their guests, thinking he was addressing the Tsarevich, asked the Duke of York whether he had come to London to transact other business, or just to attend the Wedding.

The Queen was also involved in an awkward contretemps which she resolved with touching kindness. Mr Dawson Damer, who had evidently drunk a number of loyal toasts before reaching Marl- borough House, offered Her Majesty his hand in the most cordial

manner, remarking as he did so, 'Gad! How glad I am to see you!
How well you're looking! But, I say, do forgive me – your face is, of
course, very familiar to me; but I can't for the life of me recall your
name!' The Queen grasped his proffered hand and said with a
gracious smile, 'Oh, never mind my name, Mr Damer. I'm very
glad to see you. Sit down and tell me all about yourself.'

The next day, the Queen drove to the Wedding in the new glass
State coach, accompanied by the Duchess of Teck, sublimely happy
to see her daughter make so triumphant a match. As Georgie and
May stood at the altar, the Queen 'could not but remember that *I*
had stood, where May did, fifty-three years ago, and dear Vicky
thirty-five years ago, and that the dear ones, who stood where
Georgie did, were gone from us! May these dear children's happiness
last longer!'

The Yorks spent their honeymoon at Sandringham in a house the
Prince of Wales gave them as a wedding present. It was so near the
main building that visitors could drop in at any moment. 'York
Cottage,' as it now became, was a miserable little villa barely distinguishable inside from Mr Pooter's residence in Holloway. But as
the Duke loved Sandringham better than anywhere in the world, he
regarded it as perfection. His wife, however, for whom it had not the
same hallowed associations, found it less enchanting. It was much
too small for a growing family, irredeemably hideous, and as private
as a goldfish bowl.

George's mother and sisters regarded York Cottage as a second
home and assumed they were always welcome. 'I sometimes think,'
wrote Queen Mary, looking back on the early years of her marriage,
'we were not left alone enough.' It was a charitable understatement,
for Alix was notoriously possessive, had little to do but pay visits,
and doted on her son. All her instincts were to keep him in the play-
room, while his wife tried to interest him in serious matters. Princess
May had few tastes in common with Louise, Victoria and Maud,
and was too retiring by nature to relish the boisterous life of
Sandringham.

The Prince of Wales could not conceal his disappointment that
his daughters were so plain. Some fathers might not have noticed it,
but for so experienced a connoisseur of female beauty there was no
avoiding the fact. Only Maud, her father's favourite, had inherited
any of Alix's looks and vivacity. So he never enjoyed what would
have delighted him so much, wandering through the enclosure at
Ascot with one of his girls on his arm, watching the appreciative

glances of all whom they passed. That pleasure he only experienced with his wife.

In the family and amongst friends his daughters were uninhibited enough, but they were gauche and diffident with strangers. Apart from music, in which they were well instructed, they suffered from educational deprivation. It was not their fault if they seemed silly and shallow. Their life at Sandringham was dominated by their adoring mother, who overshadowed and outshone them.

The oldest of the three girls was born in 1867 and christened Louise after her grandmother. At twenty-two she became the first member of the family to marry. Her husband, Lord Fife, was a friend and contemporary of her father. For five years he sat as a Liberal Member of Parliament before inheriting his peerage. The Prince of Wales was happy to welcome him as a son-in-law, for he was gratifyingly rich and enjoyed racing. In fact, Fife was not very agreeable. He could be amusing when he wanted, but he was contemptuous, rough and selfish, and his language was that of Billingsgate at flood tide.

For some unfathomable reason the Queen loved him dearly, although he did nothing to deserve it. Indeed, he took liberties with her which others never contemplated. Once, at a servants' ball at Balmoral, he coolly suggested they should dance a reel together. 'Her Majesty, after a moment's hesitation, consented, retired, and reappeared in a few minutes wearing – poor old lady – a short skirt. They danced together, but Macduff (doubtless invigorated by his well-loved alcohol) chose the kind of reel usually danced by sweethearts – hands locked across the bosom; and danced it in rather an improper way. Of course, the innocent old Royal Lady in the short skirt knew nothing of this, and equally, of course, nobody dared tell her; indeed if they had they would probably not have been believed.'

When the news of Louise's engagement was announced it was much criticized. Not only was Fife eighteen years older than his bride but his eccentricities were well known. Some people, however, thought it was wrong for a Princess to marry anyone less than a Prince. It is true that the Queen's daughter, another Louise, had married Lord Lorne in 1871, but the precedent proved unhappy, and long before Lorne succeeded his father as ninth Duke of Argyll, he and his wife separated.

Fife and Louise were married in 1889 in the private Chapel of Buckingham Palace. The bridegroom, who had been created a Duke for the Wedding, looked every bit forty years on, while his mother-in-law remained flawlessly youthful and could easily have been mistaken for the bride. After her marriage, the Duchess of Fife became something of a recluse and spent most of her time trying to catch trout on her husband's estates in Scotland.

Princess Victoria, who was born the year after Louise, never married and as she grew older bore the scars of spinsterhood. 'Toria', as she was called, was the most intelligent member of her family. When Queen Victoria told Bertie it was high time she married, he claimed to be powerless. 'Alix,' he said, found her daughters 'such good companions that she would not encourage them marrying, and they themselves had no inclination for it.' At different times, Toria contemplated marrying a member of the Baring family, her father's Equerry, Sir Arthur Davidson, and Lord Rosebery. But her mother insisted that she would never permit her daughter to marry a commoner, regardless of the fact that Fife was already her son-in-law.

Towards the end of her life Princess Victoria told a friend that Lord Rosebery would have been 'perfect for her, but they wouldn't let her marry him, and we *could* have been so happy.' So she remained with her mother, mostly at Sandringham. Alix loved her dearly, but none the less exploited her ruthlessly, treating her as a drudge. For one overflowing with kindness she could be surprisingly inconsiderate. Toria's cousin, the Grand Duchess Olga of Russia, thought the poor girl was treated like a 'glorified maid.' The Princess of Wales kept a bell near at hand to summon her daughter. 'Many a time a talk or a game would be broken off by a message from my Aunt Alix, and Toria would run like lightning, often to discover that her mother could not remember why she had sent for her.' The stresses and strains of her blighted life may well help account for her numerous ailments. Princess Maud, who saw how her sister was treated, once told Knollys that she 'hated the idea of leaving poor Victoria *alone* again as her life is not an easy one.' But if anyone tried to persuade 'Mother dear' that she was destroying Toria's happiness, she refused to believe it.

Princess Maud, the tomboy of the family, was born in 1869, and was Alix's fifth and last child. Like her brothers and sisters she was stiff and tongue-tied except at home. Her conversation, such as it was, was peppered with schoolboy slang. She talked about 'rotters' and 'bounders' and 'funks.' Because of her courage she was nicknamed 'Harry,' after the gallant 'little Admiral,' Harry Keppel.

What she really enjoyed were the simple, outdoor pleasures of Norfolk life: dogs, horses, bicycling and gardens.

In 1895 she became engaged to her first cousin, Prince Charles of Denmark, who was the Crown Prince Frederick's second son. Prince Charles was a charming, handsome, impecunious naval officer. He proposed to Maud during one of the family reunions at Fredensborg, and married her the following July. In 1905 King Edward played a prominent part in securing his election to the throne of Norway, which he ascended as King Haakon VII. Maud's wedding present was Appleton Farm, on the Sandringham estate, where they spent their honeymoon. She loved Norfolk and disliked Denmark. Whenever her husband was at sea she returned to Appleton, grumbling about living abroad and the hardships of being married to a naval officer. She got little sympathy from her mother, who told her that 'she must on *no* account forget that she married a *Danish* Prince and a *naval* man and *he owes* his first duty both to *his country* and his profession.' Princess Maud, Queen of Norway, died in the year of Munich, so did not live to share King Haakon's exile in the land she loved too well.

The Waleses formed so close and affectionate a circle that their critics spoke of a 'mutual admiration society.' The children, however, neither inherited nor acquired their mother's qualities, most conspicuously, as far as her daughters were concerned, her unfading loveliness. Affie's daughter, Marie, Queen of Rumania, described her 'Aunt Alix's beautiful face' as being 'dominant, triumphant, like sunshine . . . To the very end there was about Aunt Alix something invincible, something exquisite and flowerlike. She gave you the same joy as a beautiful rose or a rare orchid, or an absolutely faultless carnation . . . I especially remember her hands, long beautifully shaped hands that remained as young as her face . . . Her way of coming into a room was incomparable, her smile of welcome lit everything up . . . Everyone felt happy in her presence. She radiated!'

The Princess of Wales made people feel that they really mattered and that she preferred talking to them to anyone else in the world. To meet her was to be uplifted. The 'beloved lady' was impulsively warm-hearted. One Christmas, for example, on learning that a footman at Sandringham was homesick, she pressed a pair of cufflinks into his hands, telling him he would get his proper present later, 'but these are something personal to you from me.'

Alix's generosity was legendary. Her answer to begging letters was a five-pound note, which kept the Post Office busy. 'Thank God,' said King Edward, 'the Crown Jewels are in the Tower, otherwise the Queen would have auctioned them all off for her charities.'

Her high spirits were as spontaneous as her liberality. Frederick Ponsonby, Sir Henry's second son, describes Alix's attitude to golf, which was joyously unorthodox, and how she asked him one afternoon to partner her against Princess Victoria and Knollys. 'The Queen seemed to confuse it with hockey and was under the impression that one had to prevent the opponent putting the ball in the hole. This usually ended by a scrimmage on the green. She also thought that the person who got into the hole first won it, and asked me to hurry up and run between the strokes. It was very good fun, and we all laughed. Francis Knollys always played in a square-shaped billycock hat and a London tail coat, and hit so hard that his hat almost invariably fell off.'

In arranging her life, Alix was haphazard, unmethodical and sensationally unpunctual. Seeing that Bertie had inherited the Prince Consort's love of order, and that patience was not conspic-uous amongst his virtues, he found waiting for Alix hard to bear, although she kept him in constant practice. It never occurred to her for one moment that she might mend her ways. 'Keep him wait-ing, it will do him good!' she told Sir Sidney Greville. On one occasion, soon after she became Queen, Alix was required to assist the King in receiving a number of important deputations. The ceremony began at ten-thirty in the morning, 'but when it came to twelve o'clock there was no sign of the Queen,' although four or five separate deputations had arrived and been allotted different rooms so that they should not get mixed up. 'Soon every room was filled with eminent men in uniform, but in spite of repeated messages there was no sign of the Queen. The King in full uniform sat in the Equerries' room drumming on the table and looking out of the window with the face of a Christian martyr. Finally at ten minutes to one the Queen came down looking lovely and quite unconcerned. All she said was, "Am I late?" '

On another occasion, Alix upset the entire German railway system by keeping a 'Special' from Copenhagen to Stuttgart waiting for over an hour. The repercussions of that delay were felt as far off as Bavaria. After frenzied officials had looked at their watches for the twentieth time, Alix swept on to the station, followed by Charlotte Knollys and a cluster of agitated dogs, oblivious of the dislocation she had caused. There can be no denying that such unpunctuality was thoughtless. Prince George, who loved her dearly, told his wife that 'Mama, as I have always said, is one of the most selfish people I know.'

The strangest enigma of her character is that at one moment she could heedlessly disregard Toria's happiness, and the next would sit up all night by the bed of a dying housemaid. Even her husband sometimes complained that she suited herself at others' expense. Writing from Newmarket in 1888, the Prince told Knollys that 'having written *twice* to the Princess urging her to come to Town at latest today to go to the Royal Academy this afternoon, I got her telegram yesterday saying "Thanks for letters. Am not going till Friday. Children are anxious to stay one day longer"! To which I answered "Thought your decision going to R.A. almost public duty. Leighton will be bitterly disappointed." The Princess will not, even in a small matter like this, sacrifice the pleasure it gives her to remain at Sandringham twenty-four hours longer. I am powerless to do anything. The fact is one can hardly get any woman *ever* to understand the motto "Duty before pleasure".'

One reason Alix was reluctant to leave Sandringham was that she was becoming increasingly deaf. She had inherited otosclerosis from her mother, and her difficulty in hearing got worse after a serious bout of rheumatic fever in 1867. Sometimes she heard noises in her head like a railway train travelling at speed. Generally she succeeded in concealing her disability, sometimes talking to a dozen people at once hardly hearing a word they said. But the strain told on her, and she was happiest in the company of those she heard best.

Some people mistakenly supposed that she was unintelligent, but Lord Esher thought 'Her cleverness has always been underrated – partly because of her deafness. In point of fact she says more original things, and has more unexpected ideas than any of the family.' The more she was driven into the lonely world of deafness, the less she was able or anxious to share her husband's social life. So they tended to go their separate ways and follow their different interests. Alix's world revolved round her family, her dogs, the garden at Sandringham and her charities. Princess May was one of the few people who really understood her mother-in-law's affliction. 'She is so deaf,' wrote May to her Aunt Augusta, the Grand Duchess of Mecklenburg-Strelitz, 'that it makes me quite sad and she looks so pathetic sometimes, trying to hear what we are saying and laughing about.' Alix was deeply appreciative of the help her 'Sweet May' gave her, and once thanked her for being 'so dear and nice to me – and whenever

I am not quite *au fait* on account of my *beastly ears* you always by a *word* or even by a turn towards me make me understand – for which I am *most grateful* as nobody can know what I often have to go through.'

Much of the joy of life at Sandringham for Alix was to be surrounded by animals. She was a superlative horsewoman and adored dogs. So sensitive was she to cruelty that her brother-in-law, Tsar Alexander III, loved to tease her by putting live worms on his hook when they went out fishing together. She was particularly fond of pugs and pekineses, upon whom she bestowed a devotion which some thought ludicrous. Once, during her visit to Egypt in 1868, she was lying asleep in the stern of the steamer taking her up the Nile. Suddenly she was awakened by a cold nose belonging to a sheep, which had gnawed through a rope tethering it to the ship's rail. When she discovered that the animal was to be slaughtered next morning for luncheon, she ordered it to be shipped back to Norfolk, where it spent the rest of its days grazing round Sandringham.

On 10 March 1888, the Prince and Princess of Wales celebrated their Silver Wedding. The day before, the Kaiser died and Vicky's husband ascended the throne as Frederick III. Unhappily, he had cancer of the throat and only reigned for ninety-nine days. Because the Court went into mourning for William I, public celebrations were cancelled, but a family dinner took place at Marlborough House, which the Queen attended. It was the first time she had ever had a meal there. Alix decorated her hair for the occasion with sprays of orange blossom, in the midst of which she inserted a real orange: that the effect was lovely not ludicrous was a characteristic triumph. She was now, she said, 'no bud but the ripened fruit.'

Her bridesmaids presented her with a silver casket. 'We all looked old ladies,' said one of them 'but the Princess as fresh and young as she did on her wedding day.' The Queen echoed this sentiment. 'Alix,' she wrote in her Journal, 'was in white and silver with lovely jewels, looking more like a bride just married than the silver one of twenty-five years.' While praying God to prosper their marriage further, she felt bound to remind Him: 'To me it was not permitted to celebrate this happy anniversary with my husband Albert.' Bertie gave Alix a cross of diamonds and rubies, and a silver clock with the letters ALBERT EDWARD engraved round the dial.

The Prince was scarcely an ideal husband, and it says much for Alix's forbearance that his Silver Wedding was so happy an occasion.

Few people possessed such opportunities for philandering and he found them irresistible. But he was as constant in his devotion to his wife as he was unfaithful to her. Not only did he love her 'the best,' but, knowing how badly he sometimes treated her, felt bound to accept her shortcomings patiently. Possibly the good-tempered way in which he allowed himself to be kept waiting may be traced to a guilty conscience. 'Her lot is no easy one,' wrote Queen Victoria, 'but she is very fond of Bertie, though not blind.'

Exceptionally beautiful women sometimes protect themselves from unwanted admiration by assuming a chilly nature. Lady Antrim, one of Alix's most intimate friends, suspected the Princess of Wales was not warm enough in her relation with the Prince, and lavished more love on her children than on her husband. But be that as it may, her 'beloved hubby,' as she engagingly called him, was, according to Lord Esher, 'the love of her youth and – as I fervently believe – of all her life.'

Alix believed that envy was a major source of 'mischief and misfortune.' She practised what she preached, and 'her home remained a happy place because she refused to allow any particle of jealousy to corrode her relationship with her openly unfaithful but very loving husband.' In the 'confession-book' of a Norfolk neighbour she described her favourite employment as 'minding her own business.'

In the early days of their marriage, Alix nearly died of rheumatic fever. In his *Life and Times of Edward VII*, Sir Richard Holmes gives a touching account of the Prince of Wales's devotion. 'Nothing is so great a test of the depth and strength of married love as sickness, and it was during the serious illness of his wife that King Edward showed how kind and loving a husband he really was.' Perhaps Sir Richard was ignorant of the truth, or possibly his long service as a courtier betrayed him into tampering with it, but the fact of the matter was that the Prince behaved disgracefully. Lady Waldegrave called him a selfish brute, who only thought of amusing himself and paid not the slightest attention to his wife.

On 15 February 1867, Alix complained of severe pains and a chill: symptoms the more serious as she was soon to have a child. The Prince, however, decided that his first duty was to Windsor Races. Later that day she was found to be suffering from rheumatic fever. Only after being sent three telegrams of increasing urgency could her husband be persuaded to return to Marlborough House. On 20 February, Alix gave birth to Louise, without chloroform, which the doctors thought too risky to administer. Despite the seriousness of her illness, the Prince stayed out into the small hours evening after evening. Lady Macclesfield, who helped nurse Alix, thought his neglect outrageous. 'The Princess had another bad night, *chiefly* owing to the Prince promising to come in at 1.00 am and keeping her in a perpetual fret, refusing to take her opiate for fear she should be asleep when he came! And he never came till 3.00 am! The Duke of Cambridge is quite *furious* about it and I hear nothing but general indignation at his indifference to her and his devotion to his own amusements.' Sir William Knollys, urged on by General Grey, vainly endeavoured to persuade HRH that he was damaging his reputation by going out so often when his wife was ill. The Prince's instinct to retreat into a fool's paradise, and his anxiety to escape the depressing routine of the sickroom, are intelligible enough. But to understand is not to condone.

Alix's long illness was a landmark in her life. Apart from permanent injuries to her health, it unmistakably demonstrated that 'her husband's love had not been strong enough to keep him by her side,' and she found public neglect harder to endure than furtive infidelity. 'Now all London and all Paris knew that whilst his wife lay sick in Marlborough House the Prince had been amusing himself elsewhere.' For the rest of her life Alix had a permanently stiff knee, which she concealed when dancing or walking with a graceful, gliding movement. The 'Alexandra limp' was widely copied, so that what started as a handicap ended as a fashion.

There was little the Princess could do to overcome her deafness, apart from withdrawing to Sandringham, which she anyway thought was the best place to bring up her children. So, while Alix spent much of her time in the country, the Prince remained in London, consoling himself for her absence by breaking the bonds of matrimony whose restraining power he came to regard as 'but binding Samson with threads.' Separation, if anything, made them more affectionate. Writing from Balmoral, Ponsonby once told Knollys: 'It is astonishing how well we get on when we are far apart. Like the sailor's letter to his wife, "The further I am from you the more I love you." '

The Prince and Society

Two months after their Wedding Bertie and Alix moved into Marlborough House and the 'Great Season' of 1863 began. Neither had ever enjoyed such freedom before and they found it most exhilarating. Lady Warwick once said that the Prince was so tireless in pursuit of pleasure that he and his friends turned 'night into day.' Even in the last years of his life he would get up at seven, having gone to bed at two or three that morning. He regarded the day as eighteen hours long and hated wasting any of it. Soon after he became King he had photographs of himself scattered about Buckingham Palace so that he could sign them in spare moments.

It was often said that he sacrificed duty to pleasure, but, according to Lord Redesdale, 'The charge was completely false. However late he might stay up at some entertainment . . . he was up again at earliest dawn to attend a review at Aldershot . . . or take part in a ceremonial in some distant part of the country, where he would appear as gay and as pleased as if he was fulfilling the one ambition of his life. His strength was wonderful; he knew not fatigue . . . As a young man he seemed almost independent of sleep.' Mrs Cresswell's account of a servants' ball at Sandringham bears witness to the Prince's tireless energy. It opened with a country dance in which 'the Prince and the Princess set off with their partners, round and round, down the middle and up again, and so on to the end, the Prince the jolliest of the jolly and the life of the party, as he is wherever he goes. I never saw such amazing vitality.' He was 'his own Master of Ceremonies, signalling and sending messages to the band, arranging every dance and when to begin and when to leave off . . .

In the "Triumph" which is such an exhausting dance, he looked as if he could have gone on all night and into the middle of next week . . . He is the antidote to every text and sermon that ever was preached upon the pleasure of the world palling upon the wearied spirit . . . Almost before the dance ended, the Prince started another . . . and so on fast and furious until far into the small hours of the morning.'

Since the days of George IV, Society had looked in vain for royal patronage. King William's Court was drab, Prince Albert regarded the fashionable world with the same distaste as it felt for him, and his widow could seldom be persuaded to visit London. All that most people saw of the Queen was her head on a postage stamp. So when early in 1863, the Prince of Wales and his enchanting Princess appeared at a succession of receptions, banquets and dances, they achieved a social supremacy which lasted the rest of their lives. Disraeli described that spring and summer as a public honeymoon. Lord Palmerston invited them to Downing Street, the Lord Mayor gave a ball at the Guildhall of breath-taking magnificence, and the Brigade of Guards ended months of celebrating with an entertainment so lavish that the gold plate borrowed for the occasion was valued at three million pounds.

Following the London Season, they stayed with the Duke of Richmond for Goodwood: he was the son of the celebrated Duchess who gave the Waterloo Ball for the beauty and chivalry of Europe. From Goodwood they moved to Osborne for Cowes Regatta, thus establishing the routine the Prince followed till the end of his reign: an obligatory migration which only those insensitive to fashion dared ignore.

When the Prince sailed for India in 1876 the social life of the Capital almost ceased. Montagu Corry, Disraeli's companion and secretary, told Francis Knollys: 'London has been lifeless in the absence of the Prince! A few people have just half opened their doors to let in a few "intimes," but there has been a general absence of merry making, which I have never seen nearly equalled even in Lent.'

The Prince of Wales was of so restless and gregarious a disposition that it was rare for him to spend a quiet evening at home. In the early years of his life he had such a surfeit of reading as to lose all appetite for it. When he was not invited out, he would summon a few friends for a game of whist and supper, or venture forth in a hansom-cab to explore the night life of the Capital. He showed little discrimination about where he went or fastidiousness about the company he kept. Rumours even reached Vicky that her brother frequented disreputable places like the Cremorne Gardens, or Evans's Music Hall, once the poisoner Palmer's favourite haunts.

In 1865, Phipps wrote confidentially to Sir William Knollys asking him, 'Have you ever heard of a place in London called the "Midnight Club?" The Crown Princess told Grey that she knew that the Prince of Wales went there frequently and that the King of the Belgians had been much alarmed about it. I never heard of such a place . . . The Prince of Wales should be careful for there is a fast spreading view that he lowers himself too much in the pursuit of pleasure – and a cry of that kind, even if not entirely justified, spreads like wild fire.'

The Prince of Wales's movements during the year could be predicted with the same degree of certainty as those of the sun and moon. In January his social almanac began with a series of shooting parties at Sandringham. Then in March he would visit the French Riviera, breaking his journey in Paris. He seldom took Alix with him, preferring to travel 'en garçon.' The early summer was spent at Marlborough House and was devoted to the London Season. Next there was Goodwood and Cowes, followed by a few weeks at a German or Austrian spa. In October, he stayed at Abergeldie, near Balmoral, shooting grouse or stalking. The year ended, as it began, at Sandringham, where he invariably spent his birthday and Christmas.

Interspersed between these commitments, the Prince found time to honour most of the great houses of England with his presence. Throughout Queen Victoria's reign, the English gentry remained essentially rustic, and reluctantly visited London when urged by such necessities as seeing lawyers or placating wives. But they felt far more at home in their stables and gunrooms. They therefore evolved a pattern of Country House entertaining which combined hunting and shooting with dinners and dances: a felicitous piece of alchemy much to His Royal Highness's taste.

Dukes proved especially vulnerable to the honour of royal visits. Hardly a year went by without the Prince staying at Chatsworth with the Duke of Devonshire, Badminton with the Duke of Beaufort, Dunrobin with the Duke of Sutherland, Eaton Hall with the Duke of Westminster, or Welbeck with the Duke of Portland. Amongst others favoured with his presence, were the Alingtons at Crichel, the Brookes at Warwick, the Pembrokes at Wilton, the Lansdownes at Bowood, the Harcourts at Nuneham and Mrs James at West Dean. Considering the preparations involved, the Prince was fortunately easy to entertain, 'one of his many charms being his interest in everything and everybody . . . Few people had more joie de vivre. He enjoyed himself with the infectious gaiety of a schoolboy. That indefinable, but undeniable, gift of youth remained with him all his life.'

The social life of the Queen, such as it was, tended to be stiff and solemn. 'We subdue our voices considerably,' said Ponsonby, 'while eating the royal beef.' Lady Wolseley, accustomed to the more boisterous society of military men, described Her Majesty's dinners as 'whispery'. The Prince and Princess of Wales were less inhibited, and Marlborough House rang with sounds of revelry by night. When Major Elphinstone, soon after being appointed Comptroller to the Prince's youngest brother, Arthur, took the boy to dine at Marlborough House, he was very much 'struck by the want of ceremony shown, the Princess of Wales coming into the room calmly knitting.' The evening passed in 'a most friendly manner,' and Elphinstone assured the Queen, whom he knew to be 'rather nervous about visits to Marlborough House, that they did not stay late and that the boy was in bed by 10.15 p.m.' It must be confessed that not many who were entertained by their Royal Highnesses left so early.

'The Marlborough House Set' earned a reputation for being 'fast', and the Prince was constantly denounced for corrupting the morals of Society. Punctilious as he was in observing the majority of conventions, there was something of the Bohemian about him, as he himself admitted. Several of his friends, such as the Duke of Sutherland, whom the Queen said 'does not live as *a Duke ought*,' the Duchess of Manchester and Lord Hartington, mortified the austere classes by their love of frivolity, gambling and each other. But the Prince's charitable indulgence in choosing companions widened the scope of Society. His parents had restricted their social circle to those who obeyed the Ten Commandments, or at least the eleventh. So, Early Victorian Society was 'a very select sheepfold, fenced round by quickset hedges, and strait was the gate that led into it.' It was not only rigidly moral but strictly aristocratic: open only to those 'who were in the stud-book, however dull and dreary their minds might be.' Although 'a prodigious stickler for precedence and buttons, and the correct wearing of an order,' the Prince was unrepentantly nonconformist in pursuing pleasure, and saw no reason for depriving himself of vivacious companions merely because of defects in their social credentials.

As the Prince saw it, the significant gulf was that dividing the Queen's family from the rest of Mankind – who enjoyed a sort of equality in virtue of not being royal. He was disposed, therefore, to ignore subtle gradations of rank in a manner singularly distressing to those anxious to maintain them. Some of his guests would never have met elsewhere. It is difficult to imagine the Duke of Marlborough inviting that Prince of upholsterers, Sir John Maple, to dine at Blenheim. Nor, as the Kaiser expressed it, would all HRH's friends have chosen to go 'yachting with his grocer,' the notable philanthropist, Sir Thomas Lipton.

Shortly before he became Tsar in 1894, Nicholas visited Sandringham. 'The house-party,' he told his mother, 'was rather strange. Most of them were horse dealers, among others a Baron Hirsch. The cousins rather enjoyed the situation and kept teasing me about it; but I tried to keep away as much as I could, and not to talk. Even Aunt Alix herself was seeing many of them for the first time.' Had most of his fellow guests so much as set foot in the Summer Palace at St Petersburg they would have risked arrest.

The Prince of Wales rejoiced in the company of precisely those people who were not admitted in Society: actors, Americans, Jews and self-made men. He was for ever visiting theatres and meeting actors and actresses. When Mrs Langtry ran out of money he encouraged her to take to the Stage. In 1882 he gave a banquet at Marlborough House for the leaders of the profession. Amongst the guests were Squire Bancroft, George Grossmith, Henry Irving, Charles Wyndham and William Kendal. Newspapers describing the event particularly commended HRH's unostentatious discretion in confining the meal to nine courses. It was generally agreed that the evening had proved a triumphant success and had helped raise the social standing of actors, despite the fact that Kendal had lowered the tone by singing a vulgar song. When the Queen stayed at Sandringham in 1889, Irving and Ellen Terry presented scenes from *The Merchant of Venice*. There was nothing remarkable about that, as Her Majesty loved theatricals. But what surprised people was that, when the performance ended, Shylock and Portia joined the Prince and Princess for supper. In some great households they would have been given their meal with the housekeeper.

Americans, particularly American ladies, were almost as welcome at Marlborough House as they were eager to be invited. Since visiting the United States in 1860, the Prince had learned to admire the vivacity of its citizens. Even the most obtrusive amongst them presumed with impunity upon his tolerance and goodwill. Society was grudgingly prepared to acknowledge the existence of the New World. After all, it was some time since Columbus stumbled on it. But Jews were another matter, some thought best left in the ghetto. Not so the Prince, who counted amongst his friends the Rothschilds, the Sassoons, Sir Edward Lawson, Baron Hirsch and Sir Ernest Cassel. He was fascinated by their vast fortunes and the manner of life that went with them. Most Englishmen, however rich, hesitated to spend too lavishly for fear of being thought vulgar. But the Rothschilds were unrestrained by such scruples and would happily pay astounding sums to persuade Melba to sing, Sarah Bernhardt to recite, or Rubinstein to play. They put themselves out to please the Prince in a way which those who had less to gain from his acquaintance were not disposed to do.

Soon after HRH's marriage, Sir William Knollys consulted Lord Spencer on the wisdom of his accepting an invitation from the Rothschilds. Spencer told him that he felt confident 'that if the Prince went to a ball there, a great outcry would arise in the fine world, and I confess I think the world would for once have reason on their side, for I think the Prince ought not to accept any invitation, he ought only to visit those of undoubted position in Society. The Rothschilds are very worthy people but they especially hold their position from wealth and perhaps the accidental beauty of the first daughter they brought out. Other members of Society would complain of the Prince going to that house in preference to their own. I should be very sorry if the Prince and Princess accepted their hospitality.' The Prince, however, preferred to lead fashion than to follow it and rejected Spencer's advice.

In 1881, HRH delighted the Jewish community by attending Leopold Rothschild's wedding in a synagogue. Some of his Jewish friends, particularly Hirsch and Cassel, gave him financial advice, but not money, except, of course, for charity. And he, in his turn, helped them. 'English houses, which had been impregnable to the "bright children of the sun," as Disraeli gaily called his compatriots, were flung open when Prince Hal made them welcome.' The Queen was not so accommodating, and made her son '*dreadfully* annoyed' by refusing to invite Baron Hirsch to a State concert. Nor did Alix's sister, the Tsarina, take kindly to Bertie's Jewish friends, having caught the infection of anti-Semitism from her husband. When the Prince of Wales paid Hirsch a visit in Hungary, during which ten guns in ten days shot twenty thousand partridges, the Habsburg Archdukes were stunned: not by the size of the bag but by the faith of the host. Prince Bülow, the German Chancellor, was undoubtedly right in supposing that the Prince of Wales showed 'a marked predilection for very rich people.' HRH shared Lord Byron's view of wealth: 'Money is power and pleasure and I like it vastly.' Experience taught him that Societies which demanded breeding but denied success, of which wealth was a measure, lacked the attraction of those which reversed these values. The parvenu world of the Second Empire possessed a wit and sparkle unknown to more discriminating Courts. He was particularly intrigued by self-made men, like Sir Thomas Lipton, who was born in a Glasgow slum and made a fortune by selling Ceylon tea. In championing such friends he met bitter resistance from the Old Order. Lord Salisbury was said to have resigned as Prime Minister rather than include Lipton's name in the Coronation Honours, and the Kaiser infuriated his Uncle by refusing to meet Sir Thomas.

The Prince of Wales used his influence to open up Society, not only in search of amusing companions, but because he loved to give pleasure. Lady Paget noticed how, 'in the kindness of his heart,' whenever he gave a garden-party, he 'invited every doctor and dentist he had ever had the slightest connection with.'

Like Disraeli, with whom he had little else in common, the Prince of Wales especially delighted in the company of women. According to Margot Asquith, 'He was stimulated by their company, intrigued by their entanglements, flattered by their confidence, and valued their counsel.' One clue to his feelings may be found in the way he cut short an old English custom. Gentlemen loved after dinner to linger over their port, complaining about the price of barley, or the local Master of Foxhounds. Their wives, taking coffee in the drawing-room, felt sure they were talking bawdy. Incredible reminiscences would be exchanged about 'larks' in the Mess at Cawnpore, how Charlie Beresford gave a donkey champagne and put it in Mrs Cust's bed, or the time when Dr Keate mistakenly flogged his confirmation candidates whom he had taken for felons.

The Prince of Wales, lacking the common fund of shared experience which gave such legends meaning, tended to find them tedious. Consequently, he did not encourage gossiping over the debris of dinner, and was impatient to join the ladies. 'It would be wrong to assume,' wrote Margot Asquith, 'that the King's only interest in women was to have an "affaire" with them. That he had many "affaires" is indisputable, but there were a great many other women in his life from whom all he sought was a diverting companionship.' Margot herself was one.

Amongst the Prince's pastimes was playing cards for money and it was soon being said that he was losing heavily and encouraging others to run into debt. Lord Palmerston informed the Queen that he had heard that HRH was obliged to draw on capital to meet his losses. In fact, as Sir William told her, the Prince's financial problems arose from the cost of improving Sandringham. In 1865, Phipps sent Knollys a *'most confidential'* letter from Windsor, saying that Lord Palmerston had been staying at the Castle, and, 'in the course of conversation, mentioned to the Queen that the Prince of Wales was in the habit of playing very high at whist, and had won from Sir Gaspard Le Marchant, I think fifty pounds, when he was invited to dine at Marlborough House, which Sir Gaspard did not at all like. The Queen has been *very much* shocked at this account, the truth of which she at first positively denied, indeed she seemed really very unhappy about it, and said it had kept her awake through the nights. She was not only startled and horrified at the idea of her son gambling, but she was very much shocked at the idea of his winning money from his guests and thus giving a foundation of so extremely disagreeable a complaint.

With, I think, great good sense, she told Lord Palmerston that she had better know nothing about it, as she did not want to be the person always to bring the Prince of Wales to task for his faults. I was in a scrape for not having told HM what was going on, but I could with truth say that I was only cognisant of a general rumour that the Prince of Wales played high at whist . . . The Queen told me that I might *in confidence* tell you how horrified she had been at this revelation, and ask you whether you did not think that it was one upon which you might, from yourself as a friend, speak very seriously to him, as likely to do him more harm in public estimation than anything . . . All this comes I think from that horrible habit of sitting up so late at night, for which some exciting amusements must be found, but if it were supposed that the Prince of Wales invited Gentlemen to his house and then induced them to play for higher stakes than they liked it would do him incalculable injury.'

Six days later, Phipps wrote again, confessing that his first letter had been much ado about nothing. 'Prince Alfred has come back with an assurance from the Prince of Wales that the story of his winning from Sir G. Le Marchant is altogether false as he never played with him.' Nevertheless, Sir Charles, speaking no doubt for the Queen, hoped that the Prince of Wales would be convinced 'of the necessity of giving up this high play at whist.'

The Prince was sufficiently skilful at cards either to win, or to lose no more than he could easily afford. It was, however, repeatedly alleged that he encouraged others to play too high: Sir Gaspard, for instance. Another victim was Mr Gladstone, who, after dining with the Prince at Abergeldie, was compelled to play whist. 'I said, "For love, Sir?" He said, "Well shillings and half-a-crown on the rubber," to which I submitted.' Mr Gladstone noted that HRH had 'an immense whist memory and plays well accordingly.'

Throughout his career the Prince was harassed by unjust insinuations, harder to bear than refute. 'I am happiest,' he once wrote despairingly, when, 'like plain Mr Jones,' I can 'go to a race meeting without it being chronicled in the papers the next day that His Royal Highness the Prince of Wales has taken to gambling very seriously, and yesterday lost more money than ever he can afford to pay.'

Some of the Prince's friends claimed to have beggared themselves on his behalf, amongst them Lord Hardwicke, Lord Dupplin, Christopher Sykes, Charles Buller and Lady Warwick. But they were all naturally extravagant, and having chosen to bask in the sunshine of royalty had only themselves to blame for sunstroke.

Slender as is the evidence for the widespread suspicion that the Prince encouraged high play, there was at least one young Austrian diplomat, a certain Count Montgelas, who required four years to discharge a debt to HRH and had presumably therefore risked more than he could afford. In 1887, he enclosed a cheque for one thousand and twenty-five pounds in a letter posted from Munich. The Count began by saying that he was at last 'in a position to pay the sum which I had lost to you Sir, at play. I need hardly say that ever since that day four years ago it has been my almost daily preoccupation to amass the £1025 for which I have the honour now to enclose a cheque. On the other hand I have had to keep in mind your Royal Highness's command that I was not to pay my debt as long as my so doing would involve the necessity of my leaving the carrière. While at last I am now able to pay off my debt of honour I still remain your debtor, Sir, for the kindness your Royal Highness was graciously pleased to show me.'

The Prince and his friends looked upon cards as an innocent diversion, but many devout Victorians thought them the work of the Devil. After he became King he would often play Bridge in the Royal Train, but whenever it slowed down to pass through a station, the cards would be put away for fear of offending his pious subjects waiting on the platform, to whom he would graciously wave from the window of his carriage as if he had just been reading the *Methodist Weekly*.

The Prince's gambling was not confined to cards. The older he grew the more fascinated he became by racing, which satisfied some of his deepest instincts. Restless and craving amusement, he delighted in what he described as its 'glorious uncertainties.' Sociable and gregarious, he relished its camaraderie. However much some people regretted his fondness for racing, foremost amongst them the Queen, the crowds at Epsom and Aintree welcomed him as one of them. Perhaps their principal reason for taking him to their heart was that he possessed what Sir Edward Grey described as 'a rare, if not unique power of combining bonhomie and dignity.' Moreover, 'He had a capacity for enjoying life, which is always very attractive, but which is peculiarly so when it is combined with a positive and strong desire that everyone else should enjoy life too.' He bustled about shaking hands with everybody, recognizing everybody, putting everyone at their ease.

Henry Ponsonby, an outspoken critic of the Prince of Wales, maintained that his charm 'amounted to genius.' Indeed, he thought it was not too much to say 'that in spite of drawbacks, faults and failures, it *made* him. With a dignified presence, a fine profile and a courtly manner, he never missed saying a word to the humblest visitor, attendant or obscure official . . . No-one was left out. The appropriate remark, the telling serious phrase and the amusing joke, made all delighted even to watch him.'

At first, the Prince of Wales ran horses under other people's names as the Queen objected to his using Royal Colours. It was said that Captain Machall, who won the Grand National in 1876, was, in reality, the Prince. HRH's colours – purple, gold braid and scarlet sleeves – were first seen at Newmarket in July 1877. Lord Marcus Beresford, Charles Beresford's younger brother, advised the Prince on all racing matters. In 1883 he recommended him to send his horses to John Porter for training, starting with two fillies, Geheimniss and Junket, leased from Lady Stamford. It was apparently agreed that HRH would pay for their upkeep until 'the end of their racing careers,' that they would run under Royal Colours, and that Lady Stamford was to receive half their winnings. But 'after mature reflection,' and having taken the advice of one in whose opinion he set 'great store,' the Prince came to the conclusion 'that it would not do for me to run those two horses under my name, or under an assumed one.' He therefore suggested that Lord Alington and Sir Frederick Johnstone should take them off his hands.

Lord Alington, at HRH's request, wrote to Lady Stamford outlining the Prince's proposal and explaining what was behind it. 'The fact is HRH wishes to ask for some more money from the country and thinks the fact of his keeping race horses and its being known to the public might prejudice his chance, but all this is confidential between you and me.'

Lady Stamford felt so aggrieved by this change of plan that she instructed her solicitor, Thomas Wright of Leicester, to send his Lordship a threatening letter. Wright began by listing his client's complaints, chief of which seems to have been 'That it was distinctly stated to her by Mr Porter who was negotiating on behalf of the Prince that Geheimniss and Junket were to run in the name and colours of the Prince.' After pointing out that he would be obliged to take legal action unless they could reach some rapid agreement, he concluded by saying, 'I am sorry to add that His Royal Highness will I fear be a necessary party to any proceedings which may be taken.'

The Prince was naturally agitated and sent for Sir George Lewis, that most dexterous solicitor, who generally succeeded in settling cases out of court. Sleeping in black tin boxes which lined the walls of Lewis and Lewis, 'were papers enough to compromise half London and scandalize the other half.' When Sir George burned the lot, there could hardly have been a family of note who did not rejoice to hear it.

Only with great difficulty was Lewis able to placate Lady Stamford. 'I have spent five hours again today over this matter,' he told Francis Knollys, 'and I have seldom come across a more capricious woman than Lady S; directly one thing was settled another difficulty was interposed.' But eventually he persuaded Lady Stamford that, should she find it necessary to bring an action, it need only be against Lord Alington and Sir Frederick. HRH, on Lewis's suggestion, wrote Lady Stamford a conciliatory letter, expressing his 'deep regret at the misunderstanding that has lately occurred,' and thanking her warmly 'for the friendly feelings you have displayed in withdrawing the proceedings which at one time you thought necessary to institute.'

There is not enough evidence to apportion blame for this mysterious quarrel. All that may confidently be said is that Lady Stamford was quick to resent any injury and fickle in seeking redress, while the Prince's negotiations were of so intricate a nature as to verge on the unscrupulous. Nor was it entirely proper that a man in his position should be at such pains to delude Parliament.

In 1885, at Lord Marcus's suggestion, the Prince of Wales established a breeding stud at Sandringham. Eight years later he decided to transfer his horses for training from John Porter to Richard March. In 1896 he won the Derby with Persimmon at odds of five to one. The victory was as unexpected as it was popular and the crowds went wild with excitement. Even the policemen threw their helmets in the air. As HRH led Persimmon into the Winner's Enclosure, strangers shook him by the hand and slapped him on the back, and somebody called for 'Three cheers for the bloody Crown!' When Persimmon died in 1908 the King presented his skeleton to the Natural History Museum.

In 1900, for the only time in his life, the Prince of Wales headed the list of winning owners. In that year, 'Diamond Jubilee' – the name was Alix's inspiration – won five classic races: the Two Thousand Guineas, the Newmarket Stakes, the Eclipse Stakes, the Derby and the St Leger, and, in the same season, his Ambush II won the Grand National. This resounding series of victories was unprecedented in racing history.

In 1909 the King won the Derby with Minoru: the first time a reigning sovereign had ever won the race. When he went down to meet his horse the police were swept away as they struggled to clear his path, and the King of England was lost amidst a surging, cheering crowd. Manfully he battled through the throng, repeating in his deep guttural voice, 'Make way for the King! Make way for the King!' As he led Minoru from the Winners' Enclosure there were shouts of 'Good old Teddie,' and then somebody began singing 'God Save the King,' which was instantly taken up all round the course. The delirious, tumultuous excitement of this triumphant day, gave him the very deepest satisfaction. Apart from the pleasure and popularity he derived from racing he even succeeded in making it pay. During his career as an owner he earned over four hundred thousand pounds in stud fees and stake money.

The Prince of Wales bought Sandringham mainly because of the shooting, his other principal sporting passion. Some of his guests were astounded by his indifference to social incongruity. The Bishop of Peterborough, William Magee, who stayed over Sunday to preach, found the company 'pleasant and civil' but a 'curious mixture.' 'Two Jews, Sir Anthony de Rothschild and his daughter; an ex-Jew, Disraeli; a Roman Catholic, Colonel Higgins; an Italian duchess who is an English-woman, and her daughter, brought up a Roman Catholic and now turning Protestant; a set of young Lords and a bishop.' As early as 1866, Emily Eden told Lord Clarendon that Sandringham was 'not at all a nice young Court,' and several of HRH's neighbours objected to the motley crowd whom he invited to his Ball for the County.

Even for those with catholic tastes, there were drawbacks in staying at Sandringham, such as the bracing easterly wind that whistled round the house, or being obliged to sit up until after two in the morning, or growing accustomed to 'Sandringham Time.' The Prince borrowed the idea of advancing the clock by half an hour from the Cokes at Holkham, thus anticipating Daylight Saving by over fifty years. Some guests could never accustom themselves to leaving Sandringham at two-thirty in order to catch the two-fifteen from Wolferton Station.

An eccentricity of Sandringham's design was that the instant a guest crossed its threshold he found himself, booted and spurred, in the midst of the family. 'I arrived,' said the Bishop of Peterborough, 'just as they were all at tea in the entrance hall, and had to walk in all seedy and dishevelled from my day's journey and sit down by the Princess of Wales.' But, after watching HRH feast on poached eggs and preserved ginger, as if he were celebrating the end of Ramadan, the most timid guest felt reassured. The Prince conducted gentlemen to their rooms and gave the fire a welcoming poke, and Alix, on one occasion, tucked Mrs Gladstone into bed.

Admiral Fisher describes in his Memoirs how he evaded the reception committee in the hall and went to his room to unpack. As he stood with a boot in each hand, he heard somebody fumbling with the door handle. Thinking it was the footman allocated to him, he shouted: 'Come in; don't go humbugging with that door handle!' And in walked the King, 'with a cigar about a yard long in his mouth.'

'What on earth are you doing?' he asked.

'Unpacking, Sir.'

'Where's your servant?'

'Haven't got one, Sir.'

'Where is he?'

'Never had one, Sir; couldn't afford it.'

'Put those boots down and sit in that armchair.'

The King then talked to Fisher for so long that they were nearly late for dinner.

The Prince's guests were agreed, in the Duke of Cambridge's phrase, that 'their dear RH's are the most *charming* couple and the most delightful hosts it is possible to conceive.' Mr Gladstone spoke of the 'delicacy and kindness' with which they always received him. Edward Hamilton, the great man's Secretary, described HRH as 'a model of hosts.' 'Nothing,' he said, 'could have been kinder or more gracious than were the Prince and Princess.'

In 1884, Henry Broadhurst, the Radical MP for Stoke-on-Trent, and one of the Prince's colleagues on the Royal Commission on Housing the Working Class, was invited to stay at Sandringham, partly to give him the opportunity to see some cottages on the estate. Broadhurst describes his visit in the 'Story of his life from a Stonemason's bench to the Treasury Bench.' HRH, hearing that 'I made a rule not to dine out, and that I did not possess a dress-coat, invited me in a way I could not refuse. I spent three days at Sandringham and I can honestly say that I was never entertained more to my liking and never felt more at home when paying a visit. On my arrival His Royal Highness personally conducted me to my rooms, made a careful inspection to see that all was right and stoked the fire . . . In order to meet the difficulties in the matter of dress, dinner was served to me in my own rooms each night . . . The Princess herself, with characteristic graciousness, showed me over her beautiful dairy.' Broadhurst left Sandringham, 'with the feeling of one who had spent a weekend with an old chum of his own rank in society.'

The Prince of Wales devoted tens of thousands of pounds and a great deal of thought to improving the shooting at Sandringham. During his lifetime, the game shot in a year was increased from seven to thirty thousand head, and the largest larder in the world was built to accommodate the kill. At first, all the Prince sought from shooting was fresh air, exercise and company, but soon he became absorbed in what Sir William called, 'these competitions for the largest game bag,' the cost of which, he warned, was not only to be measured in a ledger but in 'the loss of his good name.' The Prince of Wales, like the Prince Consort before him, was dedicated to the 'battue': the wholesale slaughter of the greatest possible number of creatures, planned as a military operation. It was an alien concept requiring a foreign word to define it. 'At Sandringham,' wrote the Duke of Windsor, describing his grandfather's time, 'everything, including, I regret to say, the interests of the farmer, was subordinated to the shooting.'

For many years Mrs Cresswell, a tenant of Appleton Farm, fought a losing battle to protect her crops from the ravages of game. After abandoning the struggle, she published a book called *Eighteen Years on the Sandringham Estate* in which she listed her grievances. Nearly the whole edition was bought and burned by Edward Beck, the Prince's Norfolk agent. Somehow, a few copies escaped his vigilance, one of which found its way into the Royal Library at Windsor. If curiosity ever tempted HRH to study this poignant work, it would not have increased his love of literature. Charles Kingsley, who enjoyed a day's hunting untroubled by qualms of conscience, was so revolted by the sight of wounded hares lying thick on the ground in Wolferton Wood, writhing and screaming in agony, that he remonstrated with the Prince. As he delivered a homily on this massacre of innocents, the humbled sportsmen stood in bashful silence, their guns still smoking in their hands.

Sandringham was famous for its practical jokes: for some they were one of its terrors, for others part of its charm. It was thought tremendously funny when a wretched midshipman devoured a mince-pie made of mustard, or when a live lobster was hidden in somebody's bed. Alix was less disposed to indulge in practical jokes than to encourage rough-and-tumble games, such as tobogganing downstairs on a silver tray. Mary Bulteel, who married Henry Ponsonby, regarded the royal sense of humour with undisguised contempt. Prince Albert, she said, would go into 'fits of laughter at anything like a practical joke; for instance, if anyone caught his foot in a mat, or nearly fell into the fire or out of a window, the mirth of the whole Royal Family knew no bounds.' Lord Granville used to say that he never bothered to tell his best stories at Court, 'when pretending to pinch one's finger in the door would answer better.'

The Prince of Wales was capable of more subtle humour than that required to make an apple-pie bed, for he possessed formidable powers of mimicry and a keen sense of the ludicrous. Disliking affectation, he sometimes imitated the airs and graces of those he thought absurd. His own engaging brand of irony could be very diverting, and his happy, gurgling, contented laughter was so distinctive that it could be heard above all others in a theatre.

Charles Stamper, the 'King's Motor Mechanic,' who travelled everywhere with him and had constant opportunities to observe his foibles, noticed that 'if His Majesty were annoyed, he would show his displeasure by assuming an air of the most complete resignation.' For example, if Stamper misread a map and lost his way, the King 'would gravely deplore the manner in which misfortune singled him out for her victim,' and would 'then settle himself gently in his corner as if resigning himself to his fate. In his countenance there was written a placid acceptance of the situation and a calm expectancy of worse to come. The listless way in which he heard my apologies was inimitable. Of such gentle irony the King was a master. So exquisite was the pose he affected, that his gentlemen were often hard put to it not to smile, while sometimes the King would end up laughing in spite of himself.'

Once as they drove out of Biarritz, they passed a signpost and the King asked Stamper what it said. 'I told him "La Plage." "What does that mean?" said His Majesty. I did not know, and, since he asked me with a perfectly grave face, I quite thought he did not know either.' After consulting a small dictionary, Stamper 'turned round and told him in all seriousness that it meant "The sea-shore." At this the King burst out laughing, and I saw he had only asked me for the sake of my French.'

Always a great tease, there was nothing HRH liked better than 'chaffing his friends. But it was always done most tactfully, and in such an amusing way that everyone loved him for it, and enjoyed the chaff as much as he did himself.' When asked to Luncheon on board Sir Alan Young's yacht anchored off Cowes, he would mock his host by saying: 'I don't suppose we shall have anything decent to eat, nothing but ship's biscuits as usual?' As he knew quite well, at that very moment one of the best chefs in England was down below in the galley bestowing the final touches on quails à la grecque or stuffing snipe with foie gras. Sometimes HRH would even venture to tease those intransigent Tories, the old Duchess of Cambridge and her son, the Commander-in-Chief. Lady Geraldine Somerset relates in her diary how angry they were with him 'for heading the list of congratulations on Gladstone's birthday with a fulsome telegram to the brute. To *my* mind it is too disgusting and sickening! and *despicable*! He assured the Duke he had telegraphed in *his* name as well as his own – thank *God* it was only a joke.'

According to Wilfrid Blunt, one of the Prince of Wales's chief occupations was 'to use his social influence to compose his friends' quarrels.' Lady Warwick described him as possessing 'an almost feminine desire to put things right.' Detesting hypocrisy, he rebuked vice so gently as almost to countenance it: hence his role of Edward the Confessor. Such was his 'magically conciliatory charm' and understanding of the world, that 'everyone came to him with their troubles . . . "Tell the Prince" was the constant cry.' He never turned a deaf ear to people's problems and 'such recitals never bored him. He was by nature inquisitive – wanted to know everything about everybody – and in this way his pity, sympathy and help were brought into play.'

Neither misfortune nor disgrace persuaded the Prince of Wales to abandon his friends. 'It had been thought he might drop some of them on coming to the throne, but his heart was warmer than Prince Hal's, and he did not turn his back, when at Windsor, on the old acquaint- ances of Eastcheap.' His steadfastness through thick and thin was both a matter of principle and a deep instinct. 'I may have many faults,' he told Lord Granville in 1882, 'but I have held one great principle in life from which I will never waver, and that is loyalty to one's friends, and defending them if possible when they get into trouble. One often gets into scrapes in consequence, but I consider the risk worth running.'

When the Prince was gazetted Colonel of the Tenth Hussars, or 'The Prince of Wales's Own,' he became a close friend of its Com- manding Officer, Valentine Baker, who in 1875 was cashiered and sent to prison for allegedly kissing a young lady in a train travelling to Clapham. His case provoked elemental passions in which class hostility and moral outrage mingled. The Judge referred to 'vile passions' and a 'gross outrage,' while a Member of Parliament described Baker's behaviour as 'one of the most scandalous and atrocious crimes ever committed,' and several newspapers declared that he should have been sentenced to hard labour for his dastardly assault. Naturally, the Colonel's fair-weather friends deserted him to a man, but not the Prince, who maintained that the evidence was inconclusive and the punishment over severe. After Baker's release, HRH helped him to obtain a military post in Turkey and later pressed Gladstone to sanction his nomination as Commander-in- Chief of the Khedive's Army.

The Prince showed Dilke an equal loyalty. In 1885, Mrs Craw- ford, the wife of a Member of Parliament, told her husband that she had been Sir Charles's mistress for the past three years. It is conceivable that this confession was intended to divert suspicion from some other person. There were several perplexing features in the ensuing legal battle. Mrs Crawford, whose accusations became increasingly lurid, failed to produce the corroboratory evidence she initially promised; but Sir Charles, while protesting his innocence to the last, was unable to prove it. In one of its seasonal fits of morality the public resolved to destroy his career. Plainly no man suspected of adultery was fit to represent the burghers of Chelsea, amongst whom, presumably, such enormities were unknown.

The Prince of Wales, who had been friendly with Dilke since 1880, accepted his assurances that the charges were fabrications and did everything in his power to help him. 'I am sorry to hear that the action is likely to go against him,' HRH told Knollys. But at least it might teach 'the public in general and the Radicals in particular – that the latter are not more moral than the "bloated aristocrats!" ' From the moment Dilke fell from favour, nobody worked harder than HRH to restore him to grace. One of the first acts of his reign was to insist that Sir Charles should be readmitted to Court; and after the Liberal landslide of 1906 he urged Campbell-Bannerman to make Dilke Foreign Secretary.

Lord Charles Beresford, who for many years was estranged from the Prince by a bitter quarrel, told King George V that he would never forget 'the kindness, generosity and affection shown to me by His Majesty in those happy days gone by . . . Nothing has or ever could remove from my mind the love and devotion I bore to the most kindly hearted and generous man I ever met.' 'Warm human kindness,' said Sir Edward Grey, 'was of the very substance of the man.'

The Prince's geniality was not confined to his own circle of friends. When Madame Waddington visited Sandringham, she noticed that HRH never failed to have 'a pleasant word and smile' for 'servants, railway guards and small functionaries generally.' Not surprisingly, they thought the world of him. Stamper described his manners as unrivalled. 'His politeness was never profuse; it was always just right. Indeed, for easy grace he had no equal. Even to me, when I was off duty, he always raised his hat – taking it right off his head.' Once, when he was strolling along 'La Plage' at Newhaven, he stopped to talk to a coastguard. Afterwards, the man kept telling Stamper, 'He was so nice, he was so nice.'

Queen Victoria, who lived mostly amongst servants, held them in higher regard than did her friends and family. Her partiality for them verged on eccentricity, and she often rebuked her children and household for treating them haughtily. Her own example, she believed, was one which should be more widely followed. Sir Howard Elphinstone, Prince Arthur's Comptroller, constantly received long letters from Her Majesty complaining of the boy's offhand manner. 'Reserve is not necessary,' the Queen told Sir Howard, 'towards the *faithful devoted confidential* servants who have known him from childhood . . . If any of the Queen's sons *put* on a *tone* of *stiffness* in her presence *towards her* people when *she* does *not* do so, it is as if they *meant to show their mother* and *the Queen* that they disapproved HER MANNER.' There were 'simple little acts of courtesy and kindness,' such as shaking hands, a friendly nod, or 'an exchange of a few words on meeting,' which were much 'appreciated by *all*.'

The Prince of Wales's example was not one she often advised her family to follow, but his affability to servants was something from which they could learn. Before Prince Arthur visited Balmoral in 1873, she told Sir Howard to remind him that his eldest brother was 'always very kind, and is much beloved.' Moreover, 'stiffness' was '*not* requisite in *her* house and with her own *confidential* people, and that open frankness in those below you, when they are devoted and attached is a thing for which *you ought* to be *truly* thankful.'

Unfortunately, the Prince of Wales detested John Brown, which the Queen could not easily forgive. She never saw how her favours went to his head, or how insolent he could be. For example, he once curtly silenced Gladstone by telling him, 'You've said enough.' For some years, HRH was reluctant to visit Balmoral because he refused to share the shooting with a gillie. Soon after he became King, he gave orders that the numerous monuments the Queen had raised to her Highland servant should be destroyed, for fear they might rather recall her folly than his devotion. But coarse, rough and arrogant as Brown might be, he wore his faults on his sleeve. Nobody could call him underhand. Indeed, his rugged integrity was what first attracted the Queen.

But the Munshi, who succeeded him in the Queen's favour, was cunning and treacherous and self-seeking: no more to be trusted than a pick-pocket with a purse. Yet somehow he managed to win Her Majesty's confidence, shrewd as she normally was. So thoroughly was she deceived, that those who attempted to open her eyes, merely succeeded in making themselves suspect. The

Queen acquired Abdul Karim in the year of her Golden Jubilee. He started by waiting at table, but, tiring of menial tasks, was promoted to 'Munshi': that is, the Queen's teacher of Urdu and Hindustani. So successful was he in his task that after ten years of his instruction, the Queen addressed her Indian troops in what they were assured was their own language.

When Her Majesty told him he might join the household in the billiard room, he was given a frosty welcome. Nobody seemed anxious to fraternize with what most people regarded as a jumped-up footman, and probably impostor in the bargain. From then onwards there was nothing but trouble, as there were no bounds to the Munshi's pretensions. Before going out to India, to take up his appointment as an ADC to the Governor-General, Lord Elgin, Frederick Ponsonby was told by the Queen to visit the Munshi's father, who she had been led to believe held the rank of Surgeon-General. After much difficulty, Fritz tracked him down. Not realizing what was at stake, he told the Queen, soon after returning to England, that he had carried out her commands, and that the old man was, in fact, not in the army at all, but an apothecary at the jail in Agra. She indignantly insisted that Ponsonby had visited the wrong man, and would not speak to him for a month.

In 1890, the Duke of Connaught was amazed to see the Munshi mingling with the gentry at the Braemar games. He angrily sent for Fritz's father to enquire how such a thing could happen. 'I replied,' wrote Sir Henry, describing the incident, 'that Abdul stood where he was by the Queen's order and that if it was wrong, as I did not understand Indian etiquette and HRH did, would it not be better for him to mention it to the Queen. This entirely shut him up.'

In 1895, after Lord Wolseley succeeded the Duke of Cambridge as Commander-in-Chief, he was summoned to Balmoral. As he made the journey from Ballater station to the castle in a hired fly, he was astonished to pass the Munshi taking the air in a royal carriage. In 1897 the Queen's household went on strike when she decided to take the Munshi to France. Miss Harriet Phipps, Sir Charles's daughter, was deputed to tell Her Majesty that they would not eat with him. There was an awe-inspiring silence. The Queen became so angry that she swept everything off her desk on to the floor in a gesture of outraged majesty. In the end Lord Salisbury persuaded her that the French were 'such odd people' that they would probably laugh at the Munshi and hurt his feelings.

As befitted the son of a Surgeon-General, Abdul was given three houses. At Windsor he lived at Frogmore Cottage, near to the Mausoleum and its hallowed remains. A bungalow was built for him in the grounds of Osborne and furnished down to the last teaspoon. At Balmoral an imposing residence was placed at his disposal, sufficiently capacious to accommodate the tribe of uncles and 'aunts', nephews and nieces, who followed him from India. Every time Dr Reid was summoned to treat 'Mrs Karim' he could not but notice a different tongue was put out for inspection.

To the disgust of those acquainted with this odious Oriental, the Queen in 1894 appointed him her 'Indian Secretary,' and showed him private dispatches from the Governor General. When it became clear that State secrets were being betrayed, the Prince of Wales suggested that the Munshi might be responsible. It was a year before Lord George Hamilton, the Secretary of State for India, finally prevented the Queen showing Abdul confidential papers by threatening that it would be impossible for him to go on sending them unless she ceased to do so. After the Queen's funeral, Lord Esher noticed the Indians 'wandering about like uneasy spirits.'

The King put a peremptory end to this strange saga of innocence and intrigue. He had always considered the Munshi a fraudulent rogue, and had no regrets when he returned to his native country, complete with uncles and aunts, friends and relations. On the very day the Queen died, Lord Salisbury sent Knollys a cypher telegram about searching the Munshi's effects for letters from the Queen, which the new king was anxious to recover. The Prime Minister, before offering advice, consulted Sir Edward Bradford, the Commissioner of Police in London, whose earlier career had been spent in India, where he had fought during the Mutiny, and lost an arm after being mauled by a tiger. 'I have taken Bradford's opinion,' read the telegram, 'on the matter of the Munshi. He is strongly in favour of letting the matter rest for the present on the ground that any letters or papers which may exist have no doubt been conveyed to India where a domiciliary visit by the police would almost certainly fail to discover them. I would suggest that his advice be followed and that the Munshi be permitted to return to India. When he gets there I think that the Viceroy will probably be able to obtain the letters from him without difficulty.'

The telegram was followed by a letter from Salisbury's Private Secretary, Schomberg McDonnell, enclosing a memorandum from the Prime Minister, sent by box, being too secret to trust to the post. McDonnell explained that Lord Salisbury attached 'the greatest importance to Sir Edward Bradford's opinion as he has an expert knowledge of natives and their ways, and it certainly appears to him that the course suggested is by far the most likely to meet with success.'

The memorandum stated that Salisbury had seen Sir Edward on 21 January, and had 'discussed with him at great length what action should be taken with regard to the Munshi. Sir Edward was strongly of opinion that all the papers and letters have been removed to India; but he did not think it would be of the slightest use to attempt to find them by means of the police: natives have such extraordinary genius for hiding documents that he did not believe any domiciliary search by the police would result in the discovery of the letters: and he thought that such a search, however carefully carried out, could not fail to produce a great scandal even in India . . . What he would recommend would be that the Munshi be treated as if nothing had happened: he will probably want to return to India very soon, and Sir Edward thinks no obstacle should be placed in the way of his doing so. After his arrival there, Sir Edward thinks that the Viceroy should be instructed to send for him, or to let the head of the police see him, and persuade him to surrender the letters: if he does so, a small piece of land might be granted him: and Sir Edward anticipates that he will do so at once. Sir Edward holds very strongly that it would be a great mistake to attempt to coerce the Munshi, and that any such action could only result in a determined refusal on his part to surrender anything he may have got in the shape of letters, and probably in an attempt to make use of them.'

In April 1909, Sir Arthur Bigge, then Prince George's Private Secretary, wrote to Knollys, saying: 'You will have seen that "the Munshi" is dead – I can have no regret!' In August, he wrote again telling Knollys that 'on the strength of a letter which I shewed you from one of Queen Victoria's former servants, Ahmed Hussain, who hinted that the Munshi's family still possessed letters from the Queen, you told me that His Majesty wished me to write to the Viceroy on the subject. I have now heard from him enclosing the documents which I forward to you. He says that the result of this further enquiry is not altogether satisfactory but he doubts whether anything more can be done. You will see that Sir J. Hewett thinks the nephew is "shifty", but at the same time owing to the unpopularity of the Munshi, *if* there were existing papers his enemies would soon let the fact be known.'

The King, however, wrote to the Viceroy, Lord Minto, requesting him to make further 'discreet investigations,' as 'I am not satisfied in my mind that there may not be still letters in Queen Victoria's handwriting in their possession.' If so, he suggested they should be told to return them at once, or risk being 'the sufferers thereby.'

Amongst Knollys's Papers are three letters written by Queen Victoria to the Munshi: one in her own hand, and two headed 'true copies.' These were presumably the fish which Lord Minto caught in his trawl. The document written in the Queen's hand on Balmoral writing paper is headed: 'Extracts from the Prince of Wales's letters to the Queen in answer to hers.' The first, dated 28 September 1899, reads: 'I shall always be ready to notice and speak to the Munshi when I meet him.' The second, dated 2 October 1899, authorizes the Queen to assure Adbul Karim 'that I have no ill will against him and only trust that matters should go smoothly and quietly.' The copies are letters of slightly earlier origin. One was written in February 1894 and declared: 'I have given to the Munshi Abdul Karim (for whom I have specially written this) a gun as a present and have allowed him to wear a sword here and in India since the year 1890. Victoria RI.' The other was written in January 1896 and defined the Munshi's duties. It seems improbable that these documents were those the King sought. Certainly the one quoting his own letters might be mildly embarrassing if it fell into hostile hands, but Lord Salisbury would hardly have concerned himself on the day the Queen died with so minor a matter.

The Munshi's right to wear a sword was precisely the sort of issue about which the Prince was inclined to become obsessed. In his youth, his parents constantly complained that he took no interest in anything but clothes. Nor did his fondness for dress diminish even in middle age. In 1882, a few days after the battle of Tel-el-Kebir, Wolseley mentioned in a letter to his wife a communication he had just received from the Prince of Wales. 'His lecturing me on war amused me very much,' wrote the victorious general indignantly. 'Let him stick to tailoring that is his province, and keep his breath for his own porridge.'

The extravagant attention HRH paid to sartorial matters may well be traced to hereditary influences. The Duke of Kent, his grandfather, was so meticulous in regard to such details that those who served under him called him the 'corporal'. Queen Victoria, according to Admiral Fisher, was 'uncommon particular' about medals, and this may account for her son seeming 'to think that the correct wearing of an Order or decoration was of greater moment than the merit that had won it.'

When Queen Victoria opened the new Law Courts in Fleet Street, the Duke of Teck attended the ceremony wearing the full dress uniform of a Colonel of the British Army, a rank he had just received for his services in the Arabi campaign. The Prince suddenly assumed, in the middle of a conversation, that cold, fixed, wide-eyed stare which so unmistakably showed that something was seriously amiss. During an embarrassed silence his gaze rested on the Duke. At last he vouchsafed what was displeasing him. 'Francis,' he said, 'has got the wrong buttons!' Admiral Fisher, who perfected the art of circumspect impertinence, once came to Court in disgracefully old clothes. 'R-really Fisher,' said the King, 'that is a ver-ry old suit you are wearing.' 'Yes, Sir,' the Admiral replied, 'but you have always told me that nothing really matters but the cut.' The Prince's sensitive vigilance for sartorial lapses led to constant discoveries of discrepancies in Lord Salisbury's attire. 'As Prime Minister, Lady Salisbury wrote, her husband once went to the Palace "in a judicious mixture of two uniforms and nearly caused the death of the Heir to the Crown from consternation." Salisbury's apology to the Prince for having put on the wrong sort of trousers was masterly: "It was a dark morning and I am afraid that my mind must have been occupied by some subject of less importance." '

Henry Ponsonby was worse than Knollys in appreciating niceties of dress. In the course of a visit the Queen paid William I, she was greeted by the Kaiser and his suite in full dress uniform, but photographs of the meeting revealed Sir Henry and his assistant, Arthur Bigge, in top hats and frock coats. The Prince telegraphed Her Majesty to say how delighted he was to learn that she had met the German Emperor, and added: 'I see you were attended by Bishop Ponsonby and Dean Bigge.'

The dinner-jacket first became fashionable in 1876 when HRH took to dining in one on board HMS *Serapis* on his voyage out to India. But it was only acceptable on informal occasions amongst friends. When a daring young Guardsman 'entered the Marlborough Club in what was then a highly unconventional item of the wardrobe,' the Prince looked him up and down, as if he had rolled in manure, and addressed him thus: 'I suppose, my young friend, you are going to a costume ball.'

Not only subalterns but the mightiest in the land were liable to such rebukes. In 1908, Sir Arthur Nicolson, the British Ambassador at St Petersburg, was summoned aboard the *Victoria and Albert* to brief King Edward before his meeting with the Tsar at Reval. Towards the end of his audience, Nicolson 'observed that His Majesty's eye returned with angered insistence to the same spot,' where the badge of his Nova Scotia Baronetcy dangled from his throat. "What," grumbled King Edward, "is that bauble?" Nicolson with some pride explained that was the only hereditary Order in England. After a further brief conversation, a message came to say that the Imperial barge was approaching. 'King Edward placed his hand on Nicolson's shoulder. "Never," he said, "wear that bauble again." '

When Lord Rossmore appeared at Epsom wearing the wrong sort of hat, he was immediately caught by the Prince, who looked at him critically 'from top to toe, and then said half in jest and half in reproof: "Well, Rossmore, have you come r-r-ratting?" ' During his lifetime the Prince of Wales popularized four innovations in dress: the Norfolk Coat, the Dinner Jacket, the Homburg Hat and the practice of leaving the bottom button of waistcoats undone.

Like many inventions, that undone waistcoat was a response to sheer necessity. Sir Sidney Lee, a master of decorous understatement, described the Prince as never toying with his food. Alix was blunter and said his appetite was 'terrible'. His manner of life was precisely that which we are warned leads to a premature grave. He ate not wisely but too well. He would begin a meal with several dozen oysters and conclude it with generous helpings of plum pudding. He smoked all day, starting before breakfast, and went to bed in the early hours of the morning. But despite such habits he lived three score years and nine. It would be almost impossible to exaggerate the grave disservice he performed by not dropping dead at an early age.

It is true the Prince paid token visits to resorts such as Homburg and Marienbad, 'pour combattre l'obésité.' But he seems to have been his own doctor and his prescriptions were not rigorous. If he lost eight pounds in a month he claimed a triumph, and only needed a fortnight to put it back. During one of his last visits to Biarritz, he sat down to supper at the Hôtel du Palais. Unfortunately, he said, he seemed to have lost his appetite. Nevertheless, course after course was served and eaten by him with relish until finally, when all the other guests were gasping for breath and had long since lost all interest in food, fruit was passed round. Whereupon the King looked up and exclaimed in disappointed tones: 'Is there no cheese?'

The Queen constantly complained that the Prince and Princess of Wales lived far too restless lives. The sentiment so prettily expressed by John Howard Payne might have been written for them.

'Mid pleasures and palaces though we may roam,
   Be it never so humble, there's no place like home.'

In 1865, Phipps wrote Sir William what looks suspiciously like an 'inspired' letter: the pen was his but the views were Her Majesty's. It was a 'general opinion,' he claimed, that the Prince of Wales 'overdoes the visiting and going about.' It seemed only too probable that newspapers, by drawing attention to HRH's 'unceasing and inconsiderate pursuit of pleasure,' would encourage ill-natured comment, 'and the popularity which he has as yet undoubtedly enjoyed' might be seen to rest on no more solid ground than 'cordial manners and social good nature.' Such criticism, Phipps concluded, was not confined to the older generation. 'I hear even the young men saying that "the Prince of Wales is flying about rather too much."'

The proposition that the pursuit of pleasure 'figured disproportionately in the list of the Prince's engagements' was statistically corroborated by Arnold White in his book *Tries at Truth*. After a painstaking analysis of Court Circulars for the year 1890, he produced the following summary of HRH's social programme. 'The Prince attended, between 1 January and 30 September, 28 race meetings, 30 theatrical performances, 43 dinner parties, banquets, balls and garden-parties, together with 45 official and philanthropic ceremonies and 11 sittings of the House of Lords.'

White was one of those sociologists better acquainted with theories about society than its actual workings. The Prince, of course, was far too sophisticated a hedonist not to be bored to death by many of his engagements. That he contrived to look happy on such occasions was greatly to his credit. When the Queen was so often criticized for remaining invisible, it seems hard to complain of her son's public appearances.

Most of those who objected to the Prince's social life, assumed that it lay in his power to set the moral tone of society and that he was exercising this prerogative recklessly. It is doubtful, however, whether so small a group as the Prince and his friends possessed such influence. It is not the fly which clings to the wheel of the dynamo that generates electricity.

'The Queen and the Prince Consort,' as E. F. Benson argued, 'had for twenty years given an example of a dutiful and godly and serious life, but there is no real reason to suppose that they affected the moral tone of the country, or that adultery, drunkenness and gambling were greatly diminished in those two decades owing to their moral splendour. They set the tone of their immediate circle, but it can hardly be supposed that their domestic devotion restrained the amorous inclinations of a citizen of Windsor towards his neighbour's wife, or that a heavy drinker at Ballater would cork up his whisky bottle because the Court was abstemious, or that there was less betting at race-meetings because the Queen never put a shilling on a horse.' Either to blame or to congratulate the Prince of Wales for the ferment of social and ethical ideas which stirred during his lifetime, would be to underestimate those larger forces which work for change and to exaggerate the influence of one who was more their effect than cause.

So anxious were a group of high-minded ladies at 'the breakdown of the conventional proprieties of the seventies,' that they decided to approach the Archbishop of Canterbury to see what could be done. The 'Lambeth Penitents,' who included the Duchess of Leeds, Lady Tavistock and Lady Stanhope, invited Benson to stop the moral rot. In particular they suggested that he should reprove the Prince of Wales for the mischief he was doing. When they invited Alix to attend their devotional meetings she consulted the Queen. Naturally, Her Majesty had no objection to reclaiming the higher classes, but she thought the method suggested 'most extraordinary.' The notion of holding services on weekdays was not to her liking, besides, 'religion was not a thing to be mixed up with life.' The Lambeth Penitents achieved little, not even royal patronage, but their anxiety was genuine and the problem real.

None of the Lambeth Penitents were members of dissenting congregations, but they nevertheless represented the non-conformist conscience at a time when its influence was never more powerful. There were, however, other voices in the land. Plenty of the more robust Victorians were content to take an indulgent view of the Prince's 'pleasant little wickednesses.' For all the Prince Consort's impeccable rectitude the country never took to him, whereas his son, who did not pretend to virtue, was greatly loved and admired. The most popular sovereigns of recent centuries have been the least exemplary. Neither Henry VIII nor Charles II triumphed over temptation, but both were held in the highest esteem by their subjects. There were, moreover, consoling precedents for heirs apparent sowing a few wild oats. As Phipps sadly acknowledged, there would always be some to support the Prince through thick and thin, and 'praise him chiefly for his faults and follies.'

IV

The Prince in Trouble

There can be no advantage in pretending to virtue unless society values it. Hypocrisy only flourishes when standards are high. In permissive ages, where few things are unacceptable, there is little to hide. Because the Victorians made such strenuous moral demands they did not always practise what they preached. The dominating idea of English society was not to cultivate virtue but to avoid scandal. 'Everything was all right,' claimed Lady Warwick, 'if only it was kept quiet, hushed up, covered.'

Although it was thought necessary in the nineteenth century to maintain that marriage vows were sacred, affairs were common among fashionable people, and lovers were given adjoining rooms when staying in country houses. But if adultery was reckoned venial its advertisement was mortal: the moment they were discovered romances turned into scandals.

Those who lived by such rules invited blackmail, varying from unscrupulous pressures to criminal demands, and nobody was more vulnerable to such menaces than the Prince of Wales. The public were hungry for royal scandals and his habits were such as to provide them. The more illustrious the reputation the more potent the threat of exposure.

On 11 September 1871, HRH received a letter posted in Florence from a Pirro Benini, informing him that following the death of his sister, Madame Barucci, 'toute la correspondence de votre Altesse est en mes mains. Votre Altesse l'aurait réclamée moyennant une somme en argent de 12 à 15 cents livres sterling.' It would, he added, be very unfortunate if such intimate letters should fall into the wrong hands.

Madame Giulia Barucci was one of the most breath-taking courtesans of the Second Empire, who described herself as the 'greatest whore in the world.' She was insatiably passionate, surprisingly discreet, dazzlingly rich and devoutly religious. Like Marie Duplessis, who inspired Dumas's *La Dame aux Camélias*, she died of consumption. The Prince of Wales and his brother, the Duke of Edinburgh, were introduced to her by the Duc de Gramont during their visit to the Paris Exhibition of 1867. Her brother, Pirro, began his career as a tenor but was hooted off the stage. After some years as a solicitor's clerk, he moved to Paris in 1860 and lived off Giulia's bounty.

The Prince at once wrote to Francis Knollys, saying he had 'just received a letter from that scoundrel Benini' demanding between twelve and fifteen hundred pounds for his letters to Madame Barucci. He assured Francis that none of his letters were signed. It appeared that the blackguard had 'abstracted the letters surreptitiously,' that he was threatening the Duke of Edinburgh, and would 'stick at nothing.' Before deciding what should be done, the Prince asked Francis to consult Baron French and Monsieur Kanne. The Baron was a banker in Florence, whose son was Her Britannic Majesty's Consul in the City, and Kanne was a courier whom the Prince Consort had recommended to the Queen, and whose drawing-room was thick with signed photographs of the crowned heads of Europe.

As instructed, Knollys approached Kanne, who told him 'that nothing but money or a well arranged little Coup d'Etat – a seizure of these letters – will obtain the desired end.' After further consideration, Kanne and Knollys were inclined 'not to give any money,' but to resort to a 'coup de main,' which 'might be managed in a country like Italy.' If all else failed, Kanne wondered whether it might not be possible for somebody to 'take upon himself to be the writer of these letters, provided there is a dead certainty that *no signature*, not even initials, were attached to them.'

The Prince agreed 'that it would never do to give that scoundrel Benini any money' and tended to favour plans for seizing the letters. On 27 October, Benini wrote to the Prince saying that as he had received no reply to his previous communications, he proposed to include HRH's correspondence with his sister in a sale of her effects to be held on 9 November in her house in the Rue de la Baune.

Kanne hastened to Paris and, after a preliminary reconnaissance, concluded that Benini was 'evidently determined to sell everything as quickly as possible.' Amongst the items he saw displayed, was an album with 'portraits of the *whole* Royal family inscribed "Alfred to Giulia." I began a conversation with P.B., asked en passant to buy some portraits – answer had none. Pretended to be a collector of autographs, asked if he had some interesting signatures. Yes – a whole correspondence but could not sell it yet as he is in pourparler with the writer, but that he would sell them if they were not taken by the writer. He evidently will not part with them for a small sum. I carefully examined everything, but could not find any trace of anything coming from HRH, yet I feel convinced he has them with him.

'There are but two ways left. If the letters are not signed, nobody will buy them and the matter must be left to chance or, if this is not approved of, I propose another way. I can obtain an introduction to General Valentin who is the Ministre de Police; the letters P.B. has written to HRH sufficiently prove "Chantage" and P.B. could be imprisoned. If you approve of this you must at once send me *all* P.B.'s letters so that I can take proceedings, naturally avoiding all publicity.' Kanne hoped that it might be possible 'to induce B., under threat of imprisonment, to give up the letters. Please to let me have *immediately* a telegram simply stating either "Do Nothing" or "See Valentin." My impression is B. can do nothing. If it comes to the worst, HRH must say the letters are a forgery.'

Knollys replied to Kanne's letter, from Sandringham, saying that the Prince was 'strongly opposed to B. appearing before any tribunal (police or otherwise) as the case would then immediately get about, and he is equally disinclined to give £400, but he is at the same time willing to give any reasonable sum for the letters.' Knollys was still taken with the idea of seizing them, but conceded 'that the days for those sort of things are past.' Two days before the sale, he sent Kanne a telegram instructing him 'to buy everything with signatures. Do not see Valentin. The rest left to your judgement.' That evening, Kanne telegraphed back: 'Letters are 20. Have today seen them all. They are not signed but have A.E. Most are of delicate nature. B. wants £400. Have offered £40. No use. B. says he is determined to make money out of them.'

On 9 November, the day of Benini's sale and the Prince's thirtieth birthday, the following telegrams were exchanged between the Hôtel Bristol, in Paris, and Sandringham. 'No letter this morning. Urgency compelled me to rapid decision. Have obtained all and everything. Letter follows. Kanne.' Back came the reply: 'Your prompt action highly approved of. Knollys.' As good as his promise, Kanne sat down that very evening in the Hôtel Bristol and wrote a detailed account of his purchase. Benini at first had insisted that he would consider nothing less than £400, and threatened to advertise the letters as 'une correspondance particulière d'un Grand Seigneur,' or to sell them 'aux femmes des ces messieurs': for it turned out that he also possessed letters to his sister written by Dr Quin, the father of English homoeopathy, the Crown Prince of Denmark, and His Grace the Duke of Sutherland. Eventually, Kanne managed to purchase the whole collection for 6000 francs, about £240, which, 'considering all circumstances' was 'not too terrible.' 'I hope HRH will think I have done right in obtaining possession of all the other letters and that I have not been too liberal or easy.'

Naturally, before buying HRH's letters, Kanne studied them carefully to ensure that they were genuine. 'I first thought,' he told Knollys, 'they might be proclaimed a forgery – but when I saw them I came to the conclusion that the nature of them precluded every possibility of their being such. The writing, the intimate gossip, are sufficient proofs of identity and of being originals. At the risk of offending HRH, I *privately* for that reason mention to you, and I have good reason for doing so, that the Prince can *not* be *too careful* with his writing. Every scrape [*sic*] of his writing becomes every day of more value and importance.'

On this, as on other occasions, the Prince ignored the judicious advice of his friend Rosa Lewis: 'No letters, no lawyers and kiss my baby's bottom.' The Duke of Sutherland said of his own letters to Madame Barucci that he had seldom read anything 'more innocent or worse written,' and suggested that Knollys should publish them in his Memoirs, 'which will exceed in interest *Les Mémoires de Casanova*. Dilke will edit them, and they shall come out in weekly numbers in *Reynolds*.' As a PS he added, 'I am afraid you never met the lady in question.'

The most distressing aspect of illicit romances in the Victorian Age was that society's attitude towards unwanted children was as primitive as its means of preventing them. It was said that a considerable number of the inhabitants of Coburg bore a striking resemblance to their Sovereign, whom Ponsonby described as 'the father, nay the grandfather of many of his subjects,' and it was not unknown for people in England to claim that sons and daughters of the Prince of Wales's more intimate friends looked distinctly

Hanoverian. Often, no doubt, such similarity was pure coincidence and the inference malicious. But those who thought that Lady Susan Vane Tempest's child was the image of the Prince were not mistaken.

Lady Susan was the daughter of the fifth Duke of Newcastle, who had accompanied the Prince of Wales on his tour of Canada and the United States. Her mother, one of the Duke of Hamilton's children, ran off with a Belgian courier in 1850. Mr Gladstone, out of friend-ship for the Duke, pursued them across Europe, finally gaining access to the villa in which the fugitives were hiding by assuming a disguise. In 1860, Lady Susan Pelham-Clinton married Lord Adolphus Vane Tempest, whose father, Lord Londonderry, was Castlereagh's half-brother. His mother was a great Tory hostess, the friend of Disraeli, and an heiress in her own right. Adolphus's sister, Frances, married the seventh Duke of Marlborough, so Winston Churchill was his great-nephew.

As Susan had been one of Vicky's bridesmaids, the Queen's letters to her daughter were full of the wedding. 'Only think, Lady Susan P. Clinton has gone and married Lord Adolphus Vane, who drinks and has twice been shut up for delirium tremens. She told her father she would, as soon as she was of age! So she did and he would not allow his carriage to take her to church even; and she was given away by her brother Lord Lincoln who is very worthless I fear. It is most sad, for I fear Susan will pay dearly for it and her poor father is heartbroken about it. Lord Adolphus is a good creature . . . but between drink and his natural tendency to madness there is a sad prospect for Susan.' Apparently, Susan 'walked to church with her governess – no one but her brother there; no settlements, no trousseau, nothing and they say that at any moment he may go quite mad!' Indeed, there was 'a dreadful bon-mot' about which of the two would be 'confined first.'

Writing to the Duchess of Manchester, Lord Clarendon gave further details of the 'Susan Clinton escapade.' When the Duke learned that Lady Londonderry was actively encouraging the match, he wrote her a touching letter asking her 'whether her son was of a character or in a condition to promote the happiness of any girl . . . The hard old devil announced: she was convinced that the marriage would promote the happiness of her son which was all she had to do with.' During the ceremony, Lord Adolphus trembled so much 'that they expected a fit.' Lady Londonderry, who did not attend the service, gave a perfunctory reception, and 'the ill fated couple set off for Brighton.' During the honeymoon, Lady Susan declared herself 'the happiest of women.' Clarendon thought she 'must be among the most foolish . . . They have not made a penny of settlement on her so that if that fellow dies in one of his fits she may find herself on the pavé, unless her father took her back.'

Thirteen months later, Clarendon reported that 'Lord Adolphus Vane has been regularly mad and is so still. The Doctors say he will recover and may stand one more attack but not two.' Susan took refuge with her mother-in-law who refused to speak to her. 'I would sooner by half that she threw a glass of water in my face,' said Lady Londonderry, 'than put on that detestable passive look.' Lord Adolphus died in 1864, after a struggle with his four keepers. 'She is left penniless,' the Queen told Vicky. 'Is this not retribution? He tried to kill her last week and also the child – so that I believe it is to her a real release too!'

In 1867 the widowed Lady Susan met the Prince of Wales who did his best to console her. For the next four years they saw a good deal of each other. In late September 1871, while the Prince was at Abergeldie, he received a letter from Mrs Harriet Whatman, Susan's closest friend, who ventured to write out of a 'sense of duty and loyalty to your Person,' and from her 'deep and sincere affection and pity for a most unfortunate and unhappy lady.' 'The facts in question,' which had been revealed to HRH earlier that summer, were now within two or three months of 'the crisis.' 'The Position is a most pitiable one and most dangerous for all parties. Without *any funds* to meet the necessary expenses and to buy the discretion of servants, it is impossible to keep this sad secret.'

Mrs Whatman reminded the Prince that her 'unfortunate friend's private means were very small' so that 'the vista of expenses before her' was 'affecting her health and mind.' 'I dread,' she wrote, 'some catastrophe that may awaken public attention to facts which have hitherto been strictly confined to *my* knowledge, so strictly that not even the dearest and truest of friends Princess Edward has been admitted to the confidence.' Princess Edward was Lady Augusta Gordon Lennox, a daughter of the Duke of Richmond, who married Queen Adelaide's nephew, Prince Edward of Saxe-Weimar. 'So many persons must be included in the secret when certain Events take place and so much financial help will be required, that it is only by addressing your Royal Highness and revealing the bare Truth,' that there could be any *hope or chance* that the event in question will remain 'unheeded and unknown.'

Previously, Lady Susan had planned to discuss 'pecuniary help when she saw HRH in town,' but after his failure to pay her a visit, 'she no longer had the courage to address him on the subject of finance. Finding I *cannot* raise her to *the immediate danger of the position* and to the deadly certainty of its being revealed unless means are found to act soon so as to ensure secrecy, I have taken courage to write myself, so that you may be aware of the urgent need and danger . . . I cannot allow, in this instance, false delicacy to stand in the way of the safety and secrecy so necessary for the welfare and reputation of *all* parties concerned. I do not think it possible to surmount all difficulties incident to the event in question under the sum of two hundred and fifty pounds at the least, as it may be necessary to leave town.'

Whether in ignorance of what Mrs Whatman had done, or possibly acting in collusion, Lady Susan wrote to the Prince by the very same post. 'I cannot tell your Royal Highness,' she said, 'how *utterly miserable* I am that you should have left London without coming to see me. You have shown me *so much* kindness for the last four years that I cannot understand your having twice been in London for two days without coming to see me. What have I done to offend you?' Susan assured HRH that she had done her best 'to obey the orders your Royal Highness gave me the last time I had the happiness of seeing you, but the answer was, "*too late* and *too dangerous*."'

Discretion naturally demanded that references to the forthcoming 'event' should be shrouded in obscurity, and the word 'abortion' was never once employed. In her next letter to the Prince, Susan tried to explain why she had been rather dilatory. 'I am ready,' she assured him, 'to obey your orders in everything, and it pains me *more* than I can say that you are annoyed with me . . . Your Royal Highness blames me for not at once going to Dr C. as you desired me, but you can understand it was *most* painful to go to an *utter stranger* under such sad circumstances, when my own doctor had done everything he could for me as long as it was possible to do so with safety.' Dr C. was the Prince's own physician, Oscar Clayton, whose snobbery verged on the ludicrous. When HRH prevailed upon Gladstone to include him in an Honours List, Hamilton wrote in his Diary, 'It is to be hoped no disagreeable stories will come out about him.'

Lady Susan explained that her reason for keeping the Prince 'so long in ignorance of the fact, was, that I hoped to the last my efforts might be successful and that I need never have told you of the anxiety I have gone through. Perhaps I was wrong in keeping silence but I did it to save *you* annoyance, so please forgive me, for you little know *how* sad and unhappy I am.' In order to escape the eyes of the world she was looking for a small house to rent, either in Southend, Surbiton or Ramsgate. 'Perhaps as the latter is a seaside place it might be the safest, as people would not then wonder why I left town, but your Royal Highness must decide.' Fortunately, she had few visitors, 'except Princess Edward and Mrs Whatman, so that nobody else will know whether I am in town or not.' She concluded her letter by pointing out that, although Knollys was always most kind and helpful, there were some things she could only say to HRH personally. 'Don't *please* be angry if I *entreat* you to come and see me before I go away.'

Lady Susan was reluctant to be sent too far from London, as 'not being strong, I should be *so* afraid of being in the hands of a country doctor. Princess Edward will not be difficult to manage, as she is not suspicious and to everybody else *I am out*. My little maid's event will be about the same time as my own.'

The Prince was worried that Princess Edward might visit Lady Susan if she only moved to the suburbs. But there was no fear of that, he was told, because the Princess had '*such* a dread of infection that if I only write her a word I have a bad throat which the doctor thinks may turn to scarlet fever – *she will keep miles away*!!' Lady Susan's brother, the Duke of Newcastle, was more of a problem. She suggested that Dr Clayton should tell him she had caught rheumatic fever and needed to rest by the sea. When she finally took up residence in Wellington Crescent, Ramsgate, the Duke 'was *delighted* at her leaving town and said it would do her a world of good!!'

On 3 February 1872 Lady Susan wrote to Knollys from 20 Chapel Street in London, telling him that she had felt so '*very* unwell' after Christmas, that she made up her mind 'to come to town and consult Mr Clayton. He has not allowed me to leave my room since I returned as I may not even put my foot to the ground. He is *most* kind in coming to look after me and says it is going on all right but that I must not return to Ramsgate . . . I am *too* sorry to be obliged again to have recourse to the kindness of One who has already been so generous to me, but the expenses of two houses and the extra servants have been *very* great . . . I cannot enter into all particulars but Dr Clayton will explain all to Him when he sees Him.'

Five days later, Susan wrote to the Prince, congratulating him on his recovery from typhoid and thanking him for sending her tickets for the Thanksgiving Service at St Paul's. 'Alas! I could not go to the Cathedral but you can well believe *my heart and thoughts were there.*' The letter ended with a PS. 'Forgive such *a scrawl* my dear sir as I am a cripple on two sticks and cannot move about!!!!'

Three years later Lady Susan died, while still only a young woman, and there what is known of her history ends. But as the Prince preserved her letters for forty years, he must, in some measure, have returned the affection she evidently felt for him.

Since the days of Henry IV, no Prince of Wales had ever been summoned before a Court of Justice, so when HRH was sub-poenaed to appear as a witness in the Court of Probate and Divorce the trial was followed with mingled feelings of relish and revulsion. In 1866, Sir Charles Mordaunt, Conservative Member of Parliament for South Warwickshire, married Harriet Moncrieffe, who was barely eighteen. Her father, Sir Thomas, the Queen's neighbour at Balmoral, seemed fortunate in his daughters, all of whom were out-standingly beautiful. One married Lord Dudley and another the Duke of Atholl. In February 1869, Harriet gave birth to a premature son at Walton Hall in Warwickshire, Sir Charles's country house. The boy was apparently threatened with blindness. Partly from brooding over this misfortune, Harriet went out of her mind. On 8 March, she sent for her husband and told him: 'Charlie, you are not the father of that child; Lord Cole is the father of it, and I am the cause of its blindness.' After a few minutes, she burst into tears and said that she had been very wicked and done very wrong. When her husband asked her 'Who with?' she replied: 'With Lord Cole, Sir Frederick Johnstone, the Prince of Wales and others, often, and in open day.'

Although Harriet was evidently deranged when she made her confession, Sir Charles chose to take it at face value, which is why Rosa Lewis called him 'a dirty tyke.' On 14 March, he broke into her desk in search of corroboratory evidence, and abstracted a diary, and a number of letters, including some from the Prince of Wales and others from the great Lord Lucan. Next day, he left Walton Hall for his house in Chesham Place and never set eyes on his wretched wife again.

The 'Warwickshire Scandal' was dragged into the open on 30 April, when Lady Mordaunt was served with a writ for divorce. Her parents, however, claiming she was incapable of giving evidence, and dismissing the confessions upon which her husband relied as the ramblings of a diseased mind, entered a plea of insanity. Sir Charles's advisers professed to believe that this was merely a device to prevent their client winning his case. The legal arguments revolved round two questions: 'Did Lady Mordaunt justly accuse herself of infidelity because she had, indeed, been guilty of adultery, or did Lady Mordaunt falsely accuse herself of adultery because of "hysteria"?'

By the time the trial opened in February 1870, nobody disputed that Lady Mordaunt was mad. Indeed, she was under surveillance night and day. But the Jury had to decide whether Harriet was insane when she made her confession. After a ten-day trial, it only required a few minutes to agree that she was 'utterly unfit' to undertake her defence. Some of the evidence upon which this verdict rested was of a compelling nature. Elizabeth Hancox, who nursed Harriet throughout her confinement, recalled she was nervous and excited, given to sudden fits of weeping, and had threatened to kill the 'poor, miserable, horrid little thing' which she had brought into the world.

Another witness, describing her state of mind, said that she was 'hardly better than a beast of the field.' Sir James Simpson, who pioneered chloroform in anaesthesia, spared no revolting details of Lady Mordaunt's habits to justify his diagnosis of 'puerperal mania.' Not all the expert evidence was of equal force. One learned alienist claimed that her manner of revoking at whist demonstrated that she was of unsound mind. Various servants described how she wandered about at night, naked except for a cloak, and how she tried to smash in the door of the butler's bedroom. Physically, this once beautiful girl degenerated into a corpulent slut. But Serjeant Ballentine, Sir Charles's Counsel, maintained, without much conviction, that the plea of insanity was a conspiracy.

The Prince was only on the periphery of this sordid case, but to judge from some of the newspapers Monarchy was on trial. It is true Lady Mordaunt mentioned his name while out of her mind, but in all probability the Pope would be found guilty if such testimony was accepted. Besides, twelve good men and true had proclaimed that she was totally unfit to give evidence. It is not unknown for unbalanced females to believe that eminent men are anxious to seduce them. There were, of course, the letters Sir Charles discovered in Harriet's desk. Somehow these found their way into the newspapers before the trial began. The public, imagining in anticipation that they must be unspeakably salacious, were astonished to discover that they were such as Prince Albert himself might have sent to an elderly governess. But that they had been written at all struck some people as suspicious. During the course of the trial it transpired that the Prince had several times visited Lady Mordaunt, whom he had known from childhood, when Sir Charles was out. But to establish visits is not to prove seduction, whatever jealous husbands may infer.

The Prince was not on trial in the Divorce Court, but he was before the country, and its verdict went against him. Nevertheless, he was almost certainly innocent. When asked upon oath if there had 'ever been improper familiarity or criminal act' between himself and Lady Mordaunt, he replied, in a very firm tone, 'There has not.'

When deciding whether a man is telling the truth or committing perjury it is necessary to consider the probability of what he says and his reputation for integrity. From his earliest days the Prince was noted for straightforwardness. When he was only five years old Lady Lyttelton spoke of his 'nobleness of mind. And such truth! He inherits all his mother's.' On his ninth birthday, the Queen noted in her Journal: 'There is such good in him. He has such affectionate feeling – great truthfulness and great simplicity of character.' Dr Voisin, who taught French to the Prince, described his 'love of truth' as so developed that he was 'ready to be a witness against himself,' and Dr Becker, the Prince Consort's librarian, declared that he had scarcely ever witnessed such honesty in a child of his age. There is nothing to suggest that as he grew older his integrity diminished. Truthfulness ran in the family. 'If old Mama has a merit,' the Queen once wrote to Vicky, 'it is that of truth and the absence of all flattery.'

There was no need for the Prince to give evidence, for, had he chosen to do so, he was entitled to claim privilege. Sir Alexander Cockburn, the Lord Chief Justice, who was consulted on the wisdom of his testifying, advised him only to do so provided he could confidently face a hostile cross-examination. 'The matter appears to me to depend entirely, first, on how far Your Royal Highness can with a clear and safe conscience deny the main fact in issue, so far as you are concerned and, secondly, how far you may be constrained, when pressed, to admit circumstances calculated to detract from the credit which would otherwise be due to your denial . . . I would not, for the world, that Your Royal Highness should go into the witness-box and that your evidence should fail to command the credit and respect which ought to attach to it. I am sure that the country would be more ready to look with indulgence on what might be thought only a youthful transgression, especially with a lady apparently of such fragile virtue, than on a supposed disregard of truth in one who will one day be the fountain of justice, and in whose name the law will be administered. It must not be forgotten that a man, no matter what his station, comes forward on such an occasion under very disadvantageous circumstances, arising out of the notion that one to whom a woman has given herself up, is bound, even at the cost of committing perjury, to protect her honour.'

Cockburn warned HRH of the sort of questions he would almost certainly be asked, 'such as, for instance, the frequency and duration of your visits, and whether these were known to Her Royal Highness on the one hand, and to Sir Charles Mordaunt on the other – as also whether they were paid in your own carriage, or in a description of vehicle such as it is not usual to see the Heir Apparent to the throne riding in.' Sir Alexander felt bound to point out that, under the circumstances, many people would believe it to be probable 'that in the course of some of your visits you, Sir, yielded to the allurements of this frail and fascinating lady.'

Cockburn concluded by saying that he was not seeking to keep HRH 'from going into the witness-box' if he felt he could do so with satisfaction to his 'conscience and high sense of honour and with safety to his illustrious name and lofty position.' But he felt it was his duty to bring before him 'all the difficulties of the situation,' in the light of his 'long experience of Courts of Justice and some knowledge of the world.' The fact that the Prince, with the Lord Chief Justice's letter before him, submitted himself to cross-examination, would seem to suggest innocence.

The Queen unreservedly accepted her son's assurance that there was no truth in Lady Mordaunt's statement. When he told her what was in prospect, she sent him a telegram expressing her confidence in him. 'Bertie's appearance did great good,' she told Vicky, 'but the whole remains a painful lowering thing not because he is not innocent, for I never doubted that, but because his name ought never to have been dragged in the dirt, or mixed up with such people. He did not know more of, or admire, the unfortunate, crazy Lady Mordaunt more than he does or did other ladies.' The Queen thought Sir Charles 'a fool urged on by a bad brother and mother,' and she believed that her son had 'been vindictively and spitefully used – though why and wherefore I can't tell.' Possibly, she thought, Bertie might 'have said something about Sir C.M's usage of his wife which came back to him.' Although Alix had 'felt everything, that passed lately, deeply,' she was 'quite easy as to Bertie's conduct; only regretting his being foolish and imprudent.'

In the middle of the trial, disregarding the risk of prejudicing proceedings which were *sub judice*, *Reynolds's Newspaper* declared: 'If the Prince of Wales is an accomplice in bringing dishonour to the homestead of an English gentleman; if he assisted in rendering an honourable man miserable for life; if unbridled sensuality and lust have led him to violate the laws of honour and hospitality – then such a man, placed in the position he is, should not only be expelled from decent society, but is utterly unfit and unworthy to rule over this country.'

Considering the Prince's evidence, the Jury's verdict, the insanity of Lady Mordaunt, and his family's confidence in his innocence, the insults showered upon him seem undeserved. But then the Victorians regarded adultery as peculiarly reprehensible when it was thought to take place at tea-time. *The Law Journal* condemned his unjust treatment. 'In Constitutional countries,' it proclaimed, 'Princes are not above the law but they have the same rights and are entitled to the same consideration as other people . . . Is it allowable in the Divorce Court to treat a person as a defendant whose name is not in the suit, and who therefore cannot offer a defence? Not only were the letters of the Prince put in, but they were published in the Press even before they were read in Court. Everything that could be done seems to have been done to deprive the Prince of the protection and privilege of the Law . . . We would not keep silence if the poorest peasant in the land was so treated, and we claim for the Prince of Wales the justice that is the due of every Englishman.'

In 1891, the Prince of Wales appeared for a second time in the witness-box in what came to be known as the Baccarat Case. Normally he stayed with Christopher Sykes at Brantingham Thorpe for the St Leger, but when Sykes could no longer afford the coveted honour of entertaining him, HRH accepted an invitation to Tranby Croft, an Italianate mansion belonging to Arthur Wilson. Wilson owned 'Wilson's of Hull', a prosperous shipping line. What he lacked in refinement he made up in fortune. His wife, a Miss Smith, came from Leeds, where her father rose to be Postmaster. But such eminence was for her only a foothill of loftier ambitions, and when it became known that His Royal Highness was to honour Tranby Croft with a visit she could hardly restrain her joy. Like Edmund Hillary, on the peak of Mount Everest, she had nothing left to conquer.

The Wilsons had two daughters: Muriel and Ethel. Muriel refused an offer of marriage from Winston Churchill, whom she remembered walking up and down the drive at Tranby Croft, 'rehearsing such phrases as, "The Spanish ships I cannot see for they are not in sight," to cure him of his trouble in pronouncing the sibilant "s".' Ethel married a Mr Lycett Green, Master of the York and Ainsty Foxhounds, whose father, Sir Edward, was a manufacturer. The son of the house, Arthur Wilson junior, after a fruitless year at Magdalene, Cambridge, and a month in his father's office, retired from active life.

Amongst the guests invited to Tranby Croft were Sir William Gordon-Cumming, a Lieutenant-Colonel in the Scots Guards, Lord Coventry, Lord Edward Somerset, whose brother 'Podge' had hurriedly left the country the year before, General Owen Williams, and Berkeley Levett, a subaltern in Sir William's regiment. Sir William was a gallant soldier, outstandingly handsome, unspeakably insolent, and much fancied by the ladies. During the course of his life he made many enemies, because, as his daughter expressed it, he 'had cuckolded so many husbands' and been 'witty at the expense of so many fools.' Sir William owned forty thousand acres in Scotland and lived mainly at Gordonstoun. For twenty years he had been a close friend of the Prince, at whose suggestion he had been invited by the Wilsons.

On the first evening of his visit, when dinner was over, the Prince sat down to a game of baccarat in the smoking room. After a few hands, young Wilson, who was sitting next to Sir William, thought that he saw him increasing his stake after the cards were declared in his favour. 'My God, Berkeley, this is too hot!' he whispered to his friend. 'This man next to me is cheating.' 'My dear chap', said the subaltern, 'you must have made some mistake. It is absolutely impossible.' But, after a bit, he too saw the Colonel adding to his stake. Before retiring, Wilson spoke to his mother who was greatly distressed at the thought of a possible scandal.

Next morning, he consulted his brother-in-law, the Master of Foxhounds, who told his wife. That evening there was another game of baccarat. The Lycett Greens, who had not played the night before, joined in to watch Sir William at work. There were four members of the Wilson family seated round the table: Mrs Wilson, her son, her son-in-law and her daughter Ethel, and they all saw what they had been led to expect. The next day, 10 September, Wilson and Lycett Green told Lord Coventry that they had come to the painful conclusion that Sir William Gordon-Cumming had twice cheated at cards. In the end, after General Williams had been brought into the discussion, two decisions were reached: that the Prince of Wales would have to be told, and that, in return for a promise of secrecy, Sir William must undertake to give up playing cards.

The last person to learn of the accusations against him was Sir William himself. Lord Coventry and General Williams saw him in the 'Smoke-Room' and told him that 'a very disagreeable thing has occurred in the house. Some of the people staying here object to your manner of playing Baccarat.' Sir William indignantly denied that he had resorted to foul play and asked to see the Prince. Accordingly, after dinner, HRH, Lord Coventry, General Owen Williams and Colonel Gordon-Cumming held a brief and embarrassed meeting. Sir William 'utterly and emphatically' denied the charges, and said that he hoped that His Royal Highness did not believe he had cheated. The Prince replied, 'There are five accusers against you.' After this interview, Coventry and the general did everything in their power to persuade Sir William to sign a paper they had previously prepared. He could not hope, they said, to prove his innocence when there were so many witnesses. Besides, the only alternative to accepting their proposal, was the certainty of a prodigious scandal, involving the good name of the Prince of Wales, the honour of his regiment, and his own ruin. As the two men were old friends, and represented themselves as advising him in his own best interests, he finally agreed to sign, insisting to the last that the whole thing was a terrible mistake.

The document read as follows: 'In consideration of the promise made by the gentlemen whose names are subscribed to preserve silence with reference to an accusation which has been made with regard to my conduct at baccarat on the nights of Monday and Tuesday, the 8th and 9th September, 1890, at Tranby Croft, I will on my part solemnly undertake never to play cards again as long as I live.' His Royal Highness was the first to witness Sir William's signature and contract 'to preserve silence.' In acting as they did, Coventry and Williams seem to have been more concerned to protect the Prince from scandal than their friend from injustice.

It is surprising that men so experienced in the ways of the world could ever have conceived for one moment that the matter would end there. No secret shared by so many had any hope of surviving and the scandal at Tranby Croft was soon common gossip. Some people claimed that Sir William broke the contract by continuing to play cards, consequently releasing the signatories from their part of the bargain. In April 1891, the Prince of Wales wrote as follows to Mrs Arthur Paget. 'Perhaps you could ascertain from your French friend when he [Sir William Gordon-Cumming] played B[accarat] at Paris since Sept last, as it would always be well to know and have the exact date.' Possibly some members of the house-party betrayed the secret, from hatred of Sir William or envy of the Wilsons. But most people blamed Lady Brooke, who was said to have heard the story from the Prince. Her denials, reinforced by threats of legal action and letters to *The Times*, were not thought very convincing, and it was commonly held that the 'Babbling Brook' had let the secret out. In fact, she was one of Sir William's few loyal friends, who regarded him as 'more sinned against than sinning.' When it became clear that the whole world was discussing the Warwickshire Scandal, Sir William Gordon-Cumming instructed his solicitors to issue a writ claiming damages for slander against his five accusers.

The trial which took place from 1 to 9 June 1891, was in many respects the most sensational of the Queen's reign. The presiding judge was Sir John Duke Coleridge, the Lord Chief Justice of England, and a close friend of Sir Charles Russell who was brief for the defence. Writing to Ponsonby on 4 June, Knollys claimed, 'the Lord Chief Justice is supposed (only this of course is quite private) to be in favour of the defendants.' Sir Edward Clarke, who represented the Plaintiff, described Sir John's Charge to the Jury as a 'very fine specimen of judicial advocacy.' From first to last he believed in his client's innocence. When he published his memoirs at the end of the First World War he said that so many years had passed 'since the Baccarat Case was tried that I think I am able to form an unbiased opinion, and I think I ought to leave that opinion on record. I believe the verdict was wrong, and that Sir William Gordon-Cumming was innocent of the offence charged against him.'

Sir Edward believed that his client signed the damning document, which the defence represented as overwhelming evidence of guilt, partly because in a rash moment he succumbed to the powerful advocacy of Coventry and Williams, and partly to save the Prince of Wales from scandal. After reviewing the course of the trial, *Truth* concluded, 'No dog would be hanged on the evidence that convinced a Jury that Sir William Gordon-Cumming had cheated at cards.'

The Prince of Wales was delighted to hear that Sir Edward had been briefed. Announcing the news to Ponsonby, Knollys wrote:

'The Solicitor-General has been retained by Cumming which I am glad of as he is a gentleman and will not allow unnecessarily disagreeable questions to be asked.' That was the last good word that Marlborough House had to say for him. Subsequently, Knollys protested to Lord Salisbury's Secretary that the Prime Minister should have taken steps to protect HRH from being publicly insulted by one of the principal law officers of the Crown. During the course of his remarks in Court, Clarke hinted that Sir William had sacrificed himself to support a tottering throne, that he had been 'victimized to save the honour of a Prince who encouraged habitually an illegal game; who had jumped recklessly to a wrong conclusion on bad evidence'; and who had deliberately ignored 'Queen's Regulations.'

In an effort to establish his client's innocence, and it was possibly a measure of his own, the Solicitor-General argued that neither the Prince of Wales, nor Lord Coventry, nor General Williams, could possibly have believed that Sir William cheated at cards. Had they done so, they would never have agreed to remain silent. As a Field-Marshal in the army, HRH was naturally conversant with Article Forty-One of Queen's Regulations, which stated that 'Every Commissioned Officer of Her Majesty's Service, whose character or conduct as an officer and gentleman had been publicly impugned, must submit the case within a reasonable time to his Commanding Officer, or other competent Military Authority, for investigation.' Had HRH believed Sir William guilty, it was plainly his duty to report his suspicions to the Commander-in-Chief. To have acted otherwise, would have been to allow Colonel Gordon-Cumming 'to perform his duties as an officer and gentleman in the British Army, when it was known, and known to a Field-Marshal of the army, that he had been guilty of conduct which if mentioned to his Commanding Officer would result in an enquiry and in his ignominious expulsion from the service.' Precisely the same argument applied to Sir William's clubs. Was it possible to suppose that such honourable men as Lord Coventry, General Williams and His Royal Highness, could, for one moment, permit a blackguard, who cheated at cards, to remain a member of the Marlborough, the Carlton and the Turf?

Sir Edward told the Jury that Sir William played baccarat according to a system known as the 'coup de trois,' the principle of which was to increase the stake by a multiple of three after every winning coup. If he staked five pounds and won the coup, he would leave his original five pounds counter where it was, to which he would add the five pounds paid him by the croupier, and a further five pounds from his own counters. Without the experience to recognize the 'coup de trois' when they saw it, the defendants mistakenly supposed that Sir William was increasing his stake after the cards were declared.

In order for the banker in baccarat to decide how to play his hand he has to see what other players have staked. If anyone added a counter surreptitiously after the cards were declared the banker would be the person most likely to know. On both nights in question the Prince of Wales held the bank, and on neither occasion did he suspect malpractice, any more than did General Williams, whose sole duty was to watch the stakes and collect or pay out counters. So the only two really experienced players at Tranby Croft, who were best placed to see if things went wrong, apparently failed to notice the repeated irregularities which it was left to young Wilson to expose.

The Solicitor-General was conspicuously successful in demonstrating what novices the defendants were. Mr Lycett Green, for example, rapidly diminished in stature under cross-examination. Knollys described his evidence as 'deplorable in every way; voice, manner and matter. The fact was he completely lost his head and became so nervous that I really think if he had been asked his name he could not have told it.' It was put to him: 'Is it the practice to say what the stakes are?' 'I do not know,' he replied, 'I have not had the bank myself.' Next, he was invited to say whether the banker was influenced in his decision to stand or take another card by the amount staked by other players. His answer was inaudible. Finally, he was forced to admit that he was totally ignorant of the 'coup de trois.'

'Did you ever hear of any person playing at baccarat upon a system?'

'I cannot say.'

'Have you ever heard of a man putting down a counter – it may be for five or ten pounds – and if that wins adding to that?'

'No.'

'When he puts a counter down and wins he leaves that counter down and puts on another?'

'No. It is novel to me.'

Mrs Lycett Green was a more impressive witness than her husband, but even she was compelled to admit she had only played baccarat five or so times and that the plaintiff had taught her the game.

All Sir William's accusers, except Arthur Wilson, an acknowledged novice, expected to see foul play. 'The eye sees,' said Sir Edward, 'what it brings the expectation of seeing.' This, he suggested, explained the conjurer's success. 'You know well the old story of the humorist who stopped at the end of the Strand, and pointed to the Lion which then stood upon Northumberland House, and declared that its tail wagged.' A crowd assembled, and within three minutes half of them 'were declaring that they had seen the tail move, although it was a stone one . . . There is only one witness who says he saw anything wrong in Sir William Gordon-Cumming's play without having been told beforehand that he was going to see him cheat.' And that one witness – Arthur Wilson – had never so much as heard of the coup de trois, the system Sir William followed.

Throughout the proceedings, the Prince of Wales showed less than his usual adroitness. He seems not to have kept his head while others round him were losing theirs and blaming it on him. When Margot Asquith, whose husband was Russell's junior during the trial, asked the Duke of Devonshire what he would do if he saw one of his guests cheating at Chatsworth, he replied: 'Back him!' But the Prince was guided by less shrewd advice. For one who was so loyal to his friends, particularly in adversity, he appears to have denied Sir William Gordon-Cumming the presumption of innocence which English law demands.

But nothing he did, or failed to do, began to justify the hurricane force of the storm which raged about him. Newspapers, particularly those of a religious turn, – and 1891 was the centenary of John Wesley's death, – 'trumpeted their horror, like great moral elephants piously running amok.' The Press seemed to forget that the Lord Chief Justice had not been trying the Prince of Wales, and sentenced him more savagely than the man accused of cheating. In vain he protested that the first time he ever played cards for money was one evening at Cuddesdon in 1860 with the late Bishop Wilberforce.

The morning after the Jury found for the defendants, a leading article in *The Times* profoundly regretted 'that the Prince should have been in any way mixed up, not only in the case, but in the social circumstances which prepared the way for it.' The public, it said, was profoundly concerned and distressed by 'the discovery that the Prince should have been at the baccarat table; that the game was apparently played to please him; that it was played with his counters specially taken down for the purpose; that his "set" are a gambling, a baccarat-playing set.' The article concluded by saying that Sir William was made to sign a declaration that he would never play cards again. 'We almost wish, for the sake of English society in general, that we could learn that the result of this most unhappy case had been that the Prince of Wales had signed a similar declaration.'

Like *The Times*, the Queen deeply regretted her son's gambling and the company he kept. Indeed, she denounced both so openly, that Knollys told Ponsonby: 'The Prince of Wales desires me to say that he hopes the Queen will not allow the strong views which she entertains respecting the recent Baccarat Case to get about, as if so it will of course do him much harm.'

Of all the remonstrances he received, the most trying came from his nephew, the Kaiser. 'The Young Man,' as Bismarck called him, gratuitously took it upon himself to write his uncle a letter protesting against anyone 'holding the position of a Colonel of Prussian Hussars embroiling himself in a gambling squabble, and playing with men young enough to be his sons.'

In July 1891, W. T. Stead, the editor of the *Review of Reviews*, wrote a celebrated article for his Journal about the Prince's gambling. During the past half-century, he calculated with ruthless arithmetic, congregations throughout the world had asked God's blessing on the Royal Family, and the Prince of Wales in particular, some eight hundred and eighty million times. It now appeared that 'all the prayers of the Church for fifty years had been but as the whirling prayer wheels innumerable in pious Tibet.'

Before the storm broke, Prince George, with a sailor's eye for a falling barometer, saw trouble ahead. 'This Baccarat Scandel [*sic*] seems to have caused great excitement, what a lot of rot the papers will say about it.' Randolph Churchill offered HRH judicious consolation. 'My own experience is that praise from the Press is far less conducive to popularity than its abuse.' The correspondent of the *New York Herald* in London told Knollys that anybody would think that HRH had 'broken all The Ten Commandments at once, and murdered the Archbishop of Canterbury. A more disgraceful exhibition of ignorance and intolerance has not been witnessed in my time in England.'

The Prince's critics made great play of three aspects of his conduct: that he had taken his own set of counters with him to Tranby Croft, that he insisted on playing baccarat knowing that his host disapproved of it, and that he had no objection to the proposal to

watch Sir William's play on the night of 9 September. The Press
'howled with horror' at the discovery that the Prince possessed
counters bearing his insignia on one side and sums of money on the
other: although baccarat can no more be played without counters
than cricket without a ball. 'They say,' the Prince told Archbishop
Benson, 'that I carry about counters, as a Turk carries his prayer-
carpet. But the reason why I carry counters is to check high play.
High sums are easily named, but these counters range from five
shillings to ten pounds and that can hurt nobody.'

Much was made of HRH's callous disregard for his host's dislike
of gambling. In fact, during the course of the trial Mrs Wilson was
asked whether Sir William was the only player to stake fifteen pounds
on a coup. 'I don't think anyone,' she replied, 'until my husband
played.' Not only was he happy to take part but actually played
higher than anyone else but the plaintiff. The only shadow of
substance for the story was that a year or so before he had told his
son that he did not understand the game – which was precisely what
the Solicitor-General argued – and forbade him to play it. What he
objected to was playing baccarat badly.

The Prince knew nothing whatever of the Wilsons' suspicions until
shortly before dinner on the evening of the tenth. It was therefore
totally unjust to associate him with watching Sir William play on the
night of the ninth. While the matter was fresh in his mind, General
Williams wrote a careful account of the whole story which the
Prince and Lord Coventry confirmed was accurate. His record
clearly stated that the defendants agreed to watch Sir William's play
on the second night of his visit. But this they denied in Court.
If General Williams's record was accepted, there was no escaping the
conclusion 'that they, to avoid acknowledging conduct which everybody feels would be disgraceful, denied upon oath that which did
in fact take place.'

Sir Francis Knollys received on the Prince's behalf an impressive
number of resolutions and petitions from non-conformist bodies.
Some were discreet and deferential while others assumed the admoni-
tory tones of Old Testament prophets. All were preserved and none
were answered. Amongst them were resolutions of the Quarterly
Meeting of the United Methodist Free Church at Spalding, the
Midsummer Morning Meeting at the Abbey Road Chapel, the
Annual Meeting of the Monmouthshire Baptist Association, the
Annual Conference of the Primitive Methodist Connexion, and
sessions of the Leicestershire Sunday School Union and the Young

Men's Christian Association.

The Free Church at Spalding regarded the growth of gambling with alarm and deeply regretted that 'the Prince of Wales and other persons connected in the recent scandal, should by their example, encourage so harmful and fascinating a vice.' Some citizens of Salford spoke more in sorrow than in anger, affirming their 'loyalty to the throne' but expressing profound regret at 'learning that the Heir Apparent sometimes practises and countenances the evil habit of Gambling. They would further express the earnest hope and prayer, that, in view of the misery caused by this sin among Her Majesty's subjects, he will in future abstain from it entirely and cease to countenance it in any form.' The Primitive Methodists of Northampton, claiming to speak for a million of their fellows, begged HRH to follow more closely 'the steps of his Royal Father' and 'the example of his Royal Mother.' Quite rightly, they imagined there was no baccarat at Balmoral. At a meeting of the Young Men's Christian Association at Coventry, 'a very deep feeling laid hold of the members' to whom it was revealed that betting and gambling were 'sore evils' which eat out 'the vitals of our people' and throw 'a banefull [sic] blight on many a fair son and daughter of the Queen's subjects.' Despite W. T. Stead's head-shakings over the efficacy of public prayer, HRH graciously made a concession to the requests embodied in these resolutions. He took up bridge.

Another famous scandal in which the Prince was involved, and which looked for a time as if it would end in the Divorce Court, began during his tour of India in 1876. Disraeli described the saga as being almost as troublesome as the crisis then brewing in the Balkans. The seventh Duke of Marlborough, who married Lord Adolphus Vane Tempest's sister, Frances Anne, had two wild and troublesome sons: Lord Blandford and Lord Randolph Churchill. While still a boy, Blandford was expelled from Eton and as a young man was notorious for lechery. In 1869, he married Albertha, one of the Duke of Abercorn's seven daughters, whom he treated outrageously.

Amongst those whom the Prince took with him to India was Lord Aylesford, a racing friend and partner. 'Sporting Joe,' as his friends called him, was married to General Williams's sister, Edith. When her husband left for the East she stayed at Packington, one of their country estates. It soon became common gossip that Lord Blandford had rented a house in the neighbourhood, moved in his hunters, and had been seen leaving the Hall in the early hours of the morning.

On 20 February 1876, Lord Aylesford received a letter from Edith saying that she and Lord Blandford had decided to elope. Sporting Joe, threatening to divorce his wife and challenge her lover, hurried home. The Prince was greatly distressed by this turn of events, for all the characters in the drama were old friends.

By the same post as Aylesford heard from his wife, the Prince received a *'very private and confidential letter'* from Randolph Churchill, who, having assumed the responsibility of saving the family honour, further discredited it by the strategy he adopted. 'It has come to my notice,' he said, 'that Blandford has finally determined to act in a manner which will unhappily cast a dark cloud over his future, and also will greatly obscure the happiness of all who are intimately connected with and fond of him. I need not assure Your Royal Highness that no entreaties or arguments have been spared to prevent or even if possible delay this catastrophe. But all has been to no purpose.' Nobody, Randolph continued, could be more sensible than he was that HRH's 'great position' and his 'large experience and intimate knowledge of the world,' would lend 'to any advice or opinion' he might be prepared to offer, 'an authority that no-one else would possess . . . Your Royal Highness has not only consistently shown for many years a great friendship for Blandford, but you have also on many occasions acted with the greatest kindness to myself, besides invariably showing great interest in all that nearly concerned my family.' These circumstances emboldened Randolph 'to make the most earnest and solemn appeal to Your Royal Highness to exert all your great influence and authority to prevent any rash or hasty decision to be arrived at, or any foolish or violent actions being determined on,' by Lord Aylesford, or his brother-in-law, General Williams.

The Prince, who was busy shooting tigers, asked Francis Knollys to reply to Randolph's letter. Francis was one of Randolph's closest friends and had been his best man. 'My dear Randolph,' he wrote, 'The Prince of Wales desires me to answer your letter of 28th January. HRH has always, as you yourself say, been a true and sincere friend of Blandford's, and whenever and by whom his conduct has been called into question, no one I know could have more strenuously fought for him than the Prince. Old associations, likewise, and a long and intimate friendship, would in themselves naturally make HRH most anxious to befriend him in any matter of difficulty; but in the case to which you allude the Prince fears he can be of no use. The letter which the wife [Lady Aylesford] has written to the husband has completely cut away the ground from under the feet of both Blandford and herself, as you would be the first to acknowledge were you to see it. She expresses her intention in the strongest and most unmistakable terms of never leaving Blandford, and in fact intimates that the husband has no choice left him in the matter but to cease to consider her as his wife. Under these circumstances the Prince, as a very intimate friend of the husband's, and as a man of honor [sic], could not presume to attempt to dissuade him from adopting the course, which after mature consideration he has determined to pursue. It is indeed a sad case in every respect, and if you could see the husband, you would, I think, feel for him as much as we do. We likewise, I can assure you, my dear Randolph, feel most sincerely for you, who have always been the best and most affectionate of brothers, and the Prince fully appreciates the motives which led you to write to him.'

When Aylesford received his wife's letter, he despatched the following telegram to his mother: 'Send for the children and keep them till my return. A great misfortune has happened. Am writing by this mail.' She was naturally mystified and consulted the Princess of Wales. Alix consequently sent a cypher telegram to her husband: 'Pray let me know at once what Joe's telegram to Mother means. She is in great distress; came to me for advice. If "misfortune" alludes to B[landford] and E[dith Aylesford] no foundation as saw B here today. E in the country. Tell Joe not to take rash steps. Mother done nothing yet. Answer at once.'

'Tell Joe's mother,' the Prince replied, 'not to enquire further, but to act according to telegram. Letters by this mail will explain all. Cannot enter into particulars.' Alix, still believing the matter could be resolved if Aylesford were restrained, told the Prince in a further telegram: 'I know all about E, but things look a little better. There is a chance. Pray try your utmost to smooth matters with Joe. Hope to God all may come right yet.' But her hopes were dashed when her husband telegraphed back: 'It can never come right. If you had seen the letter you would say the same. Joe left us today. Take my advice and do not mix yourself up in the matter or you will regret it.'

Lord Lansdowne, who later became King Edward's first Foreign Secretary, was married to Maud Hamilton, Lady Blandford's sister. So, acting on Albertha's behalf, he begged the Prince of Wales to 'induce A to reconsider,' adding menacingly, 'consequences important to you as well as to him.' The Prince telegraphed back: 'A left before your telegram arrived, but could not under circumstances have attempted to alter his decision. Want to know what words "important to you as well as to him" mean. Am not aware what has occurred can affect me personally. Must beg you to explain.'

The explanation came in a letter written on 29 February, which HRH received almost a month later when he reached Suez on his way home. 'It seemed to me,' said Lansdowne, in an effort to justify his previous cryptic communication, 'that Your Royal Highness's interests, as well as those of the persons more immediately concerned, were involved. The most prominent actors in this affair are well known to be intimate friends of Your Royal Highness. It is moreover currently reported that Lady Aylesford, anticipating the danger to which she would be exposed during her husband's absence, had used every effort to prevent him from going to India, but that you had insisted on his accompanying you. Under these circumstances Your Royal Highness's name would beyond all question have figured conspicuously in the different accounts of this disagreeable story. It therefore occurred to me that it might be worth while to suggest to Your Royal Highness the prudence of inducing Aylesford to suspend his decision at all events for a time.'

The Prince of Wales was so grieved by the nature of Lord Lansdowne's intervention that he instructed Knollys to send copies of the correspondence to Lord Granville. Granville evidently persuaded Lansdowne that he had acted injudiciously, or, at the least, that it would be expedient to apologize. On 29 April, Lansdowne wrote to HRH in contrite terms, begging him to make 'some allowance for the circumstances' in which he was 'brought suddenly face to face with a calamity which threatened the prospects and happiness of my wife's sister and of her children.'

The Prince replied in his own hand, accepting Lansdowne's apology, particularly in view of 'the long friendship which has existed between yr Family and mine.' But, while forgiving him, he felt bound to point out that those whom he had consulted were agreed that the tone of Lansdowne's communications 'was most objectionable and that it was most unfair dragging my name into the deplorable occurrences which have lately happened. My greatest wish from the first was not to influence Aylesford in his actions in any way, but I was inundated on all sides by telegrams and letters from home during the close of my stay in India, which were almost more than anybody could bear. Since then I have been treated by men whom I looked upon as my friends in the most infamous manner.

I feel most deeply for poor Lady Blandford during the severe trial she has undergone, and please tell Lady Lansdowne how much I also feel for her who I know is so devoted to her sister.'

Frederick Ponsonby, who became King Edward's Assistant Private Secretary at the beginning of his reign, said that 'The King never appeared to hit it off with Lansdowne, and I was unable to guess the reason, for no one treated His Majesty with more consideration and as far as I know there had never been any real difference of opinion.' It could be that his Lordship's 'objectionable tone' was forgiven but never forgotten.

In a series of telegraphic exchanges, Randolph increased the pressure on HRH to prevent Aylesford taking precipitate action. 'There is yet a chance of matters being arranged. For God's sake use your influence to defer final decision of Aylesford's till his and your return.' 'Matters can never be arranged,' the Prince replied on Leapday 1876. 'Had you seen certain letters you would say the same. Deeply regret that this should be the case.' Randolph's next telegram introduced a note of menace. 'I know all about the letters and repeat that matters might yet be arranged quietly. If Your Royal Highness were in England you would see that a fearful family disaster might yet be avoided. For your own sake advise Aylesford to come to no hasty decision. Your Royal Highness will be held responsible generally for whatever line of conduct is adopted and is already credited with the initiative in this matter.' On 4 March, the Prince replied: 'Your telegram received today has caused me even more astonishment than your last. Have not advised A though entirely approve of line he has taken. Cannot be induced by what some people might say to persuade him to pursue a course which I as well as all here would consider most dishonorable.'

When it became clear that the Prince was proving adamant, Randolph decided to bring pressure to bear upon the Princess, to which end he enlisted the support of Henry Sturt. Sturt, a grandson of Lord Cardigan, married his first cousin, Augusta, the daughter of Lord Lucan. After nearly thirty years as a Tory MP for Dorset, Disraeli made him a peer in the New Year Honours in 1876. Lord Alington of Crichel as he became, was approached by Lady Aylesford's sisters who begged him to prevent further scandal. Consequently, out of the kindness of his heart, he agreed to accompany Randolph and Lady Aylesford to Marlborough House with a view to persuading the Princess to use her influence on her husband to stop a divorce. When the visitors were announced, Alix misheard and, thinking that

Lady Ailesbury had called, instructed the footman to show her up immediately. Surprised as she was by the deputation which appeared, there was no going back on her mistake. Lord Randolph, acting as its spokesman, told the Princess that 'being aware of peculiar and most grave matters affecting the case, he was anxious that His Royal Highness should give such advice to Lord Aylesford as to induce him not to proceed against his wife.'

Alix, alarmed by Randolph's threats and dismayed at having permitted Lady Aylesford to call on her, sent for Sir William Knollys. While they were talking things over, the Duchess of Teck was announced. Without telling her the whole story, Alix explained that she had just accidentally received the disreputable Lady Aylesford and was wondering what she should do to prevent gossip. 'Order your carriage at once,' said the Duchess, 'go straight to the Queen and tell her exactly what has happened. She will understand and entirely excuse you for any indiscretion. It will be in the Court Circular that you were with the Queen today and any comment will be silenced.' 'Her Royal Highness is giving very good advice,' said Sir William, 'pray follow it at once.' The Queen was furious with those who had sought to involve her daughter-in-law in their sordid affairs. Writing to the Prince of Wales about it, she said it was 'unpardonable of Lord Alington to draw dear Alix into it! Her dear name should never have been mixed up with such people.'

When the Prince of Wales heard that Alix had been approached, he wrote a letter to his friend Lord Hardwicke, which Lord Charles Beresford delivered by hand, asking him to represent his interests in England, to consult the Prime Minister, and to express his indignation to Randolph and Lord Alington. Hardwicke did as he was asked, and wrote HRH a fifty-page letter telling him what had happened.

On receiving HRH's instructions, Hardwicke called on Alington and Churchill and 'conveyed to each of them Your Royal Highness's great indignation at their conduct in calling on Her Royal Highness the Princess of Wales. As regards Lord Alington I can assure Your Royal Highness of his deep and sincere regret at the unwarrantable and most foolish step he took in bringing Her Royal Highness into the painful quarrel between Lord Aylesford and his wife. He will write to Your Royal Highness a full and ample apology . . . He acted on the spur of the moment without thought, and fancied that by the interference of Her Royal Highness the fatal step of an elopement might be averted. He is painfully aware of his folly . . . The fact is that Lord Alington is a very excitable man. He has always been very fond of Lady Aylesford and he was half out of his mind at the fearful future which he saw. He was called in for advice by members of her family and with the best intention in view, he took the unpardonable step of gaining an audience of Her Royal Highness.'

As regards Lord Randolph Churchill, wrote Hardwicke, 'it is a much more difficult and complicated affair.' He has 'taken a most active part' in trying to avoid the public scandal of a divorce. 'When I tell Your Royal Highness the scheme he had adopted it will be for Your Royal Highness to judge whether he is fit to move in the society of Gentlemen.' Randolph openly acknowledged 'that he was determined by every means in his power to prevent the case coming before the public and that he had those means at his disposal.' Hardwicke naturally asked what they were, on which he told him 'that letters from Your Royal Highness to Lady Aylesford written some years ago [December 1873] had been found, copies of which he had and which he was determined to use to prevent the case ever coming into Court – that these letters were of the *most compromising* character, that he had placed them in the hands of the solicitors acting for him and Blandford and that they had been submitted to the Solicitor-General for his opinion and that that opinion was that if they ever came before the public Your Royal Highness would never sit on the throne of England and that he was determined if Aylesford went into Court, that Your Royal Highness should be put into the Witness-Box etc. etc.' Hardwicke gathered that Lady Aylesford had given the letters to Lord Blandford and that he had given them to Lord Randolph. 'A more rascally or scandalous proceeding I never in the whole course of my life ever heard of, or certainly ever could have imagined.'

Hardwicke thought that Randolph would 'stick at nothing, and from the scandalous language he dared to use in my presence about Your Royal Highness, to save his family from any public exposé he will drag Your Royal Highness's name prominently forward. His line of argument is quite plain. It is this. That Your Royal Highness has been the main cause of Lady Aylesford's unfortunate step, that it was through your influence that Aylesford left his wife to accompany your Royal Highness to India, that you knew of Blandford's intimacy with Lady Aylesford before you left . . . that you rejected an imploring letter from Lady Aylesford begging of you not to take her

husband away, that in fact there was collusion between Your Royal
Highness and Aylesford to throw Lady Aylesford into the arms of
Blandford, that you had succeeded, but that having letters to prove
Your Royal Highness's own admiration for Lady Aylesford, they
would prevent any divorce by using this powerful lever in any way
they might think fit.'

After Randolph had threatened to blackmail the Prince, Hardwicke 'demanded a full and ample apology' for 'his forcing himself
upon the Princess of Wales . . . I read to him the passage in your
letter to me as regarding himself, at the same time saying it was
evidently written under great excitement, and that I could not press
the mention of Your Royal Highness having a hostile meeting with
him. In his answer which I received last night, which I enclose to
your Royal Highness, you will see the manner in which he treats my
communication.' Randolph's note read as follows: 'I can only understand HRH's letter to you as a demand for an apology or a meeting.
If I have acted indiscreetly or been guilty of the slightest disrespect
to Her RH the Pss of W by approaching her on so painful a subject
I must unreservedly offer thro' HRH the Prince of W to Her RH
the Princess my most humble and sincere apologies. This is the only
apology which circumstances warrant my offering. With regard to
a meeting no one knows better than HRH the P of Wales that a
meeting between himself and Ld R.C. is definitely out of the
question. Please convey this to HRH.'

After his interview with Randolph, Hardwicke received a letter
from Owen Williams, 'in reference to the propriety or necessity of
Aylesford taking hostile action against Blandford.' Apparently,
many of his friends felt that 'he ought to call Blandford out.' Aylesford agreed to be guided in this matter by Hardwicke and Hartington, who advised against duelling on the ground it was no longer
legal.

Later the same day, Hardwicke, quite by chance, met Aylesford
after a division in the Lords. 'He talked to me openly and frankly,'
Hardwicke reported to HRH, and said that he had 'instructed his
lawyers to proceed for a divorce.' He then discussed 'an occurrence
that took place the night before in Pratts Club where Tim
Farquharson in his midnight cups stated that Blandford and Co,
had compromising letters from Your Royal Highness in their possession written by you to Lady Aylesford. Aylesford said that he
would horse whip anyone who propagated such a scandalous false-

hood and I said "quite right".'

Hardwicke concluded his letter, which was almost as long as St Paul's Epistle to the Corinthians, with these words. 'You know how fond I am of you, how deeply I am interested in everything that concerns yr Royal Highness's welfare, that there is nothing on this earth that I would not do for you . . . If it is true as regards those *letters*, you are in the hands of most unscrupulous men, who are determined to use the knowledge they have to serve their own interests. Anything like yr Royal Highness's name coming before the public on a question of this nature would be most serious to your interests now and hereafter. You have been scandalously used by a lady and two men passing as gentlemen. We shall know how to deal with them after the storm is passed.' Disraeli expressed matters rather more succinctly. 'Blandford,' he said, 'I always thought was a scoundrel, but this brother beats him.'

On 10 April, the day after the Prince received Hardwicke's letter, he instructed Knollys to write to Sir Henry Ponsonby, sending him copies of Hardwicke's and Churchill's communications, so that they might be shown to the Queen. Knollys explained that when HRH reached Suez on his way home from India, 'he learnt of the unpardonable step which Lord Alington and Lord Randolph Churchill had taken in almost forcing their way into the Princess's presence. Feeling naturally indignant at such an insult, he wrote to Lord Hardwicke to beg him to obtain an apology from the two individuals in question. Lord Hardwicke's reply came upon the Prince like a thunderclap; and he could hardly believe in such a case of ingratitude on the part of one to whom he had always shown the most invariable kindness, nor could he have conceived it possible that Lord Randolph, to use a very mild term, could have behaved in so ungentlemanlike a manner in consequence of the Prince's refusal to mix himself up in the quarrel.

'I am authorized by the P of W to declare most solemnly that to the best of his knowledge and belief he has never in his life written a line to Lady Aylesford which could in the slightest degree be considered compromising, nor which might not be read out at Charing Cross. To show how innocent he feels on this point he has conveyed to Lord Randolph through Lord Hardwicke, his wish that copies of the letters in question should be transmitted to the Queen and the Princess . . . The P of W hopes however, and indeed feels sure, that HM with the affection she has never ceased to bestow upon him will afford him her support and assistance, and if I might humbly venture to mention such a thing, I am sure he would be much comforted were HM to send him a few kind lines or a kind telegram.'

To Hardwicke the Prince telegraphed as follows. 'Am unable sufficiently to thank you for all you have done which has my entire approval. Cannot interfere with the line A may think proper to take in the matter of a divorce. Have never in my life that I know of written letters to Lady A which might not be read by the whole world.'

Lord Randolph wrote his father a letter claiming that Hardwicke's recollection of their interview was 'inaccurate and exaggerated.' Lord Hardwicke, he said, 'came to my house to demand on the part of HRH the Prince of Wales an apology from me for having intruded upon HRH the Princess of Wales and in default of that apology Ld Hardwicke signified to me that HRH was willing to challenge me to a duel.' Randolph then told Hardwicke that 'the Divorce would most *certainly be resisted* on the ground that Lord Aylesford had by gross misconduct conduced to his wife's adultery and on the grounds that Lord Aylesford had himself frequently committed adultery . . . I told Lord Hardwicke that in the opinion of my legal advisers the evidence that HRH could give as to the reluctance with which Lady Aylesford consented to her husband's departure for India was obviously an essential part of the former portion of the defence of the Divorce Suit.

I then thought it right to warn Lord Hardwicke that there were certain letters in existence from HRH the Prince of Wales to Lady Aylesford, from the production of which letters I could not guarantee him if HRH was once placed in the Witness-Box.' Randolph denied that he had ever had the original letters in his possession, although he had been given copies, by whom he did not say. 'Viewing the exceeding gravity of the case my legal advisers had thought proper to take the opinion of one of the law officers of the Crown as to the probable effect of those letters should they ever be made public. The Solicitor-General, the highest legal authority attainable . . . considered . . . that their publication might have the most serious consequences . . . Lord Hardwicke, who treated me throughout his interview with characteristic overbearingness and excitement then permitted himself to read me a severe lecture on the impropriety of the course I had pursued and charged me with the basest ingratitude to HRH the Prince of Wales.'

The explanation for Randolph's conduct – for it can hardly be justified – was that he rushed to defend his family's honour without considering the propriety of what he was doing, that he was provoked by Aylesford telling the whole world that HRH had described Blandford as 'the greatest blackguard alive,' though that was nothing to what Randolph had been known to call him, and that he honestly, but quite mistakenly, believed that the Prince had acted in collusion with Lord Aylesford and had plotted to drive Edith into Blandford's arms.

At one stage in the quarrel, the Duchess of Marlborough wrote to the Prince pleading with him not to 'banish' Randolph from society. She admitted he had undoubtedly been 'most indiscreet in his language and forgetful of the respect due to one in your high position. But I know his motives were good and his intentions honourable, and at the time all this misery occurred he was greatly moved and excited.' Neither the Duke, she wrote, 'nor any other human being knows of my writing and nothing but my love for Randolph would induce me to trouble Your Royal Highness with this letter.'

When the Prince of Wales remarked that to the best of his recollection his correspondence with Lady Aylesford could be read out at Charing Cross or sent to the Queen, two considerations need to be borne in mind. First, that he had an exceptionally good memory so that 'the best of his recollection' was likely to be precise. Secondly, that the letters were not even three years old. Had they contained improper suggestions – rather than comments which might be so construed – he could hardly have forgotten intending them.

Clearly Randolph deceived himself, as well as others, when he bragged that he had the Crown of England in his pocket, but that is not to say, as Ponsonby pointed out to the Queen, that 'if the Prince of Wales were placed in the Witness-Box and if the letters were read and passages written in thoughtless haste were coloured by an unscrupulous Counsel' he would not succeed in representing them in a most unfavourable light. 'The Prince of Wales had evidently no evil intention in writing them and maintains they are harmless. That is quite sufficient and proves in reality they are so.'

As always, when the going was rough, the Queen was kind and generous. Ponsonby assured Knollys, in reply to his letter of 10 April, that Her Majesty 'has not the slightest doubt that the letters are not compromising from the minute she read that the Prince of Wales said so – that was sufficient. At the same time it was unfortunate there were any letters at all – added smiling that writing letters was a family failing. It would be so easy to twist sentences hurriedly written into something they did not mean . . . The Queen telegraphed at once to the Prince of Wales and really feels for his distress of mind.'

Lord Hartington, an arbiter of gentlemanly conduct, was invited by the Prime Minister to join him and the Lord Chancellor, Lord Cairns, to word a suitable apology for Lord Randolph to submit to the Prince. Cairns produced a first draft which Disraeli approved, but about which Hartington expressed one reservation. 'The only doubt I have felt is as to the passage in which it is asserted, that the statement that the letters seriously compromise the Prince of Wales is unwarranted. I think that the letters do contain expressions which are imprudent, and which, though possibly meaning nothing, are capable of a construction injurious to the character of HRH . . . If you and Mr Disraeli are satisfied that the letters do not "seriously compromise" the P of W I do not desire to raise any objection . . . The character of the letters does not as it seems to me in any way affect the impropriety of Ld R.C.'s conduct in making use of them.'

Randolph claimed that his solicitor, Mr W. Freshfield, a partner in the firm of Freshfield & Williams, who acted for the Prime Minister as well as the Bank of England, had consulted the Solicitor-General, Sir Hardinge Gifford, later Lord Halsbury, to discover what interpretation he put on HRH's letters, and Sir Hardinge had ruled that 'if they ever came before the public,' the Prince 'would never sit on the throne of England.' Naturally, the Prince was impressed, if somewhat puzzled, by so exalted an opinion, and it was not until October 1876 that the mystery was explained. 'Sir, and dear Prince,' wrote Lord Beaconsfield, 'I have seen the Solicitor-General. Far from giving the opinion of the letters imputed to him, he never saw the letters! The case put before him was an A. B. case; no names whatever given. All the stories we have heard so long, and so often, about the Solicitor-General's strong opinions (apparently quoted in Ld Blandford's last letter, in inverted commas) and the danger to the Crown of England etc. etc. are complete fabrications.' The Prince replied that he had always 'felt convinced that the statements made by Ld B and Ld R.C. concerning him [the Solicitor-General] were as false as all their other statements have been found to be – but it is most satisfactory to hear the truth from the S.G. It is a pity that there is no desert island to which these two young gentlemen? could be banished to.'

The evening after the Prince of Wales returned home from India,

Lord Hardwicke called at Marlborough House with excellent news. Lord Aylesford had told him an hour before that he had decided not to seek a divorce. Instead, he proposed to separate from his wife thus avoiding a public scandal. It was an immense relief to the Prince, who had no inclination to be cross-examined in the Witness-Box about his friendship with Lady Aylesford.

It only remained to extract appropriate apologies. As far as Alington was concerned there was no problem. He was utterly contrite and only too anxious to grovel. Almost the moment Hardwicke left him, he wrote to the Prince and Disraeli saying he would never cease to regret his 'undue precipitation' and begged forgiveness. He admitted that he had 'been guilty not only of an injudicious but a very wrong act,' which he would not attempt to justify, but which he blamed on his impulsiveness. In his letter to the Prime Minister, he further apologized for the trouble he had caused 'my dear chief and one of my sincerest friends.' The Prince, who was always quick to forgive, instantly accepted Alington's apology by telegram and letter. Within eighteen months, Alington was invited to Sandringham, and not all that long after became the Prince's partner in leasing Lady Stamford's horses.

Apologizing did not come so easily to Randolph, who was arrogant and headstrong. It was only after prolonged negotiations, involving the Prime Minister, the Lord Chancellor and Randolph's harassed parents, that he grudgingly submitted. Following the example of Queen Elizabeth, who perfected the art of evading awkward questions with 'answers answerless,' Lord Randolph explored the possibility of proffering apologies which did not apologize. On 12 July 1876, he wrote to the Prince of Wales saying that he had been informed by his father 'that Your Royal Highness utterly disclaims and contradicts' certain accusations 'which I made to Lord Hardwicke and other people, with reference to recent occurrences between Lord Blandford and Lady Aylesford. I wish therefore fully to retract them and to express my regret for having made them. With regard to certain correspondence of Your Royal Highness, copies of which were placed in my hands, I wish most emphatically to disclaim any intention of using that correspondence in any way against Your Royal Highness.' After admitting 'that it was a great indiscretion on my part' to have intruded on the Princess of Wales, he also conceded that it was possible that 'I at times expressed myself too freely and bitterly concerning events that have of late much occupied my thoughts . . . I can truly assure Your Royal Highness that I have never been unmindful of the kindness which I have often experienced from you, and it was with the bitterest regret that I found myself forced to pursue the line of conduct which has so greatly offended you, by circumstances which I could neither control or foresee. I am glad to have an opportunity of acknowledging that I have been quite misled with regard to Your Royal Highness's supposed share in recent sad events, and I venture to express a sincere hope that Your Royal Highness may be able to see your way to altering an opinion I am told you have expressed, that I have behaved towards Your Royal Highness in a dishonourable and ungentlemanlike manner.'

The Prince consulted a number of people about the wisdom of accepting an apology so expressed. Hardwicke alone advised him to do so. 'Thinking the matter over I really do think you might do a great and generous act. You can afford to forgive although you can hardly forget . . . Generosity on your part will ever rebound to your credit.' On the other hand, Ponsonby thought that Lord Randolph's letter was scarcely a free and frank apology and was 'certainly open to various constructions.' Cairns advised that the letter while 'professing to be an apology is not really an apology: it is a justification. It assumes the right of Ld R.C. to make in the first instance the charges and suggestions which he made, and it bases his retraction of and regret for these charges merely on this that (to use his own words) "he is informed by his father that HRH utterly disclaims and contradicts the accusations." ' The apology, Cairns considered, appeared to have been 'skilfully and ingeniously framed so as to avoid any admission, and even to repudiate any admission, of improper or dishonourable behaviour on the part of Lord R.C. . . . Even supposing the case is one admitting of an apology, I cannot think the present apology can be received.'

At this stage in the proceedings, the Prince of Wales decided that his best course would be to submit the negotiations to the Prime Minister, the Lord Chancellor and Lord Hartington, whose impartiality he assumed would be recognized by the Churchills, 'and whose opinion from their high position and character would be looked upon, not only by society but by the world at large, with the greatest respect.' After a good deal of discussion these three wise men produced a memorandum outlining their reasons for regarding Lord Randolph's apology of 12 July as insufficient, and suggesting a form of words which would make it acceptable. 'We are of opinion,' they wrote, 'that there is not in that letter any sufficient recognition of the gravity of the charges to which Lord Randolph Churchill has subjected himself by his conduct in recent occurrences, and we think that HRH cannot be advised to accept the apology which the letter professes to make.'

Apart from 'the very serious breach of propriety' involved in Randolph's intrusion upon the Princess of Wales, they held him guilty of 'possessing himself, either in original or copy, of private letters of the Prince of Wales,' the contents of which he had communicated to other persons; of using 'the menace that these letters would be made public through the examination of the Prince of Wales as a witness'; and 'of having stated to Lord Hardwicke . . . that the letters would seriously compromise the Prince of Wales: a statement not warranted by the letters.'

The memorandum furthermore charged Randolph with having suggested 'that the Prince of Wales was in some manner open to the imputation of having acted in collusion with Lord Aylesford in giving opportunities for impropriety of conduct on the part of Lady Aylesford,' and with using these suggestions 'as menaces to induce HRH to exercise his influence with Lord Aylesford so as to make him forego his right to proceed for a divorce.' Under such circumstances, they did not think that Churchill's conduct could 'properly form the subject of an apology in the ordinary acceptation of the term.' Nevertheless, they appended a carefully-worded retraction, which, if accepted by Lord Randolph, might, in their view, enable HRH to forgive him.

Francis Knollys forwarded this document to the Duke of Marlborough, informing him in an accompanying letter that 'HRH desires me to state that should your son write him an apology according to the exact terms and wording of the appendix he will accept it, but that he shall feel himself at liberty to make it known to his friends and acquaintances.'

Randolph was in America when he received a letter from his parents enclosing the draft of the apology which they earnestly advised him to send. On 26 August he copied it out in his own hand, but, defiant to the last, addressed it from Saratoga, where General Burgoyne had once signed what he insisted was not a capitulation but a convention. And he added an unauthorized postscript designed to annul what had gone before. It read: 'Lord Randolph Churchill having already rendered an apology to His Royal Highness the Prince of Wales for the part taken by him in recent events feels that, as a gentleman, he is bound to accept the words of the Lord Chancellor for that apology.' The Prince regarded the postscript as most ungracious but decided to ignore it. Lord Cairns told Disraeli that the PS, in his opinion, was calculated to make the 'amende' in the most 'undignified way that was possible.'

In the summer of 1876, the Prince let it be known that neither he nor the Princess would accept invitations to houses where the Churchills were received. This edict virtually destroyed Randolph and Jennie's social life. It is true that the Duchess of Manchester ignored the boycott, declaring that she held friendship higher than snobbery, and that, when John Delacour, a Yorkshire gentleman, was reproved by the Prince for continuing to associate with Lord Randolph, he courageously replied: 'Sir, I allow no man to choose my friends.' But such independence was rare. Eventually, Disraeli prevailed upon the Duke of Marlborough to accept the post of Lord-Lieutenant of Ireland to enable the family to make a dignified withdrawal from English life. Part of the arrangement was that Randolph should act as his father's private secretary. So he and Jennie and their two-year-old son, Winston, went into exile. Lord Randolph's political radicalism owed much to the bitterness provoked by his banishment from Society.

In 1884, the Prince at last agreed to meet Randolph at a dinner given by the Attorney-General, Sir Henry James. The Prime Minister, Mr Gladstone, was invited to witness the reconciliation. Two years later, the Prince dined with the Churchills at Connaught Place. Blandford, now Duke of Marlborough, was one of the party. When the electric lights went out during dinner, the Duke, who was fascinated by scientific novelties, rummaged about the cellar and managed to mend the fuse. Jennie's beauty and charm worked wonders and the evening was a splendid success. From that moment, old friendships were restored and even deepened. After Randolph rashly resigned as Chancellor of the Exchequer, destroying his political career, and throughout his last distressing illness, he had no more loyal supporters than the Prince and Princess of Wales, who showed him the utmost kindness. When Randolph died, the Prince wrote to Jennie that very day. 'The sad news reached me this morning that all was over . . . and I felt for his and your sakes it was best so . . . There was a cloud in our friendship but I am glad to think that it has long been forgotten by both of us.'

Curiously enough, after the excitement died down, the Prince chanced upon letters from Lady Aylesford which proved that there was no substance in the charge that he had compelled her husband to accompany him to India against her will. He told Knollys to send Ponsonby copies of the correspondence to show the Queen. 'Lord Blandford and Lord Randolph Churchill,' wrote Knollys, 'laid so much stress upon what they stated was fact, viz, that the Prince of Wales in spite of all that Lady Aylesford could say to the contrary, insisted on taking Lord Aylesford to India with him, that His Royal Highness thinks the Queen ought to see the two accompanying letters which he received from Lady Aylesford, and which he has only just accidentally found. You will see by letter No. 2 that Lady Aylesford gave up her opposition, and that she thought with the Prince of Wales that it would be greatly to Lord Aylesford's advantage that he should accompany His Royal Highness on the occasion in question.'

Lord Aylesford emigrated to America in 1882, where he bought twenty-seven thousand acres in Texas. Within three years, aged thirty-five, he died of drink. Lady Aylesford survived him by twelve years. For a time she and Blandford lived in France as Mr and Mrs Spencer. But in 1888, after he had inherited the Dukedom, he married an American widow, Mrs Hammersley, leaving Edith in Paris. When she died in 1897, the Prince and Princess of Wales sent a wreath to her funeral.

In 1891, the Prince permitted himself to be drawn into a further scandal in which the pattern of previous misadventures reappeared: the inevitable letter, threats of exposure, Lord Salisbury dragged in to arbitrate, adultery in high places, a social boycott, and an outraged husband. In short, the Beresford row was very much the mixture as before. But what made it dangerous was that the crisis coincided with the trauma of Tranby Croft.

Lord Charles Beresford, whose younger brother Marcus managed the Sandringham Stud, was a breezy Irish sailor. In 1882 he became a national hero when he silenced the batteries of Alexandria by taking his gunboat *Condor* so close inshore that the Egyptian guns could not be brought to bear against him. His high spirits were infectious and he made everybody laugh, even the Queen, who met him on board HMS *Thunderer* in 1887, and described him as 'beaming with fun and a trifle cracky, but clever and a good officer.'

When in 1870 the Princess of Wales was worried to death that her father might risk war against Prussia, Lord Charles brought her news of Denmark's neutrality. 'Glad to tell you, Ma'am,' he said, 'that Denmark has declared neutrality, and so has the Beadle of the Burlington Arcade. Great weight off our minds. Didn't know what either of them would do.' Once, when the Prince asked him to dine at Marlborough House, he telegraphed, 'Can't possibly. Lie follows by post.' Beresford, a founder member of the Marlborough House Set, accompanied the Prince to India in 1876, and it was he who was entrusted with the letter to Lord Hardwicke in which HRH challenged Lord Randolph to a duel.

In 1878, Lord Charles married Miss Ellen Gardner, or 'Mina' as he called her. The Prince constantly sought opportunities to further his friend's career. In 1884 he persuaded Lord Wolseley to make him his ADC during the campaign to relieve General Gordon. The following year he recommended that Lord Charles should be given the CB, and in 1886 he succeeded in getting Beresford appointed Fourth Lord of the Admiralty.

While Lord Charles was working in London, he fell in love with Lady Brooke. Frances Maynard was a great Victorian heiress, as beautiful as she was rich. In 1881 she married Lord Warwick's heir. Prince Leopold was best man, and the Prince and Princess of Wales attended the wedding. Lord Brooke, whose principal interest was fishing, regarded his wife's numerous infidelities with good-natured tolerance, just as he did her conversion to Socialism.

Lord Charles Beresford and Lady Brooke made no effort to conceal their liaison. Frances, indeed, went so far as to tell Lady Charles that she planned to elope with her husband. But the affair was short-lived and Beresford broke it off. In January 1889, Frances heard that Mina was having a baby, at which her rage and fury knew no bounds, and she wrote Lord Charles a reproachful letter accusing him of 'infidelity'. It was disgraceful, she claimed, to desert her and return to his wife. Unfortunately, Beresford had authorized Lady Charles to open his post in his absence, and consequently this astonishing effusion fell into her hands.

The Prince of Wales, when he eventually saw the letter, said it was the most shocking he had ever read. Mina deposited it with George Lewis, instructing him to threaten Lady Brooke with prosecution for libel if she gave any further annoyance. On hearing from the solicitor, Lady Brooke called at his office and demanded her letter back. 'It is my letter,' she argued, 'I wrote it.' When Mr Lewis explained that legally letters are the property of those to whom they are addressed, she decided to turn to the Prince of Wales for help. No one had a greater reputation for resolving social dilemmas, or, on occasions, creating them. Moreover, as an old friend of Charlie Beresford, he might persuade him to relinquish what she now recognized was a very foolish letter.

So she called on HRH at Marlborough House, her beautiful eyes brimming over with distress, and begged him to help her. He was not the man to refuse an appeal from so lovely a creature, and gallantly offered to come to the rescue. She confessed – as if he did not know already – that for some time she had been in love with Lord Charles to whom she had impulsively dashed off a most unfortunate letter which was now in the hands of his wife's solicitor.

The Prince of Wales went to see George Lewis and persuaded him to let him read the letter: a request which should not have been made or granted. But when HRH told him to burn the offending document, Lewis explained that he could not do so without his client's consent. Eventually Lord Charles persuaded Mina to send the letter to his brother, Lord Waterford, for safe-keeping.

The Prince, urged on by Lady Brooke, passed sentence of social death on Lady Charles, who complained to Lord Salisbury that HRH had taken up 'the cause of an "abandoned woman" against that of a perfectly blameless wife.' While Lady Brooke was seen everywhere and invited everywhere, Mina sat brooding over her wrongs in her house in Eaton Square.

Before taking up command of the cruiser *Undaunted*, Lord Charles decided to call on the Prince at Marlborough House to protest against HRH's treatment of his wife. At the best of times, the wild Irishman was no respecter of persons, but on this occasion, incensed by feelings of jealousy and guilt, his indignation overpowered him. He told the Prince that he had behaved like a blackguard in demanding to be shown Lady Brooke's letter, that he had no business whatever to interfere in a personal matter, and that his doing so had nearly caused him to be separated from his wife. Muttering threats about what would happen if Lady Charles was ill-treated in his absence, he left for the Mediterranean. Some people said that he actually struck the Prince to impart emphasis to his discourse.

In the summer of 1891 Lady Charles announced that she had decided to live abroad. Her husband therefore threatened to publish an account of all that had happened unless full amends were made. It had not escaped his notice that following Tranby Croft the Royal

Family would go to considerable lengths to hush up a further scandal.

In September, 1891, the Princess of Wales, after visiting her parents in Denmark, unexpectedly joined the Tsar and Tsarina at Livadia, where she remained to celebrate their Silver Wedding. By so doing, she missed Bertie's fiftieth birthday at Sandringham. Masculine unfaithfulness was taken for granted in the Danish Royal Family, and Alix had shown herself wonderfully gracious to a succession of rivals. But Tranby Croft and Lady Brooke between them temporarily proved too much for her.

Beresford returned to England in December, 1891 and once more accused the Prince of 'openly slighting and ignoring' Lady Charles. HRH replied that he was 'at a loss to understand how Lady Charles can imagine that I have in any way slighted or ignored her . . . Lady Charles was invited to the Garden Party at Marlborough House this last summer and I made a point on all occasions of shaking hands with her, or of bowing to her, as the opportunity presented.' There followed four frantic days of negotiation which spoiled everyone's Christmas. Even the Queen was dragged in, as Lady Charles saw fit to write to her. When Beresford threatened to hold a Press conference nobody thought he was bluffing. At the last moment Lord Salisbury succeeded in negotiating peace. It was agreed that Lady Brooke would be temporarily banished from Court, and that the Prince would write a qualified apology, regretting that circumstances had occurred which led Lady Charles Beresford to believe that it was his intention 'publicly to wound her feelings.' The offending letter which had started all the trouble was returned, and the readers of *Reynolds's Newspaper* were deprived of a succulent morsel.

Charlie Beresford soon let it be known that he was anxious to be forgiven for his part in the proceedings. The Duke of Cambridge told Knollys that he had received a letter from Beresford 'on another subject,' in which he expressed a desire 'to be *forgiven* for his conduct,' and claimed to be 'very contrite.' The Duke confessed to 'grave doubts as to the advisability of at all meeting his views. The offence was too grave to be lightly overlooked . . . In time, should Lord Charles take a calmer and altogether proper line, HRH might intimate to him that he had put aside this painful incident, but I could certainly, if I were the Prince, *never* take him into my *friendship* again, but simply treat him as an acquaintance.'

For five years the feud continued to simmer. In 1896, HRH wrote to Knollys from Cannes saying that Christopher Sykes and Adolphus FitzGeorge, the Duke of Cambridge's son, had just told him that they were 'sure that that scoundrel C.B. means mischief now that he is at large and his language about me is simply beyond words – and that he wants to make a row and vows vengeance against me. I am not looking forward to the coming London Season and expect we shall have trouble – though I know he is as great a coward as he is a bully.'

As predicted, there was trouble that summer at Ascot. 'Yesterday, Lord C.B. appeared in the Royal Enclosure,' HRH told Knollys, 'and passed close to me whilst I was talking to someone but totally ignored my existence – as I did his – I afterwards saw that gallant? sailor and blackmailer! talking to the ladies and smoking cigarettes so that his statement that I got society to boycott him is as great a lie as most of his statements! He was at the races again today and purposely passed close to me without bowing, but he bowed shortly afterwards to my son and went up to the D and Dss of Devonshire with a "hail fellow well met" kind of manner and said how glad he was to see them again. The Dss came up to me purposely to tell me this and said they were so taken aback they did not know what to do! His line evidently is to "rush" society – so to say – and show them that he intends treating me . . . with marked rudeness.'

In September, the Tsar, Nicholas II, told his 'Uncle Bertie' at Balmoral that, when he met the Kaiser on his way to Scotland, 'he was astonished to see drawn up amongst the German and Foreign Officers – Ld C.B! and said to the German Emperor "What on earth is he doing here?" The latter's answer was "Oh! he is my most intimate friend and a real good fellow!"' In telling Knollys the story the Prince remarked 'My illustrious German nephew seems a great judge of character!!!'

In June, 1897, a truce was finally arranged with the help of the Duke of Portland. It took the customary form of an exchange of letters. Beresford wrote to the Duke saying that 'On consideration of the conversation which I had with you and my brother Bill, I beg to offer an apology to HRH the Prince of Wales and express my regret for the letters which I wrote to HRH. I have also been asked by Lady Charles to apologize and express her regret for the letter which she wrote to the Queen.' Knollys then told Portland that His Royal Highness was happy to accept the apology and expression of regret which Lord Charles Beresford had offered him. The Prince sent Lady Brooke a copy of the correspondence. 'It is a great triumph,' she wrote back, 'to have received the apologies and a great relief that the episode is closed.'

This catalogue of social crises may well create a false impression of never-ending catastrophe. Accounts of volcanic eruptions tend to ignore the quiescent years. Admittedly, the Prince behaved foolishly over Sir William Gordon-Cumming and Lady Brooke. But such lapses were rare. Far more characteristic were the countless occasions when HRH settled his friends' quarrels or soothed their ruffled feelings.

V

The Prince and Politics

Soon after Bertie's sixth birthday his parents discussed his future. The Queen recorded in her Journal that Albert maintained that the boy 'ought to be accustomed early to work with and for us, to have great confidence shewn him, that he should early be initiated into the affairs of State. How true this is! So wise and right; and the more confidence we shew him the better it will be for himself, for us, and for the country.' But after the Prince Consort's death, far from implementing this 'wise and right' resolution, she constantly prevented her son playing any part in political life, so that Bagehot in his book *The English Constitution* saw fit to describe him as 'an unemployed youth.'

With sublime inconsistency, Queen Victoria encouraged the King and Queen of Prussia to give Fritz a degree of responsibility and independence that no one could persuade her to permit her son. Had some other sovereign presumed to lecture her on her duties as a parent with the same freedom as she showed to her 'dear, honoured brother' of Prussia, one can well imagine the haughty rejoinder such impudence would provoke. But then 'much of Queen Victoria's strength lay in her limitations as a logician.' Clarendon made himself very unpopular by telling the Queen that the Prince Consort would have found some regular work for his son as 'Regent of Scotland, or a Clerk in the Audit Office, or Bailiff of the Home Farm.' A major factor in the Queen's estrangement from Gladstone was his persistence in devising plans for employing the Prince of Wales. The Queen's attitude to her son was often unreasonable in every sense of the word. But having said that, there were rational grounds for refusing to share her sovereign power. Foremost amongst them was her conviction that she best understood, and consequently could best implement, the Prince Consort's policies. Even when overwhelmed with grief, she derived some consolation from continuing his work. She told Mrs Gladstone 'of the help it was to go on with his wishes, to carry out and finish his plans.'

The day after the Prince Consort's funeral, she announced her '*firm* resolve' and '*irrevocable decision*' to make his policies and intentions her law, from which '*no human power* will make me swerve.' Although for many years she ceased to perform the visible duties of Monarchy, 'she kept in her own hands every atom of the more solid functions of the Crown, and neither consulted the Prince of Wales on affairs of State or diplomatic relations with foreign countries, nor paid the smallest attention to his views . . . To open a few docks and bazaars and lay a few foundation stones was not employment for a mentally energetic man.'

In 1862, Lord Palmerston proposed that the Prince of Wales should succeed his lamented father as Master of Trinity House. The suggestion was ill received and Phipps was instructed to tell him that both Her Majesty and the Prince of Wales himself shared 'a great objection to HRH being put, for some years, into any position lately held by the Prince Consort.'

Two years later, Sir Charles wrote to Sir William Knollys informing him that the Queen desired him 'to say that she thinks that the Prince of Wales had better decline the Royal Academy dinner this year, and to say that it is a meeting which his father only attended very rarely.' Phipps ended his letter by dissociating himself from the suggestion which had inspired it. 'I am bound to obey the commands that are laid upon me, and I therefore send this message to you, to act upon as you think best. My functions however are purely ministerial and I should be glad not to appear in any way in the matter with which indeed I can have no concern.'

When Princess Helena married Prince Christian there was some surprise that the Queen should give her away. It was even rumoured that the bride's brothers objected so much to the match they they refused to do so. But the truth of the matter was as the Queen made plain to Vicky: 'I never would let one of my sons take their father's place while I live.' Ten years after the Prince Consort's death she noted in her Journal on 3 July 1871, 'Bertie remained for the Investiture. After '61 I could hardly bear the thought of anyone helping me and standing where my dearest one had always stood.'

But she added, 'as years go on I strongly feel that to lift up my son and heir and keep him in his place near me, is only what is right.'

Not until the last years of her reign would the Queen permit the Prince a regular and unrestricted supply of Foreign Office despatches and Cabinet papers. On her specific instructions, the heir to the throne was denied access to documents which circulated freely among ministers and their Private Secretaries. The royal understudy, most of whose life was spent hanging about in the wings, was not even allowed to look at his lines to prepare for the role in which destiny had cast him.

The Queen justified her decision to keep her son in ignorance by saying he was incurably indiscreet, and that 'She deprecated the discussion of national secrets over country-house dinner tables.' His letters to Lady Mordaunt and Lady Aylesford, or his intervention on behalf of Lady Brooke, were scarcely evidence of discernment. Writing in 1883 to her grand-daughter, Princess Victoria of Hesse, Her Majesty ventured to make a 'very *private* little *observation*' to the effect that 'Dear Uncle cannot keep anything to himself – but lets everything *out*.'

Frederick Ponsonby, who became King Edward's Assistant Private Secretary in 1901, says that 'When he became King and knew all the inner working of all State affairs there was no one more discreet.' But, as Prince of Wales, 'several instances could be quoted of his giving away secrets. The truth was that he was only occasionally told secrets, and while it is easy to be discreet when one knows everything, it is much more difficult to keep occasional bits of news secret.'

The root of most of the Prince's troubles may be traced to the frustration and boredom of his enforced idleness. Restless at being unoccupied, and thwarted in his desire for responsible work, he sought a variety of diversions, from assisting the Fire Brigade to playing baccarat. What was so provokingly unjust was that the Queen, having resolutely prevented him finding employment, deplored the frivolity of his mode of life. When she heard, for example, that he proposed to visit the Punchestown Races during his tour of Ireland in 1868, she told him how much she regretted it, 'as it naturally strengthens the belief, already far too prevalent, that your chief object is amusement.' There seemed no way out of the vicious circle. The Queen refused to trust the Prince with serious work because she thought him too frivolous. So he, having nothing better to do, sought amusements which justified her fears.

Even before Bertie's marriage, the Queen was convinced that he was totally unfit to succeed her. Writing to Vicky in 1859 she exclaimed: 'What would happen if I were to die next winter! One shudders to think of it: it is too awful a contemplation . . . The greatest improvement I fear will never make him fit for his position.' Twelve years later she confessed to Gladstone that 'she doubted the Prince's fitness for high functions of State.'

There were moments when Gladstone felt inclined to agree. Writing to Granville in 1873 he spoke of HRH's 'total want of political judgement either inherited or acquired.' But later, he changed his mind. In 1885, during the Prince's visit to Ireland, Gladstone 'was much struck with a little speech,' he made, 'which he concluded with the words "God protect and save Ireland." "What could have been," Mr G. said "in better taste or more apposite? It was a grand stroke. He certainly has great quickness of perception and a happy knack of always saying the right thing." ' When the Prime Minister later discussed his Irish visit with the Prince, 'Mr G. was much impressed by the sagacity of HRH.'

After Prince Albert's death, the Queen contrived to discharge her constitutional responsibilities by ceaseless correspondence. But when it came to appearing in public or entertaining visiting royalty she might as well have abdicated. Heedless of her son's qualifications for undertaking such tasks on her behalf, she preferred to neglect them than relinquish them.

As early as June 1862, Delane published an article in *The Times* urging the Queen to permit the Prince of Wales to play some part in public affairs. It was distressing to compare 'the very different measure of hospitality' England offered and received. Indeed, Claridge's rise to fame was a direct consequence of the Queen's inhospitality. During his visit to our shores, the King of Sweden stayed at the Swedish legation. 'When Prince Humbert of Italy came, Lord Palmerston had to come up from Brocket to give him a dinner, and when he went to see Windsor he had to lunch at the White Hart.' On the other hand, when the Prince of Wales visited Denmark, 'exhausted by war and merciless exactions,' he was 'received splendidly, entertained incessantly,' and asked to stay for a month. 'If the Queen,' wrote Delane, 'is still unable to entertain, let there at least be hospitality in her name.'

Because she possessed so little confidence in the Prince, she tended to confide in Princess Alice, and later Princess Helena. Knollys once told Ponsonby that HRH had remarked that 'he is not of the slightest use to the Queen; that everything he says or suggests is pooh-poohed and that his sisters and brothers are more listened to than he is.' The brother mentioned was Prince Leopold, whom the Queen regarded as the cleverest and most studious of her sons. She and Lord Beaconsfield agreed in 1876 that Leopold would assist her in the most confidential portion of her labours. Sir Charles Dilke's Private Secretary, James Bodley, was walking one day with Prince Leopold in Oxford, when the young Prince took a key from his pocket and told him: 'It is the Queen's Cabinet key which opens all the secret despatch boxes. Dizzy gave it to me, but my brother the Prince of Wales is not allowed to have one.'

Irritating as it was for HRH to see his brother, who was twelve years younger than he was, admitted to the Queen's confidence, he did not let it influence their relationship. Princess Alice, Countess of Athlone, Prince Leopold's daughter, says in her memoirs that 'Uncle Bertie was, of course, aware of the assistance which my father was giving to the Queen and knew that his younger brother had access to State papers which he, though Prince of Wales, was not allowed to see. He was understandably indignant at such treatment, and I cannot help being filled with admiration for his magnanimity, for he bore no grudge against my father and was always kindness itself to my mother and me . . . I consider he showed real greatness of spirit in his attitude towards my family.'

Sir Lionel Cust, the Surveyor and Keeper of King Edward's pictures, thought that 'the great misfortune' of the King's life 'was that his mother had lived too long . . . for the welfare of her son and successor.' Because Queen Victoria refused to take him into partnership, 'the best years of a man's life, say from forty to sixty, were to a great extent wasted.' During the Franco-Prussian War, in which the Crown Prince commanded an Army, Vicky remarked in one of her letters to the Queen, 'I am sure Bertie must envy Fritz who has such a trying, but such a useful life.' Whether intended as a hint that Bertie needed to be found worthwhile occupation, or as a rap over the knuckles for one who allegedly supported France in her struggle against Germany, the contrast was provoking.

For over a quarter of a century, the Prince of Wales directed some of his frustrated energy towards securing the right to be kept informed about affairs of State. He claimed that he knew less than the secretaries of Ministers 'about the contents of those boxes that were piled upon his Mother's desk. There was the tree of knowledge, there the fountain of wisdom; they were just out of his reach; and occasional confidences made his predicament all the more tantalizing.' Knollys considered that part of the problem was inherent in the very nature of Sovereignty. 'It has been the same thing with Heirs Apparent,' he told Arthur Bigge in 1901, 'from time immemorial, and I fear will continue to be so as long as there are monarchies.'

Lord Esher believed that the Prince of Wales's insistence upon receiving official documents as of right, 'was largely a matter of *amour propre*.' In fact, no one 'was better and more completely informed of the trend of public affairs than the Prince of Wales . . . The Prince not only heard the Government case, but he was taken into confidence by the leaders of the Opposition as well. He was speedily the best informed man in the Kingdom.' So the prolonged battle over Cabinet keys and Cabinet papers 'lacked reality, as from 1864 the Prince knew everything that was going on, and very often more than the Queen herself.' Seeing that the importance of his own work depended upon HRH being at the centre of affairs, Knollys sometimes fought the battle of the Boxes more ferociously than his master.

Even after the Queen's death, the King was sometimes kept in the dark. In October 1901, he wrote to Knollys from the Jockey Club, Newmarket, to say that he 'was much astonished at reading in today's *Times* that Sir A. Macdonnell (whose brother is a Nationalist MP) is to be appointed "Under Secretary to the Lord Lieutenant of Ireland." It seems strange that I have heard nothing on the subject from either Dudley or G. Wyndham, and should have thought the Prime Minister would have submitted it for my approval. The Government evidently consider that the Press should be earlier informed than the King ! ! ! '

Soon after his father came to the throne, Prince George set out on a tour of the Empire. During his visits to Australia and Canada he found himself hampered in talking to politicians and officials by his lack of official information about the British Government's policy. So he asked Sir Arthur Bigge, the late Queen's Private Secretary, to complain to Knollys. Bigge headed his letters: '*Private. Only for your own eye!*' After dutifully obeying his instructions, he concluded by saying: 'Does not history repeat itself? The only thing now necessary is a letter framed on those excellent models which we think ran something like this:

Marlborough House.

My dear Bigge,

The Prince of Wales desires me to let you know that he cannot help feeling rather hurt that the Queen has never consulted HRH with regard to the . . . . . . which he hears has been decided upon.

                    Yours,

                    F.K.!!'

The complaint might be familiar, but not its outcome. The moment Knollys raised the matter with King Edward, he gave instructions that his son should be sent every important Cabinet paper and Foreign Office despatch. In replying to Bigge, Knollys quite agreed 'that history repeats itself. The Duke of Cornwall will occasionally complain of the King for not telling him things, just as the latter complained of the Queen, and as without doubt little Prince Edward will complain in time to come of the Duke.' And so it came to pass, for, looking back on his years as 'King-in-Waiting,' the Duke of Windsor regretted the fact that he was never allowed 'to examine the contents of the red despatch boxes containing the submissions of the Prime Minister and the heads of the different Government departments . . . Yet, in a manner never defined, I was expected to remain conversant with all that was going on in the world.'

Even Queen Victoria sometimes protested that she was kept too much in the dark. A Lady-in-Waiting, desperate for something to say, once blurted out: 'Yesterday, Ma'am, I heard a barrel organ in the Park.' 'A barrel organ?' said the Queen indignantly. 'But I was not told. I am never told anything.' There was a stunned silence during which the assembled company contemplated the enormity of a Government which permitted a barrel organ to be played in a Royal park without informing Her Majesty.

A more serious oversight was the failure of Marlborough House to tell the Queen that the Prince of Wales intended to see Garibaldi. The first she knew of the meeting, as Phipps was quick to point out, was what she read in the newspapers. When Lord Randolph Churchill resigned in 1886, the Queen was furious to learn from *The Times* that the country required a new Chancellor of the Exchequer. As a matter of fact, Jennie learned the news in much the same way. 'Quite a surprise for you,' said Randolph, as she read about it at breakfast.

In June 1862, Lord Clarendon stayed for a couple of nights at Windsor and gave the Queen 'much wholesome advice' about developing the Prince of Wales's talents, 'by showing him correspondence and consulting him on matters of home and foreign policy, instead of treating him as a child.' He might as well have addressed his sagacious remarks to a marble bust of the late lamented Prince Consort.

During the war between Prussia and Denmark in 1864, the Prince of Wales spoke to the Foreign Secretary, Lord Russell, 'with a view to his seeing from time to time copies of the despatches.' Russell said he could only obey the Queen's 'orders on the subject,' but, in referring the matter to her, ventured to suggest that she might with advantage 'direct that despatches of interest' should be seen by the Prince.

General Grey, replying from Balmoral, told the Foreign Secretary that the Queen 'rejoices in the desire' which the Prince showed 'to know what is going on' and thought that 'it should be gratified as far as possible.' Nevertheless, she objected 'to the *principle*, which would thus be admitted, of separate and independent communication between the Prince of Wales and her Government.' Were the Prince 'to take antagonistic views on any important questions,' as, for example, over Schleswig-Holstein, 'great inconvenience, not to say injury, might be occasioned to the public service.' The Queen would, however, send HRH 'a précis of the more interesting of the despatches which come to her,' and 'such information as to the policy of her Government as she might deem right.' By this means, she would be able 'to exercise some control over what is communicated to him – a control which is very necessary, as she must tell you confidentially, that His Royal Highness is not at all times as discreet as he should be.'

Hardly a year passed without the Prince of Wales returning to the question of his access to official information, although Lord Granville told Gladstone that HRH was 'little inclined even to read what is sent him.' On those occasions when Her Majesty agreed to documents being sent to Marlborough House, the Foreign Office, in particular, proved dilatory. In October 1873, for example, Knollys complained to Ponsonby that 'as long as there was nothing in the least interesting the Foreign Office were most regular in sending Boxes to the Prince of Wales, but now that there is something going on in Europe which would really interest him, they take the greatest care not to let him have any more.'

A fortnight later, Knollys reported that 'no despatches have been sent to the Prince of Wales since I last wrote to you.' Indeed, nothing had been heard since 'Lord Augustus Loftus' most interesting despatch on the Cesarevna's chicken pox was forwarded to him in August. I must say I am curious to know the reason for this sudden cessation; and whether it is simply neglect and carelessness on the part of the Foreign Office, or whether they have repented of their former kindness.'

Again, in October 1876, during the opening stages of the crisis between Russia and Turkey, which was finally resolved by the Congress of Berlin, Knollys wrote to Ponsonby from Dunrobin, complaining that the Foreign Office had not 'sent one single Box to the Prince of Wales since the end of July and this while events of no ordinary interest are occurring. I have written to Tenterden (Permanent Under-Secretary for Foreign Affairs) on the subject, but I have done so already at least four or five times during the last year-and-a-half and the invariable result is a letter of regret and attempted explanation, and then after a short time the same thing happens again. I can hardly believe it is done on purpose, but still it looks rather like it. I wish if you have an opportunity you would say a word.'

In April 1877 the Prince was cruising off Naples in HMS *Sultan* when he received a cypher telegram urging him to return to England in view of the seriousness of the international situation. 'The Prince has no doubt that matters are "critical",' Knollys was instructed to tell Ponsonby, 'but he has no certain knowledge on the subject as the Government have not vouchsafed to send him one *single word* of information on the state of affairs since he left England, and had it not been for Prince Humbert who was good enough to place him a little *au courant* as to what was going on, and for two letters which Borthwick of the *Morning Post* wrote to me, he would have been left still more in the dark than he even is at present.'

If members of the Government suggested, as they were very fond of doing, that it was desirable for the Prince to be in England, Ponsonby could tell them 'that HRH is totally ignorant as to what is taking place. It can I think be hardly expected of him that because he gets a cypher telegram one night saying that "matters are critical" without having received any news of any sort before, that he is to rush home. It is simply treating him as if he were still travelling about with a Governor. However all this is an old story and I don't suppose that anything that can be said will alter matters. I have written on the subject over and over again to Mr Corry (Disraeli's Private Secretary) and to Tenterden, and you will see with what result. Under these circumstances, unless he receives some better reasons for altering his plans than have hitherto appeared, the Prince proposes to adhere to his intention of not returning to London before the morning of 7th May.'

During Gladstone's Second Ministry, Sir Charles Dilke, then Under-Secretary for Foreign Affairs, regularly supplied the Prince of Wales with information. When in February 1881 Sir Charles met the Prince and Princess at a dinner given by Lord Spencer, HRH spoke to him 'about his anxiety to be kept informed of foreign affairs,' as did the Princess, who told him how anxious she was about her brother, the King of Greece. So Dilke obligingly 'supplied the lack of official access to the papers by keeping the Prince privately informed from day to day in critical moments.' But such information was only fitful and haphazard, and in no way diminished the Prince's desire for regular news from Whitehall.

In the spring of 1885, Gladstone's Private Secretary, Sir Edward Walter Hamilton, met the Prince of Wales at a dinner given by Ferdinand Rothschild. 'HRH came and had a talk after dinner,' he wrote in his diary on Sunday, 10 May. 'He complains of being kept too much in the dark by the Government; and I think not without reason. He would like important decisions of the Cabinet communicated to him; and according to F. Knollys Lord Beaconsfield did latterly send the Prince an informal note of what had taken place. We had never heard of this till now. It will be entirely new to Mr G, who though always very anxious to bring the Prince forward, will not like to act behind the Queen's back. It is probable that Lord Beaconsfield acted without saying anything to HM; but he could do a good many things connected with the Queen which Mr G could not and certainly would not do. We must see what can be arranged.' The next day, Hamilton spoke to the Prime Minister, who favoured the plan of sending HRH Cabinet papers, but did 'not feel warranted to take any step without communicating first with the Queen.'

On 19 May, Gladstone went down to Windsor for a Council and 'took the opportunity of broaching the subject with HM in person, and gathered that she would prefer sending on herself at her discretion the Cabinet Report to the Prince.' But, as Hamilton pointed out, 'this would fail in its object which was to keep HRH *au fait* promptly with what was going on; for when at Balmoral she could

only let him see the Cabinet Report three or four days after date.'
By the end of the month, Hamilton's plan 'for giving the Prince of
Wales a closer insight into State secrets' had broken down. 'The
Queen would have nothing to say to the suggestion I made to
Ponsonby that the result of Cabinet deliberations should be briefly
communicated to HRH from Downing Street. She declines to
believe that Lord Beaconsfield ever made such communications;
thinks it not right that the Prime Minister should incur the responsi-
bility of what he should and what he should not tell the Prince; and
maintains that she ought to decide what should be handed on to
HRH . . . I was always afraid that the Queen would raise difficulties.
She is very jealous of anything tending to derogate her Sovereign
Powers.'

Gladstone accepted the principle 'that communications to the
Prince of Wales as to matters treated in the Cabinet should be . . .
under the immediate control of the Sovereign,' but told Ponsonby
that he thought it 'very judicious and desirable' that the Prince, 'at
this time of life,' should be admitted 'to an interior knowledge of
affairs.'

Despite the Queen's refusal to believe that Lord Beaconsfield
communicated Cabinet secrets to her son, the archives at Hughenden
provide incontestable proof that 'Disraeli kept the Prince informed
of every turn in the many critical issues which faced him' during
his last years of office. 'No doubt,' wrote Hamilton, 'Lord Beaconsfield wished to keep on good terms with both his Sovereign and the
heir apparent; and in his endeavours to please the Prince he did
not like to displease the Queen, and so he acted rather behind her
back.' Gladstone, who was more scrupulous, and necessarily more
cautious, decided henceforth to exercise a judicious indiscretion, if
not quite so extensive as that of Disraeli, at least sufficient to keep
the Prince in touch with Government policy.

During Gladstone's brief Third Ministry in 1886, which fell
because of his failure to carry Home Rule for Ireland, Lord Rosebery
was Foreign Secretary. Entirely on his own responsibility, Rosebery
sent the Prince of Wales copies of secret despatches, a practice which
Lord Salisbury continued when he became Prime Minister in
August. The situation was finally regularized in 1892 when the
Queen at last agreed that the Prince should have unrestricted access
to all official papers. He was fifty-one at the time and within nine
years of becoming King.

But it was one thing to be authorized to see despatches, and another to persuade the Foreign Office to send them. In 1895 the Prince complained: 'The *game* is *not* to let me see *any* interesting or important despatches! This has been going on for years under successive Governments. It would be far better if the FO sent me *no* more – which would be preferable to the rubbish they send!' Two years later, while he was staying at Marienbad, he received 'A large number of interesting FO Telegrams.' The only trouble was they were mostly a fortnight old. 'Every year the FO promises the same thing – but unless constantly reminded never take the trouble to send me anything.'

The Prince's concern over despatches was merely a symptom of a deeper malaise. What he really wanted was satisfying work, and nobody understood this better than Gladstone. In a letter Gladstone wrote Granville in December 1870, he looked forward 'ten, twenty, thirty, forty years hence' and decided the outlook for the Prince of Wales was a 'very melancholy one.' As he saw it, the Royal Family's 'fund of credit' was rapidly diminishing. 'To speak in rude and general terms, the Queen is invisible, and the Prince of Wales is not respected.' In such circumstances, 'the only remedial measure of which I can think is, to try to frame some plan under which the Prince, before the habits of his mind and life become so to speak rigid, shall be provided with some fair share, not of political responsibility, but of public duty.'

Gladstone's plan was that HRH should live in Ireland for part of the year, possibly replacing the Lord-Lieutenant. At the same time he hoped to encourage the Queen to make more public appearances, or, failing that, to surrender to her son such social duties as she could not, or would not perform. General Grey privately urged the Prime Minister to take a strong line with the Queen, whom he saw as a self-willed malingerer.

In 1870, when Gladstone became obsessed with what he called the 'Great Crisis of Royalty,' Republicanism looked threatening. The downfall of Napoleon inspired English republicans with new zeal. As Metternich observed, 'When France sneezes, Europe catches cold.' The Mordaunt scandal provided critics of monarchy with deadly ammunition and there were some signs that even Her Majesty no longer commanded the unwavering allegiance of her subjects. When she sought parliamentary grants to provide for her children, there were muttered complaints about 'princely paupers.' Was she not in receipt of immense sums of public money, intended to defray the cost of ceremonies she no longer performed, and to entertain exalted visitors she no longer invited?

No wonder Gladstone told his sister that before retiring, an event he anticipated by a quarter of a century, his last remaining task was to solve the 'Royalty question.' Disraeli first proposed the idea of a royal residence in Ireland, a miniature Balmoral on the banks of the Boyne. But nobody seemed anxious to bear the cost so the idea lapsed. The Prince and the Princess might have done much to inspire loyalty in Ireland had they spent as much time in that country as the Queen did in Scotland. Certainly they were rapturously welcomed when they visited Dublin in 1868. One poet wrote of the Princess that 'Treason vanished at her smile.' Alix was charmed and delighted by all she saw. She thought the countryside 'far more beautiful than Scotland,' and found the Irish full of enthusiasm, fun and warmth. She was exactly the sort of person to have felt at home in Ireland, 'with her spontaneous gaiety, her informality, her lack of logic, her love of horses, and, be it said, her want of method and her hopeless and incurable unpunctuality. As a Dane she would have understood the outlook "of a small defeated nation," brooding bitterly over its wrongs.'

In December 1871, the Prince of Wales nearly died of typhoid fever. As soon as it became clear that he would recover, Gladstone saw 'a noble and priceless opportunity to give a deeper purpose to the life spared to the nation.' Already, in June, he had approached Her Majesty at Windsor, 'on the wish expressed again and again' that there should be a royal residence in Ireland. The Queen noted in a memorandum that 'Mr Gladstone contended how important it was in *these days* to connect the *Royal Family* with *public functions* and *offices* . . . I contend that it would be wasting time in *spending* this *in Ireland*, when Scotland and England deserved it much more.' The Queen said that she believed 'the notion which had been entertained by several people of making a Royal Prince Lord-Lieutenant would be *far* the *best*. Mr. Gladstone said he thought I was right.' They then discussed the possibility of the Prince of Wales becoming her deputy at Dublin. Although Her Majesty 'doubted the wisdom of identifying the future King with Ireland,' she admitted 'it would be a good thing' if it took him 'away from the London Season.'

Gladstone sensed at once that his plan did not seem to find favour, but never recognized how strong was the Queen's aversion to Ireland. During her visit there in 1861, which included her tour of the Curragh, the Prince Consort had met with hostile demonstrations because of an infelicitous comparison he had drawn between Irish and Polish discontents. The Queen could neither forgive nor forget the insults heaped on her husband in the last months of his life.

The moment it seemed probable that the Prince would recover, Francis Knollys sent Ponsonby a noteworthy letter about HRH's future. He began by saying that it was 'most desirable that the Prince of Wales should occupy himself with some pursuit which would interest him and for which he has a *natural* inclination. Should he not be interested in the work which he undertakes, I should fear that with his disposition he might become irretrievably disgusted with business of every description. Starting from this point of view, and from an intimate knowledge of his character and tastes, I have no hesitation in saying that any scheme for employing His Royal Highness in what you call "Philanthropic Work" should be dismissed from our thoughts . . . The same objection applies to Science and Art . . . Had he any latent taste for this pursuit it would I think have developed itself long since . . . I need hardly tell you that the English nation has from time immemorial been exceedingly jealous of inter-ference by any member of the Royal Family in military affairs . . . I may also add that military affairs are at the present moment in such a state of transition, that it would be very injudicious were His Royal Highness to mix himself up with them.'

It would be much wiser for the Prince to 'lend his attention to Foreign affairs. Royal personages in all ages and of every country, have invariably been attracted by them, and History points out that they afford occupation to even the most indolent Princes. If there is one branch of Public Affairs more than another in which the Prince of Wales has manifested an interest, it is in that of the Foreign Relations of this country.' Knollys therefore suggested 'that all of the Foreign Despatches should be transmitted to him through the Queen and that they should be returned to the Foreign Office through the same channel. Any remarks which he might think proper to append to them, should be considered in the light of advice to Her Majesty, *not* to the Foreign Secretary, and he would thus fill his natural position towards her – a position which since the death of the Prince Consort has been left unoccupied.' Knollys acknowledged that studying despatches was hardly a full-time occupation, but 'a great point will have been gained if he is drawn away, in however slight a degree, from Clubs and Society, and is led, almost insensibly perhaps, to interest himself in the real business of life.'

The best employment of all for HRH 'would be to appoint him the Queen's *permanent* Deputy in Ireland, leaving all *political* matters to the Chief Secretary.' Whatever difficulties there might be, 'the present is the golden moment,' and 'the Queen and the Ministers should come to an immediate decision upon the subject, so that he may find an occupation ready for him on the very day upon which he is able to attend to business.'

Gladstone concurred with most of what 'young Knollys' wrote in his 'very businesslike' letter. 'What we want,' he told Ponsonby, was not to supply HRH 'with the means of filling a certain number of hours,' but to find him 'a central aim and purpose,' to 'mould his mind, and colour his life.' Convinced that 'Society had suffered fearfully in moral tone from the absence of a pure Court,' Gladstone thought that the Prince might inaugurate a nineteenth-century version of King Arthur's Round Table.

In making his Irish proposals Gladstone assumed that they would be acceptable to the Prince. As he told Lord Granville, 'The Duke of Cambridge long ago expressed to me his conviction, which I took to be knowledge,' of the Prince's 'readiness to go to Ireland.' But, in fact, as early as March 1872, Ponsonby warned the Queen that 'the Prince of Wales dislikes any suggestion about Ireland, and would positively refuse to go there officially in any capacity unless urged to do so by Your Majesty.' Nevertheless, 'HRH was very anxious to undertake some occupation' and 'wished to be attached to different offices of the Government so that he might be taught the business of the different departments.'

When the idea was finally abandoned, despite Gladstone's stubborn resistance, the Prince told the Queen that he 'rejoiced' to hear that it had come to nothing, as he had always 'had a very strong aversion to it.' Had he accepted the position of Lord-Lieutenant, he would have become 'the mere shadow of a shade.' It had been argued that the duties involved were easier 'than any connected with the English Government. And yet for seven hundred years English Statesmen have been engaged in this easy task and this present Government has not been wanting in making laws for Ireland, yet we hear of bloodshed and plunder at Belfast for a week, and are compelled to enforce the worst law we have copied from continental nations in gagging the Press in Dublin. I do not mean to criticize these incidents, but they scarcely bear out Mr. Gladstone's opinion on the easy task of ruling Ireland.'

The Queen mistakenly suspected that the Prime Minister's

motives were political. From the moment he learned of his electoral
victory in 1868, he plainly stated, in so far as he was capable of
plain statements, that his mission was 'to pacify Ireland.' She therefore concluded his plans for the Prince were a subtle Liberal plot.
In so thinking, she did less than justice to Gladstone's concern for
her son and the Crown.

Neither the Queen nor her Prime Minister were far behind Pius
IX in proclaiming infallibility. The possibility that they could be
mistaken was not one either of them often entertained. Illuminating
as the dialectical process is supposed to be, the collision of opposite
truths in this particular instance generated more heat than light.
'The priceless opportunity' of finding the Prince of Wales rewarding
work was lost, as also was Gladstone's reputation with the Queen.

Queen Victoria's belief that her son was politically imprudent
may be traced to his support of Denmark against Prussia. Had he
married a German and openly approved the seizure of Schleswig-
Holstein, such partisanship would have passed unnoticed. It was a
misfortune that this crisis occurred when the Prince was only twenty-
two, for he never entirely lived down his reputation of sympathizing
with a country which Britain had betrayed. In the same year he
compounded his error by visiting Garibaldi. That the Prince of
Wales should meet this dangerous revolutionary showed once more
how rash he could be, and increased the Queen's resolve that he
should play no part in politics.

From the moment Garibaldi set foot in England he received a
tremendous welcome. Only four years before, he had conquered
the Kingdom of Naples with his thousand Red Shirts and freed Italy
from a tyranny which Gladstone had denounced as the 'negation
of God erected into a system of government.' Apart from Princess
Alexandra, no foreigner had ever been greeted with such enthusiasm.
He was entertained by Palmerston, met the Archbishop of Canterbury, was received by the Provost and Fellows of Eton in School
Yard, and visited Tennyson at Farringford. The tree he planted
on that occasion still stands in the grounds.

The Queen was gravely displeased by such proceedings, and felt
'half ashamed of being the head of a nation capable of such follies.'
Writing to the Foreign Secretary, Lord Granville, she deeply regretted that 'whatever personal feeling it may have been right to
testify towards a man of remarkable honesty and singleness of
purpose, the members of her Government should have lavished
honours usually reserved for Royalty upon one who openly declares

his objects to be to lead the attacks upon Venice, Rome and Russia, with the Sovereigns of which countries the Government, in her name, profess sentiments of complete friendship and alliance. The Queen thinks that the representatives of these countries might well remonstrate at the unusual adulation shown in official quarters to one professing objects so hostile to their Royal Masters.'

In replying to Her Majesty's reprimand, Granville was forced to admit the truth of her remarks, but humbly advanced 'some countervailing considerations.' Garibaldi, he said, 'has all the qualifications for making him a popular idol in this country. He is of low extraction, he is physically and morally brave, he is a good guerrilla soldier.' He further commended himself to Englishmen by hating the Pope. 'No amount of cold water would have damped the enthusiasm of the middle and lower classes.' To some extent the 'democratic sting' had been taken out of the affair because the aristocracy had joined 'in demonstrations in his favour.' There could be no doubt that his reception would seem offensive and even ridiculous abroad. Nor could it be denied that 'There has been tomfoolery and much vulgarity, but on the whole there has also been much that is honourable to the English character.'

The Queen and her Court were as opposed to popular opinion over Garibaldi's visit as they were in supporting Prussia against Denmark. It would be discourteous to describe Queen Victoria as living in a 'fool's paradise'; suffice it therefore to say that the world as viewed from Osborne or Balmoral was unlikely to embrace the sympathies and enthusiasms of the draymen of Barclay's brewery or the denizens of Pimlico. Possibly the Queen had some inkling of Garibaldi's privately expressed purpose to encourage England to help Denmark.

The Prince of Wales, caught up in the enthusiasm of the moment, visited Garibaldi at Stafford House, the Duke of Sutherland's London residence. 'What do you think of the Prince of Wales and Garibaldi?' Disraeli asked Lady Dorothy Nevill. 'For a quasi-crowned head to call on a subject is strange – and that subject a rebel!' The Queen was horrified to hear of the visit, and complained to Vicky of 'the incredible folly and imprudence of your thoughtless eldest brother going to see him without my knowledge! It has shocked me much and his people are much to blame.'

The day after the visit, Phipps was instructed to send Sir William Knollys a letter expressing a variety of emotions from indignation to incredulity. 'You will easily believe,' he wrote 'that the announcement in *The Times* of this morning of a "visit of the Prince of Wales to Garibaldi," surprised and annoyed the Queen not a little.' It was 'an infraction of the whole system and rules of the Royal Family, who may receive strangers, but do not go to visit them, besides which a visit of this kind by one member of the Royal Family, not only compromises himself, but also the Queen and the country.' These events, said Phipps, 'are great misfortunes and make me quite unhappy.' The affair was doubly unfortunate as recently the 'Queen had been so pleased with all she had heard of the Prince of Wales . . . Then suddenly she sees such an announcement as that in today's papers, without any previous warning or notice, and felt at once hurt and aggrieved. It is impossible to over-rate the importance to each other, and to the whole family, and to the welfare of the nation, of the most cordial understanding between these two Houses, and yet sometimes it seems to me to be risked where the smallest precaution might meet any difficulty.'

General Knollys, in defending the Prince, contrived to suggest he took the matter too lightly. So the Queen decided to write to him herself. She 'was very much shocked' she said, by HRH's action, for which Sir William she felt was much to blame. Consequently she must '*insist* that no step of the *slightest political importance* shall be taken without due consultation with the Queen.' It was decidedly harsh to reproach the Prince and his Household for meeting Garibaldi, when both the Prime Minister and Foreign Secretary had lavishly entertained him.

The day following his momentous visit, the Prince told the Queen in a letter he wrote from Sandringham: 'I had to go to London yesterday for a Duchy of Cornwall Council . . . The Duke of Sutherland having written several times to General Knollys about Garibaldi, offering to bring him here, which was, of course, declined, I agreed with General Knollys that the best plan would be to call at Stafford House *quite privately*.' The Prince felt convinced that had the Queen met him she 'would have been pleased with him, as he is uncharlatanlike.' True, 'his undertakings have been certainly revolutionary, still, he is a patriot, and did not seek his own aggrandisement.' His appearance was noble and dignified, and he had 'such a quiet and gentle way of speaking – especially never of himself – that nobody could fail to be attracted to him.' He had asked a great deal about the Queen, and in reference to Denmark 'said how much he felt for all the brave soldiers who had perished in the war.'

Some days later the Prince wrote again defending his visit. His meeting with Garibaldi had been 'hailed with joy throughout the country.' The unity of Italy, in which he had always believed, was 'the avowed policy' of the Government. As for poor General Knollys, he little deserved the Queen's reproof. 'I fear he feels it very much, as he is not, and cannot be, responsible for my actions. I have now been of age for some time and am *alone* responsible, and am only too happy to bear *any* blame on my shoulders.'

The Queen's fears that Garibaldi might corrupt the allegiance of her subjects happily proved unfounded. But, within a few years of his visit, her throne was seriously threatened from a different quarter. No sooner had the Third French Republic been proclaimed on 4 September 1870, following the news of Napoleon's capitulation at Sedan, than Radicals, such as Charles Bradlaugh, the atheist agitator, Sir Charles Dilke, the Member for Chelsea, and George Odger, Shoemaker, Trade Unionist and disciple of Marx and Swinburne, demanded its instant recognition. Indeed, they went further, suggesting that Britain should follow France's salutary example. On Sunday, 19 September, a meeting was held in Trafalgar Square, during which the 'Marseillaise' was sung, red caps were hoisted on poles, and enthusiasts hailed the coming 'Republic of England.' Soon, Republican Clubs were formed up and down the country, and in April 1871 a Republican demonstration was held in Hyde Park.

Later that year, on 6 November, Sir Charles Dilke delivered a bitter attack upon Monarchy in a speech at Newcastle. What delighted the Radicals in his audience, and outraged the majority of Englishmen, was his claim that 'history and experience show that you cannot have a republic unless you possess at the same time the republican virtues . . . If you can show me a fair chance that a republic here will be free from the political corruption that hangs about the Monarchy, I say, for my part – let it come.'

Dilke's Republicanism owed more to theory than practice. 'To think and even to say that Monarchy in Western Europe is a somewhat cumbersome fiction is not to declare oneself ready to fight against it on a barricade.' Dilke added up the cost of maintaining the Royal Family and said it was not worth the money. He also indulged in mocking Her Majesty's Household, making much play of its more fanciful officials. Was the country really willing to pay for a Lord Grand Falconer, or a Lithographer-in-Ordinary? Once, when he poured scorn on the 'Court Undertaker', a man in the crowd shouted out that he ought to be found more work.

According to Lady Ely, the Queen was so distressed by Dilke's observations that she wept when she read them. Sir Charles's father, Wentworth Dilke, had helped the Prince Consort with the Great Exhibition. Some people said he was too obsequious, but the Queen formed a high opinion of him. He was one of the few people she consented to see soon after Prince Albert's death. At the time of Sir Charles's Newcastle speech, she recalled having met him as a small boy in the grounds of the Crystal Palace and stroking his head. In view of his advocacy of Republicanism, she ruefully remarked that she 'supposed she had stroked it the wrong way.'

Republican sentiment owed much to literary inspiration. Thackeray set the mood in his lectures on 'The Four Georges,' delivered during the Crimean War at fifty pounds a time. It is said that Queen Victoria so bitterly resented their sneering tone, that she refused to let him be buried in Poets' Corner. Certainly his descriptions of her Hanoverian ancestors were not calculated to inspire reverence for the dynasty. In 1870, Charles Bradlaugh, 'The Iconoclast' as he called himself, published a scurrilous pamphlet: 'George, the Prince of Wales, with Recent Contrasts and Coincidences.' Pretending to be unable to see the slightest resemblance between George IV and Prince Albert Edward, he proceeded to make a long list of discreditable similarities. It was alleged that on one occasion, the poor man's Thackeray told a Republican audience that it was his 'earnest desire that the present Prince of Wales should never dishonour this country by becoming its King.'

So serious did Republican clamour appear, that Lord Selborne thought it his duty to warn the Queen of the danger. Her Majesty, while deeply grieved by signs of disloyalty, refused to be held responsible. 'Democratic feeling,' she declared, 'is caused by the fact that the sins of the upper classes are forgiven while the lower classes are punished.'

When the Prince of Wales caught typhoid in November 1871, Republicanism was submerged under a tidal wave of loyalty. It seems virtually certain that he became infected while staying with Lord Londesborough at Scarborough. Lord Chesterfield, a fellow guest, and Charles Blegg, a stable boy who accompanied HRH on this visit, both died of the disease. Lord Londesborough was savagely criticized by the Press for permitting his drains to fall into disrepair. But it was less than just to make him the scapegoat for what was a national shortcoming. As Francis Knollys once remarked, 'There are more stinks in Royal Residences than anywhere else.' At Abergeldie a cesspool connected with a cowshed was found to be seeping into the drinking water, and a well at Sandringham was discovered to be dangerously contaminated. Prince George nearly died of typhoid while on leave there in 1891. As for the drains at Windsor, which killed the Prince Consort, Scarborough was salubrious by comparison.

When the Duke of Richmond learned of the Prince's illness, he told Knollys how dismayed he had been by 'the outrageous speeches' which Radicals had recently been making, and how he hoped and believed that HRH's 'anxious condition' would 'arouse a spirit of loyalty throughout the country.' Lady Paget recalls how during the Tichborne Trial, for which she was fortunate enough to secure a seat, the Lord Chief Justice was handed a printed placard, which he read out in Court. 'It was to the effect that the Prince of Wales had fallen a victim to virulent typhoid,' and was more or less given up for dead.

On 29 November the Queen left Windsor for Wolferton to visit her son. It was the first time she had ever been to Sandringham. 'Dear Alix and Alice met me at the door, the former looking thin and anxious, with tears in her eyes . . . I took off my things and went over to Bertie's room, and was allowed to step in from behind a screen to see him sleeping or dozing. The room was dark and only one lamp burning, so that I could not see him well. He was lying rather flat on his back, breathing very rapidly and loudly.' Inevitably, she was reminded 'so vividly and sadly of my dearest Albert's illness!' She then saw Sir William Jenner, 'who said that the breathing had all along been the one thing that caused anxiety. It was a far more violent attack than my beloved husband's was.' Her Majesty returned to Windsor on 1 December, but a week later, after a telegram from Jenner, made another 'melancholy journey' to Norfolk, which was then in deep snow. 'The Prince,' said Sir William, 'passed a very unquiet night. Temperature risen to 104. Respirations more rapid. Dr Gull and I both very anxious.'

At the height of his fever the Prince was delirious, and seems to have thought he was already King. For hours he talked or sang in several languages. The Queen was dreadfully frightened by 'his clutching at his bed-clothes and seeming to feel for things which were not there.' And the way he gasped for breath she also found 'most distressing'. Once, he took his pillows one by one and threw them about the room. During his fevered ravings he revealed so much that it was thought prudent to discourage Alix from overhearing them. In the looking-glass world of his wandering mind, he concluded she was unfaithful. 'You were my wife,' he told her, 'you are no more – you have broken your vows.'

Letters and telegrams poured into Sandringham recommending an astonishing variety of remedies which even a man in the rudest health could probably not have survived. On 10 December the Queen declared that 'the feeling shown by the whole nation is quite marvellous and most touching and striking,' showing how 'really sound and truly loyal' the people were at heart. The next day, she was woken at five in the morning with a note from Jenner, 'saying dear Bertie had had a very severe spasm, which had alarmed them very much, though it was over now. I had scarcely got the message, before Sir William returned saying there had been another. I saw him at once, and he told me the spasm had been so severe, that at any moment dear Bertie might go off, so that I had better come at once. I hurriedly got up, put on my dressing-gown, and went to the room . . . Poor dear Bertie was lying there breathing heavily, and as if he must choke at any moment.'

But the worst day of all was 13 December. The bell-ringers of St Paul's were summoned to the Cathedral to toll the Prince's death, while the newspapers hurriedly set up their 'In Memoriam' tributes. The Queen dreaded the fourteenth, the day of the month on which Prince Albert had died. As it drew closer, it filled her 'with anxious forebodings and the greatest alarm.' At one moment the Prince's life seemed threatened by 'a most frightful fit of coughing . . . Alice and I said to one another in tears, "There can be no hope." ' For hours on end the Queen sat by her son's bed, holding 'his poor hand, kissing it and stroking his arm. He turned round and looked wildly at me saying, "Who are you?" and then, "It's Mama." "Dear Child," I replied. Later he said, "It is so kind of you to come," which shows he knew me, which was most comforting to me. I sat next to the bed holding his hand, as he seemed dozing. Then once more he said, "It's so kind of you to come," and "Don't sit here for me." '

Lady Macclesfield told Lady Augusta Stanley of the Prince's 'astonishing kind heartedness and consideration' throughout his illness: 'never an unkind thing or word.' Prince Alfred also remarked on his brother's 'wonderful kindness and courtesy and consideration for everyone, even in his wanderings.'

Instead of 14 December, 'the dreadful anniversary,' dawning upon another deathbed, 'it brought the cheering news that dear

Bertie had slept quietly at intervals.' When the Queen visited him after breakfast, he kissed her hand, 'smiling in his usual way, and said, "So kind of you to come; it is the kindest thing you could do." He wanted to talk more, but I would not allow him, and left.' It seemed hardly possible to realize 'that on this *very* day our dear Bertie is getting better instead of worse! How deeply grateful we are for God's mercy!'

The Queen, whose preference was 'more and more for the simplest form of worship,' reluctantly consented, 'health permitting,' to attend a Thanksgiving Service for the recovery of her son. Disliking 'public religious displays,' she declared that the whole effect 'would be spoilt by a long fatiguing service.' Gladstone, who had shown great enthusiasm for the ceremony, was left in no doubt that going to St Paul's was 'MOST *distasteful to her feelings.*' Indeed, she thought it far from certain that the Prince 'would be able to stand the fatigue as he was suffering from his leg and had been ordered *'complete rest.'* Was his life to be sacrificed to satisfy the crowd that he had recovered from his illness?

On the morning of 27 February 1872, the Royal Family gathered at Buckingham Palace for their journey through the City to St Paul's. The Queen noted in her Journal that 'Bertie was very lame and did not look at all well.' She took him by the arm,'for he could only walk very slowly,' and helped him down to the Grand Entrance, where an open State landau was waiting. Fortunately, it stopped raining and the sun came out. Alix sat next to the Queen, and the Prince, with his eldest son on one side and his sister Beatrice on the other, sat opposite. Before the carriage drew out into the yard in front of the Palace, the centre window of the State Room opened, and the Emperor Napoleon and the Empress Eugénie stepped on to the balcony. The fugitive adventurer, who only a few months before had seemed to hold the destiny of Europe in his hands, took off his hat and bowed as the procession disappeared down the Mall.

London went mad with joy, and the Queen forgetting her reservations and 'ifs' and 'buts' was delighted by 'the wonderful enthusiasm and astounding affectionate loyalty shown. The deafening cheers never ceased the whole way and the most wonderful order was preserved. We seemed to be passing through a sea of people . . . I saw the tears in Bertie's eyes and took and pressed his hand! It was a most affecting day.' The service, however, was less to Her Majesty's liking. 'The Cathedral itself is so dull, cold, dreary, and dingy. It so badly lacks decoration and colour.' And, despite her repeated warnings, the prayers and anthems were 'too long.' They returned to the Palace by way of Oxford Street and Marble Arch. 'Even the trees were full of people,' not to mention the roof-tops. 'At Hyde Park Corner there were immense crowds, as down Constitution Hill and outside the Palace, the deafening cheering never ceasing for an instant.' The Prince of Wales returned to Marlborough House to lie exhausted on a sofa. Meanwhile, the Queen, exhilarated by her welcome, 'went upstairs and stepped out on the balcony with Beatrice and my three sons, being loudly cheered.' For the rest of the evening she could think or talk of little else than the 'wonderful demonstration of loyalty and affection, from the very highest to the lowest. Felt tired by all the emotion, but it is a day that can never be forgotten!'

A French secret agent, sent over to England to stir up sedition, reported back disconsolately that there was no chance of a revolution for at least fifty years. The historian, John Richard Green, a remote and ineffectual Republican, regarded the public rejoicing as 'simply ludicrous.' 'I am glad the Prince is better,' he told Matthew Arnold's niece, 'if only that his recovery will deliver us from a deluge of that domestic loyalty which believes the whole question of republicanism solved by the statement that the Queen is an admirable mother and that her son has an attack of typhoid.'

The Poet Laureate added an epilogue to his 'Idylls of the King.' In the course of the poem he described the British Empire as 'a crowned Republic,' with which happy paradox he turned the flank of Dilke, Chamberlain and Bradlaugh. Addressing the Queen, he recalled that unforgettable day:

> 'When pale as yet, and fever-worn, the Prince,
> Who scarce had pluck'd his flickering life again
> From halfway down the shadow of the grave,
> Passed with thee thro' thy people and their love,
> And London roll'd one tide of joy thro' all
> Her trebled millions . . . '

The Sage of Farringford spoke with the nation's voice.

Sir Charles Dilke, during the course of what began as a triumphant tour of the country, suddenly found his audiences growing hostile. Addressing a meeting at Bolton on 30 November 1871, before it was generally realized how ill the Prince was, he could not make himself heard above raucous renderings of 'Rule Britannia' and 'God Save The Queen.' A serious riot ensued during which his life was threatened. Yet only a month before he had been attracting enthusiastic crowds.

Sir Henry Cole, a professional promoter of exhibitions, who had worked with Prince Albert in 1851, sent Knollys a description on 23 June 1872, of a tour he had made of the route the Prince of Wales was to take next day before visiting the South Kensington Museum. 'I have just returned from Bethnal Green. The district is all alive and near the Museum it is a sky of flags and mottoes. I am going to have them collected. "Boots and Shoes fit for the Prince and Princess at democratic prices" is one of them. The simple loyalty of the poor people is a thing which our Botany Bay Chancellor of the Exchequer (Robert Lowe) cannot understand.' On the day itself he hastily scrawled this triumphant message. 'Communism, Republicanism and Citizen Dilke beaten hollow by loyalty thank God.'

In 1882 Dilke recanted his youthful Republicanism, partly, no doubt, because he had changed his mind, but partly in order to reconcile the Queen to his joining the Cabinet. 'There were opinions of political infancy,' he told his constituents, 'which, as one grows older, one might regard as unwise, or might prefer not to have uttered.' He went further and admitted that he had been 'rather scatter-brained' at the time of his Newcastle declaration. However unorthodox his views on Monarchy might be, even the Queen admitted that he was a sound Imperialist. A sign of his mellower view of royalty was that he became a disciple of Seeley's *Expansion of England* after reading the book on the Crown Princess's advice.

Naturally, the Prince of Wales resented criticism of the Queen, attacks upon himself, and attempts to withhold grants from his children. But that did not prevent him from seeking the friendship of his opponents. Some people thought he was almost too eager to propitiate Radicals, and too free with invitations to extremists. Even Knollys, whose instincts were 'wholly liberal,' doubted the wisdom of his meeting Michael Davitt, the Fenian leader, who in 1870 was sentenced to fifteen years' penal servitude for treason, and who supported Henry George's proposals to nationalize land. 'I am all for HRH meeting men of the most advanced opinions, but I think the line ought to be drawn at Davitt . . . I should be sorry to see the Prince trying to imitate Philippe Egalité.' As the Queen became increasingly hostile to liberals of all persuasions, and particularly those who had spoken ill of Monarchy, the Prince's unfailing courtesy towards them prevented them becoming dangerously antagonistic towards the Royal Family.

Sir Charles Dilke became the most intimate of the Prince of Wales's Radical friends. They first met at a dinner given by Lord Fife in March 1880, shortly before Dilke became Under-Secretary for Foreign Affairs in Gladstone's Second Ministry. 'On 4 March I received a note from Lord Fife,' wrote Dilke describing the encounter, 'asking me to dine with him on Friday, the 12th, to meet the Prince of Wales at the Prince's wish. The note was of such a character that it left no choice. When the dinner came off it turned out well. The Prince laid himself out to be pleasant, and talked to me nearly all the evening – chiefly about French politics and the Greek question.' HRH cultivated Sir Charles, partly because he was prepared to talk freely about foreign affairs, partly because of 'a genuine social affinity,' and partly from 'a perverse desire to know those of whom his mother disapproved.' In fact, they had much in common. They were both friends of Gambetta, who, the Prince told Wilfrid Blunt, had half converted him to Republicanism, they both believed in entente with France, they were both ardent Imperialists, and both wanted to see the Army and Navy reformed.

In 1882, when Gladstone reconstructed his Ministry after resigning as Chancellor of the Exchequer, a post he had combined with that of Prime Minister, the Prince did everything in his power to secure Sir Charles a seat in the Cabinet. In November, he invited both Dilke and Chamberlain to Sandringham to discuss Radical representation in the Government. Gladstone was most anxious to promote Dilke, whom he regarded as his likely successor. But the problem was to overcome the Queen's objection to associating with a declared republican. Like many rich people she was obsessed by imaginary poverty, and deeply resented being told by this impudent baronet that she was sufficiently prosperous to support her own children. After protracted negotiations in which Gladstone shuffled and reshuffled his Ministerial pack, Dilke was appointed President of the Local Government Board, in place of John Dodson.

The Prince played an important part in these proceedings. On 18 December, Knollys wrote to Ponsonby saying that HRH 'hears confidentially that Mr Gladstone will not force, or rather ask Mr Dodson to change his office, whereby the ministerial arrangements might be effected. HRH thinks this is a thousand pities as he is afraid serious complications may arise if it is not done. He is very anxious you should do your best to endeavour to get Mr Gladstone to give way on this point.'

Ponsonby replied that if it was proposed that he should persuade

Gladstone to force Dodson to change, it 'would be marked inter-ference. The Queen can object to any submitted arrangements but I think Ministers would dislike her proposing to force any of them to change office, or even ask them to do so.' Knollys explained that what the Prince of Wales had in mind was 'that the Queen might *suggest* to Mr Gladstone that Mr Dodson should be *invited*, for the sake of facilitating matters, to move to the Duchy of Lancaster.' In a letter headed 'Secret', Ponsonby told Knollys that 'the Dodson alternative has been suggested to the Prime Minister. The Prince of Wales's knowledge of what is going on privately makes his hints most valuable.' The problem was resolved on 23 December by Dodson agreeing to place himself in Gladstone's hands. 'I know that I have to thank His Royal Highness,' wrote Dilke, 'for a sugges-tion which has been followed out.' The Prince's intervention, in Ponsonby's phrase, proved 'opportune and important.'

When Dilke fell into political and social disgrace, the Prince of Wales remained one of his few rough-weather friends. The moment he became King he readmitted him to Court, and, as soon as the Liberals returned to power in 1905, he pressed Campbell-Bannerman to include him in his Cabinet. It is said that he only ceased to urge his claims when C-B declined to form a Government if the King insisted upon its including Sir Charles.

The most dramatic of the Prince's encounters with Radicalism took place at Birmingham on 3 November 1874. Before visiting the city he stayed with Lord Aylesford at Packington. The Mayor was Joseph Chamberlain, who made 'municipal politics the stirrup by which he mounted to the saddle.' Few other men in so short a time have exercised so great an influence on British politics. He began his career as a Radical and ended a Tory Imperialist. By abandoning Gladstone over Home Rule he split the Liberals, and then almost destroyed the Conservative Party by supporting Tariff Reform. But, as Winston Churchill wrote of him: 'No one ever in our modern history made so able an appeal to the ill-used, left-out millions.' From his entry into politics in 1870 until 1906, when a stroke all but ended his career, his word was law. 'In him – whether extreme Radical or extreme Jingo, Free Trader or Protectionist; the gal-vanizer of Liberalism or its destroyer; the colleague of Mr Gladstone or his most deadly opponent; alike in days of peace or war – the citizens of Birmingham saw only their Chief.'

Nobody in 1874 was sure how the Mayor of Birmingham would receive his Royal guests. At the time the city was a notorious strong-

hold of Radicalism, and Chamberlain had made no secret of his
Republican sympathies. Some people thought he would refuse to
shake hands with the Prince. Naturally, HRH felt apprehensive
as he stepped into the den of the 'Birmingham Lion,' while all
England waited to see what would happen. But he was immediately
reassured by seeing his host wearing a tall hat and frock coat, for
no man so ceremoniously dressed could intend mischief, even if he
sported a red camellia in his button-hole. Chamberlain, in proposing
the health of the Prince and Princess of Wales, after a luncheon in
the Town Hall, told the assembled Aldermen and citizens that
'Here in England the throne is recognized and respected as the
symbol of all constituted authority and settled government.'

Ponsonby told his mother how the Court at Balmoral watched to
see 'how Mr Chamberlain the ultra radical Mayor of Birmingham
would receive the Prince of Wales. It seems to have been most
successful and the speeches made by the Mayor were far better
than any I have read on so trite a subject as Royalty. He welcomed
them with dignity and independence.' Never again was a Republican
sentiment heard from Chamberlain's lips. Sir John Tenniel represented the celebrated meeting in a *Punch* cartoon. Chamberlain
was portrayed as a grinning lion, kneeling before the Princess and
offering her a paw. Behind his back was hidden a copy of the
Fortnightly Review A caption congratulated him on concealing
his 'red republican claws and teeth.'

When Chamberlain later became Colonial Secretary in Lord
Salisbury's Third Cabinet, the Queen rather enjoyed having him
to dine and sleep. Although 'always respectful, he never hesitated
to state his opinion. She felt it was like talking to a wild man who
had been tamed.'

Once, when the Prince and Princess were travelling to Scotland,
their train stopped at Sheffield, and somebody told them that Mr
Mundella, the Radical member for the borough, chanced to be on
the platform. Being well known for his savage attacks on Monarchy,
he was amazed to receive a message from HRH inviting him to his
carriage. After introducing him to the Princess, the Prince asked him
to tell the good people of Sheffield how sorry they were not to be able
to break their journey and spend a few days in the town. 'My dear
Mr Mundella,' he continued with the most winning courtesy, 'we
have always looked back with the greatest pleasure to the loyal and
warm-hearted welcome we received when we last visited Sheffield.'
Mundella was so enchanted by the cordiality of his reception that he

addressed his constituents that evening in these words. 'I have been commissioned by Their Royal Highnesses, the Prince and Princess of Wales, to communicate to you the following gracious message.' And he went on to tell them of his conversation with the Prince in the royal train.

The Prince's Liberal sympathies stopped short of socialism. Lady Warwick, an improbable convert to the faith, admitted she had never succeeded in arousing his interest in what to her was an 'all-absorbing subject.' He listened patiently enough to her philanthropic proposals but objected to any suggestion of levelling down. Summarizing Burke's *Reflections* in a sentence, he insisted that 'Society grows, it is not made.' Nevertheless, he remained unfailingly genial to those whose political creed he found distasteful.

When Gladstone resigned in June 1885, after being defeated on a budget amendment moved by Hicks Beach, a prolonged crisis ensued, during which the Prince of Wales took a bold initiative. As the constituencies were being redistributed at that very moment, in accordance with the Parliamentary Reform Act of the previous year, it was considered impracticable to resolve the issue by holding a General Election. Consequently, only two possibilities remained. Lord Salisbury must agree to form a Conservative Government with a minority in the Commons, or Gladstone must carry on despite his defeat. The intricate negotiations which ensued were complicated by the Queen's reluctance to leave Scotland and return south. 'The inconvenience of Her Majesty's being at Balmoral will be very great,' wrote Hamilton in his diary.

The Queen received Gladstone's telegram tendering his resignation after luncheon on 9 June. She immediately replied that she would await his promised letter, 'but would be ready to receive him to expedite matters.' Ponsonby was in London at the time, so his Assistant Secretary, Captain Bigge, telegraphed to tell him that 'the Queen expects Mr Gladstone, or, if he is not able, a deputy to come here. The Queen feels tired and wishes to benefit as much as possible from staying here, especially with so much in prospect. On account of Ascot, it would be almost impossible to reach Windsor before 20th.' The Prime Minister proved unwilling to make the journey to Balmoral, having nothing to add to his letter of resignation, and a great deal to do in London. 'Should my opinion be required,' he told the Queen, knowing how little she valued it, 'I believe I could give it best from hence.'

Hamilton, who knew how anxious the Prince was for news, wrote

Knollys a letter from Downing Street on the evening of 9 June. After explaining the reasons for Gladstone's resignation, he said that he 'greatly hoped that the Queen may be induced to accelerate her journey southwards. Without Her Majesty's presence, the political crisis cannot be tided over. I say nothing of the public inconvenience which delay will involve; but I think there will be strong feeling in the country if Her Majesty does not come within easy reach at this moment, and therefore in the interests of the Sovereign herself, I hope that notwithstanding the personal inconvenience, she may be inclined to leave Balmoral earlier than she intended.'

The next day, the Queen wrote to Gladstone, promising 'to accelerate her return' as much as she could but stressing 'the impossibility of her hurrying to Windsor.' 'The Queen declines to come down from Balmoral,' noted Hamilton in his diary on Wednesday, 10 June. 'Many disagreeable things will, I fear, be said about her, and not without reason. She is the constitutional instrument whereby alone there can be a transfer of political power; and if that instrument is not ready at hand, it is not unnatural to ask what is the use of it?'

Lord Bridport, who was in waiting at Balmoral, was instructed by Her Majesty to telegraph Ponsonby on the evening of 10 June to say that she was 'not in a state to be hurried. Has nowhere to go but Windsor where both noise and public would be dreadful. (It was Ascot Week). I am desired to ask you also to show this to the Prince of Wales.' Instead of supporting her, as she obviously expected, HRH begged her to return at once. 'In present grave ministerial crisis your presence near London earnestly desired unless you do not accept Government's resignation. Fear your position as Sovereign might be weakened by your absence. Forgive my saying this but universal feeling is so strong I could not help telegraphing.'

The Queen, shaken by her son's outspoken warning, told him she intended returning as soon as she could, 'but it is quite impossible for me to start at a moment's notice, and I must also think of my own health which is far from strong, and I must save myself as much as possible for all. Having to go to Windsor with all the gay parties round would be most trying for me.' Gladstone, who was shown a copy of the Prince's telegram, thought it 'eminently judicious' and was 'very glad, for the reasons His Royal Highness himself gave, that it was sent. The Ascot reason, were it known, would not weigh with the public. While respecting any feeling of Her Majesty in regard to that festival, they would argue that Windsor was not the only Royal Palace in the South.'

The day after the Queen received the Prince's telegram, she wrote Gladstone a fuller explanation than he had previously been vouchsafed of the circumstances which prevented her leaving Balmoral. 'With respect to the Queen's return south, she must observe first, that the Railway authorities, unless *previously* warned, do *not* consider it *safe* for her to start without some days' notice. Secondly, that the Queen is a lady nearer seventy than sixty, whose health and strength have been most severely taxed during the forty-eight years of her arduous reign, and that she is quite unable to rush about as a younger person and a man could do. And lastly it is extremely inconvenient and unpleasant from the noise and great crowds at Windsor during the Ascot Week for her to be there, and for twenty-four years the Queen has carefully avoided being there at that time. However, if she finds it necessary, the Queen will return early next week to Windsor.'

Gladstone was not persuaded by the Queen's rationalizations. He knew that she seldom appealed in vain to some authority or other, from the accommodating Dr Jenner to the Station Master at Ballater, whose professional opinions suspiciously resembled her own. Knowing that she could always find somebody to advise her to do whatever she wanted, Gladstone remained convinced that it was not beyond the resources of the London and North Eastern Railway to lay on a special train for the Queen at a few hours' notice. How simply it could be done, provided the will existed, was shown by Colonel Brabazon's brief encounter with the Station Master at Aldershot. 'Where is the London twain?' he once enquired. 'It has gone, Colonel.' 'Gone! Bwing another.'

On 12 June, Hamilton noted in his diary: 'Her Majesty does not appear to be likely to arrive for a whole week, notwithstanding the strong hints she has received from various quarters, and the timely representation of the Prince of Wales, that her continued absence would weaken the position of the throne . . . Never did a Sovereign throw away such a chance. No more popular or graceful act could have been done than if she had ordered her special train the moment she heard of the crisis and come straight to London.' When she finally 'hastened her journey a little,' returning to Windsor on 17 June, she gave it out 'that Ministerial crises must not happen again in Ascot weeks during Balmoral times.'

Before coming south, the Queen wrote to Gladstone, in what she described as 'very civil terms,' offering him a Peerage, 'as a mark of her recognition of his long and distinguished services.' Gladstone replied that he was deeply touched by Her Majesty's 'most generous letter,' and 'prized every word of it.' Nevertheless, he felt obliged to decline the gracious offer it contained, believing that any services he might still be able to render, required him to stay in the House of Commons. But, he told Lord Granville, he was so moved as to be 'almost upset' by the Queen's graciousness. 'It must have cost her much to write, and it is really a pearl of great price.'

Knowing that HRH had been foremost in advocating honours for the Prime Minister, Hamilton wrote Knollys a letter telling him 'that Mr Gladstone has been beyond measure gratified by the offer which the Queen has so graciously made to him; and, though, in conformity with a fixed resolve to take nothing himself, Mr Gladstone feels precluded from accepting that offer, the terms of the Queen's letter are very precious to him and have greatly moved him. What he feels especially is the generosity of Her Majesty. He knows very well that during the last five years he has unfortunately been obliged to do things which have not wholly commended themselves to Her Majesty; but of all the matters distasteful to himself none have been so great as those in which he has at times (and only at times) found himself to be differing from Her Majesty, for whom his regard and dutiful affection have always been very great and will I know always continue so.' Despite rejecting a Peerage, Gladstone intimated to the Prince, through Hamilton, that he would not be averse to the Garter. But, like so many of his suggestions, it did not find favour with the Queen.

On 24 June the retiring Ministers went down to Windsor. The Queen noted in her Journal that Bertie 'came to be with me during the Council, and lunched with us.' The members of the new Government were sworn in that afternoon in the Green Drawing-Room. 'Saw Lord Salisbury in Albert's room . . . Bertie left again, having kindly spent the whole afternoon at Windsor, which was the greatest help to me.' The Prince's part in the Ministerial crisis of 1885 was only a minor one, but at least the Queen welcomed his help.

In 1892 the Prince played a more prominent role by persuading Lord Rosebery to become Foreign Secretary in Gladstone's Fourth Ministry. As a result of the General Election held that summer, the Liberals returned to power with a small majority, pledged to Irish self-government. The political landscape had been transformed by Gladstone's conversion six years before to Home Rule. In the days of

Disraeli, the two parties had been distinguished by political principles, rather than social divisions:

'Beneath each banner proud to stand,
Looked up the noblest of the land.'

The Dukes of Argyll, Bedford, Devonshire and Westminster more
than matched their Tory opponents in power, prestige and wealth.
But most Liberal peers supported Union and broke with Gladstone
in 1886.

Forced to turn for support to the back streets of Glasgow and
Cardiff, Gladstone provides one of the few instances in history of a
statesman becoming progressively more radical with the passing
years. In the age of Melbourne, Macaulay had called him 'the
rising hope of the stern, unbending Tories,' but by the end of his
political career he had become 'a dangerous old fanatic' – the
description was that of his Sovereign. Writing to Ponsonby from
Balmoral on 4 June, 1892, the Queen said that 'the idea of a deluded
excited man of 82 trying to govern England and her vast Empire
with the miserable democrats under him is quite ludicrous. It is
like a bad joke!' A few days later she wrote: 'The Queen, as Sir
Henry will easily believe, is much distressed at the prospect of all the
trouble and great anxiety for the *safety* of the *country* and Empire
which these most unfortunate elections have brought about.'
Dispensing with that impartiality it was her duty to adopt, she
complained of having 'that dangerous old fanatic thrust down her
throat.' Lord Salisbury sympathized deeply with her feelings and
agreed that Gladstone's 'revolutionary appeal to the jealousy of the
poor' would 'do much harm.'

Trusting so little in the Prime Minister, the Queen resolved to
have Rosebery as Foreign Secretary. However unsound his politics
might be, he was a dependable Imperialist. During the course of the
election, Rosebery 'dreadfully disappointed and shocked' the Queen
by a speech he delivered at Edinburgh. In it, he attacked Lord
Salisbury unmercifully, and his sentiments were 'radical to a degree
to be almost communistic.' The trouble, she suspected, was that
Lady Rosebery, who had died in 1890, was 'not there to keep him
back.'

When it became clear that the Liberals had won a majority, the
Queen told Ponsonby to let Gladstone know that she would 'insist'
upon Rosebery as Foreign Secretary. 'Sir Henry may say that Lord

Rosebery is necessary to quiet the alarm of the Foreign Powers who are beginning to intrigue right and left against us, and Sir Henry may foreshadow that Mr G will find the Queen very determined and firm on *all* that *concerns* the *honour, dignity and safety* of the *vast Empire* confided to her care and which she wishes to hand down unimpaired to her children and their children's children.' Earlier she had suggested that 'Sir H who knows all these people well, could in an indirect manner' let them know that the Queen 'will *resist any* attempt' to change the foreign policy of Lord Salisbury's Government, 'to abandon our obligations towards Egypt, and any truckling to France or Russia.'

Gladstone, in fact, agreed with the Queen that Rosebery should go to the Foreign Office. The problem was to persuade him to accept. For several months he had threatened to retire from public life once the election was over. His ambitions, he said, were buried with his wife, he was plagued by insomnia, and craved solitude. What he did not say, except to a few close friends, was that Gladstone had offended him by confiding too much in Morley, and Mrs Gladstone by failing to mind her business. Fortune smiled so favourably upon Rosebery that there was something about him of the spoiled child. As William Cory wrote in one of his Eton reports, he likes 'the palm without the dust.'

As early as 13 June, before Parliament was dissolved, Rosebery's friend Edward Hamilton tried to persuade him to give up thoughts of retiring, arguing that to do so would be to desert Gladstone at the close of his career, might damage the Party irreparably, and could brand him as a traitor. He even ventured to suggest that Lady Rosebery would not have wished him to abandon politics. 'Edward Hamilton came down and dined,' wrote Rosebery in his diary, 'in a high and mighty friendly fury.' On returning to London, Hamilton failed to convince Gladstone that Rosebery proposed to retire. 'Mr G pooh-poohed the idea of his withdrawal from public life regarding him as too deeply committed.' Even the longest serving Prime Ministers have little experience of colleagues rejecting high office.

The moment the Liberals won the election, Rosebery set off in a yacht on a cruise round the West Coast of Scotland, thus preventing anyone reaching him. Earlier in the month, as the results became known, he had taken malicious pleasure in referring to '*your* victory,' or '*your* defeat.' It looked as if he might be as hard to handle as a *prima donna* refusing to go on stage. On 21 July, Hamilton wrote to

Ponsonby saying he was by 'no means sure' that Rosebery would accept the post of Foreign Secretary, and enquiring whether the Queen might write to him 'insisting on his taking the Foreign Office.'

The Queen told Ponsonby that she 'could not personally *communicate* with Lord Rosebery but indirectly something might be done through the Prince of Wales.' Sir Henry, somewhat astonished at the proposal, nevertheless replied that he thought it a 'very good one, as the Prince of Wales is a personal friend of his.'

On 31 July Rosebery formally wrote to Gladstone saying that he had no wish for office. The eighteen months he had spent in seclusion since his wife's death, convinced him that he was not intended for public life. On receiving this letter, Gladstone complained that he had never been treated so badly before. In fact, having disregarded all preliminary warnings, he had only himself to blame for this 'sudden' desertion.

On 7 August, the Prince of Wales, who was staying with Sir Alan Young at Cowes, received a letter from Knollys to say that Lord Rosebery would join the Government. The Prince replied as follows:

7 August 1892.   RYS *Aline*, Cowes.
My dear Francis,
    Thanks for your letter received this afternoon by messenger. I am indeed glad to find it is all right about Rosebery, but I wonder why he held out so long. There is no doubt he hates "Home Rule." He would not be a sensible man if he did not – but for the sake of our Foreign Relations it is most essential he should be Foreign Secretary and I only hope he will have a free hand! The Russians and French are behaving infamously to us – the moment they knew the GOM had a majority! Naturally the Queen who hates the change of Government will not give Mr G any help to form his Government but she wishes for R.
                         I am, Yrs v. sincerely,
                                    A.E.

Soon it transpired that the rejoicing was premature. After paying a short, solitary visit to Paris, 'to clear the cobwebs out of his brain,' Rosebery called on Gladstone at Carlton Gardens on 11 August. His nerves, he said, were unstrung, he had sleepless nights, and he found sustained work impossible. For three-quarters of an hour Gladstone unavailingly begged him to reconsider his decision.

On hearing what had happened, the Prince decided to write to

Rosebery himself. 'Nobody,' he told him on 14 August, 'dislikes more than I do to interfere in matters which not only do not concern me, but which might be looked upon as indiscreet; but we are such old friends and have so freely talked on so many subjects, especially regarding politics, you will, I am sure, forgive my writing to say with what deep concern I have learnt from public rumour that you are disinclined to accept office in Mr Gladstone's Government. That you may differ from him in many salient points I can easily understand and appreciate; but I, for one, who have my country's interest so deeply at heart, would deeply deplore if you were unwilling to accept the post of Secretary of State for Foreign Affairs – a post which you have filled before with such great ability, which has not only been appreciated at home, but by all foreign countries. Though I know that the Queen has no desire to press you to accept this post, which for reasons best known to yourself you are disinclined to take, still I know how much she wishes for it ... Let me therefore implore of you to accept office (if Mr Gladstone will give you a free hand in foreign affairs and not bind you to agree with him in *all* his home measures) for the Queen's sake and for that of our great Empire! Forgive me bothering you, my dear Rosebery; but I should not write so strongly if I did not feel the grave importance of your accepting office in the present serious political crisis.'

Gladstone finally resolved the problem by telling Rosebery that he proposed to submit his name to the Queen that very day 'in conformity with her wish.' Like some hesitant swimmer dreading to take the plunge, he was pushed into the water to help him make up his mind. On receiving the Prime Minister's note, Rosebery sent for Hamilton and said he could no longer resist the pressure being put upon him. He particularly mentioned the Prince of Wales's letter. In case he should change his mind, Hamilton persuaded him to draft a telegram to Gladstone. It consisted of three words: 'So be it.'

Gladstone's principal reason for remaining so long in politics was to pacify Ireland. In 1893, after eighty-five sittings, the House of Commons gave the Home Rule Bill its third reading. But the Lords rejected it by a majority of three hundred and seventy-eight, Gladstone's former colleague, the Duke of Devonshire, foremost amongst the measure's opponents. The Prime Minister wished to dissolve Parliament and appeal to the country, but found little support for the proposal. When it became clear that he could not seek a mandate to muzzle the Upper House, he toyed with thoughts of retirement. He was eighty-five, his sight and hearing were failing, and he could agree with his colleagues over neither his strategy for dissolution, nor the need for increasing naval expenditure. The Admiralty, confronted by revolutionary changes in battleship design, and growing international rivalries, wanted an additional three million pounds on the estimates. But Gladstone, believing that 'Peace' and 'Retrenchment' were the very essence of Liberalism, dismissed their unanswerable arguments as professional scare-mongering.

After a stormy Cabinet meeting held on 9 January 1894, Gladstone announced he was leaving for Biarritz. Probably he cherished the hope that he was indispensable and that his colleagues would implore him to come back on his own terms. There was a real danger that his career might end in absurdity. On 30 January, the *Pall Mall Gazette* announced that Gladstone proposed to resign at the end of the session on account of failing health, which provoked him to publish a disingenuous denial.

Hamilton told Knollys that he thought 'the contradiction most unnecessarily diffuse and sailing very near the wind of veracity. Altogether it is a most horrible mess. I should not be surprised even now if he changes his mind and makes some excuse for hanging on. But what a position! How can any of his colleagues continue to regard him with any real respect after all his solemn vows that nothing would induce him to agree to the Admiralty proposals? It is I fear a most pitiful end to a great career; and it looks as if one's worst apprehensions about his exit will be realized. I am convinced in my own mind that for the sake of his own reputation he ought most certainly to go now; and as for the party, what does it matter whether they have to face the difficulties of getting on without him immediately or a few months hence? I am going I think to make one final appeal to Biarritz.'

Soon after Gladstone returned to 10 Downing Street he prepared the Queen for his resignation in such a mysterious manner that for a time she thought he was discussing the possibility of dissolving Parliament. On 28 February, he wrote to the Prince of Wales, with 'Her Majesty's permission' to convey 'in the strictest confidence an announcement which it would grieve me if you were in the first instance to gather from the public press.' He proposed, he said, to tender his resignation to Her Majesty in the near future, 'on the ground of physical difficulties which have lately become the subject of observation and discussion . . . I desire to convey, on my own and my wife's part, our fervent thanks for the unbounded kindness which we have at all times received from Your Royal Highness and not less from the beloved Princess of Wales. The devotion of an old man is little worth: but if at any time there is the smallest service which ... Your Royal Highness may believe me capable of rendering I shall remain as much at your command as if I had continued to be an active and responsible servant of the Queen.'

'Pray accept my warmest thanks,' replied the Prince, 'for the kind letter which I have received from you today – and for giving me after the Queen the important information that you are desirous of tendering your resignation of the Premiership. After your long and valuable services to the Crown and country, I can well understand that you need the repose to which you are so fully entitled.' Nevertheless, 'Your many friends and admirers amongst which I hope I may be counted ... naturally deeply regret the step you are about to take. Both the Princess and myself are deeply touched by the kind words expressed by you concerning us. We have for a long number of years greatly valued your friendship and that of Mrs Gladstone ... Let me also assure you how greatly we value your advice on all occasions as no one in this Realm has greater knowledge and experience in public affairs than yourself, and we should never hesitate to ask it.'

On 2 March, Gladstone stayed the night at Windsor. Next morning, he handed the Queen his formal letter of resignation. No other Statesman of her reign had been Prime Minister four times or a Privy Councillor for more than half a century. But not one syllable of thanks did he receive for long and faithful service. She merely told him that she trusted he would 'be able to enjoy peace and quiet' after so many years 'of arduous labour and responsibility.' Having read her letter, he handed it to Sir Algernon West and said with a sigh: 'And this is the only record that will remain of fifty-one years as a Privy Councillor.' The sole token of his Sovereign's gratitude with which Gladstone left Windsor was a twopenny-halfpenny photograph delivered by a footman. Such heartlessness haunted his dreams, and he said that the Queen had parted with him as if she were settling a long-standing tradesman's bill. The Prince of Wales later told Margot Asquith that 'he thought it was wrong of his mother not to have said something gracious to such an old and distinguished public servant when he bade her a permanent farewell.'

The Prince of Wales's friendship with the Gladstones began when he was a child. Their eldest boy, Willie, was one of the Etonians selected by the Head Master as a companion for the Prince, and Mrs Gladstone's sister, Mary Glynne, married Lady Lyttelton's son. The great statesman made some curious concessions to Sandringham ways, such as playing whist for sixpences, tentatively puffing Havanas, and singing 'Camptown Races' while accompanying himself on a banjo: the incongruity of which so appealed to the Prince and Princess that they demanded more 'encores' than its musical merit warranted.

When Lord Ronald Gower visited Hawarden in 1896, Gladstone told him that 'no royalty he had ever met – but my experience is limited – had such charm and tact as the Prince of Wales.' Throughout his later life, he was sent a 'munificent supply' of game from the Sandringham larder, a kindness he once repaid by giving the Prince a tract he had written. One would have needed to be a devoted disciple of the great statesman to suppose that he lost by the exchange. The Prince seldom missed an opportunity to try to improve Gladstone's standing with the Queen. Two days after Princess Alice's death in 1878, HRH sent Ponsonby a consoling letter from the great man, which he thought would touch his mother. 'His Royal Highness ventures to hope,' wrote Knollys, on the Prince's behalf, 'that at this sad moment all rancour will be forgotten, and that the Queen will kindly allow you to write an acknowledge-ment to Mr Gladstone of the message which he has sent to Her Majesty through His Royal Highness.' In the margin of Knollys' letter Ponsonby noted: 'I did. H.P.'

When the Queen in the following year refused to ask Gladstone to Prince Arthur's wedding, HRH did everything in his power to persuade her to change her mind. 'The Prince of Wales,' noted Hamilton in his diary, 'who always does the right thing, has asked Mr and Mrs G to dine on Wednesday next, which I think has much pleased them. It is always to be remembered to the credit of HRH that, in connexion with that overt slight of the Queen in not bidding Mr G to the Duke of Connaught's Wedding, the Prince did his utmost to get Mr G included in the list of Royal guests.'

In 1880, the Queen tried to avoid inviting Gladstone to form a Government and the Prince of Wales was severely snubbed for his efforts to reconcile her to the inevitable. In March of that year, Lord Beaconsfield, encouraged by what turned out to be misleading by-election victories at Liverpool and Southwark, decided to go to the country. Gladstone, having retired from the Liberal leadership

after his defeat in 1874, delivered a devastating series of speeches
in Midlothian, which did much to win the election, as well as to
topple Lord Dalkeith, the sitting Conservative member, who
floundered helplessly in a torrent of thrilling rhetoric. In speech after
speech, Gladstone denounced Lord Beaconsfield and his policies
with righteous indignation. From Land's End to the Shetlands
people flocked to Midlothian 'to hear the magic voice, to watch the
eagle eye, to enjoy the superb gestures and to share in what Beaconsfield called a "pilgrimage of passion." ' Even some Liberals believed
he was inciting class war when he told a meeting at West Calder,
'I am sorry to say we cannot reckon upon the aristocracy! We
cannot reckon on what is called the landed interests! We cannot
reckon upon the clergy of the Established Church either in England
or in Scotland! We cannot reckon upon the wealth of the country,
nor upon the rank of the country! In the main these powers are
against us. We must set them down among our most determined
foes! But, gentlemen, above all these, and behind all these, there is
the nation itself. The nation is a power hard to arouse, but when
roused harder still and more hopeless to resist.'

Nobody found his triumph more distasteful and disturbing than
the Queen, who believed he was debasing politics by truckling to
the multitude. Nor was she pleased when he was more rapturously
acclaimed than she was. His whole conduct since 1876 had consisted
'of violent, passionate invective against and abuse of Lord
Beaconsfield.' Ponsonby tried to persuade her that Gladstone was
'loyal and devoted' at heart, only to be told he was nothing of the
kind. He had shown 'a most unpardonable and disgraceful spite
and personal hatred' towards a Minister 'who had restored England
to the position she had lost' when the Liberals were last in Government. His 'only excuse is – that he is not quite sane.'

When it became clear that the Tories had lost the election, the
Queen made it known that she had no intention of inviting Gladstone to form an administration. After all, he was no longer the
leader of his party. Besides, she would 'sooner abdicate than send
for or have any communication with that half-mad firebrand who would
soon ruin everything and be a Dictator. Others but herself may
submit to his democratic rule, but not the Queen.' The extravagance
of such language owed much to the conviction that Gladstone had
retired. Her Majesty's categorical refusal to contemplate him as
Prime Minister tacitly assumed that he did not aspire to office. The
moment it became clear he was resolved to head the Government,

she ate her brave words and sent for the 'People's' William.'

On 10 April 1880, the Queen 'commanded' Ponsonby to write to the Prince of Wales outlining her opinions 'on the present state of affairs . . . Mr Gladstone it is known will not desire office so that the choice of a Prime Minister lies between Lord Granville and Lord Hartington, and of these two the Queen is rather inclined to the latter, but will listen to what Lord Beaconsfield may suggest on the subject before making any decision.' The fact that Ponsonby had been instructed to inform rather than consult HRH, led Knollys to observe: 'People seem to think it odd that the Queen does not send for the P of W in a crisis like the present, so as to talk matters over with him.' But, whether or not his opinion was invited, the Prince proffered it. Assuming Gladstone would refuse an invitation to form a Government, he desired Knollys to write to Ponsonby expressing 'his earnest hope that the Queen will if possible send for Lord Hartington. HRH had a long conversation with him last night and he feels sure that Her Majesty would find his sentiments most proper and sensible. The Prince of Wales thinks that Mr Gladstone's supporters are more violent and noisy than powerful and numerous.'

Ponsonby replied that the matter was 'too important for private secretaries to correspond on' and suggested it would 'be better if HRH wrote himself to the Queen.' Acting on this advice, the Prince ventured to suggest to his 'Dearest Mama' that she should send for Lord Hartington, 'the most moderate man of the Liberal Party . . . I need hardly say that, if you wish to see me at any time, I am always at your disposal, and if I can be of the slightest use in lightening the task which is before you, or give you any assistance, or see anybody for you, I shall only be too happy to do so.'

The Queen, after consulting Lord Beaconsfield, sent for Hartington, not without reservations. His nature was too indolent and easygoing, and she had never approved of his long-standing liaison with the Duchess of Manchester. Hartington established two things which transformed the situation: Gladstone would be willing to form a Government but refused to serve under a colleague. The Prince now sought to persuade the Queen to send for him. The more she delayed, the more it might seem that she flouted the will of her people. In resisting popular clamour the Crown would be dragged into politics. It would be so much wiser to take the initiative than to have it forced upon her. One trouble was that Prince Leopold, a zealous and partisan Tory, was poisoning Her Majesty's mind against the former Liberal leader. 'The Prince of Wales feels sure,' Knollys told Granville, 'that if the Queen would only look upon Mr Gladstone as a friend instead of as the enemy of Her Majesty and the Royal Family, which Prince Leopold deliberately delights in persuading her he is, she will find him all she could wish.'

After three long conversations with Hartington at the Turf Club, HRH told Ponsonby that from all he heard he was 'strongly of the opinion that the Queen should send for Mr Gladstone.' According to Hartington, 'who saw Mr G yesterday,' nothing could have been nicer 'than the way the latter spoke of the Queen – how much he felt for her in the difficult position she was placed in, and having to part with her present Ministers, in whom she had so much confidence. From what H told me, Mr G will I am sure do all he can to meet the Queen's wishes and be conciliatory in every possible way.'

In the end, Her Majesty acknowledged she had no alternative but to send for Gladstone. But just as in ancient times the messenger who brought bad news was put to death, so now the Prince was denounced for offering good advice. 'He has *no* right to meddle,' the Queen complained to Sir Henry, 'and *never* has done so *before*. Lord Hartington must be told that the Queen cannot allow any private and intimate communications to go on between *them*, or all confidence will be *impossible*.' How far the Queen's writ ran into the further recesses of the Turf Club, and how poor Ponsonby could be expected to muzzle HRH and his friends, were matters Her Majesty had not sufficiently considered.

Gladstone was pathetically grateful for the smallest courtesies. When in 1886 HRH sent him a telegram on his birthday he said that he had never felt more sensible of the Prince's 'ever-wakeful, indefatigable kindness,' which made him 'ashamed to be the cause of giving him trouble.' And in 1889, after the Great Man was knocked down by a cab, Mrs Gladstone asked Knollys to 'express to the dear Prince and Princess of Wales, the gratitude we feel for their Royal Highnesses' most kind enquiries. They never forget us! My husband was mercifully preserved from all injury, though it is true he was knocked down completely by the shaft of a hansom. Was it not characteristic of his pluck and vigour, immediately pursuing the hansom and taking its number?' Knollys hardly exaggerated when he remarked in 1881, 'The Prince of Wales is the only friend among the members of the Royal Family whom Mr Gladstone has got, notwithstanding that he refused to enlarge the stables at Marlborough House the other day.'

Gladstone died on Ascension Day, 19 May 1898, of cancer of the mouth. Such was his exceptional vitality, that, although he was eighty-eight, he took an unconscionable time to succumb. He longed for death to release him from his protracted agony, but was only grudgingly permitted to depart. Reginald Brett organized the State Funeral in Westminster Abbey. It was his suggestion that the Eton Volunteers should form a guard of honour for one of the most illustrious statesmen ever to grace their College. The Prince of Wales asked Brett to propose him as one of the Pall-Bearers. Strangely enough, Lady Geraldine Somerset, who detested Gladstone and all his works, had prophesied years before that when heaven in its mercy 'delivered us from the curse of Gladstone's existence,' the Prince of Wales would rush up from Sandringham, 'with ten special trains and twenty extra engines, and enveloped in yards and folds of crepe, to do honour to his funeral and curry favour with the plebs.' The Service took place on Saturday, 28 May. Not only the Prince of Wales, but his son, Prince George, accompanied the coffin to its resting place in the North Transept of the Abbey, close to Disraeli's statue. After the committal, the Prince went over to Mrs Gladstone, who was seated beside her husband's grave, and took her hand and kissed it.

The Queen, incensed that her son and grandson should pay homage to a mere subject, telegraphed to discover what advice had been sought and what precedents followed. The Prince of Wales replied with terse simplicity that he had sought no advice and knew of no precedents. There was but one Gladstone.

The day after the funeral, Princess Alexandra sent 'Dearest Mrs Gladstone,' a deeply affectionate letter. 'We are thankful to think that, after all his sufferings, his last few days were peaceful and painless, and that his longing and wish to go to his "heavenly home" were granted him on the very day of Our Saviour's Ascension. It must be of some consolation to you also to feel how the whole nation mourns with you and yours the loss of that great and good man, whose name will go down in letters of gold to posterity as one of the most beautiful, upright, and disinterested characters that ever adorned the pages of history. We all individually grieve the loss of a great personal friend from whom we have received innumerable kindnesses . . . You may be sure our visit to you and your beloved husband only one little year ago, in your own beautiful home at Hawarden, will ever remain as one of our most precious and valued memories.' During this visit Gladstone took his royal visitors to see the remains of the old castle which stood in the grounds. The Princess feared the old man was over-exerting himself. When he insisted on persevering up the steep slope on which the ruins stood, she begged him not to go further, 'on account of her bad leg.'

On 2 March, the day Gladstone went down to Windsor to resign, the Queen asked the Prince of Wales to give Lord Rosebery a message saying she would like to see him to ascertain whether he would be prepared to form a Government. That she should invite HRH to undertake so confidential a commission was a belated sign of trust. The moment Gladstone formally resigned, she wrote a few lines to Lord Rosebery, urging him to accept the Premiership if even only for a short time, for the good of the country. Ponsonby personally delivered the letter and was able to tell the Queen that Rosebery had yielded to her wishes.

'My dear F,' wrote the new Prime Minister to Knollys, 'I take if it for granted that you saw Ponsonby today, but, in case you did not, I write to tell you that the Queen has charged me to form a Government, and that I have undertaken to make the attempt. There are I am happy to say internal difficulties which may cause me to fail. No one will rejoice more than I. Will you tell the Prince?'

That evening Rosebery and Hamilton dined quietly together. 'In doing what I have done today,' said Rosebery, 'I consider that it is the most daring act of my life, unless I except what I did just thirty-two years ago, which was steering the *Defiance* at Eton without ever having been on the river.'

For fifteen months Rosebery's Government retained a tenuous hold on power, most of its legislation being sabotaged by the House of Lords. Tory domination of the Upper House began during the Younger Pitt's seventeen years of office. The one hundred and forty peers he recommended to the King gave his party an unassailable majority in the Second Chamber. Throughout the nineteenth century the Conservatives could only be outvoted by so massive a creation of Liberal peers as to be both ludicrous and revolutionary. Their domination of the Lords was further increased when Home Rule drove most of Gladstone's former supporters to vote for Union. The unprecedented majority by which their Lordships had rejected the Second Home Rule Bill was a measure of the problem.

On 24 October 1894, Rosebery warned the Queen that it would 'shortly be his duty to lay before the Country' his policy on the House of Lords. 'The cry in the Liberal Party' was either to abolish it, or to withdraw its power of veto. 'Lord Rosebery does not believe these measures to be constitutionally practicable, and moreover he is in favour of a Second Chamber of some sort; though he has long believed that the House of Lords, as at present constituted, cannot continue to exist.' He therefore proposed, as a first step, that a declaratory resolution should be submitted to the Commons asserting 'the impossibility of the elected representatives of the people allowing their measures to be summarily mutilated and rejected by the House of Lords.' Plainly the Constitution could not 'long stand the strain of a permanent control exercised by a Conservative branch of the legislature on all Liberal Governments.'

The Queen sent the Prince of Wales a cypher telegram summarizing Lord Rosebery's letter, and telling him she was 'inclined to favour a dissolution sooner than consent to any step which implies tampering with the constitution, but I must first ascertain what the chances of the Unionists are, so don't mention this.' She ended by asking HRH whether he might not convey his feelings 'on this dangerous policy' to the Prime Minister, who she thought had 'behaved very ill' to her. Later the same day, the Prince telegraphed back to Balmoral: 'Quite share your feelings. Fear anything I write or say would avail nothing. He is entirely in the hands of his followers, who do not consider him extreme enough . . . Cannot give any opinion whether dissolution just now would be advisable.'

The Prince understood well enough that to attack the House of Lords was to threaten the Monarchy, as both were based on hereditary succession. No Peerage, no King. Recognizing this as he did, he remained surprisingly unmoved by Rosebery's challenge. In the short term he was right not to worry. The Government was overwhelmingly rejected in 1895. But had he foreseen the whirlwind he was to reap in the last years of his reign, when Lloyd George demanded 'Shall Peers or People rule?' he might have regarded Lord Rosebery's threats with a good deal less composure.

For all the goodwill the Prince of Wales showed Gladstone, his political views were closer to those of Lord Beaconsfield. The Liberals, he feared, were disposed to reduce Great Britain to 'Little England.' Their parsimony and pacificism, their constant cuts in naval and military estimates, their strategy of imperial withdrawal, their abandoning Gordon to his fate, in short the policies of the Midlothian campaign, left HRH as indignant as the Queen. Indeed, they rejoiced in the same brand of patriotic imperialism. 'The Prince,' wrote Dilke, is, in fact, 'a strong Conservative, and a still stronger Jingo, really agreeing in the Queen's politics, and wanting to take everything everywhere in the world and to keep everything possible.'

As the Liberals became more radical, the Prince's disenchantment with them grew. Nevertheless, he felt happier at Hawarden than Hughenden. Beaconsfield's wit and asperity left him ill at ease. Nor did he succumb to those mellifluous compliments which others found so captivating. Plenty were paid on principle: when it came to royalty the flattery was laid on with a trowel. On HRH's recovering from typhoid in 1871, Disraeli declared that the people's devotion to him 'must make a man of his sweet disposition, and noble character, happier and prouder.'

In 1875, Disraeli prevailed upon the Queen to permit HRH to visit India, succeeding where Gladstone had failed in finding him employment. Her Majesty, reluctant as ever to delegate royal duties, raised a fine crop of objections. India was too hot to be healthy. Public appearances would tire the Prince. What would happen if she were to die when he was so far away? Seeing that India was apparently quiescent, was his journey necessary? Who should have precedence, her son and heir, or her representative, the Viceroy? Would it not be simpler for the Prince to stay at home than to risk bemusing the native mind with such intransigent conundrums? She told Lord Northbrook that she had only given 'a very unwilling consent' to HRH's visit, 'for she looks with much anxiety and apprehension to so long and distant a voyage, and so long an absence of the Heir to the Throne, who moreover is no longer in that robust health which he enjoyed before his terrible illness in 1871. Nor can he bear much exercise or great fatigue (though he unfortunately takes little care of himself) with impunity.'

Such was the Queen's maternal solicitude that she plagued her son with instructions on Sunday observance, unsuitable companions, and the proper time to go to bed. She might have been less insistent upon his retiring by ten o'clock, had she known that amongst the comforts provided by the authorities in India were girls of dazzling beauty and noble birth. She was also deeply concerned over what he ate. Much as she loved her Indian Empire and attached as she was to its people, she none the less looked on Bombay Duck with pardonable suspicion. When the Prince was over thirty and the father of five children, most people would have supposed him capable of picking his way through a menu without maternal nudging. Indeed, his expanding waistline offered vivid testimony to years of dedicated gourmandizing. Consequently he looked with some displeasure on

Her Majesty's solicitous telegrams which pursued him from Government House, Calcutta, to his jungle camp at Mowleah.

The royal party set sail from Brindisi on a converted troopship, HMS *Serapis*, on 17 October 1875, and reached Bombay on the eve of the Prince's birthday. 'Thenceforward,' as Lord Charles Beresford wrote, 'the Prince's tour was an unresting progress of durbars, receptions, dinners, visits, processions, ceremonies, speeches, addresses, fireworks, entertainments, investitures, reviews, varied only by intervals of sport.' After three months of it, the Queen confessed that 'Bertie's progresses lose a little interest and are very wearing – as there is such a constant repetition of elephants – trappings – jewels – illuminations and fireworks.'

During the course of his travels, the Prince rode an elephant which in its salad days, almost a century before, had belonged to Warren Hastings. The Duke of Sutherland, whom HRH had insisted upon inviting in spite of the Queen's protests, had such a passion for railways that he climbed on to the footplate, whenever they travelled by train, and drove the engine. On one occasion, they stopped at a wayside station for some ceremony or other, for which the whole party had changed into full dress uniform, at least all save the Duke, who was nowhere to be seen. 'Where can he be?' asked the Prince, who was intolerant of delays. Beresford suggested that he might still be on the engine and went to see if he was right. 'Sure enough, the Duke was sitting on the rail, his red shirt flung open, his sun-helmet on the back of his head. In either black fist he grasped a handful of cotton waste, with which he was mopping up the perspiration of honest toil. He hurried to his carriage to change into uniform; and presently appeared, buttoning his tunic with one hand. In the other he still grasped a skein of cotton waste.' The Prince shook his head with that look of profound resignation he often assumed in the face of adversity. 'Can nothing be done?' he asked sadly.

In a letter which Francis Knollys sent Ponsonby in February 1876, from the Prince of Wales's Camp at Terai, he expressed himself in almost the same words as the Queen had used to Vicky. 'You must be tired by this time,' he wrote, 'of reading accounts of processions, levees, balls, durbars, illuminations, etc. which are all exactly alike . . . Everybody, Europeans as well as natives, imagines the Prince of Wales has come here on purpose to redress their grievances real or imaginary; that he can do anything he likes and that they have only to write to him to have everything set to rights . . . I give the same reply to everybody, that HRH is unable to interefere etc. etc. or that I must refer them to the local authorities . . . I cannot tell you how rejoiced I am that we have finished for the next three weeks with all our ceremonies, and, that we are now able to lead a "shooting coat" life . . . Nothing by the way is so tiring as going on an elephant for eight or nine hours, and when I return to camp with every part of me aching, from the top of my head to my feet, I feel inclined for one thing only: bed – instead of which I have to sit down and write replies to impossible applications. I hope that everybody in England is satisfied with what HRH has done out here. No human being I am sure could have worked harder, almost too hard sometimes in my opinion with a due regard to health, and I feel certain that the money expended on this visit will not have been spent in vain, and that the excellent impression he has made on the native Princes and Rajahs, who belong to the class it was most desirable he should conciliate, will be productive of considerable political importance.'

Beresford agreed with Knollys that the visit was 'supremely successful' and was loud in his praise of the Prince's 'zeal, ability, tact and indomitable vigour. He gave his whole mind to the enterprise; thought of everything in advance; and set aside his personal comfort and convenience from first to last.'

Corry told Knollys that he was confident that England would give the Prince 'a tremendous welcome, for the success of his visit to India,' which had equally delighted 'society, parliament and the million. I call to mind what the Duke of Cambridge said to me one day last summer. "This visit to India of the Prince will, you will see, become the most remarkable and important political event of the reign!" I believe his words will come true!'

On his way home, HRH wrote to Sir William Knollys to say that his visit to India had ended, as far as he personally was concerned, 'as satisfactorily as it commenced and I have enjoyed my stay in that wonderful and most interesting country more than I can express and have carried away the most agreeable recollections of all I have seen and heard which cannot fail to be of the greatest advantage to me now and hereafter . . . If all goes well I hope you will see this gallant old ship steaming past the Isle of Wight by the 10th or 12th of May, and I shall be dreadfully disappointed if I don't see you and Charlotte with the dear Princess and the children, standing on the bridge of the *Alberta*.'

For the few months the Prince was in India, 'The Royalty

Question,' which had rightly obsessed Gladstone, was triumphantly resolved by Disraeli, and for once HRH was given an opportunity to devote his talents to a mission of more consequence than attending a civic banquet or opening a bazaar. He had been given the task of awaking the dormant allegiance of a sub-continent, and before *Serapis* steamed out of Bombay harbour on 13 March 1876, there was no part of the Empire more devoted to the Crown.

Two disputes in 1876 between the Prince and Disraeli imposed severe strains on their friendship. The Princess was desperately disappointed when she was not allowed to accompany her husband on his tour of India, and consoled herself by wintering in Denmark with her parents. The Queen grudgingly consented to this visit, but insisted upon Alix returning in time for the State Opening of Parliament. For many years Her Majesty had refused to perform this ceremony. But in 1876, she wished to commend in person the bill foreshadowed in the Queen's Speech to make her Empress of India. Alix was so reluctant to shorten her stay abroad that she begged both the Prime Minister and her husband to persuade the Queen that there was no need for her return.

Disraeli, after receiving the Princess's appeal, consulted Lord Cairns, the Lord Chancellor, Lord Derby, the Foreign Secretary, and Lord Salisbury, the Secretary for India. They all agreed in saying she should return. 'I have the painful duty,' wrote the Prime Minister to the Prince, 'to communicate this opinion to Her Royal Highness. I fear very much that she will misunderstand my motives and conduct.'

Soon after Christmas, Sir William told Francis that the real reason it was thought necessary 'that the Princess should accompany the Queen' was 'to ensure the latter having a good reception. Disraeli told me that he had no wish that the Queen should go at all, but that if she decided to go the presence of the Princess was important . . . Mr Disraeli did not mince the matter of the Queen's unpopularity at the present moment. But, in talking, it seemed to strike him suddenly what an important point it was to ensure the Princess's presence, and from that moment he altered his tone with her.' Alix was so furious that she told Sir William that the Prime Minister was 'an old humbug.' A few days after the State Opening, Francis told Ponsonby that 'Dizzy is rather under a cloud at present with the "young court" in consequence of the part he took to bring the Princess home. I must say he as usual played, or tried to play, a double game, but that is his second nature, and he can't help it.

He likewise wrote rather absurd and most shuffling letters on the subject both to the Prince and Princess.'

Soon after the Crown took over the Government of India from the East India Company, it was suggested that the Queen should assume an Indian title. Nothing, however, was done until 1876, when Disraeli, mainly to please her, included a Royal Titles Bill in the speech from the Throne. Her Majesty was delighted by the romance of becoming Empress of India, and Lord Lytton, the new Viceroy, was convinced that the title would arouse unprecedented enthusiasm throughout the native population of the sub-continent. But the prince, who detested ostentation, was opposed to the Prime Minister's 'grandiose conceptions.' In the last year of his reign, he told Haldane that he disliked the word 'Imperial' and 'that there was too much talk of Empire now-a-days.'

To most Victorians the title 'Emperor' suggested visions of Prussian Militarism, or the dissolute Court of the Second Empire. Lord Shaftesbury spoke caustically of the bill and Granville warned the Queen, in what she described as a 'rather threatening tone,' that the measure would run into trouble. But Disraeli assured her there was no popular feeling against it. Such agitation as there was came from Liberal newspapers. He told Ponsonby 'this is a regular party move. The Opposition think they see an opportunity of damaging me and they forget that in this instance they also attack the Queen.' Corry told Francis Knollys 'that the resistance to the laying the last stone of our Empire is one of the most flimsy and factious movements ever devised. This will soon become entirely evident, I am confident, for I *know* that for every considerable petition or meeting party funds have been paying heavily.'

Neither the Queen nor the Prime Minister told the Prince of Wales anything about the Royal Titles Bill. It was a serious oversight and he was naturally incensed. It is true Sir Henry sent Knollys an account of the Bill's passage through the Commons but it hardly constituted the official intimation to which HRH was entitled.

'The discussions on the Royal Titles Bill,' wrote Ponsonby, 'have rather annoyed the Queen. When the proposal was first made to add the style of Empress to the rest of Her Majesty's titles, little was said against it and the general expressed opinion was rather in favour of it. But as time went on the proposal began to be coldly looked upon and then was attacked. The truth is that the idea got about that the Queen was to supplant her ancient title by a more modern one and that the Princes were to call themselves Imperial.

And then the Opposition rose against it. My humble opinion is that two faults were committed in the outset, viz., that Mr Disraeli neglected to consult the Opposition before bringing in the Bill and secondly that he did not sufficiently explain that the Queen had no intention whatever of changing her style, beyond adding the words Empress of India at the end of her title. Mr Disraeli snubbed those who asked for information and consequently it came to be supposed there was some hidden intention of changing Queen for Empress.'

The Queen, regretting that the Opposition had not been consulted, 'sent to Lord Granville to say she was sorry this had not been done, but hoped that he would inform his late colleagues that the Bill had been introduced at her desire and that she trusted they would support it out of respect for her. But it seems that most of the late Ministers had already raised their voices against it, thinking it purely a Tory measure, and they could not retreat . . . The Queen fears that these debates and differences of opinion will do so much harm in India, the country it was intended to benefit. I may also tell you confidentially that the Queen is very much put out by the attitude of the Liberal Party, which she thinks is as much opposed to her as to Mr Disraeli . . . It seemed a small question at first and I am sorry it has swelled into these proportions and that it has embittered parties as it has done.'

The Prince told Knollys to write to Corry saying how angry he was to learn from the newspapers about the Queen's new title. 'In no other country in the world,' Knollys protested, 'would the next heir to the throne have been treated in similar circumstances in such a manner . . . The present Prince of Wales possesses the same rights and vested interest, as regards the future of the Crown, as any of his predecessors.'

When Disraeli saw the letter, he decided to write directly to the Prince. 'It would give me real pain,' he said, 'to be considered by Your Royal Highness as wanting in dutiful and affectionate respect to you, Sir, but the matter is not altogether as, from a distance, it appears to Your Royal Highness. This addition to the Royal Titles was not in its origin a Court or Family affair, it was a political measure, ultimately decided on by Lord Salisbury and myself at Hatfield . . . Originally, we believed that all might be effected by Royal Prerogative, the titles of the Crown never having been touched by Statute, except by one of Henry 8th, which was repealed ten years afterwards . . . But it turned out, however, by the researches of the Lord Chancellor, that by the Act of Union with

Ireland, the Royal Titles had technically become statutory and we had consequently to bring the matters before Parliament . . . In conferring intimately and frequently with the Queen on this subject, I derived the conviction that Her Majesty had spoken to Your Royal Highness on this affair; because Your Royal Highness was the only one of the Royal Family to whom Her Majesty ever referred. I concluded that your additional title, Sir, as Prince Imperial of India, had been quite contemplated . . . The "Agitation", really got up for factious purposes, has been the greatest failure on record, and it has proved, after all, that this nation is not governed by newspapers.' Disraeli's final excuse was unimpressive, 'As affairs proceeded, Your Royal Highness's movements rendered any communication by post most difficult.' It may be remembered that Lady Aylesford had no problem in contacting her husband and that hardly a day passed without the Queen telegraphing her son.

The Prince personally wrote to Disraeli, acknowledging his letter and explanations. 'While thanking you for having kindly stated your reasons why you did not let me know previously of the intention of HM Govt. to add the name of Empress of India to the Queen's style, I feel bound to say that I do not feel that the facts of the case are altered. As the Queen's eldest son, I think I have some right to feel annoyed that, as stated at my desire in F. Knollys's letter to M. Corry, the announcement of the addition to the Queen's title should have been read by me in the newspapers instead of having received some intimation on the subject from the Prime Minister. I will not now enter into a discussion respecting the merits of the Bill, but as regards myself I must frankly tell you that I could never consent to the word "Imperial" being added to my name.'

The Duke of Cambridge described the Prince's treatment as 'positively *incomprehensible* and really too outrageous,' and maintained that he 'ought to be taken into confidence upon *everything*. Why he is not I cannot imagine or conceive.' The moment the Queen acknowledged that HRH had been treated inconsiderately, and furthermore said she was principally to blame, he ceased to press his grievance.

'The Royal Titles Bill,' wrote Granville to Knollys, 'is wonderfully unpopular, and I believe that the opinion that the matter has been misconducted, is not confined to the Liberals. It has lately been much rumoured that the Prince does not agree with the Queen on this subject. His popularity will be much increased by it.' HRH formally forgave the Prime Minister for ignoring him, but actions speak louder than words. For all Disraeli's extravagant praise of his 'dear and honoured Prince,' he had behaved as if he were negligible.

Randolph Churchill was probably the closest of all the Prince's political associates. Considering the bitterness of their quarrel over Blandford and Lady Aylesford, their friendship did credit to them both. Randolph's career may best be described in a metaphor from Macaulay: he went up like a rocket and came down like the stick. Churchill made his name by devastating attacks on Gladstone and Home Rule and it was widely believed that he would one day be Prime Minister. In 1886, when he was only thirty-seven, he became Chancellor of the Exchequer and Leader of the House. Apart from Pitt, no man has ever held either office so young. But, before the year was out, he destroyed his career by a wanton miscalculation.

Almost as soon as 'Lord Random,' as his enemies called him, joined Salisbury's Government, he began quarrelling with his colleagues. The Prime Minister protested that, besides presiding over the Cabinet and keeping an eye on the Foreign Office, he spent what remained of his time controlling the Queen and Randolph Churchill, and of these commitments the last was by far the most arduous. Randolph, who hardly knew what it meant to be subordinate, spoke scathingly of his Chief. Writing to Knollys in 1891, soon after hearing the news of the death of Parnell, he asked: 'When shall we get rid of that ineffable humbug Lord S? I would not mind reading his obituary notice.'

Churchill began making trouble by complaining about Lord Iddesleigh's conduct of Foreign Affairs. Admittedly his criticism was not without substance. The Foreign Secretary was no Palmerston, and his chief claim to fame was dropping dead at Lord Salisbury's feet: an accomplishment which required no particular skill. But, until this abrupt termination of his office, he pursued the traditional Tory policy of hostility towards Russia which Randolph thought senseless.

Sir Arthur Ellis, one of the Prince of Wales's Equerries, sent Knollys a diverting account of events leading to Churchill's resignation. 'I have had the opportunity,' he told him, 'of hearing "behind the sail" several details of the Randolph crisis . . . As you know, in every Cabinet there is an inner Cabinet. Into this Lord Salisbury has *not* admitted him. He found himself left out in the cold on questions especially of foreign politics.' During his short time as Chancellor, be became most unpopular, 'by cutting into old standing Treasury abuses which have been allowed to go on. I instance one economy which has raised the whirlwind against him. An old act dating from Elizabeth gave a percentage for carrying specie, which was divided amongst all sorts of people, a scandalous perquisite, the abolition of which saved the Exchequer at a stroke of the pen more than £40,000 per annum, but naturally not to the comfort of those who fattened on it. In many other similar abuses he has been *hacking and hewing:* an unpopular employment if you happen to be a *Tree.*'

The dispute which led to Randolph's precipitate resignation concerned his budget: one of the most brilliant and radical ever conceived. The trouble arose over the Chancellor insisting upon a reduction of £500,000 in the army estimates, which W. H. Smith, the War Minister, strenuously resisted. As the sum could have been found from the estimated surplus there was a simple way out of the crisis. But Churchill preferred to browbeat the Prime Minister by threatening to resign. Clearly he thought that, if Salisbury was rash enough to accept his offer, he would be swept back to power on a tide of popular feeling. In the event not a dog barked and Randolph learned that no man is indispensable. Not only had he forgotten Goschen who replaced him, but he could not appeal to the nation as budget proposals are secret. 'The difficulty now is,' wrote Ellis, 'that in this storm he is tongue-tied and can make no personal explanation.'

The Prince of Wales proposed that the Queen should 'send for Randolph and ask him to withdraw his resignation.' But Sir Henry replied 'that it would not do for Her Majesty to put herself in a position to be refused.' According to Knollys, the fact of the matter was that Randolph was no more a Conservative than was Dilke. 'All his instincts and feelings are Liberal, *very* Liberal, and I say this from having known him intimately in former days.'

No sooner had he resigned than Lord Randolph wrote to the Prince to explain his reasons for doing so. From the moment he joined the Government his political views had strongly diverged from those of his colleagues. He now thought 'that such difference of opinion, which was certain to produce weak executive action, should be brought to a close before Parliament.' The Prince forwarded Randolph's letter to the Queen, who pertinently enquired: 'Why did he take office if he thought there was such a "chasm" between him and them?' Never again would she trust 'that strange unaccountable man,' who had been unforgivably disloyal to poor Lord Salisbury, and 'a perpetual thorn in the side of his colleagues.'

The fact was that he 'expected all to bow to him, as indeed some were inclined to do.'

The Queen told Sir Henry that she thought it 'strange of the Prince of Wales' to have sent her Lord Randolph's 'most objectionable and incorrect letter,' and that it was obviously 'most undesirable and even dangerous' for HRH to have further dealings with him. When the Prince heard that the Queen had expressed disapproval of his friendship, he 'desired' Knollys to tell Ponsonby that 'Randolph does not go much into general Society, so the Prince is not likely to come across him a great deal, but he thinks it highly advisable that he should not shun public men, whatever their politics may be, and more especially when, as in Randolph's case, they are likely to come prominently to the front one day.'

So moved was HRH by the Queen's interference that he wrote to her himself, pointing out that, whether Churchill was right or wrong, he at least had 'the courage of his opinions.' Poor, and very ambitious, 'he gave up £5,000 a year in ceasing to be Chancellor of the Exchequer . . . Though I certainly do not agree in all his public views (and I have often told him so) still, I cannot help admiring many of his great qualities.'

Heedless of the Queen's warnings, the Prince and Randolph became inseparable companions, and were seen together at most of the principal race meetings. HRH was tireless in pressing the claims of his friend on anyone willing to listen. In 1888, for example, he suggested that Churchill might 'like to go out as Minister to Washington. A worse choice could easily be made.' During Randolph's last illness, when he could hardly speak or hear, the Prince invited this pathetic wreck of a once great man to stay at Sandringham, although, as Jennie confessed, 'He is quite unfit for society . . . one never knows what he may do.' His death on 24 January 1895, was a welcome release from torment.

The Golden Jubilee in 1887, celebrating the fiftieth anniversary of Her Majesty's accession, gave the Prince of Wales a splendid opportunity to exercise his talents. His most singular achievement was to overcome the Queen's aversion to what was in prospect, since nothing was more inclined to make her despondent than plans for national rejoicing. Sir Richard Holmes, the Queen's librarian at Windsor, thought the 'triumph and success of the Jubilee were due almost entirely to the energy and unfailing sense of high duty of the Prince of Wales . . . The situation brought out all those great gifts for which he was famous: his tact, his good temper, his graciousness, his knowledge of the world.'

Princes of the blood flocked to London from all corners of the globe. The visitors' book at Claridge's read like the *Almanach de Gotha*. Gorgeous Indian Maharajahs, blazing with diamonds, exotic native Princes from Africa, the Queen of Hawaii, the Kings of Saxony, Belgium, Denmark, and Greece, Crown Princes and Heirs Apparent, sons, sons-in-law and grandsons of the Queen Empress, Serene Highnesses, Princes and Princesses, complete with Ladies-in-Waiting, Equerries, servants and baggage, all had to be welcomed, found somewhere to stay, and fitted harmoniously into processions, receptions and banquets.

Nobody was better able to undertake this impossible task than the Prince. For many weeks Marlborough House was besieged by agitated functionaries clamouring for advice. Firmly and faultlessly, HRH laid down the law on Royal Salutes, Orders of Precedence, Modes of Address, uniforms, orders and protocol. But there was still some wrangling and resentment. As the Duke of Cambridge said of some of his thwarted relations, if they insisted on taking everything amiss they should never have come in the first place. Prince William of Prussia was so furious to find himself next to an African Princess at the State Dinner at Buckingham Palace that he retired to bed in a huff. Alix's father, King Christian IX, and her brother, King George of Greece, stayed at Marlborough House throughout the festivities. The Queen, who missed nothing, except seeing Mr Gladstone in the Abbey, remarked in her Journal that the King of Denmark 'had been at my Coronation when he was quite a young man.'

The summer of 1887 was exceptionally bright and beautiful. The morning of 21 June, the great day of National Thanksgiving, was cloudless and sunny. Outside Buckingham Palace the Queen could hear the crowds gathering, troops marching, and bands playing. It reminded her of the opening of the Great Exhibition. At half past eleven, she got into her gilt landau, with Vicky and Alix, to drive to the Abbey. The Prince of Wales, on his chestnut horse Vivian, rode between the Duke of Connaught and the Duke of Edinburgh, immediately in front of Her Majesty's carriage. Next came the Queen's sons-in-law. Vicky kept glancing over her shoulder at Fritz, whose days she feared were numbered. Several times the Queen clasped her hand to reassure her. The Crown Prince looked magnificent in his white uniform, silver breast-plate and eagle-crested helmet. As he saluted the crowds in acknowledgement of their greeting, it was as if Lohengrin was taking a last farewell.

When the Queen reached the Abbey, she thought of her Coronation, and of her 'beloved husband for whom this would have been such a proud day!' After the service, the Prince of Wales stepped forward and kissed her hand, at which she warmly embraced him. By the end of the day she was 'half dead with fatigue,' but *'deeply immensely* touched and gratified . . . by the wonderful and so universal enthusiasm displayed by my people, and by high and low, rich and poor . . . It shows that fifty years' *hard* work, anxiety, and care have been appreciated, and that my sympathy with the sorrowing, suffering and humble is acknowledged.'

The old Duchess of Cambridge was too infirm to watch the procession or take part in the festivities. Lady Geraldine, however, gave her a vivid description of the cavalcade of Princes clattering down Constitution Hill through cheering multitudes. It was 'the greatest and most *perfect* success ever known! The most splendid and most thrilling pageant ever seen! The most touching and magnificent display of loyalty and attachment possible to conceive. The whole thing beggars description . . . The masses and *millions* of people, *thronging* the streets like an anthill, and *every* window within sight, and every roof of every house, men hanging on to the chimneys! There was never anything seen like it! . . . It was one continuous roar of cheering from the moment she came out of the door of her palace till the instant she got back to it! Deafening.'

The festivities ended with a Naval Review off Spithead on 29 July. The Queen, on board the *Victoria and Albert*, steamed past some hundred and thirty-five vessels. It was one of the most perfect days of a flawless summer: not a cloud in the sky, or a wave disturbing the water. Even Nelson could not have felt seasick. The Empress Eugénie was one of Her Majesty's guests on the Royal Yacht. Most of the day the Prince of Wales stood by his mother's side, 'perfectly happy,' as Lady Geraldine noted, 'in a new uniform!!! having just got himself made Admiral of the Fleet!!!!' The ships were dressed with flags, the sailors cheered as only they knew how, and the thunder of countless salutes proclaimed Britannia's might. The Duke of Cambridge, admittedly only a military man, went home 'quite delighted,' believing he had just witnessed 'a marvellous display of the power and greatness of the Nation!' But more expert observers were less impressed. What had actually been exhibited was the obsolescence of the Navy.

By June 1897 the Queen had ruled longer than any other

sovereign in British history. There seemed no bounds to her Empire, nor end to her reign. Like the sun and moon, she was part of the order of nature. Held in that veneration which longevity inspires, she was beyond reproach.

Nobody was more eager than Joseph Chamberlain to make Her Majesty's Diamond Jubilee surpass all previous celebrations. It was he who persuaded Lord Salisbury that, as the Queen ruled over three hundred and fifty million people, her Empire should play a prominent part in the rejoicing. Eleven Prime Ministers of self-governing dominions were accordingly invited to join the royal procession to St Paul's. The Prince of Wales strongly supported the Colonial Secretary's proposals and did all he could to give them effect. In the ten years separating the Jubilees, he had seen the imperial constitution transformed. As more and more Colonies established their own legislatures, so the power and influence of the House of Commons declined. Some of the new assemblies looked upon the United Kingdom Parliament with suspicion, but nevertheless retained their devotion to the Crown. Queen Victoria was just as much Queen of Canada or New Zealand, as she was of Great Britain, and in their common allegiance to her they were united to one another.

It was the Prince's plan to produce a magnificent pageant which would make these facts visible to all who watched the procession, and, quite literally, bring home to the back streets of London the sublime vision of peoples of different races and religions, drawn together from all parts of the world, celebrating, as one great family, their common loyalty to the Queen. On a heroic scale the Diamond Jubilee was to be a masterpiece of imperial propaganda. It could not but have occurred to Her Majesty how poor, dear Lord Beaconsfield would have relished it, and surely it would have amused him to watch the immaculate Mr Chamberlain presiding over the revels?

There could hardly have been a more convincing demonstration of 'Queen's Weather' than on 22 June 1897, the day of the Diamond Jubilee. Early that morning the sky over London was dull and threatening. But nothing disturbed the crowd's faith that the Queen would be favoured by fine weather on the most glorious day of her life. And, just as she left Buckingham Palace, the sun burst through the clouds and never ceased to shine as she drove through the streets of her capital. The Prince of Wales, wearing a Field-Marshal's uniform, rode by Her Majesty's side. From time to time he leant towards her to call her attention to something of interest, such as a group of survivors from the Charge of the Light Brigade at Balaclava.

The procession stopped at St Paul's for a short Service of Thanksgiving. The scene was preserved for posterity by a primitive cinematograph, which the Queen thought 'very wonderful' but a 'little hazy and too rapid.' As she felt unable to manage the steps to the Cathedral, the ceremony was conducted on the pavement. When the Grand Duchess of Mecklenburg-Strelitz first heard of this particular proposal, she was amazed that 'after sixty years' reign,' nothing better could be devised than 'to thank God in the street.' Presumably she had forgotten where the Gospel was first preached.

What distinguished the Diamond Jubilee from preceding festivals, was that the procession crossed London Bridge and passed through some of the poorest districts of the capital. It was at the Prince's suggestion that this route was followed. The loyalty displayed as Her Majesty drove down the Borough Road was, in Lord Rosebery's phrase, 'deep, passionate and steadfast.' Queen Elizabeth I, in her Golden Speech, proclaimed to her 'loving subjects' that 'this I count the glory of my Crown that I have ruled with your loves.' On the evening of 22 June, 1897, nobody who had watched the Diamond Jubilee could have doubted that Monarchy in England still rested on such sure foundations.

The festivities ended on 26 June with a Naval Review. Never before in peacetime had any nation assembled such a fleet. A hundred and seventy-three warships, spaced out over thirty miles, were drawn up between Bembridge Point and the shore of Cowes. At two o'clock, the Prince of Wales, accompanied by his wife and son, set off in the Royal Yacht from Portsmouth, followed by an impressive convoy. Soon after three, the *Victoria and Albert* hoisted a signal inviting all Flag Officers aboard. Surrounded by this mighty battlefleet, whose capability for destruction was distantly hinted by the thunder of royal salutes, Princess Alexandra sat under an awning, as ever a vision of loveliness, pouring out cups of tea. Meanwhile, her guests stood awkwardly around, nibbling scones, admiring her beauty, and casting their professional eyes over the fleet in which they served.

In 1884, towards the end of Gladstone's Second Ministry, the Prince of Wales was invited to sit on a Royal Commission, under the Chairmanship of Sir Charles Dilke, concerned with housing the working classes. As the proposal for setting it up had come from

Lord Salisbury, there was no risk of involving the Prince in party squabbles. That Gladstone should propose appointing HRH was natural enough, for he constantly sought to find him public duties. That the Queen should accept his suggestion was more surprising. In fact, however, she had long felt concerned over the way the poor were housed. It was a problem to which Albert had devoted considerable attention. And when she read a pamphlet with the arresting title, 'The Bitter Cry of Outcast London,' which described what Southwark slums were like, she began to urge the Prime Minister to follow Lord Beaconsfield's example and tackle the problem by legislation.

To increase his qualifications for the work, HRH decided to see for himself some of the worst slums of Holborn and St Pancras. Having disguised himself in a 'slouch' hat and ready-made ulster, he and Lord Carrington set out in a four-wheeler to visit 'Darkest London.' What he found pained and astonished him, particularly the sight of a shivering woman and three half-naked children, huddled together on a heap of rags, dazed by cold and hunger. 'We visited some very bad places,' wrote Lord Carrington, 'but we got him back safe and sound to Marlborough House in time for luncheon.'

On 22 February 1884, the Prince of Wales delivered the only speech of substance he made to the House of Lords. Describing his recent visits to some of the poorest districts of London, he assured their Lordships 'that the condition of the poor, or rather of their dwellings, was perfectly disgraceful.' It was his 'earnest hope' that the Commission, in which he took the 'keenest and liveliest interest,' would recommend for Parliament's consideration 'measures of a drastic and thorough character.' The Prince left his listeners in no doubt how deeply disturbed he had been by seeing for himself the second of the two nations over which he would one day rule. Admittedly, and he did admit it, the London estates of the Duchy of Cornwall left much to be desired. Any comprehensive list of slum landlords would necessarily have included His Royal Highness. But the Commission loyally confined its attention to Sandringham where the Prince was justifiably proud of his improvements. 'I live in a good house myself,' he told a gathering of farmers at King's Lynn, 'and it is my wish that every labourer, when he returns home tired with his day's work, should have a comfortable home to go to.'

Dilke's work was aggravated by the diversity of his colleagues' opinions. Some seemed to believe that filth and disease were God's judgement on sin. What was wanted was pure hearts not pure water. Lord Salisbury maintained that the poor were attached to their slums and would positively resent being re-housed.

But the deepest divergence was one which perplexed most Victorian philanthropists. Loving liberty, and sensitive to the claims of individuals, they hesitated to resort to compulsory powers, without which most reforms could never be achieved. The Commissioners soon discovered that parish vestries, charged with preventing abuses, generally consisted of precisely those people most interested in preserving them.

Amongst the witnesses summoned to give evidence were Lord Shaftesbury and the Reverend A. Mearns, whose 'bitter cry' had reached the Queen. Both described scenes of unimaginable squalor: houses in which effluent overflowed down staircases, dead bodies left to rot for a week or more, vermin everywhere, unendurable stench, filth, dark, damp, helplessness and despair.

The Prince of Wales attended the Commission's meetings fitfully. Sometimes duty called him away and sometimes pleasure. But Dilke, at least, thought that he showed a devotion to the work 'quite unusual with him and he cut short his holiday and returned to London on purpose for our meeting.' Probably his principal contribution to the Commission was his presence on it. But his questions were shrewd and his sympathy generous.

The Prince approved the Commission's Report which was published in May 1885, but refused to sign an appendix proposing leasehold enfranchisement. Its tone was surprisingly radical. It suggested, for example, that Parliament should require landlords to maintain their property in habitable repair: thus threatening the Englishman's inalienable right to let his roof fall in. The brutal and inescapable facts which the Commissioners were forced to contemplate compelled them to propose measures totally inconsistent with their declared political opinions. As the Prince of Wales said at the Mansion House, on 5 November 1895, 'We are all Socialists nowa-days.'

In December 1892, Gladstone invited HRH to sit on another Royal Commission, set up to consider the problems of destitution in old age. The Prince was present at thirty-five of its forty-eight sessions, and gave up his annual spring holiday in the South of France to attend its meetings. Throughout the proceedings, he was exceptionally affable to his colleagues, particularly Broadhurst and Arch, who spoke for the working class. James Stuart, a Fellow of

Trinity and Member of Parliament for Hoxton, who was as radical as it was possible to be and yet remain in the Liberal Party, said that the Prince 'attended very regularly, and asked, when his turn came, very good questions. I thought at first that he had probably been prompted to these, but I soon found out that they were of his own initiative, and that he really had a very considerable grasp of the subjects he dealt with.' The Commission was divided between those who wanted State Pensions, contributory or non-contributory, and those who preferred to leave individuals to provide for old age by joining Friendly Societies.

The Commission's Report was published in 1895, and reflected the confusion which had bedevilled its work. The majority of members were opposed to Government-funded pensions, but some recommended a State Scheme supported by contributions. Broadhurst alone believed that people too old to earn had a right to help from their fellow citizens. The Report stirred up so much party controversy that the Prince thought it wise not to sign it. But in 1908 Broadhurst's dream came true when King Edward gave his assent to a Bill providing for Old Age Pensions.

VI

The Prince and Diplomacy

The Prince of Wales once told Gladstone's youngest son, Herbert, that when he came to the throne he proposed to be his own Foreign Minister. During his forty years of apprenticeship, he acquired a first-hand knowledge of Europe unrivalled among contemporary Sovereigns and surpassing that of all other English kings: so the years of waiting were more fruitful than most people realized. His grasp of foreign affairs was not derived from reading despatches, or from brief, formal encounters with rulers and statesmen, but from ceaseless travelling, intimate friendships, and his consequent ability to assess things for himself. Compared with him, most ministers were insular and tongue-tied.

Being one of the best-travelled men in the world, HRH recognized how misconceived was the view that there was anything 'splendid' in Britain's isolation. Sir Edward Grey, who was Foreign Secretary from 1905 to 1916, seldom ventured to cross the Channel and refused to converse in such faltering French as Winchester had taught him. But the King spoke it faultlessly. Madame Steinheil went so far as to say that he was almost too grammatical. Moreover, he was equally fluent in German, having spoken it since childhood. Throughout his life, HRH cultivated the friendship of foreign ambassadors in London, such as M. Waddington, French Ambassador from 1883 to 1893, Count Karolyi, the Austrian Ambassador from 1878 to 1899, and M. de Staal, Russian ambassador from 1884 to 1902. The Danish Minister, M. Falbe, was often invited to Marlborough House and Sandringham, while the Prince and Princess enjoyed his lavish hospitality at Luton Hoo. Whatever the

Queen or Disraeli might think about HRH's 'chitter chatter,' Prince Bülow, who later became Imperial Chancellor of Germany, described him as 'so cautious and clever that he often enticed their secrets out of foreigners, while he himself never said anything that he did not want to say.'

Until the destruction of the Russian, German and Austrian Empires at the end of the First World War, the rulers of Europe were principally responsible for their country's foreign policy. Writing to King Edward VII in December 1901, the Kaiser boasted that he was 'the sole arbiter and master of German foreign policy.' The Government and Country, so he said, '*must* follow me even if I have to "face the musik".' [*sic*]. As constitutional monarchs, neither Queen Victoria nor Edward VII possessed such powers. But they, nevertheless, exercised a greater influence over their fellow Sovereigns, most of whom were relations, than did their Ministers. The Kaiser was far more in awe of his grandmother than of Rosebery or Salisbury. In no other political sphere were British Governments compelled to leave the Royal Family so wide a discretion. They could not prevent the Prince of Wales from visiting his father-in-law, the King of Denmark, his sister-in-law, the Empress of Russia, his brother-in-law, the King of Greece, or his Imperial German nephew. And what was discussed, or possibly agreed, at such meetings, was not within their competence.

Throughout the nineteenth century diplomacy was conducted in secret, and was imposed upon, rather than decided by, the peoples of Europe. In so far as Foreign Policy revolved round dynastic antagonisms or alliances, decisions were reached at family gatherings, not ministerial conferences. Most rulers would have regarded the intervention of mere subjects in their personal affairs as impudent meddling. Given that Britain could not instruct the Great Powers how to conduct their diplomacy, and given the pre-eminence accorded to Queen Victoria by her fellow Sovereigns, her ministers could not but concede to her the status she had won. Consequently, no royal prerogative offered wider scope.

The Queen's family was deeply divided between those who supported and those who suspected Germany. Soon after Prince Albert's death, the Queen told the King of Prussia that while she lived she would dedicate herself to preserving 'the best understanding between our two countries, and to carrying on 'as my beloved Angel would have wished!' But she did not even succeed in persuading the Prince of Wales to forgive Bismarck for attacking Christian IX in 1864.

During the Seven Weeks' War her two daughters found themselves enemies, for Fritz was the hero of Königgrätz, while Alice's husband, the Grand Duke of Hesse, fought for Francis Joseph. The Queen herself was torn between sympathy for her first cousin, George V, the blind King of Hanover, who was driven from his kingdom, and the victorious Prussians who deprived him of his heritage. 'The poor things,' wrote Vicky of Austria's allies, 'have broken their own necks. Oh! how cruel it is to have one's heart and one's head thus set at right-angles!'

In 1870, predictably enough, the Queen supported Prussia. Accepting the general opinion that France would win the war, she told her 'poor, dear, beloved child,' the Crown Princess, that words were 'far too weak to say all I feel for you, or what I think of my neighbours!!!' Napoleon's conduct she thought iniquitous. 'My whole heart and my fervent prayers are with beloved Germany!' She told Sir Theodore Martin that 'it was merciful the beloved Prince was taken, for had he lived I could never have prevented him from joining the German Armies.' When news came through of the victories of Metz and Sedan and the capitulation of the Emperor, it looked to the Queen as if God's hand was at work in humbling his Empire.

After the proclamation of the Second Reich in 1871, the Queen became increasingly aware that it threatened the peace of Europe. She particularly distrusted Bismarck, whom she regarded as authoritarian and aggressive. The Prince Consort's dream, which she and Vicky shared, of a liberal, peace-loving Germany, closely allied to England, cultured, enlightened and prosperous, was slowly becoming a nightmare, for all the Imperial Chancellor had to offer was 'blood and iron.'

The Prince of Wales was a great deal more sensitive to German affronts than the Queen. She could not but look with charity upon Albert's native land, while he saw Prussia through Alix's eyes. The family was also divided in its feelings towards Russia. The crisis which started in 1876 with the revolt of successive Balkan states against Turkish oppression, appeared to Lord Beaconsfield to be partly inspired by the Tsar. It was consequently his policy to shore up the Ottoman Empire to frustrate such knavish tricks. But the cruelty with which the Sultan crushed the rebels in Bulgaria provoked Gladstone to demand that his troops withdraw, 'bag and baggage,' from the provinces they had 'desolated and profaned.' Seizing this opportunity, Russia declared war, allegedly to save her

Christian neighbours, but, as the Queen, Prince and Prime Minister believed, in fact to achieve her old ambition to capture Constantinople.

Alix took Dagmar's part and supported her father-in-law, Alexander II, and Affie, having recently married the Tsar's daughter, joined in denouncing Lord Beaconsfield. Not only the Royal Family but the country was divided, between those who suspected Russia of threatening British interests, as at the time of the Crimean War, and those who accepted her own version of events, that she was struggling to protect Christian minorities in the Ottoman Empire from bestial persecution. The penalty of dynastic marriages was strife within families. As the Queen wrote in 1870: 'These divided interests . . . are quite unbearable. Human nature is not made for such fearful trials – especially not mothers' and wives' hearts.'

Sometimes, as in 1876, the Prince of Wales shared the Queen's hostile feelings towards Russia, but, as Germany grew more menacing, he increasingly favoured the possibility of friendship. Even towards Germany, his attitude only became inflexible during the last years of his life. Despite his distrust of Bismarck, he looked forward to the day when his brother-in-law succeeded to the imperial throne, dismissed the Chancellor, and governed Germany in close accord with England: thus fulfilling the Prince Consort's dream of reviving the alliance which had sealed Napoleon's fate at Waterloo. It was only after his nephew became Emperor and began demanding a place in the sun, that the Prince gradually became convinced that Europe was drifting towards war and that the British Empire was threatened. But it was not until some time after the death of the Emperor Frederick that HRH began to despair of the possibility of friendship with Germany.

However much HRH's feelings towards the Kaiser and the Tsar might alter with changing circumstances, his love of France was constant and indestructible. From his first golden memory of Napoleon III at St Cloud, during the Crimean War, to his last visit to Biarritz within ten days of his death, the enchantment never diminished. In 1878, the French President, Marshal MacMahon, held a Great Exhibition in Paris. For nearly three weeks the Prince stayed at the Hôtel Bristol to attend the inaugural ceremonies and to supervise the British Section, over which he presided. In the course of one of the many speeches he was called upon to make, he nailed his French colours to the mast in uncompromising terms. '*Permettez-moi de vous dire et de dire à la France entière que la prospérité de ce pays et celle de la Grande-Bretagne ont un intérêt essentiellement réciproque.'* Bülow described HRH's speech at the opening ceremony as giving 'exaggerated utterance to his love of France.'

Above all, the Prince of Wales loved Paris, where he soon became a familiar and popular figure. As he took his seat at a restaurant, or entered his box at a theatre, a discreet whisper of *'Prince de Galles'* might register his arrival. But Parisians respected his privacy and left him to live as he pleased, without comment or censure.

The idea of an *Entente Cordiale* was in the Prince's mind as early as 1866: indeed he minted the phrase. The conspicuous part he played in turning those words into a reality was possibly his greatest achievement. A few days before war broke out between Prussia and Austria, HRH dined with M. Drouyn, the French Ambassador in London. During the evening, he confessed that his sympathies were with Austria in the conflict which threatened. 'The general interests of Europe,' he suggested, 'could best be served by an *"entente"* between France and England.' If both countries acted together, peace might still be preserved. In reporting this conversation to his Government, the Ambassador carefully noted the Prince's precise phrase.

The Queen was fascinated by the Emperor Napoleon and treated him chivalrously during his last exile in England, but she and the Prince Consort were strongly opposed to his Italian campaign in 1859. From then onwards, she regarded her erstwhile ally as a dangerous adventurer. 'Nothing annoyed dear Papa more,' she told Vicky in September 1870, 'than the abject court paid to the Emperor, and the way in which we were forced to flatter and humour him . . . When in '59 in spite of all our endeavours and warnings, he made war in Italy against Austria and deceived us, Papa was most indignant and broke off all friendly, personal intercourse . . . Your elder brothers unfortunately were carried away by that horrid Paris (beautiful though you may think it) and that frivolous and immoral court did frightful harm to English society (that Papa knew and saw) and was very bad for Bertie and Affie. The fearful extravagance and luxury, the utter want of seriousness and principle in everything – the many crimes in France all show a rottenness which was sure to crumble and fall.' When Paris finally capitulated to the Germans in 1871, the Queen wrote: 'Surely that Sodom and Gomorrah as Papa called it deserves to be crushed.'

The Prince of Wales took a very different view of life in the Second Empire and enjoyed all it had to offer. While attending the opening of the Paris Exhibition in 1867, he contrived to entertain himself in ways which pained Sir William. 'The accounts I subsequently had of this visit,' Knollys noted disapprovingly, 'were very unsatisfactory, supper after the opera with some of the female Paris notorieties, etc. etc.' The very things about imperial Paris which the Queen found most deplorable, were precisely those which recommended it to her son.

On 15 July 1870, while the Prince was giving a dinner party at Marlborough House, at which Delane, the editor of *The Times*, was a guest, a messenger came with a telegram from Printing House Square, announcing that France had declared war on Germany. The very next day, the Crown Princess wrote to the Queen to say that Count Bernstorff, the Prussian Ambassador in London, had sent a despatch to Berlin reporting that the Prince of Wales had told Count Apponyi, the Austrian Ambassador, of his delight that Austria was 'going to join with the French – and his hope that we should fare ill. This he is said to have loudly expressed at a dinner of the French ambassador's. Perhaps it is exaggerated, but, of course, it is a story related everywhere.'

The Queen at once wrote back: 'That story about Bertie is quite untrue – so he declares and he is furious with Bernstorff who certainly is a shocking mischief maker.' Two days later, she wrote again to say that Count Apponyi was 'furious – as B. never spoke to him about political matters.' She told Vicky that she hoped that the King would recall Bernstorff after his 'abominable and outrageous' conduct. 'He has done incalculable mischief by all the gossip and lies he has invariably retailed and sent to Berlin to poison all your ears.' Until a more sympathetic Ambassador was appointed, 'no good understanding could exist between the two countries.' But, for all her protests, Bernstorff remained at his post until removed by a mightier hand than the Kaiser's.

As soon as he became aware of Bernstorff's accusations, the Prince of Wales sent Francis Knollys to see the Ambassador to deny that he had ever expressed 'satisfaction at the idea that the Prussians would be unsuccessful in the approaching war.' Indeed, his family connections with Prussia would not allow of such sentiments. Although Bernstorff professed to accept HRH's assurances, Bismarck repeatedly asserted 'that Prussian aspirations had a foe in the heir to the British Crown.'

Four days after the outbreak of hostilities, the Queen told Gladstone that she was sleepless with anxiety, because '*all* her nearest and dearest and all she holds most dear next to her own beloved country' were 'in danger of life and home. It is a dreadful thing and makes one feel that Foreign Connections are a great misfortune.' While at any moment Vicky and Alice might be taken prisoner by the French, the Queen felt 'bound' to tell the Prime Minister that the Princess of Wales was 'very violent in her anti-Prussianism,' that her mother was 'very intriguing,' and her husband 'very imprudent.'

It was not necessary for the Prince of Wales to say or do anything to provoke attack. At one and the same time he was criticized for showing excessive sympathy for both combatants. While his mother and sister abused him for partiality to the French, Parliament and the newspapers reproached him for sending a friendly message to Fritz.

During the summer of 1870, as one French defeat followed another, the Prince longed 'to be of use,' and begged the Queen to let him try to negotiate a peace between the King of Prussia and the Emperor Napoleon. 'I cannot bear sitting here and doing nothing,' he wrote from Abergeldie on 21 August, 'whilst all this bloodshed is going on. How I wish you could send me with letters to the Emperor and King of Prussia . . . I would gladly go any distance, as I cannot help feeling restless when so many one knows and likes are exposed to such dangers.' But the Queen replied unkindly that 'even if he were personally fitted for such a very difficult task' his position 'would make it impossible.'

Early in 1871, General Gallifet, one of the Prince's closest friends in the French Army, predicted that if the Germans insisted on retaining Alsace and Lorraine, 'France would in due time seek to reverse the annexation.' But the Queen was reluctant to believe that Germany's victory threatened the peace of Europe. 'A powerful Germany,' she told the Prince in September 1870, 'can never be dangerous to England, but the very reverse, and our great object should therefore be to have her friendly and cordial towards us.' Throughout the war, she looked upon France as the aggressor. The conflict she saw as one between 'Civilization, liberty, order and unity,' as characterized by Prussia, and 'despotism, corruption, immorality and aggression,' as represented by France. When Dr Macleod in a sermon at Balmoral referred to Frenchmen as 'reaping the reward of wickedness, vanity and sensuality,' the Queen nodded her head to show her approval.

She was not alone in her looking-glass world. The Prince Consort had foreseen the 'necessity that this vainglorious and immoral people should be put down.' And Thomas Carlyle, whose hero was Frederick the Great, declared that the triumph of Prussia was 'the hopefullest fact' that had occurred in his lifetime. Even when the King of Prussia was proclaimed Emperor of Germany, amidst the smoking ruins of Paris, Carlyle still thought that Europe had nothing to fear in losing a mistress and finding a master.

The chivalrous manner in which the Prince of Wales treated the fallen Bonapartes exposed him to criticism from both France's enemies and her new Republican government. As soon as the Prince heard that the Empress had escaped to England, in Sir John Burgoyne's yacht, *Gazelle*, he offered her Chiswick House, which the Duke of Devonshire had lent him some years before. In his letter to the Empress, written from Dunrobin, he spoke of his happy memories of the kindness and friendship the Imperial family had shown him since 1855. '*La Princesse et moi ayant pensé qu'une résidence près de Londres Vous serait agréable, j'ose offrir à V.M. notre Maison de campagne "Chiswick" qui serait entièrement à la disposition de V.M. et nous serions bien heureux si Vous l'accepteriez.*'

Lord Granville, the Foreign Secretary, thought HRH's offer imprudent, and feared it might prejudice England's relations with France. The Empress, however, declined it, having already taken Camden Place, Chislehurst. The moment the Prince and Princess returned from Scotland, they paid her a visit and did what they could to console her. Two years later, on 9 January 1873, the Emperor died after a long illness and several operations.

The Prince paid the Empress two visits before the funeral, on 11 January, and three days later, when the Emperor lay in state. The Queen told Vicky on 14 January that she had 'just heard by telegraph that Bertie, Affie and Christian have been (by my desire) to Chislehurst to pay a last mark of personal respect to him who was excessively kind to them always and who lay in state today!' The Prince, his brother and brother-in-law, were conducted into the hall of Camden Place by the Prince Imperial, then a boy of sixteen. The Emperor lay in an open satin-lined coffin, dressed in full uniform. Some people mistakenly imagined that he had died of jaundice because in the process of embalming his face had turned yellow. The next day he was buried in St Mary's Church on Chislehurst Common.

The Prince Imperial became a cadet at the Royal Military Academy at Woolwich. When he passed out seventh of his year, Queen Victoria congratulated the Empress on 'the success of the dear young Prince.' In 1879 he applied to go to South Africa to fight the Zulus. Disraeli, at first, discouraged the proposal, but the young man was so insistent that he eventually consented. The Queen told the Duke of Cambridge how touched she was by the Prince's desire 'to serve with my brave troops,' but as he was 'very venture-some,' it must clearly be understood that he was merely a 'spectator'.

The Prince of Wales took as great an interest in the boy as did Her Majesty, and helped negotiate permission for him to see the fighting. As, in fact, did the Empress, who at first welcomed obstruc-tion. But when she saw her son's despair she changed her mind, and 'went herself to the War Office, unknown to anyone, to ask if nothing could still be arranged for him to go in some way or another.'

On 1 June, the Prince Imperial was killed after being ambushed by Zulu warriors. The Duke of Cambridge found it 'quite inexplic-able' that 'the Prince should have been allowed to get into so exposed a position.' And what made matters worse was that the youth had seemingly been deserted by his escort. 'It is incredible,' wrote the Queen in her Journal, 'that there was not one who remained behind to try to save this precious life.' It was 'too dreadful' that the poor boy should have been left to his fate by British soldiers. The Prince of Wales was deeply distressed by the news, and told his mother that he could not 'get the poor little Prince Imperial' out of his thoughts, and that he regarded 'his untimely and horrible death as a most dreadful catastrophe.' As for the 'poor, poor Empress, what has she to live for now? Nothing. Her last hopes, her last interest in life is at an end. It is really too dreadful, too awful.' Unhappily, the episode was 'a blot on our army in South Africa.' Had he lived, HRH believed, the young Bonaparte 'would have proved an admirable Sovereign,' and a great ally of England like his father.

The Empress decided that her son's body should be brought back to Chislehurst. The Government was anxious not to offend Repub-lican France by paying undue attention to Napoleon's family, but the Prince of Wales insisted that the highest honour should be paid to one who had died in Her Majesty's service. As the warship bearing the remains of the Prince Imperial steamed up the Channel, twenty-three minute-guns were fired from Spithead, one for each year of his life. The funeral was held on 12 July and the Queen watched the procession. Before the service, she visited the *Chapelle Ardente*, which 'was beautifully arranged, all hung with white, and burning candles all round.' Soon afterwards, she 'saw the coffin borne out by ten Artillery Officers, preceded by the clergy, one priest carrying the crucifix on high.' Her four sons were amongst the pall-bearers, paying an unprecedented tribute to the fallen dynasty. Lord Beaconsfield, who feared that the Royal Family had made too much of the funeral, said he hoped that the French Government would share their satisfaction with these last rites.

For some time after France's defeat in 1871, it looked doubtful whether the Third Republic would survive. Naturally, the Prince of Wales was no Republican, and, while realistic hopes could be entertained of alternative forms of government, he was tempted to indulge them. But by 1878 he concluded that the majority of Frenchmen were wholeheartedly committed to the regime, which he therefore decided to support.

In 1876 the French Government let it be known to the Foreign Office that they very much hoped the Prince would become President of the British Section of the Paris International Exhibition, planned for the spring of 1878. Having been brought up by his father to rejoice in Exhibitions, he willingly undertook the task, and spared neither time nor effort to make his country's share in the enterprise a triumph. Once the British Pavilion was built in the Champs-Elysées, he constantly visited Paris to supervise proceedings. Both in public speeches and in private conversations, he took the opportunity to encourage friendly relations. Inevitably, in advocating *entente* he sanctioned Republicanism.

Soon after the opening of the Exhibition, the Prince of Wales met Gambetta, the most notable French statesman of the day, whose cardinal principle after 1871 was: '*La Prussianisme voilà l'ennemi.*' M. Delcassé, who later played a prominent part in the Anglo–French *entente* of 1904, told a colleague, while its terms were being discussed, that he had long worked for such an alliance, but that the idea was not his. 'I got it from Gambetta,' he admitted, 'and my only ambition is to continue his work.'

The two men met for the first time on 6 May 1878, at a dinner at the Quai d'Orsay. Lord Lyons, the British Ambassador in Paris, introduced them. Many years afterwards, the King told M. Paoli, the special Commissioner of Police who guarded him in France, that Gambetta had struck him 'as so vulgar in his manner and so careless of his appearance that I asked myself if this was really the man who had discovered the means of exercising an irresistible fascination over the minds of crowds. Then we talked. Gambetta expounded his ideas and his plans; and the captivating charm of his eloquence made me forget the physical repulsion with which he inspired me:

I was "carried away" in my turn, like the others . . . He was a great politician and a wonderful master of words.' During their conversation they soon discovered how much they shared in common. Gambetta stressed his wish for the closest understanding between their two countries. The Prince replied he had been a friend of France since his visit as a boy.

The understanding for which the Prince worked during the Paris Exhibition, almost foundered in consequence of Lord Beaconsfield's foreign policy. It was announced on the eve of the Congress of Berlin that Britain had signed a defensive alliance with Turkey in return for the cession of Cyprus. In France the news was greeted with indignation and was seen as a threat to her influence in Egypt and the eastern Mediterranean. So great was the indignation that Lord Lyons urged HRH to postpone his proposed visit to Paris in July. But the Prince, far from avoiding the issue, was resolved to assure Gambetta that there was no cause for concern. Accordingly, he invited him to luncheon at the *Café des Anglais*, whose chef, M. Duclere, was described by Rossini as 'the Mozart of Cooking.'

Some accounts of the meal suggest that it began awkwardly because Gambetta was not at his ease, while the Prince was distressed by his guest's boots and frock-coat. But when the time came for brandy and cigars, the tension relaxed. Gambetta discovered that the Prince was one of the best-informed men he had ever met, and HRH recognized that his friend's lucidity, wit and brilliance had not been exaggerated. They were still engaged in animated discussion at six o'clock that evening. So successful was this mission, that Lord Lyons informed the Foreign Secretary that the Prince had 'acquitted himself with great skill,' and that Gambetta 'was extremely pleased with the interview.'

Until Gambetta's death in 1882, he and the Prince frequently discussed European politics. He loves our country, said the Frenchmen, 'at once "*gaîment et sérieusement*," and his dream of the future is an "*entente*" with us.' Twenty years before such an understanding was finally accomplished, the Prince and Gambetta were discussing it over supper at the *Café des Anglais*. Gambetta believed that he saw in his royal friend 'the makings of a great statesman,' and thought him particularly far-sighted in not sharing 'the hostility of a section of the English nation against Russia.' If all Princes, he told HRH, were like you, there would be no need of republics.

The problems of achieving an understanding between Britain and France increased towards the end of the nineteenth century. In particular, Colonial rivalries imposed a cumulative strain on friendly relations. General Wolseley's defeat of Arabi at Tel-el-Kebir in September 1882 turned Egypt into a British dependency. For the next twenty years France was antagonized by the occupation of a part of Africa which she had dominated herself since the Battle of the Pyramids. When Sir Evelyn Baring became virtual dictator of Egypt, with the unassuming title of 'Consul-General,' hardly a vestige of French influence remained. Elsewhere, as in Madagascar and Tonkin, conflict threatened. By 1883, ill-feeling against Britain was so intense that the Prince of Wales abandoned his visit to Paris that spring. But worse was to come.

In 1896, Lord Salisbury ordered Kitchener to reconquer the Sudan. After two years, fighting, the campaign was concluded by the Battle of Omdurman. Henceforth, proclaimed the Prime Minister, for the benefit of France, Sudanese territory would revert to Egyptian rule: an arrangement he described as 'not open to discussion.' In September, 1898, Captain Marchand, a French explorer, planted the tricolour at Fashoda, on the White Nile. When Salisbury was told what had happened, he instructed Kitchener to insist that Marchand should haul down his flag and withdraw. For some days the two men confronted one another, exchanging demands and refusals. The crisis was finally resolved when the Captain was ordered by the Quai d'Orsay to retire as gracefully as circumstances permitted. This conciliatory gesture was inspired by M. Delcassé, who had recently become Foreign Minister. The French, however, were slow to recognize the wisdom of his policy and quick to resent the humiliation of surrender.

The outbreak of the Boer War in September 1899 provoked worldwide indignation and demonstrated how isolated Britain had become. Had Lord Salisbury submitted to President Kruger's demands and abandoned the Uitlanders to their fate, he would have presided over the break-up of the British Empire. But all that most countries saw was a mighty Empire, which for centuries had boasted of being the land of the free, endeavouring to crush a valiant handful of rebels and put them behind barbed wire. Nowhere more than in France did this spectacle inspire a passionate sense of outrage. French newspapers tirelessly attacked the British Government and savagely ridiculed the Queen and the Prince.

During President Kruger's visit to France in November 1900, sympathy for the Boers and hatred of England reached a frenzied crescendo. When Lord Rosebery and Lady Warwick attended the first night of Rostand's great drama *L'Aiglon*, written specially for Sarah Bernhardt, they were greeted with shouts from the audience of '*A bas les Anglais! Vivent les Boers!*' and had to be hustled out of the theatre by the back way.

Even the Prince of Wales, an unfailing friend of France, was hissed, jeered and abused. General Owen Williams told Knollys that he thought it might be unwise for HRH to attend the opening of the Paris Exhibition in the spring of 1900, in view of widespread hostility towards England. 'My dear Francis,' he wrote, 'you are a model of discretion and will decide as to whether the Prince of Wales ought not to know something more of what is going on in Paris than is gathered from the papers, for I feel sure that *if he were only aware* of the atrocious caricatures of the Queen that are published there, and eagerly bought up by the populace, he would at once decline to have anything to do with their Exhibition. I can only tell you that one of these caricatures is so abominably indecent, and obscene, that the police suppressed it. It was too bad to describe, the letter press on a par. Of course people will try to minimize these attacks to HRH, for, if he knew of them, he would perforce be obliged to resign his position with regard to the Exhibition of Paris next year. The worst of the case is that these insults are only repudiated by the Government in a half-hearted sort of way, and not at all by the rest of the nation, from the Highest to the Lowest. In fact the members of the clubs are as bad as those they would describe as canaille. The question is whether the Prince ought not be acquainted with the *facts*.'

General Williams was not alone in warning HRH of the threatening mood of public opinion in Paris. Colonel Henry Mapleson, who having retired from the Royal Artillery devoted himself to promoting Italian Opera, sent Knollys a number of scurrilous pamphlets so that he might see for himself what was being written and read. In an accompanying letter he explained that 'living in Paris and moving constantly in all parts of the City and mixing with all sections of the community,' he was in a position to 'state with absolute truth and free from all bias and exaggeration, that the anti-English feeling here is most intense in character and is shewn in every possible way. Far from diminishing, I find it on the increase.' Obviously, the newspapers had 'done much to fan the smouldering antipathy for *perfide Albion* into a fierce flame,' but 'people who do not pay any attention to the press are the most vindictive!'

In acknowledging Mapleson's letter, Knollys referred to more favourable opinions from the British Embassy in Paris and English-men travelling in France. But the Colonel 'respectfully' pointed out by way of reply, 'that the majority of English people travelling on the Continent follow a beaten track, and visit Hotels and patronize establishments more or less dependent on Anglo-American travellers and consequently it is not in these places that they can correctly gauge the true feeling of the French population . . . The proprietors of the French newspapers are coining money by constantly attacking England, and their increased circulation is proof positive that the majority here endorse the action of the Press. Whenever there is a *report* of a Boer victory, the habitués of the Boulevard cafés are mad with delight and any English looking people, who happen to be in these places, are accosted with the most insulting epithets.'

Lord Salisbury tried to persuade the Prince of Wales to attend the inaugural ceremonies of the Paris Exhibition, on the ground that his doing so would help to improve relations. But the Prince rejected the Prime Minister's advice, for fear he might seem to condone the disgusting abuse directed against the Queen. The bitter hostility which was felt by France for England at the beginning of King Edward's reign, is a measure of the diplomatic revolution he helped to achieve within three years of his accession.

Until the death of his brother-in-law, the Emperor Frederick, in 1888, the Prince of Wales looked forward to the day when Vicky and Fritz would realize their aspirations: liberal and constitutional government at home, and close friendship with England abroad. In so far as anything could reconcile HRH to Bismarck, it was the hope that his days were numbered. But, when the Chancellor was finally dismissed, it was not so that Fritz might replace him with a more enlightened minister, but in order that William II could rule with-out restraint. From the moment the Kaiser 'dropped the Pilot' and steered his 'new course,' the Prince became increasingly dismayed by the erratic antics of his nephew. But, even as late as 1901, he referred to the two countries as 'natural allies.'

The Prince visited Germany a great deal less often than France, partly because he shared Vicky's dislike of its stiff and joyless Court. But such were his winning ways, that few Germans recognized how thoroughly they bored him, and the British Ambassador in Berlin, Lord Odo Russell, wished he would come more often. 'The Prince's visit to Potsdam,' he told Knollys in 1874, 'has proved an immense success, and the oftener His Royal Highess can exercise his personal influence in Germany, the better for our international relations. He carries everything before him and fascinates everyone he speaks to. Only the other night the Station Master at Cologne was saying to me: "Of all the Royal Princes we have known, none is so beloved, so popular or so respected as the Prince of Wales." And this sentiment I have heard expressed in every class of society the Prince has approached.'

When Prince Bismarck sent his son, Count Herbert, on a mission to England in 1882, in an effort to establish better relations, he was repeatedly invited to Marlborough House and Sandringham. 'No one knows better than you,' the Count told Knollys, 'how kindly I have been received in England and that it is His Royal Highness to whom I am especially indebted for it.' After staying at Abergeldie for a week in the autumn of 1884, he managed to leave his cap and some handkerchiefs behind. Writing to Knollys in an effort to retrieve them, he became quite effusive for one whose pen was so often dipped in vitriol. 'I cannot tell you how much I enjoyed my visit on the Deeside: everybody was so kind to me that I never felt happier in my life.' But, courteous and hospitable as the Prince was, he regarded his guest with suspicion, and some years later had occasion to describe him as a 'scoundrel whose ingratitude for all the kindness I have shown him for so many years knows no bounds.'

The Crown Princess was unpopular in Prussia, partly because she seldom bothered to conceal the high regard in which she held her native land, partly because she supported liberalism in a reactionary and authoritarian state, and partly because she was said to dominate Fritz and fill his head with foolish notions. The fact that she was brilliantly clever, outstandingly well-read and exceptionally artistic, counted for little in Court and military circles. In opposing Bismarck, she made a ruthless enemy, who waged war against her without chivalry or scruple. He even encouraged Prince William to think of his mother as an alien Princess, of malign if not treasonable disposition, who conspired with her foreign relations to deprive Germany of its rightful place in the world.

Nobody understood Vicky's difficulties better than the Prince, who showed her unfailing affection. Whenever they met, she wrote of 'his dear kind face' wearing 'its beaming expression,' and her letters glowed in the 'sunshine' of his visits. In the early days of her widowhood, she told her daughter Sophie that it was 'a great joy having dear Uncle Bertie near. There is not a kinder brother in the world, and I cling to him in my loneliness very much.'

She loved him the more for his being so fond of her husband, to whom he became increasingly attached. 'Never forget Uncle Fritz,' he told his son, Prince George. 'He was one of the finest and noblest characters ever known; if he had a fault, he was *too* good for this world.' In thanking Vicky for the birthday present she sent him in 1888, he told her that nothing could have given him 'greater pleasure than the medallion of our beloved Fritz. The likeness is admirable and I shall greatly value it as representing the best and noblest of men, whose kindness and affection towards me never ceased ever since I knew him.'

Fritz was often accused of becoming a liberal because of Vicky's persuasion, but she merely fortified a faith he already possessed. Before they were married, the Queen noted with approval that her son-in-law-to-be was determined to resist the 'Old traditional doctrine' of the Junkers. His death was much more than a family tragedy, for he shared his wife's dedication to Anglo-German friendship, and the 1914 War would have been inconceivable had Frederick III lived as long as his father.

Throughout Fritz's last dreadful illness, as he slowly died from cancer of the throat, amidst the unseemly wrangles of his doctors, the Prince of Wales overflowed with solicitude for his and Vicky's suffering. In February 1888 he paid them a visit at San Remo, where the Crown Princess had taken her husband in search of sunshine. He found her bewildered by the conflicting advice of seven querulous physicians, and besieged by reporters who bribed her servants, scrutinized her through telescopes, and were altogether brash and unfeeling. 'I have been here since Monday,' he told Knollys, 'and though my Brother-in-law's progress is slow it is I think satisfactory. I see him twice a day – and he talks a little – but I fear suffers great discomfort. His courage and fortitude is *beyond* all praise. My poor sister has a terribly difficult time to go through, but she bears up bravely and her spirits are wonderful – which is all important. It is a great pity that the English and German doctors are so antagonistic one with the other. That is the great difficulty of the situation and the patient has to suffer in consequence.'

Fritz's father died on 8 March 1888, so his reign of ninety-nine days began in Italy. By then he could no longer speak, but his first actions as Emperor eloquently proclaimed his feelings. He took off his Order of the Black Eagle and lovingly bestowed it on Vicky. Next, he sent Queen Victoria a telegram, assuring her of his 'devoted affection' and 'earnest desire for a close and lasting friendship between our two nations.' Before they left for Berlin, Vicky scribbled

her mother a hurried note. Already she knew in her heart that
Fritz's days were numbered. It was so hard, she wrote, that he was
'succeeding his father as a sick and stricken man.' She prayed that
'he might be spared to be a blessing to his people and to Europe.
How much good he might have done!'

As soon as the Prince of Wales heard that the Old Kaiser was
dead, he wrote to his sister to say: 'My thoughts as you can imagine
are entirely with you and dear Fritz. God grant that the long journey
may do dear Fritz no harm. Mama sends me over to the Funeral
which of course I should have attended anyhow and I shall perhaps
bring Eddy with me. Though of course the poor old Emperor's death
is very sad, still I must offer you and Fritz my sincerest congratulations on having become Emperor and Empress.'

During his visit to Germany for the funeral of William I, the
Prince recognized that Fritz's illness was mortal and hope for his
recovery illusory. 'I return home,' he told Knollys, 'with a heavy
heart as God knows if I shall ever see my dear and excellent Brother-
in-law again. It is almost only a matter of time. How long or how
short I cannot say – but he is doomed. All know it here and above all
my poor sister, who is heart broken.'

In fact, they met once more at the end of May, when Fritz's son
Prince Henry was married to Alice's daughter Irene. The Emperor
had less than three weeks to live, but insisted on being present at the
ceremony, which took place in the rococo chapel at Charlottenburg.
He wore the blue ribbon of the Garter and an order which he had
been given by the Grand Duke of Hesse, the bride's father. Although
obviously pale and wasted, he still looked every inch a king. The
sight of the dying man struggling for breath while attempting to hide
his infirmity, was pitiful to watch. He was greatly fatigued by the
ceremony and ran a high temperature that evening. Probably the
final decline of His Majesty's health could be reckoned from that day.
Old Field-Marshal Moltke told a friend after the service, 'I have
seen many brave men, but none as brave as the Emperor has shown
himself today!'

Fritz died on 15 June 1888, and his funeral took place three days
later on the seventy-third anniversary of the Battle of Waterloo. It
was one of the rare occasions upon which Alix accompanied her
husband to Germany. It is true the Queen begged her to go, but she
felt deeply for Vicky, whose 'plans and ambitions' were crushed,
and who had 'nothing left but remembrance of the past.'

After the ceremonies had taken place, the Prince hurriedly wrote

Group at Rumpenheim, August 1865, including the Prince and Princess of Wales, Augusta, Duchess of Cambridge (in window, left), Duke of Cambridge (in light suit and dark bowler hat), Hereditary Grand Duke (seated, in light suit and light bowler) and Hereditary Grand Duchess (on balcony in light dress) of Mecklenburg-Strelitz, Princess Mary of Cambridge (standing, right, with eyes cast down).

Three children of Edward VII. *Bauerle*.

Portrait of Queen Alexandra. *Fildes*.

The family of King Christian IX and Queen Louise of Denmark, 1883. *Tuxen.*

Shooting party in Windsor Great Park, November 1867.
Left to right : General Grey, Major Grey, General Seymour, Prince of Wales, Prince Christian of Schleswig-Holstein, Sir James Clark.

Alexandra, Princess of Wales and her three daughters at Sandringham, January 1882.
Left to right : Princess Victoria, Princess Louise and Princess Maud.

Shooting party at Abergeldie,
1871. *Zichy*.

Prince George (later
King George V), 1872.
Sant.

The Prince of Wales dressed as the Lord of the Isles at the Waverley Ball, 1871.

an account of them for the Queen, so that Lord Lorne, who was
returning to England that night, could deliver the letter next day.
At 8.30 that morning, he and Alix had left the British Embassy in
Berlin, where they were staying with Sir Edward and Lady Malet,
for Friedrichskron. They were at once shown into a room 'where all
the family were assembled,' and received by William and Dona.
'Our meeting with them, especially with Charlotte, Henry and Irene
was very trying . . . We then all walked in procession behind the
hearse to the Friedenskirche . . . The most touching incident was
dear Fritz's chestnut horse "Worth" (which he rode at the battle)
being led by two grooms close behind the hearse, and he was continually neighing . . .

'After the blessing was given many of us approached the coffin and
knelt down in silent prayer. After that we all separated, and I felt
on leaving the church that I had parted from the noblest and best
man I had ever known, except my ever-to-be-lamented father.' A short
time after the funeral, 'poor dear Vicky and her three girls arrived
from Bornstadt, where they had attended a private special service
during the funeral at Potsdam. My meeting with darling Vicky was
heartrending and she cried and sobbed like a child, then got calm,
and could speak of dear Fritz and his last moments which were,
thank God, peaceful and painless.'

When Vicky visited Sandringham in 1891 she was deeply touched
by her brother's memorial to Fritz, which was 'so good and so *like*
his dear noble face, so manly and calm.' She told her daughter,
Sophie, how 'nice and good of Uncle Bertie,' it was 'to erect this
little monument to our dear one's memory' in the church where they
worshipped each Sunday.

Soon after the Emperor's death, a painful controversy broke out
between Sir Morrell Mackenzie, the English specialist in whom
Vicky and Fritz had shown the greatest trust, and the German
doctors he virtually displaced. Ostensibly, the dispute was confined
to questions of treatment and diagnosis. But Bismarck exploited the
quarrel in order to discredit the Dowager Empress. In the first
instance, Fritz's own doctors had proposed consulting Mackenzie,
but later it was alleged that the Crown Princess had summoned him
because she distrusted the Court physicians. It was further suggested
that Mackenzie had diagnosed cancer too late and hence was
responsible for his patient's death. It would be interesting to know
how his detractors would have cured a malignant growth.

The Prince of Wales was distressed by these 'lamentable' wrangles, and told Vicky that Sir William Gull, 'who came to see us a few days ago, said that as alas! dear Fritz was no more what was the use of a fight with the doctors about the illness, who was right or who was wrong. Undoubtedly all did their best, but it was undignified and wrong to quarrel over the grave of one who all wished to save.'

Although Vicky remained unshakably loyal to Mackenzie, through all the battles which raged around him, and in which he joined with more zeal than discretion, her brother formed a less favourable impression of his wisdom and integrity. Knollys was convinced that Sir Morrell was 'not only a most awful liar, but likewise a very blundering and unnecessary one.' Although he expected to be invited to Sandringham, the Prince of Wales had 'at last become disgusted with him' and showed little disposition to ask him. Nor was Lady Mackenzie to be trusted. Ponsonby reported that the Queen thought her 'a very dangerous woman.' There was no knowing, he added, 'what secret she might reveal about the Royal laundry.'

Vicky herself was savagely attacked by several German newspapers in the first years of her widowhood. Setting aside considerations of chivalry, as we are bound to do if we wish to understand Bismarck, it remains difficult to explain why the Dowager Empress was so viciously reviled. She herself believed that it was partly to excite dislike against everything English.

The Queen wished Lord Salisbury to complain to Bismarck about some of the more outrageous attacks on her daughter appearing in Germany, but he thought it wiser to take no notice of them, as it was impossible to hold the Chancellor 'responsible for what appeared in a newspaper.' Ponsonby told Knollys that he thought that 'the Empress agrees in this view. She says it is only part of the general plan to attack all her friends, Geffken, Roggenbach, Freytag and Morier: to endeavour to prove them traitors and then show the Emperor that he should distrust his mother who has such friends.'

In several letters the Prince of Wales deplored the way Vicky was slandered. 'I always had the greatest contempt and dislike of the Press,' he told her, 'though of course one cannot exist without it, but ever since dear Fritz's illness it has come out quite disgracefully. *The Times* correspondent at Berlin [Charles Lowe] is really a horrible fellow and mischievous beyond measure. When he does not invent anything himself he inserts extracts from other newspapers in the most disagreeable manner.' A few days later he assured her: 'I fully share all your bitter feelings against the Press as they are also my

own. The way that horrid man Mr Lowe behaves is really too disgraceful. I shall seek out an early opportunity to let Mr Buckle [the
Editor of *The Times*] know your feelings on the subject.'

When Vicky paid her first visit to England after Fritz's death,
she spent her birthday at Windsor. The Prince at the time was at
Sandringham, so sent 'two lines' to tell her how much she would be
in his mind on 'tomorrow's dear anniversary – though you will miss
the one who was nearest and dearest to you in life. Still you will be
able to spend your birthday in your old home at least quietly and
undisturbed, and God knows *you* need such a repose after the terrible
mental and physical worry you have endured so long. Try and
forget while you are in your own country those who persecuted you
so unmercifully in your adopted country – all I can say is shame on
them!'

So far from seeking to console his widowed mother, William added
to her grief. He belonged to a generation which had grown up under
Bismarck and shared his intolerance of those liberal ideals which
Vicky and Fritz held sacred. As William grew older, he became less
agreeable. By the time he was sixteen he had the makings of a
singularly awkward adolescent. Sometimes he was so petulant and
dogmatic that his mother felt like a hen who had hatched an ugly
duckling. The Queen, having had nine children of her own, foresaw
trouble. She warned of children's 'greatest object being to do
precisely what their parents do not wish and have anxiously tried
to prevent!'

Like the Queen, Vicky made the mistake of trying to make her
eldest son follow in his father's footsteps. Admittedly, she recognized
the error of her ways. 'One must guard against the fault,' she wrote,
'of being annoyed with one's children for not being what one wished
and hoped. One must learn to abandon dreams and take things as
they come and characters as they are – one cannot quarrel with
nature.'

Those who lived through the creation of the German Empire, and
watched the invincible Prussian army parade before their Emperor
in Berlin, may possibly be forgiven for becoming over-excited by the
triumphs of imperialism. Certainly the boy born to be Kaiser was
deeply affected by the war of 1870, which he followed eagerly on a
map, and by the rejoicing which greeted his grandfather's proclamation at Versailles.

Prince William's uncritical patriotism provoked him to challenge
his parents. Why were they so reluctant to praise the Chancellor for

all he had done for Germany? Why had his mother wept on learning that Napoleon III had died? The more he contradicted his father, or called his mother a socialist for reading *Das Kapital*, the deeper the rift between him and his parents grew. Vicky, who was amazingly well-informed and knew what rubbish her son was talking, found it intolerable to live at close quarters with one who was never mistaken. She reproached him for being vain, reactionary, self-assertive, arrogant, and ignorant: while he accused her of stubbornly clinging to discredited ideals, of obstructing Bismarck, and of obsequious, if not treasonable, dependence on England. He once told General Waldersee that his mother conspired with Queen Victoria against the interests of Germany, and that she tried to make 'Anglophils of her children.' Vicky believed that her son's 'deplorable friends,' and 'all the nonsense with which his head has been so systematically stuffed,' had poisoned his mind. But above all, she blamed Bismarck. When the Chancellor in 1890 discovered that William proposed to dismiss him, he begged the Empress Frederick to intercede. 'I can do nothing,' she is said to have replied. 'You, yourself, Prince Bismarck, have destroyed my influence with my son.'

The Kaiser looked upon England with conflicting emotions of hatred, fear, envy and admiration. Once, when his nose was bleeding profusely, he refused to try to stop it, saying he preferred to lose every drop of English blood in his body. He often spoke of his English relations as 'the damned family' and of his contempt for a nation of thieves and traffickers. But the very intensity of his feelings betrayed unrequited love. He was obsessed by England, he copied England, he denounced England, and in his heart he could not help being fond of England. When in 1918 he arrived as a fugitive in Holland, the first thing he asked for was 'a cup of really good English tea.'

William's strenuous efforts to ingratiate himself with Englishmen were pathetically misdirected. Instead of respecting their silence and reserve he became garrulous and flamboyant. Amongst those bred to conceal their feelings, he was as incongruous as a clown turning somersaults in a mortuary. Nevertheless, he assured an audience at the Guildhall in 1891 that he always felt at home in their beautiful country, and twenty years later amazed Theodore Roosevelt by telling him: 'I adore England.'

William's egotism was prodigious, even for an Emperor. His favourite pronouns were 'I' and 'My'. He constantly talked about 'My Army,' 'My Navy,' 'My Ports,' or 'My Chancellor': but never 'My mistakes' for those were his ministers'. Such was his self-esteem that he insisted on being surrounded by paintings and photographs of himself. One was so challenging that General Gallifet described it as 'less a portrait than a declaration of War.' But his most obtrusive characteristic was his compulsive exhibitionism. An indulgent admirer once remarked that the Kaiser's trouble was that he wanted to be the bride at every wedding and the corpse at every funeral. He particularly fancied himself in the role of Frederick the Great, and once placing his hand on his heart proclaimed: 'He is not dead, he lives here.' But then, as Churchill said, 'If you are the summit of a volcano, the least you can do is to smoke.'

Dramatic and impulsive by nature, the Kaiser was given the nickname: 'William the Sudden.' Throughout his career he continually surprised even those who knew him best by his feverish and capricious changes of policy. Before he was eight months old, Vicky declared he was 'never quiet a minute,' and that she had seldom seen 'such a bit of quicksilver.' After he had been Kaiser for three years, Randolph Churchill complained: 'It is impossible for Europe to be tranquil so long as that excitable young Emperor keeps gallivanting about. Why can't he live quietly like the Emperor of Russia and the Emperor of Austria do?'

William was a classic schizophrenic. At one moment, he would triumphantly defy the world; in the next, he would crumble and collapse. It is difficult to decide which of the two Kaisers was the most contemptible: the excitable, blustering, bullying War Lord, ludicrously bragging of his genius, inviting comparison with Frederick the Great, vain, flamboyant, loud-mouthed, insensitive and threatening; or the hesitant, tearful, touchy, pathetic creature, who in sudden moments of truth lost faith in his own acting.

The Prince of Wales was almost the perfect uncle: generous, affectionate and anxious to see everyone happy. At first, he thought Prince William a charming boy. In 1874 he persuaded Alix to accompany him to Berlin to attend his nephew's confirmation, at which 'Willy went through his examination admirably.' After the ceremony, he took the sacrament with Vicky and Fritz and their son. She regarded it as 'a great comfort and happiness' to have her brother with her. 'Dear Bertie is *all* kindness,' she told her mother, 'so considerate, so amiable and affectionate – so kindly accepting all that we can do for his comfort or entertainment, which alas is not much. He is as amiable a guest as he is a host, and this is saying a *great* deal!'

Four years later, when Vicky's daughter Charlotte married Prince

Bernhard of Meiningen, the Prince of Wales was present, and, in describing the family gathering for the Queen, he wrote it would be 'impossible to find two nicer boys than William and Henry.' In 1880 Prince William became engaged to Princess Augusta Victoria of Schleswig-Holstein-Sonderburg-Augustenburg. Her father, Duke Frederick, was the elder brother of Queen Victoria's son-in-law, Prince Christian.

The Prince of Wales, but not the Princess, attended William's wedding, by which time relations between the two were showing signs of strain. The Prince was disturbed by William's brusque military ways, growing chauvinism and estrangement from Vicky and Fritz. For his part, the bridegroom was coming to regard his Uncle Bertie as a corrupting influence on his parents. Their worsening relationship deteriorated rapidly in 1884, when the family was bitterly divided over the proposed marriage between Prince Alexander of Battenberg and the Crown Princess's daughter, Princess Victoria. William opposed the plan, despite the fact that Queen Victoria and his mother approved it, and particularly resented his uncle's reputed role of 'matchmaker-in-chief.'

In 1885 the Prince of Wales's confidence in his nephew was shattered for ever, when Dagmar told him of William's clumsy efforts to poison the Tsar's mind. In a series of letters, written in English, the young man represented his Uncle Bertie as trying to incite Germany to wage war on Russia. In June, 1884, he warned Alexander III that the Prince's visit to Berlin 'has yielded and is still bringing extraordinary fruit, which will continue to multiply under the hands of my mother and the Queen of England. But these English have accidentally forgotten that *I* exist. And I swear to you my dear cousin, that anything I can do for You and Your country I will do.' When Prince William visited England for the Queen's Jubilee in 1887, he complained that his uncle ostentatiously ignored him while hardly ever leaving Fritz.

When William succeeded his father as Emperor, the Prince of Wales became increasingly anxious about him. Sometimes he merely found him absurd, and spoke light-heartedly of 'my illustrious nephew' or 'William the Great.' But the way the young Kaiser treated his widowed mother disgusted him. 'His conduct towards you,' he told her in November 1888, 'is simply revolting. But alas! he lacks the feelings and usages of a gentleman! Qualities which his ever to be regretted father and also his grandfather possessed to a high degree.' HRH found it some consolation that 'Master William is getting into a nice scrape with the Press, and the time may come quicker than he expects when he will be taught that neither Germany nor Prussia will stand an autocrat at the end of the 19th Century.' In 1892 the Prince advised Knollys to read the April number of *The Contemporary Review*, in which there was a pungent attack on the Kaiser. 'How furious my imperial nephew would be if he read it – but I have advised my sister to do so.'

Bülow believed that the 'complete cleavage between Uncle and Nephew' was 'brought about by the events of the ninety-nine days of the year of mourning, 1888, by the attempt of the then Prince William to persuade his father to abdicate at San Remo, by the ugly scenes between son and mother at the father's death-bed, and by the undutiful behaviour of the son to his mother after his father's death.' One of the late Emperor's last acts had been to re-christen the *Neue Palais*: 'Friedrichskron.' Almost the first order William gave on becoming Kaiser was that the old name should be restored, as if to show how little he valued his father's memory. Although Fritz begged his son 'as a filial duty' to approve his sister's marriage, no sooner had he succeeded than he forbade the wedding.

The Princess of Wales was deeply incensed by the Kaiser's behaviour, and shared and encouraged her husband's feelings of outrage. Most of all she deplored his treatment of his mother. 'Instead,' she wrote in August 1888, 'of William being a comfort and support to her, he has quite gone over to Bismarck and Co, who entirely overlook and crush her. Which is too infamous.' Charlotte Knollys later told Bülow that the Princess of Wales looked on her nephew Willy as 'inwardly our enemy.' She was not for one moment deceived by his 'assurances of love and affection. His heartless treatment of his dying father and his behaviour to his mother show that he has as little heart as he has political common-sense.'

The Kaiser believed that his Uncle was always intriguing against him, mainly because he assessed the conduct of others in terms of his own behaviour. But, in fact, the Prince repeatedly urged his sister to remain on good terms with her son. Nine days after Fritz's funeral, he told her how well he knew her 'endless difficulties with W., but you must not be disheartened dearest Vicky and try to surmount them – above all if possible try and have some influence with him, so that he may not be entirely at the mercy of those in whose political opinions you cannot agree.'

Two days later he wrote again to say that 'sad as our recent journey was, it was a labour of love, but we felt we could never

adequately express to you *how* deeply we felt for you in your irreparable sorrow. Your loss is one different to every one else under
similar circumstances as not only is it the loss of a beloved husband,
counsellor and friend which can never be replaced, but the great
interests in life and of your adopted country were absorbed with him
for the last thirty years. Now that is gone!' But rather than live in the
past, the Prince argued, she still had 'a mission to fulfil, namely to
strive that the great deeds and noble principles in which the beloved
Fritz excelled may not be lost sight of. That you have bitter feelings
about people and things is indeed not to be wondered at, after what
you have told me and all I have heard, but I would beg you dearest
sister, to endeavour to dispel these feelings as much as you possibly
can, hard as it must necessarily be for you. Above all things endeavour to have influence over W. This is I know no easy task, but
do not despair, do not give up the hope that eventually the example
and views of his ever to be regretted father may yet be an example
to him in the difficult task which he has to fulfil. Let no estrangement exist between you both, and remember he is his father's eldest
son, and your first born. All those that love you and wish you well,
not only your relations but your friends and those who are dearly
attached to you, wish this I know.'

Later that year, the Prince told Vicky that he was dreadfully
grieved by the way she had been treated. 'Prince Bismarck is like
Mephistopheles behind W. urging him to do things which must be
painful and distasteful to you, and bolstered up by the son Herbert
Bismarck and many others no doubt, and when one knows that the
Official Press is the mouthpiece and in the pay of the Wilhelm
Strasse, it is doubly galling and bitter for you to bear. Still I would
urge – and do so more strongly than ever, not to quarrel with W.
whatever happens. His not answering letters is not a good sign, but
the more you can transmit business with him by word of mouth, the
better . . . If as you say there is a party who wish to get rid of you
and drive you away from the country, I hope you will not play their
game. Show them you have only contempt for the abominable way
they behave . . . I cannot find words, dearest Vicky, to express to
you what I feel on the subject. Only don't let them think that they
irritate you as that will punish them more than anything.'

In November 1888, when Vicky was staying at Windsor, her
brother wrote from Sandringham thanking her for two 'kind and
affectionate' letters. 'You know,' he said, 'what my feelings are for
you, dearest sister, and have ever been, and though I am not

demonstrative by nature, my feelings are none the less sincere. It was a real pleasure for me to bring you over from Flushing and to feel that I might perhaps be of some small comfort to you. And now you are in a haven of rest, and though alas! nothing can really assuage your overwhelming sorrow or bring back the one you loved so well, still you are in your old home once more and surrounded by your nearest and dearest relations which must be soothing to your broken and bleeding heart. Pray think no more of William's rudeness to me. I feel sure that in time all will come right. He is headstrong and wilful and my only regret is that he should listen to and be guided by the pernicious advice of such bad men.'

Queen Victoria, the Empress Frederick and the Prince of Wales were distressed by the brevity of the Kaiser's mourning for his father. Hardly had Fritz been dead a fortnight before his son began planning to meet the Tsar. 'If this somewhat hurried visit to Russia,' the Prince wrote to Vicky, brings about 'good relations between the two countries we shall have no reason to regret it, but owing to the deep mourning it seems to me very soon to undertake a visit which to a certain extent must be in state.' But William had lurked long enough in the wings, and now he was playing the leading role nothing could keep him from strutting into the limelight.

In 1888 Francis Joseph invited the Prince of Wales to attend the autumn military manoeuvres of the Austrian Army. When the Prince learned that the Kaiser would be visiting the Emperor at the same time, he sent him two letters expressing pleasure at the prospect of their meeting. Neither message was answered or acknowledged. On 11 September, the day after HRH arrived in Vienna, he was told that his presence in the city during the Kaiser's visit would be unacceptable to his nephew. He was utterly taken aback, as he had recently parted from William the best of friends. But to avoid embarrassing Francis Joseph he agreed to visit Rumania while the two Emperors met.

The Queen was furious when she heard what had happened, and told her grand-daughter, Princess Victoria of Hesse, that 'Willy had behaved most outrageously to Uncle Bertie.' In the month following the Vienna affront, Count Hatzfeldt, the German Ambassador in London, saw Lord Salisbury and 'read or rather translated into French a long minute of Prince Bismarck's,' which 'explained at some length the political reasons which made the presence of the Prince of Wales at Vienna, together with the two Emperors, inadvisable. The gist of his argument was that it would irritate the Emperor of Russia, at a moment when matters were very delicate.' The Chancellor went on to hint at 'three grounds of offence.' First, that the Prince was reported as saying 'that if the Emperor Frederick had lived he would have made concessions as to Alsace, as to North Schleswig, and as to the claims of the Duke of Cumberland.' Second, that the Prince and Princess had urged the latter claims personally on Prince Bismarck. Third, that the Prince treated the Kaiser 'as an Uncle treats a nephew, instead of recognizing that he was an Emperor who, though young, had still been of age for some time.'

As soon as Lord Salisbury's account of his conversation with Count Hatzfeldt reached Balmoral, the Queen told him that it was 'simply absurd that the Emperor of Russia, the Princess of Wales's own brother-in-law (and who never expected the Princess to treat him otherwise, having the good sense to feel a great relief in the intimacy which exists between near relations, as opposed to formal etiquette,) should have been angry at the Uncle and Nephew meeting.' As for 'the Prince's not treating his nephew as Emperor; that is really too *vulgar* and too absurd, as well as untrue, almost *to be believed*. We have always been very intimate with our grandson and nephew, and to pretend that he is to be treated *in private* as well as in public as "his Imperial Majesty" is *perfect madness*! He has been treated just as we should have treated his beloved father and even grandfather, and as the Queen *herself* was always treated by her dear Uncle King Leopold. *If* he has *such* notions, he had better *never* come *here*. The Queen will not swallow this affront.' The Kaiser's behaviour showed 'a very unhealthy and unnatural state of mind; and he *must* be made to feel that his grandmother and Uncle will not stand such insolence. The Prince of Wales must *not* submit to such treatment. As regards the political relations of the two Governments, the Queen quite agrees that that should not be affected (if possible) by these miserable personal quarrels; but the Queen much *fears* that, with such a hot-headed, conceited, and wrongheaded young man, devoid of all feelings, this may at ANY moment become impossible.'

Vicky was most distressed by the way her son had treated his Uncle Bertie. It was some weeks before her brother told her the full story, not wishing to add to her troubles. Finally, on 31 October 1888, after the newspapers had made a field day of the matter, he sent her a long letter describing what had happened. 'You know, dearest Vicky,' he wrote, 'how I have taken William's part and stuck up for him in the family, and what is the result of all this?

When I proposed to meet him at Vienna on his recent visit there, he expressed a strong wish through his Ambassador that I should not, and on his arrival there expressed himself to the Emperor, and others, in unmeasured terms about me, and accused me of every kind of thing. Every statement was false and he must have known it. Needless to say he was aided and abetted by that scoundrel Herbert Bismarck . . . Of course I did not wish to place the kind Emperor of Austria in an unpleasant position, so I spent in Rumania the time your son was at Vienna. When he saw Sir A. Paget he never asked after Mama nor gave any message for me . . . It pains me to write all this to you, dearest Vicky, *his* mother, but it is now my duty to do so. Till he makes some apology for the gross insult he has heaped upon me in a foreign country, I must naturally cease having any further acquaintance with him.'

As Vicky told the Queen, she 'had no idea of what happened at Vienna' until she received Bertie's letter. 'I am so ashamed and so indignant. Any want of respect or gratitude or courtesy to Bertie from a son of mine I resent most deeply, as he has been the very kindest of uncles to all my children. Here Bertie was blamed for having left Vienna, in order not to see William, and to be purposely uncivil to him!'

In 1891 the Kaiser paid his first state visit to England. After staying with the Queen for four days at Windsor, Buckingham Palace was put at his disposal, and the Prince of Wales played a prominent part in welcoming him. On 10 July, he was present at the Guildhall when William was given the Freedom of the City and told the assembled company that in so far as it lay in his power he intended 'to maintain the historical friendship between our two nations. My aim, above all, is the maintenance of peace.' Not a year passed between 1890 and 1895 without the Kaiser paying Queen Victoria a visit. The hints he repeatedly dropped that Britain should join the Triple Alliance between Germany, Austria and Italy, were so blatantly indelicate as to defeat their own end. It was typical of him that when Lord Salisbury in 1895 showed some signs of considering such a partnership he chose to rebuff him.

Baron Eckardstein, who for many years was First Secretary at the German Embassy in London, described the Kaiser's 'perpetual visits to England' as 'politically unjudicious.' His clumsy attempts to win Britain's friendship produced a 'contrary effect to what was intended.' Those who were supposed to be attracted were, in fact, repelled, while Russia and France, imagining an Anglo-German alliance would soon be signed, hastened to reach agreement.

Unfortunately, the Kaiser acquired a taste for visiting Cowes, where his habitual solecisms got on his Uncle's nerves. As Commodore of the Royal Yacht Squadron, HRH resented his nephew's interference. At the conclusion of William's visit in 1893, Knollys told Algernon West, 'The German Emperor's visit has been a great success, and he enjoyed it immensely; so much so indeed, that I am afraid it will tempt him to repeat his visit very frequently.'

Until the Kaiser began dominating the racing by building *Meteor I* and *Meteor II* to outclass the Prince of Wales's *Britannia*, HRH much enjoyed spending August on the Solent. But when, in his own phrase, his nephew began behaving as if he were 'Boss of Cowes,' he grew disillusioned. There is, of course, nothing like sport for promoting ill-will. In 1897, unable to compete with his nephew's extravagance, and tired of the bickering which the German challenge provoked, HRH sold *Britannia*. 'The regatta at Cowes,' he complained, 'was once a pleasant holiday for me, but, now that the Kaiser has taken command there, it is nothing but a nuisance.'

Undoubtedly, the Prince's exasperation partly arose from envy, conscious or unconscious. While he was hardly ever consulted, the world hung on his nephew's lightest word. While he was obliged to seek his mother's permission to cross the Channel, the Kaiser was only answerable to God, with whom he had long since reached an understanding. But HRH was by no means alone in blaming the Emperor for turning a friendly regatta into something approaching war. In 1897, members of the Royal Yacht Squadron were horrified to read a telegram from the German Emperor, pinned up on their Notice Board, which accused the Committee of gross mismanagement, and ended by saying 'your handicaps are simply appalling.'

The naval escort which accompanied the *Hohenzollern* to the Solent in 1895 included two new cruisers: the *Wörth* and the *Weissenburg*. The day after the Emperor arrived was the twenty-fifth anniversary of Wörth. So he boarded the warship named after the battle, and harangued its crew in terms which could not fail to give offence in France. Such sabre-rattling was also resented in England. The peace and calm of the Regatta was the last occasion for discordant speeches. It was a time for bands playing excerpts from *Iolanthe* and *HMS Pinafore*, for tea on the lawn of the Royal Yacht Squadron, for dinners and dances, for flags fluttering in the breeze, for midnight assignations. And suddenly into this summer idyll crashed the Kaiser, with his brash, provocative tirades, his menacing battle cruisers, his grievances about handicapping, and his indecent insistence on winning everything in sight. It was like an inebriated wrestler attempting to dance *Swan Lake*.

No amount of diplomacy could ever succeed in repairing the damage done to Anglo-German relations by the Kruger Telegram. In an effort to further his dream of uniting the whole of South Africa under British Rule, Cecil Rhodes secretly encouraged Jameson's attempt to overthrow President Kruger. On 30 December 1895, Dr Jameson invaded the Transvaal with six hundred irregular troops. Three days later he surrendered at Conje to a superior force of Afrikaners and his ill-judged expedition ended in ignominy.

Germany's colonial ambitions and economic interests encouraged the Kaiser to side with the Boers, particularly as 'he attributed the Jameson Raid to his Uncle, the Prince of Wales, and to the latter's two capitalist friends, Beit and Sir Ernest Cassel.' On 3 January 1896, the Kaiser presided over a conference to which the Chancellor and Foreign Minister were summoned. He began the meeting by proposing that troops should be sent to Pretoria and that the Transvaal should be made a German Protectorate. Prince Hohenlohe pointed out that such a policy 'would mean war with England.' In the end, it was agreed that the Kaiser should send Kruger a telegram of encouragement and goodwill. 'I express my sincere congratulations,' it read, 'that, supported by your people without appealing for the help of friendly Powers, you have succeeded by your own energetic action against armed bands which invaded your country as disturbers of the peace and have thus been enabled to restore peace and safeguard the independence of the country against attacks from the outside.'

The Kaiser's telegram produced an explosion of anger in England. 'The nation will never forget this telegram,' proclaimed the *Morning Post*, 'and it will always bear it in mind in the future orientation of its policy.' William's mischievous meddling and double-dealing were furiously resented. Having for years paraded his love and loyalty whenever he visited England, he had now demonstrated by his action the worthlessness of his words. In 1913, Sir Edward Goschen, then British Ambassador in Germany, told a colleague 'that the impression made in England by the Kruger Telegram could never be entirely forgotten.' The First Royal Dragoons, of which the Emperor had recently been made Colonel, were so disgusted by the honour, that they cut his portrait in pieces and threw it on the fire.

The Prince of Wales did not lag behind public opinion in deploring his nephew's 'spontaneous outburst,' which betrayed his 'true feelings.' The moment he read the 'shameful telegram' he requested the Queen to give the offender a 'good snubbing.' Knollys was 'desired' to write to Sir Arthur Bigge to say that HRH felt sure that 'the Queen looks upon the German Emperor's message to President Kruger as a most gratuitous act of unfriendliness.' Moreover, 'considering the Emperor's relationship with her Majesty, the professions which he has always made as to his love for this country, and the appointments which he holds both in the English Army and Navy, he has shown in addition the worst possible good taste and good feeling in congratulating the Boers.'

The Queen believed 'it would not do' to snub the Kaiser, and told the Prince that 'sharp, cutting answers and remarks only irritate and do harm.' As 'William's faults come from impetuousness as well as conceit' the most powerful weapons were 'calmness and firmness.' Both the letter she wrote the Kaiser, and her willingness to accept his improbable excuses, without, as Lord Salisbury expressed it, 'enquiring too narrowly into the truth of them,' showed that she practised what she preached.

Ten years after the Vienna incident, another bitter dispute broke out between Uncle and Nephew. It concerned Admiral Senden, whose aggressive manners and unfailing tactlessness earned him many enemies. When the Admiral accompanied the Emperor to Cowes, he constantly boasted of the immense fleet Germany was building. But, despite his offensive ways, he was often chosen to undertake missions to England. It was he, for example, who delivered the Kaiser's letter to the Queen justifying his telegram to Kruger.

One morning in February 1898, the Prince of Wales chanced to meet Senden in the Equerries' Room at Marlborough House and being busy treated him somewhat curtly. The Kaiser, regarding the alleged incident as a personal affront, descended on Lascelles at the British Embassy in Berlin, complained bitterly of Senden's ill-treatment, and demanded that Lord Salisbury should hear of his protest.

On 23 February, the Prince of Wales wrote Lascelles a 'most private and confidential letter,' discussing his meeting with Senden and what had followed. 'You may indeed,' he began, 'have been "much taken aback by the German Emperor's surprise visit" to you on the 19th, but the communication he thought fit to make to you concerning myself has astonished me even more than it has you. I have always been on most friendly terms with Admiral Senden, and whenever we have met have treated him as an old acquaintance. It was through me that he was made an Hon Member of R.Y. Squadron as I thought it would please the Emperor and be agreeable to the Admiral during his frequent visits to England. Why therefore he should have deliberately tried to make mischief between me and the Emperor by making statements which are not true is simply incomprehensible to me!

'It was purely accident when I met him in the Equerries' Room where I had come to speak to Sir S. Clarke, and was quite surprised to see the Admiral there. Of course his name would have been sent up to me, but as I met him downstairs we had a friendly talk. I asked as I always should do after the Emperor and Empress. We talked a little about yachting and I told him our Secretary of the R.Y.S. Mr. Grant, was retiring from ill health. He then asked if he could do any commissions for me at Berlin to which I answered in the negative and I added that I was writing to the Empress Frederick by Royal Messenger. This is all that passed and I wished him goodbye.

'After what has occurred I must beg of you to let Admiral Senden know that in future I can have no more communication with him of any kind. I deny *in toto* that I was uncivil in any way, and his statements are positively untrue and I greatly resent them as a positive insult to myself. Nobody is more anxious for friendly relations with the Emperor than I am – though on more than one occasion I have been "highly tried" . . . How is it possible that good relations may be maintained if persons who have access to the Emperor bring him garbled accounts of interviews? I think I have the character of being civil to everybody, so what object should I have to be the reverse to one who I know possessed the Emperor's confidence?

'I will not write further on this disagreeable subject, which has pained and annoyed me more than words can express, and leave the whole matter in your hands. Of course my letter is strictly private but when you have the opportunity I hope you will make its contents known to the Emperor. He is a powerful Sovereign I know. But I am his Uncle and his Mother's eldest Brother and I cannot submit to the treatment I have met with.'

Lascelles requested an audience with the Kaiser in order to tell him what the Prince had said. In the belief that 'it is best to speak plainly on delicate subjects,' he read him the whole of HRH's letter 'without omitting a single word. His Majesty interrupted me more than once . . . When I came to the statement that Your Royal

Highness had "on more than one occasion been highly tried," the
Emperor said with a laugh that he had always thought it had been
the other way up. His Majesty frowned but did not say anything
when I read with some emphasis the passage about persons having
access to His Majesty bringing garbled accounts of interviews. When
I read the last paragraph of Your Royal Highness' letter, the
Emperor began to speak but I hastily interrupted him by observing
that *mutatis mutandis* His Majesty had used nearly the same words in
his conversation with me on the 19th ultimo. He then said that he
knew that the Prince of Wales was his Uncle and his Mother's
Brother and looked upon him as a silly boy, but that His Royal
Highness seemed to forget that the silly boy had become German
Emperor, and had the interests of the Empire to consider even before
those of his family relations.'

In 1899, the Kaiser suggested that he and the Empress should pay
a State visit to England. His proposal was welcome to the Government who felt it would show the world 'that the alleged coalition in favour of the Boers had no real existence.' Besides, Chamberlain was eager to explore the possibility of coming to terms with
Germany. But resentment over Admiral Senden, which had been
dormant for several months, erupted with such violence as to
threaten the Emperor's visit. When the Prince of Wales noticed the
Admiral's name amongst those his nephew intended to bring to
England, he immediately sent for Baron Eckardstein and asked him
to do what he could to persuade the Kaiser to change his mind.
When the Baron broached the matter, William replied: 'If I go to
England at all this autumn I shall take who I like with me.' In the
end, the Duchess of Devonshire persuaded the Prince to withdraw
his objections, provided the Admiral apologized, and was not
amongst those accompanying the Kaiser to Sandringham.

The Kaiser, the Kaiserin, two of their sons, and the Foreign
Minister, Count Bülow, arrived at Portsmouth on the *Hohenzollern* on
19 November 1899, some six weeks after the outbreak of the South
African War. The great majority of the German people objected to
their visit, which the Empress had done her utmost to prevent. She
had never cared for her English connections, she believed that the
British Government would exploit the occasion so as to make it
appear to endorse their 'oppression' of the Boers, and she feared that
William would succumb to one of his sudden infatuations for
England.

The Royal Family warmly welcomed their visitors, for the

country was sadly in need of friends, and not a single incident ruffled the reunion. Even Admiral Senden was temporarily chastened. During the Kaiser's three-day visit to Sandringham, Alix stifled her feelings, and did what she could to make his stay a success, although she hated having him in her house. But when she discovered that amongst his retinue was a barber whose sole duty it was to curl his moustache, she shook with laughter and called him a fool. As far as possible, the Prince avoided controversy. But when Uncle and Nephew talked politics, Bülow was reminded 'of a fat malicious tom-cat playing with a shrewmouse.'

The more aggressive German policy became, the more the Prince revised his views of Russia. During the Crimean War, when Lord Raglan commanded the British Army besieging Sebastopol, he sometimes forgot that Napoleon was his ally. Having served his military apprenticeship under Wellington in the Peninsular, he tended to speak of the enemy as the 'French'. Similarly, the Prince as a boy had been taught to regard Russia as the principal threat to England's peace and prosperity, and old habits die hard. With Gibbs's help, he had followed Lord Lucan's exploits and stuck flags on a map to trace the progress of the Allies. Political prejudices, planted by Palmerston and nurtured by Disraeli, proved difficult to uproot. Russia's 'historic mission' to dominate the Dardanelles and Bosphorus so as to secure an outlet into the Mediterranean, her envious glances across the frontier of Afghanistan, her efforts to infiltrate Persia at Britain's expense, kept fear and suspicion alive. Throughout the Eastern Crisis, which ended in the Congress of Berlin, the Prince supported Disraeli in striving to curb Russia. Ten years later, he joined the Queen in condemning the Tsar's 'barbaric, Asiatic, tyrannical' treatment of Prince Alexander of Battenberg. But even when Anglo-Russian relations were at their worst, family feeling diminished ill will and held out hope for the future. After all, Alix's sister, Dagmar, was daughter-in-law to Alexander II, wife to Alexander III and mother to Nicholas II. The Queen's grand-daughter, Princess Alexandra of Hesse, became the last Empress of Russia, and the Duke of Edinburgh married the Grand Duchess Marie, the only daughter of Alexander II. The Prince of Wales frequently visited Russia, or met its Royal Family under his father-in-law's roof. When eventually German threats compelled Britain to seek the Tsar's friendship, the King could draw on a fund of goodwill built up over many years.

The Prince first visited Russia in 1866, when he attended Dagmar's

wedding to the Tsarevich. She was most anxious for him to come as
so few of her family would be there. Alix was having another child
and could not risk the journey. Queen Victoria would have preferred
her son to send one of his gentlemen to represent him. It was 'perfectly natural,' she told him, that he wanted to see Russia and 'to be
present at the marriage of dear Alix's sister, and that Dagmar
should wish to see her kind brother-in-law's face at so trying a time.'
But it was 'a bad time of the year' for travelling, and besides he was
'always running about the country, and all of *us*, would like to see
you a little more stationary.'

Before setting out in October, the Prince told Lord Derby that 'he
should only be too happy to be the means in any way of promoting
the *entente cordiale* between Russia and our own country.' On 9
November, the Prince's twenty-fifth birthday, the Grand Duchess
Marie Feodorovna, as Dagmar became on being received into the
Orthodox Church, married her giant of a Cossack. The splendour
and magnificence of the various ceremonies was such as could only
be seen in Holy Russia. The Prince stayed for a month in St Petersburg and was lavishly entertained. Indeed, he was made so welcome
that tongues began to wag. It was a dazzling experience, but there
was something disconsolate in the ritual diversions of St Petersburg,
which shone with the cold light of the moon not the warm glow of
the sun. The Prince preferred the reckless vulgarity of the parvenu
Second Empire, where pleasure was sought with uninhibited
abandon. The Court of the Tsar was gorgeous, noble and stately, but
it was also exceedingly dull.

In 1874 the Duke of Edinburgh married the Grand Duchess Marie,
the only daughter of Alexander II. Both Dagmar and Alix favoured
the alliance, which they saw as a blow to Germany. The Queen was
anxious for Affie to marry, for, as is the way of sailors, he kept a lady
in Malta. The sooner he settled down the less 'scrapes' there might
be. But she was far from convinced he had found the right bride.
Unfortunately, Marie's head would be filled with '*half oriental*
Russian notions,' her family were arrogant and 'false', and there were
painful religious differences. Indeed, it would be 'the first departure
since 200 years nearly from the practice of our family since the
Revolution of '88! We must be very firm – or else we may pack up –
and call back the descendants of the Stuarts.' When the Queen told
Vicky in April 1873 that she would soon have a sister-in-law
belonging to the Russian Orthodox Church, she broke the news
with the words: 'The murder is out.'

Neither the marriage nor the bridegroom was popular in England. The Queen herself admitted her son had an 'ungracious, reserved manner,' which made him 'so little liked.' On the back of an invitation which Knollys sent Ponsonby, inviting him to dine with the Prince of Wales on board the *Osborne*, Sir Henry wrote: 'Sir H. Keppel expostulated on the merits of the Duke of Edinburgh "No officer knows his duty better or is more devoted to it" – and yet – well no-one likes him – why?' Possibly his trouble was that he too closely resembled his reprobate Uncle, Ernest II of Coburg. He was rude, touchy, wilful, unscrupulous, improvident and unfaithful. Besides which he took to the bottle and no one could trust him, except to make mischief. Even his mother once called him a 'slippery youth.'

Although the Queen disliked the principle of one of her children marrying a Russian, she soon came to look on her daughter-in-law as a treasure. After her first visit to Balmoral, she told Vicky, 'I have formed a high opinion of her; her wonderfully even, cheerful satisfied temper – her kind and indulgent disposition, free from bigotry and intolerance, and her serious, intelligent mind – so entirely free from everything fast – and so full of occupation and interest in everything makes her a most agreeable companion. Everyone must like her. But alas! Not one likes him! I fear that will never get better.'

The Prince and Princess of Wales, Prince Arthur, the best man, Vicky and Fritz, attended the wedding, which took place at St Petersburg on 23 January 1874. First there was an Orthodox ceremony in the Winter Palace, and then an Anglican Service conducted by Dean Stanley. The Dean's wife, Lady Augusta, was astonished by the mixture of squalor and magnificence in which the Tsar lived. On the one hand, he was surrounded by avenues of flunkeys, miles of corridors, hung with 'frowning old Tsars,' and acres of halls. But on the other, dust and dirt abounded, and his palaces were filled with such stenches that Lady Emma Osborne suspected that there was a dead mujik concealed under the floor-boards of her bedroom. The marriage was not a happy one. The Duke treated his wife like a stowaway found in the hold of his ship. For her part, the Duchess detested the English climate, deplored English cooking, and resented the fact that the Princess of Wales was given precedence over her. Soon after she settled at Clarence House, war almost broke out between Russia and England. But, at least, her wayward husband took her part, much to the Queen's dismay. 'I am grieved to say,' she wrote in 1877, that Affie 'has become most imprudent in his language and I only hope he does not make mischief. It is very awkward with this Russian relationship just now. This is what I always feared and dreaded.'

In the summer of 1875, Bosnia and Herzegovina, two persecuted provinces in the Ottoman Empire, rebelled against the Sultan, who had totally failed to implement any of the reforms which he had promised to make at the end of the Crimean War. Early the following year, Abdul Aziz was murdered. His successor, Abdul the Damned, confronted with further rebellions in Serbia and Bulgaria, suppressed them with ferocious severity. The atrocities committed by his irregular 'Bashi-Bazouks' brought Gladstone out of retirement in a whirlwind of righteous fury. His displeasure was partly directed against Turkish barbarism, but some was reserved for Disraeli, whose policy seemed to countenance it. On 6 September 1876, Gladstone published one of the most incendiary pamphlets ever written: 'The Bulgarian Horrors and the Question of the East.' It contained the demand that the Turks should be cleared out 'bag and baggage from the Province they have desolated and profaned.' Seldom, if ever, had Englishmen shown such excitement at the fate of a far-off country.

Some of the indignation which Gladstone intended to arouse against the Prime Minister and Abdul the Damned rebounded like a boomerang. Disraeli regarded Gladstone's intervention as unpatriotic and ill-judged. Touching as was his concern for the Bulgarian populace, he was, in effect, providing the Tsar with a pretext for declaring war on the Sultan and seizing the Straits. In a misguided fit of morality, not wholly divorced from expectations of party advantage, the Liberal leader seemed positively anxious to surrender the hard-won gains of the Crimean War and expose the British Empire to precisely those threats which previous Statesmen had laboured to avert. As for his pamphlet, Disraeli dismissed it as 'vindictive and ill-written,' and 'of all the Bulgarian horrors, perhaps the greatest.'

The Prince of Wales told Disraeli that he deeply deplored 'the present agitation over the so-called Bulgarian atrocities, which is so prevalent throughout the country. It must, I fear, weaken the hands of the government, who are so anxious to do all in their power to obtain peace.' He was convinced that Gladstone's success in campaigning against the Sultan, merely emboldened Russia to increase her demands. In making this point to the Queen he was preaching to the converted. 'The speeches of Mr Gladstone,' he told her, 'have given Russia more confidence, who now pours more officers, men and money into Serbia, and will not allow them to treat for peace. It is really too bad, and makes my blood boil with indignation.'

In April 1877, no doubt with Gladstone's rhetoric ringing reassuringly in his ears, the Tsar declared war on Turkey and advanced on Constantinople. By the following March he had signed the Treaty of San Stephano, whose terms reflected the decisiveness of his victory. But Russia had gained more than either Britain or Austria could accept, and the Congress of Berlin was held to deprive Alexander of the fruits of his victory. As the threat to our interests in the Eastern Mediterranean became increasingly obvious, the Bulgarian atrocities were forgotten, and the mood was such as to enable Disraeli to revert to the country's traditional policy of shoring up the Ottoman Empire.

In April 1877, Algernon Borthwick, proprietor and editor of the *Morning Post*, wrote to Knollys to say that: 'Public feeling in England is becoming excited every hour more distinctly against the obvious perfidy of Russia, whose real attack is upon ourselves and not upon Turkey.' In this serious crisis, 'Lord Beaconsfield quite understands the Russian plans and is prepared to meet them as Lord Palmerston would have done, but he is thwarted by some of his colleagues who are not so keen sighted.' Lord Salisbury, after discussing the Eastern question with the Prince, told his wife that the 'Turkophil party' had no more zealous supporters than HRH: a view shared by the Russian Ambassador Count Schouvaloff, who described the Prince in a despatch to St Petersburg as 'the most Turkish of all Englishmen.'

The Queen doubted whether the Congress of Berlin would suffice to solve the problems which it had been summoned to consider. She maintained that no arrangement would be lasting '*without fighting*, and giving those detestable Russians a good beating . . . They will always *hate us* and we can never trust them.' The Queen regarded Russia as a 'horrid, corrupt country,' whose climate was miserable, whose society was 'pernicious' and whose government was 'wicked, villainous and atrocious.' It was no surprise to her that the mischievous Mr Gladstone encouraged the Tsar's ambitions, while dear Lord Beaconsfield, who shared her dread of Russia's intrigues, ordered the fleet to Constantinople and despatched troops to Malta. As for Alexander III, for whom she felt '*such* a dislike,' he was nothing more than a 'violent Asiatic, full of hate, passion and tyranny.'

England's alliance with Russia in 1907 was finally achieved

because both countries felt threatened by the policies of William II. The differences which had divided them for so long began to seem less significant than the common danger confronting them. But even in Fritz's lifetime, the Prince of Wales showed signs of overcoming his traditional distrust of St Petersburg. In 1884, M. de Staal became Russian Ambassador in London, a post he occupied for the next eighteen years. His outstanding intelligence and charm soon made him a popular figure in English Society and a constant guest at Marlborough House and Sandringham. Under his influence, the Prince was gradually persuaded to look with less disfavour on his country.

Sir Robert Morier was another diplomat who sought to revise HRH's opinion of Russia. Morier began his career in Germany, where his liberal views as much disgusted Bismarck as they delighted the Crown Princess. Lady Paget described him as 'very stout and very clever,' and once went so far as to call him a 'fat old elephant.' But, nevertheless, she acknowledged his 'wit and readiness,' and the fact that he 'danced beautifully in spite of his huge size.' Wherever he went, 'his loud and boisterous laughter could be heard through two or three rooms,' as he stood in the centre of an admiring circle, 'mopping his head and shining face' with a handkerchief.

Soon after Sir Robert was sent to St Petersburg in 1884, the Queen became convinced that he had succumbed to Russian blandishments, and she told Lord Salisbury that he should have appointed somebody like Sir Augustus Paget brought up in the old traditions. But the Prince's confidence in his friend and protégé remained unshaken, and he increasingly came to accept Sir Robert's view that Bismarck's imperialism could be contained by Anglo-Russian co-operation.

In 1887, Lord Randolph Churchill paid a private visit to Russia, which he soon transformed into an unauthorized programme for promoting better relations between the British Government, which he in no sense represented, and the Tsar, to whom he was given a letter of introduction by the Princess of Wales. It was not long before the Chancelleries of Europe echoed with rumours about Lord Randolph's mission, to which they attributed a political significance it did not possess. Both the Queen and Lord Salisbury deplored the way in which the erstwhile Chancellor of the Exchequer, seemingly with HRH's approval, proclaimed a goodwill towards Russia which neither of them felt. Nor were they best pleased when the Tsar invited Churchill to Gatschina to discuss Anglo-Russian relations.

'On Monday last,' Randolph told the Prince, 'we were received by their Majesties. I thought her Majesty the Empress looked wonderfully well and really not a day older than when I saw her in 1873 at Cowes. It would seem that perpetual youth is the prerogative of the Royal Family of Denmark. With the Emperor I had a long conversation. He asked much about English men and matters and about the state of parties . . . I thought that H.M. seemed most pacifically inclined, and this view is confirmed by what I hear in other quarters.' Churchill was left in no doubt as to the Tsar's 'extreme desire for friendly relations with England.'

The Prince, made only too aware that Her Majesty held him partly responsible for Lord Randolph's mission, insisted that his 'visit has no political object of any kind.' He simply 'wanted to be out of England till Parliament met, so as to avoid making speeches at meetings; though he entirely supports Lord Salisbury's Government, and I own I regret that he is not asked to rejoin it, because, in spite of his many faults and constant errors of judgement, he is very clever and undoubtedly a power in the country.' But the Queen was unable to understand her son's 'high opinion of a man who is clever undoubtedly, but who is devoid of all principle, who holds the most insular and dangerous doctrines on foreign affairs, who is very impulsive and utterly unreliable.'

After dismissing Bismarck in 1890, the Kaiser told the world he proposed to steer a 'new course.' The Chancellor's policy had, in his own words, been based on 'friendship with Russia.' But within ten days of his fall from power, his successor refused to renew the Reinsurance Treaty which Bismarck had signed with Alexander III in 1887. The moment it became clear at St Petersburg that there was no further prospect of remaining Germany's ally, Russia began looking to France as a possible partner. It is some measure of the extent of the Kaiser's blunders that the 'New Course' drove the Tsar of all the Russias into the arms of the Third Republic. When Alexander stood at attention on board the *Standart*, while an Imperial band welcomed his French guests by playing the 'Marseillaise', the battle hymn of Revolution, he ended that era of history in which a succession of Holy Alliances and Leagues of Emperors had looked, and not looked in vain, to the rulers of Russia to protect monarchical institutions, indeed Christianity itself, from those atheistical and republican doctrines with which France infected Europe.

In September 1894, Alexander was found to be suffering from nephritis. His doctors suggested that he should be moved to Livadia, his summer palace in the Crimea, but nothing could save him, young and strong as he was. Dagmar sent Alix a despairing telegram on 30 October, and the next day, the Prince and Princess of Wales, accompanied by Lord Carrington, Sir Arthur Ellis, one of the Prince's Equerries, and Charlotte Knollys, set out for Russia. On 5 November, the anniversary of Inkerman, Charlotte wrote to her brother from Livadia describing the journey and what they found on arrival. 'We heard of the poor Emperor's death at Vienna where we stopped to dine. We continued our journey at 10 o'clock and after two more *very* cold nights in the train reached Odessa on Saturday morning. There to our dismay we found a *very* high sea. But the Princess would go on. Fortunately, we had an "armed cruiser" of 6,000 tons so felt the motion much less. I am sure the *Osborne* would have turned a regular summersault (I do not know how to spell it) or shaken herself and us to pieces if she had been in a sea like that . . . You may imagine how sad everything and everybody is here: funeral services twice a day and the whole population as black as crows. On Thursday the body is to be taken to Moscow to lie in state there for twenty-four hours as they say otherwise the people would not believe he was really dead . . . The poor Emperor's end came suddenly. He was sitting in his armchair, fully dressed, holding the Empress's hand and a moment before had said he felt better, then he gave one sigh, his head fell back against the Empress and all was over. The Empress remained sitting with her hand still in his till she fainted dead away.'

Sir Arthur Ellis wrote to Knollys by the same post to say that 'the confusion, indecision and bustle reminds me of the masterly inactivity and fussiness of Windsor Castle, even worse. Plans are changed every hour.' The number of services he was required to attend drove him to despair. 'I hardly recognize the Prince of Wales or myself, kneeling in full uniform with each a long lighted taper, on our knees twice a day, at these eternal masses for the dead, the "*Chanteurs de la cour*" singing their mournful dirges too beautifully . . . He died very bravely in a chair, encouraging all around him to be calm and not to give way and quite willing to die. The Duchess of Edinburgh arrived that day and had the folly to say to his face: "Thank God I've arrived in time to see you once more." He signed scores of documents up to the day before, and was conscious to the last and facing his fate like a man.' One of the last things he did was to write Alix a farewell letter in case he did not live long enough to see her.

On 8 November, the Russian Imperial Family, accompanied by the

Prince and Princess of Wales, and Sir Arthur grumbling about the thirty-nine masses he had attended, which he seemed to regard as a personal affront, set off on a three-day journey to Moscow in the Imperial train. The weather in the Crimea was like spring on the Riviera, but when they reached Moscow there was snow on the ground. As they passed through the Ukraine, peasants lined the track to pay their last respects. The Prince wrote to Francis from the Kremlin to say that he had spent his 'ancient birthday in the train travelling over the "Steppes." It is the third time for twenty-five years that you have not spent the 9th with me! We both feel that we are of some use and comfort to the poor Empress and her children in their grief. The Princess is of immense comfort to her sister. I am sure without her she would have completely broken down but she is wonderfully calm and resigned. The young Emperor is quite touching in his deference and regard for her and hardly likes to assume his new position. It is such a contrast to another Emperor and his conduct to his mother!'

From Moscow the coffin was taken to St Petersburg. Charlotte could not 'help feeling that if the poor man knows what is going on he will be glad when they leave his poor body in peace. Services are always held twice a day and all the near relations kiss his face which is only like a disfigured *mask* by this time.' The last service was held on 19 November. 'We have just come back from the Funeral,' wrote Charlotte to Francis, 'and I am trying to get off a few lines to you by this post. It was a very trying and fatiguing ceremony. I left at 9.45 and did not get back till 1.30, having stood for three whole hours in the church without moving, while the service was being performed in a language I could not understand. It was most affecting to see the Empress take a last farewell of her husband before the coffin was finally closed. Over and over again she kissed his poor face and hands and then when she had torn herself away, she came back again to kiss him *once* more. The Princess seems everything to her, sleeps always in her room and supports and comforts her.'

The Prince, Charlotte reported, 'has won good opinions here and people are very much edified by the way in which he *crosses* himself, just they say as if he had done it all his life. I think he considers it part of his Russian Uniform of which he is very proud.' In an earlier letter, she told her brother that HRH was 'making a very good impression on *every*body, he is never in the way and is so kind and civil to all the suite and even to the servants. The Princess keeps well. She sleeps in the Empress's room and never leaves her for a moment and is in fact everything to her.'

Exactly a week after his father's funeral, the young Emperor married Princess Alexandra of Hesse, Princess Alice's daughter. They had first met when she visited Russia for her sister Ella's wedding to the Grand Duke Serge. In April 1894, the Tsarevich, having at last overcome the Princess's reluctance to change her religion, proposed and was accepted. The new Tsarina had been brought up to detest Prussia, which during the 'Seven Weeks' War' of 1866 had seized Hesse from her father, the Grand Duke. Consequently the Prince of Wales entertained high hopes that his niece would resist German influence at the Court at St Petersburg, while working for better relations with England. Moreover, there were grounds for believing that Nicholas was well disposed. Charlotte told Francis she was perfectly certain 'that England has a great personal friend in the young Emperor,' which 'was shown in so many little ways. For instance every single German attendant whether Gentlemen, ladies or servants leave Russia the day after the wedding, the only exception being made in favour of Princess Alexandra's English maid.' Charlotte was premature in foreseeing a diplomatic revolution merely because Alix's maid stayed on at the Winter Palace: although the Chancelleries of Europe were perfectly capable of jumping to such conclusions. Nevertheless, the prospects of better relations were plainly improving, and the Prince only stayed in Russia as long as he did in the hope of exploiting them further.

Nicholas and Alexandra were married on the Dowager Empress's birthday, 26 November, and for that day the Court came out of mourning. The Tsar was dressed in the uniform of his Hussars, and according to Charlotte Knollys, looked 'dreadfully pale and worn,' as well he might with the cares of Russia on his not very broad shoulders. 'The new Empress,' reported Sir Arthur, 'looked really lovely and bows so gracefully and prettily. The Duchess of York could take a few lessons from her and get rid of that *shy nod* which offends so much. I think the Duke of York is rather bored here and pining to get back to shoot.'

General Ellis was right. Prince George was indeed anxious to return to his guns and coverts. But he also disliked being separated from his 'shy' Duchess, to whom he wrote: 'I never saw two people more in love with each other. I told them both that I could not wish them more than they should be as happy as you and I were together. Was that right?' Throughout the tragic vicissitudes of the Tsar and Tsarina's lives, from the obsequious deference of Tsarskoe Selo, to the rough obscenities of Tobolsk, whether rich, magnificent and powerful, or poor, depressed and humbled, their love for each other endured without faltering, from the moment they took their marriage vows in the Winter Palace, until death did them part in the cellar at Ekaterinburg.

Before returning to England, Sir Arthur Ellis sent Knollys a final report from St Petersburg. 'The young Tsar,' he wrote, 'is properly occupied as old Staal says in directing all his energies to the creation of a new Tsarevitch – *"La meilleure politique."* He is very natural, unassuming and unpretentious, with a good heart. Most anxious to do right, he has already shown his intentions (rather mildly in truth) but shocking the Ultra Tories here. I mean divesting himself of the protective soldiery and placing himself at the mercy of the populace . . . No doubt great changes are looming and mistakes will be made. But anything is better than the repressive policy of the former reign. The young people always talk English together and he constantly has reproved friends of his who spoke of her as a German Princess saying "She is *English* remember".'

Sir Arthur went on to complain with more candour than courtesy of Her Majesty's insatiable appetite for news from Russia. 'That old tiresome woman at Windsor Castle telegraphs hungry for *more* letters and I have written at great length, the feeblest platitudes nine times. It is quite superfluous since Carrington, your sister, Wernher and Lascelles all have equally to write – to say nothing of the papers who are sickeningly overflowing with details. The cipher telegraphing correspondence would make you laugh. She is gluttonous over that d–d blue cipher book. I could not help expostulating with Ponsonby for sending some utterly useless platitudes in cipher. "I hope you and dear Alix and George are perfectly well and not fatigued with the exertions" – in cipher!! How silly!! The mountain in labour and out crept a mouse.'

In the course of his letter, the General expressed his contempt for the singular deference – evidently not infectious – with which Lord Carrington regarded Her Majesty. 'Charles Carrington leaves this evening. I am sorry he goes, for his companionship at public functions has been pleasant. But quite *entre nous* he is *so* impressed by the Queen!! her *greatness*, her *goodness* and the greatness and importance of her Lord Chamberlain, that there have been times when I have had difficulty in *not* laughing in his face. One thing amused me, he said that going to Windsor for a Privy Council he never permitted any member to smoke en route in the train "out of deference to the Queen," but when I told him J. Brown always had a short black cavendish clay in private with her, he said "That was different." You would think she was made of different flesh and blood to ordinary womankind to hear him talk and the fulsome telegrams he sent her were comic simply – almost like prayers to the *Bon Dieu!! This between ourselves* for otherwise and vis a vis the P of W he has been perfectly natural and like his old self.'

The Prince of Wales returned to England delighted with the excellence of his relations with the new ruler of Russia. Lord Rosebery, who had recently succeeded Gladstone as Prime Minister, congratulated him on his mission in such laudatory language as to suggest he had been taking lessons from the Lord Chamberlain. 'I am anxious,' he wrote, 'to be among the first to welcome your Royal Highness home, and to express my deep sense of the good and patriotic work that you have accomplished since you left England. Never has your Royal Highness stood so high in the national esteem as today, for never have you had such an opportunity. That at last has come and has enabled you to justify the highest anticipations, and to render a signal service to your country as well as to Russia and the peace of the world.'

In the autumn of 1896, Queen Victoria invited the Tsar and Tsarina, and their infant daughter, the Grand Duchess Olga, to visit her at Balmoral. The Prince of Wales, anxious to show the world, and especially the Kaiser, how cordial England's relations were with Russia, prevailed on the Queen to permit him to welcome her visitors with all possible ceremony. He also proposed that Lord Salisbury and M. de Staal should be invited to meet the Tsar.

During what Bigge called the 'Russian occupation,' Balmoral was so full that four laundry maids were obliged to share a bed, and the footmen's quarters were as packed as the hold of a slave ship. But their occupants were not without consolation. Before leaving the castle, the Tsar handed the Master of the Household a thousand pounds to be distributed among the servants. Such Oriental munificence more than compensated for a few days' overcrowding.

On Sunday 27 September, the entire party staying at Balmoral was driven to church at Crathie, the Queen refusing to be dismayed either by the tempestuous weather, or the variety of her guests' religious convictions. 'The most awful stormy morning,' wrote Lady Lytton, 'but all was arranged for going to kirk so we all went and got no harm in shut carriages for Her Majesty never gives in. It was very interesting seeing the two pews full of the Royalties and the

Emperor and Empress standing by the Queen even in the Scotch kirk, where all is simple and reverend.'

On 3 October, the last day of the visit, the Queen and her guests 'were all photographed by Downey by the new cinematograph process, which makes moving pictures by winding off a reel of film. We were walking up and down, and the children jumping about.' Afterwards, Nicky and Alix planted a tree, took a drive to Invercauld, dined *en famille,* and left at ten that evening, to the Queen's 'great regret,' as she was 'so fond of them both.'

Lady Lytton was full of praise for the Prince of Wales, whom she described as 'very jolly' in the evening, and 'the greatest help all the time.' If anything, he was possibly too zealous when it came to outdoor pursuits. 'From the very first day,' Nicky complained to his mother, 'my uncles took charge of me. They seem to think it necessary to take me out shooting all day long. The weather is awful, rain and wind every day and on top of it no luck at all – I haven't killed a stag yet.' It is said that during his visit he only contrived to shoot a brace of grouse. Fortunately, he was permitted a brief respite from such gruelling pleasures when the Prince paid a rapid visit to Newmarket to watch Persimmon run in the Jockey Club Stakes. The Queen told Lady Lytton that she disliked her son racing, 'and that it encouraged it so much in others, and that the Prince Consort was so against it, and quite distressed when the Prince even put into a lottery. But it makes the Prince happy, and is perhaps a better excitement than others.'

Politically speaking, the visit was indecisive, particularly as contentious issues were mostly avoided. But, after the Tsar returned to Russia, he often wrote to his 'Dearest Uncle Bertie,' exchanging family gossip. Such letters were written in faultless English, and ended: 'Ever your most loving nephew, Nicky.'

The Kaiser did his best to poison relations between Russia and England. Shrewdly suspecting as much, the Queen decided to warn Nicky that her grandson was not to be trusted. 'I feel I must tell you,' she wrote from Windsor in March 1899, 'something which you *ought* to know and perhaps do not. It is, I am sorry to say, that William takes every opportunity of impressing upon Sir F. Lascelles that Russia is doing all in her power to work against us . . . I need not say that I do not believe a word of this, neither do Lord Salisbury nor Sir F. Lascelles. But I am afraid William may go and tell things against us to you, just as he does about you to us. If so, pray tell me openly and confidentially. It is so important that we should under-

stand each other, and that such mischievous and unstraightforward
proceedings should be put a stop to. You are so true yourself, that I
am sure you will be shocked at this.'

Two months after the outbreak of the Boer War, the military
situation in South Africa looked critical. During 'Black Week' in
December 1899, Lord Methuen was defeated at Magersfontein,
General Gatacre at Stormberg, and Sir Redvers Buller at Colenso.
Anticipating the demise of the British Empire, reports of whose
death were decidedly premature, the Kaiser proposed to Count
Osten-Sacken, the Russian Ambassador in Berlin, that the Tsar
should 'order his armies against India,' while Germany ensured 'that
none should stir in Europe.' He further suggested that France might
be persuaded to join an alliance which would put an end to England's
'imperialist cupidity.' The conspiracy came to nothing. It was one
thing to express sympathy for the Boers and another to risk war on
their behalf. Moreover, both France and Russia had learned to
beware of the Kaiser, especially when offering them Egypt and
India as gifts.

Such was the hostility aroused towards England by events in
South Africa, that the Prince of Wales decided to spend the spring
of 1900 in Denmark and not at Biarritz. While travelling to
Copenhagen via Ostend and Brussels, he was nearly killed by a
young anarchist. Seven attempts were made on the life of the
Queen, but only one on the Prince. This took place at the Gare du
Nord, Brussels, at 5.30 in the afternoon, on 4 April. A Belgian youth,
Jean Baptiste Sipido, jumped on the footboard of the royal carriage
as it steamed out of the station and fired several shots through the
open window of the Prince's compartment. One bullet lodged in the
back of the seat between the Prince and Princess. The occupants of
the carriage, including Miss Charlotte Knollys, remained imper-
turbably calm, except for Alix's lap dog, which shivered with fright.
HRH described his would-be assassin as '*un pauvre fou*,' and
observed how fortunate it was that anarchists were such poor shots:
it was almost inconceivable to miss at a range of six feet.

'The incident in Brussels,' wrote the Prince to Knollys, who
seldom accompanied HRH on his trips abroad, 'cannot have failed
to make a sensation at home. My escape was simply wonderful as
the man fired at two yards from me. Fortunately he was a bad shot
and had an indifferent pistol in the bargain.' The Prince was
disposed to blame Dr Leyds, the Secretary of State for the Transvaal,
whose propaganda 'made the Press on the continent so violent

against us, and induced the Anarchists to take action as was exemplified last week. The Princess was most courageous and we were none the worse and finished the journey most comfortably. The positive inundation of telegrams and letters has been simply terrific.'

Sipido, who was only a boy of fifteen, never showed the slightest remorse for having attempted to kill the Prince. Indeed, he maintained that he deserved to be shot because of the thousands of Boers for whose deaths he was responsible. It appears that Sipido credited HRH with precisely that influence over policy which he had struggled so long to achieve. The authorities in Brussels were suspiciously feeble, for they not only permitted Sipido to escape, but seemed reluctant to pursue him.

'The behaviour of the Belgians,' according to the Kaiser, was 'simply outrageous, and people in Germany are utterly at a loss to understand the meaning. Either their laws are ridiculous, or the jury are a set of d----d bl---y scoundrels.' The moment he first heard the news of the attempt on his uncle's life, he called on the British Embassy to convey his congratulations on HRH's escape. As it was only eight o'clock in the morning, the ambassador was obliged to receive the 'All Highest' in dressing-gown and pyjamas. The Kaiser, to whom pyjamas were a novelty, almost forgot the purpose of his visit in his astonishment at Lascelles's attire.

In point of courage the Prince was the equal of any of his ancestors. Lord Redesdale wrote of 'his wonderful courage and coolness. It never seemed to occur to him that there could be such a thing as danger.' In 1907, after serious outbreaks of labour troubles in Paris, the *Gendarmerie* begged the King not to leave his motor. But he only smiled at their fears. 'Who would hurt me in Paris?' he asked, as he joined the crowds on the pavement.

The King and Diplomacy

On 17 January 1901, Queen Victoria suffered a mild stroke at Osborne and it was thought wise to send for her children. The Duke of Connaught received the telegram advising him to return while he was staying in Berlin. The moment the Kaiser learned of his grandmother's illness, he told his uncle that he proposed to return with him to England. Prince Arthur, who of all the Royal Family was best-disposed to his nephew, tried tactfully to suggest that he might not be welcome. But William insisted that as the Queen's eldest grandson his place was by her side. 'The Old Trouper,' as Sarah Bernhardt called him, instinctively hogged the limelight. It was he who drove the Imperial Train to Flushing, and he who took the helm of the ship in which they crossed the Channel. Throughout the journey, he appeared to be in exalted spirits, and was so full of fun and jokes that nobody would have guessed the nature of his mission. His suite attributed his good humour to separation from the Empress, but his own explanation was that 'Uncle Arthur is so downhearted we must cheer him up.'

Forty years before, the Queen had told Vicky that to die 'peacefully surrounded by all one's children is indeed a great blessing and an enviable end.' But later, she changed her mind, and described it as 'very dreadful' to have crowds of relations hovering round. 'That I shall insist is never the case if I am dying. It is awful.'

The Prince of Wales reached Osborne on the morning of 19 January, but returned to London next day to meet the Kaiser. On the 21st he was back by his mother's bedside. Apart from some difficulty in breathing, there were no distressing signs of illness. Sometimes her mind wandered but for most of the time she slept. The day before she died she asked Sir James Reid whether she was better. When he said that she was, she asked eagerly: 'Then may I have Turi?' The dog was fetched and allowed to lie on the bed beside her.

There were times when she seemed to confuse her grandson with Fritz, but shortly before she died she recognized the Prince of Wales and held out her arms to him murmuring 'Bertie!' He embraced her lovingly and was then so overcome that he hurriedly withdrew. Some said that this was the last word she uttered, but others thought they heard her calling 'Albert.' During the afternoon of 22 January, Bishop Davidson remained by her bed praying and reading hymns. Most of the time the Queen showed no signs of awareness, but when he came to the last verse of 'Lead Kindly Light,' her favourite hymn, he saw she had grasped its meaning.

'And with the morn those Angel faces smile,
Which I have loved long since and lost awhile.'

While the Bishop was offering Her Majesty the consolations of religion, Arthur Balfour, the leader of the House of Commons, was sitting in the Equerries' Room trying to sort out some of the constitutional problems which were arising. What was to be done about a number of documents urgently requiring her signature? He was astounded by the mountain of Despatch Boxes which had piled up during the week in which the Queen ceased to attend to them: impressive testimony to a lifetime of hard labour. The problem was solved just after half-past six when the Prince of Wales became King.

The Queen died, surrounded by children and grandchildren, who shortly before had called out their names, as if to arouse her from that eternal sleep into which she was peacefully drifting. When the news was announced to the waiting journalists outside, they leapt on bicycles and raced to the Post Office at Cowes, shouting as they hurtled past, 'Queen dead! Queen dead!' Such unbecoming hubbub was entirely foreign to the Queen's hushed and 'whispery' Court, or the calm and peace which still surrounded her as she lay in the palatial seaside villa which she and Albert had built on the shores of the Solent.

Repeatedly the Kaiser in writing to the King recalled his vigil at Osborne. As late as February 1906, he was disposed to dwell on the 'silent hour we watched and prayed at her bedside, when the spirit of that great Sovereign Lady passed away as she drew her last breath in my arms.' Princess Beatrice, however, maintained that her

mother died in the arms of a nurse, and Princess Louise told Lord
Esher, less than three weeks after the event, that 'The King knelt at
the side of the bed. The German Emperor stood silently at the head,'
while Doctor Reid 'passed his arm round her and supported her.'

When Vicky heard her mother was dying she desperately wanted
to see her once more, but was too ill to travel. Ever since 1898, she
had known that she was suffering from cancer of the spine. But she
kept the fact secret as long as she possibly could so as not to distress
her family. The Queen never discovered that her daughter was
troubled by anything worse than lumbago. For two years the
Empress endured agonizing pain, which even morphia could only
briefly mitigate. Her courage was such that weak, wasted and
tortured as she was, she somehow contrived to live an almost normal
life, until she could neither eat, nor sleep, nor move. On 23 January,
Vicky's daughter, Princess Margaret, broke the news to her that
Queen Victoria was dead. That evening, she wrote in her diary how
desolate the world would be without her 'sweet darling beloved
Mama; the best of mothers and the greatest of Queens, our centre
and help and support – all seems a blank, a terrible awful dream.
Realize it one cannot.' The page of Vicky's journal on which these
words are written is smudged and stained with tears.

The Queen, who, as the Prince of Wales once said, 'loved funerals,'
left him two detailed memoranda, dated October 1897 and January
1898, about how she wished to be buried. She wanted a military
funeral, there were to be no undertakers, and she preferred white to
black. Accordingly, the Kaiser measured her for her coffin, and
the King and the Duke of Connaught lifted her into it, covering her
face with her wedding veil. They were astonished to find how light
she was.

After lying in state for ten days at Osborne, on Friday, 1 February,
the journey to Windsor began. The sun shone brilliantly and the
Solent was quiet and calm: 'Queen's Weather' to the last. The
coffin, covered in white and gold, with the Imperial Crown at its
head, was placed on the quarterdeck of the *Alberta* where it was
guarded by five admirals, Lady Lytton and Miss Harriet Phipps,
who had once withstood the Queen's fury when she told her the
Household declined to dine with the Munshi. The *Victoria and
Albert*, with the King and Queen on board, sailed astern of the
Alberta, escorted by the *Osborne*, the *Hohenzollern* and the Admiralty
yacht *Enchantress*. The *Alberta*, with its convoy of mourners, steamed
slowly through two long lines of warships, stretching from Cowes to

Portsmouth. To the east of this mighty fleet, the huge battleship *Hatsuse* lay at anchor, sent there by the Mikado as a last tribute.

Soon after the procession left Trinity Pier behind it, the King sent for the Captain of his yacht and demanded to know why the Royal Standard was flying at half-mast. 'The Queen is dead, Sir,' was all he could find to say although it seemed obvious enough. 'The King of England lives,' replied His Majesty, and the Standard was hoisted to the truck. As the *Alberta* glided through this vast array of ships, guns thundered their salutes, guards of honour presented arms and the melancholy strains of the funeral march drifted across the water. By the time *Alberta* approached Portsmouth, to anchor under the shadow of the *Victory*, silent crowds could be seen lining the shore and the sun began to set in a wild blaze of glory. It was the sort of scene Turner loved to paint.

The following morning, the Queen's body was taken from Portsmouth to Victoria. Lady Lytton sat by the coffin, and when she peeped out from behind the drawn blinds of the compartment she saw people kneeling beside the track, as the Prince of Wales had done when he travelled in Alexander III's Funeral Train to Moscow. From Victoria, the coffin was taken to Paddington Station.

Colonel John St. Aubyn, the Officer in Command of the First Battalion Grenadier Guards, was in charge of the troops in the vicinity of Victoria Street and Buckingham Palace Road. At about eleven-fifteen, he caught sight of the gun-carriage, drawn by eight cream-coloured horses, in full state harness, 'with a kind of purple wreath on their manes and withers,' forming 'the most magnificent equipage' he had ever seen. 'Some people,' he wrote, 'thought the white horses inappropriate, but, as they never conveyed anyone but the Queen during her life, I do not think so myself. The coffin covered with a white pall, and with the Crown, the orbs, the sceptre and the collar of the Garter on it, passed within a couple of yards of me. Although my head was bent, I could see the King, the Emperor, and the Duke of Connaught, followed by the other Kings and Princes and their suites, and the carriages with the Queen and Princesses and other Royalties, as the procession moved by very slowly.'

When the coffin arrived at Windsor and was placed on the gun carriage waiting to take it to St George's Chapel, the horses, which had been standing in the cold for about an hour and a half, kicked and plunged so violently that they broke part of the harness, making it impossible to proceed. At one moment it seemed probable that they would upset the coffin. The Royal Artillery Officer in Charge later told Colonel St. Aubyn that 'what gave way was a steel pin in the swingle bar. He said he had been out in South Africa and seen artillery harness subjected to every kind of strain, and had known many traces and other parts of the harness break, but never this pin – which in this case was brand new, just out of Woolwich. There was probably a flaw in the steel.'

While this drama was going on in the Station Yard, the front of the Procession was marching up Windsor High Street, past the statue of the Queen put up at the time of her Diamond Jubilee. It was eventually halted by a non-commissioned officer sent by Fritz Ponsonby's order. Prince Louis of Battenberg suggested that, if the traces could not be repaired, the naval Guard of Honour could drag the gun-carriage to St George's. Ponsonby, having obtained the King's permission to adopt this proposal, ordered the Captain of the Naval Guard to pile arms and bring his men to the gun-carriage. When the Artillery team were instructed to get their horses clear, they held a whispered conference and appealed to the King. 'Right or wrong,' he decreed, 'let Ponsonby manage everything; we shall never get on if there are two people giving contradictory orders.'

So the Artillery men grudgingly withdrew, while the sailors took charge and, with that ingenuity for which the Senior Service is famous, contrived to manhandle the gun-carriage through the streets of Windsor to the steps of St George's Chapel. Meanwhile, the congregation inside, who were at a loss to understand why the service had not begun, shivered with cold, for whoever stoked the boiler evidently shared the late Queen's dislike of heat. 'At last, the West Doors were flung open, and up the steep steps was borne the casket containing the dead Queen's body: the extreme shortness of it struck one with pathetic insistence; almost a child's coffin this.'

For the next two nights it remained in the Albert Memorial Chapel, beside the recumbent effigies of the Prince Consort in armour, the Duke of Clarence in Hussar uniform, and the Duke of Albany in Highland dress. On it were placed the Crown, two orbs, one of them Queen Elizabeth's, the sceptre and the collar of the Garter. Day and night four officers stood motionless on guard, a duty shared alternately by the Grenadiers and the First Life Guards. As the hour struck, reliefs of officers marched up the Chapel in slow time with carried swords, 'till they came opposite the officers they were to relieve, when they halted and fronted towards them. They all then presented arms, and the senior of the old guard said to the new: "I commit to your charge the body of her late Majesty Queen Victoria, Queen of Great Britain and Ireland, Empress of India, together with the Regalia of the British Empire." The two reliefs then changed places: the old relief marching out in slow time with carried swords, and the new slowly reversing swords, and then standing at ease leaning on them with bent heads.'

The Dean of Windsor and Bishop Davidson held a short service for the Royal Family at six on Sunday evening. Madame Albani sang two anthems, accompanied by a harmonium. Davidson thought her voice 'too strong for the place.' Shortly before this service was held, Colonel St. Aubyn was told by a verger that the Royal Family was waiting outside for the King. 'I stood opposite the door standing at ease,' he wrote in his account of his 'last three days of duty in the presence of Queen Victoria.' When the Royal Party appeared he came to attention. 'The King of Greece came first, and then the King, the Emperor and many others whom I could not distinguish. The King when he saw the officers round the coffin came and said to me: "I do not wish the officers to watch while we are in the Chapel, will you tell them to go?" I saluted, said "Sir," went up to the coffin, told the officers and we all marched out in slow time.'

The service took about half an hour. 'Then the doors opened and the King and Queen came out followed by the rest of the Royalties. I gave the word to present arms to the officers and saluted with the hand myself. The King came up to me and held out his hand. I prepared to kneel and kiss it, but before I had got down – a matter of some difficulty in a tight uniform and a bearskin – he checked me and said: "I thank you and your comrades for having done your duty so well." I said, "It has been a great privilege Sir." Then the Queen turned back and held out her hand, which I kissed, going as near to kneeling as I could.'

During the course of that Sunday, two Eton boys, Shane Leslie and his cousin, Hugh Frewen, persuaded a verger to let them look at the Queen's coffin. They found the Chapel suffocated in flowers. So much so, that 'The sweet and sickly air smelt like laughing gas and the soldiers toppled over from time to time under the fumes.' Hugh wrote a poem describing the scene for the *Eton College Chronicle.* Somebody showed it to the King, who 'was kind enough to express a wish that Frewen would one day become his Poet Laureate.'

The Queen's final journey, down the Long Walk to the Mausoleum at Frogmore, took place after luncheon on the afternoon of 4 February. Many of those who walked behind her coffin had accompanied her during her lifetime on this pilgrimage, for when she resided at Windsor during her widowhood she never allowed a day to pass without visiting that hallowed spot. Over the door of the Royal Shrine was a brass tablet inscribed: 'His mourning widow, Victoria the Queen, directed that all that is mortal of Prince Albert be placed in this sepulchre. A.D. 1862. Farewell, beloved! Here, at last, will I rest with thee; with thee in Christ will I rise again.' And now that day had come. As the family left Frogmore it started to snow. Even the elements it seemed were conspiring to give the Queen her white funeral.

The King might well have been forgiven had he not shown much grief for his loss. There was a time when his mother had hardly troubled to conceal her aversion for him. After the Prince Consort's death, she admitted to Lord Clarendon that it 'disturbed her to see him in the room.' Throughout his youth, the Prince was constantly reminded that his slow progress was breaking his parents' hearts. Indeed, the Queen subjected the wretched boy to such a deluge of criticism that the moral barometer at Windsor seemed permanently stuck at 'stormy.' She told him that he was idle, listless, weak, unfeeling, restless, contradictory, indiscreet, noisy, and unsupportable with younger children.

It would be misleading to regard the Queen's first outbursts of frenzied grief as considered judgements or her last word. In 1869 she said, 'I am sure no Heir-Apparent ever was so nice and unpretending as dear Bertie is,' and hardly a 9 November passed without her proclaiming how fortunate she was to have such a good and affectionate son. Towards the end of her life, the Queen and Prince might often be seen sitting together rocking with laughter over some family joke. It was evident from all he did and said that he greatly admired his mother, and with that discriminating forgetfulness which is the measure of a generous mind he held her memory sacred.

In foreign affairs, there was no Minister of the Crown, with the possible exception of Lord Salisbury, who could claim to advise the King in virtue of his superior knowledge or experience. Naturally, he needed to be told what policies the Government intended to pursue, but in contrast to his lifelong study of Europe, his intimate relations with its rulers, his outstanding facility for languages, and his firsthand knowledge of the Continent, most politicians seemed parochial, ignorant and tongue-tied. There were Ministers, of course, itching to lecture him on matters they did not understand, just as there are schoolboys happy to tell the Astronomer Royal how to identify Jupiter. But that did not alter the fact that His Majesty was in a better position to instruct them than they him.

The King soon established an informal Cabinet of his own, to list whose names is to demonstrate his skill in recognizing talent: Knollys, Esher, Fisher, Bertie, Hardinge, Spring Rice. Moreover, he always took the closest interest in diplomatic appointments, often pressing the claims of those who won his confidence. Spring Rice became Minister to Persia 'entirely due' to the King, who 'insisted upon it with Lord Landsdowne.' Similarly, Sir Francis Bertie gratefully acknowledged that he owed being sent to Paris to 'His Majesty's gracious advocacy.' Lord Esher spoke of the King's 'unerring judgement of men – and women' as a 'supreme gift.' In forming his opinions, 'he never allowed his likes and dislikes to interfere,' and 'he saw through all attempts to cajole or mislead him.'

When King Edward came to the throne, Britain had no allies and, apart from a preference for remaining isolated, no consistent foreign policy. Problems were resolved as they presented themselves in what seemed the most practical manner. In 1902, Sir Thomas Sanderson, then permanent Under-Secretary for Foreign Affairs, admitted that after Count Hatzfeldt had complained that he was incapable of understanding the principles governing British foreign policy, he had told him that 'he ought to know that we have not got a policy and work from hand to mouth.'

Ever since 1894, Europe had been divided into two armed camps: The Triple Alliance, consisting of Germany, Austria and Italy; and the Dual Alliance signed that year by Russia and France. At one moment during the South African War it seemed possible that both groups might combine in an effort to save the Boers.

The problem facing British Statesmen at the turn of the century, was whether to remain aloof, or to throw in their lot with Germany or France. The Prime Minister remained a powerful advocate of isolation. In the first months of the new reign, he drafted a Memorandum challenging the view that it was dangerous not to have allies. What certainly would be unwise, he argued, would be to incur 'novel and most onerous obligations,' merely in order to guard against perils which might not threaten. Besides, even assuming that there were cogent arguments for joining a European alliance, 'The British Government cannot undertake to declare war, for any purpose, unless it is a purpose of which the electors of this country would approve. If the Government promised to declare war for an object which did not commend itself to public opinion, the promise would be repudiated, and the Government would be turned out. I do not see how, in common honesty, we could invite other nations to rely upon our aid in a struggle, when we have no means whatever of knowing what may be the humour of our people in circumstances which cannot be foreseen.'

Some of Lord Salisbury's colleagues believed that his policy did not sufficiently allow for changing circumstances. While Bismarck remained Chancellor of Imperial Germany, proclaiming he governed a 'sated power,' Britain was relatively secure. But the Kaiser's ambitions in Baghdad, the Balkans, the Persian Gulf, Africa and the Far East, and, above all, his plan to construct a powerful German Navy, created a new situation. When the battleships envisaged in the Naval Laws of 1898 and 1900 were in commission, Britain's supremacy at sea would be challenged and isolation could become dangerous. As far as the King was concerned he was too good a European to see any particular virtue in insular policies.

After the 'Khaki election' of October 1900, Lord Salisbury, who had hitherto been his own Foreign Secretary, appointed Lord Lansdowne to take his place at the Foreign Office. Two years later, Arthur Balfour succeeded his uncle as Prime Minister. The King never felt entirely at ease with any of these statesmen. Lansdowne, in particular, seemed to regard 'the whole domain of the Foreign Office as his private property,' and treated the King like a poacher.

Lansdowne was descended from Lord Shelburne, the Prime Minister who was driven from office in 1783 by the 'infamous coalition' of Fox and North. His maternal grandfather, Count de Flahault, was one of Napoleon's generals and a natural son of Talleyrand. Lansdowne was sent to Eton, where Balfour was his fag, and Balliol, while Jowett was its Master. In 1876 he incensed the Prince of Wales by his injudicious intervention on behalf of Lady Blandford, his wife's sister.

Like the Duke of Devonshire, Lansdowne began his political career as a Whig but later joined the Conservatives. Besides Bowood, a large estate in Scotland and Lansdowne House, he owned some hundred and twenty thousand acres in County Kerry. It is hardly surprising, therefore, that he had little sympathy for the Liberal Land Bill of 1881, which offered Irish tenants three 'F's': Fair rent, Free sale and Fixity of tenure. In 1883 Gladstone appointed him Governor-General of Canada, and four years later Lord Salisbury made him Viceroy of India.

As Secretary of State for War from 1895 to 1900, Lansdowne was widely blamed for Britain's reverses in South Africa. Towards the end of the Boer War, Queen Victoria suggested he should take over the Foreign Office. In expressing his gratitude to Her Majesty for this mark of her confidence, he told her that he valued it the more 'because he does not disguise from himself that as Secretary of State for War he must often have seemed to Your Majesty to fall short of Your Majesty's expectations.' The *National Review* described Lansdowne's promotion as 'a first rate joke of Lord Salisbury's – one of the most cynical acts of our time,' and the *Daily Mail*, written according to the Prime Minister 'by office boys for office boys,' declared that it was 'a thoroughly bad precedent that a Minister who had failed in one office should be rewarded by promotion to a higher and even more important office.' Since Lansdowne's appointment can hardly have been based on his past success, it must presumably be attributed to his powerful political standing in the Unionist Party.

A last attempt to reach Anglo-German understanding was made early in 1901. For a time it looked the most promising of such negotiations, but in the end proved no more successful than the discussions begun by Bismarck in 1875, Lord Salisbury in 1895, and Chamberlain in 1898 and 1899. This final failure was a turning point in history, partly because it compelled Britain to choose between remaining isolated or seeking alliance with France or Russia, and partly because unresolved differences between the two countries aggravated ill-feeling.

On 9 January 1901, the Duchess of Devonshire invited Eckardstein to Chatsworth from the twelfth to the eighteenth. 'Pray come without fail,' she wrote, 'as the Duke has several urgent political questions to discuss with you. You will also find here Joseph Chamberlain.' During his visit, he discussed outstanding international questions and Anglo-German relations. After dinner on 16 January, he had a long conversation with the two Ministers in the library at Chatsworth, during which they 'definitely formulated their position.' Immediately after returning to London, Eckardstein reported to Bülow, the new Imperial Chancellor, that he had just met Chamberlain 'at the country house of the Duke of Devonshire' and that in the course of discussion, the Colonial Secretary told him that 'he and his friends in the Cabinet had made up their minds that the day of a policy of "splendid isolation" was over for England. England must look about for allies for the future. The choice was either Russia and France or the Triple Alliance.' Preferring the latter to the former, he 'would do everything to bring about a gradual advance in this direction . . . But should a permanent partnership with Germany prove unrealizable, he would then support an association with Russia.'

The Kaiser's visit to his grandmother in January 1901 made a deep impression in England, and the goodwill thus created assisted negotiations. Eckardstein, acting for Count Hatzfeldt, who was too ill to play any part in the Imperial visit, met the Emperor on board the Dutch Mail Boat in which he and the Duke of Connaught crossed the Channel. On their way back to London, Eckardstein told the Kaiser about his conversations at Chatsworth.

During his stay in England, the Kaiser's relations with his Uncle were exceptionally cordial. King Edward told Vicky on 1 February that her son 'was kindness itself and touching in his devotion, without a shade of brusquerie or selfishness.' A few days later he referred to 'William's touching and simple demeanour, up to the last,' which would 'never be forgotten by me or anyone.' One of the first acts of the King's reign was to bestow the Order of the Garter on the Crown Prince of Germany. At the same time he made the Kaiser a Field-Marshal of the British Army, and his brother Prince Henry a Vice-Admiral of the Fleet. When Eckardstein returned to London from Osborne, he reported to Berlin that 'the most cordial relations conceivable prevail, not only between the Kaiser and the King, but also with the Queen and other members of the Royal Family.'

On the day the Emperor left for home, he informed a favoured audience at Marlborough House that Providence had decreed that 'two nations which have produced such men as Shakespeare, Schiller, Luther and Goethe must have a great future before them; I believe that the two Teutonic nations will, bit by bit, learn to know each other better, and that they will stand together to help in keeping the peace of the world. We ought to form an Anglo-German alliance, you to keep the seas while we would be responsible for the land; with such an alliance, not a mouse could stir in Europe without permission.'

At the end of February, the King paid a visit to Vicky at Friedrichshof. During his stay he saw rather more of the Kaiser than he had expected, but their meetings remained friendly, although his patience had been tried on the journey by hearing the Boer National Anthem sung wherever he went. His Majesty was only accompanied by Fritz Ponsonby, his Assistant Private Secretary, and Sir Francis

Laking, who might be able he hoped to persuade the German doctors to increase the meagre doses of morphia they prescribed for the Empress Frederick. He took the view that it was right to risk shortening a doomed life in an effort to relieve intolerable suffering.

On the last evening of her brother's visit, the Empress gave Fritz, her godson, two large boxes of letters to take back to England. Apart from insisting that she did not 'want a soul to know that they have been taken away,' she left no instructions what was to be done with them once they had left Germany. In 1928, Fritz, believing he was acting in accordance with her wishes, published a selection of them. The Kaiser, then an exile in Holland, tried to prevent the book coming out, for he did not cut a very agreeable figure in its pages. But the controversial work appeared, and allowed 'the Empress's own words to provide the answer to those cruel and slanderous accusations' from which her memory suffered.

Lord Lansdowne looked with more favour upon the possibility of signing an agreement with Germany than did the Prime Minister. The Foreign Office even drew up a draft convention which suggested that if either of the signatories were attacked by two or more powers, the other would come to its rescue. Lord Salisbury thought these proposals offered a poor bargain as it was far more probable that Germany would be invaded than Britain. His reservations were shared by Holstein, the Head of the Political Section of the Wilhelm-strasse: a sinister, morbid man, who preferred to work in the dark than to face the light. When Chamberlain warned in 1901 that 'if we could not find support in one camp we must seek it in another,' Holstein regarded the threat as 'rubbish and humbug.'

In the summer of 1901, the Empress Frederick died, welcoming death as a happy issue from affliction. Queen Alexandra, bringing a wreath of flowers from Windsor, the home her sister-in-law had loved so well, accompanied King Edward to Potsdam, where Vicky was laid to rest beside Fritz in the Mausoleum in the Friedenskirche. The King found the Kaiser's insistence on exploiting the occasion for military display most distasteful.

Ten days after the ceremony at Potsdam, the King and the Kaiser met at Wilhelmshöhe, near Homburg. After luncheon, during which the Emperor was in high spirits, he and the King and Sir Frank Lascelles went into the garden to settle the future of Europe. The meeting was not a success. The Kaiser resurrected the phrase 'perfidious Albion,' and obliged the King to question the sincerity of his protestations of friendship. Germany, William said, wanted

Britain to commit herself to the Triple Alliance. Vague affirmations were not enough. What was wanted was a Treaty, ratified by Parliament. His technique savoured less of seduction than rape. Like some tempestuous lover, he demanded the ultimate concession before even holding hands.

Early in February 1902, the King gave an official dinner at Marlborough House for Foreign Ambassadors and his own Ministers. After dinner, Eckardstein noticed Chamberlain and the French Ambassador heading for the billiard room. Hard as he tried, he could not hear what they said, apart from two words: 'Morocco' and 'Egypt'. From that moment, he was convinced that Chamberlain was resolved to seek partnership with France: the alternative he had always envisaged should discussions with the Wilhelmstrasse break down.

Just as Eckardstein was about to go home, he was intercepted by an equerry who said that the King would like to see him privately. His Majesty, who had changed into more comfortable clothes, was in excellent spirits. After offering him a whisky-and-soda and a cigar, he expressed his concern about 'the renewed abuse of England in the German Press and the unfriendly and sarcastic remarks of Count Bülow in the Reichstag.' These, he said, had aroused so much resentment among his Ministers and in public opinion 'that for a long time at least there can be no more any question of Great Britain and Germany working together.' The King hinted that France was pressing England to come to an agreement, and as all the Government wanted was 'peace and quiet and to live on a friendly footing with all other countries,' it would probably be best to reach such a settlement. 'If the Kaiser now writes me long letters assuring me of his friendship for England, I cannot, I am sorry to say, give much weight to what he says.'

As far as negotiations with Germany were concerned, the King endorsed Lord Lansdowne's foreign policy. But in 1902 a serious dispute broke out between them over the Shah of Persia. Early that year, Lansdowne instructed Sir Arthur Hardinge, the British Minister in Tehran, to persuade the Shah to visit England. The imperial fly, however, showed little desire to walk into Lansdowne's parlour. Sir Arthur finally overcame his resistance by virtually promising him the Garter. In so doing he greatly exceeded his brief, for the distinction was not his to bestow.

King Edward, obsessed by such things, was justly indignant to learn what Sir Arthur had done. Queen Victoria had admittedly given the Garter to the Shah's father, but the King now proclaimed that he had no intention of being bound by precedent, and that he refused to confer a specifically Christian Order of Chivalry upon an infidel. He therefore proposed that the Shah should be told before leaving for England that he could expect the GCVO or the GCB but not the Garter.

Lansdowne suggested that His Majesty in giving these instructions had not fully realized 'that if such an intimation were to be made, the Shah would probably abandon his visit,' which 'would be most unfortunate and detrimental to the interests of this country.' The Foreign Secretary respectfully questioned the King's contention that the best way of reaching agreement with Persia was by coming to terms with Russia. 'I would venture to say that although His Majesty's anticipations may prove correct, the policy is not one which has yet been recommended by his advisers . . . It would to my mind be most regrettable if the Shah's visit were to fall through owing to a seeming rebuff.'

On 20 August, Lansdowne accompanied the Shah to Portsmouth to have luncheon on board the *Victoria and Albert*. The journey was something of an ordeal as the fêted guest kept stopping the train in order to be sick. Nor was conversation made easy by a musical box which nobody knew how to silence. After luncheon, Lansdowne presented the King with a memorandum in which he suggested that the Statutes of the Order of the Garter should be amended in such a manner as to make it possible to bestow it on those who did not belong to the Christian Faith. Somehow, the Foreign Secretary gained the impression that the King had approved his proposals, whereas, in fact, he had only agreed to consider the document.

On returning to London, Lansdowne instructed Messrs Garrard, the Court Jewellers, to design a special version of the Garter star and badge suitable for infidels, which he proposed could be accomplished by omitting the Cross of St George. Next, he wrote to the King requesting him to make arrangements for conferring the new insignia on the Shah before he returned home, and told the Persian Minister that His Majesty had graciously consented to bestow the coveted honour upon his master.

The King was still on board the *Victoria and Albert* berthed in Pembroke Dock, when he received the Foreign Secretary's letter enclosing Garrard's designs for a non-Christian insignia of the Garter. He was so outraged that he flung the package out of the porthole of his cabin. By a singular chance it fell into a steam pinnace moored alongside the Royal Yacht and was retrieved by a stoker. The King then sent for Fritz Ponsonby and dictated a furious letter to Lord Lansdowne, pointing out that he had never approved of the Shah being given the Garter, that he would not hear of omitting the Cross of St George, and that he strongly objected to having his prerogative usurped. It was, moreover, unheard of for one Sovereign to dictate to another what decoration he should be given. 'If the Shah leaves this Country in the sulks, like a spoilt child, because he cannot get what he wants, it cannot be helped.' Lansdowne replied that the mistake was entirely his, as he had clearly misunderstood what the King had said. Under the circumstances, having assured the Shah he would be given the Garter, he had no alternative but to place his resignation in the King's hands.

Knollys recommended the King to withstand Lansdowne's pressure, and Lord Curzon ruled that it was wrong in principle to confer the Garter on an infidel. But the Duke of Devonshire advised Balfour to support his Foreign Secretary. Accordingly, Balfour sent the King a dexterous letter in which he said that they were concerned 'with the not unfamiliar problem of having to deal with a public servant who, by mistake, had exceeded his instructions. The question in such cases inevitably arises, is he to be "thrown over", or is he not?' Lord Lansdowne, 'erroneously believing himself to be authorized by Your Majesty, has pledged Your Majesty to bestow the Garter on the Shah – has indeed pledged Your Majesty repeatedly and explicitly. If he be prevented from carrying out these pledges what will be his position?' Then Balfour, taking the pin from his grenade, posed one further question. If the Foreign Secretary resigned, 'could the matter stop there in these days of Governmental solidarity?'

In this urbane fashion the Prime Minister threatened the King with a constitutional crisis unless he agreed to surrender. Balfour furthermore pointed out that even if Lord Lansdowne were disavowed, it would hardly dispose of the commitment into which he had entered. While it might be a 'relatively small matter' to offend the Shah, we could not afford to appear to act dishonourably. 'Our well-known fidelity to our engagements is one of our few trumps. We must not waste it.' Such was the force of these arguments that the King consented to a special mission being sent to Tehran to invest the Shah with the insignia of the Order upon which he had set his heart.

Even before Anglo-German discussions finally broke down, Britain began to look elsewhere for an ally. Her choice fell upon Japan, which shared her anxiety to check Russian expansion in Central and North-Eastern Asia. Some years before, Japan had attacked China, seized Korea and captured Port Arthur. By the Treaty of Shimonoseki of 1895 the Government at Peking was forced to surrender these and other territories to the Mikado. Whereupon Germany, Russia and France, all of whom had interests in that part of the world, intervened and compelled the victor to disgorge most of his conquests. The Treaty of Shimonoseki was Japan's San Stefano, while China was the sick man of the Orient over whose corpse the vultures hovered.

As Britain had taken no part in these predatory proceedings, she retained Japan's goodwill: a matter of some consequence when the two island Empires began negotiating in the summer of 1901. In August of that year, the Japanese Ambassador, Baron Hayashi, started tentative discussions with Lord Lansdowne. While Hayashi was negotiating in London, the Foreign Office in Tokyo was exploring the alternative possibility of coming to terms with the Tsar. To this end, Marquis Ito, a former Japanese Prime Minister, headed a mission to St Petersburg. Lansdowne, however, refused to continue negotiating while Japan insisted upon the simultaneous pursuit of contradictory policies. Ito was consequently diverted to London where a Treaty was soon concluded.

The King at first felt some reservations about England becoming an ally of Japan. But such doubts as he had were soon dispelled when he saw what might be gained. Nobody was more insistent than His Majesty that Ito must be cordially welcomed, and he travelled up from Sandringham on Christmas Eve to meet his guest in person. After all the fuss that had been made of him in St Petersburg and Berlin, it was necessary to show him every possible civility.

The Anglo-Japanese Treaty was formally signed on 30 January 1902. If Japan were involved in a war against more than one Power to defend Korea, Britain agreed to come to her help. On the same conditions, Japan promised to assist Britain in defence of her interests in China. In the more probable event of a war between Russia and Japan, Britain undertook to remain benevolently neutral. Finally, both signatories offered each other naval facilities, such as the use of docks and harbours. The most important consequence of the Treaty for Europe was that it marked the end of Britain's isolation.

As soon as it became clear that Anglo-German agreement was unattainable, Britain began to explore the possibility of coming to

terms with France: a task made easier in May 1902 by the signing
of peace in South Africa. Two notable Frenchmen had long advocated *entente*: the Foreign Secretary, Delcassé, and Paul Cambon,
the French Ambassador to the Court of St James. Following his
conversation with Chamberlain at Marlborough House, Cambon
sent Lansdowne a letter listing the points he wished to discuss in the
hope of achieving agreement.

On 10 February 1902, the Ambassador sat next to King Edward
at dinner at Buckingham Palace. During the course of their conversation the King told him: 'Lansdowne has shown me your letter. It
is excellent. We must go on.' In fact, for some months, His Majesty's
illness and coronation prevented him giving further thought to
Anglo-French relations. It was not until early in 1903 that he started
to plan the most important journey 'undertaken by any British
Sovereign in modern times.'

The King's journey to Lisbon, Rome and Paris in the spring of
1903, owed nothing whatever to any of his Ministers. He alone
decided that he wished to pay a State Visit abroad. He alone chose
when to go, where to go, and with whom to go. He planned every
detail himself with such meticulous secrecy that even the Queen and
Knollys for a time knew nothing of what was in prospect. Fritz
Ponsonby, who accompanied the King on the tour, only learned
after leaving Lisbon that they were later going to Paris. Even then
he was warned to keep this knowledge to himself. Neither the Prime
Minister, nor the Foreign Secretary were told about the journey
until it was more or less planned. When some Ministers expressed
misgivings they were courteously ignored. After the King's progress
proved a triumphant success, several people were eager to share the
credit. But those at the time who were in a position to know, agreed
with Delcassé that it was 'the King, and the King alone, who conceived the scheme of a visit to Paris.' Count Metternich, Hatzfeldt's
successor as German Ambassador in London, told Bülow in June
1903, that he knew 'for certain' that the visit of King Edward to
Paris was 'the result of his own initiative.'

The first person the King consulted was not Lord Lansdowne, but
the Marquis de Soveral, the Portuguese Minister in London. Luis
de Soveral achieved a unique eminence in Edwardian Society.
Apart from the King, he was the most sought-after guest in England.
His popularity rested upon his wit, charm, and tact, for he was
neither rich nor particularly well connected. The ladies, with whom
he incessantly flirted, adored him. From the moment he came to

London in 1884, the Prince and Princess of Wales fell under his spell and soon began treating him as a member of their family. Once the Marquis's name was mistakenly left off a list of guests for Sandringham and the King asked him why he had waited for an invitation. 'Well Sir,' said de Soveral, 'I had got as far as my door when your command arrived.' On 1 March 1903, King Edward summoned him for a private talk at the Palace and told him he planned to visit the King of Italy and the French President, M. Loubet. He then asked him to discover from King Carlos whether it would be agreeable for him to call at Lisbon.

The moment de Soveral returned to the Portuguese Legation, he sent a 'highly confidential' cypher telegram to King Carlos. In it, he quoted the King as saying: 'Political considerations of the highest order oblige me to pay a visit to the King of Italy in Rome and the President of the French Republic in Paris . . . I have decided – if this is agreeable to the King of Portugal – to begin at Lisbon where I would sail directly . . . H.M. the King asked me to maintain the utmost secrecy about this. Here nobody suspects a thing; not even the Queen herself.' Extreme discretion was necessary partly because King Edward was anxious that his Ministers should learn of his proposed European tour from his own lips, and partly because he had no wish to offend either Russia or Germany by ill-timed disclosures.

Preliminary negotiations over the King's visit to Loubet were privately undertaken by Colonel Stuart-Wortley, the Military Attaché to the British Embassy in Paris, and a friend of the President. Sir Edmund Monson, the Ambassador, was at first neither consulted nor informed. In order to ensure privacy, communications from London were sent to the Colonel's house in the Rue de la Faisanderie. Stuart-Wortley's wife was never told from whom these secret letters came, but she suspected that they were written by either the King or de Soveral.

Loubet showed 'unmistakable delight' at the King's suggested visit, which he believed 'would do an amount of good which is probably not realized in England . . . In this capital, His Majesty, while Prince of Wales, has acquired an exceptional personal popularity; and he would find, when he returned here, that this feeling was as warm as ever.' The President insisted that 'he could not lay too much stress on the influence which the King's presence in Paris would have on friendly relations between the two peoples.' When Monson was let into the secret, he endorsed Loubet's view that the King could expect a friendly reception, and that his visit would cause considerable pleasure to all classes in France.

The King's Ministers looked on the venture with various degrees of misgiving. Lord Londonderry was said to oppose the whole idea and the Prime Minister was thought to have doubts. Lord Lansdowne at first referred to the Paris visit as 'quite an informal affair,' but when Monson asked Knollys how the King wanted to be received, he was told: 'as officially as possible, and that the more honours that were paid to him the better it would be.' Several times, the Foreign Secretary warned that the King might meet a hostile reception. It was certainly true that many seemed slow to recognize that peace had been signed with the Boers for almost a year. 'It was a poorly kept secret,' wrote Lord Redesdale, 'well known to all those who were in any way behind the scenes at the time, that the King's Ministers were very much averse to his paying those visits officially as King of England.'

Instead of inviting the Foreign Secretary or a Minister of the Crown to accompany him on the voyage, the King took Charles Hardinge, then Assistant Under-Secretary for Foreign Affairs. Hardinge was given the title of 'Minister Plenipotentiary' and performed the duties of a diplomatic aide-de-camp. Some said he had only been selected because his wife was one of Queen Alexandra's Ladies-in-Waiting, but, as Fritz Ponsonby recognized, his choice was in fact yet one more example of the King's 'unerring judgement of men.' The distinction of Hardinge's subsequent career proved how right His Majesty was: Ambassador to St Petersburg and Paris, Viceroy of India and Permanent Under-Secretary of State for the Foreign Office.

Lord Lansdowne was 'very unwilling' to consent to Hardinge's 'unusual' appointment and only gave his consent a week before he was due to sail. At best, it was a startling innovation, at worst, a breach of the Constitution. Whenever Queen Victoria was not in London, whether she was at Windsor, Balmoral, Cannes or Cimiez, she was invariably accompanied by a Minister of the Crown. When George IV held private communications with foreign Ministers, Canning successfully insisted upon being present at such interviews. Sir William Anson asserts in his study of *The Law and Custom of the Constitution* that the Sovereign 'does not constitutionally take independent action in foreign affairs; everything that passes between him and foreign Princes or Ministers should be known to his own Ministers who are responsible to the people for policy and to the law for acts done.' It was therefore to stand precedents on their heads –

often the best place for them – for King Edward to visit the President of the Third Republic and to hold conversations with M. Delcassé with only the Portuguese Minister and Charles Hardinge present. It is true that Hardinge was under instructions to send full reports of all that took place to the Foreign Office, but that only offered Lord Lansdowne such consolation as is to be derived from learning of *faits accomplis*. It was like telling a man trapped under the ruins of his house that he had been buried by an earthquake.

The King set sail from Portsmouth in the *Victoria and Albert* on Tuesday, 31 March 1903. Two days later, he was rowed ashore at Lisbon in a State Barge manned by eighty oarsmen. Endless trouble had been taken to make the visitors comfortable. Bathrooms were specially installed in the Necessidades Palace, and the guests were called with tea in the morning and provided with whisky-and-soda at night. When the King was presented with an address by the two houses of the Cortes he gracefully alluded to the ancient alliance which had bound Britain to Portugal since the days of Charles II. Before leaving England he had asked Sir Thomas Sanderson to send him copies of all treaties with Portugal, so his spontaneous remarks were based on detailed briefing. The visit to Lisbon was received with excited enthusiasm and gave new life to an old friendship.

On 7 April, the King set sail for Naples, by way of Gibraltar and Malta. Ponsonby sent the Italian authorities a telegram announcing that His Majesty would be arriving incognito, 'which seemed rather absurd as no other human being in the world could come with eight battleships, four cruisers, four destroyers, and a dispatch vessel.' Of course, whether he described himself as Lord Renfrew, the Earl of Chester, or Duke of Lancaster, whether he was accompanied by a battlefleet or a single Equerry, he was likely to be recognized. After all, his profile was on every stamp and coin. Indeed, he was not necessarily best pleased if his disguise proved too successful. When he dined under an assumed title at a restaurant, he quickly became impatient if expected to wait his turn. Once, when visiting a friend without warning, a servant asked for his name. 'You ought to know me,' said the King. 'I know you. Last year you were the third footman with the Duchess of Manchester.' During his stay in Naples, the King insisted on visiting its slums, which provoked Hardinge to lecture him on the folly of needlessly exposing himself to danger. 'I spoke to him very seriously,' Hardinge told his wife. 'He was very nice, thanked me, said that I was quite right and that he would not do it again.'

From Naples the King took a train to Rome: the first English Sovereign to set foot in the Eternal City since King Ethelwulf visited it in the ninth century. In a felicitous speech at the Quirinal, he recalled the happy months he had spent in Italy in the winter of 1859, and spoke of the common love of liberty the two countries shared. The King's custom of speaking off the cuff was a measure of his freedom from ministerial restraint. On this particular occasion, Ponsonby, who had taught himself shorthand, took down the King's remarks as he made them. His Majesty, in the enthusiasm of the moment, referred to England and Italy as having 'often fought side by side.' As Fritz could only recall a single instance of such companionship in arms, he took the liberty of omitting the word 'often.'

During his visit to Rome, the King was anxious to pay a courtesy visit to Pope Leo XIII, who was then ninety-three. On three previous occasions, he had met Pius IX, and could see no reason for departing from such precedents. Nor had he any desire to offend his Roman Catholic subjects merely in order to gratify Protestant bigotry. Political parties and religious denominations might base their appeals on sectional interests, but King Edward saw it as the Sovereign's duty to transcend faction and represent the nation. Fisher once ventured to congratulate His Majesty on his adroitness in 'sending to ask after Keir Hardie's stomach-ache! By Jove, he went for me like a mad bull! "You don't understand me! I am the King of ALL the people!" '

Balfour, scenting controversy, tried to discourage the visit, arguing that the head of the Anglican Church should eschew the Pope. Unreasonable as Protestant intolerance might be, it was wisest not to provoke it. The King, however, was disposed to be more courageous. After reading a sheaf of resolutions, telegrams and letters sent by Protestant Societies, he told Ponsonby that 'he did not intend to be guided by such narrow-minded people.'

In the end, it was arranged that His Majesty, acting on his own initiative, would privately visit the Pope, thus enabling the Cabinet to disclaim responsibility. The audience took place on the afternoon of 29 April and discussion ranged from reminiscences of Leo's visit to London in 1846, to the problems of Venezuela and Somaliland. During the interview, the Pope thanked the King for the tolerance shown to Roman Catholics throughout the British Empire. The meeting was welcomed by Italians, but distressed those whose Christian charity stopped at the Vatican.

The principal purpose of the King's journey was to visit neither

Lisbon nor Rome, but Paris: a fact he concealed by leaving it to the last. In spite of the President's assurances, nobody could be sure how well he would be received. Disputes over Siam, Fashoda and South Africa had gravely damaged Anglo-French relations. Some Parisian newspapers in their zeal to encourage ill-will, saw fit to remind their readers of the trial of Joan of Arc. His Majesty was accustomed to being blamed for most of the world's misfortunes but hardly felt responsible for what happened in Rouen in 1431.

When the Royal Train steamed into the Bois de Boulogne on 1 May, and the King stepped out on to the platform in the spring sunshine, the success of his venture was by no means certain. The procession from the railway station to the British Embassy was watched without much enthusiasm, while groups of protesters shouted: 'Vivent les Boers!' Their cries were lost on the King who could not hear them above the clatter of his escort of cuirassiers. But Delcassé, who shared a carriage with Hardinge, tried to avert his attention from these unfortunate demonstrations by repeating without much conviction: 'Quel enthousiasme, quel enthousiasme!'

Ponsonby, whose position in the procession was that from which the Duke of Plaza Toro led his army, 'received anything but a pleasant ovation,' for, by the time he passed, 'the cheers had become jeers.' Provoked by the scarlet coat of his uniform, the crowd showered him with witticisms, most of which he was unable to understand. When somebody said to the King, 'The French don't like us,' he merely replied, 'Why should they?' That evening, he made a speech which started the thaw. 'It is hardly necessary,' he began, 'for me to say with what sincere pleasure I find myself once more in Paris, which, as you know, I have very frequently visited in the past with a pleasure that continually increases, with an affection strengthened by old and happy associations.' He went on to say that he trusted that the days of conflict were over, and that future historians, in alluding to Anglo-French relations in the twentieth century, would only record peaceful progress and friendly rivalry. 'A Divine Providence has designed that France should be our near neighbour, and, I hope, always a dear friend. There are no two countries in the world whose mutual prosperity is more dependent on each other.' The King could hardly have identified himself more forthrightly with the policy of *entente*.

That evening, he visited the Théâtre Français to see Maurice Donnay's play *L'Autre Danger*. During the interval, he insisted on mingling with the crowds in the foyer to greet old friends, much to the dismay of the police who hoped to confine him to the Presidential box. Amongst those he recognized was Mlle Jeanne Granier, a well-known actress. As soon as he saw her, he held out his hand and said 'Oh, Mademoiselle, I remember how I applauded you in London. You personified there all the grace, all the esprit of France.' Soon all Paris seemed to have heard of this encounter.

The next morning, after watching a review at Vincennes, the King attended a reception at the Hôtel de Ville, where he made an irresistible speech which went straight to the hearts of his audience. 'I shall never forget my visit to your charming city,' he said, 'and I can assure you it is with the greatest pleasure that I return each time to Paris, where I am treated exactly as if I were at home.' That afternoon, he drove out to Longchamps for a race meeting, specially arranged by the Jockey Club of which he had long been a member. An outsider, John Bull, won the 'Prix Diamond Jubilee.' In the evening, he dined at the Elysée Palace, where he went out of his way to be agreeable to Prince Radolin, the German Ambassador to Paris. The day's entertainment was completed with a visit to the Opéra. The King, as he sat between Monsieur and Madame Loubet, after a long day and a ten-course dinner, washed down with Château Haut Brion 1877 and Château d'Yquem 1874, fought a partially successful battle against sleep. When he finally drove back to the Embassy late that night, the streets were lined with wildly cheering crowds, shouting 'Vive le Roi!' 'Vive L'Angleterre!'

As if to prove that he meant what he said about feeling at home in Paris, the King next morning walked to the Anglican Church in the Rue d'Aguesseau for Matins. After the service, he attended a luncheon given in his honour by Delcassé at the Quai d'Orsay. When the meal was over, the two men retired for a private discussion, during which His Majesty warned Delcassé not to trust the Kaiser, whom he described as 'mad and malicious.' Besides emphasizing once more his desire for friendship and understanding, he expressed a hope of reaching agreement with France's partner, Russia. As a result of the King's public utterances and private assurances, Delcassé decided that England meant what she said. The diplomatic exchanges which followed the Paris visit derived from that conviction.

In the afternoon, Sir Edmund Monson gave a Garden Party in the Embassy grounds for English residents in Paris, and the King planted a chestnut tree to commemorate his visit. In the evening,

President Loubet came to dinner, but being a day of rest there were no speeches, only some light music. The next morning, Monday, 4 May, the King took his departure, driving with Loubet to the Gare des Invalides. The streets were lined with excited crowds: cheering, waving, shouting, 'Vive notre Roi!' It had taken over a hundred and fifty thousand Germans several months to capture Paris in 1871. In 1903 it took one man four days.

President Loubet and M. Delcassé returned the King's visit four months later. There was the usual round of banquets at Buckingham Palace and the Guildhall, a visit to Windsor and a review at Aldershot. On 7 July, Delcassé called on Lord Lansdowne at the Foreign Office to discuss the possibility of resolving outstanding conflicts and signing a treaty of friendship. Cambon also arranged for the French Foreign Minister to sit next to Chamberlain at a dinner he was giving that evening at the Embassy. The President won the hearts of the English people by seeming so pleased with all that was done for him. Cambon reported that 'Never for fifty years, has the head of a foreign state been the object in this country of such ovations.'

Apart from meeting Lansdowne and Chamberlain, the French Foreign Minister had a long conversation with the King, in the course of which they agreed that it was 'necessary to organize a vast coalition which could stand up to Germany.' Delcassé, who regarded King Edward as 'sensible, practical and thoughtful,' was particularly impressed by his assertion that Russia was 'indispensable' if Germany was to be kept in awe of Europe.

Soon after Delcassé's visit to the Foreign Office, Lord Lansdowne and Cambon began to negotiate in earnest, particularly concentrating on differences in Egypt and Morocco. They were sufficiently successful for Lansdowne to prepare a draft agreement to put before the Cabinet. In April the following year, Britain and France signed three separate conventions. All the terms were immediately made public, except for five articles relating to Morocco. The Germans, however, soon knew enough about the secret provisions to represent them as a grievance.

'Today,' wrote M. Paléologue in his Journal, on Friday, 8 April 1904, 'Paul Cambon, our Ambassador in London, and Lord Lansdowne, Secretary of State for Foreign Affairs, signed the Anglo-French agreement . . . This great diplomatic achievement embraces innumerable problems and solves them in the most equitable spirit. Every subject of difference and dispute between the two countries has been dealt with . . . We are to give up Egypt to England in return for which she gives up Morocco to us. The agreement which has just been concluded does not merely liquidate the past; it opens a new era in Anglo-French relations.'

In 1915, after reading a book on the *Origins of the War* by Holland Rose, Balfour wrote Lansdowne a letter saying he was 'much surprised to see that he quite confidently attributes the policy of the *entente* to Edward VII, thus embodying in a serious historical work a foolish piece of gossip which prevailed at the time of King Edward's death, and perhaps before. Now, so far as I remember, during the years which you and I were his Ministers, he never made an important suggestion of any sort on large questions of policy.' Indeed, Balfour thought he might 'write privately to Rose and tell him the facts.'

Arthur Balfour walked with Kings without taking Kipling's advice about keeping the common touch. As a statesman, he was aloof, fastidious and cynical. So ignorant was he of the ways of the world that he once asked Beatrice Webb to explain the term 'Trade Union.' As His Majesty took considerable care to keep his intentions secret, it is hardly surprising that Balfour failed to recognize the extent to which the King's journey was made on his own initiative. It would, however, be a mistake to suppose that the letter he wrote Lord Lansdowne proves that King Edward was little more than a decorative nonentity.

It is, of course, true that some of the King's contemporaries, the Kaiser foremost amongst them, were tempted to overestimate the part he played in foreign policy. But to recognize their mistake is not to suggest that His Majesty was a ventriloquist's dummy obediently reproducing his master's voice. In so far as he faithfully echoed the views of his Ministers, it was partly because he acknowledged his constitutional duty to accept their advice. But more often than not, he had long supported the measures they recommended. While Balfour was still studying Cicero at Eton, and Lansdowne enjoying the leisurely life of an Oxford undergraduate, the Prince of Wales was telling the French Ambassador that 'the general interests of Europe could best be served by an *entente* between England and France.'

If Balfour could not recall the King making 'an important suggestion of any sort on large questions of policy,' it was possibly because he spent too much time on metaphysics, and not enough on reading newspapers, which he claimed never to open. But, following his lead, subsequent writers have suggested that the King 'had neither the inclination, the industry nor the ability to play a decisive role in international affairs,' that his approach to problems was too impulsive and personal, that he failed to recognize the significance of social and economic forces, and that his reputation was founded on 'myth'. In his *History of England from 1870 to 1914*, Ensor argued that 'King Edward did not exercise over British Foreign Policy the influence often popularly attributed to him,' and claimed that the *entente* 'was the work of Cambon, Lansdowne and Delcassé.'

In a sense, it is idle to dispute the origins of a policy which was a natural response to German provocation. Need one enquire too closely why the householder arms himself with a poker when he hears an intruder prowling about downstairs? But, at the same time, it would be laughable to pretend that the appearance of Lord Lansdowne or Mr Balfour in the Champs Elysées would magically have transformed French opinion overnight. As Cambon remarked, 'any clerk at the Foreign Office could draw up a treaty,' but there was no one other than the King 'who could have succeeded in producing the right atmosphere for a rapprochement.'

Before accepting the Prime Minister's grudging estimate of his Sovereign's services, it is worth considering what other people thought. For example, Sir Edmund Monson, who watched the King at work, told Lord Lansdowne that the visit has been 'a success more complete than the most sanguine optimist could have foreseen.' This he attributed to the King's personal charm, his popularity in Paris as Prince of Wales, and his indefatigable readiness to undertake an 'overcharged programme.'

Within a week of the event, the Belgian Minister in Paris reported back to Brussels that the 'impression produced in France by King Edward VII's visit could not be better . . . Seldom has such a complete change of attitude been seen as that which has taken place in this country during the last fortnight towards England and her Sovereign.'

Hardinge, who was presumably in a better position to judge the King's achievement than those who were left at home, wrote an account of His Majesty's visit to Paris while it was still fresh in his mind. His account concludes with this verdict: 'It only remains for the writer of this record to state his conviction that the success of the King's journey and the happy results which may confidently be anticipated therefrom, are entirely due to His Majesty's own personality, to his courteous tact, to his frank and genial manner, and to his unrivalled knowledge of men and of the world.' At the end of his long life, Lord Hardinge of Penshurst, looking back on the events of 1903, had no cause to revise his opinion. 'It is almost impossible,' he wrote in his Memoirs, 'to measure the success and importance from a political point of view of the King's visit to Paris . . . Honour to whom honour is due, and the honour of the improvement in Anglo-French relations was due entirely to the initiative and political flair of King Edward.' Had he listened to his Ministers 'he would never have gone to Paris.'

Neither Salisbury, nor Lansdowne, nor Grey travelled much in Europe, so it was left to the King to create goodwill abroad. After his death, one speaker in the House of Commons claimed that 'His Majesty did what no minister, no cabinet, no ambassadors, neither treaty, nor protocols, nor understandings, no debates, no banquets, and no speeches were able to perform. He by his personality, and by his personality alone, brought home to the minds of millions on the continent the friendly feeling of the country.' This eloquent tribute to the King's achievement, came from the Leader of the Opposition: Arthur James Balfour.

The war which broke out between Russia and Japan in February 1904, involving the Tsar in defeat and revolution, meant, for a time at least, that Germany could attack France without having to fight on two fronts, Russia being too heavily committed in the East to intervene in the West. By the time of the *entente*, Count Schlieffen, the German Chief of Staff, had perfected his plan for massing the German Armies in the West to attack France through Belgium, and argued 'in favour of the earliest possible thorough clearing up with France at arms.'

The German Government was naturally tempted to take Schlieffen's advice, but the Kaiser, for all his bluster, was in the last resort timid, and would not risk the war which was the logical continuation of his policy. He was, moreover, bewildered by the conflicting counsel he received from his Admirals and Generals. The soldiers were always eager to mobilize and fight, but the sailors demanded more time to enlarge the Kiel Canal and to construct battleships. Schlieffen was ready for war in 1904, but Tirpitz needed a further ten years to complete his naval programme.

Until the *entente* was accomplished, Holstein regarded its possibility as too remote to take seriously. He thought that whenever he chose, he could make his own terms with England. No sooner was he proved wrong, than he made the mistake of assuming that

Britain would never risk the bones of a single Grenadier to save the Third Republic. 'We can take it for granted,' he claimed, 'that British diplomatic support' as envisaged in Article Nine of the Anglo-French Convention on Morocco, 'will remain platonic.'

Nobody could question Germany's right to intervene over Morocco. Not only was she one of the signatories of the Madrid Convention of 1880 by which the powers of Europe endeavoured to settle its future, but she had a growing commercial stake in the country. In the autumn of 1904 the British Minister in Tangier, Sir Arthur Nicolson, was told by his German colleague 'that his Government did not consider that the Anglo-French Agreement had any official existence: it had not been officially communicated to the German Government, and had not consequently been officially accepted by them. France and Great Britain were of course at liberty to settle their own differences, but these were matters between those two countries alone, and in no wise affected the rights and interests of third parties.'

Early the following year, Germany embarked upon one of the most ill-judged adventures in its history. For some months, the Sultan of Morocco, Abdul Aziz, had shown an increasing resentment of France upon whose military, administrative and economic assistance he largely depended. So, in March 1905, Bülow and Holstein proposed that His Imperial Majesty, who was just setting out on a spring cruise in the Mediterranean, should land at Tangier and promise the Sultan German support in maintaining his sovereignty. On 31 March, after a fearfully rough passage from Lisbon, the Kaiser anchored off Tangier and went ashore. He did not much enjoy his ride to the legation on a white Barbary stallion of uncertain temper, through streets lined with what he took to be Spanish anarchists, French and Italian riff-raff, and wild-eyed natives. It made him long for those meticulous processions he so much enjoyed in Berlin. Fastidious diplomats, disposed to distrust even judicious public utterances, regarded the Kaiser's speech to a dejected body of some twenty 'brave pioneers of German commerce' as outrageously flamboyant. But Bülow was delighted by the dramatic manner in which the Emperor William had flung down the gauntlet.

The King described William's conduct as a 'gratuitous insult' to Britain and France. 'The clumsy theatrical part of it would make one laugh were the matter not a serious one.' The trouble was that nobody told his nephew how ridiculous he made himself. 'I have tried to get on with him and shall nominally do my best to the end –

but trust him – never. He is *utterly* false, and the bitterest foe that England possesses!'

Delcassé was 'positively cheerful' when he heard about 'William's trumpet-blast at Tangier,' because he believed that 'nothing could have a more salutary effect on the English.' Had the crisis started at Metz or Strasbourg not a dog would have stirred. 'But for a German ship to come and fly the Hohenzollern standard off the Moroccan coast, right opposite Gibraltar – do you think the English can stand that?'

On 19 April the French Chamber debated the Moroccan crisis and Delcassé was savagely attacked particularly by Socialist deputies. The Left in politics, in reckless innocence of the harsher realities of history, often suppose that they have only to roll over on their backs like puppies, dangling their paws engagingly in the air, to resist attack. Such, however, was the strength of opposition to Delcassé that he sent in his resignation. It was only with great difficulty that M. Rouvier, the Prime Minister, finally persuaded him to withdraw it.

When rumours reached the King of what was happening, he sent Delcassé a telegram urging him 'very strongly' to retain his portfolio, and saying he 'personally would greatly regret' his departure, in view of their 'confident and steadfast relations,' as well as the 'great authority' he possessed 'for the settlement of outstanding questions.' Lansdowne described His Majesty's decision to send this message as a 'very unusual step.' It was, in fact, unprecedented for an English King to communicate with a Minister of a foreign government, without consulting his own advisers or the appropriate Head of State. But the King's intervention was nothing to that of the Kaiser, who, six weeks later, secured the Foreign Minister's dismissal by threatening war.

On his way back to England from his Mediterranean cruise, King Edward spent from 29 April to 5 May in Paris. Throughout that week he did everything in his power to demonstrate his support for the *entente* and its principal architect. On 30 April he dined with President Loubet at the Elysée, and was loud in his praise of the Foreign Minister's policy. Three days later, after luncheon with his old friend the Marquis de Breteuil, the King took Delcassé aside and talked to him for an hour, encouraging him to stick to his guns, but at the same time to do what he could to improve relations with Germany. 'My Government,' he promised, 'will give you every assistance in its power.' It was during the King's visit to Paris that

Delcassé became convinced that if France was attacked by Germany, Britain would come to her aid. Eckardstein, who happened to be in Paris at the time, reported back to Bülow that the King had left no doubt that France could depend on England's support and had conspicuously reaffirmed the solidarity of the *entente*.

Early in June 1905, Prince Radolin told Rouvier that so long as M. Delcassé remained in office there was no possibility of an improvement in Franco-German relations. He furthermore suggested that unless France accepted a Moroccan conference she risked attack. Rouvier was so terrified by these threats that he warned President Loubet that war might break out at any moment. The Cabinet, he said, would have to decide between his policy of conciliation and Delcassé's belief that Bülow was only bluffing. When the Foreign Minister discovered that not one of his colleagues supported his policy of rejecting German demands, he was obliged to resign once more.

Delcassé's fall from power was welcomed in Germany with universal rejoicing and Bülow was made a Count. But as France soon learned, the reward of appeasement is not peace. They had paid the danegeld, but they did not get rid of the Dane. The Germans interpreted Rouvier's abject surrender as proof of weakness, and so increased their demands. Prince Radolin next insisted that the Prime Minister must accept a Moroccan Conference. This also he felt bound to do, and arrangements were made for the Great Powers to meet at Algeciras in January.

The King's quarrels with the Kaiser in 1905 reflected the political dissensions which divided their countries. Even before the Tangier Incident, the King went out of his way to advertise his support of France. In March, he cancelled the Prince of Wales's visit to the Crown Prince's wedding: ostensibly, because the King of Spain would be in England at the time; in reality, because of growing international strain. That summer, the King refused to visit his nephew at Homburg, although he was only a few miles away 'combating obesity' at Marienbad.

The Kaiser took his revenge by refusing to permit his son to visit Windsor, offering the same excuse as the King had employed on behalf of the Prince of Wales: a visit from King Alfonso. 'I was indeed sorry,' King Edward wrote to the Crown Prince, 'and at the same time surprised to learn from your letter that you and Cecile are unable to pay us a visit at Windsor which we had all so looked forward to. As you write that "unhappily your Papa objects to your coming to England this year," there is nothing more to be said on the subject. Another year it will probably be the same story as I have reason to believe that your father does not like your coming to England.'

William was furious when he was shown this letter, and addressed Lascelles at 'great length' on the subject, protesting that 'the remarks about himself amounted almost to a personal insult. It seemed as if the King was seeking a quarrel with him, and he cited other instances which he considered gave him grounds for complaint.' The Kaiser authorized Lascelles to state he regretted the unsatisfactory nature of his relations with the King, 'but he could not admit the fault was his.'

On 13 September, Sir Frank sent the King a fuller account of his nephew's grievances. The invitation to the Crown Prince should have been addressed to the head of the House of Hohenzollern, not to the young man himself. The Kaiser hesitated to permit his son to visit England, because when he had previously done so there had been 'unseemly romping in unlighted corridors,' and one young lady had gone so far as to take off a slipper. The King's refusal to meet the Kaiser on his return to England from Marienbad had been taken in Germany as an insult. 'The whole tone of the German Emperor's language to Lascelles,' wrote the King to Knollys, 'is one of peevish complaint against me. I consider it wholly uncalled for. The real truth is that he was jealous at my asking his son at all.'

Knollys told Lascelles that the Kaiser could 'hardly expect a formal reply to all the points which he raised.' His Majesty therefore thought 'that if the Emperor asks whether you have heard from him on the subject of what he said to you, that you should answer in general terms, saying that the King never has had, and has not at the present moment, any possible wish to quarrel with him (why indeed should he?) and on the contrary he is anxious to keep on the best of terms with him, that with respect to a meeting it would give him much pleasure to have one, if possible, next year, provided that there was a more friendly feeling between the two countries than now unhappily exists.'

When the Liberals came into office in December 1905, Campbell-Bannerman appointed Sir Edward Grey to succeed Lord Lansdowne. Most of his first weeks at the Foreign Office were spent in electioneering, but as soon as he became Foreign Secretary he made it clear that the new Government would continue the *entente*. Sir Edward's 'ignorance of foreign affairs was really astonishing, knowing as he did no foreign language, and having made hardly as much as a holiday tour in Europe.' Naturally, he was bound to be guided by the department of which he was head, and the prevailing wisdom of the Foreign Office overwhelmingly favoured friendship with France and Russia. The new generation of diplomats, men such as Hardinge, Bertie and Mallet, all of whom owed their positions to the King, shared a common distrust of Bülow and Holstein, and a common faith in the wisdom of the *entente*.

Shortly before Christmas 1905, the King of Spain, Alfonso XIII, warned the French Military Attaché in Madrid that Germany planned to attack France in the near future. Only the month before, the Kaiser had urged him to concentrate two hundred thousand men on the Pyrenees, 'in view of a Franco-German war.' When Rouvier heard of these suspicions, he immediately instructed Cambon to pass on the warning to the King, 'who has given us such strong proof of his friendship.' Rouvier believed that 'a talk with Edward VII' was 'both necessary and urgent,' but, in view of the elections, 'it would be premature to mention the matter to the British Government.' The French Prime Minister evidently did not subscribe to Mr Balfour's estimate of His Majesty's importance.

On 20 December, Cambon read King Edward some crucial passages from the Madrid report. Having heard all he had to say the King asked: 'Have you mentioned this to Sir Edward Grey?' The Ambassador replied that the 'communication was not intended for the British Government. Royal confidences are not to be noised abroad and we cannot give the King of Spain away.' While not denying the truth of that assertion, the King remained anxious to 'find some means of letting Grey know, and Campbell-Bannerman too.'

As the audience drew to a close, Cambon broached the subject of a military alliance. 'Your Majesty may remember,' he said, 'that, at the beginning of last June, this serious question was the subject of secret discussions between Lord Lansdowne and myself. They were interrupted by M. Delcassé's fall: I don't know whether the new Cabinet would be disposed to resume them, and I am wondering whether I should ask my government for appropriate instructions.' 'By all means do so,' said the King, 'it would be very useful.' When Rouvier received Cambon's account of his audience, he at once sent him the following telegram: 'I am of the opinion that you should go ahead with the conversations, as King Edward advised you.'

In accordance with his instructions, the French Ambassador saw Sir Edward Grey at the Foreign Office on 10 January 1906, with a view to discovering what support France might expect from a Liberal Government at the Algeciras Conference, due to begin the following week, and what assistance, if any, would be forthcoming should negotiations break down and his country be invaded. He began by 'citing the King's strong opinions' for seeking the interview, and went on to say that when he was last in Paris M. Rouvier had spoken to him 'on the importance of arriving at an understanding as to the course which would be taken by France and Great Britain' in the event of the discussions at Algeciras 'terminating in a rupture between France and Germany.' Probably the Kaiser did not actually want a war, but the policies he pursued might make one unavoidable. Grey replied that he could make no promises without consulting his colleagues. Nevertheless, it was his 'personal opinion that if France were to be attacked by Germany in consequence of a question arising out of the agreement which our predecessors had recently concluded with the French Government, public opinion in England would be strongly moved in favour of France.'

Before the Algeciras Conference opened on 16 January 1906, the King personally promised Cambon that Britain would do her utmost to help France. 'Tell us what you wish on each point, and we will support you without restriction or reserve.' Grey said much the same in a private letter to Nicolson, whom Lansdowne had chosen to represent Britain at Algeciras. 'The Morocco Conference,' he wrote, 'is going to be difficult if not critical. As far as I can discover the Germans will refuse altogether to concede to France the special position in Morocco which we have promised to help her to obtain. If she can succeed in getting this with our help it will be a great success for the Anglo-French *entente*. If she fails the prestige of the *entente* will suffer and its vitality will be diminished. Our main object therefore must be to help France to carry her point at the Conference.'

As soon as the Conference began, the Germans discovered how isolated they had become. Even their partner, Italy, would not support them. It was generally believed that Bülow and Holstein were only interested in finding a pretext for waging war with France, and nobody particularly wished to become their accomplice. When the terms of the Algeciras Agreement were signed on 6 April, Morocco's independence was reaffirmed, but the reality of French control remained unchanged. The Kaiser was deeply disappointed. In the margin of a despatch which maintained that Britain gained most at Algeciras, he wrote: 'Correct!' Sir Arthur

The Prince of Wales at an ice hockey match at Sandringham, February 1895.

Sir Francis Knollys, c. 1900.

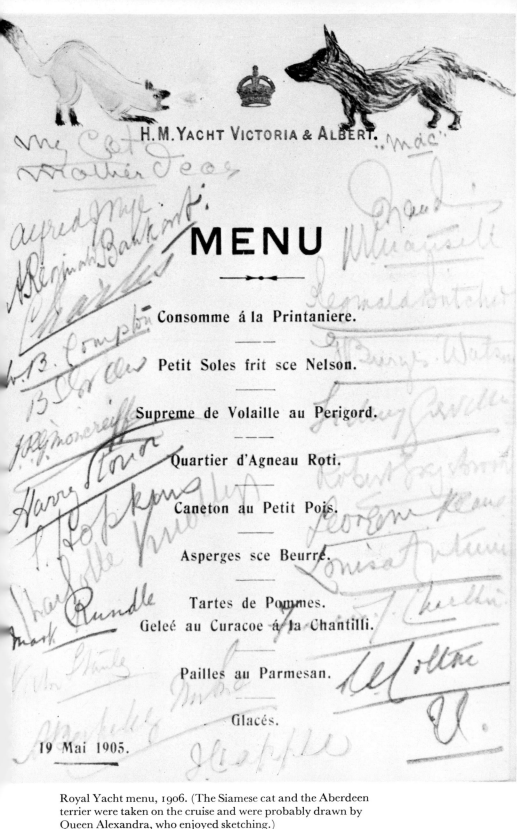

MENU

H. M. YACHT VICTORIA & ALBERT.

Consomme á la Printaniere.

———

Petit Soles frit sce Nelson.

———

Supreme de Volaille au Perigord.

———

Quartier d'Agneau Roti.

———

Caneton au Petit Pois.

———

Asperges sce Beurré.

———

Tartes de Pommes.
Geleé au Curacoe á la Chantilli.

———

Pailles au Parmesan.

———

Glacés.

19 Mai 1905.

Royal Yacht menu, 1906. (The Siamese cat and the Aberdeen
terrier were taken on the cruise and were probably drawn by
Queen Alexandra, who enjoyed sketching.)

Picnic on Monkey Island, 1905, with King Edward VII (centre), Prince Edward (in sailor suit), Princess Victoria (next to him), Hon. Harry Legge (facing camera, near silver teapot), Hon. Charlotte Knollys (back view, at end of table), Marquis de Soveral (far left of picture, at end of table).

Group, Friedrichshof, 1906, including King Edward VII, Kaiser William II, Crown Prince Constantine (wearing white trousers) and Crown Princess Sophie (in striped costume) of Greece, Prince Frederick Charles of Hesse-Cassel (in background, centre, wearing light uniform with dark collar) and Margaret, Princess Frederick Charles of Hesse-Cassel (centre in group of three ladies).

King Edward VII opening the South African Exhibition, February 1907,
accompanied by Queen Alexandra, the Prince and Princess of Wales, Princess
Christian of Schleswig-Holstein, Princess Louise, Duchess of Argyll, the Duke
of Argyll.

King Edward in Algiers, 1905. Frederick Ponsonby is holding a checked cap
and Hon. Harry Stonor is standing (second left).

King Edward VII with Tsar Nicholas II at Reval, June 1908.

King Edward VII (in cape) and George, Prince of Wales
(back view) with attendant, shooting in Scotland.

Nicolson could have asked for no better tribute. Two days before the Conference concluded, Bülow dismissed Holstein, in the hope of diverting blame from himself.

The Moroccan incident was, in Winston Churchill's phrase, 'the first milestone to Armageddon.' From then onwards, Europe endured the agony of a succession of disputes, each threatening to plunge the world into war, but each somehow resolved, until Austria's ultimatum to Serbia in July 1914 precipitated a crisis which could not be settled peacefully. Unhappily, the relentless logic of the alliance system involved the major powers of Europe in every passing squabble. German pressure at Algeciras proved totally counterproductive. Far from destroying the *entente*, it obliged the Liberals to contemplate military action.

In January 1906, the King wrote the Kaiser a conciliatory letter congratulating him on his birthday. After the strains of the previous years, he was anxious to be on better terms with his nephew. Having expressed his desire that the Algeciras Conference would guarantee peace and justice, he spoke of his concern 'that the feeling between our two countries may be on the best footing. We are – my dear William – such old friends and near relations that I feel sure that the affectionate feelings which have always existed may invariably continue.'

The Kaiser was delighted with the King's letter which 'breathed such an atmosphere of kindness and warm, sympathetic friendship' that it constitututed 'the most cherished gift among my presents.' It had been, he claimed, his 'life's endeavour and ideal' to work in 'mutual good understanding' with England for the peace and wellbeing of the world.

In August 1906, King Edward met the Kaiser at Friedrichshof, but not before Dona had mischievously written to Bülow to say that she thought that the King 'ought to visit the Emperor in one of his own castles, if not in his own capital . . . Why can't the fat old gentleman manage to get as far as Wilhelmshöhe?' The meeting was cordial, the King avoiding controversial subjects, and the Kaiser being in the 'best possible spirits.' The Emperor seemed pleased to see his uncle again, and told Bülow that everything passed off to his complete satisfaction, while the King was relieved that no discordant note had been struck and that his nephew had done his best to be agreeable.

The two Sovereigns met twice in 1907: once at Wilhelmshöhe, a palace near Cassel, where the King stayed the night of 14 August on his way to Marienbad, and once in November when William paid a state visit to England. On arriving at the railway station at Cassel, His Majesty was met by the German Emperor, the Imperial Chancellor and an impressive array of Staff Officers. Bands played, there were incessant royal salutes and the whole thing was wonderfully organized down to the last geranium. But instead of being given luncheon on arrival at the Palace there was another parade, and the famished King was obliged to take the salute while half the German Army marched past.

During his visit, the King avoided discussing politics with William but honoured the Chancellor with a long conversation. 'The idea on which he laid particular emphasis,' said Bülow, 'was that, in proportion as the Press on both sides of the Channel became more foolish, and the two peoples, or at least a minority in either, more unreasonable, the more it behoved the governments to keep a clear head. He assured me once again . . . that now, as always, his most fervent wish was Anglo-German "peace and goodwill".'

The state visit of the Emperor and Empress was somewhat overdue, as the King had been almost seven years on the throne before inviting them. At the last moment, within ten days of his expected arrival, the Kaiser sent a telegram saying that he was suffering 'from bronchitis and acute cough,' the after-effects 'of a very virulent attack of influenza,' which left him 'quite unable to meet the strain of the programme so kindly prepared for me.' The King at once replied: 'Your telegram has greatly upset me as your not coming to England would be a terrible disappointment to us all – my family and the British nation. Beg of you to consider your decision and trust you may be much better next week. We will lessen the programme as much as you like.'

After receiving this telegram, and a letter from Bülow emphasizing the damage he might do to Anglo-German relations, particularly as the British Ambassador had seen him in the very rudest of health galloping down the Central Avenue of Berlin surrounded by aides-de-camp, William made a miraculous recovery and said he was ready for anything. The Chancellor attributed the Emperor's short-lived indisposition to his fear that he would be badly received in England because of the impending trial of his friend Count Eulenburg. The Count was accused on highly suspect evidence of unnatural vices. But the scandal lost none of its impact because most of the testimony was perjured. Eulenburg's real offence was not his reputed passion for a Munich boatman some quarter of a century before, but that Holstein held him responsible for his downfall in 1906.

The Kaiser and Kaiserin arrived at Portsmouth on 11 November in the *Hohenzollern*. The official part of their visit lasted a week and was spent at Windsor. It was fortunate the invalid had made so complete a recovery for the King had arranged a taxing programme of festivities. During a state banquet in the Waterloo Chamber, held on the second evening of the visit, His Majesty made a teasing reference to his nephew's recent illness. 'For a long time we had hoped to receive this visit, but recently we had feared that, owing to indisposition, it would not take place; but, fortunately, their Majesties are now both looking in such good health that I can only hope their stay in England, however short, will much benefit them.' The week was spent amidst a galaxy of royal relations. The gold plate was brought out, and the Yeomen of the Guard, and the Kaiser's 'memories of bygone days,' foremost amongst them 'the figure of my revered grandmother,' whose image, he said, was engraved on his heart. And there were countless other recollections taking him back to the earliest days of his childhood, 'spent under the roof and within the walls of this grand old Windsor Castle.'

The Kaiserin returned home once the Windsor visit was over, but the Kaiser stayed on privately with Colonel Stuart-Wortley at Highcliffe Castle, on the Hampshire coast. While he was there, he had several conversations with his host in an effort 'to remove the obstinate misconceptions' which prevailed about 'his feelings towards England.' After his return to Germany he boasted that he had mended the windows his people had broken.

Sir Frank Lascelles was due to retire in 1908, after twelve years as British Ambassador in Germany. No other diplomatic post involved so many royal rows. Sir Frank was repeatedly required to convey offensive messages between the King and the Kaiser. If he reported what was said too faithfully, he was reproached for causing ill-feeling. If he was too diplomatic, the King or the Kaiser accused him of not representing their grievances with sufficient force. King Edward, in particular, came increasingly to feel that he did not stand up to his nephew. 'Lascelles is out of favour now with the King,' noted Wilfrid Blunt in his diary in June 1908, 'as being too German in his sentiments.'

Such were the problems of finding a successor to Lascelles acceptable to the Emperor, that the King suggested a meeting. 'I propose making my annual cure at Marienbad next month,' he wrote on 13 July. 'I should be very glad if it suited you to give me a rendezvous on 11 August at Friedrichshof. I could arrive in the morning and stay till after dinner.'

Sir Edward Grey, hoping that the King would try to persuade the Kaiser to agree to a joint reduction in naval expenditure, presented His Majesty with two lengthy documents explaining that while the British Government would not dream 'of questioning the right of Germany to build as large a navy as she thinks necessary for her own purposes,' it had, nevertheless, to be faced that her rate of naval construction would necessitate 'a new British programme to be begun next year.' Hardinge believed that the fact that the British Government 'for the first time in history' had seen fit to brief a King 'to act as their spokesman,' was 'indisputable proof' of the confidence they felt in his wisdom and tact.

In the end, after a three-hour conversation with William, the King left the problems of disarmament to Hardinge. The Kaiser was so furious with the latter for venturing to interfere with Germany's naval programme, that the King's instinct to avoid the issue was clearly justified. The series of explosions which ensued, when Sir Charles sailed into the minefield, showed how dangerous it was to navigate in such waters. After their meeting, the Kaiser told the Tsar that 'Uncle Bertie was all sunshine and in very good humour. He intends visiting Berlin officially with Aunt Alix next year.'

It was agreed that Sir Edward Goschen, the younger brother of the Chancellor whom Randolph forgot, should succeed Lascelles. Goschen would cheerfully have declined the invitation to lie on a bed of nails had King Edward not begged him to accept. Steed, who met him soon after his appointment was announced, found him almost in tears. 'I shall have to go,' he said, 'I cannot refuse the King. But I am certain my mission to Berlin will end in failure, for there will be no means of avoiding catastrophe.'

A few weeks after the Friedrichshof meeting, the King, in common with most of Europe, was astonished to read an account of an interview with the Kaiser which appeared in the *Daily Telegraph* on 28 October 1908. It was one of the greatest scoops in the history of journalism. Before the First World War, when diplomacy was conducted in secret, and Sovereigns were not obliged to expose their private lives to public scrutiny, it was unprecedented for a newspaper to publish an interview with one so august as his Imperial Majesty. So when the *Daily Telegraph* published an article headed: 'The German Emperor and England – Personal Interview – Frank Statement of World Policy – Proofs of Friendship' it created tremendous excitement. The Tsar, for example, could talk of little else when he met the British Ambassador some days later, and a copy of the article, heavily scored with a blue pencil, lay open on a table.

There are sometimes moments, claimed the anonymous correspondent, 'when a calculated indiscretion proves of the highest public service, and it is for that reason that I have decided to make known the substance of a recent conversation which it was my privilege to have with His Majesty the German Emperor. I do so in the hope that it may help to remove the obstinate misconception of the character of the Kaiser's feelings towards England.'

Part of the interest shown in the article when it was first published lay in identifying its author. It was, in fact, none other than Colonel Stuart-Wortley, who helped the King arrange his visit to Paris in 1903, and who only the year before had invited the Kaiser to Highcliffe. He was a friend of Sir Harry Lawson, whose father, Lord Burnham, had started the *Daily Telegraph*, virtually the only newspaper in the country to show sympathy for Germany. Not only did the Kaiser correct proofs of the article in his own hand, but he asked Bülow to approve its publication: an unusual precaution in one so impetuous. The Chancellor returned the manuscript with a few trivial amendments. But the moment the storm broke, the 'Eel', as he was nicknamed, tried to wriggle out of his part in the proceedings by claiming that he had been too busy to read the article himself.

'You English are mad, mad as March hares,' the *Telegraph* quoted the Kaiser as saying. 'What has come over you that you are so completely given over to suspicions quite unworthy of a great nation? What more can I do than I have done? Have I ever been false to my word? Falsehood and prevarication are alien to my nature.' Considering that he was one of the most compulsive liars of his age, such protestations were empty. Few men, he said, had been worse misjudged than he had. Throughout his reign, he had constantly shown the friendliest feelings for England. Not only had he refused the requests of Russia and France to join them in saving the Boers, but he had handed their confidential notes to the Queen who had deposited them in the archives at Windsor. During Britain's darkest hour in her war in South Africa, he had sent his grandmother a plan of campaign, which was precisely that adopted by Lord Roberts. That, too, might be found in the Royal Archives. As for the German Navy, so far from constituting the remotest threat to England, it was purely designed to protect his growing commerce.

Three days after the interview was printed, Sir Frank Lascelles wrote to Knollys to say that its author did 'not seem sufficiently acquainted with the Emperor to make allowances for the exaggeration in which His Majesty habitually indulges.' The King, who was shown the letter, underlined these words in pencil, and added an exclamation mark at the end. It seems that despite Colonel Stuart-Wortley's admirable intentions, very few Englishmen revised their opinion of the Kaiser, and most people thought his protestations ridiculous.

It was, however, in Germany that the article made most impact. The great majority of the Emperor's subjects sympathized with the Boers, and were incensed to learn that he had drawn up a 'plan of campaign' to help the British Army. Besides, why needlessly alienate France and Russia by telling them how he betrayed their confidences? Both in the Reichstag and the Press the question was raised whether the Kaiser was fit to rule. William was helpless, shattered and humbled. He beseeched Bülow to save him and talked of abdicating.

The Chancellor's conduct throughout the crisis showed that his one anxiety was to save himself. When this became clear to the Kaiser by the summer of 1909, he summoned up his courage and dismissed him. Bülow devoted the last twenty years of his life to writing his Memoirs. Through four massive volumes and many thousand pages, his recollections smoulder with hatred, rage and malice. Having ruthlessly betrayed those with whom, and for whom, he worked, he now attributed his downfall to the treachery of colleagues. To read his Memoirs is to glimpse the disease which destroyed the Second Reich.

Having given such grave offence by stressing his friendship for England, the Kaiser decided to put matters right by giving a further interview. In a three-hour audience, he harangued Dr William Hale, an American clergyman visiting Berlin, on the way he was misunderstood. During the course of a rambling disquisition, he apparently said that his Army and Navy were ready for war with England and the sooner it came the better. He spoke with scathing contempt of King Edward, and bitterly reproached Britain's misdeeds in Egypt, India and South Africa. He ended by claiming that the future of civilization depended upon the United States and Germany.

The Wilhelmstrasse denounced Dr Hale's account of his discussion with the Emperor as a 'baseless invention,' and did what it could to smother its publication. Meanwhile, Count Metternich informed the King that the Kaiser emphatically denied the truth of Dr Hale's assertion. Publicly, the King felt bound to accept what his nephew said, but privately he remained convinced that the words attributed to him were perfectly correct. 'I know the German Emperor hates me,' he told Knollys, 'and never loses an opportunity of saying so (behind my back), whilst I have always been kind and nice to him.'

The strength of pacifist sentiment in the Government caused the King as much anxiety as the vagaries of the Kaiser. At least with his knowledge and approval, if not on his initiative, Lord Esher, on 8 November 1908, invited Colonel Huguet, the French Military Attaché in London, to visit him secretly at Orchard Lea, his house near Windsor. In an exceedingly confidential briefing, he told the Colonel that the Cabinet was divided into two groups. One, headed by Asquith, Grey and Haldane favoured giving France all possible assistance in the event of war with Germany. But the other, which looked to Lloyd George and Winston Churchill, inclined to believe that Britain should stand aside. King Edward, said Esher, strongly opposed 'progressive and pacifist elements,' but the final decision belonged to the Government.

The Chancellor of the Exchequer, Lloyd George, had never so much as set foot in William's domains before he visited Germany in 1908 to study its system of National Insurance. But soon he was telling his fellow countrymen to trust the Kaiser, cut back expenditure on battleships, and divert the money saved to social reforms. World-wide publicity was given to his assertion that 'the only way to relieve the tension of Europe' was by Anglo-German understanding. In short, all was for the best in the best of all possible worlds. As he read Lloyd George's speeches, the King could not but wonder whether the Chancellor should not have a word with Hardinge on the Kaiser's willingness to reduce the size of his fleet, or, better still, stick to income tax and death duties, leaving Foreign Affairs to Sir Edward Grey.

Between 1908 and 1911, Lloyd George looked to Churchill for support. In several speeches, as compelling as they were irresponsible, Winston attacked those who warned of a German threat. On 17 August 1908, the very day on which his engagement was announced, he told a miners' rally at Swansea: 'I have been astonished and grieved to read much of the wild language which has been used lately by people who ought to know better about our relations with Germany. I think it is greatly to be deprecated that persons should try to spread the belief in this country that war between Great Britain and Germany is inevitable ... There is no collision of primary interests – big, important interests – between Great Britain and Germany in any quarter of the globe. Why, they are among our very best customers . . . Although there may be snapping and snarling in the newspapers and in the London Clubs, these two great peoples have nothing to fight about, have no prize to fight for, and have no place to fight in.'

In further speeches, this incongruous keeper of the Liberal conscience denounced 'the braggart call for sensational expenditure on armaments,' which he traced to 'a false lying panic started in the party interests of the Conservatives.' He poured ridicule on what he christened the 'Dreadnought fear-all school,' promising that, like his father before him, he would never permit the 'agitations of ignorant, interested and excited hotheads' to persuade him to support public expenditure upon armaments in support of an 'aggressive and Jingo policy.'

The ruling class in Edwardian England were slow to forgive Churchill. Lloyd George's politics were such as they expected from a small-time solicitor from Criccieth. But Winston's radicalism betrayed his friends and family. It was all very fine for him to affect the common touch, but when he wearied of the rough-and-tumble of the hustings, or found the stench of Oldham too obnoxious, he could always retire to the calm of Blenheim to contemplate a fresh assault on Dukes, or meet Lord Curzon at dinner.

It would seem that the King felt something of this prejudice, for in 1907 he wrote to the Prince of Wales: 'As for Mr Churchill he is *almost more* of a cad in office than he was in opposition.' On the other hand, he later remarked to Lord Esher that Winston was even younger in spirit than in years, and he thought it possible he might change a great deal. Hardinge told Knollys in 1909 that Grey was convinced 'that Winston and Lloyd George would ruin the party,' and for good measure he added his own opinion, which was that Churchill's speeches were 'ungentlemanlike' and his presence in the Government 'a disgrace.'

In August 1908, the King wrote to the Foreign Secretary asking why the Prime Minister permitted Lloyd George and Winston Churchill to make irresponsible speeches on Foreign Affairs, and advised him to reprove them for trespassing on his territory. He believed that, as well as an increasing threat from Germany, there was also a growing danger that Liberals like Lloyd George would lull Englishmen into a false sense of security. It was with astonishment and concern that he watched the Chancellor's spectacular excursions into diplomacy, about which he knew little or nothing.

The King's long-delayed visit to Berlin took place early in 1909. Neither the King nor the Queen wanted to go, Alix particularly resenting being 'dragged' to Germany. The Kaiser, however, told the Tsar he was anxious to improve relations with England, and that he looked forward to receiving Uncle Bertie, 'not only because I am gratified to have him and Aunt Alix over here, but also because I expect the visit to have useful results for the peace of the world.'

When the royal train steamed into the Lehrter Bahnhof on the morning of 9 February, the Emperor and Empress, Bülow, Tirpitz, Metternich and several members of the Imperial family were waiting to receive them. The ceremony had been meticulously rehearsed and the welcoming party was drawn up precisely where the King's carriage stopped. Unfortunately, His Majesty decided to alight from the Queen's compartment, some hundred yards away: so the Kaiser, the Kaiserin, the assembled Princes and Princesses, and other dignitaries present, were obliged to hurry down the platform in a most undignified manner. Alix, who looked young enough to be Dona's daughter, although she was many years older than the Empress, was not as sorry as she ought to have been that she had made her host look absurd.

During the State drive through the streets of Berlin, the coach in which she and the Kaiserin travelled suddenly came to a stop, the horses refusing to move another inch. In the end, the royal ladies were obliged to transfer to a less ornate carriage to complete the journey. Meanwhile, the King and the Kaiser waited apprehensively in the Palace Courtyard, dreading what might have happened. The terrible fate of Alexander II could not have been far from their minds. When the rest of the procession finally arrived, the Kaiser was almost beside himself with fury, having been pathetically eager to show his uncle how well they did such things in Germany. But as Napoleon remarked: *'du sublime au ridicule il n'y a qu'un pas.'*

The Emperor did his best to make the visit a success. He had pictures of Copenhagen and Sandringham hung in Aunt Alix's room, and a portrait of Queen Victoria in the King's study. There was a gala dinner at the Palace, a family luncheon, a Court Ball, Supper with the Crown Prince, luncheon at the British Embassy, an evening at the Opera, a visit to the Rathaus, not to mention a number of other diversions. The King, who normally spent February on the Riviera, had a wretched cold, an incessant cough, and, as one young Englishman said, looked 'very seedy, poor old dear.'

King Edward won the hearts of the City Fathers when he visited the Town Hall by appearing delighted with all the arrangements they made, by proposing a toast to the people of Berlin in a speech delivered in faultless German, by putting the starchiest alderman at his ease, and by radiating such warmth and geniality that those who basked in its glow spoke of the sunshine of his presence: a trite enough cliché, but one to which people seemed irresistibly drawn.

Shortly after the luncheon the King gave at the British Embassy on 10 February, he was seized with a dreadful fit of coughing. He was talking to Princess Daisy of Pless, when he fell back half-conscious on the sofa, dropping his burning cigar on the carpet. As he lay there, fighting for breath, the Princess struggled to unfasten his collar and prayed that he would not die. By the time the Queen arrived, the King had recovered enough to undo the top buttons of his uniform. In less than quarter of an hour, His Majesty rejoined his guests and assured them there was no cause for concern. As if to prove the truth of what he said, he lit a fresh cigar. In fact, as he well knew, he was suffering from chronic bronchitis and his days were numbered.

The King had no intention of throwing away such goodwill as his visit might inspire by risking controversy. Count Metternich warned his colleagues in Berlin that political discussions would be 'highly inappropriate.' It was recognized that the King had always been reluctant to raise important issues with his nephew, so it was understood that the occasion was purely social. Then, quite unexpectedly, and at the last possible moment, the King suddenly tackled the most sensitive issue of all: the size of the German Navy. Conceivably he sensed that this was his last opportunity to prevail upon the Kaiser to settle so vexed a dispute. The only known account of their conversation, written for Bülow by the Emperor, suggests that the King was exceptionally conciliatory. Naturally, he would not have wished to embark on a battle royal just before taking his leave, but it is hardly credible that he was quite so accommodating as the Kaiser would have us believe.

The two Sovereigns embraced, the King climbed into his carriage, the whistle blew, and as the train drew out of the station, he saw his 'Imperial Nephew' for the last time, standing on the platform, every inch a Hohenzollern. Their meeting had not been particularly fruitful. Ponsonby believed that the Kaiser had done his best to make it agreeable, but got the impression that the majority of Germans hated the English almost as much as the Queen hated them. So it would seem that the magnificent hospitality lavished on the visitors was no more than a splendid but empty charade.

Until the Bosnian crisis of 1908, the King's relations with the Emperor Francis Joseph could hardly have been more harmonious. The Austrian Emperor was the doyen of Sovereigns, having come to the throne in 1848, the Year of Revolutions. In his youth, the Prince of Wales frequently visited the Habsburg dominions and saw a good deal of the Crown Prince Rudolph. He had first met Francis Joseph in 1862 when he stayed at Vienna with Colonel Bruce on his way to Egypt.

When King Edward suggested he might pay a state visit to Vienna in August 1903, the Emperor was delighted. Not since the days when Richard Coeur de Lion was thrown into prison at Durrenstein, on his way home from Jerusalem, had the Austrians been given an opportunity to welcome a King of England. There were the customary exchanges of uniforms, courtesies, speeches, toasts, visits to the Opera, banquets and balls. Nothing could have passed off better according to the British Ambassador in Vienna.

In 1904 they met again at Marienbad, where the King was taking the cure. They dined together in the restaurant of the Weimar Hotel, His Majesty having arranged for a consignment of grouse to be sent out from Balmoral. The following August they met at Bad Ischl, a delightful spa high up in the mountains, surrounded by forests abounding in game. After a pleasant luncheon, the King and the Emperor took an afternoon drive, during which they discussed the Kaiser, Morocco, and the Sultan's treatment of Christians in Macedonia. On returning to Marienbad, the King told Cassel in a letter: 'I stayed a few hours at Ischl on my way here to pay the E a visit and found H.M. in excellent health and we had some very interesting conversations. Would to God that some other sovereigns were as sensible as he is!'

Regardless of rumours to the contrary, the King's first three meetings with Francis Joseph possessed no political significance, other than that attached to any display of goodwill. But, when the two Sovereigns met once more in August 1907, King Edward requested that Baron von Aehrenthal, Austria's Foreign Minister, should be invited. The King and Hardinge arrived at Bad Ischl having just met the Kaiser at Wilhelmshöhe. Instead of fifty thousand troops lining the streets, they were welcomed by hundreds of children who showered them with alpine flowers. Their drive through the town was a carnival not a parade, and almost the only people in uniform were the Fire Brigade.

During his visit, the King had political discussions with both the Emperor and Baron von Aehrenthal. Their tone was wholly conciliatory, and he repeatedly stressed the traditional friendship and common interests which bound their countries together. Official communiqués did not exaggerate when they spoke of complete accord.

One of the Emperor's aides-de-camp, Baron Margutti, later alleged that King Edward tried to detach his master from Germany. A major penalty of secret diplomacy was that it enabled mischievous persons to put their own construction on what such meetings signified. When a picture appeared in a newspaper of King Edward in earnest conversation with Campbell-Bannerman at Marienbad, an enterprising sub-editor printed the words 'Is it Peace or War?' beneath it. Curiously enough, the Prime Minister happened to recall what the King was actually saying at the time. He was asking Sir Henry whether he thought halibut tasted better boiled or baked.

The King and the Emperor met for the last time in August 1908. There were more festivities than usual as Francis Joseph was celebrating the diamond jubilee of his reign. During his brief stay at Bad Ischl King Edward persuaded the Emperor to take his first ride in a horseless carriage. The vehicle chosen was a Züst, a German–Belgian venture. King Edward requested the Emperor to climb aboard first. 'No, no,' he said, 'you go ahead, you know more about it.' Although it was mid-August, the old man was given a blanket to keep off the chill, and some cotton wool to put in his ears to drown the roar of the engine. Evidently they expected to hear more than the ticking of the clock. His drive lasted for eighty minutes and on one stretch of road they briefly touched thirty miles an hour.

As Hardinge's efforts at Friedrichshof to persuade the Kaiser to cut down his navy had only succeeded in provoking an outburst of indignation, it occurred to the King that a more subtle way to prevail upon his nephew would be to persuade Francis Joseph to have a word with him. The Emperor, however, showed no anxiety to grapple with his ally. His reluctance to intercede was natural enough. For thirty years his foreign policy had been based on the treaty he signed with Bismarck in 1879, and he saw no reason to risk his life's work merely to help Asquith build fewer battleships. As the King himself had ducked the issue twenty-four hours before, he could hardly blame the Emperor for doing the same. The King left

Ischl well satisfied with the cordial way in which he had been received. 'Everything went off capitally,' Hardinge told Knollys. 'The old Emperor is the dearest and most courteous old gentleman that lives.'

When King Edward returned to Marienbad, Wickham Steed, *The Times* correspondent at Vienna, warned him that Austria was contemplating annexing Bosnia and Herzegovina. 'I cannot believe that,' said the King. 'It would upset the whole of Europe. What proof have you? The Emperor Francis Joseph gave me no hint of anything of the sort. No, I cannot believe that.' Steed assured the King that his suspicions were founded on what in the past had proved highly reliable sources. But His Majesty remained sceptical. 'I still think you are wrong,' he insisted. 'Surely the Emperor would have said something to me?'

The final decision to annex the two provinces was taken on 18 August, the Emperor's seventy-eighth birthday, and publicly announced on 6 October. Count Mensdorff, the Austrian Ambassador in London, was instructed to hand the King a letter from the Emperor the day before the news was to be published. At least His Majesty was to be spared learning about it from *The Times*. The King was deeply offended by the way in which Francis Joseph had kept him in the dark. Mensdorff received a distinctly chilly welcome. Lord Redesdale, who was at Balmoral at the time, said that His Majesty was terribly upset, indeed he had 'never seen him so moved. He had paid the Emperor of Austria a visit at Ischl less than two months before. The meeting had been friendly and affectionate . . . The two sovereigns and their two statesmen had discussed the Eastern question – especially the Balkan difficulties – with the utmost apparent intimacy, and the King left Ischl in the full assurance that there was no cloud on the horizon. Now, without a word of warning, all was changed.'

The Bosnian crisis convinced the King of the danger of world war as it seemed to suggest that Francis Joseph was becoming as aggressive as the Kaiser. In April 1909, he asked the Prime Minister 'whether in framing the Budget the Cabinet took into consideration the possible (but the King hoped improbable) event of a European war. The income tax, which always has been regarded as a war tax, now stands so high for unearned incomes over a certain amount that any increase would have a most disastrous effect.' Like most of his subjects he willed the end but resented the means. The intolerable burden of tax which so distressed His Majesty was levied at one shilling and seven pence in the pound on incomes of eighteen thousand per annum.

From 1903 until 1909, the King spent part of his summer at Marienbad, following in the footsteps of Goethe, Chopin and Wagner. Previously, he had taken the waters at Homburg which was convenient for Friedrichshof, but after Vicky's death he deserted the German spa, whose dictatorial regulations he had begun to find irksome. Moreover, as Marienbad was in the Austrian Empire it was not exposed to sudden visits from the Kaiser. Campbell-Bannerman, who began visiting the Spa soon after the Franco-Prussian War, when it was still hardly known, complained to Herbert Gladstone in 1899: 'I do not know how it comes to pass, but in this small society of English people, quite half of the ladies either have already been, or are qualifying themselves for being, divorced: and a considerable number of the men are helping.' Such deplorable laxity did not deter the King. Indeed, some people said it accounted for his patronage.

King Edward first visited Marienbad in 1897, and, in so doing, turned it into a bustling royal resort, much to the dismay of those who for many years had looked on it as a sanctuary. Campbell-Bannerman was quick to recognize the danger. 'We have seen a new realization,' he wrote in 1899, 'of the saying that "wheresoever the eagle is there will the carcasses be gathered together." Whether on account of the Prince's presence or not, the English and American society here has contained an extraordinary number of tainted ladies – including five divorcees and about ten others of various degrees of doubtfulness. The decent people were almost in a minority and we thought of wearing our marriage certificates as a sort of order outside our coats.'

The King did not subject himself to a severe regime while taking his cure. Although he regularly drank the water, whose virtue was said to derive from Sulphate of Soda, he was not so rigorous when it came to restricting his diet. The undiminished appetite with which he devoured trout, grouse, aubergines and peaches, showed exceptional confidence in the efficacy of Marienbad's springs. And such weight as he contrived to lose was rapidly restored when he returned home and succumbed to the irresistible genius of his French chef. Ponsonby, who always accompanied His Majesty to Marienbad, said that nowhere else in the world had he seen so many fat people.

The King always stayed at the 'Weimar,' a Grand Hotel whose façade resembled a French provincial Opera House. Throughout his visit he assumed the title of Duke of Lancaster, although on the

Emperor's birthday he dressed as an Austrian Field-Marshal and once more became the King. The resort was not much patronized by the English gentry, who were mostly occupied shooting grouse during its high season. But people like Lloyd George, Haldane, Pinero, Fisher, Rosebery, and Oscar Browning, who were either not gentlemen, or did not regard 'the Twelfth' as a red-letter day, flocked to this 'Pool of Bethesda.' For Browning, whose proudest boast was that he had seen three Emperors in their baths, Marienbad was Mecca. To mingle with monarchs while losing superfluous weight was to glimpse the sublime.

When the King visited Marienbad the Hotel Weimar became a Continental Court. It was at Marienbad, for example, that the King came to recognize how much he had in common with Campbell-Bannerman. At the beginning of his reign he had regarded him as little better than a traitor, whose opposition to the Boer War was subversive and disloyal. When Sir Henry delivered a speech in the Holborn Restaurant to the National Reform Union, in which he described the scorched-earth policy in South Africa as barbaric, he was accused of insulting the British Army and of siding with its enemies. By 1905, Campbell-Bannerman's outspokenness could be seen in a more charitable light, and the King decided to get to know him better. That summer at Marienbad he saw a good deal of Sir Henry, and was delighted to discover that he spoke French like a native, endlessly read French novels, was an old friend of Princess Bonaparte, and rejoiced in Parisian life. According to Fritz, the King had expected Sir Henry to be 'prosy and heavy, but found to his surprise that he was quite light in hand with a dry sense of humour. He told several amusing stories and was very good company.'

The King had several conversations with Georges Clemenceau, Prime Minister of France from 1906 to 1909, during his last three visits to Marienbad. As Prince of Wales he had counted Clemenceau amongst his French friends. No man could be more confidently relied on to speak his mind fearlessly. He did not earn his title 'the Tiger' for nothing. When he visited England in 1884, Queen Victoria told Sir Henry Ponsonby to write to Knollys expressing the 'hope that the Prince of Wales will not meet M. Clemenceau at dinner or elsewhere while he is in London.'

Their first meeting at Marienbad took place in August 1907. As soon as the King heard that he was staying at Carlsbad, he invited him to luncheon at the Hotel Weimar. Throughout the meal,

Clemenceau furtively fed Caesar, the King's wire-haired terrier, and chaffed his owner for infringing the quarantine laws. *'Mais puisque c'est moi qui les fais,'* was His Majesty's reply.

After luncheon, the discussion turned to more serious themes: not that risking rabies was a trivial matter. Clemenceau's invitation was much appreciated in France, and was one of those courtesies which helped consolidate the *entente*. Sir Edward Grey regarded the meeting as being 'specially opportune' after the King's recent visits to the German and Austrian Emperors. 'It has given great satisfaction in France and has allayed any susceptibilities or suspicions, to which the French are too prone, that might otherwise have been aroused.'

The following August, Clemenceau was once again invited to luncheon with the King. What he and his fellow countrymen wanted to know, he asked the King without ceremony, was what Britain would do to help them if German armies crossed their frontiers? No doubt the Navy would destroy the Kaiser's fleet. But in 1870 the Prussians had hardly any ships, yet they captured Paris just the same. The British Army was not prepared for a sudden war, despite the fact that German Strategy was known to demand a lightning break-through in the west. If help was to be effective, it must be immediate, and fully equipped armies cannot be improvised at the last moment. *'Ce n'est pas à Trafalgar, qui était une bien brillante victoire navale, mais à Waterloo, qui était une bien petite bataille, que l'Angleterre à cassé le cou a Napoléon.'*

The last time the two men met was in August 1909. Clemenceau reverted once more to the theme that it was not enough for Britain to expand her fleet, and was clearly concerned that the Liberals might leave the Republic to fight alone. But even supposing a hundred thousand British troops were sent to France to help stem the tide, they would be hopelessly outnumbered. Assuming the Germans followed the Schlieffen plan, the weight of their attack would be such as to drive the British Army back to the Channel ports. His parting words to the King were: *'Surtout, Sire, soignez votre Armée.'*

The more Britain felt threatened by Germany and Austria, the clearer became the need to reach an agreement with Russia. Nothing short of a Triple *entente* would suffice to withstand the Triple Alliance. As early as 1903, the King told Delcassé, during his state visit to Paris, that he was convinced that a better understanding with the Tsar was the logical corollary of improved relations with France. When they met again in July, King Edward insisted that Russia was 'indispensable if Germany is to be kept in awe of us. I can only beg you, Monsieur le Ministre, to make your allies in St Petersburg realize that from now onwards France, England and Russia must go hand in hand. If you do that, you will have done great work for the world's freedom.'

In November 1903, Count Benckendorff, the new Russian Ambassador, was invited to dine and sleep at Windsor, and was 'much impressed by the earnestness of the King's conversation with him in favour of a friendly understanding.' A fortnight after the Anglo-French Agreement was signed, Hardinge told Sir Francis Bertie that the King was determined 'to bring off a similar arrangement with Russia.'

On 10 February 1904, the Mikado declared war on the Tsar to defend his interests in Manchuria and Korea. Anticipating diplomatic formalities, Admiral Togo launched a midnight torpedo attack on a Russian squadron at Port Arthur, sinking two battleships and a cruiser. The authorities at Pearl Harbor in 1941 had less excuse for being taken unaware when this strategy was repeated.

The Russo-Japanese war put a dangerous strain on the *entente*. In an effort to be conciliatory, King Edward told the Tsar that he would personally ensure that his Government remained strictly neutral in the war in the Far East, and Queen Alexandra wrote to explain that just because Britain had a treaty with Japan there was no question of collusion against Russia. It was almost impossible to avoid being disingenuous in endeavouring to reconcile the incompatible demands of promising Japan the support she was entitled to expect, while dispelling the fears of France and Russia. However much the King protested to the Tsar that his attitude was 'scrupulously correct,' the Kaiser's stories of Uncle Bertie's perfidy carried conviction.

Despite the setback to Anglo-Russian relations resulting from the war, the King contrived to make progress even in 1904. In the spring of that year, while visiting Denmark to celebrate Christian IX's eighty-sixth birthday, he formed an important friendship with Russia's Minister to Copenhagen, Baron Alexander Isvolsky, who two years later became the Tsar's Foreign Secretary. They first met at a luncheon at the British Embassy given on 14 April. The King told Isvolsky that he was convinced that the *entente*, signed a few days before, would benefit not only England and France but all

Europe. The success with which long-standing differences had been resolved, led him to hope that it might be possible to achieve '*une entente analogue avec la Russie.*' To reach such an agreement had always been '*l'objet de mes plus sincère désirs,*' as he had made clear to the Emperor and Count Benckendorff. His new ambassador to St Petersburg, Sir Charles Hardinge, had been instructed to establish the most cordial relations with the Russian Government and to find a solution to all outstanding differences which had hitherto kept their countries apart. The King deplored the fact that the Japanese War could not but delay the realization of his dream, but he stressed that his Government had done what it could to restrain Japan, and was still seeking ways of resolving the crisis.

In the hope of restoring his shattered fortunes in the Pacific, the Tsar, urged on by the Kaiser, despatched his Baltic Fleet to the Far East to sweep Admiral Togo from the sea. On 21 October, the ninety-ninth anniversary of Trafalgar, Admiral Rozhdestvensky, in command of a battlefleet of thirty-five warships, encountered a number of Hull trawlers fishing off the Dogger Bank. These he mistook in the dark for Japanese torpedo boats and promptly opened fire. It was the last naval victory of his career. One trawler was sunk with the loss of its captain and a deck hand, and other ships were seriously damaged. The Russian Armada, fearful of being attacked, steamed on, without even attempting to offer assistance.

This amazing blunder must partly be attributed to incompetent seamanship and wretched morale. When the squadron had weighed anchor at the start of its voyage round the world, there was such hopeless confusion that the ships were obliged to return to their moorings and start again. The officers complained, not without justice, that they were beaten before they set out. Most evenings, to drown their sorrows, they drank not wisely but too well. Indeed, Count Radolin believed that vodka played no small part in the Dogger Bank incident. 'If it were not for the loss of life,' wrote the King to his sailor son, 'one would laugh at the Russians for being such damned fools.'

When Nicholas heard the news he telegraphed the King to say that he deplored the 'loss of lives of innocent fishermen. Having had many warnings that Japanese were lurking in fishing smacks and other vessels for purpose of destroying our squadron on its way out, great precautions were ordered to be taken, especially by night, whenever any vessels or boat came in sight. Trust no complications will arise between our countries owing to this occurrence.' He also mentioned that he had heard of the 'sad incident in the North Sea' through a 'foreign source.'

It was inconceivable to the King that the Russian Admiral should not have sent a report home, so he replied: 'I have received your telegram and am surprised that only through a foreign source you heard of the untoward incident which occurred in the North Sea. Knowing your kind heart I felt sure you would deplore the loss of innocent lives. But what has caused me and my country so painful an impression is that your squadron did not stop to offer assistance to the wounded, as searchlights must have revealed to your Admiral that the ships were British fishing vessels.' The King suggested to Lansdowne that 'if the Russian admiral continues on his way without even communicating with his own Government, we really have a right to stop him.'

While King Edward endorsed the Government's policy of demanding reparations, he thought the language of the British Press too violent. In the end, what Lord Rosebery called the 'unspeakable outrage' was referred to an International Commission of Inquiry which ordered Russia to pay £65,000 compensation. But the episode naturally proved a setback for Anglo-Russian relations and caused great anxiety in France.

While The Hague Court was resolving the Dogger Bank dispute, Admiral Rozhdestvensky sailed past the Cape of Good Hope into the Indian Ocean and on to the French island of Madagascar, where he dropped anchor. For three months, he scoured the world's shipyards in search of battleships to reinforce his navy, while German merchantmen supplied the fleet with fresh stocks of coal. When the Russians finally steamed into the Strait of Tsushima, between Japan and Korea, on 27 May 1905, they were intercepted by Admiral Togo. Within forty-five minutes, Rozhdestvensky had lost eight battleships, seven cruisers and six destroyers. Russia's devastating defeat compelled the Tsar to sue for peace, which was signed on 5 September at Portsmouth, New Hampshire. Considering how decisively he had been defeated, the terms obtained were surprisingly favourable. Nevertheless, Russia in 1905 was impoverished, battered and humbled.

During the war, William renewed his efforts to detach the Tsar from France and to discourage rapprochement with England. In a series of secret letters, he told Nicky that the *Entente cordiale* was a revival of the 'Crimean Combination' against Russia. Meanwhile, he assured Lascelles that he wanted nothing more than Anglo-

German friendship. Nobody who has made a synoptic study of the Kaiser's correspondence can blame the King for thinking him equivocal.

In January 1906, Hardinge succeeded Sir Thomas Sanderson as Permanent Under-Secretary at the Foreign Office. The King was naturally delighted to have his protégé in so important a post. The Tsar told Sir Charles, on bidding him farewell, that he depended upon him to continue working for Anglo-Russian friendship when he took up his new appointment. Hardinge promised to do his 'level best', and explained that one of the reasons which had induced him 'to give up the Embassy at St Petersburg' was his belief that he could be of most use impressing his views 'on people at home.'

In October 1905, before he became Foreign Secretary, Grey insisted that if a Liberal government were elected it would not introduce 'new and unwelcome change in foreign policy.' In his opinion, Russia's estrangement from Britain had 'its roots not in the present but solely in the past.' It was the business of both Governments to try to establish better relations. In February 1906, he told his friend Spring Rice that he was 'impatient to see Russia re-established as a factor in European politics,' and the following month he agreed with Count Benckendorff to work for an understanding.

On 28 March, Sir Edward told Knollys that he had received 'more than one intimation' that the Tsar felt that his visit to Balmoral in 1896 had never been returned, 'and that he very much wants the King to visit him.' Russian ministers had made it clear 'that with every disposition on their part to improve relations with England no real progress will be made unless the Tsar puts his hand to it. And this he will not do as long as he remains unvisited. An *entente* with Russia is now possible, and it is the thing most to be desired in our foreign policy. It will complete and strengthen the *entente* with France and add very much to the comfort and strength of our position. But it all depends upon the Tsar and he depends upon the King.'

Sir Arthur Nicolson, Hardinge's successor at St Petersburg, approached his task with 'considerable misgivings.' He was under no illusion how hard it would be to overcome a legacy of hostility and suspicion which dated back to the days of the Crimean War. Personally, he was 'most anxious to see removed all causes of difference between us and Russia,' many of which he believed 'were caused by simple misunderstanding of each other.' But German influence was predominant in Court and Government circles, and it was widely believed that Japan would never have dared to go to war without Britain's encouragement. Moreover, Sir Arthur foresaw that public opinion at home could hamper negotiations. Those who saw Russia as 'a ruthless and barbarous autocratic state' might prove slow to see the advantages of allying with the Tsar.

Count Benckendorff, after a brief return to Russia in March 1906, came back with an invitation for His Majesty to pay a state visit some time later that year. But the King favoured delay, partly because the Kaiser would be incensed if he were to visit St Petersburg before Berlin, and partly because he thought it better to wait until it seemed probable that negotiations would succeed. The last thing he wanted was the publicity of failure. 'I honestly confess,' he wrote in a memorandum of 22 March, 'that I can see no particular object in visiting the Emperor in Russia this year. The country is in a very unsettled state and will, I fear, not improve for some time to come. I hardly think that the country at home would much approve of my going there for a while. I have no desire to play the part of the German Emperor, who always meddles in other people's business.' So, for the time being, the suggestion was not pursued further.

Soon after taking up residence at St Petersburg, Nicolson invited Sir Donald Wallace, an old friend and recognized authority on Russian affairs, to stay at the Embassy. They were troubled times as revolution broke out in October 1905. Wallace sent Knollys a series of penetrating letters, intended, of course, for the King, describing what was happening. His Majesty's Information Service was of an exceptionally high order.

In August 1906, Wallace told Knollys: 'Things are in a very critical condition. So far as we know, the serious mutiny at Sveaborg is not yet supressed, and as I write, news has come in that fighting is going on in the streets of Cronstadt, while disorders of a less serious kind are taking place all over the country. Though the new Prime Minister, Stolypin, is an intelligent, energetic man and most anxious to introduce reasonable reforms, I do not feel that he will long remain master of the situation because the forces of disorder are powerful and wide-spread, and the administrative machine, never very efficient, has been thrown out of gear by the events of the last eighteen months.

'For this lamentable state of things, the Duma, in my opinion, is partly to blame. Instead of improving matters it made them worse. The moderate majority – the so-called Constitutional Democrats or Cadets – had a splendid chance and recklessly threw it away. If they had at once come forward as the champions of order and legality and offered to co-operate with the Government in a series of practical reforms, much good work might have been done in an orderly pacific way. Instead of this they refused to condemn political assassination and bomb-throwing . . . They were for the most part men of the well-intentioned, pedantic, professional type who imagine that a great Empire can be governed and wild popular passions restrained by abstract philosophical principles and ingenious political theories.

The first article of their political programme, which they proclaimed from the house-tops, was a general amnesty. All the arrested or exiled political assassins and bomb-throwers were to be immediately let loose, in the hope that they would become at once orderly members of society and supporters of an orderly constitutional regime. Imagine an English government, at a moment of intense seditious agitation in Ireland, liberating all the imprisoned Fenians! And yet, these "Cadets" must know very well that what the imprisoned assassins and bomb-throwers want is not a Constitutional Government but the Socialist Republic. They have never made any secret of their aspirations and intentions.' The Socialists 'know clearly what they want and are ready to use all the means in their power to attain their ends. They far surpass their rivals in determination, energy and perseverence, and that is, in my opinion, the most alarming feature of the situation.'

After sixteen months of patient negotiation, the Anglo-Russian Convention was signed on 23 September 1907. Although the agreement was seen as uniting Russia, France and Britain in a Triple Alliance, its terms were limited to resolving outstanding disputes which had antagonized the signatories for the last half-century in Afghanistan, Persia and Tibet. Most people in England welcomed the Treaty, but many Radicals saw it as implicitly condoning Tsarist tyranny. A number of politicians and writers, including Bernard Shaw, Ramsay MacDonald and John Galsworthy, wrote a letter to *The Times* deploring 'an arrangement which, for a very dubious and temporary advantage,' pandered to Russian despotism. 'The English people,' said Henry Nevinson, 'are being trapped by a Liberal Foreign Office into some sort of alliance with the forces of Russian tyranny.' Among the 'temporary advantages' of which Shaw and his friends spoke, were fifteen million men whom the Russians mobilized in 1914.

The news of the Anglo-Russian Convention left the Wilhelmstrasse resentful and dismayed, although for a time they affected indifference towards it. Holstein had always insisted that such a thing could never happen, but he underestimated his own genius for reconciling his enemies. The Kaiser saw in the *entente* further proof of his Uncle's Machiavellian diplomacy and his strategy of encircling Germany. 'When taken all round,' he wrote, 'it is aimed at us.'

For four years, the King had worked for Anglo-Russian understanding, indeed Hardinge described it as 'the triumph of King Edward's policy of which the Anglo-French *entente* was the first step.' Sir Charles himself, of course, played an invaluable part in negotiations, but the brunt was borne by Nicolson. As the King acknowledged: 'Nicolson deserves the greatest praise for having carried out these most difficult negotiations with such skill and perseverance. His recent negotiations and his triumph at Algeciras place him in the front rank of our diplomats.'

Soon after the Convention had been signed, the King proposed a meeting with the Tsar in June 1908. When rumours began flying round Europe that the real purpose of his visit was to negotiate a naval and military alliance, Grey made a statement to the Commons explaining that His Majesty's journey to Russia was just such a state visit as he had paid to the Austrian Emperor, the Kings of Italy and Portugal, and the President of the French Republic. The Government had no intention whatever of contracting another treaty. Sir Edward's bland assurances neither soothed German apprehensions nor allayed Radical protests. Ramsay MacDonald condemned the prospective visit as 'an insult to England,' while Keir Hardie spoke of 'consorting with murderers.'

There was even a debate in the House of Commons, held on 4 June, to discuss the wisdom of the King 'hobnobbing' with a 'bloodstained creature' like the Tsar. The House was half empty. Some members, no doubt, preferred watching cricket on Upper Club to listening to Keir Hardie: but then there is no accounting for tastes. Much play was made of political suspects thrown into prison or sent to Siberia. Balfour supported Grey and argued that friendship with Russia would help preserve peace.

The King's visit was partly a family affair. The Tsarina was, after all, his niece, and Nicky was Alix's nephew. He was consequently furious to be told that he was 'condoning atrocities' by meeting them. So angry was he, that he refused to invite Keir Hardie, Victor Grayson and Arthur Ponsonby to a Royal Garden Party at Windsor. Ponsonby protested that his exclusion was an insult to his constituents 'and an attempt by the Sovereign to influence votes of members by social pressure,' and Keir Hardie told his constituents at Merthyr Tydfil that the King had kept outside politics since the days of Charles I and that he had better remain outside! This may have been good advice but it was bad history. By no stretch of the imagination could James II or George III or even Queen Victoria be described as 'outside politics.'

On Saturday, 6 June, the *Victoria and Albert* set out from Portsmouth on its voyage to Reval. The King was accompanied by the Queen, Princess Victoria, Sir Charles Hardinge, Sir Arthur Nicolson, who was returning to Russia after a spell of leave, Charlotte Knollys, Fritz Ponsonby, Admiral Fisher and Sir John French. The North Sea was so rough that only the most intrepid sailors dared to emerge from their cabins. At Kiel they were met by Prince Henry of Prussia and the entire German North Sea Fleet, which, as Hardinge reported to Grey, 'gave food for reflection upon the recent German naval programme of construction, while the intricate evolutions of the torpedo flotilla, which excited the admiration of all the naval officers on board the royal yacht, served as a useful object-lesson of the efficiency of the German Navy.'

The Royal Yacht anchored off Reval on Tuesday morning, 9 June, in glorious sunshine. The King, dressed in the uniform of the Kieff Dragoons, summoned Sir Arthur Nicolson to his cabin for a last-moment briefing. They sat facing one another in chintz armchairs, while His Majesty fired off a fusillade of questions. What was the present direction of Russian policy? Who were the members of the Tsar's staff and what was their history? How well did Stolypin and Isvolsky get on together? What was the relationship between the recently signed Convention and the Franco-Russian Treaty of 1894? Would the Emperor be in the uniform of the Scots Greys or that of a Russian Admiral? Did Stolypin speak French, German or English? Would it be wise to make no mention of the Duma? What were its present relations with the Government? Would the Emperor be likely to mention Britain's alliance with Japan, and, if so, what line should he take? Further questions followed about Russia's finances, Russia's railways, the condition of Russia's army and navy, and Russia's writers, musicians and scientists. Stolypin later told Nicolson that he was amazed at the King's grasp of his country's affairs. '*On voit bien*,' he declared, '*que c'est un homme d'état.*'

Protocol required the King to pay the first visit, but the Tsar thought it more fitting to meet his uncle and aunt on board the

Victoria and Albert. As soon as the Royal Yacht dropped anchor, a pinnace was seen heading towards it, containing the Tsar and Tsarina, the Dowager Empress, the Imperial children, and the Queen of the Hellenes, a grand-daughter of Nicholas I and Queen Alexandra's sister-in-law. After affectionate greetings, the English visitors were escorted back to the *Standart,* where the Guard of Honour was drawn up to receive them. The King gave the Russian sailors the traditional greeting: 'Good morning, my children,' to which they replied 'God save the King.' The royal families and their suites then stood around exchanging pleasantries, listening to the band, and munching caviare sandwiches washed down with kirsch, which Ponsonby thought tasted like boot polish.

That evening the Tsar gave a State Banquet to which, amongst others, he invited Stolypin, Isvolsky and Benckendorff. In proposing the King's health in a carefully prepared speech, delivered in the flawless English he had learned from his tutor, Charles Heath, the Tsar said that he trusted their meeting would strengthen 'the many and strong ties which unite our houses,' would draw their two countries closer together, and would help to promote the peace of the world. King Edward's sentiments were so similar that had the two Sovereigns been schoolboys they would almost certainly have been in trouble for copying each other's work.

Throughout the visit, the Tsar seemed happy and at ease, but the Tsarina was nervous and distraught. Perhaps she was worrying about Alexis. One evening, Hardinge, finding the festivities on board the *Standart* a trifle overpowering, wandered off in search of a few moments' tranquillity. As he strolled along the deck, he heard somebody sobbing, and found the Empress in a deck chair weeping uncontrollably. When he offered to help, she said there was nothing that anyone could do and asked to be left alone.

Fisher, who told Fritz Ponsonby that the ten days he spent on the Royal Yacht were the happiest of his career, was the life and soul of the party. Had he not been an Admiral of the Fleet he would have made a superlative court jester. After dinner, on the second night of the visit, Fisher told the band on the *Victoria and Albert* to play the waltz from *The Merry Widow,* which he proceeded to dance with the Grand Duchess Olga, with his hands behind his head. 'How about Siberia for me?' he asked her in the middle of the performance. The King told him that he must try to remember he was no longer a midshipman, and even the Tsarina was seen to smile at Fisher's antics. Next, by royal command, the First Sea Lord danced a hornpipe, and there were so many 'encores' that he was finally too exhausted to go on.

The King had several conversations with Stolypin, who told Hardinge he was 'fascinated' by His Majesty, and could see why he was 'regarded as the first statesman in Europe.' King Edward spoke of 'the prospects of agriculture; the pacific aims of the Anglo-Russian Convention; the marvellous progress made in the Russian railway system; the improved relations between Russia and Germany; the gratifying collaboration between the Government and Duma; the flourishing state of Russian finances; the amazing reforms introduced into the army and navy; how magnificent the Emperor looked in his uniform of the Scots Greys; how gratified he was, how really gratified to meet them.'

When the King met Isvolsky he told him how well he remembered their conversation at Copenhagen in 1904, and how much the Anglo-Russian *entente* owed to his diplomatic skill. The Tsar's ministers could not but warm to a Sovereign who so evidently appreciated them. It was part of the King's magic that nobody left his presence without being raised in his own esteem. On the second day at Reval, the King made the Emperor an Admiral of the Fleet, an unexpected honour which pleased him immensely. During dinner that night, in the course of proposing the King's health, the Tsar returned the compliment by inviting His Majesty to become an Admiral of the Russian Navy. Seeing that with the exception of one cruiser it lay at the bottom of the Pacific, it was the thought which counted.

The Tsar's principal aide-de-camp, Prince Orloff, told Fisher that the King at Reval 'changed the atmosphere of Russian feelings towards England from suspicion to cordial trust.' And the Tsar himself 'repeatedly expressed his great satisfaction at the visit of the King and Queen, which, he said, sealed and confirmed the intention and spirit of the Anglo-Russian Agreement.'

But, although everything was sunshine at Reval, there was thunder in Downing Street. On 10 June, Asquith wrote Knollys a letter headed 'Secret', in which he complained that he had just 'received a cypher telegram from Hardinge announcing that the King had appointed the Tsar an honorary Admiral of the British Fleet and expressing a hope that this step would meet with the approval of the Government. Without, for the moment, giving any opinion as to the wisdom or otherwise of this proposal, I feel bound to point out that it would have been more in accordance with constitutional practice, and with the accepted conditions of ministerial responsibility, if before His Majesty's departure, some intimation had been given to me and my colleagues, that it was in contemplation. We are now placed face to face with a *fait accompli*, in regard to which we have had no opportunity of consultation or decision. I must defer sending any answer until I can see and consult Sir E. Grey. The Cabinet, which is clearly entitled to a voice in such matters, cannot be conveniently assembled before Monday. As you know well, this Russian visit has from the first been a delicate affair: We have done our best to remove apprehension and doubts, but where such grave issues are involved, I should not be doing my duty, if I did not suggest, and even urge, the desirability of preliminary notice.'

The Kaiser made no attempt to conceal his disgust at his uncle's meeting with the Tsar. The fact that Fisher and French accompanied the King on his visit to Russia was widely construed as proof that the Convention of 1907 possessed a strategic significance. The Kaiser declared at a review of the Cavalry Guard at Döberitz, that Russia, France and England were plainly 'encircling' the Fatherland.

So certain was the German Emperor that a secret agreement had been reached that he would not believe that the two Sovereigns had avoided politics, that Reval was a family reunion, that there were no surreptitious understandings, and that Fisher had occupied himself dancing hornpipes. Even had he been drawing up plans to 'Copenhagen' the German Navy, it is difficult to see how the Russians with their one cruiser could have given him much assistance.

Germany's central position in Europe was of immense military advantage. In so far as she was 'encircled,' it was entirely her own doing. By alienating her neighbours, she provoked them to unite, and by allying with Austria antagonized Russia. The Triple Entente was a direct reaction to Germany's *Weltpolitik*.

It is difficult to assess the King's contribution to the foreign policy of his reign, because there is no reliable means of measuring influence. But it would be a great mistake to confuse the intangible for the negligible. The King, unlike Queen Victoria, greatly preferred meeting people to writing letters. So the effect of his personality was more often felt in conversation than correspondence. It is impossible to trace precisely in what manner and to what degree the constant support he gave men like Grey, Nicolson and Hardinge, to which they all bore tribute, changed the course of history. But the encouragement and friendship he offered Delcassé and Isvolsky, the trust he inspired in the Tsar, despite the Kaiser's efforts to destroy it, the loyalty he evoked from the citizens of Paris, the confidence reposed in him by his own subjects, were evidence of shrewd and suave diplomacy.

The historian is fortunate in possessing hindsight. What for King Edward was a mysterious future is for us a well-mapped past. Looking back from the last quarter of the twentieth century to its first decade, we can see that if Britain was to survive the approaching Armageddon she must have powerful allies. Above all, she needed to recognize the threat confronting her. While Lloyd George and Winston Churchill told their audiences to trust the Kaiser, to economize on armaments, and to prefer pensions to guns, the King was preaching vigilance, demanding battleships and promoting the Triple Entente: in short, tirelessly advocating precisely those policies which saved us in 1914.

VIII

The King and the Conservatives

The morning after Queen Victoria died, the King left Osborne for London to attend a meeting of the Privy Council at St James's Palace. The Archbishop of Canterbury, Dr Temple, administered the traditional oath of Sovereignty, after which King Edward said a few words of his own. He did so without notes and without consulting anybody, having decided what he proposed to say in the train from Portsmouth to Victoria. In the course of his remarks, he announced that he wished to be known as Edward VII.

The Queen had made it perfectly clear in a letter she wrote in 1864 that she intended him to take the title 'Albert Edward.' 'Respecting your names,' she said, 'I wish to repeat, that it was beloved Papa's wish, as well as mine, that you should be called by *both*, when you become King.' The Prince replied that he quite understood the Queen's wishes about his bearing his two names, 'although no English Sovereign has ever done so yet, and you will agree with me that it would not be pleasant to be like "Louis Napoleon," "Victor Emmanuel," "Charles Albert" etc., although no doubt there is no absolute reason why it should not be so.'

There the matter rested for thirty-seven years, until the day after the Queen ceased to be in a position to enforce her will. Nobody took down the King's speech in shorthand, but Lord Rosebery was sufficiently impressed by it to produce a faithful summary. 'My first and melancholy duty,' said His Majesty, 'is to announce to you the death of my beloved mother, the Queen, and I know how deeply you, the whole nation, and I think I may say the whole world, sympathizes with me in the irreparable loss we have all sustained.

I need hardly say that my constant endeavour will be always to walk in her footsteps. In undertaking the heavy load which now devolves upon me, I am fully determined to be a constitutional Sovereign in the strictest sense of the word, and as long as there is breath in my body, to work for the good and amelioration of my people. I have resolved to be known by the name of Edward, which has been borne by six of my ancestors. In doing so I do not undervalue the name of Albert, which I inherit from my ever-lamented great and wise father, who by universal consent is I think deservedly known by the name of Albert the Good, and I desire that his name should stand alone.'

Soon after Queen Victoria's death, a Commission was set up to enquire into the King's finances so as to advise the Government on the Civil List. It consisted of Mr Balfour, representing the Conservatives, Sir William Harcourt, representing the Liberals, and Sir John Maple, Baron Eckardstein's father-in-law, representing the King's millionaire friends who advised him on business matters. Knollys told the Commission that it was his 'happy duty' to inform them 'that, for the first time in English history, the heir-apparent comes forward to claim his right to the throne unencumbered by a single penny of debt.'

On 25 June 1901, a bill was passed raising the Civil List by £85,000 to £470,000. During his reign, the King's finances were so well administered that all his requirements were met out of income, thus satisfying Mr Micawber's recipe for happiness. Two courtiers were responsible for this state of affairs: Lord Farquhar, the Master of the Royal Household, and Sir Dighton Probyn, Keeper of the Privy Purse. Farquhar was ambitious if haphazard in handling money. Indeed, some people suspected he was too ingenious in making it multiply. In the summer of 1905, he persuaded Knollys to become a Director of 'Siberian Proprietary Mines Limited,' a speculative venture of dubious integrity. Under such patronage the company's shares soared to sixteen pounds, but it was not long before they plunged to a realistic level. Farquhar was said to have made £70,000 by timely buying and selling, in which respect he was more fortunate than other investors.

If Farquhar was the most Edwardian of the King's courtiers, Sir Dighton was eminently Victorian, and not the remotest hint of impropriety was ever linked with his name. He began his career as a soldier, served in India, won the Victoria Cross for valour during the

Mutiny, and formed 'Probyn's Horse.' In 1877 he succeeded Sir William Knollys as Comptroller of the Prince of Wales's Household. After King Edward's death he remained Queen Alexandra's Treasurer, in which post he merited another medal for his valiant campaign against prodigal generosity. He died at Sandringham in 1924 having served the family for fifty-two years.

When it came to investment, the King looked to Sir Ernest Cassel, whose Midas touch turned everything to gold. Cassel, the son of a German Jew, started life in Cologne and left school at fourteen. He was little more than a boy when he came to London to make his fortune. Within a quarter of a century he had become a multi-millionaire. His activities ranged from financing the Mexican Central Railway, issuing loans to the Government of China, financing the construction of the Aswan Dam, building the first London Underground, and helping establish the National Banks of Turkey and Egypt. In 1878 he married Annette Maxwell, a Roman Catholic from Darlington, and became a naturalized British subject.

Cassel met the Prince of Wales in 1896 and soon became one of his closest friends. For all his immense fortune, which he spent liberally, giving two million pounds to charity during his lifetime, Sir Ernest remained simple, blunt, and austere in the midst of plenty. The King deeply admired the genius and tenacity of this prince of entrepreneurs, who seemed to know better than the Foreign Office what was going on in the world.

Sir Ernest made many enemies, partly because of his origins, partly because he was terse and undiplomatic, and partly because some people found his success intolerable. His critics suggested he subsidized the King: hence the honours showered upon him. In fact, what he seems to have done was to manage the royal investments in such a way that all profits went to the King, while losses were met by his adviser.

It would be wrong to suppose that the friendship between the two men depended on Cassel's usefulness to the King. If that had been all there was to it, they need only have met on a strictly professional basis. In truth, each helped the other. But Cassel's social standing was naturally enhanced by royal patronage. His Majesty, for example, agreed to be godfather to Cassel's grand-daughter, Edwina Ashley, who married Lord Louis Mountbatten. Confusion often arose because Sir Ernest looked remarkably like his Sovereign. Mrs Keppel's daughter, Sonia, who was under strict instructions to curtsy to the King whenever she saw him, also curtsied to Cassel to be on the safe side.

Throughout his reign, the King insisted that his Ministers must keep him informed on matters great or small. In March 1903, Mr Balfour attended a dinner of Nonconformist Unionists and addressed them, amongst other things, on defending the Empire. The next day the King read an account of his speech in *The Times* and wrote to tell him that as he took 'such a deep interest in the welfare of this country and especially in all matters connected with its defence, he was naturally much surprised, and he might even say pained, to have received no information on the subject.'

Chamberlain was guilty in the summer of 1901 of a more serious oversight when he failed to let the King see a Proclamation issued by Lord Kitchener, then Commander-in-Chief in South Africa, concerning his policy of scorched earth and concentration camps. Knollys sent the Colonial Secretary the sort of letter he had been writing for thirty years. 'The King desires me to let you know he has been greatly surprised that Lord Kitchener's Proclamation should not have been submitted to him, and that the first he should have known of it should have been through the newspapers. He feels sure that you will agree with him that this is not right, and that as the Head of the State he has reason to complain that such omission should have occurred, even though it was only the result of an oversight.'

Chamberlain instantly apologized saying that he 'was under the impression that the correspondence containing the draft proclamation had been sent to Your Majesty at the same time as to Lord Salisbury and the Cabinet, and he is grieved to find that by a most regrettable oversight this was not done. He has now again given definite instruction that all papers of similar importance are to be sent to Your Majesty and he trusts that Your Majesty will be pleased to overlook this unfortunate incident.'

Evidently the King was only partially satisfied, for, when Knollys replied to Chamberlain's apology, he dwelt more on the enormity of the offence than what had been pleaded by way of mitigation. 'The King has received Mr Chamberlain's letter of the 12th inst., regretting that a copy of Lord Kitchener's Proclamation was not laid before him before it was published. The King regrets the so-called "oversight" very deeply as the document was of considerable importance and created much comment all over the world. It is to be hoped that in future His Majesty's Government will not be guilty of a similar error as it places the King in a very false position and he cannot afford being treated as a cypher by his Ministers.'

Soon after coming to the throne the King decided that it would be inappropriate to be crowned until peace was signed in South Africa. In the end, it was agreed to hold the Coronation on 26 June 1902. Much to the King's disgust, the Kaiser refused to permit the Crown Prince to attend the ceremony. King Edward was anxious that the Coronation honours should be national rather than political, and obtained Lord Salisbury's agreement to offer peerages to prominent Liberals, including his own Private Secretary, Sir Francis Knollys.

In June 1902, he instituted the 'Order of Merit,' so as to 'reward in a special manner officers of the Navy and Army, and civilians distinguished in Arts, Sciences, and Literature.' It was inspired by Frederick the Great's Order *Pour le Mérite*. Lord Roberts, Lord Wolseley, Lord Kitchener, Lord Kelvin, Lord Lister, Morley, Lecky and G. F. Watts, were among the first to receive the honour. Later in the reign, Admiral Fisher, Admiral Togo and Miss Florence Nightingale were admitted to the Order.

Twelve days before the Coronation was to take place, the King caught a chill at Aldershot. On 16 June he returned to Windsor, where his doctor, Sir Francis Laking, recommended a milk diet and plenty of rest. The Press was told that His Majesty was suffering from a severe attack of lumbago. On 23 June, the King returned to London, driving from Paddington Station to Buckingham Palace in an open carriage, with an escort of Household Cavalry. It had been suggested that he should travel from Windsor by road but he refused to disappoint the crowd.

That afternoon, having obtained a second opinion from Sir Thomas Barlow, Laking told the King that he was suffering from Perityphilitis (inflammation of the appendix), that an operation was imperative, and that the Coronation would have to be postponed. But the King, although wretchedly ill and in great pain, would not hear of it. After a furious argument he ordered Laking to leave the room. But Sir Francis stood his ground and told the King that if he did not have his appendix removed he would die in the Abbey, if not before. Eventually, the King agreed to take his doctors' advice.

The Duchess of Sermoneta, who came over from Rome for the Coronation, learned at Dover that her journey was wasted. As she sat in her compartment in the station, she heard the guard walking along the train, 'giving bad news to us all: "The King is very ill," he said, "they have had to operate on him, and the Coronation is put off indefinitely." This dramatic announcement was a shock to everyone, and total strangers entered into excited conversation.'

The operation began soon after midday on 24 June in a bedroom at Buckingham Palace. There was every reason to fear its outcome. The surgeon, Sir Frederick Treves, later told Princess Victoria that 'his firm conviction was that His Majesty would die during the operation.' The King himself feared he had cancer of the stomach, seeing that both Vicky and Affie had died of that disease. The operation took forty minutes and was a complete success, but had it been delayed the King could not have survived.

Most of his convalescence was spent on board the *Victoria and Albert*. Sometimes, when the Queen came to talk to him, he pretended to be asleep, because the effort of trying to make her hear tired him so much. Lord Esher was invited to stay on the yacht to help amuse the patient. 'I was sent for by the King,' he wrote on 27 July, 'and sat with him for two hours. He is very comfortable, dressed in his yacht clothes, with a white cap, and looking wonderfully well. He *sits* up now – in a huge chair specially constructed – and he reads and writes all day, quite happily, not a bit bored. He is on a very sparse diet – hardly anything – and he is proud of a reduction of eight inches round the waist, and a loss of certainly two stone in weight. His face is improved – and grown younger – much fined down. He is to be allowed to stand up on Tuesday, just five weeks from the operation . . . Treves thinks him a much healthier man than before the operation.'

King Edward was touchingly grateful and considerate to those who looked after him. Soon after he came round from the anaesthetic he told Treves he proposed to make him a Baronet in case he had a relapse and the honour was overlooked. Not only was Miss Haines, his Irish nurse, made the first Matron of the Officers' Home at Osborne, but when he visited Ireland in 1903 he asked to meet her parents to tell them how much he appreciated all she had done for him.

Most of the clergy saw the King's illness as evidence of Divine intervention and sought the origins of appendicitis in theology. The Bishop of Stepney suggested that the Country had been approaching the Coronation 'with undue levity and that the call has come in this postponement to remember the Lord our God.' The Bishop of Southampton advanced the theory 'that we had been too much absorbed in thoughts of Imperial greatness and earthly prosperity.' The Bishop of London, preaching in the Chapel Royal, suspected that the Coronation had become 'too much a great show' and 'too little a great national sacrament.' Cardinal Vaughan declared that 'the finger of God has appeared in the midst of national rejoicing to call the thoughts of all men to Himself.'

Nobody recognized more clearly than the King the expense and inconvenience of postponing the Coronation: hence his courageous desire to struggle on. The Ritz and Claridge's emptied overnight as their royal visitors forlornly returned home. It was even suggested by some who could scarcely have recognized the sacramental significance of the ceremony, that a substitute should be found to take the King's place. One monthly magazine went to considerable expense to retrieve copies of an issue containing an article on 'How I Saw the Coronation by a Peer's daughter.'

The postponement of the Coronation created a crisis in the royal kitchen where M. Menager had been preparing a banquet for two hundred and fifty guests. He had arranged a menu of fourteen courses, and ordered two thousand five hundred plump quails, three hundred legs of mutton, and huge quantities of sturgeon, foie gras, caviare, asparagus and strawberries. While upstairs the King lay at death's door, downstairs the servants packed hampers of food to be distributed to the poor. Possibly the inhabitants of Whitechapel may have found *consommé de faisan aux quenelles*, sole poached in Chablis and garnished with oysters and prawns, or snipe stuffed with foie gras, a trifle rich for their taste.

The Coronation eventually took place on 9 August, less than seven weeks after the King's operation. Before leaving for the Abbey, he sent for his grandchildren so that they might see him in his robes. 'Good morning, children,' he said, as they gazed at him wide-eyed and overawed, 'am I not a funny-looking old man?' Legend has it, that Queen Alexandra was late as usual, and that the King finally 'burst into her room, watch in hand, remonstrating, "My dear Alix, if you don't come immediately you won't be crowned Queen." ' The procession set out from Buckingham Palace shortly before eleven o'clock, and the crowds, delighted to see the King looking so well, shouted and cheered without ceasing. Half an hour later, the golden coach, drawn by eight cream-coloured horses, reached the west door of the Abbey. Inside, the congregation heard a fanfare of trumpets and bells pealing. Their long vigil was over. On the King's instructions, a special pew was reserved for

Sarah Bernhardt, Mrs Keppel, and a number of other decorative ladies, whose only claim to an invitation was His Majesty's esteem. Some irreverent wit dubbed it: 'The King's Loose Box.' The scholars of Westminster, deceived by a preliminary stirring of clergy, prematurely hailed their Sovereign. When a few minutes later the King appeared in the choir, the boys, determined not to repeat their mistake, gave a decidedly half-hearted rendering of their ritual cry: 'Vivat Rex Eduardus! Vivat Rex Eduardus! Vivat! Vivat! Vivat!'

Archbishop Temple, whose contribution to *Essays and Reviews* over forty years before had exposed him to charges of heresy, was so blind that the service had to be printed for him on special cards. Even these did not prevent him making several blunders, such as adjuring the King to give his special protection to 'widowers'. Prince Edward noticed his tutor, Mr Hansell, kneeling 'with his eyes closed and his lips moving as in prayer.' Afterwards, Finch, the Prince's valet, said he felt sure that Hansell 'was praying not for the King but that the Archbishop would last through the service.'

Shortly before the supreme moment was reached, the aged Primate showed increasing signs of infirmity. As he returned from the altar with the Imperial Crown he nearly stumbled. It was only with an agonizing effort that he raised it on high, with trembling hands, before placing it on the King's head, and even then he would have put it on the wrong way round, had His Majesty not gently helped him adjust it.

The Archbishop was the first to pay homage. Kneeling before his Sovereign he promised to be 'faithful and true,' and to 'acknowledge the service of the lands I claim to hold of you, as in right of the Church. So help me God.' He then spontaneously added: 'God bless you Sir; God be with you Sir.' As he struggled to rise, his strength failed him, and though King Edward rose from his throne and took him by the hands to support him, he would have fallen if three bishops kneeling near by had not sprung to his rescue. A few minutes later, the Bishop of Winchester, Randall Davidson, asked him whether he wanted help, only to be told to 'Go away!'

Within four months of the Coronation, Temple was dead, and the man whose assistance he had so peremptorily rejected succeeded him as Primate of All England. The King had known the new Archbishop since 1883, when he became Dean of Windsor, and looked on him as a trusted friend. But he feared he was sometimes indecisive. At the foot of a letter which Davidson wrote in the summer of 1906, King Edward noted: 'This is a very "shilly shally" letter from a good but not strong man either physically or morally.' In so saying, he must have forgotten Davidson's resolute resistance to Queen Victoria in 1884 when she threatened to publish a memoir of John Brown. On that occasion the new Dean preferred to risk his career rather than let her persist in anything so injudicious.

During the last forty years of her reign, Queen Victoria preserved her various residences as shrines to the Prince Consort and even the smallest change was frowned upon. Rooms which had been fashionable at the time of the Great Exhibition of 1851 looked eccentric half a century later. The Queen had spent most of her widowhood at Osborne or Balmoral, both pre-eminently the work of Prince Albert, and visited London as rarely as she could. Buckingham Palace was consequently drab, neglected and uncomfortable. It had neither central heating nor electric light. Moreover, like Windsor, it possessed few bathrooms or lavatories, so that royal visitors needed to possess medieval habits. Alix's sister, Dagmar, once complained that staying there was like living out of doors.

When Lionel Cust, the Surveyor of the King's Pictures, was asked to collect the Queen and Prince Consort's personal belongings, so that His Majesty might consider what should become of them, he found himself 'alone in the rooms once occupied by Prince Albert, still apparently much the same as when he last used them . . . In the drawers of the desk were many loose papers, including two or three early letters of an intimate family nature.' In the room where the Prince died at Windsor his medicine glass was still on the bedside table.

The King supervised every detail of the modernization and redecoration of his palaces, seldom consulting Alix. He was assisted by the Comptroller of the Lord Chamberlain's Department, Sir Arthur Ellis, the Master of the Household, Lord Farquhar, the Secretary of the Office of Works, Lord Esher, and Lionel Cust. Together, 'they explored each palace from end to end in order to decide what alterations and improvements might be necessary to make the Palace into a suitable residence for the Sovereign and his Court at the beginning of the twentieth century.'

Much of the actual work was carried out under the King's eye. 'Offer it up,' he would instruct the workmen, as they groaned under the weight of a life-size portrait of some royal predecessor, and then, standing back, he would put his head on one side and contemplate the arrangement. 'That is not amiss,' he would say, once he was satisfied, and the carpenters would mark the wall so as to know precisely where to hang it. He greatly enjoyed showing his guests his treasures, but never pretended to knowledge he did not possess, and 'more than once confided to Cust, with that peculiar thickening of his r's, that he did not know much about ar-r-t, but did think he knew something about ar-r-angement.'

Both at Windsor and at Buckingham Palace the King decided to take over his father's rooms, which were stripped of those relics of the past to which his mother had clung so tenaciously. It was as if Albert's ghost was being exorcized with bell, book and candle.

During the summer of 1902, Buckingham Palace, which had so long been shrouded in dust sheets, became once more the scene of dazzling entertainments, splendid ceremonies, and delightful dinner parties. Queen Victoria's dreary 'Drawing Rooms' were replaced by Evening Courts which were much more enjoyable. In 1903, the King and Queen held a State Ball at Windsor: the first for sixty years. Her late Majesty took a sombre view of the diversions of her subjects, and once even wrote to the Editor of *The Times* deploring their frivolity. But now there were cakes and ale, and a King disposed to rejoice. So, young men, who were soon to lie sprawled on the battlefields of Flanders, danced until dawn and made love by the light of the moon.

The King decided he could not possibly afford to keep up Osborne as well as Balmoral, Sandringham, Windsor and Buckingham Palace. He therefore handed over the outbuildings to the Admiralty as a College for Naval Cadets, to replace the old training ship *Britannia*, moored off Dartmouth. The stable block of the Great House was to be used for their training, and the paddocks given over to football and cricket. Most of the remaining buildings were converted into a convalescent home for Army and Navy Officers. The King's sisters shrilly reminded him of their beloved Mama's wishes, but failed to persuade him to change his mind. Two Kings, King Edward VIII and King George VI, were among the College's earlier students.

The King first encountered Reginald Brett as a Cambridge undergraduate, just after the Franco-Prussian War. Brett, who succeeded his father as Lord Esher in 1899, became a close friend of Albert Grey, and through his influence was invited to Marlborough House. But it was not until 1897, when Brett and the Prince of Wales worked together on plans for the Diamond Jubilee, that their friendship really began. Having finished with Eton and Trinity,

Brett, a hesitant Liberal with Conservative roots and instincts, became Lord Hartington's Private Secretary and Member for Falmouth. Finding himself unsuited to the rough-and-tumble of the hustings, he retired from politics in 1885 to Orchard Lea, a house he built himself on the outskirts of Windsor. In 1879 he married Eleanor van de Weyer, daughter of the Belgian Ambassador to London. Brett's wife brought him into Queen Victoria's inner circle. In 1895 he became Secretary to the Office of Works, in which post he became involved in the Diamond Jubilee, Queen Victoria's funeral and King Edward's Coronation.

Soon Esher acquired a unique position of his own as an intermediary between the Sovereign and his Ministers. Few men can ever have refused so many glittering prizes. He was asked to write Disraeli's life and refused. He was asked to edit the *Daily News* and said no. He was offered the Secretaryship of War by the Tories (1903), and the Viceroyalty of India by the Liberals (1908), and rejected both. Nothing could lure him to take the stage for he believed that his gifts were best exercised behind the scenes. As early as 1902 his friend, Lord Rosebery, called him a 'Grand Vizier.'

Esher's genius for companionship enabled him to influence affairs by means of his friendships, and he was regularly to be seen at Brooks's dining with Fisher, Soveral and Knollys. In 1905, Carrington noted in his diary that he 'has a wonderful footing in Buckingham Palace' and 'seems to be able to run about as he likes.' In common with most of the King's close associates, he profoundly distrusted the Kaiser. Writing to Knollys in May 1908, he confessed 'I dislike *all* Germans.'

In 1901 King Edward appointed Esher Deputy-Constable and Lieutenant-Governor of Windsor Castle. The most arduous but rewarding of his duties were concerned with the Royal Archives. In the process of sorting out Queen Victoria's correspondence, at the King's special request, he gradually acquired an unrivalled insight into constitutional lore. So, whenever nineteenth-century precedents became relevant to contemporary problems, Esher was able to quote chapter and verse. As the Lieutenant-Governor resolutely refused access to the Archives, he was able to make exclusive use of their secrets. 'His position as a political éminence grise to Edward VII and George V in successive crises involving the powers and prerogatives of the Sovereign rested on this basis.'

Esher further exploited his enviable responsibility for the late Queen's papers by publishing the letters and diaries she wrote before coming to the throne, with the title *The Girlhood of Queen Victoria*. He was also co-editor with Arthur Benson of the first three volumes of *The Letters of Queen Victoria* which covered the years from her accession to the death of the Prince Consort. On the strength of the material at his disposal, Esher encouraged the King to defend the prerogatives of the Crown from slow erosion or direct assault.

Some of Esher's missions on His Majesty's behalf gave offence in official circles. When the Kaiser in 1908 took exception to Esher's remarks on the size of the German Navy, he expressed astonishment that such liberties were permitted to 'the man who looked after the drains at Windsor.' In fact, Esher had resigned from the Office of Works six years before, and as a member of the Committee of Imperial Defence had every right to speak on maritime matters. Nevertheless, the German Emperor's resentment echoed the view of Whitehall. Lord Mersey noted in his diary on 20 July 1907, that Esher was ' "mal vu" at the FO as he is supposed to repeat things to the King, which Grey resents.'

Sir Charles Hardinge, when Permanent Under-Secretary at the Foreign Office, strongly resisted what seemed to him unauthorized interference. In June 1906, for example, Esher sent Sir Charles a telegram asking for 'a short statement of what has been done in the matter of the Baghdad Railway, for the King's information.' Hardinge replied the same day as follows: 'I have shown your telegram of this morning to Sir E. Grey and I regret that I am unable to comply with your request and give you the information which you have asked for. Any information which the King may desire on foreign politics, will always, as heretofore, be gladly supplied if HM will make known his commands through one of his Private Secretaries.'

By the same post, Sir Charles wrote to Knollys, to prepare him 'in case Esher says anything to the King on the subject.' His letter shows how indignant he felt. 'The enclosed telegram,' it began, 'which I received this morning fairly astonished me, and might cause a very inconvenient precedent. I submitted it at once to Sir E. Grey and I enclose you a copy of the letter which I have written to Esher with Grey's approval. We cannot possibly admit Esher's interference in Foreign Office affairs and if the King wants information on any subject we look to receive a request for it through the proper channel which is yourself . . . If this system of supplying memoranda to Esher were followed, any number of people might make the same request, and Sir E. Grey feels very strongly that Esher is not the proper channel between him and the King. I feel certain that you will agree.'

The King, however, saw no reason to comply with Foreign Office procedures if it suited him better to follow some other course. Nor did he think it was proper for Grey or Hardinge to decide what agents he might, or might not, employ. As James I once told the House of Commons, he was an old and experienced King and would not be taught his office.

The month after King Edward died, *The World* published a series of articles attacking Lord Esher's 'mysterious power.' It was evidently anxious to ensure that George V would not depend on him. 'Prime Ministers or First Sea Lords,' it claimed, 'may come and go, but he goes on for ever.' Hostility towards Esher largely derived from envy of his influence. A King's favourite is often nobody else's. But the fact that he was unaccountable to Parliament was reasonable cause for anxiety. Certainly this 'man outside the constitution' wielded power 'beyond the reach of effective criticism.' *The World* therefore suggested that Esher's position should be clearly defined in a White Paper and that he should be required to answer questions in the House of Lords. Such parliamentary scrutiny was the 'historic and well-tried antidote to abuse of power.'

Brodrick spoke for most of his colleagues when he complained of the way in which Esher 'dined with the King alone,' or was seen leaving the Palace 'at unusual hours.' The consequence of these furtive encounters soon became clear. 'By the time any decision had come to the point when the Cabinet could lay it before the Sovereign, the issue had been largely prejudged, on the incomplete premises of an observer who had no official status. In other words Esher, whether intentionally or not, had constituted himself the unofficial adviser of the Crown.'

Secure in the King's confidence, Esher shrugged off attacks, and seldom went out of his way to placate enemies. One of his strongest points 'was that he never minded who got credit for any measure he devised so long as it was adopted by the authorities.' Sir Lionel Cust, 'looking back after an interval of twenty-five years,' gave it as his 'considered opinion that the remarkable influence which Lord Esher exercised over King Edward VII in the early years of the reign, was well applied, of great assistance to the King and of benefit to the nation at large.' In many respects Esher's relation to King Edward resembled that of Count Eulenburg's to the Kaiser. Both disliked responsibility, both shared the gift of keeping their Sovereigns amused, both were brilliant and artistic, both preferred the back stairs to the front door, both worked in feminine ways, and both were suspected of Grecian vices.

In 1898, just when the Prince of Wales was growing tired of Lady Warwick, he dined at Portman Square with Lord Albemarle's son George Keppel, and instantly fell under the spell of his enchanting wife, Alice. She was twenty-nine at the time and the Prince was fifty-seven. That evening changed the rest of his life, for he had found the most perfect mistress in the history of royal infidelity. For the next twelve years she remained what Mensdorff called 'La Favorita'. Wherever His Majesty went, she too was invited. Only three bastions of morality let down the portcullis and would not let her pass: the Duke of Norfolk at Arundel, the Duke of Portland at Welbeck, and Lord Salisbury at Hatfield.

George Keppel accepted the situation as if it were perfectly natural to share his wife with his Sovereign. There was something distinctly feudal in his acceptance of seigniorial rights. On the rare occasions when Alice was snubbed because of her liaison, the King's instinct was to destroy the offender as he had once crushed Randolph Churchill. But such was the generosity of her nature that she invariably persuaded him to do nothing.

Alix's attitude towards 'La Favorita' is popularly supposed 'to have been one of almost superhuman charity and forbearance.' Certainly, 'she could rise to heroic heights, but there were moments when she was less saintly.' On learning that Mrs Keppel had arrived at Cowes, the Duchess of York wrote to Prince George: 'What a pity Mrs G. K. is again to the fore! How annoyed Mama will be.' Once, as Alix looked out of a window at Sandringham, she saw the King and Mrs Keppel returning from a drive in an open carriage. She herself had never lost her graceful figure, but Alice Keppel, her junior by twenty-five years, was already plump. The sight of these two stout persons sitting solemnly side by side was too much for her, and she sent for Charlotte Knollys to share the joke.

Alice Keppel was good-natured, humorous and discreet. She smoked cigarettes through a long holder, and spoke in a deep, throaty voice. Her zest for life was infectious and she was gay without being frivolous. Nobody had fewer enemies and there was nothing self-seeking about her. She loved the King for himself and understood his moods. Hence the skill with which she handled him. Once, when they were playing bridge together – and His Majesty was recognized to be more formidable as a partner than an opponent – he began to get angry with her for muddling her cards. She remained, however, unmoved, excusing herself on the ground that she 'never could tell a King from a Knave.'

Politically, she supported the Liberals, and counted Lloyd George and Asquith among her friends. When Asquith resigned in 1916 and had nowhere to go after leaving Downing Street, she told Margot that she hoped they would stay with her for as long as they wished, and gave them her own bedroom and sitting-room to make them comfortable.

On the whole, His Majesty's humblest subjects took to Mrs Keppel. One morning, when Lord Alington called to take her for a drive in Hyde Park, she insisted on being shown his slum property in the East End of London. After the tour was over, she thanked him for her outing, but added with just a suspicion of menace, 'next year there will be such a difference I am sure.'

All Europe knew she was the King's mistress, and when she travelled abroad she was treated as if she were royal. Immediately after King Edward's death, Hardinge wrote a private note on what he described as 'a delicate matter upon which I am in a position to speak with authority. Everybody knew of the friendship that existed between King Edward and Mrs George Keppel, which was intelligible in view of the lady's good looks, vivacity and cleverness . . . I would like here to pay a tribute to her wonderful discretion, and to the excellent influence which she always exercised upon the King. She never utilized her knowledge to her own advantage, or to that of her friends; and I never heard her repeat an unkind word to anybody. There were one or two occasions when the King was in disagreement with the Foreign Office, and I was able, through her, to advise the King with a view to the policy of the Government being accepted. She was very loyal to the King and patriotic at the same time. It would have been difficult to find any other lady who would have filled the part of friend to King Edward with the same loyalty and discretion.' Mrs Keppel lived through two world wars, retaining to the end her love of life, her stately beauty and her warm heart.

In the very same month in which the Prince met Mrs Keppel, he also struck up a friendship with Miss Agnes Keyser, a middle-aged lady some ten years younger than he was. She, and her younger

sister, Fanny, opened a Hospital for Officers at the time of the
Boer War, in their own house, 17 Grosvenor Crescent, just behind
Buckingham Palace. Rich as she was, she needed additional re-
sources, so the King persuaded Sir Ernest Cassel, Lord Rothschild,
Lord Burnham, Arthur Sassoon, and a few other friends, to set
up a trust for her. The hospital became known as 'King Edward's
Hospital for Officers,' and the entire royal family lent it their
support. Rosa Lewis, who did not often pay compliments to other
women, praised the way this formidable matron persuaded the
King to 'induce his snob friends to dole out.'

In fact, it had not proved difficult, for His Majesty's interest in
medical matters was famous. In 1908 he told Sir Frederick Treves
that his greatest ambition was 'not to quit this world till a real
cure for cancer has been found,' and said that he felt 'convinced
that radium will be the means of doing so!' Throughout his life the
King cultivated the society of doctors and surgeons. He learned, for
instance, from Pasteur's own lips to recognize the extent to which
disease was caused by germs. In 1888, he summoned a meeting to
found a National Association for the Prevention of Consumption.
When he laid the foundation stone of a new wing of the Brompton
Hospital, he asked 'If consumption is a preventible disease, why is it
not prevented?'

Agnes Keyser offered the King the peace and comfort of the
nursery. When they dined alone together, the conversation was as
wholesome as the cooking. The dishes she saw fit to set before the
King were Irish stew and rice pudding. Like a devoted nanny, she
grumbled about his voracious appetite, his liking for rich food, and
those wretched cigars which aggravated his bronchitis. Her house
was an ever-open refuge as her duties kept her at home. The night
before the Prince travelled to Osborne in January 1901 to see his
mother for the last time, he spent the evening at Grosvenor Crescent.
Had Alix not been at Sandringham he would probably have
remained at Marlborough House. But, as it was, he had supper with
Sister Agnes, and afterwards sat by the fire and told her how utterly
unworthy he felt to succeed the Queen.

Of all the King's companions none was more faithful than
Caesar, his long-haired, white-coated fox terrier. It is true he was
neither aristocratic nor strictly speaking handsome, but he had
what the French call *La beauté du diable*, and made up for lack
of looks by engaging ways. He was mischievous, cheerful and deeply
attached to the King, who would often ask him: 'Do you like your

old master?' At night he slept curled up in an armchair beside the King's bed, and every morning, Wellard, the second footman, washed and combed him. Caesar might be seen wherever His Majesty went, trotting behind him down the Rue de la Paix, or strolling along the beach at Biarritz. On his collar was engraved the legend: 'I am Caesar, the King's dog.' And there was something about his jaunty air which seemed to suggest he had read the inscription.

When the King travelled by road, Caesar would generally sit on the back seat. Once, when His Majesty was taking coffee in the garden of the Café Glatzen, Stamper heard terrible screams and rushed to see what was happening. He found the King shouting, 'Caesar! Come here! Come here, you bad dog.' But the terrier was too intent upon chasing a white peacock to answer his master's summons. In the end, Stamper managed to catch him and bring him back and he was sentenced to solitary confinement in the car. 'His Majesty never beat Caesar. The dog and he were devoted to one another, and it was a picture to see him standing shaking his stick at the dog, when he had done wrong. "You naughty dog," he would say very slowly. "You naughty, naughty dog." And Caesar would wag his tail.'

Stamper, 'the King's Motor Mechanic,' maintained His Majesty was one of the earliest pioneers of the road. At the beginning of his reign, motoring was regarded as an inferior pastime, unworthy of Royal patronage. But as soon as it was discovered that the King possessed several cars, it became respectable to own them. Queen Victoria frowned on horseless carriages, and was not amused to see a photograph of her eldest son, sitting in an open motor, wearing a tall hat which had blown over his nose. 'I hope,' she told her Master of the Horse, 'you will never allow any of those horrible machines to be used in my stables. I am told that they smell exceedingly nasty, and are very shaky and disagreeable conveyances altogether.'

The King was always interested in anything new and willing to experiment. In a sense, motoring may be seen as a return to a first love, since in younger days he had often joined the Duke of Sutherland on the footplate. He liked to be driven fast and was very proud to have travelled at sixty miles an hour on the Brighton road. 'Fine run, Stamper,' he would say, 'fine run,' if he reached his destination without a breakdown. The King's cars were distinguished by their claret colour and absence of number plates. But although they were always stylish and well appointed, they were never ostentatious. Such calculated restraint was the King's doing. 'Pomp out of place he could not endure.'

In 1913, Stamper, encouraged by Dornford Yates to put down his spanner and take up his pen, wrote his recollections. They provide a telling portrait of the King, whom he found 'kind and appreciative to a degree, strict, but not stern, often quick-tempered, though his anger had gone – not passed, but gone – almost before it was there, and he was never unreasonable, but always ready to hear an explanation. He had a wide sympathy and a generous nature. Resolute and strong-willed, he was a man who formed powerful opinions, and to his opinions he would stick with all the determination in the world, unless and until he was shown that he was wrong, when he would instantly give way in the most frank and handsome manner imaginable . . . I never saw him depressed, he had a keen sense of humour, his energy was quite tireless, and he simply did not know the meaning of the word "fear".'

It was often said that the King spoke with a German accent, but Stamper denied that he 'did anything of the kind.' Indeed, 'he spoke the fairest English in the world,' although his voice was deep and gruff. After years of trying to make Alix hear him, he tended to shout, and his pronunciation was syllabic. For example, he pronounced the word interest, 'in-ter-est.'

Stamper was deeply impressed by the King's vitality, and noticed as time went on, 'so far from waning, his energy seemed to wax.' Although in the last years of his life his hair turned grey, his step remained noticeably sprightly. 'If he had a destination of any kind, his pace was invariably brisk,' and 'he was in or out of a car or a train in a moment. All his movements were smart, and all he did he did quickly. He spoke rapidly, ate fast, thought apace. He even smoked hard. Speed was of the very essence of his nature.'

Lord Ormathwaite, one of His Majesty's Gentlemen Ushers, wrote of his life at Court, that his main recollection of King Edward 'goes back to his amazing simplicity. This great King, grandiose and magnificent in so many outward ways, yet had the inward simplicity of a little child.' His gift for putting people at their ease owed much to this characteristic. But he could be very forbidding if he wished, and those who ventured to traverse treacherous ground were called to order with a chilling stare.

The King was not easy to shock, for he had never sought the sheltered life, but he had a strict regard for social propriety.

When he was Prince of Wales he complained to the Lord Chamberlain, his friend Carrington, about a play called 'The Gaiety Girl,' which mocked Holy Orders. Carrington assured the Prince that he would at once give instructions 'that the clergyman must, as represented, be taken out of the piece.' In this sort of play, he went on to explain, 'there is so much "gagging" and alteration, that the piece is an entirely different one in many cases to the one sent in: and I am very sorry indeed that the Prince of Wales should have had such reason to complain.' In a later letter, Carrington asked Knollys 'to kindly always let him know if he heard anything wrong,' and he would 'see to it at once. I have given directions to pass no more burlesque parsons.'

The passing of the years did nothing to diminish the King's peppery temper. Even as a child Lady Lyttelton described him as 'passionate and determined enough for an autocrat,' and towards the end of his life he became, if anything, more liable to sudden gusts of anger. Ponsonby could never quite understand why King Edward made people so frightened of him, but he claimed 'that even his most intimate friends were all terrified of him.' At one moment, he was like an affectionate, purring kitten, and, the next, like a tiger, growling and showing his claws. Ponsonby's daughter thought the King in his own way, 'just as formidable as his mother, with the difference that, whereas she struck terror by icy sarcasm, he made himself felt by roaring in a loud, guttural voice. His angry bellow, once heard, could never be forgotten.'

Besides being short-tempered, the King was exceptionally restless and betrayed his impatience by tapping his foot, drumming his fingers or fiddling with the cutlery. Not the least of his trials was the agony he endured being kept waiting by Alix. Playing bridge always tested his temper, as he brought to the game 'a royal acquisitiveness and desire to lead, which neither the cards nor his modicum of skill could always gratify.' If the rubbers fell to his opponents, his spirits sank, and it became disagreeably evident that His Majesty was displeased. Once, at Balmoral, Balfour, while partnering the King, made an ill-judged declaration, and endeavoured to extricate himself by saying: 'Sir, there remains but one thing to be done. Please send me to bed.'

Margot Asquith, a brilliant, wayward and outspoken lady, who was no respecter of persons, and whose comments on Royalty were sometimes so stark as to be savage, gave it as her opinion that 'a kinder, more considerate and courteous man than King Edward never existed.' She might even have joined his Court, as when she was twenty Knollys asked her to marry him. At the time, she thought his great age – he was then thirty-five – 'must have affected his reason.' However, when she declined, 'the expression on his face was more one of relief than disappointment.'

Fritz Ponsonby, who began his career as a courtier working for Queen Victoria, found the King 'far more considerate and human.' It was rare for the Queen to consider her Household's feelings, 'and it never occurred to her to ascertain whether any wish of hers might cause inconvenience, whereas King Edward was always thinking of small acts of kindness.' Virtually all His Majesty's servants shared Ponsonby's opinion. Sir Seymour Fortescue, for example, who became an Equerry in 1893, and served the King 'for the next seventeen years, until the day of his death – to me the saddest day I have ever known,' found him 'the kindest and most considerate of masters that ever a man was fortunate enough to serve.'

In looking back on his early life, Churchill wrote of 'the extra-ordinary kindness and consideration for young people which the Prince of Wales always showed.' When Winston published his first book, *The Malakand Field Force*, the Prince of Wales told him: 'I cannot resist writing a few lines to congratulate you on the success of your book! I have read it with the greatest possible interest, and I think the descriptions and the language generally excellent. Everybody is reading it, and I only hear it spoken of with praise.'

The King was always anxious to express his compassion in practical ways. In 1904, for instance, during Cowes Regatta, he heard that his old friend, Mrs Arthur Paget, had fallen down a lift shaft. The moment the news reached him he wrote to her husband asking: 'Is there anything I can send her? Flowers or fruit or both? Has she a table to put across the bed for reading?' After Christopher Sykes fell on hard times, ruined by royal entertaining, the Prince told Knollys: 'I shall be furious if he gives me a birthday present as I do not wish him – with his reduced income – to spend a farthing on my account. I am sure to have his best wishes and that is quite sufficient.'

The King's kindness was not confined to those of whom he was fond. Few people exasperated him more than Arnold-Forster, whom he described on different occasions as 'not quite a gentleman,' 'hopeless,' and as 'obstinate as a mule.' Nevertheless, when the

Conservatives resigned in 1905, Arnold-Forster told the King that if he had achieved 'any small measure of success' at the War Office, it was in 'a large degree due to the unfailing encouragement and kindness he had received from His Majesty. Mr Arnold-Forster looks back with singular pleasure on the fact that he has never left the King's presence without feeling cheered and helped, and he is deeply conscious of the generous consideration that has been accorded to him.'

To the end of his days, King Edward took great pleasure in giving presents. 'It was this trait in his character that induced him to give so many decorations. He liked the obvious pleasure it gave the recipient.' One day, his private detective, Xavier Paoli, ventured to admire a tiny match-box engraved with a crown which the King wore on his watch-chain. Instantly, His Majesty unfastened it and said: 'Accept it my dear Paoli as a souvenir. I should like you to have it.'

The King's godson, Sir Edward Grey, maintained that 'warm human kindness was of the very substance of the man. The misfortune or unhappiness of anyone he knew caused him real discomfort; and he would do anything in his power to relieve it.' In 1910, a few days after King Edward died, Lord Charles Beresford, who had once quarrelled with him so violently over Lady Brooke's letter, wrote to George V to say that he would never forget the late King's 'kindness, generosity and affection in those happy years gone by. Nothing has or ever could remove from my mind the love and devotion I bore to the most kind-hearted and generous man I ever met.'

The King's 'astonishing memory of persons and names,' which Stanley remarked on in 1862, hardly ever failed him. Shortly after Holman Hunt completed his painting of London Bridge on the night of the Prince's wedding, His Royal Highness visited his studio to see it. After examining it minutely, he suddenly singled out Mr Combe's figure, which the artist had depicted in the crowd. 'I know that man!' he exclaimed. 'Wait a minute. I have seen him in the hunting-field with Lord Macclesfield's hounds. He rides a clever pony about fourteen hands high, and his beard blows over his shoulders. He is the head of a house at Oxford and not a College. Yes I remember now – it's the Printing Press.' His Majesty rarely needed to be briefed about people's careers: he knew already. Hence the gratifying feeling he conveyed to those he met that they were of such consequence in the world as to have left their mark on their Sovereign.

In July 1902 Lord Salisbury resigned on account of failing health. Some people suspected that his resignation was the result of a serious difference with King Edward respecting foreign policy. The Prime Minister, it was said, regarded the King as trespassing on his own special province and preferred to surrender office than independence. It was also rumoured that His Majesty had included some such name as Cassel or Lipton in the Coronation honours, to which Salisbury took objection. But, considering the Prime Minister was too ill to attend the Coronation, and indeed died within thirteen months of resigning, it would seem over-ingenious to seek alternative explanations to the one he gave at the time.

The King was not greatly distressed by Salisbury's departure. There was a certain intellectual aloofness about him which he found forbidding, and few of their tastes and pastimes coincided. The Prime Minister was utterly indifferent to fashionable society, deficient in small talk and careless about attire. His insular outlook discouraged the search for allies which the King deemed essential, and he was the only British statesman whose age, experience, reputation and authority overshadowed that of his Sovereign.

The King, on Lord Salisbury's advice, invited Arthur Balfour to succeed his uncle as Prime Minister. While Balfour was in his last year at Eton, William Cory wrote of him: 'He philosophizes in his youth, he will philosophize to the end.' Cory also predicted his pupil would one day occupy the highest office under the Crown. For a quarter of a century, between 1880 and 1905, the apogee of the British Empire, eminent Etonians presided over its destiny: Gladstone, Rosebery, Salisbury and Balfour.

From Eton, Balfour went to Trinity College, Cambridge, joined Randolph Churchill's 'Fourth Party,' and was appointed Chief Secretary for Ireland, where his ruthless policy earned him the epithet 'Bloody Balfour.' Between 1891 and 1892, and again between 1895 and 1902, he was Leader of the House and as such contrived to remain serenely unmoved by the rough-and-tumble of politics. As Ramsay MacDonald said: 'He saw a great deal of life from afar.' For all his Draconian reputation, the new Prime Minister looked doleful and apprehensive. Winston Churchill, who knew him well, described him as 'the best-mannered man I ever met – easy, courteous, patient, considerate, in every society and with great and small alike . . . His presence was a pleasure and his conversation a treat.'

King Edward was seldom entirely at ease with Balfour, who held irreverent views on the sacredness of monarchy. Neither his dialectical acrobatics nor his sceptical detachment appealed to His Majesty, who thought him distant, vague and indolent. Nor could he rid himself of the suspicion that Balfour regarded him with the same disdain he showed for public opinion. Even Queen Victoria had been a little in awe of her Chief Irish Secretary, whose formidable intellectual powers she found intimidating.

Balfour spent much of his time as Prime Minister struggling to prevent his administration from disintegrating. For half a century after the battle to repeal the Corn Laws, the principle of Free Trade had been accepted by all political parties. So long as Britain remained the 'Workshop of the World,' exporting more than she imported, it would have been rash to have provoked retaliatory tariffs by a policy of protection. But by the beginning of King Edward's reign, foreign manufacturers began flooding Britain's markets. Changing circumstances required a re-appraisal of traditional policies.

In the spring of 1903, Chamberlain told Herbert Gladstone that he had grown weary of the old controversies. 'You can burn your leaflets,' he said, 'we are going to talk about something else.' On 15 May, he delivered a speech from the Birmingham Town Hall, the capital of his empire, in which he deeply divided his party. Having just returned from a tour of South Africa, he challenged the principle of Free Trade, which, so he claimed, was ignorantly misinterpreted by a small remnant of Little Englanders. Unless the British Empire was held together with fiscal ties, it threatened to break apart. Imperial preference was in reality a system of free trade within the King's dominions. Tariff reform would protect British industry from an influx of cheap foreign manufactures, while at the same time uniting the Colonies. Chamberlain proclaimed that preferential duties within the Empire were the great issue of the day, which would at one stroke unite the Commonwealth, maintain employment, increase prosperity, provide new markets, cut the cost of living and create an additional source of revenue to finance social reform. It would also, of course, involve taxing food.

The morning after Chamberlain's speech, Asquith burst into Margot's bedroom with *The Times* in his hand. 'Wonderful news today,' he said, 'and it is only a question of time when we shall sweep this country.' If Chamberlain united the Liberals in defence of a cardinal tenet of their faith, by the same token he split his own party, many of whom feared to jettison free trade. Vainly attempting to hold his Cabinet together, Balfour resorted to formulas of such intricate subtlety that one back-bench Liberal commented: 'We are to have a ministry of balance, a government of philosophic doubt.'

Chamberlain recognized that it would take several years to convert the country. However strenuously he maintained that 'Tariff Reform means work for all,' he met with resistance to taxing food: 'the big loaf' against 'the little loaf.' King Edward's instinct was to leave well alone. During his formative years, the principle and practice of *laissez-faire* had found triumphant expression, and he now saw little reason to abandon free trade. Nevertheless, he had no desire to see Balfour's Government disintegrate in the first year of its life. So, on 8 August 1903, he wrote to ask the Prime Minister: 'Would it not be possible to refer the whole matter to a Royal Commission?' The question was of far 'too serious a character for any Cabinet to arrive at a just conclusion in one or two meetings, but if the Royal Commission were appointed without loss of time, consisting of the ablest men in the country, and thoroughly conversant with so difficult a problem, it would relieve Mr Balfour and the Cabinet of a great responsibility.' Balfour, however, rejected the King's proposal.

In September, Chamberlain resigned so as to be free to advocate his policies. His Majesty described his loss to the Government and to the Country as 'a very serious one. No Minister of the Crown could have worked harder or more conscientiously than Mr Chamberlain has in drawing the Colonies closer together with the Mother Country.' Not only did Balfour lose his Colonial Secretary, but the Chancellor of the Exchequer, Charles Ritchie, the Secretary of State for India, Lord George Hamilton, and the Lord President of the Council, the Duke of Devonshire, all vehement opponents of protection, also decided to leave the Government. When the King heard of their resignations, he invited the Prime Minister to Balmoral to discuss the crisis. 'I cannot approve of resignations being announced,' he told him, 'until I have thoroughly discussed the matter with you . . . It would not look well in the eyes of the Public that a matter of such importance should be settled without my seeing the Prime Minister.' But by the time the King's telegram reached Balfour, he had already given the news to the Press.

Some weeks before the reconstruction of the Government, the

King attended a gala performance at Covent Garden, in honour of President Loubet's visit to England. During the interval, His Majesty discussed the 'Motor Regulation Bill' with several Cabinet Ministers. It was absolutely right, he said, to 'tax the rich, but never the poor.' 'Especially their food, I hope, sir,' interposed the Chancellor of the Exchequer. 'Yes, yes, never tax the poor man's food. I will never give my assent to a bill taxing necessary food, and I do not care who knows that I have said so.' As the King returned to the Royal Box, the Duke of Devonshire whispered to Lord Balfour of Burleigh, 'Very good, we must send him on the stump.'

In the summer of 1903, while the Conservatives were engaged in tearing themselves apart over tariff reform, the King visited Ireland for the first time in his reign, landing at Kingstown on 21 July. Whatever grievances the Irish might nurture, they were determined to demonstrate their loyalty to the Crown. George Wyndham, the Irish Chief Secretary, described their Majesties passing through 'an interminable lane of frenzied enthusiasm. The King perfectly calm among dancing dervishes and horses mad with fear and excitement, bowing and smiling and waving his hands to the ragamuffins in the branches.' Wherever he went, he 'laughed, thanked us all and beamed enough to melt an iceberg.'

During this visit Wyndham presented over eighty deputations to their Majesties. Although they were supposed to present addresses, 'they did everything but that: shook the King's hand and marched off with address under arm, were retrieved and address extracted.' Wyndham could hardly find words to 'express the kindness and coolness of the King' who coached them in a reassuring whisper. 'Hand me the address,' he would say, and then accepted it 'as if gratified by finding such adepts in Court ceremonial.' Sometimes those presented to the King became so confused as to forget their set speeches. When they stammered some apology, he would shake them by the hand, murmuring: 'That's all right, quite all right. I quite understand, quite understand.'

The following spring the King and Queen returned to Ireland once more, thus spending longer there in the first three years of the reign than Queen Victoria in over half a century. But its problems were too intractable to be resolved by gracious gestures. Nevertheless, the loyalty and goodwill their Majesties evoked created a favourable climate for conciliation. Unfortunately, Balfour was too obsessed with political survival to exploit the King's magic.

Since the King's visit to India in 1875, he had always shown a personal concern for its welfare, and fully supported Balfour's decision in December 1903 to invite Lord Curzon to remain Viceroy for two more years in view of the distinguished manner in which the great Proconsul had represented the Crown. Some months before, at Curzon's insistence, Lord Kitchener had been appointed Commander-in-Chief of the Indian Army. It was not long, however, before they became involved in a series of furious disputes, principally over civilian interference in military matters. Kitchener protested about the dual control of the Indian Army, whereby executive power was vested in the Commander-in-Chief, but administrative decisions were left to the Indian Government. The bureaucracy which evolved to meet the demands of the system struck Kitchener as absurd. Two departments, for example, sat in the same building writing each other ten thousand letters a year. If only Gilbert had made this arrangement the theme of one of his operas it could hardly have survived the scrutiny of the Savoy Theatre. But Curzon argued that the machinery worked well enough, that it was sanctified by tradition, and that Kitchener's proposed reforms would lead to military dictatorship.

Both men solicited support for their views from political friends in England, and neither hesitated to avail himself of the assistance of the Press. Consequently the shots which were fired at Simla rang around Whitehall. On the merits of the dispute Churchill believed that there was 'no question that Curzon was right. But in craft, in slow intrigue, in strength of personality, in doubtful dangerous manoeuvres, the soldier beat the politician every time.' So, in the end, 'the Government of Curzon's own friends and the Secretary of State, Mr Brodrick, almost his best friend, pronounced against him, and pronounced against him in error.'

At the end of May 1905, Brodrick produced a report which unanimously recommended that the military aspects of army administration should be left exclusively to the Commander-in-Chief, a conclusion which Kitchener greeted with undisguised delight. King Edward supported the view that the General responsible for defending India should be given the power to carry out that task. It was always his instinct, once the right man had been found, to leave him as far as possible to work things out for himself. 'We soldiers,' Haig told Lord Knollys, 'certainly owe the King a great deal of gratitude for the important share he has taken in bringing about this satisfactory change.'

Even before Brodrick's report reached him, Curzon believed that his former friend was undermining his authority. Early in June 1905, Knollys received a 'very private and confidential' letter from Viceregal Lodge, Simla, complaining that Brodrick was placing the Viceroy in 'a false almost humiliating position.' 'For five years,' wrote Curzon, 'I worked without difficulty or friction with George Hamilton who knew a good deal about India and understood how to handle the Government of India. Now all is changed. The Secretary of State is continually interfering in matters of which he knows nothing, and exerting his authority in a manner which often leaves me in doubt whether there is any advantage in having either a Viceroy or a Government of India at all. I may therefore at any moment be driven to resignation for there comes a time at which one cannot perpetually go on being treated as I now am.' The letter ended with the request: 'Please show this to *nobody*, it is for your eyes alone.'

When the King was at Marienbad that August he learned that the Viceroy had carried out his threat, and at once sent him 'a truly consoling and gracious message.' Although the King took the view that the military authorities in India were justified in resisting civilian control, he was eager to see Curzon rewarded for his services. On 1 September, Knollys sent Balfour the following telegram: 'The King desires me to inform you that he thinks Viceroy of India should be offered an Earldom and at once. He hopes that considering Viceroy of India's character such an offer made immediately might soothe his feelings.' But Balfour maintained that it would be a serious mistake so to time the recognition of Curzon's services 'as to suggest that it was in the remotest degree connected with his action in the Curzon-Kitchener dispute.' The King reluctantly accepted this argument, and begged the returning Viceroy 'in the interests of the British Empire at large and especially as regards India, not to enter into any further controversy regarding the different issues with my Government which compelled you to resign.'

Before leaving India, Curzon thanked Knollys for a 'truly sympathetic letter,' and said that 'the kindness and gracious consideration' he had received 'at the hands of His Majesty the King' was a thing he could never forget. 'His first telegram to me from Marienbad and his later telegram from Balmoral, are documents such as a subject can rarely have received from his Sovereign, and they will remain among my most precious possessions. Deserted by all or nearly all my old friends at home, and misrepresented to a degree of which few are aware, and which I have been powerless to check, you can imagine how consoling it has been to me to think that the King, whom it has been my pride to serve, should have apprehended the facts with so quick an insight, and should have extended to me so noble-minded and generous a support. I can never forget his magnanimity to my dying day.' It is no mean tribute to the loyalty King Edward inspired in his foremost servants that although he supported Kitchener's struggle for independence, he retained Curzon's gratitude.

Throughout his reign the King was forced to fight a rearguard action in defence of his prerogatives, and there was no more persistent trespasser on this hallowed ground than Arthur James Balfour. In common with Queen Victoria, King Edward attached the greatest importance to the discretionary authority vested in the Crown, and Ministers who treated him as 'a mere signing machine' were soon shown the error of their ways. The royal prerogative consisted of a residual legacy of powers belonging to the Sovereign which had not been assumed by the King's Ministers. In the absence of any written Constitution, the precise nature and extent of such powers might be variously interpreted, as was demonstrated in the seventeenth century in the conflicts between the Stuarts and their Parliaments.

As King Edward saw it, his principal prerogatives were those of pardoning prisoners, summoning and dissolving Parliament, selecting and dismissing Ministers, declaring War or Peace, making treaties, ceding territory, creating peers, and appointing Bishops and Judges. In most of these instances, it had become customary for the King to exercise his prerogative on the advice of the Prime Minister. 'The functions of the Monarch,' wrote Lord Esher, with all the authority of one who had dug deep in the Royal Archives, 'are those of influence and criticism, a restraining rather than impelling power. Our people are essentially conservative and they are very suspicious of "initiative." It is usually that quality in a government which precipitates a fall.'

Balfour grudgingly acknowledged that the King was entitled to be told of government decisions, and the reasons which led to their being taken, but denied his right to be informed of preliminary discussions, or of differences which took place before agreement was reached. Consequently, he saw fit to deprive the King of confidential papers produced while policies were in process of maturing, a ruling which found little favour at Buckingham Palace, and which gravely encroached upon what Bagehot listed as the Sovereign's 'three rights – the right to be consulted, the right to encourage, the right to warn.'

Balfour further encroached on the royal prerogative by maintaining that the Prime Minister had the right to choose or dismiss Ministers without the King's consent. Before leaving office, he even claimed that the Ministry of the day was entitled to insist on a dissolution if a majority in the Commons desired an election.

In July 1905, Balfour was defeated by four votes when Redmond succeeded in carrying a hostile amendment. The Liberals maintained it was his duty to resign, but Balfour argued that 'There was only one plain test whether the Government can carry on the business of the Country, and that plain test is, whether the House of Commons support them.' The King regarded this proposition as totally unacceptable because it took no account whatever of the Sovereign's responsibility for summoning and dissolving Parliaments. Nor did he care for the unrepentant effrontery with which the Prime Minister advanced novel doctrines as if they were sanctioned by long-established custom.

In November 1905, Chamberlain delivered a speech at Bristol in which he charged the Prime Minister with refusing to face fiscal issues. For several months the Opposition had been proclaiming that the Emperor had no clothes, and now the foremost of his erstwhile lieutenants publicly admitted as much. In the same month, Campbell-Bannerman told an audience at Stirling that if his party won the next election he did not intend to bring forward a measure for Home Rule during the life of the next Parliament. Nevertheless, he proposed 'step by step' to move in that direction. Two days later, Lord Rosebery attacked him for having revived the issue. 'Emphatically, explicitly and once for all,' he told an audience at Bodmin, 'I cannot serve under that banner.' Balfour, miscalculating the extent to which Rosebery's ill-judged defection would tear the Liberals apart, decided to resign, fondly hoping that he had paid out enough rope with which they would hang themselves. But when the trap dropped it was Balfour who swung at the end of the noose.

The King and the Liberals

On the afternoon of 4 December 1905, the King came up from Sandringham to receive the Prime Minister's resignation. A few minutes after Balfour returned to Downing Street, Knollys wrote Campbell-Bannerman the following letter.

> Buckingham Palace
> 4 Dec. 1905
> 4.45
>
> Dear Sir Henry,
>   Mr Balfour has just placed his resignation and that of the Government in the hands of the King, I am desired by His Majesty to acquaint you that he would be glad too if you would have the goodness to come to Buckingham Palace at a quarter to eleven o'clock tomorrow (Tuesday) morning.
>
> Believe me,
> Yours vy truly,
> Knollys

The haste with which this communication was sent evidently betrayed the impeccable Knollys into more than one solecism.

Immediately after his audience with the King, Sir Henry described what took place to Asquith. 'His Majesty had been most amiable and expressed himself delighted at hearing he would undertake to form a government. He warned him, however, that being Prime Minister and leading the Commons at the same time would be heavy work, and added: "We are not as young as we were, Sir Henry!" He suggested he should go to the Lords, to which Campbell-Bannerman answered that no doubt he would ultimately be obliged to do this, but that he would prefer starting in the Commons if only for a short time. The King, instead of pushing the matter, seemed to fall in very pleasantly with the idea and shook him warmly by the hand. Knowing that he ought to kneel and kiss hands, C-B advanced and waited, but the King interrupted by some commonplace remark; when he had finished speaking, C-B again advanced meaning to kneel, but the King only wrung his hand, at which he felt the interview was over, as to have another try would have been grotesque. He retired from the presence of His Majesty to Lord Knollys's room and told him he feared he had never kissed hands at all, to which Lord Knollys replied that it did not matter.'

In earlier days the King had felt serious misgivings about his new Prime Minister, who only four years before had publicly deplored the Government's 'most unworthy policy of enforcing unconditional surrender upon those who were to be their loyal and contented subjects in the new colonies.' But even worse was his celebrated criticism of the methods employed by the British Army in fighting the Boers. Tired of complacent excuses about War being War, or being told that the campaign was virtually at an end, Sir Henry posed the question: 'When was a War not a War?' and solved the problem by suggesting 'When it was carried on by *methods of barbarism* in South Africa.' For all the King's cordiality, it was some time before he could bring himself to forgive this remark. Furthermore, His Majesty suspected, and not without justice, that Campbell-Bannerman was one of the more leisurely of mankind. His political indolence may be explained, if not excused, by his scepticism about the benefits of legislating. Arthur Ponsonby, who saw his methods of working at close quarters, acknowledged that Campbell-Bannerman was too easygoing, and remembered him once confessing that he had never read a Bill or Blue Book through.

It was common knowledge that the King was exceptionally tolerant of advanced opinions. Moreover, Sir Henry was one of those reassuring Radicals who owned a castle in Scotland and a house in Belgrave Square. His passion for France was a further recommendation as far as the King was concerned. He loved it so much that he would sometimes take a return ticket on a channel steamer just to have luncheon in Calais.

In June 1905, Lord Carrington arranged a dinner to give the King an opportunity of meeting Campbell-Bannerman. They got on famously and talked until one in the morning. 'If we come in,' said Carrington at the end of the evening, 'Sir Henry will make your Majesty a first-rate Prime Minister.' That summer at Marienbad the King went out of his way to cultivate the Liberal leader. Sir Henry he found was excellent company and displayed the rugged straightforwardness which Queen Victoria found so attractive in John Brown. For his part, Campbell-Bannerman was surprised to discover what 'a wise and excellent' Sovereign King Edward was, confounding 'in the most amazing way all those who doubted his qualities as a ruler and his capacity as a statesman.'

Campbell-Bannerman's administration was exceptionally talented, unavoidably inexperienced, and almost too rich in its diversity. One of its more eccentric members was John Burns, the first working man to sit in a Cabinet. When the Prime Minister invited him to become President of the Local Government Board, he congratulated him on 'the most popular appointment' he had made. In fact, Burns did little to keep the red flag flying, and became increasingly out of touch with those whose interests he was supposed to be representing. His greatest service to the Government was that his presence in it broadened the base of its popular appeal. His role was less that of a commanding officer than a regimental mascot.

If Burns was to be believed, he enjoyed the entire confidence of the King. 'Me and 'im get on first rate together,' he proclaimed with pardonable hyperbole. Fastidiously courteous to all whom he encountered, His Majesty, nevertheless, regarded his President of the Local Government Board with more apprehension than relish. He was especially nervous lest JB might turn up at his first Court function in some unsuitable garb. Burns, however, appeared in a perfectly-fitting gold coat, made by the King's tailor, for whom he had worked in his youth as an errand boy.

Of greater concern to King Edward, were Burns's speeches. His long apprenticeship in opposition had conditioned him to protest, and he frequently forgot that as a Member of the Government he shared a collective responsibility for the policies it pursued. Moreover, he did not find it easy to break the habit of Radical rhetoric. While fighting the election, Burns told audiences up and down the country that he favoured the destruction of the House of Lords, regardless of the fact that such sweeping constitutional reform played no part in the Government's programme. The King at once protested to the Prime Minister, pointing out that as he had 'so recently recommended several prominent members of the House of Commons to be peers' he was 'somewhat surprised that a member of the Cabinet should have made this declaration.'

Campbell-Bannerman said he could well understand His Majesty's 'surprise on reading the phrases in Mr John Burns's address. He will communicate with Mr Burns at once and inform him that Your Majesty has directed his attention to the matter, and that it is incumbent upon a Cabinet Minister to refrain from the expression of extreme views unless with the consent and leave of the head of Your Majesty's Government. Sir Henry Campbell-Bannerman would beg humbly to express his regret that Your Majesty should have been thus troubled, and he hopes that Your Majesty will excuse the error that has been committed, which is due solely to the inexperience in official responsibility of the Minister concerned.'

Parliament was dissolved on 8 January 1906, and the merits of free trade and tariff reform were debated from one end of the country to the other. Beatrice Webb recognized that the Liberal victory was essentially Conservative, the working class preferring the familiar tradition of free trade to a revolutionary tariff policy. When it came to auctioning social reforms, Balfour was dramatically outbid by a party willing 'to give and not to count the cost.' Much play was made by the Liberals of Milner's policy of employing Chinese workers in the Rand Gold Mines under a system of indenture. This so-called 'Chinese slavery' became a magnificent electoral asset, well calculated to horrify trade unionists, to discredit Balfour, and to expose the ugly face of Imperialism.

As the election results became known, King Edward wrote to the Prince of Wales to say that 'The Liberal, or, rather, Radical wave has simply swamped the Unionists.' There were 377 Liberals in the new House of Commons, giving them a majority of 84 over a combined Opposition of 157 Conservatives, 83 Irish Nationalists and 53 assorted Labour Members. Amongst a distinguished array of statesmen buried under the rubble of this electoral earthquake, were Balfour and Brodrick. Writing to Knollys on 17 January 1906, the former Prime Minister described his crushing defeat as 'something more important than the swing of the pendulum or all the squabbles about free trade and fiscal reform. We are face to face (no doubt in milder form) with the Socialistic difficulties which loom so large on the continent. Unless I am greatly mistaken, the election of 1906 inaugurates a new era.'

In 1832, the Duke of Wellington remarked of the reformed Commons: 'I never saw so many shocking bad hats in my life.' In much the same spirit, Knollys complained to Esher that 'the old idea that the House of Commons was an assemblage of "gentlemen" has quite passed away.' Even one of the Westminster policemen observed to Philip Snowden that he noticed a great change in the new Members. The electoral reforms of 1867 and 1884 were evidently beginning to bear fruit. Up and down the country, supposedly safe Conservative seats had crumbled, and Liberal candidates, who would not have risked sixpence on their chances of success, were astonished to be elected. Nearly half the Members of the 1906 House of Commons were newcomers.

After the Government had been in power for nine months, Esher gave Knollys an account of 'a very interesting talk' he had had with John Morley, Secretary of State for India. He discovered that Morley was 'genuinely fond of his India Office work and engrossed in its details. Of course, contact with the absorbing machinery of government in India, has broadened his sympathy for Imperial responsibilities.' Moreover, he was 'keenly alive to the preponderating elements of ignorance and disregard of the greater national interests in the present House of Commons.' It only required, so he said, 'A very little; a word or two spoken rashly' to 'throw our majority into the "perish India school".' Morley remembered saying to Gladstone that if he withdrew his influence from the Parliament of 1880, 'it might rush into wild excesses: but in his opinion, the Parliament of 1880 was Conservative when compared with this one. Evidently, he thinks the present majority so ill instructed, and so stupidly sentimental that only a few experienced men, C-B, Asquith, Grey, himself and Haldane, stand between the government of the country and anarchy. Perhaps I have slightly coloured his language, but this is the essence of what he said, in his cold didactic style. "Mr G" he said, "would have silenced Lloyd George or dismissed him from office. C-B – much as he would like to – can do neither; and that is the difference between the two epochs".'

Although the King liked Campbell-Bannerman a good deal better than Balfour, and once told Knollys it would be 'a bad day for the country' if anything happened to him, he had as much, if not more, reason to complain of the inadequate information his new Prime Minister vouchsafed him. Sir Henry's letter to His Majesty provoked irritated marginal comments such as: 'The information as usual is meagre,' 'What valuable information!' 'A very brief account!' When Knollys complained that 'the Prime Minister's reports of Cabinet proceedings were really making a fool of the King' and that 'there is no use in Ministers *liking* the King if he is treated like a puppet,' Esher told him that nobody could 'make a silk purse out of a sow's ear.'

'Your Majesty,' wrote Esher in April 1906, after Campbell-Bannerman had been Prime Minister for four months, 'has noticed that the communications from the Prime Minister are few and somewhat trivial. From what he has seen of the way the Government business is managed, Viscount Esher believes the reason of this to be that the Prime Minister has aged a good deal lately, and finds it even more difficult than hitherto to fix his attention upon details. Never a laborious man, his disinclination to master troublesome subjects has now given place to impossibility, and Viscount Esher believes that the main reason why he writes so meagrely to Your Majesty is that he has very little to tell. The work of the Government, even on large questions of policy, is carried on in the various departments, practically without reference to the Prime Minister.

A year later, Esher noted in his Journal: 'I have had a letter from Francis Knollys complaining of the meagre information sent to the King by C-B. He asks what can be done? It is not easy to advise. C-B is too old not to be incurable. The indolence of age is upon him. I don't for a moment believe that he wishes to keep the King in the dark, but he cannot bring himself to write. It thoroughly bores him ... The result is sad, both in the interests of tradition and the Monarchy. In the interests of both, the practice which prevailed under the Queen should be adhered to, because the position of the Sovereign should be altogether independent of the personality of the Monarch, if the Monarchy is to stand. The King's . . . office should be as sacred as his person, and C-B is lowering the former.'

The King was also distressed by Campbell-Bannerman's parliamentary bad manners, and could not be made to understand that no self-respecting Radical could risk being thought too courteous. Balfour returned to the House in March, having been found a seat for the City of London. His first speech as Leader of the Opposition was a pitiful exercise in sophistry: all footwork and no punches. It only took the Prime Minister a couple of minutes to leave his opponent writhing on the canvas. 'The right honourable gentleman,' he said, 'is like the Bourbons. He has learned nothing. He comes back to this new House of Commons with the same airy graces – the same subtle dialectics – and the same light and frivolous way of dealing with great questions. He little knows the temper of the new House of Commons if he thinks those methods will prevail here. The right honourable gentleman has . . . asked certain questions which he seemed to think were posers . . . I have no direct answer to give to them. They are utterly futile, nonsensical and misleading . . . I say, enough of this foolery . . . Move your amendments and let us get to business.' The cheers of Sir Henry's Liberal supporters might almost have been heard at Lambeth, and even the Conservatives conceded that he had won a notable victory. But the King, writing to the Prince of Wales, told him that the debates in the House of Commons were not dignified. 'The PM having so large a majority does not care what he says or does and the rudeness of his language is deplorable.'

Not long after the Liberals were returned to power in 1906, disputes broke out between the two Houses of Parliament. One of the first measures to come under attack was a bill to modify controversial features of the 1902 Education Act, Balfour's principal legislative achievement. Regardless of the mandate its sponsors claimed to possess, the House of Lords amended it out of existence.

King Edward had long maintained that neither the Monarchy nor the House of Lords should be dragged into party politics, and that as both derived their authority from the hereditary principle, to challenge either was to challenge both. The House of Lords, having rejected Liberal measures with conspicuous partisanship, could hardly claim immunity from counter-attack by pretending to be impartial. Whenever possible, the King, as the custodian of the Constitution, sought to encourage harmony, fearing that squabbles between the Houses of Parliament would dispel the mystique surrounding government. But even His Majesty's conciliatory gifts failed to persuade Conservative peers to vote for Radical bills.

In an effort to reach a compromise, King Edward invited the Archbishop, Randall Davidson, and the Prime Minister, to stay a few days at Windsor in the middle of November. The two men held several discussions about what Campbell-Bannerman called a 'very bad business.' More than once he protested that he could not restrain his backbenchers, leaving Davidson persuaded that he was 'terribly in the hands of the more popular force among his followers,' and that he greatly under-rated the bill's 'anti-Church' character.

Despite all King Edward's efforts to prevent a constitutional conflict, Lord Lansdowne and his colleagues persisted in their strategy. Campbell-Bannerman was consequently confronted with the choice of trying to recover the original measure by stripping off layer after layer of destructive amendments, or of refusing to accept any of them, a much less laborious process. On 8 December, he told the King that the Cabinet had agreed to reject the Lords' amendments *en bloc*, rather than try to modify a mutilated bill. The King replied that he could not see much sign on the Government's part of the 'spirit of concession,' and that he was afraid from what Sir Henry said 'that the chances of a compromise are not very bright.'

A few days before Christmas, Lord Lansdowne's motion that the House of Lords 'do insist upon their amendments to which the Commons had disagreed,' was carried by 132 votes to 52. Campbell-Bannerman contemplated taking up the gauntlet and holding a general election on the issue, but in the end decided that, if battle was to be joined, it would be wiser to fight on more favourable ground. On 20 December, the Prime Minister told the Commons that he proposed to drop the bill, but warned their Lordships that they had won a Pyrrhic victory.

After the electoral landslide of 1906, Campbell-Bannerman had an overall majority of 84, but on most issues he could rely on the votes of the Irish Nationalists and Labour Party, which enlarged it to over 200. The Conservative majority in the House of Lords, however, was even more overwhelming. Only 83 Peers out of a total of 602 claimed to be Government supporters.

On 15 January 1906, before the full extent of the Conservative defeat was recognized, Balfour announced in a speech at Nottingham that he proposed to ensure that 'the great Unionist Party should still control, whether in power or whether in Opposition, the destinies of this great Empire.' Two months later, he told Lord Lansdowne that it was vital that Conservatives 'in the two Houses shall not work as two separate armies, but shall co-operate in a common plan of campaign.' The King, impatient of party intrigue, doubted the wisdom of Tory strategy, and warned Balfour that in exploiting his majority in the Lords he risked aggravating ill-feeling between the Houses, increasing demands for constitutional change, and rendering conciliation impossible.

When Campbell-Bannerman decided against holding an election in December 1906, at a moment when Churchill and Lloyd George expressed themselves willing to fight, he was only postponing the day of battle not surrendering. If some elated Conservatives persuaded themselves that the Liberals were on the run, the King had no such illusions. Before leaving Paris for Biarritz in March 1907, he remarked to Knollys: 'I hope the Prime Minister will not abolish the House before I return.'

Apart from Balfour, nobody did more than Lloyd George to ensure that the House of Lords remained politically controversial. The instant the kettle threatened to go off the boil, up went the Celtic gas. As early as September 1906, in a speech at Llanelly, he expressed his readiness to diminish the power of what he sarcastically described as 'that exalted Chamber.' The King regarded such language as sacrilege and protested to the Prime Minister, who assured him that he had 'admonished' the offender 'to avoid such a tone in future.' Lloyd George, he remarked, 'is essentially a fighting man, and has not yet learned that once he gets inside an office his sword and spear should only be used on extreme occasions, and with the consent of his colleagues.'

His Majesty was only partly convinced by Sir Henry's explanations. In particular, he remained deeply sceptical about the suggestion that as Lloyd George's speech had been delivered in Welsh, the translation might be at fault. What the President of the Board of Trade had been reported as saying was unmistakably authentic. Despite his Sovereign's displeasure, Lloyd George proceeded to tell the Palmerston Club at Oxford that the foremost issue of the day was 'whether the country is to be governed by the King and his Peers or by the King and his people.'

Lloyd George's remarks provoked instant protest from Sandringham. 'Dear Sir Henry,' wrote Knollys on 3 December, 'The King desires me to point out to you that Mr Lloyd George brought in His Majesty's name in the speech which he made against the House of Lords at Oxford. The King sees it is useless to attempt to prevent Mr Lloyd George from committing breaches of good taste and propriety by abstaining from attacking, as a Cabinet Minister, that branch of the legislature, though His Majesty has more than once protested to you against them ... But His Majesty feels that he has a right, and it is one on which he intends to insist, that Mr Lloyd George shall not introduce the Sovereign's name into these violent tirades of his, and he asks you as Prime Minister to be so good as to take the necessary steps to prevent a repetition of this violation of constitutional practice, and of good taste.'

In the 'King's Speech,' at the opening of Parliament in February 1907, reference was made to 'serious questions' affecting the working of the Constitution, which had 'arisen from unfortunate differences between the two Houses.' A committee was set up to examine solutions of the difficulty, but its recommendations were so intricate that the Prime Minister revived Bright's proposal that the House of Lords should only be granted a temporary power of veto. In June, Sir Henry moved a resolution in the House of Commons: 'That, in order to give effect to the will of the people as expressed by their elected representatives, it is necessary that the power of the other House to alter or reject bills passed by this House should be so restricted by Law as to secure that within the limits of a single Parliament the final decision of the Commons shall prevail.'

In the course of his remarks, Sir Henry spoke scathingly of Balfour, 'at the winding of whose horn the portcullis over the way comes rattling down.' No other Leader of the Opposition, he claimed, had committed what he could only describe as the 'treachery of openly calling in the other House to override this House.' It had become impossible to doubt that the Second Chamber was 'being utilized as a mere *annexe* of the Unionist Party . . . One begins to doubt, in fact – I certainly doubt – whether he or his party have ever fully accepted representative institutions.'

In what F. E. Smith described as 'a brilliant and rancorous speech,' Winston Churchill declared that 'the general election of 1906 was the most vehement expression of public opinion which this generation has any knowledge of; and that expression of public force was countered . . . by the most arbitrary and uncompromising assertion of aristocratic privilege.' The Upper House was 'one-sided, hereditary, unpurged, irresponsible, absentee.'

Despite a rising tide of radical fury, and despite the fact that the House of Lords mangled or destroyed two Scottish Land Bills in August, Campbell-Bannerman hesitated to give legislative effect to his June resolution. In September, he spent a brief holiday at Balmoral, during which he was reminded once more that the dispute between the two Houses was of grave concern to the King. But that did not discourage him from telling an audience at Edinburgh that unless the Lords ceased to reject bills which the Commons had passed with enormous majorities, he would be compelled to seek a mandate from the Country to curb their powers. Soon after, he became mortally ill, and was forced to leave others to finish the fight.

Both the King and Campbell-Bannerman took a great deal of trouble over appointing bishops and deans, a subject upon which they tended to disagree. Sir Henry, himself a Presbyterian, believed it was time to give Evangelicals 'a turn.' His Patronage Secretary, Henry Higgs, noticed that the Prime Minister did not care for the notion which prevailed on the Episcopal Bench that bishops should be scholars and gentlemen. 'I have no patience,' he said, 'with professors of a religion founded by fishermen who think that the higher posts in the Church must be preserved for the highly-born and the highly educated. I have little doubt that St Peter dropped his h's and that Our Saviour's Sermon on the Mount was uttered in the broadest Galilean dialect.' As Lord Hugh Cecil once remarked: 'Our Lord was not a gentleman.'

The most troublesome appointment with which Campbell-Bannerman had to deal was the Bishopric of Chichester. So many clergy in the diocese had gone over to Rome that a strong man was needed to diminish the rate of conversions. In November 1907, the Prime Minister wrote to Knollys explaining the problems of filling the vacant see. 'The peculiarity of the case is that in certain residential towns – Brighton, Worthing, Eastbourne – sacerdotalism has under the late bishop been allowed to go to extremes.' Within the last dozen years, 'no fewer than seventeen vicars or curates have gone over to the Roman Church. There is therefore a strong demand for a stalwart Evangelical, but this would in my opinion be a great mistake: the evil must be grappled with by someone more congenial but who will lend no countenance to illegalities. Such a man I believe is the Rev. H. Russell Wakefield.'

The King, however, was far from convinced, and told Knollys that he would 'like to have the Archbishop of Canterbury's opinion' concerning the Prime Minister's candidate for Chichester. It was clear, wrote His Majesty, that the new bishop 'should neither be a High or Low Churchman – but if a Broad Churchman he would probably do.' Nevertheless, he could not help wondering whether it was 'a good qualification for a bishop that Mr Wakefield had twice been Mayor of Marylebone?'

As the Archbishop shared the King's misgivings about Russell Wakefield, Knollys told the Prime Minister, as tactfully as he could, to think again. 'The King,' he wrote on 23 November, 'is always very reluctant to disagree with any recommendation of yours, but he has his own views as to the qualifications required for the higher appointments in the Church, and he is afraid he must ask you to be so good as to submit the name of some other clergyman for the Bishopric of Chichester.'

Campbell-Bannerman's Patronage Secretary regarded Knollys's

letter as a 'sinister document,' and wrote Sir Henry a memorandum explaining his objections to it. 'The selection of the Bishop is an Act-of-State which the Reformation cut off from the Church and handed over to the Head of the Nation . . . Responsible as you are, your advice ought not to need the concurrence of the Primate.' Indeed, State patronage arose in the first instance from 'our horror of being priest ridden,' and the constitution consequently gave the Archbishop no voice in choosing his colleagues. 'It is bad enough that he should cripple your legislation without blocking your executive action.' Higgs objected even more strongly to Knollys's assertion that His Majesty had 'his own views' on ecclesiastical appointments. 'I feel pretty sure,' wrote the exasperated secretary, ʋthat these views are something like this – "Above all things get a gentleman!' "

On his way to Biarritz, Campbell-Bannerman wrote to Knollys once more, telling him of his 'great perplexity about the Chichester vacancy. To speak quite frankly (but quite confidentially) my difficulties are these. There has undoubtedly been great dissatisfaction with the stamp of men generally put on the bench lately: not only on the ground of the section of the Church they were taken from but also because of their poor intellectual equipment. I am therefore averse from continuing the same stamp of nominee, however excellent they may be in certain respects. Again I cannot recommend to the King for elevation to the bench any one who is, or has the reputation of being, sacerdotal in his views and practices. Besides purely ecclesiastical considerations, I cannot disregard political aspects. If these are to count for nothing where is my *raison d'être* in the matter? Say what we like, politics do come in: and if clergymen in the Church who support the Liberals (and they are many) see flagrant and active opponents of the Government promoted over their heads, they will naturally be discouraged and have a sense of injustice. Not that I would make politics the test or reward of political action; but of course I should like to see some representation of my opinions on the Bench of Bishops.'

In the end the problem was resolved by the appointment of Dr Ridgeway, Dean of Carlisle, a moderate Churchman whom Sir Henry described as 'broadminded, devout, active, affable.'

The King, so far from being afraid of High Churchmen, often accompanied Alix to All Saints, Margaret Street, which was renowned for the excellence of its music and the splendour of its ritual. Services at Sandringham, while hardly Tractarian, were not conducted in ignorance of the fact that the Prayer Book's liturgy derived from the Catholic tradition of pre-Reformation England. In matters of religion, as in much else, King Edward favoured compromise. His subjects belonged to so many different faiths, that he did not wish to identify himself too exclusively even with Anglicanism. When King Carlos of Portugal and the Crown Prince were shot by left-wing assassins in February 1907, His Majesty attended a Requiem Mass in their memory at St James's Church, Spanish Place, having driven there with the Queen and a Sovereign's Escort. The *Protestant Alliance* declared that even James II had hesitated to attend the Mass in State, but the King ignored their protests, preferring to be guided by his own unerring instinct.

Another matter about which the King and Campbell-Bannerman were unable to agree was Suffragettes. His Majesty regarded their conduct as 'outrageous' and told Sir Henry that their 'militancy does their cause (for which I have no sympathy) much harm.' He was, however, in favour of Mrs Sidney Webb and Miss Octavia Hill being made members of the Poor Law Commission set up in 1905. The Prime Minister, on the other hand, looked on the movement with dilatory benevolence, but refused to commit himself on the subject in his Election Manifesto. In March 1907, he supported a private member's bill to give women the vote, but it was talked out by several of his colleagues. 'Thank heaven those dreadful women have not yet been enfranchised,' wrote the King to the Prince of Wales. 'It would have been far more dignified if the PM had not spoken on the bill – or backed it up. But he appears to wish to stand well with everyone!'

The last years of King Edward's reign saw an alarming growth of direct action. It seemed that there were increasing numbers of people who despaired of the parliamentary process and looked to strikes and demonstrations to secure their ends. Even a group of Duchesses caught the infection and exhorted the public not to 'lick stamps' so strongly were they opposed to National Insurance. 'Were there now to be *two* classes in the land,' demanded Lloyd George, '*one* class which could obey the laws if they liked; the *other* which must obey whether they liked it or not?' If legislation to insure people against poverty and misery was to be optional, 'was the law for the preservation of game to be optional? Was the payment of rent to be optional?' When Mrs Pankhurst and her followers failed to persuade the Government to give them votes, they took to the streets to further their demands. When the Unionists proved unable to get their way over Ireland, they armed Ulster. When working men wanted higher wages, they threatened a general strike. The King became increasingly disturbed by violence and unrest. Perhaps Balfour was right in supposing that England had caught the Continental disease, which had 'produced massacres in St Petersburg, riots in Vienna, and Socialist processions in Berlin.' It is not only in retrospect that the splendours of Edwardian England seem fleeting and insubstantial. The King himself believed that his grandson would never reign and that the red flag would flutter above the Mall.

After speaking at Bristol on 14 November 1907, Campbell-Bannerman suffered the first of a series of heart attacks. The King advised him to convalesce at Biarritz. Sir Henry returned to Downing Street in January, but retired to bed the following month with what was called 'influenza'. Asquith took over the Government in his absence, thus being cast in the role of Crown Prince. Already Knollys was contemplating the succession. As early as 4 January 1908, he told Austen Chamberlain that many Liberals appeared to believe 'that if anything happened to C-B the Party would go to smash in six months.' He maintained that 'Grey was the best man to succeed him,' that the choice lay with the King, and that of course he might send for Grey, and overrule Grey's personal objections. 'Personally,' he added, 'I like Asquith, and I like Mrs Asquith, though some people don't; but I don't think he is quite the right stamp of man for Prime Minister.'

Later that January, Esher told Knollys that 'should the Prime Minister die or retire, his loss will be more felt than ever, because his influence over the strong Liberal sections of the Party can alone keep those sections under restraint . . . The danger for the coming year or two is that a Liberal Government, in order to avoid a great secession in Parliament, and facing with a timid spirit socialistic demands, may yield to the pressure of the wire pullers, and starve the naval and military votes for the purpose of giving large doles to semi-socialistic experiments. It makes one doubt whether Grey or Asquith could, even if they would, be strong enough to stem this torrent. They command a certain section in the House of Commons, but carry little weight in the Country . . . For this reason, I think that in addition to Grey and Asquith, it is worth your while to consider Morley as a possible successor to the PM. He is beyond all cavil and reproach a strong representative trusted radical. He is known to be a strong opponent of socialism in every form, and this has not weakened his power in the councils of the Liberal Party. He could, with impunity, do things which neither Grey nor Asquith could do, and be certain of support from the Party. Of course, there are all sorts of drawbacks, but I only write this because it has come home to me very strongly in the last few days, that he may have to be thought of as "in the running".'

Two days before leaving for Biarritz on 5 March 1908, the King told Asquith that 'he had quite made up his mind' to send for him 'in the event of anything happening to Campbell-Bannerman, or of his sending in his resignation . . . He said be thought C-B very useful so long as he was equal to the job, as making things smooth and keeping people together. But it was evident he was breaking up, and we must provide for the future.' During this audience, the King told Asquith that, if Sir Henry resigned before Easter, he would have to come out to Biarritz to kiss hands.

Asquith, the son of a Yorkshire farmer, was a self-made man. Not that the King held that against him, for he shared Samuel Smiles's reverence for those who rose to eminence from humble origins. After a spectacular career at the City of London School, Asquith went to Balliol, joining the college the very term that Jowett became its Master. In 1876 he was called to the Bar and appeared as a junior counsel on behalf of Parnell and against Sir William Gordon-Cumming. Ten years later he became a Member of Parliament as an ardent disciple of Gladstone.

Before going abroad, the King drove to Downing Street, which he approached from the garden gate in the Horse Guards in the hope of arriving unnoticed. Campbell-Bannerman was deeply touched by the visit. Vaughan Nash, his Private Secretary, told Knollys: 'The King appeared on Wednesday . . . He stopped about twenty minutes and Sir H was none the worse for it . . . But I was glad when the old place fell back into its proper gloom and quietude.' During their conversation, the King urged Sir Henry, provided his strength permitted, to postpone all thought of resignation until after Easter. Queen Alexandra sent the Prime Minister some flowers. On the accompanying card she wrote: 'A few violets I brought back from Windsor in the hopes that they may cheer the poor patient. With heartfelt wishes for a speedy recovery.'

The King himself was far from well: hence his anxiety to stay at Biarritz as long as possible. Past experience proved that the sea air and spring sunshine did wonders for his bronchitis. So concerned were his doctors about his condition that they urged him to stay abroad for six weeks rather than three. This he agreed to do, but nothing would persuade him to let them issue a bulletin.

In the middle of March, the Prime Minister showed signs of wishing to resign, and King Edward instructed Sir Arthur Davidson, who temporarily found himself combining the roles of secretary and equerry, to tell Nash to impress on Sir Henry the King's 'earnest hope that he will not think of resigning before Easter. Apart from any political considerations, the King feels sure that it would react injuriously on Sir Henry's health and might retard his recovery.'

On March 17, Knollys wrote to the King to say that he feared that Sir H. Campbell-Bannerman would 'not now last long. Owing to Your Majesty having seen Mr Asquith before you went abroad, everything ought to run easily and smoothly when the office of Prime Minister becomes vacant. It will be a very simple affair as he will now have simply to go to Biarritz, "kiss hands" and then come home again. As he told Your Majesty that he proposed to make no alterations whatever at first, he will merely become Prime Minister in addition to being Chancellor of the Exchequer: a similar course was adopted by Mr Pitt, Mr Canning and Mr Gladstone. There will be no complication or difficulties of any description as there will be no names to submit to you and no "shuffling of the cards." May I remind Your Majesty that the Queen summoned Lord Russell to Balmoral *the day after* Lord Palmerston's death and that she did not wait for the funeral.'

The King wrote back four days later to say that he quite agreed 'that when the worst occurs to the poor Prime Minister, which I much fear will not be long in coming, Asquith should come out here *alone* to discuss matters and "kiss hands".' After deploring 'all the pernicious bills that are being brought in,' he said that he very much doubted that Asquith would 'be able to keep his Government and Party in order as C-B did. He has neither the strength or ability. C-B was a great gentleman and poor Asquith is so deplorably common not to say vulgar! Oh! for the shades of Canning, Pitt and Gladstone!'

On 23 March, Knollys told the King that he had heard that Asquith was now contemplating 'a regular reconstruction of the Government.' If this turned out to be true, he was afraid that it would be bound to inconvenience His Majesty, 'as there will have to be a meeting of the Privy Council under his auspices, "kissing of hands" etc. etc.'

Two days later, Knollys wrote again to say that he had seen Asquith that morning 'and the following is what he told me, but he begged me to consider they were his present ideas only, and that he might not be able to carry them all out. He thinks that Lord Elgin should retire. He is of no use either in the Cabinet (Colonial Secretary) or in the House of Lords. That Lord Tweedmouth (Admiralty) should be moved to another office. He looks upon him as being quite unequal to the work of his present office. That Lord Ripon and Sir H. Fowler should go. That Mr Lloyd George should succeed him (Mr Asquith) as Chancellor of the Exchequer. Lord Crewe to go to the Colonies and to be Lord Privy Seal. Lord Tweedmouth to be President of the Council. Mr McKenna to be First Lord of the Admiralty and Mr Runciman, Financial Secretary of the Treasury, to be Minister of Education. Possibly Mr Burns, who has offended many of his own side, to be President of the Board of Trade, and in that case Mr W. Churchill to go to the Local Government Board with a seat in the Cabinet, but if Mr Burns is not moved, Mr W. Churchill would then become President of the Board of Trade.

Mr Asquith is anxious that the reconstruction should take place as soon as possible as he says the present situation is becoming very demoralizing and when the proper moment comes, he proposes to go to Biarritz, with Your Majesty's permission, and talk matters over and make his submissions. He is very anxious that the changes should all be effected before the House of Commons meets again after the recess which will be on 27 April.

As I mentioned in my last letter these changes will involve a meeting of the Privy Council, delivering up "Seals of Office" and "kissing of hands." I am afraid it will cause Your Majesty much inconvenience, but I do not see how it could be done without your presence in England before you start for the northern courts. I am sure Your Majesty will agree that it would not look well should there be a meeting of the Privy Council in Paris at the Embassy . . . No one knows better than Your Majesty how necessary it is for the Sovereign in these democratic days to be very careful how he acts in matters of state, and the formation and reconstruction of a Government is the most important of all the duties of a King.'

The King replied that it seemed 'rather dreadful that the Chancellor of the Exchequer has already such decided views as to the changes he contemplates in the Cabinet when he becomes Prime Minister, whilst the present head of the Government is still alive! It reminds one of a dying animal with the vultures hovering about him. However he must I suppose look to the future. He certainly seems to have drastic intentions relative to some of his colleagues. When the time comes for him to come out and inform me of his proposals, it will be time enough for me to discuss them with him – as it is my right to do. If he is anxious that I should express my views *now* regarding his contemplated changes, I have no objection to your telling him that they shall have my fullest consideration, and very probably I shall agree to some of the changes he is anxious to make . . . At the same time, even in these democratic days, I do not see the necessity of going over to England merely to hold a Council and receive and give Seals of Office. That could all be perfectly accomplished at Paris at my Embassy which is British ground.' The King added this postscript. 'Should Mr McKenna be considered to be the most able First Lord of the Admiralty, I should insist on Sir John Fisher remaining "First Sea Lord" or the dangers Britain would incur would be too great!'

Knollys was deeply troubled by the King's unwillingness to return to England, which he feared might gravely damage his reputation. It would be most unfortunate if His Majesty should seem to prefer to bask in the sun at Biarritz than to kiss hands with ministers.

Knollys's fears were confirmed by a confidential letter Lord Crewe wrote him towards the end of March. 'I saw Asquith this morning,' wrote Crewe, 'and impressed upon him the necessity of speaking *quite plainly* on the subject of the King's return to London. He is as convinced as you or I can be of the importance of this, and will say so. On the other hand it is a rather difficult and delicate matter for him to lay stress on the consideration which is really the strongest, i.e., the view which would generally be taken of His Majesty's absence from England, in such close proximity, on such an occasion. But no doubt you have been able to set this aspect clearly before him: being away from England at the moment he may not of himself give it due weight.'

Knollys assured Asquith on 30 March that he had written to His Majesty recommending 'that he should come home towards the middle of April for the necessary Privy Council and kissing of hands; and I pointed out to him that it would not look at all well that these ceremonies should take place at Paris . . . When you see him, I hope you will urge upon him as strongly as possible the propriety of his coming back. I am *sure* he ought to return, and I have gone as far, and perhaps further, in what I have said to him than I am entitled to go. But of course he will attach far more weight to your opinion on this subject, speaking as Prime Minister, than to mine.'

Asquith agreed that it was of 'the utmost importance that the King should return to London, and if and when the opportunity comes, I shall not fail to urge this view upon him as strongly as I can.' Much to Knollys's relief, Sir Arthur reported from Biarritz 'that Mrs George Keppel told me last night that when motoring with the King in the afternoon she said something casually with reference to C-B and asked if his death would make any alterations to his plans. He said he could not say, but he meant to do whatever the future Prime Minister suggested.'

By the end of March it was no longer possible to doubt that Campbell-Bannerman was dying. Doctor Dawson told Knollys that he had been summoned to examine the Prime Minister and had been forced to the conclusion that 'under no circumstances' could he ever again do public work. Indeed 'his condition necessitated his resignation as soon as possible.' The quicker he gave up office the less strain it would be. On 1 April, Campbell-Bannerman sent in his resignation, partly on medical advice, and partly because he recognized the problems of carrying on the Government with an invalid for Prime Minister.

The King, however, in a last effort to persuade him to change his mind, sent Knollys a telegram saying: 'I am most anxious that he should not resign until the Easter Vacation.' Knollys replied that he believed 'the leading members of the Cabinet feel it to be very difficult to carry on the Government any longer under present conditions as confusion and embarrassment in consequence exist . . . Under these circumstances would not Your Majesty be placing yourself in a false position if you pressed for delay of resignation?'

Bowing to the inevitable, the King telegraphed Campbell-Bannerman: 'Have received your letter with sincere regret. Under the circumstances I have no alternative but to accept your resignation as I see that it would be a relief to your mind, and, I hope, help to improve your health, when once the strain and anxiety of your position is removed.' The same day he wrote Sir Henry a letter in which he expressed his 'sincere regret that the intercourse we have had with one another ever since you became Prime Minister is at an end, as it has always been a great pleasure and satisfaction to me to do business with you at all times.'

By the same post, the King sent Knollys a copy of this correspondence and mentioned in a covering note that he had 'thought of offering the Prime Minister a Peerage,' but feeling sure 'he would not accept it,' had changed his mind. Besides, His Majesty doubted whether 'the measures he has brought forward in Parliament have been worthy of any reward.' Campbell-Bannerman died at Downing Street on 22 April, and five days later made his last journey north from Euston, to be buried beside his wife, Charlotte, in the churchyard at Belmont.

When Queen Victoria refused to leave Balmoral after Gladstone's resignation in 1885, the Prince of Wales sent her a telegram beseeching her to return and expressing the fear that her position as Sovereign would be weakened by her absence. He must therefore have been perfectly well aware of the dangers of lingering at Biarritz. But the truth of the matter was that he was far from well, and perhaps would have been wiser to have let his doctors say so. His heart was overtaxed, he was liable to alarming fits of choking, and his bronchial attacks were becoming increasingly grave. Earlier in his reign, he would have refused to listen to his doctors, would have told them that they knew nothing of the Constitution, and ordered the yacht to Calais. After all, it was only with the greatest difficulty that they persuaded him to postpone his Coronation. That he was now prepared to take their advice is the measure of his infirmity. Besides, when the King told Ponsonby early in March 'to sound Asquith and ask him privately whether he had any objection to coming out to Biarritz,' he replied 'that he would be glad to come out as it would be an advantage to be abroad during the difficult time of forming a Cabinet.'

On the evening of 6 April 1908, Asquith drove to Charing Cross Station and caught the boat train for Paris. The newspapers noted that he wore a thick overcoat and a travelling cap pulled down over his eyes. He reached Biarritz late the following evening and was granted an audience with the King on the morning of 8 April. As he told Margot in a letter written later that day: 'I put on a frock coat, and escorted by Fritz and old Stanley Clarke went to the King who was similarly attired. I presented him with a written resignation of the office of Chancellor of the Exchequer; and he then said "I appoint you Prime Minister and First Lord of the Treasury" whereupon I knelt down and kissed his hand. *Voilà tout!* He then asked me to come into the next room and breakfast with him. We were quite alone for an hour and I went over all the appointments with him. He made no objection to any of them and discussed the various men very freely and with a good deal of shrewdness.'

The news that the King had summoned Asquith to Biarritz was ill-received in England. When rumours of the visit reached Printing House Square, Buckle wrote incredulously to Asquith to find out if they were true, because, as he said, it was 'so unlike His Majesty's usual consideration for his ministers and for public business.' Under the circumstances he might have guessed the true explanation of events, instead of publishing a damaging denunciation of his Sovereign. *The Times* leader was written by Colonel Repington: a disgruntled officer who was obliged to resign from his regiment for unbecoming conduct, and never forgave the King for refusing to reinstate him. *The Times* began by asserting that it was 'a very wide departure from hitherto unbroken precedent' for 'this high constitutional function intimately bound up with the most delicate adjustments of our political system' to have taken place abroad. 'It may perhaps be regarded as a picturesque and graceful tribute to the reality of the *entente* with our French friends that the King and the Prime Minister should find themselves so much at home in their beautiful country as to be able to transact the most important constitutional business on French soil. Still the precedent is not one to be followed . . . Circumstances are doubtless conceivable in which it might be necessary to resort to this mode of transacting constitutional business, but in this case we are glad to believe that His Majesty is in excellent health. No other plea but that of necessity can be regarded as entirely adequate at a time when the importance of keeping the constitutional function of the Crown fully in evidence cannot be exaggerated.' One newspaper even proclaimed that the episode had more in common with the custom of the Angevins than twentieth-century Monarchy.

It is difficult to believe that when Asquith saw the King at Biarritz he failed to notice how ill he was, or that nobody mentioned to him how anxious the doctors were to prevent His Majesty travelling back to England: where it was still so cold that the Prime Minister had found it necessary to wrap himself in a thick overcoat before leaving for France. It was all very well for Browning to write 'Oh to be in England, now that April's there,' but Sir Francis Laking was most emphatic that the climate of Biarritz suited his patient a great deal better. Only the month before, Asquith had told Ponsonby that he positively welcomed the excuse to get away from Downing Street, but now did nothing whatever to save his Sovereign from attack. 'It is no wonder that a Prime Minister who could not protect his King from the wholly undeserved reproach of having slighted the constitution, should never enjoy his confidence.'

Nothing was worse for the King's bronchitis than the mists and fogs of London. As early as 1905, Sir Felix Semon, a pulmonary specialist, begged him to winter in the South of France. In February 1907, he felt so wretched that he seriously considered abdicating. Like his father, he was inclined to be fatalistic about illness. On this occasion, his doctors decided to prepare a detailed statement of his condition which they entrusted to Knollys. His Majesty's bronchial attacks, they said, 'were rarely accompanied by any rise in temperature but generally were extremely obstinate. Moreover, by their long duration, by their causing confinement to the house, by their interference with sleep resulting from the nocturnal attacks of coughing, and by their generally depressing effect, they usually considerably reduced for a time the King's strength. In a man of his age and stout build there was, of course, always the apprehension that in one of these coughing attacks some important blood vessel might give away, and this anxiety was now increased by the fact that a tendency to haemorrhage was manifest.' They warned 'that His Majesty's health, even when it appears excellent to the world at large, unfortunately always is in a somewhat precarious state,' and that it could not be gainsaid 'that either a more rapid progress of any of the degenerative changes now at work or an acute complication of any kind may bring about, apparently suddenly, very serious results.'

Asquith's relations with the King began badly and grew worse as the Government became more radical. The Palace was sensitively vigilant over the distribution of honours and Knollys pounded Nash with critical broadsides. In July 1908, for example, he was desired to say that a gentleman who had been recommended for a Knighthood was a 'bankrupt hatter.' Ministerial speeches were the theme of a regular correspondence, Lloyd George and Winston Churchill proving persistent and impenitent offenders. Knollys, who liked and even admired Asquith, did what he could to preserve peace, and when obliged to convey His Majesty's displeasure to the Prime Minister, subtly contrived to do so with such pungency as to suggest that it need not be taken too solemnly. For all their differences, the King treated Asquith with never failing courtesy. The last time he saw the Prime Minister he was, in fact, disgusted with him, and dreaded the interview, but Asquith afterwards told Margot: 'I had a good talk with the King and found him most reasonable.'

Long before Lloyd George persuaded Asquith to make him Chancellor of the Exchequer, the King was convinced he was dangerous. As President of the Board of Trade he had repeatedly given offence by assaults on the House of Lords, by proposing the appointment of a Minister for Wales without the remotest authority for so doing, and by dragging the Sovereign's name into politics. Lloyd George's oratory, inspired by the hope that the poor should inherit the earth, was less rapturously received at Buckingham Palace than in Limehouse. His wonderful flow of eloquence, his musical cadences, his devastating ridicule, his capacity for identifying himself with the 'left-out millions,' his preaching of class war, were familiar enough ingredients of radical rhetoric, but what struck many as revolutionary was to hear them proclaimed by the Chancellor of the Exchequer speaking with all the authority of a Minister of the Crown.

By 1909 the Liberals were rapidly losing support in the country as by-elections demonstrated. Lloyd George was therefore required to devise a budget which would help restore the Government's popularity. Needing to finance old age pensions and increase naval estimates, he was forced to put up taxes. But, as many Liberals doubted the wisdom of building more Dreadnoughts, it was vital to raise the money in ways they would find attractive. There is nothing like vindictive taxation for restoring party morale.

Some writers have argued that Lloyd George believed that the House of Lords would be bound to accept his Finance Bill, but others have suggested that it was specifically designed to tempt them to reject it. Having forced their Lordships on to highly vulnerable ground, the Government could then appeal from the Peers to the people. Just as the King had a technical right to refuse his assent to bills, so the Upper House was theoretically entitled to vote against a budget. But, as they had refrained from so doing for over two centuries, it was more or less taken for granted that the practice was dead, not dormant.

In March, Asquith told the King that the Government had decided to raise an additional revenue of fifteen million pounds to pay for battleships and old age pensions. They proposed to find the money by increasing the standard rate of income tax by two pence, by introducing a super-tax of sixpence on incomes of over five thousand pounds, and by making a distinction between 'earned' and 'unearned' income so as to tax the latter more heavily. As interest on savings was deemed to be 'unearned,' some people said that thrift was being penalized. It was further proposed to increase the duty on drink, which especially grieved the Irish and the Brewers, and to levy a development tax of half a penny in the pound on land, a reversion duty of two shillings in the pound on the enhanced value of property at the end of a lease, and a Mineral Rights duty of five per cent. The expense of collecting some of these taxes proved so considerable that they were abandoned soon after the war. Certainly the forecasts of ruin they inspired bore little relation to the pitiful revenue they yielded.

Lloyd George presented his 'People's Budget' to the House of Commons on 29 April 1909, in a four-hour speech, which he read as if he hardly understood what he was saying, pausing at commas and rushing past full stops. Considering the brilliance with which it was later defended, its début was disappointing. 'This is a War Budget,' he declared in his peroration. 'It is for raising money to wage implacable warfare against poverty and squalidness.'

Lloyd George's battle against poverty, struck many of his opponents as primarily a campaign against property and capital. Moreover, it was suspiciously socialistic since it implied that budgets were not merely intended to defray the costs of government but to redistribute wealth. Philip Snowden's approval was the kiss of death. Although the Budget was postponed by a ferocious parliamentary battle, land values instantly fell. The activities of the 'Budget League,' presided over by Churchill, were hardly calculated to inspire confidence in property. The 'Land Song' with which they concluded their meetings, posed the question:

'Why should we be beggars with the ballot in our hand? God gave the Land for the people!'

Such sentiments were not what the Duke of Marlborough wished to hear as he ruefully surveyed his ancestral acres. Nor was he consoled by the fact that his cousin led the singing.

The Conservative Party obligingly enabled the Chancellor to represent their opposition as an attempt by the prosperous classes to evade their fair share of taxes. In an even more formidable campaign than Chamberlain's 'unauthorized programme,' Lloyd George denounced his critics, particularly the Peers, as protagonists of monopoly and privilege. When the Lords rejected his budget he added the charge that they had defied the Constitution to save their pockets. Lord Rosebery described the Chancellor's proposals as 'inquisitorial and tyrannical.' What he had introduced was less a budget than 'a revolution,' underlying which might be seen the 'deep, subtle, insidious danger of socialism.' Sir Edward Carson believed that it meant 'the beginning of the end of all rights of property' and Lord Lansdowne described it as 'a monument of reckless and improvident finance.' The Duke of Buccleuch claimed to be so impoverished that he could no longer afford a guinea subscription to a Dumfriesshire football club.

The King, as a great landowner, naturally felt misgivings about Lloyd George's taxes, but, nevertheless, deplored the damage done by 'foolish and mean speeches' in defence of wealth and property. Some of the radical language employed to defend the Budget he thought even more objectionable. On 30 July 1909, Lloyd George, addressing an audience at Limehouse, particularly picked on Dukes as a symbol of exploitation and cited the huge profits they made as justification for taxing them. 'Ah! The Dukes!' he said. They all knew the Dukes, especially in the East End! Now there was the well-known case of the Duke of Northumberland. A County Council wanted to buy a small plot of land as a site for the school to train the children who in due course would become the men labouring on that Duke's property. The rent was insignificant; his contribution to the rates on the basis of, say, thirty shillings an acre. What did the Duke demand for it for a school? Nine hundred pounds an acre! Well, if it was worth nine hundred pounds, let His Grace pay taxes on nine hundred pounds! 'We are placing the burdens,' the Chancellor concluded, 'on the broadest shoulders. Why should I put burdens on the people? I am one of the children of the people. I was brought up amongst them, I know their trials, and God forbid that I should add one grain of trouble to the anxieties which they bear with such patience and fortitude. When the Prime Minister did me the honour of inviting me to take charge of the National Exchequer at a time of great difficulty, I made up my mind that, in framing my Budget, no cupboard should be barer, no lot should be harder to bear. By that test, I challenge them to judge the Budget.'

The King, after studying the Chancellor's Limehouse speech, which for better or worse constituted a new departure in politics, instructed Knollys to complain to Lord Crewe, the Lord Privy Seal, about Ministers of the Crown inciting class war. 'The King is so seriously annoyed with Lloyd George's Limehouse speech, that when he sees Asquith tomorrow he intends to speak very strongly to him on the subject . . . The King thinks he ought to protest in the most vigorous terms against one of his principal Ministers making such a speech . . . full of false statements, of socialism in its worst and most insidious form and of virulent abuse against one particular class, which can only have the effect of setting "class against class" and of stirring up the worst passions of his audience. It is hardly necessary perhaps to allude to its gross vulgarity. The King cannot understand how Asquith can tacitly allow certain of his colleagues to make speeches that would not have been tolerated by any Prime Minister until within the last few years.'

Crewe replied that he need hardly tell Knollys how distressed he was to learn 'that the King should take so serious a view of this speech by one of His Majesty's Ministers and a colleague of my own . . . I have always deprecated and disapproved of the class of speech to which this belongs, by whomever made . . . The fashion of making speeches of this sort was originally set by Chamberlain, and it has been followed ever since by other politicians of the same type. To them the temptations of the platform are very strong, and responsible speeches seem to them dull.' Crewe acknowledged that the personal nature of Lloyd George's remarks was indefensible, but would not admit 'that the statements of fact which he made were false.' It was 'only fair to remember that both he and the Government generally have been the target for any number of random charges of brigandage and the like.' So far from appeasing the King, Crewe's letter seems to have compounded the offence. In a curt reply, Knollys told him that His Majesty 'regrets that his relations with some of the members of the present Cabinet should be increasingly the reverse of harmonious.'

Probably prompted by Asquith, Lloyd George wrote the King a letter of apology, in which he expressed his 'great regret' that he had earned His Majesty's disapproval. 'The Chancellor of the Exchequer, however, has found himself subjected to a storm of hostile criticism, the virulence of which, he ventures to think, is without parallel in the history of financial legislation in this country.' For this reason, he 'ventured to submit that in his recent speech, the first public speech which he has made since the introduction of the Budget, he was justified in retorting upon his opponents in language which fell short of much that has been said and repeated on the other side.'

The King wrote back from the *Victoria and Albert* at Cowes, explaining that he had not intended to express an opinion on the Budget, but only the language used by the Chancellor in defending it, 'which the King thinks was calculated to set class against class and to influence the passions of the working and lower orders against people who happen to be owners of property. The King readily admits that the Chancellor of the Exchequer has been attacked by some members of the opposition with much violence, and he regrets it, but he must remind him that though those gentlemen may have passed the fair limits of attack, they are private members and do not hold a high office in the Government.' It was because Lloyd George held 'one of the most important offices under the Crown' that the King, 'with much regret,' had felt it his duty 'to remonstrate with the Prime Minister against the tone of the Chancellor of the Exchequer's speech . . . The King, in conclusion, must give the Chancellor of the Exchequer every credit for the patience and perfect temper which he has shown, under considerable provocation, during the debates on the Budget.'

Winston Churchill was almost as active as Lloyd George in hurling abuse at Dukes, whom he described in a speech at Leicester on 4 September as 'unfortunate individuals, who ought to lead quiet, delicate, sheltered lives, far from the madding crowd's ignoble strife . . . Do not let us be too hard on them. It is poor sport – almost like teasing goldfish . . . These ornamental creatures blunder on every hook they see, and there is no sport whatever in trying to catch them. It would be barbarous to leave them gasping on the bank of public ridicule upon which they have landed themselves. Let us put them back gently, tenderly into their fountains – and if a few bright gold scales have been rubbed off in what the Prime Minister calls the variegated handling they have received, they will soon get over it.'

Such remarks seemed unforgivable in certain circles. Lloyd George's Radicalism was, at least, intelligible, but few could understand why Churchill seemed so anxious to betray the class from which he sprang. Knollys wrote to *The Times* denouncing the Leicester speech. 'He and the King,' wrote Winston, 'must really have gone mad . . . This looks to me like a rather remarkable Royal intervention and shows the bitterness which is felt in those circles.'

Confronted with a budget which a former Liberal Prime Minister had pronounced to be revolutionary and socialist, the Lords asked themselves two questions: Were they legally entitled to veto a

Finance Bill, and, if so, would it be wise? Reginald McKenna, the First Lord of the Admiralty, told the King that it would be contrary to established constitutional practice for the House of Lords to vote against a budget. 'No two principles, he urged, were more firmly settled in the Constitution than that the House of Commons is alone responsible for taxation and that it is only by a vote in that House that the life of the Government of the day can be terminated. Yet the action of the Lords in rejecting a Finance Bill would amount to a denial of both these principles . . . He pointed out that a Finance Bill had never yet been thrown out by the Lords, and that the rejection of the present one would be "the first step in a revolution".'

The King was not wholly convinced by McKenna's doctrines, but, nevertheless, believed it would be wrong for the Lords to reject the Budget, if only because it would force the House of Commons to seek to restrict their powers. Historians and lawyers held conflicting views on the rights and wrongs of the issue. Dicey and Anson agreed that it would be legitimate for the Upper House to reject a Finance Bill, but Sir Frederick Pollock thought that to do so would be 'the most audacious attempt to subvert the foundations of Parliamentary Government since the revolution of 1688.' On 4 October 1909, Esher noted in his journal while staying at Balmoral: 'I sat next the King at dinner tonight. We talked a good deal about the Budget and the House of Lords. He is strongly opposed to the Lords throwing out the Bill.'

The King's close advisers shared his opinions that the Lords should pass the Budget. Esher told Knollys that 'The vital question which has got to be answered by the House of Lords is, whether the bill shall or shall not pass: whether it shall be rejected, with all the accompaniment of disturbance financial and political, or whether it shall go through, on the understanding that the first unionist majority shall reverse the land clauses . . . When you think of the great collateral issues involved, the conflict between the two houses of Parliament, the doubtful constitutional proceeding involved in the Lords touching the Budget, the warnings of Lord Salisbury, the want of precedent, the whole situation too perilously resembles that of 1640 for my taste. If I were Mr Balfour, I should solemnly warn the country, that the day I was given a majority, I should reverse the policy of Lloyd George, but I should let the Budget pass.'

Knollys wrote a memorandum for the King on 12 September, in which he expressed his opinion 'that certain members of the Cabinet are prepared to go all lengths in order to secure a success over the House of Lords, and to adopt the most unscrupulous measures to achieve that object.' It was clear that the Government would 'not be satisfied with a temporary victory' but would seek support from Radicals and Socialists to bring in 'a Bill with the purpose of crippling the power of the House of Lords.' Knollys therefore ventured to suggest that His Majesty should write to the Prime Minister saying that he regarded 'the matter as being of too serious and important a nature to be dealt with by means of a correspondence and that he hopes Mr Asquith may in consequence be able, notwithstanding his Parliamentary duties, to come to Balmoral for a few days with the object of giving His Majesty an opportunity of discussing the question personally with him in detail. Should the House of Lords reject the Finance Bill a constitutional and political crisis would arise, graver than any which has been seen since the days of the great Reform Bill of 1832.'

During the crisis, Knollys not only corresponded with the Prime Minister but with Margot as well. Margot began the correspondence by sending him a letter dated 7-30 a.m. 16 September and written in pencil. 'If the Lords throw out the Budget,' she wrote, 'things will be *very serious*. None of the other side realize what it will mean, nor do they any of them understand the Budget. You hear them say "country places will be shut up and sold etc." This Budget does not *touch* country places that are not near towns. *No* agricultural country (in which most of our friends have their country seats) is touched by this Budget.'

Margot regarded criticism of the Finance Bill as 'grossly and ridiculously exaggerated. As Sir Edgar Vincent said: "The land taxes are very mild and will hurt *no* one." There was the same shrieking over the Death Duties and there has been more luxury and riches and higher prices paid and wages given every year since. The other side when they get in can *always* alter these taxes. If the Lords pass the Budget, they finish up for ever our cries against the House of Lords. If they reject the Budget, our majority will be much bigger and they will make Lloyd George a hero which would not be good for him . . . It will be a bad day for our Royal Family and for England when money gets grasped into a few hands like in America. Old Queen Victoria was very wise when she said (if she ever *did*!!) "Look after the Crown and the people and the aristocracy will look after themselves".' Knollys sent Margot's letter to Esher, who returned it with the comment that 'the good lady writes wildly and deserves your courteous rebuke.'

One good reason for regarding the Budget as socialist, Knollys replied, was that Labour members welcomed it as such. 'There is I think no doubt that among certain classes an uneasy feeling exists (it may be quite uncalled for, but there it is) and I know as a *fact* that one man, who is a friend of mine, has already sent abroad for the purpose of investment, very large sums of money, and that a firm of Stockbrokers, whom I know, have been entrusted by their clients with no less a sum than fourteen millions with orders to invest it abroad. I am, as you know, a Liberal, and whenever I have been in the House of Lords, I have invariably voted for the Government ever since they have been in office; but I, like many other Liberals, feel anxious as to the presence in the Cabinet of two men who are thought to exercise a dangerous pressure on their colleagues, to say nothing of the violence of their speeches.'

Knollys, however, agreed with Mrs Asquith that the House of Lords would be making 'a very great mistake' if it rejected the Budget, and told her that he intended 'to vote for the Government should the rejection of the Finance Bill be moved.' It was only because they were 'such very old friends' that he had written so candidly stating his 'own *individual views.*'

For several months nobody knew for certain whether Lord Lansdowne and his colleagues proposed to reject the Budget. But towards the end of September, after a long talk with J. S. Sandars, Balfour's Private Secretary, Esher warned Knollys that this was what was intended. Lansdowne, it appeared, 'was in favour of amending the Bill – but has given way. Mr Balfour reluctantly (I think) has come to the conclusion that the straightest and best course, was to say "This is a *new* policy, which we think disastrous. The country must decide the issue. If the constituencies approve, then the House of Lords has nothing more to say. The Government has been in office four years. They had no socialistic mandate. It is only fair to the people that they should have a say. If the House of Lords shrinks from referring such a question to the nation, it is useless as a second chamber, and had better go." That is, in short, the policy of the Opposition.

'I still think it is a *gamble*. And I am sure gambling in politics rarely succeeds. If the Budget were allowed to go through, its unpopularity with *all* classes would become certain. It would not make the poorer classes better off in the course of the next two years, and the middle and upper classes would writhe under the army of "inspectors" and the sheafs of "returns" which would be

flung at them. The upshot would be a *large* unionist majority.'
But by rejecting the Budget, the Lords would provoke the Liberal
Party to tamper with their powers, with the result that in the long
run 'The House of Lords, as we know it, will disappear.'

In order to prevent a constitutional crisis, the King tried to
persuade the Conservatives to pass the Budget. In October, he saw
Asquith at Balmoral and asked him 'Whether he thought he was
well within constitutional lines in taking upon himself to give
advice to and, if necessary, put pressure upon the Tory leaders at
this juncture.' Asquith replied that he thought 'what he was doing,
and proposing to do, perfectly correct from a constitutional point
of view.' The King said 'that in that case, he would not hesitate
to see both Balfour and Lansdowne on his return to London.'

Just in case the House of Lords suddenly came to its senses, Lloyd
George delivered a series of speeches at Newcastle over the weekend
of 9 – 11 October, designed to ensure it committed political suicide
while its balance of mind was disturbed. The Chancellor warned
the Lords, in the confident expectation that they would not heed
his advice, to consider what they were doing. 'The Peers may
decree a Revolution but the People will direct it . . . It will be asked
why five hundred ordinary men, chosen accidentally from among
the unemployed, should override the judgement – the deliberate
judgement – of millions of people who are engaged in the industry
which makes the wealth of the country. It will be asked who or-
dained that a few should have the land of Britain as a perquisite?
Who made ten thousand people owners of the soil, and the rest of us
trespassers in the land of our birth? These are questions that will be
asked. The answers are charged with peril for the order of things
that the Peers represent. But they are fraught with rare and refresh-
ing fruit for the parched lips of the multitude.'

On his return to London from Balmoral, the King sent for Balfour
and Lansdowne on 12 October 1909, and tried to persuade them to
let the Budget pass, if only to avoid a constitutional crisis. They
were somewhat disingenuous in claiming that no decision had been
reached, omitting to mention they both favoured rejection. The
King thought them 'stiff and uncommunicative,' and very much
doubted 'whether any result of importance' would accrue from his
conversation. It was particularly regrettable that one of his rare
failures as a mediator should have occurred over a matter of such
consequence.

The following day, Esher wrote Knollys a letter in which he

told him that Haldane had made it clear that if the Lords rejected the Budget, 'it would lead, beyond all question, to a change in the constitution of the country. Home Rule divided the Liberal Party. But upon the question of the Budget and the veto of the House of Lords the Party was united. That would be bound to mean, sooner or later, that the veto would go. Lloyd George's speeches, whatever *we* may think of them, appeal (just as Gladstone's and Chamberlain's did) to the sporting instincts of his party, and he is becoming every day a more formidable force in politics. It is no use blinding ourselves to this fact, whether we like it or not.' Esher described the Chancellor as having 'knocked out Winston Churchill,' which was all to the good, as he felt sure Lloyd George would 'prove more amenable in the long run. A man of that class is always easier to deal with when once he is "arrivé", than a man sprung from the "upper" class. He is less dangerous, in spite of his flaming language. Most of that is mere Celtic gas.' The King wrote on the top of his letter: 'I agree with main points. E.R.'

Amongst those who took it upon themselves to advise the King, was Lord Hugh Cecil, who thought that he should dismiss Asquith and send for Rosebery. On 11 October, he put this proposal to Knollys in a *private and confidential* letter. 'I am conscious,' he wrote, 'that in venturing to write to you as I am about to do, I am doing what in ordinary circumstances might be properly censurable as an impertinence, and may even as things are incur your disapprobation. I console myself with thinking that at the worst you can put my letter in the fire and dismiss it from your mind.

'It seems clear that we are approaching a political crisis of great gravity. The Lords are as far as I can hear almost certainly going to destroy the Budget. It may be that they are imprudent and that they would do better to pass it; but things are as they are.' In the election which the Government would be bound to fight, 'no means must be omitted to secure a Unionist majority, or at worst a very great reduction of the present Liberal majority.' Although nobody could be sure what the electors might do, 'it seems to me certain that Lord Rosebery is more likely to lead them against the Budget and in defence of the Lords than any other man. I am not of course forgetful of Mr Balfour's great powers: but those powers are rather parliamentary than popular.' For fear of being thought 'audacious and impertinent,' Cecil refrained from discussing how a Ministry headed by Rosebery might come into being, but he conceived of it as comprising 'men of all shades of thought,' resting 'as our ancestors said on a broad bottom.'

Knollys could hardly have failed to recognize the perilous novelty of advising the King to dismiss a Prime Minister whose party enjoyed a decisive majority in the Commons. Moreover, he knew only too well how irresolute Rosebery could be. But for all that he showed Cecil's letter to the King. In answering it, he raised the objection of 'Lord Rosebery's want of nerve,' to which Lord Hugh replied: 'Frankness is best in matters of importance – so let me say that what I rely on in my own mind is that Lord R would probably include me in his Government and that I could make up for this single defect in his qualifications for the task. I have mentioned my ideas on these topics to no one – not even to my brothers – except Lord R and yourself. Nor does Lord R know of my communications with you.'

Rosebery listed four main objections to Cecil's proposals. First, he did not believe that the King would agree to take the necessary initiative. Secondly, he doubted whether ministers would be willing to serve under him. Thirdly, he was 'wholly sceptical' of his influence in the country, and finally he looked upon office with 'abhorrence.' He acknowledged, however, that he had 'always thought that the right outcome of this crisis was a united anti-socialist temporary government.'

Before the month was out, Cecil sent Knollys a final letter suggesting that Balfour might approach the plan 'more favourably if he did not know that it came from me. For one thing he has known me since childhood – and that makes it difficult to treat my ideas as quite "grown up." For another, he knows that I have been very much against him over the fiscal controversy. But even if it came to him from a less suspect source he could hardly be much pleased with it, since it depends on the proposition that Rosebery is a more inspiring figure to the masses than he is. Nevertheless I think he might be willing as a matter of patriotism to give Rosebery every support.'

The House of Commons finally passed the Finance Bill on the night of 5 November, after the Opposition had forced over five hundred and fifty divisions. Some three weeks later, Knollys told Asquith that, if the Lords rejected the measure, it would be 'almost an impossibility' to create a sufficient number of Peers to ensure the success of subsequent legislation. On 30 November, after six days of debate, the Lords threw out the Budget by a majority of two hundred and seventy-five votes. All that day, bemused 'backwoodsmen' wandered about the Palace of Westminster as if lost in a maze.

But when it came to the division they knew what to do.

The Chancellor rejoiced to see his bait swallowed hook, line and sinker. 'Their greed has overborne their craft,' he exclaimed triumphantly, 'and we have got them!' Knollys was restrained from voting by the King, but told Sir Almeric Fitzroy, Clerk to the Privy Council, 'that he thought the Lords mad.' Three days after the bill's rejection, Asquith proposed the motion 'That the action of the House of Lords in refusing to pass into law the financial provision made by the House for the service of the year is a breach of the Constitution and a usurpation of the rights of the Commons.' It was carried by a majority of over two hundred.

Acting on Asquith's advice, the King dissolved Parliament on 15 December 1909, and a bitter campaign followed to decide 'Shall Peers or People rule?' Put that way, the answer seemed self-evident. In the nineteenth century, Members of the Upper House were forbidden to play an active part in elections. But now for the first time Standing Orders were amended, and noble Lords flung themselves recklessly into the fray. Their sudden liberty, far from advancing their cause, seemed as damaging to their interests as the Act which permitted prisoners to give evidence on their own behalf proved to accused persons.

With the best will in the world – a commodity in short supply in 1909 – it is difficult to see how His Majesty's name could have been kept out of politics. By rejecting Lloyd George's Budget, the House of Lords virtually compelled Asquith to seek to reduce their powers. But how could he prevent them from exercising their veto upon legislation designed to restrict it? The obvious solution to the problem was to persuade the King to employ his prerogative to create a sufficient number of Peers to swamp Lord Lansdowne's majority. But how would he react to a request to pursue such a policy? Would he feel constitutionally bound to follow the Prime Minister's advice, or would he insist upon deciding for himself how honours should be awarded?

Naturally there was no easy way of resolving such issues without reference to King Edward. The fact could not be escaped that the royal prerogative was at the centre of the problem, that it would be impossible to prevent its mysteries being exposed to debate, and that in exercising it, or in declining to exercise it, His Majesty would appear to favour one party over the other. It was because he anticipated this dilemma that he urged the Opposition to pass the Budget.

On 15 December, the day Parliament was dissolved, Knollys

told Nash that 'the King had come to the conclusion that he would not be justified in creating new peers (say three hundred) until after a second general election and that he, Lord K, thought the Prime Minister should know of this now,' though for the present he would suggest that the matter should go no further. In insisting upon a second election the King asserted a new constitutional doctrine: not an unreasonable thing to do in a novel situation. Nor was it possible to criticize him for seeking a mandate from the country – unless it be reckoned a fault to trust the people.

More than once during the election Lloyd George was almost engulfed by the fury he aroused. After addressing the citizens of Grimsby, he was obliged to leave by a side door, climb a wall and cross a railway line, so as to escape a crowd who seemed anxious to burn down the hall, preferably with him in it. Nothing, he assured crowded audiences, would persuade him to serve in a Liberal Government unless it were made possible for the House of Commons to pass legislation 'with, or without, the consent of the Second Chamber.'

Early on in the campaign, Lloyd George appeared to suggest that the Prime Minister was in possession of a 'guarantee' from the King to create enough Peers to ensure the Government a majority in the Lords. Asquith himself created the same impression in a speech he made at the Albert Hall on 10 December. The next Liberal Government, he told a crowd of ten thousand supporters, would not assume office unless it secured 'the safeguards which experience has shown to be necessary for the legislative utility and honour of the party of progress.' In so saying, he seems to have taken the King's consent for granted, for he never mentioned the matter to him, although Knollys had warned him only a fortnight before that it would be 'almost an impossibility' to agree to such a request.

As a result of the campaign, the Liberals won 275 seats, the Unionists 273, the Irish Nationalists 83, and the Labour Party 40. On at least two issues the Government could depend on a majority of over a hundred: Home Rule for Ireland and restricting the Lords' veto. Asquith had received a bitter but not fatal rebuff.

Randall Davidson, shortly after the election, saw King Edward and offered his services as a mediator should they ever be required. 'An hour might very easily come in the near future,' he told Knollys, 'when it might be useful to have somebody at hand who knows the political leaders intimately and who yet stands quite outside political strifes and parties. I am anxious that you should know that I am wholly available at a few hours' notice.' Davidson disclaimed the faintest desire to be either 'a wire-puller or a diplomat in such an imbroglio,' but he felt 'more and more the difficulty which must now surround the King's position and the likelihood that the Prime Minister may be tempted to get out of his own perplexities by throwing an unfair responsibility upon the King.' He hoped and believed that Asquith was 'too strong a man to yield to that temptation,' but the possibility could not be ruled out, hence his offer of help.

On 20 February 1910, during the debate on the Address, the Prime Minister admitted to an astonished House of Commons that he stood before them without the King's promise to create enough Liberal Peers to ensure the passing of Government Bills. 'It is the duty of responsible politicians,' he said 'as long as possible, and as far as possible, to keep the name of the Sovereign and the prerogatives of the Crown outside the domain of party politics . . . To ask, in advance, for a blank authority, for an indefinite exercise of the royal prerogative in regard to a measure which has never been submitted to, or approved by, the House of Commons, is a request which, in my judgement, no constitutional statesman can properly make, and is a concession which the Sovereign cannot be expected to grant.' These remarks which were music to the King's ears, 'provoked cries of disappointment from even loyal members of the Party.' It had been widely assumed that the battle was almost over, but now it appeared the campaign had hardly begun.

In the first weeks of 1910, the King's violent fits of coughing, from which it sometimes seemed he could not hope to recover, so alarmed his doctors that they begged him to winter abroad. At first, he refused to take their advice on the ground that he could not leave London while the constitutional crisis remained unresolved. But eventually, with Asquith's help, they prevailed upon him to go, and early in March he set out for Biarritz. Balfour, in fact, maintained that it would prove to his advantage to be prevented from seeing his Ministers. It was clear to those who knew him that worry and distress contributed to his ill-health.

Even at Biarritz the King could not escape politics. For some weeks it seemed possible that divisions within the Cabinet might bring the Government down. 'It may interest you to know,' wrote Hardinge to Knollys on 22 March, 'that Grey of his own initiative told me this morning that all the Cabinet are at sixes and sevens and that he does not see how they can possibly get over the next three weeks without breaking up. He is evidently very disgusted with Winston for having declared that he would not object to a Single Chamber Government.'

The distant prospect did not lend enchantment, as the King made plain to Knollys. 'The way the Government is going on,' he told him, 'is really a perfect scandal and I am positively ashamed to have any dealings with them. Out of silly spite against the House of Lords they are making a most disgraceful mess of the finances of the country. What can be in worse taste than the speeches of Lloyd George and Winston Churchill! That a man occupying the position of Chancellor of the Exchequer could make the style of speech he was guilty of at the Gladstone League, surpasses everything. I don't see how we can (under such a Government as the present one) hold together! It is all very serious and very sad. The word "socialism" is now the motto inscribed on the Liberal Banner!'

On 9 April, the King wrote to Knollys saying: 'I do not suppose the Prime Minister will suggest my making a quantity of Peers, but should he do so I should certainly decline as I would far sooner be unpopular than ridiculous.' Four days later he received a letter from Asquith who explained that the Government was confronted with the problem that the Irish members, led by Redmond, upon whose votes they depended for their majority, declined to support the Budget, unless the Chancellor withdrew his increased duties on whiskey. 'After full consideration,' wrote Asquith, 'Your Majesty's advisers are strongly and unanimously of opinion that to purchase the Irish vote by such a concession would be a discreditable transaction.' The Prime Minister warned the King that this refusal to grant concessions could lead to the downfall of the Government.

Partly on principle, but partly to win the support of the Irish, for whom the passing of Home Rule was of far greater consequence than the details of a Finance Bill, the Cabinet had agreed upon three resolutions for reforming the House of Lords. Should these be rejected, it would become the Prime Minister's duty 'to tender advice to the Crown as to the necessary steps – whether by the exercise of the Prerogative, or by a *refererendum ad hoc*, or otherwise – to be taken to ensure that the policy, approved by the House of Commons by large majorities, shall be given statutory effect in this Parliament.' Asquith concluded his ultimatum with the pious wish that 'as far as possible, the name of the Crown should be kept out of the arena of party politics.' This sentiment struck the King as sheer hypocrisy. His prerogative was at the heart of the matter, and could no more be evaded than the attributes of God in a discussion of the Trinity.

Esher told the King that the Government were attempting 'to purchase the assent of the Irish representatives to a Budget of which they disapprove, and the price given is to threaten Your Majesty, with a view ultimately of inducing Your Majesty to assist in a coup d'état.' Esher's note to Knollys provided a more pungent version of events. 'Bribe or blackmail (whichever you like) for the Irish. The *price* – a menace to the Sovereign. A pretty pass.'

Asquith outlined the Government's policy in a speech he made to the House on 14 April. If the Parliament Bill was rejected, he said, he would feel it his duty to tender advice to the Crown as to the steps which would need to be taken to give it statutory effect. When pressed for a more precise definition of this cryptic utterance, he replied: 'Wait and see.' One member proffered alternative advice: 'Ask Redmond.'

As Asquith proposed that the King's pledge was to be given 'in this Parliament,' he seems to have ignored the condition His Majesty made about seeking the country's consent for so drastic an exercise of his prerogative. Knollys believed that the King had been betrayed, and told Esher that the Prime Minister was about 'to commit the greatest outrage which has ever been committed since England became a Constitutional Monarchy.' If he were King, he would 'rather abdicate than agree to it.' It was, however, some consolation to know 'that if the King appealed to Balfour on the "creation" business, he would not hesitate to respond by accepting office.'

The King at Biarritz studied not only the Prime Minister's letter of 13 April, but the speech he made next day. Both expositions of Government policy filled him with disgust. 'Why don't the *moderate Liberals*,' he asked Knollys, 'state that, if the Government continues their socialism and arbitrary ways, they cannot support them? The Prime Minister at the end of his letter to me distinctly says that he and the Cabinet agree "The name of the Crown should be kept out of the arena of party controversy." Yet in his speech in the House of Commons he talks of "We shall feel it our duty to tender advice to the Crown" and "What the precise form of that advice will be it will of course not be right for me to say now." Evidently by that it is supposed he is going to ask me to swamp the House of Lords by a quantity of Peers. As I told you in my last letter I positively decline doing this. Besides I have previously been given to

understand I should *not* be called upon to agree to this preposterous measure. Certainly the Prime Minister, and many of his
colleagues, assured me so but now they are in the hands of Redmond
and Co. they do not seem to be their own masters. Matters are
getting into terrible muddle and the way the Government is behaving is simply disgusting.'

Because the King died before Asquith formally submitted his
request, some writers have argued that it is impossible to say what
his reaction would have been. But in the light of his own statements
it seems probable that he would have persisted in seeking the view
of the country, either by means of a general election, or, as the
Prime Minister himself had suggested, a referendum. He repeatedly
told Knollys that he regarded Asquith's demand as 'preposterous',
that he would prefer to become 'unpopular than ridiculous,' and
that he 'positively declined' to comply with so drastic a plan, unless
required to do so by the nation. In so saying, he had the fervent
support of Balfour, Esher and Knollys. Moreover, at no time in
his reign was he less disposed to take the advice of his Ministers,
who had alienated him to a dangerous degree.

Writing to Knollys on 22 April about his return to London, the
King said that 'Should it be the intention of the Prime Minister,
Lloyd George and Mr Churchill to meet me at Victoria Station,
it would be a *great* relief for me if they did *not*, and as I may arrive
at about five I put in the plea that they cannot absent themselves
from the House of Commons at that time. I suppose however I
shall have to see the PM the following day, and I do not look forward
to it.' His Majesty went on to say that he felt '*most* acutely' the way
in which his Ministers had treated him, 'especially the Prime Minister.
I wish them to understand that I look upon them with the greatest
disfavour and can no more be on friendly terms with them. They
are not only ruining the country but maltreat me personally and I
can neither forgive or forget it. They are all so puffed up with self-
conceit that they think they can do no wrong, but the old idea
has been that the Sovereign can do no wrong!'

Three days before the King returned to London the Prince of
Wales told Knollys that his father seemed 'very angry with the PM
and the Government and rightly so, as I must say they have treated
him very shabbily . . . One can see by his letters how worried
he is by everything.'

Knollys was so distressed by the Prime Minister's insistence upon
reforming the House of Lords during the lifetime of the present

Parliament, that he decided to take up the Archbishop's offer of assistance. On the afternoon of 27 April, Balfour, Esher and Knollys met secretly at Lambeth to discuss the constitutional deadlock. Davidson maintained that the King was under no obligation to acquiesce in 'schemes of this absolutely novel and, in the quiet sense, revolutionary character, on the mere ground that the Prime Minister proposing them has, for the moment, a small or even a large Parliamentary majority.' He inclined to the view that the King should take 'the public into his confidence as regards the exercise of his own responsibility.' Knollys 'summed up the discussion by making it clear that Mr Balfour would, if His Majesty refused the "advice" of his present ministers, come to the King's assistance in order to dissolve Parliament, and that there was no objection to the King's proposing a compromise if any reasonable basis could be found.'

The day after King Edward returned to London the House of Lords passed the Budget. A week later a stunned nation learned of his death. By common consent, his successor was permitted a brief respite, and an attempt was made to solve the constitutional crisis by an all-party conference. When this broke down in November, Asquith asked the new King to dissolve Parliament and give him a secret pledge to create enough Peers to destroy the Conservative majority in the Lords should it prove necessary to do so. He furthermore insisted that he was bound by the statement he made on 14 April in which he told the Commons that he would resign if he failed to obtain the necessary guarantees. Not only did he refuse to permit the King to consult Balfour and Lansdowne, but threatened to fight an election on the basis of 'The King and the Peers against the People.' They 'behaved disgracefully to me,' said His Majesty with commendable restraint.

Sir Arthur Bigge advised King George to risk Asquith's resignation and turn down his request. He maintained that the Prime Minister should trust the Sovereign to act constitutionally and that it was an insult to demand that he should commit himself in advance. But Knollys, whom the King had appointed as joint Private Secretary, took an opposite view. The King, he said, must be seen to act impartially. Besides, if Asquith was driven to resign, Balfour would not be prepared to form a government.

Knollys may well have hoped that the secrecy surrounding the King's pledge would prevent the Crown being dragged into the electoral arena. But his sudden conversion to a policy of surrender astonished Bigge. 'In less than 48 hours,' he wrote, 'Lord Knollys's mind has been entirely changed as he was adamant as to any assurance being given; today he strongly urges the King to come to a secret understanding and tells me that by advocating resignation, rather than agree to any understanding, I am exposing the King and the Monarchy to the gravest dangers. He told the King he was convinced his late Majesty would have followed his advice. This quoting what a dead person would do is to me most unfair, if not improper, especially to the King, who has such a high opinion of his father's judgement.'

Two questions arise from Knollys's sudden volte-face. What persuaded him to change his mind so rapidly and drastically? What made him tell the King that Balfour would not be prepared to form a government? It is possible that he was over-persuaded by Asquith, an old friend and a gifted negotiator. It might, however, be argued that his second thoughts were wiser than his first. It can hardly be wrong to advise a constitutional Sovereign to be guided by his Prime Minister. It is also conceivable that there was some misunderstanding over what Knollys actually said. It was plainly his duty to point out that, given the balance of forces in the House, Balfour could not possibly form a government commanding a majority.

The second general election of 1910 produced almost exactly the same result as the first. Soon after it became known that Asquith had obtained the King's consent to destroy Lansdowne's majority, the House of Lords passed the Parliament Bill, but not before many Conservative Peers attempted to die in the last ditch rather than capitulate. Party feelings ran high, and Knollys was bitterly reproached by the Opposition for his part in their defeat.

Even the King came to have second thoughts on the wisdom of what he had done, and seems to have adopted the Conservative view of the advice Knollys gave him. Towards the end of 1913, his attention was drawn to a note on the Lambeth Conference which recorded that 'Mr Balfour made it quite clear that he would be prepared to form a Government to prevent the King being put in the position contemplated by the demand for the creation of Peers.' After studying this document, he added and signed the following Minute:

'It was not until late in the year 1913 that the foregoing letters and memoranda came into my possession. The knowledge of their contents would, undoubtedly, have had an important bearing and influence with regard to Mr Asquith's request for guarantees on 16 November 1910.' Before this discovery was made, Knollys had already resigned, largely because of the discord provoked in the Royal Household by the constitutional crisis. It was a wretched conclusion to forty years of devotion to the Crown and a high price to pay for being right.

On the day Knollys retired he received a letter from King George V saying: 'I wish to send you these few lines, as I could not tell you *all* I felt when I saw you this morning. I have known you ever since I can remember anyone or anything. You are my oldest friend and the one whose advice I have so often sought and never in vain. When you were with my dear Father, you never failed to give me help and assistance, however often I asked. Your 47 years with my Father was one long faithful service of devotion, and no one knows better than I do the trust and reliance he placed in you and how much it was justified. I remain always my dear Francis your very affectionate and grateful old friend, George R.I.'

The King and the Services

King Edward played so active a part in reforms of the army and navy, that many senior officers would have preferred him to have taken less interest in them. It might well be argued that his foremost service to the country was the support he gave Admiral Fisher in dragging the Victorian navy into the twentieth century.

British seamen had never been seriously challenged since the days of Nelson. It is therefore little wonder that they became dangerously complacent and hostile to innovation: hazardous instincts to acquire in an age of technical change. Just as Wolseley battled with 'bow and arrow' generals, so Fisher was faced with 'fossil' admirals, brought up in the days of sail and far from reconciled to their passing.

On paper, the Royal Navy remained the most formidable in the world, but the striking-power of its ships was less impressive than their number. Throughout the Age of Apathy, senior officers lacked the incentive of war experience to persuade them to alter their ways. Those who recognized that drastic reforms were necessary to meet the German threat were bitterly resisted by others who saw no need for them. It so happened that the birth pangs of the modern navy exactly coincided with King Edward's reign.

The desire to build a powerful fleet became an obsession with the Kaiser, although neither his grandfather nor Bismarck could see the slightest need for one. Indeed, they knew full well that Germany could barely afford its army, let alone a navy. There were, of course, a few plausible arguments for a programme of naval expansion, and nobody deployed them more skilfully than Admiral Tirpitz, but the

Kaiser's main concern was his own prestige. Bülow believed he was prepared to sacrifice everything to his desire to build more and more battleships.

The Empress Frederick was quick to see that her son's ambition would be bound to antagonize England, and overstrain German resources. 'With so huge an army,' she told her mother in 1894, 'an unduly and disproportionately large navy seems to me a mistake, both from an economical and political point of view. William's one idea is to have a navy, but this is really pure madness and folly.'

In the early years of his reign, the Kaiser's ministers did their best to discourage his naval ambitions. The Reichstag, they claimed, would never agree to vote the necessary funds. But in 1897, when he appointed Admiral Tirpitz as Secretary of State for the Navy, he found a man after his own heart. It was true, the Admiral told him, the public was hostile, but that was because it was ignorant. What was required was intensive education, and to that end he launched the 'Navy League,' paid for by Krupp and patronized by the Emperor. Soon the country was deluged with naval propaganda. No argument for building battleships, good, bad or indifferent, was left to rust unused.

The first fruit of Tirpitz's campaign was harvested in 1898, when the Reichstag passed a bill authorizing the construction of nineteen battleships and forty cruisers by 1903. Two years later, a second Navy Law was passed, providing for the construction of a larger fleet over a longer period. Acceptance of the Navy Law of 1900 became an article of faith. The Kaiser often spoke of it as if it were one of the forces of destiny.

Apart from a handful of naval experts, King Edward was one of the first Englishmen to recognize just how dangerous German rivalry was becoming. When he visited Kiel in June 1904, the Kaiser, despite the efforts of Bülow and Tirpitz to discourage him, paraded the entire German Fleet before his uncle's eyes. The impression it made on the King was deep and lasting. He was not one to wade through pages of Admiralty statistics, but, having seen for himself those long lines of battleships, and having been lectured by his nephew on their speed and fire-power, he took the point.

Nobody did more than Admiral Fisher to bring home to King Edward just how serious the German challenge was. When Fisher joined the navy in 1854, his first ship was HMS *Victory*, Nelson's flagship at Trafalgar. The Commander-in-Chief, Plymouth, Sir William Parker, invited the fourteen-year-old midshipman to dinner, and fascinated him with his recollections of Lord Nelson, for he was the last serving officer to belong to the 'band of brothers.' Nor had conditions of service greatly changed since the time of George III. On his first day aboard, he saw eight men flogged, and fainted at the sight. Fisher's frenzied energy, his single-mindedness, his administrative genius, his broad vision, and his abrasive patriotism, earned him rapid promotion and made him many enemies.

When King Edward came to the throne, Fisher was Commander-in-Chief of the Mediterranean Fleet. Early in 1901, the First Lord of the Admiralty, Lord Selborne, visited Malta, and was so impressed by the Admiral's views on how best to modernize the navy, so captivated by his charm, and so delighted with the striking improvement in the efficiency and morale of the ships under his command, that he resolved to bring him back to England to give him the opportunity to put his ideas into practice. From 1904 until 1910, Fisher was First Sea Lord, in which post, at a crucial moment in naval history, he proved his ability to translate bold and imaginative plans into triumphant realities.

Fisher's letters and conversations owed much to the thought and language of the Bible. When Lord Esher, his close friend and fellow conspirator, learned of his death in 1920, he wrote in his Journal: 'I heard late last night that poor dear old Jackie had gone aloft. Well, he had many crowded hours of glorious life and few men have ever enjoyed the press and lull of battle more than he. He elbowed his way through love and war with a directness and self-confidence that never blenched at any obstacle . . . Jackie was a Maccabean – a true believer in the God of Battles, in the Jahveh of the ancient Hebrews. His Bible was the Old Testament, which he knew by heart, without a dash of the New in his disposition.'

Ten years before the outbreak of the First World War, Fisher saw it coming. In the Spring of 1908 he went so far as to predict that hostilities would begin in the late summer of 1914, a calculation based on the fact that work on enlarging the Kiel canal would be finished, and that Tirpitz would have built enough ships to risk war. In considering this prophecy it should be remembered that Winston Churchill, a year later, told the miners of Swansea that talk of war was 'nonsense'.

Fisher returned to England at the end of 1901 to become Second Sea Lord. In 1903 he became Commander-in-Chief, Portsmouth, and the following year returned to the Admiralty as First Sea Lord. During King Edward's reign, he radically transformed the navy by improving training and conditions of service, re-designing capital ships, scrapping obsolete vessels, strategically redistributing resources, and reorganizing the Reserve Fleet.

Fisher began by concentrating his attention on the instruction of Officer Cadets. The traditional system, under which both the King's sons had been trained, was to send boys of about fifteen for three terms on board *Britannia*, an old wooden ship moored off Dartmouth, followed by a further term on the training cruiser *Isis*, after which their formal education was deemed to be complete. In 1903 Fisher and Selborne introduced a totally new scheme based on the public school system. Boys began the new course before they were thirteen at the Naval College at Osborne, from which they transferred to the Senior College at Dartmouth. Candidates were selected by interview and a written exam based on Common Entrance. Fisher failed to persuade the Government to pay cadets' fees, a proposal which led the King to call him a Socialist.

The army's reverses in South Africa compelled the Government and War Office to learn from their mistakes. But there was no comparable calamity to force the Navy to change its ways. It was Fisher's supreme achievement to goad the Admiralty into the sort of review of the Service normally reserved for a defeat, and to shatter the legacy of complacency and confusion which rendered such reappraisal necessary.

After a few months as First Sea Lord, Fisher persuaded the Admiralty to build a revolutionary new battleship, displacing eighteen thousand tons and possessing a main armament of ten twelve-inch guns, a speed of twenty-one knots and turbine propulsion. Bismarck once told the Reichstag 'We Germans fear God and no one else in the world.' Fisher transposed this maxim into a motto of his own: 'Fear God and dread nought.' It was this which suggested the name by which the new class of battleship was ever after known. Its design was so advanced that it rendered its rivals obsolete overnight. The *Dreadnought* was constructed with unprecedented speed. Her sea trials began in October 1906, only a year after the first plate of her keel had been laid at Portsmouth Dockyard. She instantly justified her designers' expectations and all but silenced her critics.

The new ships offered better amenities for those who served in them. More spacious messdecks, the provision of bakeries, larger galleys and more varied meals, helped to make life aboard tolerable. Dr Johnson's advice that no man should go to sea who had contrivance enough to get himself into a gaol, ceased to apply. On the lower deck, improved conditions were universally ascribed to 'Jackie' Fisher. Officers might squabble over the merits of his reforms, but the seamen and stokers of the navy were behind him to a man.

Because the *Dreadnought* made older ships obsolete, Fisher saw little point in retaining those which served no effective purpose. By scrapping them, not only could estimates be reduced but nobody could be tempted to rely on worthless vessels. The First Sea Lord divided the navy into three categories: 'Sheep,' 'Llamas' and 'Goats.' 'Sheep' were deemed battleworthy, 'Goats' were broken up or sold, and 'Llamas' reserved for further consideration, some ending up as depot ships and others being sent to the scrap yards. At the foot of a list of what looked an imposing fleet, Fisher wrote in his bold hand: 'Scrap the lot.'

Such drastic measures were just what the navy needed, but not what many senior officers wanted. The 'Sheep' and 'Goat' policy was applied with equal ruthlessness to the Reserve Fleet. Sixty venerable warships were sold or broken up, and the remainder reorganized into squadrons, manned by nucleus crews, and ready for active service at short notice. By saving the cost of preserving worthless ships, more could be spent on building Dreadnoughts.

It was not enough to modernize the navy without redistributing its resources to meet the strategic demands of a new era. For much of his career, Fisher had doubted the wisdom of stationing small squadrons all over the world to police the Empire and protect trade. Basing his plans on the axiom that the gravest threat to Britain came from the Kaiser and Tirpitz, he concentrated the navy's strength in the North Sea and English Channel. In 1908, he pointed out to Esher that Mahan described 'the unobtrusive way in which eighty-six per cent of the British guns are trained on Germany as a masterpiece of Fleet distribution! I won't tell you what the German Emperor says. Isn't it curious how little the British people realize what Providence does for them? Germany has to keep *three millions* of soldiers to be the first military power and to maintain her existence. England only takes *128,000 men* to do the same with her Navy.'

Many senior officers were bitterly opposed to the new 'Home Fleet,' partly because the thinking behind it was little understood. It was essential for diplomatic and strategic reasons to disguise the extent to which Fleet dispositions had Germany in mind. Public explanations were therefore impossible. The Prince of Wales, a senior officer with considerable experience of the service, was only won over to Fisher's proposals by a full exposition of them. 'Our only possible enemy is Germany,' wrote the First Sea Lord in October 1906. 'Germany keeps her *whole* Fleet always concentrated within a few hours of England. We must therefore keep a Fleet twice as powerful within a few hours of Germany . . . The politicians and the diplomats will not be the people the public will hang if the British Navy fails to annihilate the whole German Fleet and gobble up every single one of these 842 German merchant steamers now daily on the Ocean! NO!! – it will be the Sea Lords!!!'

Even before Fisher became First Sea Lord, he told Esher that the most effective way of disposing of Tirpitz's navy would be to destroy it before it grew too strong. To act otherwise would be like saying that one preferred to fight a tiger than its cub. In March 1908, he had a long, secret conversation with the King, in which he attempted to convince His Majesty that the navy should follow the precedent set by Nelson in April 1801 when he sank the Danish Fleet in the harbour of Copenhagen. As war with Germany was a virtual certainty, why leave her to choose the most propitious moment to start it? The King, however, told him he must be mad to contemplate such an initiative, and would not hear of the idea of waging war without first declaring it.

It was one of King Edward's traits to place his entire reliance on selected individuals whose good sense particularly impressed him. As Fisher remarked to Esher, His Majesty 'never failed in his judgement on whose opinion to rely.' Ceaseless efforts were made to destroy Fisher's reputation with the King, who remained serenely unmoved by the most atrocious slanders. Indeed, wrote Jackie, 'he quite enjoyed the numberless communications he got . . . I was a Malay! I was the son of a Cingalese Princess – hence my cunning and duplicity! I had formed a syndicate and bought all the lands round Rosyth before the Government fixed on it as a Naval Base – hence my wealth! How the King enjoyed my showing him my private income as given to the Income-Tax Commissioners,' which amounted to £382 6s 11d, after tax and annuities were deducted.

Esher once told Fisher how 'simply magnificently' the King had behaved towards him. 'Your enemies were very clamorous in the gate at one moment, and almost anyone might have been forgiven had they been shaken. But H.M. *never was*! I must say that no-one that I have ever met is a more loyal friend. We have all tried him sometimes, I fear, but it never seems to detach him from those to whom he has once given his confidence.'

Fisher's reforms stirred up such bitter opposition, that he needed powerful political support. Both Lord Cawdor, the Conservative First Lord who succeeded Selborne in March 1905, and Lord Tweedmouth, his Liberal successor, were men of straw. Tweedmouth became so unpredictable that in April 1908 Asquith decided to move him. Soon after, he was found to be suffering from cerebral disease and his eccentricities were explained. At a crucial time, Fisher was forced to rely on a Prime Minister who was mortally ill and a First Lord whose mind was unhinged. Under these circumstances, he depended upon the King not merely for encouragement but for survival.

'When Your Majesty,' he wrote in October 1907, ' "backed up" the First Sea Lord against naval opposition to the *Dreadnought*, and when Your Majesty launched her, went to sea in her, witnessed her battle practice (which surpassed all records), it just simply shut up the mouths of the revilers as effectively as those lions were kept from eating Daniel! *And they would have eaten me but for Your Majesty!*' Despite the exuberance of Fisher's style, what he said was none the less true, for the help the King gave him was indispensable and unfailing. Had he been left to his own devices he must have foundered. His ruthless treatment of opponents and the violence of his enthusiasms were such as to attract devoted disciples or deadly enemies. One could no more remain indifferent to Jackie Fisher than to a hurricane.

Queen Alexandra, one of Admiral Fisher's most ardent partisans, shared the King's admiration and affection for him. They had much in common. Both had a certain childlike simplicity and directness. Both 'spoke, wrote and thought in large type italics.' Both were 'enthusiastic, impetuous, single-minded.' Both were upheld by 'a firm, uncomplicated, religious faith,' and both 'loved laughter and laughed at the same jokes.' Above all, they nurtured a common hatred of Germany. When the First Sea Lord spoke of Britain's 'betrayal of Denmark,' and claimed he could capture the Kiel canal and recover Schleswig and Holstein, she prayed that the Government would let him do so. Fisher always referred to her as 'Blessed Queen Alexandra,' while she addressed him as 'Dear Admiral Jack,' or, after 1909, as 'My beloved Lord Fisher.'

It would have been no more possible for Fisher to have reformed the navy without making enemies, than for Shylock to cut off his pound of flesh without shedding blood. As he often observed: 'The pruning knife ain't pleasant for fossils and ineffectives.' He had made it his task to rouse the navy from its torpor, which demanded pungency not tact. Only by being 'ruthless, relentless and remorseless' could he clear away obstructions. All who resisted him were treated as traitors. 'I will make their wives widows,' he proclaimed ferociously, 'their children fatherless and their homes dunghills.' The ruined careers of those who opposed him bore ominous testimony to the sincerity of his intentions, 'and many grisly examples of Admirals and Captains eating out their hearts "on the beach" showed that he meant what he said.'

The King repeatedly endeavoured to restrain Admiral Fisher's combative language, and once had to reproach him for shaking his fist in his face. Esher shared His Majesty's reservations. 'Pray be Machiavellian,' he wrote in 1906, 'and play upon the delicate instrument of public opinion with your fingers and not with your feet – however tempting the latter may be.'

Many naval officers looked on their service careers as a lifelong holiday, and deeply resented the new fashion of stressing professional duties. When ships were transferred from the Mediterranean to home waters there were howls of protest because of the diminished amenities the North Sea had to offer. A rearguard action against reform was fought in the drawing-rooms of Belgravia, the Duchesses defiantly arraying themselves behind those obstructing change. But the King and Queen's massive social support enabled the First Sea Lord to carry the day. Their Majesties were like Dreadnoughts scattering lesser battleships.

From the moment Fisher began to transform the navy, he found himself opposed by 'pre-historic' admirals, trained in the days of sail, such as Lord Charles Scott, Penrose Fitzgerald, Vesey Hamilton and Captain Hedworth Lambton, the Saviour of Ladysmith. These aristocratic 'mandarins' were reinforced by retired 'fossils', like Admiral Field. A majority of officers, more particularly the junior ones, fervently admired Fisher. 'The Blue Water School,' as they were called, included Prince Louis of Battenberg, Jellicoe, Percy Scott, Bacon and Madden, all of whom reached the highest ranks in the service. The opposition, initially led by Admiral Sir Reginald Custance, poured scorn on Fisher's schemes, and earned from their author such unflattering titles as 'Yellow Admirals' and the 'Blue Funk School.'

Fisher was unshakeably convinced that the defence of the Empire could be entrusted to the navy, and that money required for building battleships should be found by reducing the size of the army. He detested Haldane, whom he called a 'soapy jesuit,' and regarded the War Office with envy, and suspicion. It is hardly surprising therefore that the military authorities were never numbered amongst the First Sea Lord's most willing associates.

In September 1908, he wrote to his 'dear friend,' Esher, who envisaged a more exalted role for the army, to say that '*millions* of soldiers – *millions* and *millions* of them, are no use to us unless we have absolute undoubted supremacy at sea because it would be *starvation* not *invasion* that would bring us to our knees if we lost command of the sea. *Germany can pour 3 million soldiers into England!* Can you contemplate any Army scheme that would give us *3 million* soldiers as highly trained as the German Army, and, if so, what the cost? There is only so much money that even this rich country can possibly spend on the Army and Navy. So keep the Navy supreme and give the balance to the Army! (*but that is not the prevailing idea at this moment!*) If you tamper with the Navy – it naturally leads to an agitation for increasing the Army to make us safe against invasion. *But no British Army you could desire would be adequate against 3 million German soldiers if the command of the sea was lost.*'

Drastic reforms necessarily generate heat. The most diplomatic of First Sea Lords could not have avoided ill feeling. But Fisher was partly to blame for creating such angry dissension that the navy split into warring factions. His nature was combative and he spoiled for a fight. 'I entered the Navy penniless, friendless and forlorn,' he would point out to his critics. 'I have had to fight like hell, and fighting like hell has made me what I am.' Drunk with delight of battle, he never troubled to cultivate the gentler art of persuasion. Unfortunately, but not unnaturally, the first casualty of his tempestuous career was the *esprit de corps* of the service he loved so well. The King, who hated discord, asked Captain Bacon 'Whether the schemes could not perhaps have been launched with less friction?' He recognized, of course, 'that the Navy was ultra-conservative and hated reforms.' Nevertheless, both he and the Prince of Wales were much upset by the feeling of 'unrest' in the Fleet.

In 1904 the King made Fisher his Principal Naval Aide-de-Camp, a post which carried a special right of access to the Sovereign. Soon their official relationship grew into a deep personal friendship. The King was enchanted by the Admiral's reckless letters, 'dashed off red-hot as they left his mind.' But for all their imprudent violence they were generous and affectionate. Those he addressed to Esher began 'My beloved Friend,' and concluded with some such farewell as 'Till charcoal sprouts,' or 'Yours till Hell freezes.' When Winston Churchill started working on his account of *The World Crisis*, he found it impossible to re-read Fisher's letters 'without sentiments of strong regard for him, his fiery soul, his volcanic energy, his deep creative mind, his fierce outspoken hatred, his love of England.'

These qualities, combined with unquestioning loyalty to the throne, proved irresistible to its occupant, who rejoiced in the Admiral's companionship. Once, during a tedious luncheon party, Fisher was heard to remark to the King: 'Pretty dull this, Sir, hadn't I better give them a song?' On another occasion, during dinner at Carlsbad, the King warned a young lady, with whom Sir John was engaged in lively conversation, 'You had better be careful of these sailors, you know the saying they have a wife in every port.' Fisher, trusting to the immunity granted Court Jesters, shouted across the table, 'Wouldn't you, Sir, have loved to be a sailor?' For an instant there was a stunned silence, and then the King burst out laughing.

At one time, when Fisher's enemies were baying for his blood, King Edward told him he was 'The best hated man in the British Empire.' 'Perhaps I am,' he admitted. 'Do you know I am the only friend you have?' the King persisted. 'Your Majesty is no doubt right,' replied the Admiral, 'but you have backed the winner.'

Three days after the King's death, Queen Alexandra sent for Fisher, who was shown into a room where she stood alone with her dead husband. It was a most trying moment for both of them. She took the Admiral's hand in hers, and speaking with deep emotion told him how much King Edward had loved him. The affection was mutual. 'It is curious,' Jackie told Esher in June 1911, 'that I can't get over the personal great blank I feel in the death of our late blessed Friend King Edward! There was something in the charm of his heart that still chains one to his memory.'

Early in 1905, Balfour decided to make Selborne Governor-General of South Africa, and to appoint Walter Long to succeed him at the Admiralty. On 3 March, Fisher sent Knollys a draft of the letter of resignation he proposed to send the Prime Minister. In it he said that Sir Andrew Noble, chairman of Armstrong, Whitworth and Company, had just invited him to become President of 'an immense combination of the greatest shipbuilding, armour plate and gun making firms in the country,' with twenty thousand a year and virtually dictatorial powers. Moreover, he was not prepared to work with Long whom he suspected of sympathizing with the Yellow Admirals.

The King told Balfour it would be mad to let him go. In the end, Lord Cawdor, an enterprising Chairman of the Great Western Railway, succeeded Selborne, and Fisher was made an additional Admiral of the Fleet. The First Sea Lord was a poor man and turned down a fortune to remain at his post. His Majesty's influence was never exercised to greater effect than in persuading him that his country needed him at the Admiralty.

After Campbell-Bannerman's triumph in 1906, the majority of his supporters deluded themselves into believing that the dangers confronting the nation were greatly exaggerated and that its defences were stronger than they were. The wish to dispense with the cost of Dreadnoughts fathered the thought that the Admiralty's demands were excessive. The Germans rejoiced at the Liberals' landslide victory and prayed that nothing would discourage them from starving the army and navy. A hard core of Liberals were convinced pacifists, such as Morley and Burns, who resigned in August 1914. Almost half the party opposed the Anglo-Russian *entente*, for no spoon was long enough with which to sup with the Tsar. Had it not been for the perspicacity of the King, the watchfulness of the Press, and the vigilance of men like Fisher and Lord Roberts, the politicians of the day would probably have so weakened the services as to invite defeat.

Early in 1908, the Reichstag passed a Third Naval Act, increasing expenditure on shipbuilding by twenty per cent, and bringing the strength of the fleet up to thirty-seven battleships by 1914. Consequently, several English newspapers demanded more Dreadnoughts, and an 'Imperial Maritime League' was started to press for a public enquiry into the Government's naval economies. When Lord Esher was invited to join its Council, he was so dismayed by its hostility to Fisher, that he sent *The Times* a copy of his reply. 'There is not a man in Germany,' he wrote, 'from the Emperor downwards, who would not welcome the fall of Sir John Fisher, and for this reason only, apart from all others, I must beg to decline your invitation.'

The Kaiser, after reading Lord Esher's letter, decided to write privately to the First Lord, refuting the aspersions it contained, and endeavouring to allay anxieties aroused by the Naval Bill. Recognizing how unusual it was for a Sovereign to correspond with a foreign subject, he informed King Edward of his action. His Majesty's reply was not such as to encourage further correspondence. 'My dear William,' it read, 'I have received your letter of the 14th inst. in which you have informed me that you have written a letter to Lord Tweedmouth relative to the German naval programme in which you have detected some uneasiness in the British press. Your writing to my First Lord of the Admiralty is a "new departure", and I do not see how he can prevent our press from calling attention to the great increase in building of German ships of war, which necessitates our increasing our Navy also. Believe me, Your affectionate Uncle, Edward R.'

The King, who always hated a fuss, told Esher he deeply regretted the publication of his letter to the Navy League. But, when they next met, His Majesty treated the episode as a joke. 'If the German Emperor comes over here,' he said, 'we must hide you away, or send you on a bicycle tour.'

Edward Marjoribanks, who succeeded his father as Lord Tweedmouth in 1894, showed little prospect of an outstanding political career in his salad days, except perhaps in marrying Randolph Churchill's sister, Fanny. Having been publicly expelled from Harrow for locking a boy in a cupboard and leaving him there to starve to death – the story is possibly apocryphal, as even in those heedless days it is difficult to believe that the authorities were so negligent as not to notice the victim's absence – he became the ringleader of a gang of Oxford vandals who broke into Christ Church Library and burned a number of valuable manuscripts. Before his own role in these proceedings was discovered, he told his friends that nobody who claimed to be a gentleman could possibly have taken part in so outrageous an enterprise. This sublime impudence was the first sign he showed of possessing a flair for politics. In 1892 he became Gladstone's Chief Whip, and in December 1905, Campbell-Bannerman appointed him First Lord. 'Neptune only knows how he got there,' commented Lord Vansittart, 'for he patently was potty.'

Esher's letter, the Emperor told Tweedmouth, was 'a piece of unmitigated balderdash, and had created immense merriment in the circles of those "who know".' It was 'absolutely nonsensical and untrue' that the German Naval Bill was meant as a challenge to Britain. 'The German Fleet is built against nobody at all. It is solely built for Germany's needs in relation with that country's rapidly growing trade.' Nobody questioned Britain's right to build a hundred battleships, and the Germans were equally entitled to decide for themselves the size of the Fleet they desired. Perpetual newspaper references to the 'German danger' were 'utterly unworthy' of a nation possessing 'a world-wide Empire and a mighty Navy.'

Tweedmouth was so excited by receiving a letter from the Kaiser that he gossiped about it everywhere, finally entrusting the precious document to a young lady he chanced to fancy. Eventually the manuscript found its way into the hands of the *Morning Post*, who were prevailed upon not to publish it. Not until October 1914, when Anglo-German relations were past repair, was it finally printed.

As a result of the First Lord's incessant chatter, everyone knew of the letter. But the fact that he betrayed details of the naval estimates in the reply he sent the Kaiser was successfully kept quiet. Several newspapers expressed disapproval at the German Emperor's unwarranted interference, and the Prince of Wales wondered what his cousin would have said had King Edward written a private letter to Tirpitz. Just as the dust was settling, Tweedmouth wrote Knollys a letter proposing that His Majesty should join fifteen of his unmarried nieces in staging a bright but 'proper' variety entertainment. The King minuted at the foot of the invitation: 'This is very sad but explains his extraordinary behaviour on so many occasions.'

Tweedmouth was succeeded by Reginald McKenna, who had rowed for Cambridge in the year of the Silver Jubilee. Asquith told Knollys that the new First Lord 'was a very able man and quite sound on the question of keeping up the Navy.' But Fisher was apprehensive because McKenna's reputation at the Treasury threatened ruthless economy. 'I saw Asquith,' the Admiral told Knollys. 'He was exceedingly friendly and asked me if I would agree to McKenna as he had promised the King (so I understood) to see me on the subject . . . He said "I know you fought McKenna when he was at the Treasury but you'll find him all right and the very best man you could have." So I said no more.' Two days later, Fisher told Esher: 'I can't tell you how very nice Asquith was to me and I feel absolutely sure it is all due to the King. (*God bless him!!!*) He kept me when I wanted to go and took me out to the doorstep . . . St Paul was the greatest persecutor of the Christians but when he got into office (was converted I mean) he was greater than all the Apostles put together. So may be St McKenna!'

McKenna soon showed signs of conversion. Within weeks of taking office, he was won over to the Admiralty's demand for more Dreadnoughts, and found himself eating every word he had spoken at the

Treasury. He was one of those people who gave a stubborn loyalty to whatever department he served. Having transferred his allegiance to the navy, he supported increased estimates with just the same zeal with which he had recently resisted them.

Feuds between Fisher and his adversaries grew increasingly bitter when Lord Charles Beresford headed the 'Syndicate of Discontent.' An Irish eccentric in the grand tradition, he loved a scrap as much as the First Sea Lord. When it seemed possible that he might be ordered to attack the Russian Fleet, which had fired on British trawlers off the Dogger Bank, he planned to engage it with only part of the force at his disposal, claiming he thought it unsporting to fight with the odds too heavily in his favour. Fisher's appointment in 1905, as an additional Admiral of the Fleet, blasted Beresford's chances of succeeding him as First Sea Lord, a post which his admirers, amongst whom Lord Charles himself must be numbered, thought him pre-eminently qualified to fill.

As Commander-in-Chief of the Channel Fleet, Beresford publicly denounced the Admiralty's plans for redeploying its resources, describing its proposals as 'a fraud upon the public and a danger to the Empire.' The Home Fleet he considered had been established with the sole purpose of diminishing the importance of his command. Others might see it as a response to the growing threat from Germany, but for him it was plainly part of a personal vendetta. Prince Louis of Battenberg, who never doubted that Sir John Fisher was a 'truly great man,' none the less blamed him for starting the 'pernicious partisanship' which he thought so damaging to the navy, and believed that 'his hatred of C.B.' had induced him 'to maintain for the past two years an organization of our Home forces which was indefensible.'

On 4 November 1907, Beresford ordered the Channel Fleet to curtail its manoeuvres and 'paint ship' off Portland, in preparation for the Kaiser's forthcoming visit to Spithead. The Captain of the *Roxburgh* requested Sir Percy Scott, the Rear-Admiral in command of the First Cruiser Squadron, for permission to complete the gunnery exercise in which he was engaged. Scott, who was widely known to be an admirer of Fisher, signalled: 'Paintwork appears to be more in demand than gunnery so you better come in to make yourself look pretty by the 8th.' When Beresford heard of the message he was furious, although it was precisely the sort of thing he might himself have said. Not only did he publicly reprimand the Rear-Admiral, but sent a signal to all captains under his command describing Sir

Percy's conduct as 'contemptuous in tone and insubordinate in character.'

Every wardroom and messdeck in the Fleet took sides over the 'paintwork' controversy, news of which soon reached the journalists gathered at Portsmouth awaiting the Kaiser's visit. *The Times* correspondent demurely announced that Lord Charles Beresford and Sir Percy Scott were reported to be 'at variance,' but lesser newspapers were not so diplomatic. In itself, the episode was obviously trifling. Nevertheless, it symbolized two vital principles. The first was the primary importance of preparing the navy for War. Were guns never to be fired for fear they might become dirty, or, worse still, wear out? Were ships never to hold night manoeuvres in case they collided in the dark? The second principle concerned the divided loyalties which were tearing the navy apart. Unseemly squabbles between high-ranking officers were conducive to neither discipline nor harmony, two qualities for which the Senior Service had hitherto been renowned.

King Edward was the most forgiving of men, but in spite of his formal reconciliation with Beresford in 1896, their relationship could not but be overshadowed by recollections of their quarrel. His Majesty's affection for Fisher, and his faith in his reforms, naturally disposed him to take his part. For all that, he went out of his way to treat Beresford justly. Shortly before he died, he told Bigge that he thought Lord Charles had done 'as much good to the Navy so far as training and the sailoring part of it, as Fisher may have done in organization.' Beresford, however, was convinced that the King's mind was being poisoned against him. 'History,' he told Knollys in January 1908, 'abounds with stories of men holding high command having been put out of favour with their Sovereign through false reports and innuendoes made about them during their absence on duty. I have suffered from the most cowardly and treacherous stabs in the back during the last two years owing to false statements made publicly and privately.' But as in the same letter he refers to being 'quite delighted to get so kind a message from the King,' his enemies presumably had not proved wholly successful.

So scrupulous was the King in his official dealings with Beresford, that in 1906 he conferred the Grand Cross of the Royal Victorian Order upon him, and in 1908 accepted his invitation to review the Channel Fleet. After the King and Queen's visit to his flagship, HMS *King Edward VII*, he told them he would never forget their 'kindness and charm,' which reminded him 'so clearly of those happy days gone by which can never be effaced from my memory.' The King replied by expressing 'the great pleasure and satisfaction which it gave the Queen and myself to visit the Channel Squadron under your command. You may indeed be proud to command such a splendid Fleet, and their appearance and efficiency made a deep impression on all who saw them.'

During a Court Levee at St James's Palace in May 1908, Fisher was talking to Churchill and Lloyd George when, according to Admiral Slade, an eyewitness, Beresford 'shook hands with Lloyd George and Winston, but when Sir John put out his hand he turned his back on him, just like a naughty schoolboy.' The incident took place 'in full view of the King and before the Ministers and C.B.'s Naval officers . . . It is all over the fleet.' The deference shown towards Beresford by Asquith and his colleagues, suggests that they were afraid of the fiery Irishman and overawed by his social eminence. In his time, Lord Charles threatened the King, Prime Minister and First Sea Lord with exposure in the Press, and such was his popularity with the country that, when he spoke of appealing to the public, politicians panicked at the prospect. After his unparalleled display of insubordination in turning his back on the First Sea Lord, King Edward thought the Government a pack of cowards for not ordering him to haul down his flag. Esher shared the King's opinion, and told Knollys that he doubted whether McKenna possessed 'the pluck' to deal with the insolent admiral. 'If he should have the moral courage, it would not surprise me if, later on, he found occasion to say farewell to Jackie also.'

In September 1908, Fisher complained to Esher that Lord Charles was once more 'stirring up his quarrel with Percy Scott,' and had 'written officially to the Admiralty renewing the strife that was supposed to be ended by the removal of Percy Scott to another command. The fact is he thinks everyone is frightened of him and certainly he has been treated as if this were the case. Hedworth Lambton said to me just before leaving for China "Seize Beresford by the scruff of the neck and kick him out and like all Irishmen he will go under at once. It's all pure brag." Anyhow, it is simply disastrous this parleying with mutiny and we shall have a catastrophe before long! Sneaks and traitors are doing a fine business in ruining the discipline of the Navy and the authority of the Admiralty.'

McKenna, showing more courage than Esher expected, obtained his colleagues' sanction to dismiss Lord Charles, on the ground that his conduct towards the First Sea Lord was subversive of discipline.

It was consequently announced on 15 February 1909, that Beresford would retire from his command in March and that the Channel Fleet was to be incorporated into the Home Fleet. It was, as had been predicted, a Pyrrhic victory for Fisher.

King Edward approved the decision, but feared the rebel Admiral might 'give trouble and annoyance.' His foreboding was rapidly justified. When Beresford hauled down his flag, he was carried shoulder high through the streets of Portsmouth, and was so exhilarated by demonstrations of popular support that he called on Asquith at Downing Street and warned him that he proposed to stump the country in an effort to overthrow the Government, unless it set up a Court of Enquiry to investigate his complaints against the Admiralty. Asquith agreed to do so, informing Lord Charles that 'Statements so grave upon matters vital to the national safety proceeding from an officer of your eminence and of your long and distinguished service clearly call for prompt and thorough examination.'

The Committee, as originally nominated, consisted of Haldane, Grey, Crewe, Esher and Admiral Sir Arthur Wilson. In reporting its membership to the King, Asquith referred to Wilson as possessing an authority in the navy 'probably greater than that of any other officer.' 'As you say,' wrote the King in reply to the Prime Minister's letter, 'the allegations are of so grave a nature' that your proposal to set up a Committee of Enquiry 'meets with my highest approval. The appointment of Admiral of the Fleet Sir Arthur Wilson to be a member of the Committee is an excellent one, as his views will be of the greatest value being one of the most distinguished Officers of the Navy.' Beresford, however, objected to Wilson and Esher, whose names were withdrawn in deference to his views.

Beresford had been pressing for an enquiry since the beginning of 1908, when he was still a serving officer. But Lord Tweedmouth refused to countenance the proposal and told Knollys 'that if a Government were to order an outside enquiry into the Admiralty, the Board would have no choice but at once to resign. It would be ten times worse if they proposed to call officers under Admiralty command to give evidence before such an enquiry.' He was fortified in so saying by a memorandum which Esher prepared for the King. 'The Board of Admiralty,' he wrote, 'is the supreme Naval authority, wielding the powers of the King and of the Executive Government. Every great Admiral, Lord Howe, Hood, St Vincent and Nelson, have had to obey and have obeyed the orders of the Board. There has been "grumbling" at times, but no *serious* case of intrigue or insubordination. The act of the Board, in consequence of Lord Hood's mild remonstrance in 1795, when his Flag was hauled down, extinguished insubordinate complaints – at the cost, no doubt, of some hardship to that distinguished Admiral. The responsibility of the Board of Admiralty does not relieve the Executive Government, (who are the King's advisers), from *their* responsibility for the efficiency and proper distribution of the Fleets. If a Government were to agree to a "public enquiry" into the *policy* of the Board of Admiralty, it would be in fact an enquiry into the policy of the Government. Either the Board of Admiralty should be supported, (and insubordination incidentally crushed), or the Government should appoint a new Board.'

While the Committee considered the evidence, all England took sides. The King, *The Times*, the *Daily Telegraph*, the *Observer*, and half the navy, including most of its ablest officers, supported Fisher. 'Society,' a majority of Beresford's contemporaries, the *Daily Express* and *Daily Mail* opposed him. A naval friend of the First Sea Lord, who called at Lord Charles's house in Grosvenor Place to leave his card, was inadvertently shown into the dining-room by the butler, where he found a committee of Admirals gathered round the table plotting Fisher's downfall.

Although the Prince of Wales treated the King's views with reverence, he was won over to Beresford. In vain his father warned him that Lord Charles's concern for the navy was all 'bosh' and a 'form of self-advertisement.' What finally turned Prince George against Fisher was his discovery that for several years the First Sea Lord had secretly corresponded with Captain Bacon, one of Beresford's subordinates. The Prince was not alone in regarding this as a form of spying, nor in thinking that Fisher was foisting misguided reforms on the navy. In such matters his instincts were deeply Conservative, and he was just the sort of officer whom the First Lord was liable to incense.

When Fisher heard that Asquith had yielded to Beresford's demands he wanted to resign, but the King ordered him to stay at his post. 'I shall of course obey His Majesty,' he told Ponsonby, 'but it is almost past belief how Beresford has been pandered to.' As ever, King Edward remained steadfast. 'Fisher shall not be kicked out,' he told Knollys, 'in spite of the Cabinet, the Press and Charles Beresford.'

When Asquith's Committee published its findings in August 1909, it was so half-hearted in its defence of the Admiralty that Beresford claimed the victory. As soon as Fisher read the Report, he wrote to Ponsonby who was at Marienbad with the King. 'Five great men signed it. *They are five great cowards!* Glorified milk and water! and Mr. "Facing-bothways" in excelsis! But *where* is the *kernel* namely *Discipline?* Echo answers "where"! An Admiral flouts the Admiralty and only some soft words are said of his not recognizing "the paramount authority of the Admiralty"! But what of the damnable statement as to the Admiralty not giving its confidence to Beresford? How could the Admiralty give their confidence to an Admiral who within 24 hours of assuming his command began writing mutinous letters!' The King, after reading these remarks, minuted: 'J.F. has indeed every reason to feel more than deeply hurt at pandering to C.B!'

Knollys received a considerable number of letters critical of the Committee's findings. 'As you say,' wrote Esher, 'the Committee were terrified of C.B. and *still are*! But it makes one perfectly furious to find men who should be grateful for all the enormous hard work they have got out of Fisher, letting him down, as they have done. Why should anyone try to work hard for the country when those who represent it treat you as if you were working solely for yourself? No wonder Jackie is sore.' Nor did Charles Hardinge think much of the Beresford report. 'It was a miserable attempt to conciliate everybody which satisfied nobody. I think Fisher and the Admiralty have certainly reason to complain at the criticisms passed on their want of co-operation with Beresford. One cannot co-operate with a man who refuses to work with you and who is puffed up with his own pride and self-importance.'

In September, the King invited McKenna to Balmoral, and Fisher told Knollys how delighted he was by His Majesty's splendid gesture. '*Just the exact right thing!* It will delight McKenna and will go far to neutralize the bad blow given by the Beresford Committee to the Admiralty. McKenna is in a ticklish position as you say and I expect he will feel bound out of loyalty to his colleagues to defend in some measure what Asquith has done, (though in his heart he knows Asquith is a coward and no fighter) and will talk to His Majesty in duty bound of Asquith's political sagacity in framing the Beresford report as he did . . . If the Committee had smashed Beresford in their report and proved him out of his own mouth a blatant liar and imbecile in his ignorance of the Naval situation (as was clearly shown by the evidence), I say if the Committee had done this, Beresford would have been so utterly discredited that he would have disappeared, but now he poses as the one man the country looks to for the Navy being kept straight and cites the Committee in his favour. But I need not weary you with more on this as your excellent letter puts it in a nutshell. "If Beresford declares publicly that the report was favourable to him, it must be unfavourable to the Admiralty." '

Early in 1909 it appeared that the Germans were not only increasing the number of warships they planned to build under the 1908 Law, but were also accelerating the rate at which they were being constructed. To meet this threat, the Admiralty sought authority to lay down six rather than four Dreadnoughts, a figure they later increased to eight.

Balfour was greatly concerned by increasing competition and pointed out in the House of Commons that by the spring of 1912 Germany might well possess twenty-one battleships to Britain's twenty. Although the Prime Minister reluctantly proclaimed his willingness to contemplate naval increases, which to appease his radical supporters he described as 'a horrible, devastating and sterilizing expenditure,' the feeling remained that he was neglecting national security.

The King shared Balfour's anxiety and told Fisher that he was 'very much disturbed at the revelations' which had been made in the House of Commons debate on the vote of censure moved on 29 March, accusing the Government of endangering the security of the Empire and relying on too small a margin of superiority over other fleets. He was 'much annoyed' to have been left unaware of the German increase in shipbuilding when he was at Berlin in February. Under the circumstances, he sincerely hoped that 'eight Dreadnoughts' would be forthcoming. Lloyd George and Churchill refused to accept the Admiralty's arguments, insisting that four Dreadnoughts would meet the country's needs, while the Conservatives coined the slogan: 'We want eight and we won't wait.'

Fisher was delighted with the resolute way in which McKenna fought the Admiralty's battles, and begged Knollys to be sure that the King gave the First Lord every support and encouragement. In February, he sent him a letter 'of the most confidential and secret character,' the contents of which he trusted His Majesty would be 'graciously pleased not to divulge.' The Sea Lords, he said, had told McKenna that they would 'not accept four ships but must have *six*. We have made out the Navy estimates to put in *eight* ships with authority to push on the first *four* and order *everything* for the last four . . . Really we can only build *six*, as we can't make gun mountings for more, but we are going for *eight* so as to get on to the utmost! My belief is that *finally* the approved arrangement will be *six* ships as we originally said. I have had two long visits from Sir E. Grey at my house *and he quite understands we are not going to accept four ships*! All the same I am excessively glad the King is going to see McKenna tonight and I hope His Majesty will be graciously pleased to pat him on the back for he has behaved splendidly and the Prime Minister disgracefully. He *is as weak as water*! Grey is a rock. McKenna is writing an ultimatum to Asquith at this present moment telling him of the final and absolute determination of the Board of Admiralty.'

The Cabinet was so hopelessly divided over the number of Dreadnoughts to sanction that it remained deadlocked for well over a month. Grey, Haldane, Crewe and Runciman supported McKenna and the Admiralty. Lloyd George, Churchill, Harcourt, Burns and Morley agreed that four Dreadnoughts were more than enough. The Chancellor even suggested that the Reichstag had only accelerated its building programme to relieve unemployment. He and his colleagues seemed less afraid of possible German aggression than the political consequences of increasing expenditure to meet it.

One day in February 1909, Esher was walking back to the India Office with Morley, discussing the naval crisis, when they happened to meet Winston Churchill. He asked me, Esher reported to Knollys, 'to tell Jackie, that he was "as fond of him as ever," but that he, Winston, could not recede, and that six Dreadnoughts meant *his* retirement. He said that he thought Jackie might take this to be bluff, but he was serious. Evidently he thinks Lloyd George would also retire . . . On the other hand Haldane says four Dreadnoughts would mean that Grey and he would go! My impression is that six will win. If not the Government will be hopelessly discredited in Europe and in this country.'

On 24 February, Asquith succeeded in finding a compromise which satisfied McKenna and Grey as well as Lloyd George and Churchill. That evening he wrote the King a letter giving details of his 'concordat.' It provided for four new Dreadnoughts to be laid down in the ensuing financial year, 'for an Act of Parliament to be passed this session providing for a programme of Naval construction so calculated as to keep us always ahead of the German programme,' and for 'power to be given in the Act to make forward contracts for the ships of next year, so that the Government will be able (if so advised), next Autumn, to place orders for four additional Dreadnoughts, to be laid down not later than 1st April 1910.' Five months later it was agreed with surprisingly little opposition that the case for four additional Dreadnoughts was established. The Admiralty, wrote Churchill of this curious solution, originally 'demanded six ships: the economists offered four: and we finally compromised on eight.' One explanation of the Chancellor's ultimate surrender, if such it was, may be seen in a letter which Esher wrote Knollys while the battle was still raging. Lloyd George, he claimed, was 'far more reasonable than Winston and less combative. *Au fond* the man is an Imperialist, and built on the Chamberlain lines. *He* understands the situation as regards the Navy. I don't, for a moment, say that he will desert Winston and Morley and Co., but he is much more inclined to give way than they are, and if they do give way, it will be due to him.'

On the King's birthday, 9 November 1909, Fisher was given a peerage, and took the title Lord Fisher of Kilverstone. His Majesty had wished to give him a higher honour, but Asquith pointed out that even Nelson had not been so rewarded after destroying Napoleon's fleet at Aboukir Bay. Fisher, who had naturally not seen the Downing Street correspondence, grumbled at becoming 'a common or garden Peer, like the man who makes linoleum or lends money for elections.' At least, he said, they might have made him a Viscount like 'a successful brewer.'

After several consultations with McKenna and Esher, and in view of the impending general election, Fisher decided to resign in January 1910. When Beresford heard the news, he suggested a toast: 'To the death of fraud, espionage, intimidation, corruption, tyranny and self-interest, which have been a nightmare over the finest service in the world for the last four years.'

Fisher's reforms were achieved at a high price. 'The spirit of unity, which Nelson had epitomized a century earlier with his "Band of Brothers", had been torn and shattered, and the wounds lingered on until the common perils of war with Germany healed them in 1914.' Fisher's distrust of the War Office, and his obstinate conviction that the army's only use was as 'a bullet fired by the navy,' did little to promote co-operation between the Services. While Fisher was First Sea Lord nobody seemed to know what the Admiralty's war plans were. He believed that victory could best be won by unexpected attack: hence battle plans should be left to the First Sea Lord working in total secrecy. But senior officers protested that it was not only the enemy who would be taken by surprise. His strategic plans, in so far as they were ever divulged, were so outrageous that it is difficult to decide whether they were daring and imaginative, or wild and hare-brained. He once proposed, for example, that a squadron of war-ships should be sent to Devil's Island, cut the cable to France, and kidnap Dreyfus: a strategy worthy of Dumas.

What distinguished Fisher's reforms and commended them to Liberal governments was that they were initially achieved with reduced estimates. He believed that so far from economies dimin-ishing efficiency they could even contribute to it. 'Swollen estimates engender parasites both in men and ships which hamper the fighting qualities of the fleet.' When in 1918 the German navy surrendered and steamed into Scapa Flow, every clerk in the Admiralty was invited to watch, but nobody thought of asking the former First Sea Lord. Nor did anyone think of listening to his warning that 'we have stopped the war too soon.' Writing in 1923, Churchill proclaimed that there was 'no doubt whatever that Fisher was right in nine-tenths of what he fought for. His great reforms sustained the power of the Royal Navy at the most critical period in its history . . . It was Fisher who hoisted the storm-signal and beat all hands to quarters.'

The army needed reform even more than the navy. As fighting in South Africa dragged on for eighteen months into the King's reign, even the War Office began to suspect that something must be wrong. Britain's military exploits at Magersfontein, Colenso and Stormberg, appeared to vindicate Sir Charles Dilke's judgement that the army was better prepared for the parade-ground than the battle-field. Nevertheless, in some quarters, Lord Kitchener was criticized for prosecuting the war too vigorously and for refusing to stop short of unconditional surrender.

The King repeatedly expressed his belief that the Commander-in-Chief should be given a free hand in the field. In September 1901, Sir Arthur Davidson wrote to Brodrick, Lord Lansdowne's suc-cessor at the War Office, to say that His Majesty was 'greatly con-cerned with regard to the position of Lord Kitchener in South Africa, who is seriously hampered in his military operations by con-siderations forced upon him from the Colonial Office point of view which effectually prevent his carrying out in their entirety military plans which must necessarily include the restriction of liberty of action in places where this freedom has been grossly abused . . . The King sees the many great difficulties which surrounded both Mr Chamberlain and Lord Milner (High Commissioner for South

Africa) in giving Lord Kitchener a free hand, but His Majesty thinks that at present Lord Kitchener is not accorded enough freedom of action, and he, therefore, hopes you will bring your influence, as Head of the Military Department, to bear on Mr Chamberlain to induce him to see how impossible it is to expect Lord Kitchener to conclude the War unless he is allowed to adopt means which will effectively prevent his adversaries from replenishing their supplies of men and material. The King thinks that unless something of this sort is done Lord Kitchener will resign, which would have both morally and materially a disastrous effect, and which ought, therefore, at any cost to be averted.'

Sir Douglas Haig maintained that it needed a 'military disaster' to get the country and politicians, let alone the majority of senior officers, to admit the need for reforms. Certainly the Boer War exposed massive deficiencies in staff work, weapons, and training. As early as August 1901, King Edward urged a 'searching' enquiry 'into the many blunders we had made in South Africa,' and, in October 1902, he told Brodrick that 'very great reforms' were 'essential' both in the army and the War Office, as a direct outcome of recent defeats. Sir Sidney Lee went so far as to describe His Majesty as heading 'the advance guard of army reformers,' and Esher maintained that if the British Army were better prepared for the next war than the last, the nation would 'owe it to the King.' On different occasions His Majesty spoke of the War Office as 'a mutual admiration society,' described the shortcomings of its Intelligence branch as 'one of those scandals which ought to hang Lords Lansdowne and Wolseley,' and said that 'should the War Office refuse to cleanse the "Augean Stable" they must be forced to do so.' These views were so similar to those expressed by Lord Esher that they clearly owed much to his advocacy.

In April 1902, the Government decided to hold an investigation into the military shortcomings revealed by the South African War. The King, although favouring an enquiry, nevertheless opposed Lord Salisbury's plan for a Royal Commission, mainly because he believed that publication of its report would harm the army 'in the eyes of the civilized world.' It was, of course, to be hoped that we might 'profit by the many mistakes which have doubtless occurred during the campaign,' but no good could come from encouraging ridicule and abuse. 'This system of "washing one's dirty linen in public" the late Queen had a horror of, and the King shares the views of his beloved Mother.' Despite the objections of his late and living Sovereigns, Salisbury declined to abandon his plan for a Royal Commission, which sat under the chairmanship of Lord Elgin. At least His Majesty's suggestion that Lord Esher should be a member met with the Prime Minister's approval. Although the Commission's Report, published in August 1903, confined itself to analysis, offering no proposals for specific reforms, the glaring defects it exposed in military administration strengthened demands for change.

In listing the army's problems the King was inclined to include the Minister of War. Brodrick, like Curzon, was a product of Eton and Balliol. The King regarded him as too eager to interfere, too ready to overrule his military advisers, particularly Lord Roberts, the Commander-in-Chief, and too disposed to assume responsibilities he should either have shared or delegated. Brodrick was so distressed by the King's displeasure that he wrote him a long letter outlining the problems of his office and hinting that criticism increased them. In thus protesting, he paid a telling tribute to the King's marksmanship, since arrows which miss their target spill no blood.

When King Edward came to the throne, he saw more of Brodrick than any other Minister, apart from Lord Salisbury. Indeed, Campbell-Bannerman told the Government Whips 'that if the name of the Secretary for War was seen so often in the papers as having been in audience at the Palace, he would call attention to it in the House of Commons in relation to the constitutional government of the Army!' From the start, the King 'made it clear that he wished to be consulted about all questions of Army policy, and notably about appointments.' Furthermore, 'he wished to be apprised before any Cabinet decision was taken on any important military changes.' Brodrick relates in his Memoirs that he received letters from Knollys 'on questions of promotion, appointments and War honours,' at the rate of one a day during the first two months of the reign. 'The King felt that the Sovereign should no longer be a registry office, but should in many cases initiate action. His interest extended even to the promotion of civil servants within the War Department.' While Brodrick's oblique reference to Queen Victoria as a 'registry office' did less than justice to her omniscient concern for the army, it was certainly true that His Majesty shared her resolve to scrutinize appointments with meticulous care.

After Chamberlain, Ritchie and Lord George Hamilton resigned in September 1903, Balfour was forced to re-construct his Cabinet, and decided to transfer Brodrick to the India Office. On the 21st of the month, Esher was summoned to Balmoral for what he assumed was his usual week's stalking. But the moment he arrived the King asked him to go to the War Office. 'Of course I was taken aback,' Esher told his son, Maurice, 'and put several objections, which are obvious, and finally said I would think it over. Certainly I shall refuse. It is not my line to go back into politics and become identified with party strife.'

The Prime Minister did all he could to persuade Esher to join his Government. 'We had a long talk. I told him that I was sure it would be a mistake, that I was not a politician, and that I could not undertake to ally myself to a party.' Later, the King made a further attempt to overcome Esher's resistance. 'This was the most trying interview of all, and he was pathetic and entreating . . . But I was firm, and finally he admitted that perhaps I might be right.'

Generally, Balfour appointed his friends and relations to Ministerial posts. Consequently, the Government of Great Britain resembled a family partnership. On the few occasions when he strayed from the path of nepotism, he invariably stumbled into a political morass. His choice of Arnold-Forster as Secretary of State for War proved characteristically misguided. Arnold-Forster was a grandson of Dr Arnold. As both his parents died young, he was brought up by Jane Arnold, who married W. E. Forster, Gladstone's great Minister of Education. After being sent to Rugby and University College, Oxford, he was called to the Bar, acted as Private Secretary to his adopted father, whose surname he added to his own, entered publishing, wrote a number of works of instruction, and became a Unionist Member of Parliament. In 1901, Lord Salisbury made him Secretary to the Admiralty, where his industry and intelligence brought him to Fisher's notice.

Arnold-Forster was the victim of his antecedents and suffered from most of the occupational diseases to which schoolmasters are heir: he was opinionated, didactic and so assured of his infallibility that it was said that he could give His Holiness the Pope 'two stones and a licking.' Even his virtues were carried to such extremes as to threaten to turn into vices. Such, for example, was his frenzied passion for business that he drove his principal actuary mad. Sir Almeric Fitzroy described him as entering upon his task 'with the enthusiasm of the apostle and the spirit of the martyr.' Moreover, he possessed an unerring tactlessness which won him gratuitous enemies. As Esher told Knollys, he was 'extraordinarily sensitive to the smallest criticism,' 'Very touchy and querulous,' and 'a pedant with no knowledge of the World.'

King Edward, who never cared for the appointment, told Balfour that the Secretary of State lacked polish, and that it seemed improbable that his intellectual qualities would compensate for his gaucherie. The Prime Minister agreed that 'Mr Forster's *manner* is not his strong point,' and said that he could not but admit the force of His Majesty's criticism. Nevertheless, he possessed, and was '*known* to possess,' exceptional knowledge, 'untiring industry and a burning zeal for reform.'

Lord Elgin's report on the South African War had confined its attention to diagnosis, so it still remained to decide on appropriate cures. The King suggested appointing a committee of three, under Lord Esher's chairmanship, to advise on the reorganization of the War Office. He also proposed inviting Fisher to serve. The last member of the trio was Colonel Sir George Clarke, then Governor of Victoria, a shrewd, open-minded soldier and administrator. Fisher strongly supported Sir George's claims as he was known to favour 'the Naval Basis for the organization of the Army,' and was prepared to reduce military estimates so as to spend more on battleships. Here was a 'blue water' man after the Admiral's own heart. 'Humbly submit,' he telegraphed to Knollys 'he is absolutely indispensable, so please press his inclusion in the committee, which of no use without him.' By the time Clarke reached England, Fisher and Esher had completed their report. Fortunately, he found no difficulty in endorsing it: after all he had been carefully chosen as likely to share their opinions. As Esher once confessed, the most harmonious and expeditious committees are those whose members agree in advance what conclusions they ought to reach.

'The dauntless three,' or as Campbell-Bannerman called them, 'the damnable dictatorial domineering Trio,' sent the King a first report in January 1904. They made five principal proposals. First, they suggested that the Committee of Imperial Defence, established the previous year, should be greatly enlarged and given a permanent Secretariat. Secondly, they recommended the creation of a General Staff. Thirdly, they advocated a drastic reconstruction of the War Office, involving the formation of an Army Council on the lines of the Board of Admiralty. Fourthly, they planned to abolish the post of Commander-in-Chief, which for half a century had led to rivalry between the War Office and Horse Guards. As Esher told the King, 'Your Majesty is the natural head of the Army all over the World.' Finally, they suggested appointing an Inspector-General to carry out such duties as had formerly belonged to the Commander-in-Chief and had not been transferred to the Army Council.

The Committee handed their report to the Prime Minister on 26 February, having finished it in as many months as Lord Hartington had needed years to produce a similar document. The King felt convinced 'that the results of their deliberations and inquiries' would prove of 'great benefit to the Army,' and was gratified by their suggestion that the Duke of Connaught should become the first Inspector-General. Lord Roberts, Sir John French, Sir Douglas Haig, and the majority of junior officers, supported Esher's proposals. But Kitchener was bitterly hostile, resenting civilian interference, and deploring the abolition of the post of Commander-in-Chief, to which he aspired. Nevertheless, it was generally agreed that the report was bold, imaginative and admirably presented. Balfour took a close interest in army reform and supported Esher so vigorously that many of the Committee's proposals were implemented before its findings were published. On 6 February, for example, the names of the new Army Council were announced, and Lord Roberts, the last Commander-in-Chief, laid down his office.

The King, as head of the army, never hesitated to raise matters on his own initiative. In October 1903, he wrote to Lord Roberts about training senior officers, reminding him that Lord Elgin's Commission blamed many of the reverses in South Africa on their inexperience in handling large forces. The First Army Corps at Aldershot, he pointed out, was supposedly being trained 'with a view to being ready at any moment to be sent on active service.' But nearly all the brigades had no brigadiers and would only receive one on mobilization. 'The King much doubts the wisdom of spending large sums of money in training men if the officers who will lead them in war are not trained at the same time.'

There were occasions when the King's obsessive concern with buttons and buckles led him to forget that there was more to soldiering than uniforms and accoutrements. He needed Sir Percy Scott to remind him that gunnery was as vital as looking 'pretty.' But, trivial as some of his comments may seem, they were by no means all foolish. After all, a greater soldier than King Edward once proclaimed that men are led by baubles. When the War Office got khaki 'on the brain,' His Majesty intervened to restrain its enthusiasm for doing away with all that was splendid and gorgeous and dressing soldiers in shoddy. Of course it was 'more invisible than blue and red, and admirably adapted to those climates where there is but little vegetation and chiefly dust and mud,' but regiments on home duty should be permitted to wear more distinctive uniforms. When King Edward learned that it had been decided to abolish the red pugaree worn by the Duke of Cornwall's Light Infantry, he instructed Ponsonby to protest to the Quartermaster-General on the grounds that the matter had not been submitted to him, that the Regiment had been granted this head-dress as a token of their gallantry in the American War of Independence, and that he could see no objection to their continuing to wear it while not on active service. 'The King knows you agree with him in thinking that every-thing possible should be done to keep up these historical distinctions which are so precious to a Regiment.' In the end it was agreed that the pugaree might be worn 'to perpetuate the distinctive red tuft granted to the 46th Regiment for gallantry in the field in 1777.'

Arnold-Forster was reluctantly compelled to reduce the size of the army in response to political pressures. Sir Arthur Bigge, himself a former soldier, told Knollys that after reading the War Minister's proposals he felt inclined to rub his eyes 'wondering if I am dream-ing.' It was difficult to believe that the same party was in power 'that held office from 1895 until the end of the South African War, for I call to mind the strenuous efforts, earnest representations and the endless negotiations which were brought into play in order to induce the country and Parliament to sanction the increase to the Army of a few Battalions. I think I am correct in saying that Lord Lansdowne and Mr Brodrick declared that the extra Battalions they respectively asked for were essential to the safety of the Empire. With my own hand I wrote a letter to the Commander-in-Chief in the Queen's name appealing to the patriotism of those officers and men who had served in the Army to return to the Colours.

'The same Government which has passed through such bitter and costly experiences, now proposes to abolish at least fourteen bat-talions of the line. Were Lansdowne, Brodrick, Wolseley, Wood, Buller all wrong? The German Emperor at a review at Aldershot said to me "I have told my Staff to take particular notice of the Horse Artillery for there is nothing like it in the world: but what funny people you are, I hear you are going to abolish some of the batteries. I quite see that the cost of the Army must be reduced, but this could be done by reducing the strength of the battalions, to say five hundred men. But for heaven's sake leave the Cadres! You can easily expand from five hundred to eight hundred or a thousand in time of war, but the creation of new regiments is no easy matter." Forgive this long letter. But I was so long behind the scenes and always took great interest in Army matters that I confess feeling alarmed at what is foreshadowed by Mr. A. Forster's new scheme.'

Arnold-Forster made the fatal but not uncommon mistake of failing to keep King Edward sufficiently informed. Consequently Knollys was instructed to send him letters of pained protest. Irritated by such criticism, he noted in his Diary: 'I suppose soon I shan't be able to ask my private secretary to tea without consulting the King, the Cabinet, Lord Esher and the Committee of Defence.'

In order to brief Knollys, Esher prepared a memorandum describing Queen Victoria's relations with various War Ministers, 'taking a few volumes haphazard from the collection of Army papers at Windsor.' These showed 'how fully the Queen was kept informed, and how frequently questions put by her to her Ministers led to a reconsideration of some nomination or proposal, which had been rather too hastily agreed upon by the military authorities of the day. For it is not solely in the interests of the Crown's prerogative that upon all military questions the Sovereign should be kept informed, and the King's approval sought. It is in the interests of the Army, that a Permanent Authority, beyond the reach of parliamentary and professional pressure, should exercise the very important functions of criticism and control. The questions which the Sovereign may think it necessary to put to a Minister, sometimes give trouble, and the Ministers have been restive in past times under these criticisms, but I have rarely come across a case where the fact of having to put *on paper* a reasoned argument for an appointment or for a proposal, has not led either to a statement so clear and strong as at once to carry the point, or a reconsideration of a step which had been hastily taken and which, but for the interference of the Sovereign, would have been final and productive of injury to the service.

'Arnold-Forster, who, of course, has had a very limited experience, thinks that an interview now and again with the King, during which he *argues* some question of principle with which he is engrossed at the moment, is a fulfilment of the duty which the Secretary of State for War owes to the Sovereign. If that were to be admitted, the Army would very seriously suffer. The King – if the old tradition is to be maintained – should require all proposed appointments of any importance, and all changes of any importance, affecting the organization, discipline or administration of the Army, to be laid before him *in good time*, in order that H.M. may understand and approve them before they are put into force . . . I am afraid this is rather a pedantic letter, and I am conscious that it reads like a portion of a Constitutional Treatise, but I feel very strongly the great importance of the considerations which you urged in your letter to the Secretary of State and which I think he has failed to realize.'

While Lord Esher's Committee transformed the War Office, Arnold-Forster devoted his attention to other defects exposed by Lord Elgin's Commission. By July 1905 he was finally ready to announce his proposed reforms to the House of Commons. The King, who had been sent details of them in June, was unimpressed, and told Balfour that he was 'strongly of opinion that what the Army, especially the Officers throughout the Army, requires at the present time, is a period free from disturbance and constant change. The King could understand the necessity for a large plan of Army Reform, based on clear and definite principles . . . But the King must view with regret proposals which are admittedly "half measures," of a tentative character, the urgent necessity for which is not apparent, and which are not calculated to reassure the officers and men of the Army, who have been disturbed by the uncertain prospects held out to them under the various projects which the Secretary of State has foreshadowed from time to time as imminent. The King cannot withhold his consent from the proposals which he is advised by the Cabinet to approve, but he cannot conceal his strong misgivings as to the effect which the announcement will have upon the Army.'

Shortly before Balfour resigned, Lord Roberts warned his fellow peers that Britain's armed forces 'were absolutely unfitted and unprepared for War.' Although Fisher declared that invasion was inconceivable, provided the Fleet remained supreme, Roberts believed that it would be possible to land some sixty thousand men in a sudden 'Bolt-from-the-Blue.' Both he, the King and Esher agreed that a volunteer army was bound to fall short of our needs in a major war.

Haldane, having aspired to become Lord Chancellor, was dismayed to be asked to succeed Arnold-Forster, as the War Office was known as a graveyard of reputations. Nevertheless, he turned out to be the greatest Secretary of State since Cardwell. Haldane was educated at Edinburgh and Göttingen, became a lawyer, wrote books on philosophy and represented East Lothian for over quarter of a century. Having championed the army during the Boer War against his Liberal colleagues, he was one of the few leading members of the party accepted in military circles. Unlike Brodrick and Arnold-

Forster, who arrived at the War Office with cut-and-dried plans for reform, Haldane began with a thorough review of the problems likely to face him. Gifted as he was as a writer, he was no orator. His matter was admirable, but his delivery emptied the House. H. G. Wells, with the effrontery of a pot reproaching a kettle, likened his voice to a beast in pain.

The new Secretary of State was an ardent admirer of Germany. He slept with Goethe under his pillow, translated Schopenhauer into English, and was profoundly influenced by Hegel. 'Since the days of antiquity,' he once said, 'no nation had brought forth so proud a line of great thinkers as those who gazed at the smoking ruins Napoleon had left in his wake.'

In the summer of 1906, Haldane was invited by the Kaiser to attend army manoeuvres near Berlin. Before paying this visit, he decided to spend a short holiday at Marienbad, where the King went out of his way to invite him to dinner, picnics and drives in the country. On one occasion, he instructed Haldane to buy an Austrian hat so that they might drink coffee together disguised as natives. The Minister became 'much attached' to the King, who asked for Haldane's name to be added to the 'list of dinner and weekend guests he liked to meet.' Indeed, so intrigued was he by the clarity of Haldane's mind that he told the Kaiser he was 'one of the cleverest men in England.' Looking back on his relations with King Edward, Haldane described them as unusually close 'as between Minister and Sovereign.' His Majesty 'was one of the few outside the professional soldiers who understood what I was trying to do for his army, and without his constant support and advice I could not have done what I have done.'

Haldane began his career at the War Office by telling his colleagues that what he had in mind was an 'Hegelian Army': a prospect calculated to dismay both friend and foe. In practice, he was guided by three basic principles. First, that home defence depended upon the navy, but that, nevertheless, some troops must be available to destroy such enemy forces as might contrive to land. Second, that we needed an expeditionary force to assist our allies in Europe. Third, that it was imperative to reorganize the Militia, Yeomanry and Volunteers as potential front line troops. Whatever means were contemplated to achieve these ends would have to satisfy Winston Churchill and Lloyd George. Most of the radical members of Haldane's party looked on the army with deep distrust, supposing it to be Conservative, incompetent and costly. Like

Fisher, he could only hope to achieve improvements by promising economies. But he also had to contend with the argument that the best method of financing Dreadnoughts was to cut back military estimates.

Haldane was less disposed than most to believe that Germany threatened the peace of Europe, but he still saw it as his duty to provide for that possibility. In so doing, he was wholeheartedly supported by the King and Campbell-Bannerman, who had himself been Secretary of State for War in Gladstone's last two ministries. Above all, Lord Esher played a vital, if invisible, role in instigating and implementing Haldane's schemes. Between them they created the Territorial Army, a reserve of fourteen infantry divisions and fourteen mounted brigades, which only required a few weeks' intensive training to be ready for war.

The King was indefatigable in supporting the Territorials. Indeed, Knollys questioned the wisdom of showing such public enthusiasm for measures which savoured of party politics. But, heedless of all warnings, he presented Colours to newly formed battalions and held innumerable levees for Territorial Officers. In October 1907, he summoned the Lord-Lieutenants of England, Scotland and Wales to Buckingham Palace, and urged them to use their influence in launching County Associations and to do everything in their power to help the Secretary of State. Haldane wrote the King a deeply grateful letter 'for the great influence given to the movement for the organization of a Territorial Army by the example which Your Majesty has shown to the Lieutenants of the Counties. Mr Haldane believes that they have quitted your Majesty's presence with a new sense of their responsibility and with a greatly heightened realization of the nature of the national effort in which their King has summoned them to bear a notable part.'

The magnitude of Haldane's reforms may be judged by the torrent of criticism they attracted. The Militia, the most ancient reserve force of the Crown, resented proposals for change and obstructed reorganization. Lord Kitchener dismissed Esher's schemes as those of a military illiterate, and said that Haldane's 'Town Clerk's Army' was better equipped for picnics on Salisbury Plain than withstanding a resolute enemy. In the event of war in Europe, the Germans would 'walk through the French line like partridge.' It was absurd to imagine that we could depend upon a handful of volunteers to defeat millions of conscripts.

Lord Roberts combined criticism of Haldane's reforms with a

public campaign for compulsory military service. But, despite the force of his arguments, no political party dared support conscription. To have done so would have courted electoral suicide. King Edward sympathized with what Lord Roberts said, but thought him unwise to stir up fears of invasion. Just as Tirpitz had talked of threats from England when seeking to build his fleet, so Lord Roberts spoke of German aggression to justify his views. Naturally such language gravely damaged relations with the Kaiser. So much so, that the King sent Knollys to beg the Field-Marshal to be more diplomatic, and give the voluntary principle a full and fair trial. If it succeeded, our military problems were solved. If it failed, nothing could show more clearly the need for compulsion.

No sooner had Asquith become Prime Minister than Lloyd George and Churchill began clamouring for drastic reductions in military expenditure. There was precious little love lost between Haldane and the Chancellor. Lloyd George called his colleague the 'Minister of Slaughter,' and Haldane spoke of Lloyd George as 'unbalanced'. On Waterloo Day, 1908, Churchill circulated a memorandum in which he maintained that the army was too large and that the 'Expeditionary Force was not justified by any legitimate need of British policy.' Such an initiative coming from the President of the Board of Trade was unusual, and led Esher to observe: 'He thinks himself Napoleon.' The army, according to Churchill, was only intended for 'minor emergencies.' In the event of the navy failing to stop an invasion, 'whether doubled or halved the Army would not be able to cope.'

The King privately encouraged Haldane to stand firm against such attacks, and admired the dexterity with which he defended his estimates. 'I saw Haldane this morning,' Esher told Knollys on 22 May. 'He realizes that he is on the threshold of a desperate struggle. His determination is fixed, and he will not assent to any reduction *at all* in the personnel of the Army. His view is that the irreducible minimum has been reached. He has a strong case, and, if the Cabinet decides against him, he will resign at once. From this he declares nothing will induce him to swerve. The forces arrayed against him are considerable because of the reputation – quite undeserved so far – in the Country of the Chancellor of the Exchequer and of Churchill.'

Soon after going to the War Office, Haldane created a new command with its Headquarters at Malta. The King, believing the arrangement would further 'the military federation of the Empire,' pressed the Duke of Connaught to become the first Commander-in-

Chief at Valetta. The Duke was most reluctant to comply, believing the strategy ill-conceived and the post superfluous, but in the end deferred to his brother's wishes. Experience of the Mediterranean command confirmed HRH's fears, and he soon began complaining that the experiment had failed and that the arrangement was proving wasteful and inefficient. Finally, in July 1909, he told the Prime Minister that he proposed to resign in October. 'I was I hope civil,' wrote Asquith to Knollys, 'but I gave him no ground whatever for supposing that I did anything but deplore his action. I am really sorry that the Duke (under whatever influences) should show himself so inaccessible to reason.'

The King was furious, and harsh things were said on either side. The Duke alleged that the King was envious of his popularity in England and wanted him out of the country. The King maintained that his brother spent so much time on leave that Haldane's scheme had never been given a chance. In replying to the Prime Minister's letter announcing HRH's decision to resign, His Majesty claimed to be 'much annoyed at his brother's persistent obstinacy,' and said that the Duke 'must now consider his military career at an end.'

Haldane, still believing that the command was a matter of 'high strategy,' offered it to Lord Kitchener, who turned it down. So the King was prevailed on to send him the following telegram: 'I much hope that you will accept the proposal which should reach you today from Mr. Haldane. This proposal is strongly supported both by myself and all my Ministers. I take a personal interest in the matter and attach great importance to your acceptance. Edward R.' 'I am very grateful to Your Majesty,' Kitchener replied, 'for the consideration you have given to my case and I am telegraphing to Mr Haldane in the sense Your Majesty wishes.'

Soon Kitchener, like the Duke of Connaught before him, realized that Haldane had blundered and after a time convinced the King that the Malta command was a 'damned rotten billet.' His Majesty sought to make amends by securing his brother's appointment as Governor-General of Canada, and by urging Asquith to make Kitchener Viceroy of India.

Haldane's reforms were so thorough that he even made allowance for *dix minutes d'arrêt* during which an expeditionary force could drink cups of tea after disembarking in France. Throughout his five years at the War Office, he was attacked by the Conservatives for not doing enough, and by his 'supporters' for doing too much. Most radicals 'could see nothing but criminal folly in a government of the left mending instead of ending our military system.' The King's support for his schemes was therefore especially valuable. Indeed, it could be argued that His Majesty's concern for the armed services was almost as important as his diplomatic ventures.

Britain was far better prepared for war in 1914 than in 1793, 1854 or 1899. So much so, that Sir John Fortescue spoke of the British Expeditionary Force as being 'perfect to the last detail,' and 'incomparably the finest army which ever set sail from England.' Yet, as Clemenceau repeatedly pointed out, a hundred thousand men were not enough. Until England had 'a national army worthy of the name' the *entente* would not save France. He did less than justice to the Territorials when he called them 'a plaything,' but he was right to warn King Edward to nurture his Army.

Like Fisher, Haldane was one of the principal architects of victory and like Fisher his country showed him base ingratitude. To their everlasting shame, the Conservatives insisted in 1915 that he should be left out of the Coalition Government because of his 'pro-German sympathies.' It was unforgivable that friends like Grey and Asquith yielded to ignorant clamour, but it was even more disgraceful that the Opposition, who had watched him laboriously reorganize the British Army, should ever have voiced the demand. At least Haig recognized what soldiers owed him. Immediately he returned from France after the Armistice, he went to the house in Queen Anne's Gate 'where Haldane lay forgotten and neglected, and there left a copy of his Dispatches inscribed "to the greatest of British War Ministers".'

XI

〰〰〰〰〰〰〰〰〰〰〰〰〰〰〰〰〰〰〰〰〰〰〰

Death of the King

The King's last illness began in March 1910 while he was staying in Paris on his way to Biarritz. It seems that he caught a chill while watching Edmond Rostand's *Chantecler*, with which he was 'dreadfully disappointed.' 'I never saw anything so stupid and childish and more like a Pantomime!' he told Prince George. 'The heat of the theatre was awful and I contrived to get a chill with a threatening of bronchitis.' In fact, on returning from the theatre he had felt so ill that Sir James Reid feared he might die and stayed with him all night. After a time the air of Biarritz began to work its wonders, but the King still suffered from bronchitis and seemed worried and out of sorts. The evening before he returned to England, he stood on the verandah of his hotel, gazing out to sea, and spoke of leaving next day, 'perhaps for good.'

King Edward arrived back in London on 27 April in excellent spirits and looking better for his holiday. That evening he visited Covent Garden to hear Tetrazzini sing Gilda in *Rigoletto*, one of his favourite operas. Lord Redesdale saw him take his usual corner place in the omnibus box, and sit there alone. 'Then he got up, and I heard him give a great sigh. He opened the door of the box, lingered for a little in the doorway, with a very sad expression on his face – so unlike himself – took a last look at the house, as if to bid it farewell, and then went out.'

Having stayed two days in London, during which he saw several of his Ministers, he travelled down to Sandringham. After Church on Sunday morning, he spent a long time wandering round the gardens, although it was cold, windy and wet. When he returned to

Buckingham Palace on 2 May, he was suffering from a chill, but dined out that evening with Agnes Keyser at Grosvenor Crescent. Next morning, after a night of severe bronchial attacks, his doctors tried to persuade him to rest, but nothing would induce him to remain in bed or to give up transacting business. During a visit from Sir Francis Hopwood, the Permanent Under-Secretary of the Colonial Office, the King was seized with a terrible fit of choking. Sir Francis begged him to rest, saying there was not a man in his Empire who would continue to work when so obviously ill. But His Majesty would not listen. 'I shall work to the end,' he said. 'Of what use is it to be alive if one cannot work?'

Queen Alexandra was spending a short holiday at Corfu when she heard that the King was unwell. Without realizing just how ill he was, she decided to return. On landing at Dover on 5 May, Princess Victoria was handed a letter from her brother asking her to prepare their mother for the worst, and to warn her that the King was in no condition to meet her at the station. The Queen seemed unable to grasp the gravity of the situation, until she actually saw her husband hunched up in a chair, battling for breath and looking tired and grey. As soon as the returned travellers came into his room, he smiled and welcomed them home. But, hard as he tried, he could not conceal his difficulty in speaking. Somehow he managed to ask a few questions about their journey, and said he hoped that they had not come back because of him. When he noticed Princess Victoria glancing anxiously at a cylinder of oxygen, he reassured her by saying 'I have had this often.'

At first, he refused to consent to a bulletin being published, but gave way when the Prince of Wales pointed out that people would wonder what had prevented him from meeting the Queen at the station. At seven-thirty in the evening of 5 May, a bulletin was issued with His Majesty's approval, saying that he was suffering 'from bronchitis and that his condition causes some anxiety.'

Next morning, Friday 6 May, the King felt 'wretchedly ill,' and only contrived to smoke half a cigar. Nevertheless, he could not be prevented from dressing in a frock coat to receive Sir Ernest Cassel. Both Sir Francis Laking and the Queen begged Sir Ernest to try to prevent the King talking too much and to make his visit brief. Later that day, Cassel told his daughter how His Majesty, ill as he was, insisted upon 'rising from his chair to shake hands with me. He looked as if he had suffered great pain, and spoke indistinctly. His kindly smile came out as he congratulated me on having you brought home so much improved in health. He said, "I am very seedy, but I wanted to see you. Tell your daughter how glad I am that she had safely got home and that I hope she will be careful and patient so as to recover complete health." He then talked about other matters, and I had to ask his leave to go as I felt it was not good for him to go on speaking . . . Sir James Reid told me he had dressed on purpose to receive me, and they could not stop him.'

As soon as the Archbishop of Canterbury learned that the King was seriously ill, he hurried to Buckingham Palace. During the course of the day, he had some quiet and he hoped helpful talk both with the Prince of Wales and 'poor Knollys, whose grief was most touching.' As the day drew on, the King began to lose consciousness, but in lucid moments recognized he was dying. 'I shall not give in,' he was heard to mutter, 'I shall work to the end.' The Queen, in a gesture of heroic magnanimity, sent for Mrs Keppel to give her the opportunity to take her last farewell. When the end was evidently approaching, the Archbishop said the Commendatory Prayer, and a few moments afterwards the King ceased to breathe. 'I have seldom or never seen a quieter passing of the river,' wrote Davidson of his vigil. Hawkins, the King's second valet, said that His Majesty had often expressed a presentiment that he would die on a Friday.

It was later rumoured that Edward VII, like Charles II before him, had died a Roman Catholic. Supposedly, Father Forster, the Priest-in-Charge of St Edward's, Westminster, within whose parish the Royal residences lay, had administered the last sacrament and received him into the Church. It greatly amused Forster to be held responsible for so dramatic a conversion. He did, however, admit 'that in old days, whenever King Edward had Catholic guests at Marlborough House, he was invited to bring them the Sacrament. On such occasions the Prince and Princess of Wales, as they were, always met him at the door and conducted him upstairs with lighted tapers.'

The King's death at the time seemed very sudden. The outcry raised only two years before when he wished to remain at Biarritz, showed that the public had little idea how ill he was. In fact, the problem was not so much to account for the King's death as to explain how he lived so long, considering what he ate, drank and smoked.

Writing from Yokohama on 7 May, Sir Felix Semon told Knollys that his thoughts went back 'to that morning three years ago, when

Sir Francis Laking and I handed you that report, which I strongly felt it my *duty* to make and which had been so sadly justified by the course of events! I don't think anybody will call me an "alarmist" now! How I wish the King instead of going home direct from Biarritz, had, as usual during the last few years, made a Mediterranean trip and returned much later than he did! But I suppose, the political constellation rendered that course impossible. It is too sad to speculate upon what might have been.'

The King's body remained in the bedroom in which he died for over a week. Neither King George nor his mother could be persuaded for several days to fix the date of the funeral. Later, the Queen told Theodore Roosevelt, who chanced to be visiting Europe at the time, 'They took him away from me, they took him away from me. You see, he was so wonderfully preserved. It must have been the oxygen they gave him before he died. It was most extraordinary – but they took him away from me.'

Queen Alexandra sent for King Edward's old friends so that they might take a last look at him before he was put in his coffin. 'Today I said goodbye to our dear King,' wrote Esher in his Journal on 10 May. 'The Queen sent for me, and there she was, in a simple black dress with nothing to mark specially her widowhood, and moving gently about his room as if he were a child asleep. The King was lying on the bed in which he always slept. His head was inclined gently to one side. No appearance of pain or death. There was even a glow on his face and the usual happy smile of the dead who die peacefully. The Queen talked for half an hour, just as she has always talked to me, with only a slight diminution of her natural gaiety, but with a tenderness which betrayed all the love in her soul, and oh! so natural feeling that she had got him there altogether to herself. In a way she seemed, and is, I am convinced, happy. It is the womanly happiness of complete possession of the man who was the love of her youth, and – as I fervently believe – all her life. She talked much of their ultimate resting place together and of the impending hour when they take him away from her. Once she said, "What is to become of me?" Round the room were all the things just as he had last used them, with his hats hanging on the pegs as he loved them to do.'

Ponsonby was in the country when the King died and was sent for by the Queen. As soon as he arrived at the Palace, she took him to the King's bedroom. 'The blinds were down and there was a screen round the bed, so that at first I could see nothing, but when we came round it I saw the poor King lying apparently asleep. I was very much awed and hardly liked to speak except in a whisper, but the Queen spoke quite naturally and said how peaceful he looked and that it was a comfort to think he had suffered no pain. She said she felt as if she had been turned into stone, unable to cry, unable to grasp the meaning of it all, and incapable of doing anything. She added that she would like to go and hide in the country, but there was this terrible State Funeral and all the dreadful arrangements that had to be made.'

At last, on the evening of Saturday, 14 May, the King's remains were transferred to an oak coffin and placed on a purple catafalque in the Throne Room of Buckingham Palace, with the Royal Standard draped over it, and the Crown, Sceptre and Orb at its head and foot.

Until King Edward's death it was not the custom for Sovereigns to lie in state. It is true that the coffin of George III was placed in St George's Chapel the day before his funeral, but otherwise there was no precedent for the decision that 'the remains of his late Majesty King Edward VII of blessed memory' should lie in state in Westminster Hall from 17–20 May. The King's coffin was carried down the Mall to Westminster on a gun-carriage drawn by eight black horses, while bells tolled and batteries of guns in Hyde Park fired a farewell salute. As the procession left Buckingham Palace, the Royal Standard was hoisted once more, visibly asserting the dictum: 'The King is dead. Long live the King!'

George V, dressed in the uniform of an Admiral, walked alone behind the gun-carriage, followed by Prince Edward and Prince Albert, then naval cadets at Osborne, and Queen Alexandra and her sister, the Dowager Empress of Russia, who rode in a state coach. 'The whole proceedings were, by universal consent, regarded as dignified, simple, devotional and impressive.'

On reaching Westminster Hall King Edward's coffin was placed near the spot where Charles I had been sentenced to death. In its nine hundred years of history never before had so many people passed under its roof in so short a time. The waiting crowd stretched back to Chelsea Bridge, and silent mourners braved hours of torrential rain before filing past the catafalque. In three days, some half a million people paid this last tribute to King Edward.

On 20 May, the King's coffin left Westminster Hall on its final journey to Windsor. By one o'clock in the morning the streets of London were lined with people. In the words of a funeral ballad sold to the waiting crowds:

'A King he was from head to sole,
Loved by his people one and all.'

After a stormy night, the clouds cleared and the sun shone brilliantly all morning. Following primitive funeral customs, Queen Alexandra gave instructions that her husband's favourite charger, 'Kildare', should follow behind the coffin, and then 'Caesar', led by a Highlander.

When, later that month, Esher called on Francis and Charlotte Knollys at Buckingham Palace, he noted that 'Caesar the dear King's dog came to tea. He won't go near the Queen – and waits all day for his master, wandering about the house.' The sight of the faithful terrier trotting behind the gun-carriage, surrounded by Kings and Queens and Princes, led even those 'unused to the melting mood,' to reach for their handkerchiefs. Caesar became such a national hero that an enterprising publisher brought out a Memoir of the late King entitled: *Where's Master?*

Shortly after the funeral, Margot Asquith visited the Queen Mother. Noticing a large photograph of Caesar, she said: 'Poor little dog. His devotion to your King, Ma'am, touched every spectator.' 'Horrid little dog!' came the unexpected reply. 'He never went near my poor husband when he was ill!' 'But Ma'am,' said Margot, 'the day you took my husband to see the King when he was dead, the dog was lying at his feet.' 'For warmth, my dear,' she replied.

In addition to a glittering cavalcade of Princes, resplendent in scarlet and gold, nine Sovereigns rode in the procession, every one of whom was related to King Edward. King George V was his son, the Kaiser his nephew, King George I of Greece and King Frederick VIII of Denmark were brothers-in-law, King Haakon of Norway a son-in-law, King Manuel II of Portugal, King Ferdinand I of Bulgaria and King Albert I of the Belgians were Coburg cousins of varying degrees of remoteness, and King Alfonso XIII of Spain had married his niece, Princess Ena. A procession of carriages followed the Kings and Princes, containing the Queen Mother, the Dowager Empress of Russia, Queen Mary, the late King's daughters, Theodore Roosevelt and the French Foreign Minister. In the twelfth and last coach sat a sorrowful figure whom few spectators recognized, and whose humble place concealed his true importance. Nobody understood this better than Lord Rosebery, who sent Knollys the following note when he heard of the King's death. 'In this terrible calamity, public and private, after the family I think most of you. It is half your life gone;

but you can look back to forty years of unstinted and absolute devotion, and loyal service such as I think has rarely been given by man to man. That must be some comfort to you.'

Soon after the Royal Train steamed into Windsor Station, a hundred sailors from HMS *Excellent*, the gunnery school which Fisher had once commanded, dragged the gun-carriage up the hill to St George's Chapel, following the accidental precedent of 1901. Inside the Chapel, Queen Alexandra, leaning on a stick, stood near the place where Archbishop Longley had married her almost half a century before. 'The minor canons seemed lost to all sense of the dignity of the ceremonial on which they were engaged and were occupied in craning their necks forward in every posture of idle curiosity, in order to obtain a view of what was passing outside the building; the choir followed their example, and shaped into a huddled mob, while the Dean of Windsor, whose duty it was, as their leader and head, to see that order prevailed, deserted his place for a seat among the spectators, where he became absorbed in conversation with a lady.'

Towards the close of the service, King Edward's coffin was lowered into the Chancel Crypt, to rest beside that of the Duke of Clarence. The ceremony ended with the Archbishop scattering three handfuls of dust into the void below, and the Garter King of Arms proclaiming to one of the most exalted congregations ever assembled, that it had pleased 'Almighty God to take out of this transitory life into his Divine Mercy the late Most High, Most Mighty, and Most Excellent Monarch, Edward VII, by the Grace of God, of the United Kingdom of Great Britain and Ireland and of the British Dominions beyond the Seas, King, Defender of the Faith, Emperor of India, and Sovereign of the Most Noble Order of the Garter.'

After the funeral, the congregation were given a magnificent luncheon in St George's Hall, during which 'the Kaiser seized the opportunity to take the French Ambassador aside and – with the King's food scarcely out of his throat and the King's wine scarcely dry on his lips – made a sinister suggestion as to the possibility of France siding with Germany in the eventuality of Germany challenging England, a suggestion which M. Paul Cambon diplomatically affected to misunderstand.'

For several weeks after the King's death, Lord Knollys received countless letters consoling him for his loss and paying tribute to his loyalty and devotion. Nobody could speak with more authority than Lord Esher, who told him: 'The world wide tributes of the past week have been very wonderful, and you must have got some little consolation from them. To me they appear, if you will let me say so, in some measure a recognition of your life's work. Perhaps no-one will ever know quite what you were to the King, but I think I have guessed.'

Another letter which gave Knollys special pleasure came from Sir Charles Hardinge, who assured him that 'Ever since the terrible catastrophe of Friday night my thoughts have been with you, dear friend, the most intimate and almost lifelong friend and adviser of our beloved King. For you the loss of him is far greater than for almost anybody else, but I hope and trust that a loyal duty performed with an absolutely single-minded devotion, which should be an example to us all, may afford you some consolation and comfort in the terrible loss that we all, and you in particular, have sustained in the death of our King. Unhappy as I am at the loss of a master who was always so good and kind to me, I feel how insignificant my loss is compared with yours, and I wanted to write you a few lines to tell you of my very deep and heartfelt sympathy. May God help you to bear the blow.'

Knollys also received a generous letter from Lord Charles Beresford. 'My dear Francis,' wrote the Admiral, 'No-one in the Empire will feel the terrible loss it has sustained more than yourself. After the long years of affectionate devotion to the late King to find him gone from you for ever is an irreparable, a cruel and a crushing blow. Your tact, skill and sound advice given to the late King must often have been invaluable to him and as I wrote to you once before has never been appreciated in its full merit by the Country, but your many friends know well what the Empire owes to you. Poor old Francis. I have known you many years and have always found you the same. Your life has been devoted to the welfare of the King and Country. Believe me when I tell you how sincerely and affectionately I feel for you in a sorrow that will take all your fortitude and strength to bear. You may derive some small consolation from the knowledge that all your friends can never forget your splendid services and affectionate devotion to our poor dead King. I remain my dear Francis, Yours ever, Charlie Beresford.'

Lord Farquhar, the Master of the Household, also wrote Knollys a touching letter. 'My dear Francis,' he said, 'I feel I must write to you before I go to bed. I am afraid to say all I want to you for fear of breaking down, but that my whole heart is with you in this great sorrow I am sure you know . . . It must be a comfort for you to recognize that you have ever been by far the best, the most devoted, the most valuable and the most loyal servant our good and great king ever had and in his great name yours will always be associated by those who know the truth. This is what I want to say to you and may God bless you.'

Some newspaper eulogies of the late King were so absurdly extravagant as to pass belief. But Wilfrid Scawen Blunt privately reached a verdict devoid of deference or sentiment. 'Today,' he noted in his Journal on 20 May, 'the King was buried, and I hope the Country will return to comparative sanity, for at present it is in delirium. He might have been a Solon and a Franeis of Assisi combined if the characters drawn of him were true. In no print has there been the smallest allusion to any of his pleasant little wickednesses . . . Yet all the bishops and priests, Catholic, Protestant, and Non-Conformist, join in giving him a glorious place in heaven . . . For myself I think he performed his duties well. He had a passion for pageantry and ceremonial and dressing up, and he was never tired of putting on uniforms and taking them off, and receiving princes and ambassadors and opening museums and hospitals, and attending cattle shows and military shows and shows of every kind, while every night of his life he was to be seen at theatres and operas and music-halls. Thus he was always before the public and had come to have the popularity of an actor who plays his part in a variety of costumes, and always well.

'Abroad, too, there is no doubt he had a very great reputation. His little Bohemian tastes made him beloved at Paris, and he had enough of the "grand seigneur" to carry it off. He did not affect to be virtuous, and all sorts of publicans and sinners found their place at his table . . . He quarrelled with nobody and always forgave. He disliked family scandals, and spent much of his time patching up those of the Court and whitening its sepulchres . . .

'It was the same with his peace-making diplomacy. He liked to be well received wherever he went, and to be on good terms with all the world. He was essentially a cosmopolitan, and without racial prejudice, and he cared as much for popularity abroad as at home. This made him anxious to compose international quarrels. He wanted an easy life, and that everybody should be friends with everybody . . . He knew Europe well, and exactly what foreigners thought of England. The knowledge was of use to him and to our Foreign Office, especially under such insular Secretaries of State as Arthur Balfour and Edward Grey.'

King Edward's qualities were easily discernible even from afar. It was only necessary to be a short time in his company to be aware of his *joie de vivre*, his infectious gaiety, his interest in everything and everybody, his boyish energy and winning charm. Perhaps the tribute which would most have astonished his parents was paid him by Asquith in the House of Commons, when he spoke of the King's strong and abiding sense of his regal responsibilities. 'His duty to the State always came first. There was no better man of business; no man by whom the humdrum obligations – punctuality, method, preciseness and economy of time and speech – were more keenly recognized or more severely practised . . . Wherever he was, whatever may have been his preoccupations, in the transactions of the State there were never any arrears, never any trace of confusion, and never any moment of avoidable delay.' King Edward was open in all his dealings, candid in giving opinions, and steadfast in keeping his word. But above all, as Lord Hugh Cecil said, he was 'one of the most lovable of human beings.'

No man was less likely than Edward VII to pretend to be more virtuous than he was. He freely acknowledged his failure to observe the seventh commandment as rigidly as he should. What is less well known is how faithfully he kept the other nine. It is said that a man may best be judged by his friends, so Lord Esher shall have the last word. 'I have known all the great men of my time in this land of ours, and many beyond it. He was the most kingly of them all.'

Cap Martin Hotel
April 8.th

My dear Francis,

I am sending you [Waddington's?]
original letter & the
copy of my answer
to him — also the
copy of a letter he wrote
[...] [Lord?] B. Please keep
these & if you like show
them to S. McDonnell.
Now let me thank
you for yours of 5.th &
in the main I quite
agree with every word
you have written.
After receiving W's letter
I took 3 or 4 days to
consider well — what
I should answer.
I consulted nobody
but felt that a

Prince of Wales to Sir Francis Knollys. 8 April [1892].

Cap Martin Hotel
April 8th

My dear Francis,
I am sending you Waterford's
original letter and the
copy of my answer
to him – also the
copy of a letter he wrote
to Lady B. Please keep
these and if you like show
them to S. McDonnell.
Now let me thank
you for yours of 5th and
in the main I quite
agree with every word
you have written.
After receiving W's letter
I took 3 or 4 days to
consider well what
I should answer.
I consulted *nobody*
but felt that a

Chronology

1841	November 9th	Prince of Wales born.
1842	January 25th	Prince of Wales christened.
1849	April	Birch becomes Prince's tutor.
1852	January	Gibbs appointed Prince's tutor.
1855	August	Prince visits Paris with parents.
1858	April 1st	Prince confirmed.
1858	November	Gibbs retires.
1858	November	Colonel Bruce becomes Prince's Governor.
1859	January	Prince visits Italy.
1859	July	Prince at Edinburgh University.
1859	October	Prince goes to Oxford.
1860	July	Prince's State tour of Canada.
1860	September	Prince visits United States.
1860	November	Prince returns to Oxford.
1861	January	Prince goes to Cambridge.
1861	July	Prince trains at Curragh.
1861	September 24th	Prince meets Alix at Speyer.
1861	December 14th	Prince Consort dies.
1862	February	Prince sets out on Eastern tour.
1862	September 9th	Prince proposes to Alix.
1863	March 10th	Prince marries Alix.
1864	January 8th	Birth of Prince Albert Victor.
1864	February	Prussia declares war on Denmark.
1865	June 3rd	Prince George born.
1866	November 9th	Prince attends Dagmar's wedding.
1867	February 20th	Louise born.
1868	April	Prince and Alix visit Ireland.
1868	July 6th	Victoria born.
1869	November 26th	Maud born.
1870	February 23rd	Prince at Mordaunt Trial.
1871	September	Lady Susan Vane Tempest confined.
1871	November	Benini sells back letters from Prince.
1871	November	Prince catches typhoid.
1872	February 27th	Thanksgiving for Prince's recovery.
1874	January 23rd	Prince attends Affie's wedding at St Petersburg.
1875	October	Prince sets sail in *Serapis* for India.
1876	April	Royal Titles Bill.
1876	May	Prince returns from India.
1878	May	Prince attends Paris Exhibition.

1881	February 27th	Prince attends wedding of Prince William of Prussia.
1884		Prince on Royal Commission on working-class housing.
1887	June 21st	Queen Victoria's Golden Jubilee.
1888	March 9th	Fritz succeeds his father as Frederick III.
1888	March 10th	Prince celebrates his Silver Wedding.
1888	June 15th	Death of Frederick III.
1888	September	Kaiser refuses to meet Prince at Vienna.
1889	July 27th	Louise marries Fife.
1890	September	Prince at Tranby Croft.
1891		Prince quarrels with Lord Charles Beresford.
1891	June	Trial of Sir William Gordon-Cumming.
1891	July	William II pays first State Visit to England.
1891	November 9th	Alexandra remains at Livadia for Prince's fiftieth birthday.
1891	December 3rd	Eddy becomes engaged to Princess Mary of Teck.
1892	January 14th	Eddy dies at Sandringham.
1892		Prince on Royal Commission examining Old Age Pensions.
1893	July 6th	Prince George marries Princess Mary of Teck.
1894	November	Prince and Princess attend funeral of Alexander III.
1896	July 22nd	Maud marries Prince Charles of Denmark.
1896	September	Prince helps entertain Nicholas II at Balmoral.
1897	June	Queen Victoria's Diamond Jubilee.
1899	October 12th	Outbreak of Boer War.
1900	April 4th	Sipido attempts to assassinate Prince.
1901	January 22nd	Queen Victoria dies.
1901	February	King visits Empress Frederick.
1901	August 5th	Empress Frederick dies.
1901	August 11th	King meets Kaiser at Wilhelmshöhe.
1901	December 24th	King meets Marquis Ito.
1902	January 30th	Anglo-Japanese Treaty signed.
1902	May 31st	Boers surrender.
1902	June 24th	King's appendix removed.
1902	August	Shah of Persia visits England.
1902	August 9th	King Edward's Coronation.
1903	April 2nd	King visits Lisbon.
1903	April 29th	King visits Pope Leo XIII.
1903	May 1st	King visits Paris.
1903	July	Loubet and Delcassé visit England.
1903	July	King and Queen visit Ireland.
1903	August	King pays Francis Joseph a State Visit.
1904	February 10th	Mikado declares War on Tsar.
1904	April	King meets Isvolsky in Copenhagen.
1904	April 8th	Anglo-French Conventions signed.
1904	October 21st	Dogger Bank incident.
1905	March 31st	Kaiser's Tangier visit.
1905	May 27th	Admiral Togo destroys Russian Fleet.
1905	August	Curzon resigns as Governor-General of India.
1905	December 4th	Balfour resigns.

1905	December 5th	Campbell-Bannerman forms Liberal Government.
1906	April 6th	Algeciras Agreement signed.
1906	August	King and Kaiser meet at Friedrichshof.
1907	August	King meets Kaiser at Wilhelmshöhe.
1907	August	King meets Francis Joseph at Bad Ischl.
1907	September 23rd	Anglo-Russian Convention signed.
1907	November	Kaiser pays first State Visit to King.
1908	April 1st	Campbell-Bannerman resigns.
1908	June	King meets Tsar at Reval.
1908	August	King meets Kaiser at Friedrichshof.
1908	August	King meets Francis Joseph at Bad Ischl.
1908	October 6th	Austria annexes Bosnia–Herzegovina.
1909	February	King visits Kaiser at Berlin.
1909	April 29th	Lloyd George presents 'People's Budget'.
1909	November 30th	Lords reject Budget.
1909	December 15th	Parliament dissolved.
1910	January	Asquith wins election with reduced majority.
1910	March 9th	King at Biarritz.
1910	May 6th	King Edward dies.
1910	May 20th	King Edward's funeral.

Select Bibliography

A full bibliography of King Edward VII would require a volume of its own. The choice of a 'Select Bibliography' must be capricious. The following list includes every work quoted in the text, but omits most standard histories, and many well-known biographies of Victorian and Edwardian statesmen. Nevertheless, half a loaf is better than no bread, and the works listed below should help readers explore the life and times of Edward VII in further detail. Abbreviated titles used in Source References are indicated in italics.

ADAMS, WILLIAM SCOVELL. 'Edwardian Heritage: A Study in British History, 1901–6.' London: F. Muller, 1949; New York: Kraus Reprint, 1971.

AIRLIE, MABEL FRANCES ELIZABETH (GORE) OGILBY, COUNTESS OF. 'Thatched with Gold: Memoirs.' London: Hutchinson, 1962.

ALBERT, CONSORT OF QUEEN VICTORIA. 'Letters of the Prince Consort, 1831–61.' Selected and edited by Dr Kurt Jagow and translated by E. T. S. Dugdale. Published by authority of His Majesty the King. London: J. Murray, 1938; New York: E. P. Dutton & Co, 1938.

ALBERT, CONSORT OF QUEEN VICTORIA. 'The Prince and his Brother: Two Hundred New Letters.' Edited by Hector Bolitho. London: Cobden-Sanderson, 1933; New York: D. Appleton-Century-Co, 1934.

ALICE, PRINCESS OF GREAT BRITAIN. 'For My Grandchildren: Some Reminiscences of Her Royal Highness Princess Alice, Countess of Athlone.' London: Evans Bros, 1966; Cleveland: World Publishing Co, 1967.

AMES, WINSLOW. 'Prince Albert and Victorian Taste.' London: Chapman & Hall, 1967; New York: Viking Press, 1968.

ANDREW, CHRISTOPHER. 'Théophile Delcassé and the Making of the *Entente Cordiale*: A Reappraisal of French Foreign Policy, 1898–1905.' London: Macmillan, 1968; New York: St Martin's Press, 1968.

ANDREWS, ALLEN. 'The Follies of King Edward VII.' London: Lexington, 1975.

ANTRIM, LOUISA JANE GREY, LADY. 'Recollections of Louisa, Countess of Antrim.' Shipston-on-Stour: The King's Stone Press, 1937.

ARONSON, THEO. 'A *Family* of Kings: The Descendants of Christian IX of Denmark.' London: Cassell, 1976.

ARONSON, THEO. '*Grandmama* of Europe: The Crowned Descendants of Queen Victoria.' London: Cassell, 1973; Indianapolis: Bobbs-Merrill Co, 1974.

ARONSON, THEO. 'Queen Victoria and the *Bonapartes*.' London: Cassell, 1972; Indianapolis: Bobbs-Merrill Co, 1972.

ARTHUR, SIR GEORGE COMPTON ARCHIBALD. 'Concerning Queen Victoria and her *Son*.' London: R. Hale, Ltd, 1943.

ARTHUR, SIR GEORGE COMPTON ARCHIBALD. 'Not Worth *Reading.*' London and New York: Longmans, Green and Co, 1938.

ARTHUR, SIR GEORGE COMPTON ARCHIBALD. 'Queen *Alexandra.*' London: Chapman & Hall, 1934.

ASHWELL, ARTHUR RAWSON. 'Life of the Right Reverend Samuel Wilberforce, DD, Lord Bishop of Oxford and afterwards of Winchester, with Selections from his Diaries and Correspondence.' London: J. Murray, 1880; New York: E. P. Dutton & Co, 1883.

ASKWITH, HON. BETTY. 'The Lytteltons: A Family Chronicle of the 19th Century.' London: Chatto & Windus, 1975.

ASKWITH, GEORGE RANKEN ASKWITH, BARON. 'Lord James of Hereford.' London: E. Benn Ltd, 1930.

ASTON, SIR GEORGE GREY. 'His Royal Highness the Duke of Connaught and Strathearn: A Life and Intimate Study.' London: G. G. Harrap & Co, 1929.

BACON, SIR REGINALD HUGH SPENCER. 'The Life of Lord Fisher of Kilverstone, Admiral of the Fleet.' London: Hodder & Stoughton, 1929; Garden City, New York: Doubleday, Doran & Co, 1929.

BALFOUR, ARTHUR JAMES BALFOUR, 1ST EARL OF. 'Chapters of Autobiography.' Edited by Mrs Edgar Dugdale. London: Cassell, 1930.

BALFOUR, MICHAEL. 'The Kaiser and His Times.' London: Cresset, 1964; New York: W. W. Norton, 1972.

BARKER, DUDLEY. 'Prominent Edwardians.' London: Allen & Unwin, 1969; New York: Atheneum, 1969.

BATTISCOMBE, GEORGINA. '*Mrs Gladstone*: The Portrait of a Marriage.' London: Constable, 1956; Boston: Houghton Mifflin, 1957.

BATTISCOMBE, GEORGINA. 'Queen *Alexandra.*' London: Constable, 1969; Boston: Houghton Mifflin, 1969.

BEACONSFIELD, BENJAMIN DISRAELI, 1ST EARL OF. 'The Letters of Disraeli to Lady Chesterfield and Lady Bradford.' Edited by the Marquis of Zetland. London: E. Benn, 1929; New York: D. Appleton & Co, 1929.

BEAL, ERICA. 'Royal Cavalcade.' London: S. Paul & Co, 1939.

BEAVAN, ARTHUR HENRY. 'Marlborough House and its Occupants, Present and Past.' London: F. V. White & Co, 1896.

[BEETON, SAMUEL ORCHART]. '*The Siliad*: or The Siege of the Seats.' London: Ward, Lock and Tyler, 1874.

BELL, GEORGE KENNEDY ALLEN, BP. OF CHICHESTER. 'Randall Davidson, Archbishop of Canterbury.' London: Oxford University Press, H. Milford, 1935.

BENNETT, DAPHNE. 'Vicky: Princess and Royal German Empress.' London: Collins, Harvill, 1971; New York: St Martin's Press, 1972.

BENNETT, GEOFFREY MARTIN. 'Charlie B: A Biography of Admiral Lord Beresford of Metemmeh and Curraghmore, GCB, GCVO, LL, DCL.' London: Daunay, 1968.

BENSON, EDWARD FREDERIC. '*As We Were*: A Victorian Peep Show.' London: Longmans, Green & Co, 1930; Norwood, Pa.: Norwood Editions, nd.

BENSON, EDWARD FREDERIC. '*Daughters* of Queen Victoria.' London: Cassell, 1938. ———. 'Queen Victoria's Daughters.' New York: Appleton-Century Co, 1938; Norwood, Pa.: Norwood Editions, nd.

BENSON, EDWARD FREDERIC. 'The *Kaiser* and the English Relations.' London and New York: Longmans, Green & Co, 1936.

BENSON, EDWARD FREDERIC. 'King *Edward VII*. An Appreciation.' London and New York: Longmans, Green & Co, 1933.

BENSON, EDWARD FREDERIC. 'Queen *Victoria*.' London: Longmans, Green & Co, 1935; New York: Grosset & Dunlap, 1935.

BERESFORD, CHARLES WILLIAM DE LA POER BERESFORD, 1ST BARON. 'The Memoirs of Admiral Lord Charles Beresford. Written by Himself.' London: Methuen, 1914; Boston: Little, Brown, 1914.

BLAKE, ROBERT. 'Disraeli.' London: Eyre & Spottiswoode, 1966; New York: St Martin's Press, 1967.

BLUNDEN, MARGARET. 'The Countess of Warwick. A Biography.' London: Cassell, 1967.

BLUNT, WILFRED SCAWEN. 'My Diaries. Being a Personal Narrative of Events, 1888–1914.' London: M. Secker, 1919; New York: A. A. Knopf, 1921.

BOLITHO, HECTOR. '*Albert*, Prince Consort.' London: M. Parrish, 1964; Indianapolis: Bobbs-Merrill Co, 1965.

BOLITHO, HECTOR. 'The *Reign* of Queen Victoria.' New York: Macmillan, 1948; London: Collins, 1949.

BOLITHO, HECTOR. 'Victoria, the *Widow*, and Her Son.' London: Cobden-Sanderson, 1934; New York: D. Appleton-Century Co, 1934.

BONNAR, HYPATIA (BRADLAUGH). 'Charles Bradlaugh: A Record of His Life and Work.' By his daughter, with an account of his parliamentary struggles, politics and teachings by John M. Robertson. London: T. Fisher Unwin, 1894.

BOURNE, KENNETH. 'Foreign Policy of Victorian England, 1830–1902.' London and New York: Oxford University Press, 1970.

BRADLAUGH, CHARLES. 'George, Prince of Wales, with Recent Contrasts and Coincidences.' London: Austin, 18—.

BROADHURST, HENRY. 'Henry Broadhurst, MP: the Story of His Life from a Stonemason's Bench to the Treasury Bench, Told by Himself.' With an Introduction by Augustine Birrell, KC. London: Hutchinson & Co, 1901.

BROADLEY, ALEXANDER MEYRICK. 'The Boyhood of a Great King, 1841–58: an Account of the Early Years of the Life of His Majesty King Edward VII.' London and New York: Harper & Bros, 1906.

BROOK-SHEPHERD, GORDON. 'Uncle of Europe: The Social and Diplomatic Life of Edward VII.' London: Collins, 1975; New York: Harcourt Brace Jovanovich, 1976.

BROUGH, JAMES. 'The Prince and the Lily.' London: Hodder & Stoughton, 1974; New York: Coward-McCann, 1975.

BRUCE, HENRY JAMES. 'Silken Dalliance.' London: Constable, 1946.

BUCHANAN, MERIEL. 'Queen Victoria's Relations.' London: Cassell, 1954.

BÜLOW, BERNHARD HEINRICH MARTIN KARL, FÜRST VON. 'Memoirs.' 4 vols. London and New York: Putnam, 1931–2; Boston: Little, Brown, 1931–2.

BUSCH, MORITZ. 'Bismarck; Some Secret Pages of His History.' Being a diary kept by Dr Moritz Busch during twenty-five years' official and private intercourse with the great Chancellor. London and New York: The Macmillan Co, 1898; New York: AMS Press, 1970; St Clair Shores, Mich.: Scholarly Press, 1971.

CECIL, GWENDOLIN. 'Life of Robert, Marquis of Salisbury.' By his daughter. London: Hodder and Stoughton, 1932; New York: Kraus Reprint Co, nd.

CHURCHILL, JENNIE (JEROME) LADY RANDOLPH CHURCHILL. 'The Reminiscences of Lady Randolph Churchill.' By Mrs George Corwallis-West. London: Edward Arnold, 1908; New York: The Century Co, 1908; New York: Kraus Reprint Co, 1972.

CHURCHILL, PEREGRINE, AND MITCHELL, JULIAN. 'Jennie, Lady Randolph Churchill: A Portrait with Letters.' London: Collins, 1974; New York: St Martin's Press, 1975.

CHURCHILL, RANDOLPH S. 'Winston S. Churchill.' London: Heinemann, 1966–7; Boston: Houghton Mifflin, 1966–7.

CHURCHILL, SIR WINSTON LEONARD SPENCER. '*Great* Contemporaries.' London: Butterworth, 1937; New York: G. P. Putnam's Sons, 1937; New York: Arno, nd.; Chicago: University of Chicago Press, 1974.

CHURCHILL, SIR WINSTON LEONARD SPENCER, 'Lord *Randolph* Churchill.' London and New York: The Macmillan Co, 1906.

CHURCHILL, SIR WINSTON LEONARD SPENCER. 'My Early *Life*: A Roving Commission.' London: Butterworth, 1930; New York: Manor Books, 1972.

CHURCHILL, SIR WINSTON LEONARD SPENCER. 'The World *Crisis*.' 4 vols. London: T. Butterworth, 1923–9; New York: C. Scribner's Sons, 1923–9.

CLARKE, SIR EDWARD GEORGE. 'The Story of My Life.' London: J. Murray, 1918; New York: E. P. Dutton, 1919.

COLSON, PERCY. 'Victorian *Portraits*.' London: Rich and Cowan, 1932; New York: Arno, nd.

CORNWALLIS-WEST, GEORGE FREDERICK MYDDLETON. 'Edwardian *Hey-Days*: or A Little About a Lot of Things.' London and New York: Putnam, 1930; Brooklyn, New York: Beekman Pubs., 1975; New York: British Book Centre, 1975; Boston: Charles River Books, 1977.

CORTI, EGON CAESAR, CONTE. 'The English Empress: A Study in the Relations between Queen Victoria and Her Eldest Daughter, Empress Frederick of Germany.' With an introduction by Wolfgang, Prince of Hesse and translated by E. M. Hodgson. London: Cassell, 1957.

COWLES, VIRGINIA SPENCER. '*Edward VII* and His Circle.' London: H. Hamilton, 1956.

COWLES, VIRGINIA. 'The *Kaiser*.' London: Collins, 1963; New York: Harper & Row, 1964.

CRESSWELL, MRS GEORGE. 'Eighteen Years on the Sandringham Estate.' Temple, 1888.

CREWE, ROBERT OFFLEY ASHBURTON CREWE-MILNES, 1ST MARQUIS OF, 'Lord Rosebery.' London: J. Murray, 1931.

CROFT-COOKE, RUPERT. 'Feasting with Panthers: A New Consideration of Some Late Victorian Writers.' London: W. H. Allen, 1967; New York: Holt, Rinehart & Winston, 1968.

CUST, SIR LIONEL HENRY. 'King Edward VII and His Court: Some Reminiscences.' London: J. Murray, 1930; New York: E. P. Dutton, 1930.

DANGERFIELD, GEORGE. 'Victoria's Heir: the Education of a Prince.' London: Constable, 1941; New York: Harcourt, Brace, 1941.

DASENT, ARTHUR IRWIN. 'John Thadeus Delane, Editor of "The Times"; His

Life and Correspondence.' London: J. Murray, 1908; New York: C. Scribner's Sons, 1908.

'The Dictionary of National Biography,' founded in 1882 by George Smith; edited by Sir Leslie Stephen and Sir Sidney Lee; from the earliest times to 1900. "Edward VII'. Article 1912. London: Oxford University Press, 1921–7

DREW, MARY (GLADSTONE). 'Catherine Gladstone.' By her daughter. London: Nisbet & Co, 1919.

DREW, MARY (GLADSTONE). 'Mary Gladstone (Mrs Drew); Her Diaries and Letters.' Edited by Lucy Masterman. London: Methuen & Co, 1930.

DUFF, DAVID. 'Albert and Victoria.' London: Tandem, 1973.

————. 'Victoria and Albert.' New York: Taplinger, 1972.

DUFF, DAVID. 'Hessian Tapestry.' London: Muller, 1967.

DUFF, DAVID. 'Whisper Louise: Edward VII and Mrs Cresswell.' London: Muller, 1974; Levittown, New York: Transatlantic Arts, 1975.

DUGDALE, BLANCHE E. 'Arthur James Balfour, First Earl of Balfour.' London: Hutchinson, 1936; Westport, Ct., Greenwood Press, nd.; Norwood, Pa.: Norwood Editions, nd.

ECKARDSTEIN, HERMANN, FREIHERR VON. 'Ten Years at the Court of St James', 1895–1905.' Translated and edited by George Young. London: T. Butterworth, 1921; New York: E. P. Dutton, 1922.

EDWARD VII, KING OF GREAT BRITAIN. 'Personal Letters of King Edward VII, together with Extracts from the Correspondence of Queen Alexandra, the Duke of Albany and General Sir Arthur and Lady Paget.' Edited by Lieut.-Col. J. P. C. Sewell. London: Hutchinson & Co., 1931

EDWARD VII, KING OF GREAT BRITAIN. 'A Royal Correspondence; Letters of King Edward VII and King George V to Admiral Sir Henry F. Stephenson.' Edited by John Stephenson. London: Macmillan & Co., 1938.

EDWARD VIII, KING OF GREAT BRITAIN. 'The Crown and the People, 1902–53.' London: Cassell, 1953; New York: Funk & Wagnalls, 1954.

EDWARD VIII, KING OF GREAT BRITAIN. 'A Family Album.' By HRH the Duke of Windsor. London: Cassell, 1960.

EDWARD VIII, KING OF GREAT BRITAIN. 'A King's Story; the Memoirs of HRH the Duke of Windsor.' London: Cassell, 1951; New York: Putnam, 1951.

EDWARDS, WILLIAM HAYDEN. 'The Tragedy of Edward VII: a Psychological Study.' London: V. Gollancz Ltd, 1928; New York: Dodd, Mead, 1928.

EMDEN, PAUL HERMAN. 'Behind the Throne.' London: Hodder & Stoughton, 1934.

ENSOR, ROBERT C. 'England, 1870–1914.' London and New York: Oxford University Press, 1936.

ERNLE, ROWLAND EDMUND PROTHERO, BARON. 'Whippingham to Westminster: The Reminiscences of Lord Ernle.' With an introduction by Lord Kennet and a concluding note by Sir A. Daniel Hall. London: J. Murray, 1938.

ESCOTT, THOMAS HAY SWEET. 'King Edward and His Court.' London: T. F. Unwin, 1903; Philadelphia: G. W. Jacobs & Co, 1908.

ESCOTT, THOMAS HAY SWEET. 'Society in the New Reign.' By a Foreign Resident. London: Unwin, 1904.

ESHER, REGINALD BALIOL BRETT, 2ND VISCOUNT. 'Cloud-capp'd Towers.' London: J. Murray, 1927.

ESHER, REGINALD BALIOL BRETT, 2ND VISCOUNT. 'The *Influence* of King Edward and Essays on Other Subjects.' London: J. Murray, 1915.

ESHER, REGINALD BALIOL BRETT, 2ND VISCOUNT. '*Journals* and Letters.' Edited by Maurice V. Brett. 4 vols. London: I. Nicholson & Watson Ltd, 1934–8.

EYCK, FRANK. 'The Prince Consort: a Political Biography.' London: Chatto & Windus, 1959; Boston: Houghton Mifflin, 1959.

FARRER, JAMES ANSON. 'England Under Edward VII.' London: G. Allen & Unwin, 1922.

[FIELD, JULIAN OSGOOD]. '*Uncensored* Recollections.' London: E. Nash & Grayson Ltd, 1924; Philadelphia: Lippincott, 1924.

[FIELD, JULIAN OSGOOD]. 'More Uncensored *Recollections*.' London: E. Nash & Grayson Ltd, 1926; New York: Harper & Bros, 1926.

[FIELD, JULIAN OSGOOD]. '*Things* I Shouldn't Tell.' London: E. Nash & Grayson Ltd, 1924; Philadelphia: Lippincott, 1925.

FIELDING, DAPHNE. 'The Duchess of Jermyn Street: The Life and Good Times of Rosa Lewis and the Cavendish Hotel.' London: Eyre & Spottiswoode, 1964; New York: Penguin, 1978.

FISHER, GRAHAM AND HEATHER. 'Bertie and Alix: Anatomy of a Marriage.' London: R. Hale, 1974.

FISHER, JOHN ARBUTHNOT FISHER, BARON. 'Fear God and *Dread Nought*: The Correspondence of Admiral of the Fleet Lord Fisher of Kilverstone.' Selected and edited by Arthur J. Marder. 3 vols. London: Cape, 1952–9.

FISHER, JOHN ARBUTHNOT FISHER, BARON. 'Memories.' By the Admiral of the Fleet, Lord Fisher. London: Hodder & Stoughton, 1919.

————. 'Memories and Records.' New York: George H. Doran Co, 1920.

FITZMAURICE, EDMOND GEORGE PETTY-FITZMAURICE, 1ST BARON. 'The Life of Granville George Leveson Gower, Second Earl of Granville, KG, 1815–91.' London and New York: Longmans, Green & Co, 1905.

FITZROY, SIR ALMERIC WILLIAM. 'Memoirs.' London: Hutchinson & Co, 1925; New York: G. H. Doran, 1925.

FORBES, LADY ANGELA SELINA BIANCA (ST CLAIR-ERSKINE). 'Memories and Base Details.' London: Hutchinson & Co, 1921; New York: G. H. Doran, 1922.

FORTESCUE, JOHN WILLIAM. 'History of the British Army.' 13 vols. London: Macmillan, 1910–30; New York: AMS Press, 1976.

FORTESCUE, SIR SEYMOUR JOHN. 'Looking Back.' London and New York: Longmans, Green & Co, 1920.

FRANCE. Commission de Publication des Documents Relatifs aux Origines de la Guerre de 1914. 'Documents Diplomatique Français (1871–1914).' 41 vols. Paris: Impr. Nationale, 1929–59.

FRASER, PETER. 'Lord Esher: a Political Biography.' London: Hart-Davis MacGibbon, 1973.

FULFORD, ROGER. 'The Prince *Consort*.' London: Macmillan, 1949.

FULFORD, ROGER. 'Queen *Victoria*.' London: Collins, 1951.

GAVIN, CATHERINE IRVINE. 'Edward the Seventh, a Biography.' London: J. Cape, 1941.

GERNSHEIM, ALISON AND HELMUT. 'Edward VII and Queen Alexandra: A Biography in Word and Picture.' London: Muller, 1962.

GIBBS, FREDERICK WAYMOUTH. 'The Education of a Prince: Extracts from the Diaries of F. W. Gibbs, 1851–6.' Cornhill Magazine, 986: 105–119.

GLADSTONE, WILLIAM EWART. 'The Political Correspondence of Mr Gladstone and Lord Granville, 1876–86.' Edited by Agatha Ramm. Oxford: Clarendon Press, 1962.

GOLLIN, ALFRED M. 'Balfour's Burden; Arthur Balfour and Imperial Preference.' London: A. Blond, 1965.

GORDON-CUMMING, SIR WILLIAM GORDON, BART. 'The Baccarat Case, Gordon-Cumming vs. Wilson and Others.' Edited by W. Teignmouth Shore. Edinburgh and London: W. Hodge & Co, 1932.

GORE, JOHN. 'Edwardian Scrapbook.' London: Evans Bros, 1951.

GOSCHEN, GEORGE JOACHIM GOSCHEN, VISCOUNT. 'Lord Goschen and His Friends (the Goschen Letters).' Edited by Percy Colson; introduction by Sir Shane Leslie, Bart. London and New York: Hutchinson, 1946.

GOWER, LORD RONALD CHARLES SUTHERLAND. 'My Reminiscences.' London: K. Paul, Trench & Co, 1883; Boston: Roberts, 1884; New York: C. Scribner's Sons, 1884.

GOWER, LORD RONALD CHARLES SUTHERLAND. 'Old Diaries, 1881–1901.' London: J. Murray, 1902; New York: Scribners, 1902.

GREAT BRITAIN. Foreign Office. 'British Documents on the Origins of the War, 1898–1914.' Edited by G. P. Gooch and Harold Temperley. 11 vols. London: HM Stationery Office, 1926–38; New York: Johnson Reprint Corp, nd.

GREEN, JOHN RICHARD. 'Letters of John Richard Green.' Edited by Leslie Stephen. New York and London: The Macmillan Co, 1901.

GREVILLE, CHARLES CAVENDISH FULKE. 'The Greville Memoirs: A Journal of the Reigns of King George IV and King William IV 1814–70.' Edited by Lytton Strachey and Roger Fulford. London: Macmillan, 1938.

GREY, CHARLES. 'The Early Years of His Royal Highness the Prince Consort.' London: Smith Elder, 1867; London: Kimber, 1967.

GREY, EDWARD GREY, 1ST VISCOUNT. 'Twenty-five Years, 1892–1916.' London: Hodder & Stoughton, 1925; New York: F. A. Stokes Co, 1925.

GUEST, IVOR FORBES. 'Napoleon III in England.' London: British Technical & General Press, 1952.

GWYNN, STEPHEN LUCIUS. 'The Life of the Rt Hon Sir Charles Dilke, Bart.' Begun by Stephen Gwynn and completed and edited by Gertrude M. Tuckwell. London: J. Murray, 1917; New York: The Macmillan Co, 1917.

HALDANE, RICHARD BURDON HALDANE, 1ST VISCOUNT. 'An Autobiography.' London: Hodder & Stoughton, 1929.

HAMILTON, SIR EDWARD WALTER. 'The Diary of Sir Edward Walter Hamilton, 1880–5.' Edited by Dudley W. R. Bahlman. Oxford: Clarendon Press, 1972.

HAMILTON, LORD FREDERICK SPENCER. 'The Vanished World of Yesterday.' London: Hodder & Stoughton, 1950.

HARDIE, FRANK. 'The Political Influence of the British Monarchy, 1868–1952.' London: Batsford, 1970; New York: Harper & Row, 1970.

HARDIE, FRANK. 'The Political Influence of Queen Victoria, 1861–1901.' London: Frank Cass & Co, 1963; New York: Humanities Press, 1963.

HARDINGE, CHARLES HARDINGE, BARON. 'Old Diplomacy; the Reminiscences of Lord Hardinge of Penshurst.' London: J. Murray, 1947.

HARDMAN, SIR WILLIAM. 'A Mid-Victorian Pepys; the Letters and Memoirs of Sir William Hardman.' Annotated and edited by S. M. Ellis. London: C. Palmer, 1923; New York: George H. Doran Co., 1923; Philadelphia: Richard West, 1973.

HARRISON, MICHAEL. '*Clarence*: The Life of HRH the Duke of Clarence and Avondale, 1864–92.' London: W. H. Allen, 1972.

HARRISON, MICHAEL. 'Painful *Details*: Twelve Victorian Scandals.' London: M. Parrish, 1962.

HASTINGS, SIR PATRICK. 'Famous and Infamous Cases'. London: Heinemann, 1950; New York: Roy Pubs, 1954.

HAVERS, ROBERT MICHAEL OLDFIELD, 'The Royal Baccarat Scandal.' Kimber, 1977.

HIBBERT, CHRISTOPHER. 'Edward VII: A Portrait.' London: A. Lane, 1976.

HIRST, FRANCIS WRIGLEY. 'In the Golden Days.' London: F. Muller, 1974.

HOHENLOHE-SCHILLINGSFÜRST, CHLODWIG KARL VIKTOR, FÜRST ZU 'Memoirs of Prince Chlodwig of Hohenlohe-Schillingsfuerst.' Authorized by Prince Alexander of Hohenlohe-Schillingsfuerst and edited by Friedrich Curtius. English edition supervised by George W. Chrystal. London: Heinemann, 1906; New York: The Macmillan Co, 1906.

HOLMES, SIR RICHARD RIVINGTON. 'Edward VII, His Life and Times.' London: The Amalgamated Press Ltd, 1910–11.

HOLSTEIN, FRIEDRICH VON. 'The Holstein Papers.' Edited by Norman Rich and M. H. Fisher. 4 vols. Cambridge, England: Cambridge University Press, 1955–63.

HOUGH, RICHARD ALEXANDER. 'Advice to a *Granddaughter*.' London: Heinemann, 1975; New York: Simon & Schuster, 1976.

HOUGH, RICHARD ALEXANDER. 'First *Sea Lord*: An Authorized Biography of Admiral Lord Fisher.' London: Allen & Unwin, 1969.

————. 'Admiral of the Fleet: the Life of John Fisher.' New York: Macmillan, 1970.

HOUGH, RICHARD ALEXANDER. '*Louis* and Victoria: The First Mountbattens.' London: Hutchinson, 1974.

————. 'The Mountbattens: The Illustrious Family who, through Birth and Marriage, from Queen Victoria and the Last of Tsars to Queen Elizabeth II, enriched Europe's Royal Houses.' New York: E. P. Dutton, 1975.

HUNT, WILLIAM HOLMAN. 'Pre-Raphaelitism and the Pre-Raphaelite Brotherhood.' London: Chapman and Hall, 1905–6; New York: AMS Press, nd.

HYDE, HARFORD MONTGOMERY. 'The *Cleveland* Street Scandal.' London: W. H. Allen, 1976.

HYDE, HARFORD MONTGOMERY. 'Their Good *Names*: Twelve Cases of Libel and Slander with Some Introductory Reflections on the Law.' London: H. Hamilton, 1970.

JAMES, ROBERT RHODES. 'Lord *Randolph* Churchill.' London: Weidenfeld & Nicolson, 1959.

————. 'Lord Randolph Churchill: Winston Churchill's Father.' New York: A. S. Barnes, 1960.

JAMES, ROBERT RHODES. '*Rosebery*, a Biography of Archibald Philip, Fifth Earl of Rosebery.' London: Weidenfeld & Nicolson, 1963; New York: Macmillan, 1964.

JENKINS, ROY. '*Asquith*.' London: Collins, 1964; New York: Chilmark Press, 1965.

JENKINS, ROY. 'Mr. Balfour's *Poodle*.' London: Collins, 1968; New York: Chilmark, 1968.

JENKINS, ROY. 'Sir Charles *Dilke*: a Victorian Tragedy.' London: Collins, 1958.

————. 'Victorian Scandal: a Biography of the Right Honorable Gentleman Sir Charles Dilke.' New York: Chilmark Press, 1965.

JUDD, DENIS. 'Edward VII: A Pictorial Biography.' London: Macdonald & Jane's, 1975.

JULLIAN, PHILLIPPE, 'Edward and the Edwardians.' Translated by Peter Dawnay. London: Sidgwick and Jackson, 1967; New York: Viking, 1967.

KENNEDY, AUBREY LEO. 'My Dear *Duchess*: Social and Political Letters to the Duchess of Manchester, 1858–69.' London: J. Murray, 1956.

KENNEDY, AUBREY LEO. '*Salisbury*, 1830–1903: Portrait of a Statesman.' London: J. Murray, 1953.

KEPPEL, SONIA. 'Edwardian Daughter.' London: H. Hamilton, 1958; New York: British Book Centre, 1959.

'King Edward The Seventh.' London: T. Nelson & Sons, 191–.

'King Edward VII, Biographical and Personal Sketches with Anecdotes.' By Sir Edward Dicey and Others. London: Skeffington & Son, 1910.

LANG, THEO. 'My Darling Daisy.' London: Michael Joseph, 1966.

————. 'The Darling Daisy Affair.' New York: Atheneum, 1966.

LANGTRY, LILY. 'The Days I Knew.' With a foreword by Richard le Gallienne. London: Hutchinson & Co, 1925; New York: George H. Doran, 1925.

LEE, SIR SIDNEY. 'King *Edward VII*: A Biography.' New York: The Macmillan Co, 1925–7.

LEE, SIR SIDNEY. 'Queen *Victoria*, A Biography.' London: Smith, Elder & Co, 1902; New York: The Macmillan Co, 1903.

LEGGE, EDWARD. 'King Edward in His True *Colours*.' With appreciations of Edward VII by Comte d'Haussonville and A. Vambéry. London: E. Nash, 1912; Boston: Small, Maynard, 1913.

LEGGE, EDWARD. 'More About King *Edward*.' London: E. Nash, 1913; Boston: Small, Maynard, 1914.

LEGGE, EDWARD. 'King Edward, the *Kaiser* and the War.' London: G. Richards Ltd, 1917.

LEGGE, EDWARD. 'King *George* and the Royal Family.' London: G. Richards Ltd, 1918.

LESLIE, ANITA. '*Edwardians* in Love.' London: Hutchinson, 1972.

LESLIE, ANITA. '*Jennie*: The Life of Lady Randolph Churchill.' London: Hutchinson, 1969.

————. 'Lady Randolph Churchill: The Story of Jennie Jerome.' New York: Scribner, 1969.

LESLIE, ANITA. 'The Remarkable Mr *Jerome*.' New York: Holt, 1954.

LESLIE, SIR SHANE, BART. 'The End of a *Chapter*.' London: Constable, 1916; New York: C. Scribner's Sons, 1916.

LESLIE, SIR SHANE, BART. 'The *Film* of Memory.' London: M. Joseph Ltd, 1938.

LESLIE, SIR SHANE, BART. 'Men Were *Different*: Five Studies in Late Victorian Biography.' London: M. Joseph, 1937.

LIDDELL, ADOLPHUS GEORGE CHARLES. 'Notes from the Life of an Ordinary Mortal: Being a Record of Things Done, Seen and Heard at School, College, and in the World during the Latter Half of the 19th Century.' London: J. Murray, 1911.

LONDONDERRY, EDITH HELEN (CHAPLIN) VANE-TEMPEST-STEWART, MARCHIONESS. 'Henry Chaplin: a Memoir.' Prepared by his daughter. London: Macmillan & Co, 1926.

LONGFORD, ELIZABETH (HARMAN) PACKENHAM, COUNTESS OF. 'Victoria R. I.' London: Weidenfeld & Nicolson, 1964.

————. 'Queen Victoria: Born to Succeed.' New York: Harper, 1964.

LYTTELTON, SARAH (SPENCER) LYTTELTON, BARONESS. 'Correspondence.' Edited by her great-granddaughter the Hon. Mrs Hugh Wyndham. London: J. Murray, 1912; New York: Scribner, 1912.

LYTTON, EDITH (VILLIERS) BULWER-LYTTON, COUNTESS. 'Lady Lytton's Court Diary, 1895–9.' Edited by Mary Lutyens. London: Hart-Davis, 1961.

MCCLINTOCK, MARY HOWARD (ELPHINSTONE). 'The Queen Thanks Sir Howard: The Life of Major-General Sir Howard Elphinstone VC, KCB, CMG.' By his daughter. London: J. Murray, 1945.

MACDONAGH, MICHAEL. 'The English King: A Study of the Monarchy and the Royal Family, Historical, Constitutional and Social.' London: E. Benn Ltd, 1929; New York: J. Cape & H. Smith, 1929.

MACDONNELL, JOHN COTTER. 'Life and Correspondence of William Connor Magee, Archbishop of York.' London: Isbister & Co, 1896.

MACKAY, RUDDOCK F. 'Fisher of Kilverstone.' Oxford: Clarendon Press, 1973.

MCKENNA, STEPHEN. 'Reginald McKenna 1863–1943, a Memoir.' London: Eyre & Spottiswoode, 1948.

MACLEOD, DONALD. 'Memoir of Norman Macleod.' By his brother. London: Daldy, Isbister & Co, 1876; New York: C. Scribner's Sons, 1876.

MADOL, HANS ROGER. '*Christian IX*.' Compiled from unpublished documents and memoirs. Translated by E. O. Lorimer. London: Collins, 1939.

MADOL, HANS ROGER. 'The Private Life of Queen *Alexandra* as Viewed by Her Friends.' London: Hutchinson, 1940.

MAGNUS, SIR PHILIP MONTEFIORE, BART. 'King *Edward the Seventh*.' London: J. Murray, 1964; New York: E. P. Dutton, 1964.

MAGNUS, SIR PHILIP MONTEFIORE, BART. '*Gladstone*: A Biography.' London: J. Murray, 1960; New York: E. P. Dutton, 1960.

MAGNUS, SIR PHILIP MONTEFIORE, BART. '*Kitchener*: Portrait of an Imperialist.' London: J. Murray, 1958; New York: E. P. Dutton, 1958.

MALLET, MARIE CONSTANCE (ADEANE), LADY. 'Life with Queen Victoria: Letters from Court.' Edited by Victor Mallet. London: J. Murray, 1968; Boston: Houghton Mifflin, 1968.

MALMESBURY, JAMES HOWARD HARRIS, 3RD EARL OF. 'Memoirs of an Ex-Minister: An Autobiography.' London: Longmans, Green & Co, 1884; New York: Scribner & Welford, 1885.

MARDER, ARTHUR JACOB. 'British Naval *Policy*, 1880–1905: the Anatomy of British Sea Power.' London: Putnam & Co, 1941.

————. 'The Anatomy of British Sea Power: A History of British Naval Policy in the Pre-Dreadnought Era, 1880–1905.' New York: A. A. Knopf, 1940.

MARDER, ARTHUR JACOB. 'From the Dreadnought to *Scapa Flow*: The Royal Navy in the Fisher Era, 1904–19.' London and New York: Oxford University Press, 1965–6.

MARIE, CONSORT OF FERDINAND I, KING OF RUMANIA. 'The Story of My Life.' London: Cassell & Co, 1934; New York: C. Scribner's Sons, 1934.

MARIE LOUISE, PRINCESS. 'My Memories of Six Reigns.' London: Evans Bros, 1956; New York: Dutton, 1957.

MARTIN, RALPH G. 'Jennie: The Life of Lady Randolph Churchill.' Englewood Cliffs, N.J.: Prentice-Hall, 1969–71.

————. 'Lady Randolph Churchill: A Biography.' London: Cassell, 1969–71.

MARTIN, SIR THEODORE. 'The Life of His Royal Highness the Prince Consort.' 5 vols. London: Smith, Elder & Co, 1875–80; New York: Appleton, 1875–80.

MAURICE, SIR FREDERICK BARTON. 'Haldane: The Life of Viscount Haldane of Cloan KT, OM.' London: Faber & Faber Ltd, 1937–9.

MAURICE, ANDRÉ. 'King Edward and His Times.' Translated by Hamish Miles. London: Cassell & Co, 1933.

————. 'The Edwardian Era.' New York: D. Appleton-Century Co, 1933.

MAXWELL, SIR HERBERT EUSTACE, 7TH BART. 'The Life and Letters of George William Frederick, Fourth Earl of Clarendon, KG, GCB.' London: E. Arnold, 1913.

'Memoirs of Baron Stockmar by His Son.' Translated by Georgina Müller and edited by K. Müller. London: Longmans, 1872.

[MENZIES, AMY CHARLOTTE (BEWICKE)]. 'Memories *Discreet* and Indiscreet by a Woman of No Importance.' London: H. Jenkins Ltd, 1917; New York: E. P. Dutton & Co, 1917.

MERSEY, CLIVE BIGHAM, 2ND VISCOUNT. 'A Picture of Life, 1872–1940.' London: J. Murray, 1941.

MIDDLEMASS, ROBERT KEITH. 'The Life and Good Times of Edward VII.' With an introduction by Antonia Fraser. London: Weidenfeld & Nicolson, 1972; Garden City, New York: Doubleday, 1972.

MIDLETON, WILLIAM ST JOHN FREMANTLE BRODRICK, 1ST EARL OF. 'Records and Reactions, 1856–1939.' London: J. Murray, 1939; New York: E. P. Dutton, 1939.

MINNEY, RUBEIGH JAMES. 'The Edwardian Age.' London: Cassell, 1964; Boston: Little, Brown, 1965.

MONGER, GEORGE W. 'The End of Isolation: British Foreign Policy, 1900–7.' London: Nelson, 1963.

MONYPENNY, WILLIAM FLAVELLE AND BUCKLE, GEORGE EARLE. 'The Life of Benjamin Disraeli, Earl of Beaconsfield.' Rev. ed. London: Murray, 1929; New York: Russell & Russell, 1968.

MORLEY, JOHN MORLEY, VISCOUNT. 'The Life of William Ewart *Gladstone*.' 3 vols. London: Macmillan & Co, 1903; New York: The Macmillan Co, 1903.

MORLEY, JOHN MORLEY, VISCOUNT. '*Recollections*.' New York: The Macmillan Co, 1917; London: Macmillan, 1918.

MORRIS, A. J. ANTHONY. 'Radicalism against War, 1906–14: The Advocacy of Peace and Retrenchment.' London: Longman, 1972; Totowa, N.J.: Rowman & Littlefield, 1974.

MÜNZ, SIGMUND. 'King Edward VII at Marienbad: Political and Social Life at the Bohemian Spas.' London: Hutchinson & Co, 1934.

NAPIER, ELMA. 'Youth Is a Blunder.' London: J. Cape, 1948.

NEVILL, LADY DOROTHY FANNY (WALPOLE). 'The Reminiscences of Lady Dorothy Nevill.' Edited by her Son Ralph Nevill. London: Edward Arnold, 1906.

NEVILL, LADY DOROTHY FANNY (WALPOLE). 'Under Five Reigns.' London: Methuen, 1910; New York: John Lane Co, 1910.

NEWSOME, DAVID. 'A History of Wellington College, 1859–1959.' London: J. Murray, 1959.

NEWTON, THOMAS WODEHOUSE LEGH, 2ND BARON. 'Lord *Lansdowne*.' London: Macmillan & Co, 1929.

NEWTON, THOMAS WODEHOUSE LEGH, 2ND BARON. 'Lord *Lyons*: A Record of British Diplomacy.' London: E. Arnold, 1913; New York: Longmans, Green & Co, 1913.

NEWTON, THOMAS WODEHOUSE LEGH, 2ND BARON. '*Retrospection*.' London: J. Murray, 1941.

NICHOLAS II, EMPEROR OF RUSSIA. 'The Letters of Tsar Nicholas II and Empress Marie: Being the Confidential Correspondence between Nicholas II, Last of the Tsars, and His Mother, Dowager Empress Maria Feodorovna.' Edited by Edward J. Bing. London: I. Nicholson & Watson Ltd, 1937.

NICOLSON, HAROLD. 'King *George the Fifth*: His Life and Reign.' London: Constable, 1952; Garden City, New York: Doubleday, 1953.

NICOLSON, HAROLD. 'Sir Arthur Nicolson, Bart., First Lord *Carnock*: A Study in the Old Diplomacy.' London: Constable & Co, 1930.

————. 'Portrait of a Diplomatist: Being the Life of Sir Arthur Nicolson, First Lord Carnock, and a Study of the Origins of the Great War.' Boston: Houghton Mifflin, 1930.

NOEL, GERARD. 'Princess Alice: Queen Victoria's Forgotten Daughter.' London: Constable, 1974.

NOWELL-SMITH, SIMON HARCOURT. 'Edwardian England, 1901–14.' London and New York: Oxford University Press, 1964.

ORMATHWAITE, ARTHUR HENRY JOHN WALSH, BARON. 'When I was at Court.' By Lord Ormathwaite, GCVO, Master of Ceremonies to King Edward VII and King George V. London: Hutchinson & Co, 1937.

OWEN, FRANK. 'Tempestuous Journey: Lloyd George, His Life and Times.' London: Hutchinson, 1954; New York: McGraw-Hill, 1955.

OXFORD AND ASQUITH, HERBERT HENRY ASQUITH, 1ST EARL OF. 'Fifty Years of British *Parliament*.' London: Cassell, 1926; Boston: Little, Brown & Co, 1926.

OXFORD AND ASQUITH, HERBERT HENRY ASQUITH, 1ST EARL OF. 'Memories and *Reflections*, 1852–1927.' London: Cassell, 1928; Boston, Little, Brown & Co, 1928.

OXFORD AND ASQUITH, MARGOT ASQUITH, COUNTESS OF. 'An *Autobiography*.' London: T. Butterworth, 1920–22; New York: George H. Doran Co, 1920–22.

OXFORD AND ASQUITH, MARGOT ASQUITH, COUNTESS OF. 'More *Memories*.' London: Cassell, 1933.

————. 'More or Less about Myself.' New York: E. P. Dutton & Co, 1934.

PAGET, WALPURGA EHRENGARDE HELENA (VON HOHENTHAL), LADY. 'Embassies of Other Days, and Further Recollections.' London: Hutchinson, 1923; New York: George H. Doran, 1923.

PALÉOLOGUE, GEORGES MAURICE. 'The Turning Point: Three Critical Years, 1904–6.' Translated by F. Appleby Holt. London: Hutchinson & Co, 1935.

PAOLI, XAVIER. 'My Royal Clients.' Translated by Alexander Teixeira de Mattos. London: Hodder & Stoughton, 1911.

————. 'Their Majesties as I Knew Them: Personal Reminiscences of the Kings and Queens of Europe.' New York: Sturgis & Walton Co, 1911.

PEARSALL, RONALD. 'The Worm in the Bud: The World of Victorian Sexuality.' London: Weidenfeld & Nicolson, 1969; New York: Macmillan, 1969.

PEARSON, HESKETH. 'Labby (the Life and Character of Henry Labouchere).' London: H. Hamilton, 1936; New York: Harper & Bros, 1937.

PEARSON, JOHN. 'Edward the Rake.' London: Weidenfeld & Nicolson, 1975.

PETRIE, SIR CHARLES. 'The Life and Letters of the Right Hon. Sir Austen Chamberlain, KG, PC, MP.' London: Cassell, 1939–40.

PETRIE, SIR CHARLES. 'Scenes of Edwardian Life.' London: Eyre & Spottiswoode, 1965; New York: W. W. Norton, 1965.

PLESS, MARY THERESA OLIVIA (CORNWALLIS-WEST), FÜRSTIN VON. 'From My Private Diary.' London: J. Murray, 1931.

PONSONBY, ARTHUR PONSONBY, BARON. 'Henry Ponsonby, Queen Victoria's Private Secretary: His Life from His Letters.' By his son. London: Macmillan, 1942; New York: Macmillan, 1944.

PONSONBY, FREDERICK EDWARD GREY, BARON SYSONBY. 'Recollections of Three Reigns.' Prepared for the press with notes and an introductory memoir by Colin Welch. London: Eyre & Spottiswoode, 1951; New York: Dutton, 1952.

PONSONBY, FREDERICK EDWARD GREY, BARON SYSONBY. 'Sidelights on Queen Victoria.' London: Macmillan & Co, 1930; New York: Sears Pub. Co, 1930.

PONSONBY, SIR JOHN. 'The Ponsonby Family.' London: The Medici Society, 1929.

PONSONBY, MARY ELIZABETH (BULTEEL), LADY. 'Mary Ponsonby: A Memoir, Some Letters, and a Journal.' Edited by her daughter Magdalen Ponsonby. London: J. Murray, 1927.

————. 'A Lady in Waiting to Queen Victoria, Being Some Letters, and a Journal of Lady Ponsonby.' New York: J. H. Sears & Co, 1927.

POPE-HENNESSY, JAMES. 'Lord Crewe 1858–1945: The Likeness of a Liberal.' London: Constable, 1955.

POPE-HENNESSY, JAMES. 'Queen Mary, 1867–1953.' London: G. Allen & Unwin, 1959; New York: Knopf, 1960.

PORTLAND, WILLIAMS JOHN ARTHUR CHARLES JAMES CAVENDISH-BENTINCK, 6TH EARL OF. 'Men, Women and Things: Memories of the Duke of Portland.' London: Faber & Faber, 1937.

POUND, REGINALD. 'Albert: A Biography of the Prince Consort.' London: Joseph, 1973; New York: Simon & Schuster, 1974.

PRIESTLEY, J. B. 'The Edwardians.' London: Heinemann, 1970; New York: Harper & Row, 1970.

RADZIWILL, CATHERINE, PRINCESS. 'The Empress Frederick.' London: Cassell, 1934; New York: H. Holt, 1934.

RAMM, AGATHA. 'Sir Robert *Morier*: Envoy and Ambassador in the Age of Imperialism, 1876–93.' Oxford: Clarendon Press, 1973.

READ, DONALD. 'Edwardian England, 1901–15: Society and Politics.' London: Harrap, 1972.

REDESDALE, ALGERNON BERTRAM FREEMAN-MITFORD, BARON. '*Further* Memories.' With an introduction by Edmund Gosse. London: Hutchinson, 1917; New York: E. P. Dutton, 1917.

REDESDALE, ALGERNON BERTRAM FREEMAN-MITFORD, BARON. 'King *Edward VII*, a Memory.' London: Privately printed by Ballantyne Press, 1915.

REDESDALE, ALGERNON BERTRAM FREEMAN-MITFORD, BARON. '*Memories*.' London: Hutchinson, 1915; New York: E. P. Dutton, 1916.

RENNELL, JAMES RENNELL RODD, BARON. 'Social and Diplomatic Memories.' 3 vols. London: E. Arnold, 1922–5.

RICHARDSON, JOANNA. 'The Courtesans: The Demi-monde in 19th Century France.' London: Weidenfeld & Nicolson, 1967; New York: World. 1967.

RIDLEY, JASPER GODWIN. 'Lord Palmerston.' London: Constable, 1970; New York: Dutton, 1971.

ROBY, KINLEY E. 'The King, the Press and the People: A Study of King Edward VII.' London: Barrie and Jenkins, 1975.

ROLO, P. J. V. 'Entente Cordiale: The Origins and Negotiation of the Anglo-French Agreements of 8 April 1904.' London: Macmillan, 1969; New York: St Martin's Press, 1969.

ROOSEVELT, THEODORE. 'Cowboys and Kings, Three Great Letters.' Cambridge, Mass.: Harvard University Press, 1938; New York: Kraus Reprint, 1968.

ROSE, KENNETH. 'The Later *Cecils*.' London: Weidenfeld & Nicolson, 1945.

ROSE, KENNETH. 'Superior Person: A Portrait of Curzon and His Circle in Late Victorian England.' London: Weidenfeld & Nicolson, 1969; New York: Weybright and Talley, 1970.

ROSSMORE, DERRICK WARNER WILLIAM WESTENRA, 5TH BARON. 'Things I Can Tell.' London: E. Nash, 1912; New York: George H. Doran, 1912.

RUSSELL, SIR WILLIAM HOWARD. 'The Prince of Wales Tour: A Diary in India; with Some Account of Visits of His Royal Highness to the Courts of Greece, Egypt, Spain and Portugal.' London: S. Low, Marston, Searle and Rivington, 1877; New York: R. Worthington, 1877.

ST AUBYN, GILES. 'The Royal George, 1819–1904: The Life of HRH Prince George, Duke of Cambridge.' London: Constable, 1963; New York: Knopf, 1964.

SEMON, SIR FELIX. 'The Autobiography of Sir Felix Semon.' Edited by Henry C. Semon and Thomas A. McIntyre. London: Jarrolds Ltd, 1926.

SERMONETA, VITTORIA (COLONNA) CAETANI, DUCHESSA DI. 'Things Past.' With a Foreword by Robert Hickens. London: Hutchinson, 1929; New York: D. Appleton & Co, 1929.

SMALLEY, GEORGE W. 'Anglo-American Memories.' London: Duckworth, 1911; Philadelphia: Richard West, 1973.

'Some Letters from a Man of No Importance, 1895–1914.' London: J. Cape, 1928.

SOMMER, DUDLEY. 'Haldane of Cloan: His Life and Times, 1856–1928.' London: G. Allen & Unwin, 1960.

SPENDER, J. A. 'A Life of the Right Honourable *Sir Henry* Campbell-Bannerman.' London: Hodder & Stoughton, 1923; Boston: Houghton Mifflin, 1924; New York: Kraus Reprint, nd.

SPENDER, J. A. and ASQUITH, CYRIL. 'Life of Lord Oxford and Asquith.' London: Hutchinson, 1932.

SPENDER, J. A. '*Men* and Things.' London: Cassell, 1937; Plainview, N.J.: Books for Libraries, nd.

SPRING RICE, SIR CECIL ARTHUR. 'The Letters and Friendships of Sir Cecil *Spring Rice*: A Record.' Edited by Stephen Gwynn. London: Constable, 1929; Boston: Houghton Mifflin, 1929; New York: Arno, nd.; Westport, Ct.: Greenwood, nd.

STAMPER, CHARLES WILLIAM. 'What I Know: Reminiscences of Five Years' Personal Attendance Upon His Late Majesty King Edward the Seventh.' London: Mills & Boon Ltd, 1913.

STANLEY, ARTHUR PENRHYN, 'A Victorian *Dean*: A Memoir of Arthur Stanley, Dean of Westminster, with Many New and Unpublished Letters.' Edited by the Dean of Windsor and Hector Bolitho. London: Chatto & Windus, 1930.

STANLEY, LADY AUGUSTA FREDERICA ELIZABETH (BRUCE). 'Letters of Lady Augusta *Stanley*, a Young Lady at Court, 1849–63.' Edited by the Dean of Windsor and Hector Bolitho. London: Gerald Howe, 1927; New York: George H. Doran Co, 1927.

STANLEY, LADY AUGUSTA FREDERICA ELIZABETH (BRUCE). '*Later Letters* of Lady Augusta Stanley, 1864–76, including many Unpublished Letters to and from Queen Victoria and Correspondence with Dean Stanley, Her Sister, Lady Frances Baillie and Others.' Edited by the Dean of Windsor and Hector Bolitho. London: J. Cape, 1929.

STEED, HENRY WICKHAM. 'Through Thirty Years, 1892–1922: A Personal Narrative.' London: W. Heinemann Ltd, 1924; Garden City, New York: Doubleday, Page & Co, 1924.

STEINER, ZARA S. 'The Foreign Office and Foreign Policy, 1898–1914.' London and New York: Cambridge University Press, 1970.

STOCKMAR, ERNST ALFRED CHRISTIAN, FREIHERR VON. 'Memories of Baron Stockmar.' By his son Baron E. von Stockmar. Translated by G. A. M. Edited by F. Max Muller. London: Longmans, Green & Co, 1872; Boston & New York: Lee & Shepard, 1873.

STOECKL, AGNES, BARONESS DE. 'Not All Vanity.' Edited by George Kinnaird. London: J. Murray, 1952; New York: Scribner, 1952.

STUART, JAMES. 'Reminiscences.' London: Printed for private circulation at the Chiswick Press, 1911.

SUFFIELD, CHARLES HARBORD, BARON. 'My Memories, 1830–1913.' Edited by Alys Lowth, London: H. Jenkins Ltd, 1913.

SYKES, CHRISTOPHER. 'Four Studies in Loyalty.' London: Collins, 1946.

[THOMPSON, EDWARD RAYMOND]. 'Portraits of the New Century (the First Ten Years).' By E. T. Raymond. London: E. Benn Ltd, 1928; Garden City, New York: Doubleday, Doran, 1928.

THORNTON-COOK, ELSIE (PRENTYS). 'Kings in the Making; the Princes of Wales.' London: J. Murray, 1931.

TOLLEMACHE, HON. LIONEL ARTHUR. 'Talks with Mr Gladstone.' London and New York: Longmans, Green & Co, 1898.

TREVELYAN, M. 'Grey of Fallodon: Being the Life of Sir Edward Grey, afterwards Viscount Grey of Fallodon.' London: Longmans, 1937; Atlantic Highlands, N.J.: Humanities Press, 1948.

TROWBRIDGE, WILLIAM RUTHERFORD HAYES. 'Queen Alexandra: A Study of Royalty.' With an introduction by Walburga, Lady Paget. London: T. F. Unwin Ltd, 1921.

TSCHUMI, GABRIEL. 'Royal Chef: Recollections of a Life in Royal Households from Queen Victoria to Queen Mary.' London: W. Kimber, 1954.

TUCHMAN, BARBARA (WERTHAM). 'The Proud Tower.' New York: Macmillan, 1966; London: Hamish Hamilton, 1966.

VANSITTART, ROBERT GILBERT VANSITTART, BARON. 'The Mist Procession: the Autobiography Lord Vansittart.' London: Hutchinson, 1958.

VICTORIA, CONSORT OF FREDERICK III, GERMAN EMPEROR. 'The Empress Frederick writes to Sophie, Her Daughter, Crown Princess and later Queen of the Hellenes: Letters 1889–1901.' Edited by Arthur Gould Lee, with an introduction by Her Majesty Queen Helen, Queen Mother of Romania. London: Faber & Faber, 1955.

VICTORIA, CONSORT OF FREDERICK III, GERMAN EMPEROR. 'Letters of the Empress Frederick.' Edited by the Right Honourable Sir Frederick Ponsonby. London: Macmillan & Co, 1929.

VICTORIA. PRINCESS OF PRUSSIA. 'Queen *Victoria* at Windsor and Balmoral: Letters from Her Granddaughter, Princess Victoria of Prussia, June 1889.' Edited by James Pope-Hennessy. London: Allen & Unwin, 1959.

VICTORIA, QUEEN. '*Darling* Child: Private Correspondence of Queen Victoria and the Crown Princess of Prussia, 1871–8.' Edited by Roger Fulford. London: Evans Bros, 1976.

VICTORIA, QUEEN. 'Dear and Honoured Lady: The Correspondence between Queen Victoria and Alfred Tennyson.' Edited by Hope Dyson and Charles Tennyson. London: Macmillan, 1969; Rutherford, N.J.: Fairleigh Dickinson University Press, 1971.

VICTORIA, QUEEN. '*Dearest* Child: Letters between Queen Victoria and the Princess Royal, 1858–61.' Edited by Roger Fulford. London: Evans Bros, 1964; New York: Holt, Rinehart & Winston, 1965.

VICTORIA, QUEEN. 'Dearest *Mama*: Letters between Queen Victoria and the Crown Princess of Prussia, 1861–4.' Edited by Roger Fulford. London: Evans Bros, 1968; New York: Holt, Rinehart & Winston, 1968.

VICTORIA, QUEEN. '*Further* Letters of Queen Victoria, from the Archives of the House of Brandenburg-Prussia.' Translated by Mrs J. Pudney and Lord Sudley and edited by Hector Bolitho. London: T. Butterworth, 1938.

————. 'Letters of Queen Victoria.' New Haven: Yale University Press, 1938.

VICTORIA, QUEEN. 'Leaves from a Journal: a Record of the Visit of the Emperor and Empress of the French to the Queen, and of the Visit of the Queen and HRH, the Prince Consort, to the Emperor of the French, 1855.' With an introduction by Raymond Mortimer. London: A. Deutsch, 1961; New York: Farrar, Straus & Cudahy, 1961.

VICTORIA, QUEEN. 'The Letters of Queen Victoria, a Selection from Her Majesty's Correspondence between the Years 1837 and 1861.' Published by authority of His Majesty the King; edited by Arthur Chistopher Benson and Viscount Esher. 3 Vols. London: J. Murray, 1907; New York: Longmans, Green & Co, 1907.

VICTORIA, QUEEN. 'The Letters of Queen Victoria, a Selection from Her Majesty's Correspondence and Journal between the Years 1862 and 1878.' Second series. Published by authority of His Majesty the King; edited by George Earle Buckle. 3 vols. London: J. Murray, 1926–8; New York: Longmans, Green & Co, 1926–8.

VICTORIA, QUEEN. 'The Letters of Queen Victoria, a Selection from Her Majesty's Correspondence and Journal between the Years 1886 and 1901.' Third series. Published by authority of His Majesty the King; edited by George Earle Buckle. 3 vols. London: J. Murray, 1930–2.

VICTORIA, QUEEN. 'The Queen and Mr Gladstone.' Edited by Philip Guedalla. London: Hodder & Stoughton, 1933; Garden City, New York: Doubleday, Doran & Co, 1934.

VICTORIA, QUEEN. 'Regina v. Palmerston: the Correspondence between Queen Victoria and Her Foreign and Prime Minister, 1837–65.' Edited by Brian Connell. Garden City, New York: Doubleday, 1961; London: Evans Bros, 1962.

VICTORIA, QUEEN. 'Your Dear Letter: Private Correspondence of Queen Victoria and the Crown Princess of Prussia, 1865–71.' Edited by Roger Fulford. London: Evans Bros, 1971; New York: Scribner, 1971.

VILLIERS, ELIZABETH, pseud. 'Queen Alexandra, the Well-beloved.' London: Stanley Paul & Co, 1925.

VILLIERS, GEORGE. 'A Vanished Victorian, Being the Life of George Villiers, Fourth Earl of Clarendon, 1800–70.' By his grandson. London: Eyre & Spottiswoode, 1938.

VINCENT, JAMES EDMUND. 'His Royal Highness Duke of Clarence and Avondale: a Memoir.' Written by authority. London: J. Murray, 1899.

VORRES, IAN. 'The Last Grand Duchess: Her Imperial Highness Grand Duchess Olga Alexandrovna, 1 June 1882–24 November 1960.' London: Hutchinson, 1964; New York: Scribner, 1965.

WADDINGTON, MARY ALSOP (KING). 'Letters of a Diplomat's Wife, 1883–1900.' London: Smith, Elder & Co, 1903; New York: C. Scribner's Sons, 1903.

WALDERSEE, ALFRED HEINRICH KARL LUDWIG, GRAF VON, 'A Field-Marshal's Memoirs: From the Diary, Correspondence and Reminiscences of Alfred, Count von Waldersee.' Condensed and translated by Frederic Whyte. London: Hutchinson & Co, 1924.

WARWICK, FRANCES EVELYN (MAYNARD) GREVILLE, COUNTESS OF. 'Afterthoughts.' London: Cassell & Co, 1931.

WARWICK, FRANCES EVELYN (MAYNARD) GREVILLE, COUNTESS OF. 'Life's Ebb and Flow.' London: Hutchinson & Co, 1929; New York: W. Morrow & Co, 1929.

WATSON, ALFRED EDWARD THOMAS. 'King Edward VII as a Sportsman.' With an introduction and a chapter on 'yachting' by Captain the Hon. Sir Seymour Fortescue. London and New York: Longmans, Green & Co, 1911.

WELCOME, JOHN, pseud. 'Cheating at Cards: The Cases in Court.' London: Faber & Faber, 1963.
————. 'Great Scandals of Cheating at Cards: Famous Court Cases.' New York: Horizon Press, 1964.
WEST, SIR ALGERNON EDWARD. '*Recollections*, 1832–86.' New York and London: Harper & Bros, 1899.
WEST, SIR ALGERNON EDWARD. 'The Private *Diaries* of the Rt. Hon. Sir Algernon Edward West, GCB.' London: J. Murray, 1922; New York: Dutton, 1922.
WESTMINSTER, LOELIA (PONSONBY) GROSVENOR, DUCHESS OF, 'Grace and Favour: the Memoirs of Loelia, Duchess of Westminster.' London: Weidenfeld & Nicolson, 1961.
WILHELM II, GERMAN EMPEROR. 'The Kaiser's Letters to the Tsar.' Copied from government archives in Petrograd, and brought from Russia by Isaac Don Levine. Edited with an introduction by N. F. Grant. London: Hodder & Stoughton, 1920.
WILHELM II, GERMAN EMPEROR. 'My *Ancestors*.' Translated by W. W. Zambra. London: W. Heinemann Ltd, 1929.
WILHELM II, GERMAN EMPEROR. 'My Early *Life*.' New York: George H. Doran Co, 1926; London: Methuen, 1926.
WILHELM II, GERMAN EMPEROR. '*My Memoirs*: 1878–1918.' London: Cassell & Co, 1922.
————. 'The Kaiser's Memoirs, Wilhelm II, Emperor of Germany, 1888–1918.' English translation by Thomas R. Ybarra. New York: Harper & Bros, 1922.
WILLIAMS, FLORENCE. 'It Was Such Fun.' By Mrs Hwfa Williams with an introduction by Lady Sybil Grant. London: Hutchinson, 1935.
WILSON, JOHN. 'CB: A Life of Sir Henry Campbell-Bannerman.' London: Constable, 1973; New York: St Martin's Press, 1974.
WOODHAM-SMITH, CECIL BLANCHE (FITZGERALD). 'Queen Victoria, Her Life and Times.' London: Hamish Hamilton, 1972.
————. 'Queen Victoria from Her Birth to the Death of the Prince Consort.' New York: Knopf, 1972.
WOODWARD, ERNEST LLEWELLYN. 'Great Britain and the German Navy.' London: Oxford University Press, 1935; Hamden, Conn: The Shoe String Press-Archon Books, 1964.
WORTHAM, HUGH EVELYN. 'The Delightful *Profession*: Edward VII, a Study in Kingship.' London: J. Cape, 1931.
————. 'Edward VII, Man and King.' Boston: Little, Brown & Co, 1931.
WORTHAM, HUGH EVELYN. '*Edward VII*.' New York: The Macmillan Co, 1933; London: Duckworth, 1933.
WYNDHAM, GEORGE. 'Life and Letters of George Wyndham.' By Guy Wyndham and J. W. Mackail. London: Hutchinson, 1925.

YOUNG, KENNETH. 'Arthur James Balfour: the Happy Life of the Politician, Prime Minister, Statesman and Philosopher, 1848–1930.' London: Bell, 1963; Chester Spring, Pa.: Dufour Editions, 1963.

Source References

Source references are prefaced by the number of the page on which the source is quoted. Line numbers indicate where quotations begin in the text. Catch phrases follow to help describe and identify such passages.

Since the Knollys Papers have not yet been calendared, I have adopted the policy of identifying all sources *other* than those which come from this collection. It may therefore be assumed that unattributed quotations come from Knollys's correspondence, or are not of sufficient consequence to require source references.

For the sake of brevity, books are referred to by their authors rather than titles. Thus Adams, W. *Edwardian Heritage* is described as 'Adams'. When more than one of an author's works appears in the Select Bibliography, shortened titles are used to distinguish between them. On this principle, Aronson's *Grandmama of Europe* is referred to as 'Aronson. *Grandmama*'. These abbreviations of title appear in the Select Bibliography.

Roman numerals are used to indicate Volume numbers, or the first, second or third series of the *Letters of Queen Victoria*.

CHAPTER ONE

15:10   Queen's suffering. Fulford. *Dearest.* 165.
16:26   Puseyites. *Q.V.L.* I. i. 450.
16:38   'Albert junior'. *Q.V.L.* I. i. 458, 460, 594.
17:24   Royal nursery. Emden. 67
17:27   Over anxiety. Fulford. *Letter.* 319.
17:36   Education. *Q.V.L.* I. i. 458.
17:41   Smoking. Fulford. *Consort.* 261.
18:22   Stockmar. Nicolson. *George V.* 14.
18:38   Infant education. Martin, T. ii. 175.
19:1   Bad advice. Longford. 217.
19:2   Difficult position. Martin, T. ii. 176.
19:6   Moral upbringing. Fulford. *Consort.* 251.
19:9   Hanoverian profligacy. Martin, T. ii. 170, 175–7.
19:22   Living examples. Martin, T. ii. 170, 175.
19:25   Perfect man. Fulford. *Consort.* 254.
19:33   Great uncles. Strachey and Fulford. v. 98.
20:26   Pusey views. Askwith, B. 79.

20:27   Lady Lyttelton. Askwith, B. 80, 84.
21:7   Albert at play. Fulford. *Consort.* 95.
21:16   No compensation. Victoria, Queen. *Further.* 75.
21:23   Hereditary antipathy. Strachey and Fulford. vi. 9.
21:29   Caricature. Fulford. *Dearest.* 187.
22:8   News. Noel. 36
22:13   Autocrat. Askwith, B. 83.
22:19   Inattention. Woodham-Smith. 266.
22:33   Intelligence. Askwith, B. 83.
22:37   World's welfare. Martin, T. ii. 175.
22:40   Parents' anxiety. Esher. *Influence.* 7.
23:16   Human Prince. Esher. *Towers.* 155–6.
23:29   Hohenlohe's opinion. Curtius. i. 87.
23:37   'Fallacious formula'. Benson. *Edward VII.* 33.
24:5   Bad influences. Nicolson. *George V.* 14.
24:17   Wellington College. Newsome. 78.
24:27   Friends. Benson. *Edward VII.* 34.
24:32   Granville's View. Fitzmaurice. i. 224.
24:39   Solecisms. Magnus. *Edward VII.* 42.
25:11   Etonian visitors. Benson. *Edward VII.* 21.
25:16   Parents' refusal. McClintock. 43.
25:19   Hawtrey's complaint. Gibbs. 117.
25:30   Educational ideals. Martin, T. ii. 184–5.
26:2   Samuel Wilberforce. Strachey and Fulford. v. 197.
26:6   Possible tutor. Wyndham. 335–6.
26:22   Henry Birch. Martin, T. ii. 174.
26:35   Perfect choice. Askwith, B. 84.
27:17   'Morbid feelings'. Woodham-Smith. 335.
27:19   Rare holiday. Holmes. i. 64.
27:28   Puseyism. Woodham-Smith. 335.
27:36   Queen on Birch. Gibbs. 115.
28:6   Prince's affection. Woodham-Smith. 335.
28:11   Parting presents. Lee. *Edward VII.* i. 29–30.
28:17   Prince downcast. Gibbs. 106.
28:20   Birch's living. Jagow. 182.
28:30   Prince's character. Magnus. *Edward VII.* 7–8.
29:28   Gibbs's character. Gibbs. 105.
30:19   Tantrums. Gibbs. 111, 113.
30:39   King on Gibbs. Esher. *Journals.* ii. 368.
31:3   Gibbs's departure. Fulford. *Dearest.* 143.
31:11   Lindsay on Gibbs. Woodham-Smith. 403–4.
31:22   Gibbs's failure. Fulford. *Dearest.* 142, 144.
31:30   Feared Father. Magnus. *Edward VII.* 14.
32:5   'Nameless youth'. Fulford. *Dearest.* 231.
32:13   Over-scolding. Baillie. *Later Letters.* 153.
32:25   Severity resented. Strachey and Fulford. vii. 389.
32:30   Forgiving nature. Magnus. *Edward VII.* 8.
32:38   'Adored' Father. Field. *Recollections.* 21.
32:39   Affectionate relations. Fulford. *Consort.* 262.

33:8 Share lectures. Corti. 50.
33:16 Intellect atrophied. Corti. 50.
34:10 Loyalty to Coburg. Grey, C. 244.
34:19 Anglo-German friendship. Eckardstein. 54.
34:27 'German element'. Fulford. *Mama.* 142.
34:40 Climb trees! Magnus. *Edward VII.* 10–11.
35:21 Unsuitable upbringing. Fulford. *Consort.* 258–9.
36:12 St Cloud. Mortimer. 81.
36:23 Paris visit. *Q.V.L.* I. iii. 172, 175–6.
36:36 Napoleon III. Strachey and Fulford. vii. 156–7.
36:40 Napoleon's charm. *Q.V.L.* I. iii. 176–8.
37:19 Napoleon and Bertie. Mortimer. 85.
37:26 Promised land. Aronson. *Bonapartes.* 67.
37:38 Napoleon's tomb. Martin, T. iii. 337–8.
38:16 Happy visit. *Q.V.L.* I. iii. 174–5.
38:20 Versailles ball. Mortimer. 124–8.
39:15 Prince's faith. Wortham. *Profession.* 398.
39:28 Prince's companions. Martin, T. iv. 206.
40:10 Bruce's authority. Esher. *Influence.* 10.
40:13 Regard for Bruce. Fulford. *Dearest.* 157.
40:16 Excellent companion. Bolitho. *Brother.* 205.
40:24 Equerry's duties. Redesdale. *Memories.* i. 167.
40:28 Albert's Memorandum. Esher. *Influence.* 12–15.
41:13 White Lodge. Esher. *Towers.* 158.
41:27 Birthday letter. Strachey and Fulford. vii. 383.
41:35 Life's duties. Esher. *Influence.* 9–10.
42:11 Provincial tour. Broadley. 332.
42:38 'Squalid debauch'. Magnus. *Edward VII.* 21.
43:9 Visits Metternich. Magnus. *Edward VII.* 22.
43:11 Sad look. Lee. *Edward VII.* i. 44.
43:19 Silent on Art. Fulford. *Dearest.* 152.
43:37 Rome. Wortham. *Profession.* 57.
44:14 Pius IX. *Q.V.L.* I. iii. 41.
44:34 'Effeminate' parting. Windsor. *Album.* 30.
44:39 'Odious' Oxford. Fulford. *Darling.* 160.
45:7 'Place for *study*'. Esher. *Influence.* 19–20.
45:36 'Monkish place'. Fulford. *Dearest.* 215.
45:40 'Lazybones'. Corti. 59.
46:6 Liddell's opinion. Bolitho. *Reign.* 164.
46:39 Newfoundland triumph. Martin, T. v. 149.
46:41 Newcastle's reports. Martin, T. v. 237.
47:7 Albert's scepticism. Martin, T. v. 191.
47:11 Self-satisfaction. Lee. *Edward VII.* i. 90.
47:28 Gratifying success. Martin, T. v. 240–1.
47:39 New York Ball. Lee. *Edward VII.* i. 103.
48:22 Queen's praise. Corti. 63.
48:26 Buchanan's praise. Martin, T. v. 243.
48:35 Intolerable restraints. Lee. *Edward VII.* i. 112.
49:11 Kingsley. Fulford. *Dearest.* 309.

49:13   Kingsley's affection. Lee. *Edward VII.* i. 116.
49:24   'Lolling'. McClintock. 42.
50:5   Army prohibited. Magnus. *Edward VII.* 23.
50:12   Curragh programme. Woodham-Smith. 414–15.
50:28   Imperfect drill. Magnus. *Edward VII.* 47.
50:37   Talking 'shop'. Lee. *Edward VII.* i. 110.
51:29   Albert 'too perfect'. Fulford. *Letter.* 207.
51:33   Bertie forgiven. Fulford. *Mama.* 132.
51:40   Albert broken-hearted. *Q.V.L.* II. i. 113.
52:29   Albert's remonstrance. Battiscombe. *Alexandra.* 29.
52:32   'Horrible prospects'. Woodham-Smith. 416.
53:10   Albert's distress. Woodham-Smith. 417–18.
53:28   'Eton volunteers'. Fulford. *Dearest.* 370.
53:33   Call of Duty. Baillie. *Dean.* 90.
53:38   'Never despair'. Fulford. *Consort.* 270.
54:10   'Feverish cold'. Woodham-Smith. 423.
54:25   Unfit physicians. Maxwell. ii. 253.
54:30   'Great worry'. Woodham-Smith. 425.
54:32   'Excessive excitement'. Fulford. *Consort.* 271.
55:7   'Crisis over'. Longford. 299.
55:12   Albert's passing. Baillie. *Stanley.* 245.
55:20   Queen's despair. Woodham-Smith. 429.
55:26   Bertie's promise. Longford. 301.
55:32   Queen's plea. McClintock. 47.
56:11   Albert disliked. Ames, W. 175.
56:17   Albert's wishes. Lee. *Edward VII.* i. 128.
56:23   Albert's guidance. *Q.V.L.* II. i. 31–2.
56:36   Albert's 'memorials'. Victoria, Queen. *Further.* 154, 129.
56:41   *'Firm* resolve'. *Q.V.L.* I. iii. 606.
57:7   'Papa's plan'. Fulford. *Mama.* 67.
58:2   Clarendon distressed. Villiers. 315, 313.
58:5   Bad relations. Kennedy. *Duchess.* 180–1.
58:14   'Sad truth'. Fulford. *Mama.* 33, 40, 43–4.
58:24   Bertie's 'fall'. Magnus. *Edward VII.* 52–3.
58:31   'Dutiful son'. *Q.V.L.* I.. i. 14.
58:38   'Good son'. Bolitho. *Widow.* 226.
58:39   'Pleasant visit'. *Q.V.L.* III. i. 354–5.
59:3   'Improving' company. Lee. *Edward VII.* i. 130.
59:9   Stanley 'unclerical'. Fulford. *Mama.* 95.
59:37   'Tumbledown Temples'. Baillie. *Dean.* 183–5, 125.
60:6   Stanley's verdict. Baillie. *Dean.* 140, 184–5.
60:23   'Horrid Paris'. Fulford. *Letter.* 299–300.
60:38   'Greatly improved'. *Q.V.L.* II. i. 34, 39.
61:10   Bruce's death. Fulford. *Mama.* 89.
61:19   General Knollys. *Q.V.L.* II. i. 41–2.

CHAPTER TWO

63:2   Bertie's marriage. Fulford. *Dearest.* 82.
63:10   'Keep from mischief'. Paget. i. 124.
63:12   'Arranged' marriage. Corti. 72.
63:18   Princesses scarce. Fulford. *Dearest.* 323.
64:1   Princess Augusta. Battiscombe. *Alexandra.* 16.
64:5   Possible brides. Fulford. *Dearest.* 313–14, 293, 309, 223–4, 311.
64:23   Princess Alexandra. Fulford. *Dearest.* 289, 292, 291.
65:22   Cambridge cousins. Fulford. *Dearest.* 353, 351–2.
66:6   Rumpenheim. Queen to Leopold. 23. vii. 63. Royal Archives. Y. 110. 4.
66:16   Wally at Windsor. Paget. i. 139.
66:28   Albert enchanted. Fulford. *Mama.* 104.
66:30   'Danish beauty'. Fulford. *Dearest.* 308, 323.
66:39   Nurse's report. Fulford. *Dearest.* 321–2
67:9   Vicky bewitched. Fulford. *Dearest.* 337–8, 341.
67:23   Fritz approves. Battiscombe. *Alexandra.* 23.
67:36   Speyer meeting. Magnus. *Edward VII.* 48.
67:40   Bertie 'pleased'. Fulford. *Dearest.* 350–1.
68:7   Bertie remiss. Fulford. *Dearest.* 353, 356.
68:21   'Marry early'. Fulford. *Mama.* 43.
68:29   Sudden 'fear'. Fulford. *Dearest.* 357.
68:35   Windsor proposal. Magnus. *Edward VII.* 50.
69:15   'Sacred duty'. Fulford. *Mama.* 38.
69:19   Cesarewitch. Fulford. *Mama.* 54.
69:23   Alix 'entrapped'. Battiscombe. *Alexandra.* 31.
69:29   Uncle George. Fulford. *Mama.* 82–4.
70:7   Alix's suitability. Fulford. *Mama.* 44.
70:23   Queen's tears. Paget. i. 159.
70:30   'Trying moment'. *Q.V.L.* II. i. 43.
70:35   High praise. Battiscombe. *Alexandra.* 36.
70:40   'Papa's blessing'. Battiscombe. *Alexandra.* 36.
71:6   'Happy letter'. Magnus. *Edward VII.* 58–9.
71:27   Absurd supposition. Battiscombe. *Alexandra.* 37.
71:32   Bertie in love. Magnus. *Edward VII.* 60.
71:36   Queen pleased. Baillie. *Stanley.* 269.
71:41   Alix's love. Kennedy. *Duchess.* 214.
72:14   'First parting'. Battiscombe. *Alexandra.* 39.
72:24   Forbidden visit. Paget. i. 161.
72:40   Queen's 'horror'. Magnus. *Edward VII.* 61.
73:16   Mothers-in-law. Wortham. *Profession.* 95.
73:29   Alix lands. Baillie. *Stanley.* 272.
73:34   Queen's 'satisfaction'. *Q.V.L.* II. i. 46.
73:40   Alix 'inspected'. Bell. i. 119.
74:13   Queen cheered. Battiscombe. *Alexandra.* 41.
74:22   Pious books. Baillie. *Stanley.* 273.
74:24   Alix's virtues. Fulford. *Mama.* 130–1.
74:33   Former times. Fulford. *Mama.* 131.
75:7   'German element'. Fulford. *Mama.* 126, 301, 323.

76:5   'No Lent'. Arthur. *Alexandra*. 37.
76:8   'Very Catholic'. Battiscombe. *Alexandra*. 42–3.
77:3   Huge crowd. Paget. i. 166.
77:7   Shabby Cortège. Malmesbury. 572.
77:23   Civic worthies. Ellis. 268.
78:8   Queen's welcome. *Q.V.L.* II. i. 72.
78:22   Wilberforce's text. Arthur. *Alexandra*. 43.
78:29   'Touching moment'. Magnus. *Edward VII*. 67.
78:38   Eton visit. Liddell. 46.
79:12   Alix stoned. *Eton and Windsor Gazette*. 13. v. 75.
79:18   Fireworks. Churchill. *Randolph*. 7.
79:22   Unhappy wedding. Fulford. *Mama*. 84, 173, 175.
80:2   Queen's 'moans'. Longford. 380.
80:3   Self indulgence. Magnus. *Gladstone*. 200.
80:15   Princess Mary. Kennedy. *Duchess*. 210.
80:36   Agonizing moments. *Q.V.L.* II. i. 75, 73.
80:41   Jenny Lind. Macleod. 319.
81:4   Prince's appearance. Kennedy. *Duchess*. 214.
81:15   Kingsley impressed. Lee. *D.N.B.* 561.
81:17   Stanley's reaction. Baillie. *Dean*. 216.
81:20   Bride late. Kennedy. *Duchess*. 214.
81:24   Bride's appearance. Kennedy. *Duchess*. 214, 210.
81:27   Wilberforce moved. Ashwell. iii. 89.
81:34   'A fine affair'. Lee. *D.N.B.* 561.
81:38   Queen's embrace. *Q.V.L.* II. i. 76.
82:3   'Second Balaclava'. Churchill. *Randolph*. 8.
82:23   Frogmore visit. *Q.V.L.* II. i. 77.
82:32   Bertie 'radiant'. Fulford. *Mama*. 180.
82:39   'Loved best'. Battiscombe. *Alexandra*. 71.
85:8   Prince's gambling. Magnus. *Edward VII*. 128.
85:15   'Friendly hint'. *Q.V.L.* II. ii. 352.
86:8   'Extra expenses'. Balham. i. 204.
87:5   'Guelpho's' lament. Anon. *The Siliad*. 233.
87:20   'Ample means'. *Q.V.L.* III. i. 516.
88:40   'Actress friends'. James. *Rosebery*. 57.
89:5   Knollys' influence. Warwick. *Afterthoughts*. 30.
89:28   Sovereign's secretaries. Asquith. *Memories*. 226.
89:41   Unrivalled discretion. Legge. *King Edward*. 180–1.
90:21   Palmerston's warning. Bourne. 369.
90:27   Denmark deserted. Tollemache. 129.
90:31   'Horrible war'. Lee. *Edward VII*. i. 250–2.
91:2   Queen 'grieved'. *Q.V.L.* II. i. 206–7.
91:19   Alix 'unhappy'. Fulford. *Mama*. 287.
91:36   'Unjust avarice'. Corti. 127.
92:16   'Violent partisanship'. *Q.V.L.* II. i. 190–1.
92:22   Clarendon's interview. *Q.V.L.* II. i. 194.
92:30   Queen's suffering. Fulford. *Mama*. 300–1, 323.
93:18   'No respect'. Fulford. *Mama*. 16.
93:21   Albert's dictum. *Q.V.L.* II. i. 218.

93:24   'Stockmar right'. Battiscombe. *Alexandra*. 68.
94:3   'Bestial Germans'. Bülow. *Memoirs*. i. 338.
94:4   'Hateful Huns'. Arthur. *Reading*. 166.
94:6   'Georgie boy'. Battiscombe. *Alexandra*. 176.
94:11   Aunt Alix. Lee. 171.
94:18   Dagmar's hatred. Beal. 402.
95:16   Danes ill-used. Paget. i. 183–4.
95:24   German visit. Magnus. *Edward VII*. 87.
96:19   Fredensborg boring. Gernsheim. 51.
96:31   'So rude'. Benson. *As We Were*. 162.
98:3   Alix's lodging. Magnus. *Edward VII*. 86.
98:30   '*Deeds of valour*'. Lee. *Edward VII*. i. 256.
98:40   'Married daughter'. *Q.V.L.* II. i. 85.
99:10   'Poor Lenchen'. Fulford. *Mama*. 311.
99:20   Consent withheld. Madol. *Christian IX*. 174.
99:35   Christian's appearance. Fulford. *Letter*. 56–7.
100:3   '*Abominable* marriage'. Battiscombe. *Alexandra*. 78.
100:14   Alice's opposition. Fulford. *Letter*. Intro. xv.
100:16   Alice 'jealous'. Noel. 120.
100:34   Family pleads. Battiscombe. *Alexandra*. 77–8.
101:10   Bertie 'amiable'. Fulford. *Letter*. 47.
101:22   'Old Christian'. Battiscombe. *Alexandra*. 165.
101:25   Confidence lost. Battiscombe. *Alexandra*. 78.
101:29   Atrocious rumours. Fulford. *Letter*. 76.
101:37   Lenchen's wedding. Fulford. *Letter*. 82, 78.
102:12   'Great simplicity'. Battiscombe. *Alexandra*. 122.
102:19   Over strictness. Battiscombe. *Alexandra*. 121.
102:23   'Rampaging' children. Battiscombe. *Alexandra*. 122–3.
102:28   'Unaffected' Princesses. Bahlman. ii. 542.
102:35   Mother love. Nicolson. *George V*. 50.
103:1   'Big kiss'. Battiscombe. *Alexandra*. 143.
103:3   Royal diminutives. Marie, Queen. i. 43.
104:2   Eddy 'dawdly'. Battiscombe. *Alexandra*. 163.
104:20   Eddy's '*ignorance*'. Diary. 19. i. 85, 4. xi. 87, 5. xi. 85. Royal Archives.
104:29   No reader. Magnus. *Edward VII*. 178.
104:35   'Elementary movement'. St. Aubyn. 299.
105:5   '*Who tells?*' Pope-Hennessy. *Mary*. 193.
105:31   'Deservedly drowned'. *Truth*. May, 1890.
105:39   'Greatest position'. Longford. 512.
106:23   Princess Hélène. Pope-Hennessy. *Mary*. 196–7.
107:1   'Royal Idyll'. Young 468.
107:11   Grandmama helps. Pope-Hennessy. *Mary*. 198.
107:33   Balfour reports. Young. 122–3.
110:2   May approved. Pope-Hennessy. *Mary*. 207–8, 242.
110:20   'Poor Eddy'. Pope-Hennessy. *Mary*. 222.
111:2   Final moments. Pope-Hennessy. *Mary*. 222, 226.
111:15   'One more link'. Pope-Hennessy. *Mary*. 226.
111:26   Royal 'harem'. Ponsonby, A. 359.
112:6   Father and son. Cust. 33.

112:8   'Ill-judged chaff'. Asquith. *Memories*. 238.
113:10   '*No-one* else'. Nicolson. *George V*. 47.
113:12   'Sailor prince'. Paget. ii. 396.
113:39   Dawson Damer. Field. *Uncensored*. 262.
114:10   Queen remembers. *Q.V.L*. III. ii. 275.
114:26   Family visits. Battiscombe. *Alexandra*. 198.
115:21   Royal reel. Field. *Uncensored*. 206–7.
116:10   'Good companions'. Battiscombe. *Alexandra*. 200.
116:19   Rosebery 'perfect'. Leslie. *Edwardians*. 291.
116:24   'Glorified maid'. Vorres. 53.
117:14   Maud reproached. Battiscombe. *Alexandra*. 200.
117:24   Aunt Alix. Marie, Queen. i. 43–4.
117:37   Footman's present. Battiscombe. *Alexandra*. 202.
118:1   Crown Jewels. Jullian. 206.
118:8   Unorthodox golf. Ponsonby. *Recollections*. 137.
118:21   'Keep him waiting'. Airlie. 106.
118:24   Queen late. Ponsonby. *Recollections*. 105.
119:1   Alix 'selfish'. Battiscombe. *Alexandra*. 240.
119:28   'Cleverness underrated'. Esher. *Journals*. i. 346.
119:40   'Sweet May'. Pope-Hennessy. *Mary*. 328.
120:29   'Ripened fruit'. Battiscombe. *Alexandra*. 174.
120:30   'Old ladies'. Holmes. ii. 370.
120:33   Queen on Alix. *Q.V.L*. III. i. 391.
121:7   'Not blind'. Battiscombe. *Alexandra*. 70.
121:14   'Beloved hubby'. Esher. *Journals*. iii. 1.
121:18   Happy home. Battiscombe. *Alexandra*. 138.
121:21   'Confession-book'. Bevan. 191.
121-25   'Married love'. Holmes. ii. 374.
122:3   Outrageous neglect. Battiscombe. *Alexandra*. 83.
122:17   'Husband's love'. Battiscombe. *Alexandra*. 86.

CHAPTER THREE

123:12   False charge. Redesdale. *Edward VII*. 17–18.
123:21   Sandringham ball. Cresswell. 169–71.
126:3   'Joie de vivre'. Forbes. 66.
126:9   'Royal beef'. Bahlman. ii. 515.
126:16   'Calmly knitting'. McClintock. 77.
126:34   'Select sheepfold'. Benson. *Edward VII*. 151–2.
127:13   House-party. Bing. 84.
128:34   'English houses'. Benson. *Edward VII*. 153.
128:37   Prince annoyed. Magnus. *Edward VII*. 219.
129:4   'Rich people'. Bülow. ii. 183.
129:20   Kind heart. Paget. ii. 293.
129:25   Female companionship. Minney. 72.
129:39   'Affaires'. Minney. 72.
131:7   Gladstone submits. Morley. *Gladstone*. ii. 378.
131:13   'Mr Jones'. Watson. 120.

132:10   'Glorious uncertainty'. Lee. *Edward VII*. i. 578.
132:15   'Bonhomie'. Grey, Visct. ii. 14–15.
132:23   Prince's charm. Ponsonby, A. 109.
133:26   Compromising secrets. Smalley. i. 268.
135:2   'Pleasant' company. Macdonnell. i. 293.
135:22   Bishop's arrival. Macdonnell. i. 294.
135:34   Fisher unpacks. Cowles. *Edward VII*. 316–17.
136:6   '*Charming* couple'. St. Aubyn. 163.
136:8   'Kindness'. Morley. *Gladstone*. iii. 385.
136:10   'Model hosts'. Bahlman. ii. 542.
136:16   Broadhurst's visit. Broadhurst. 149–50, 153.
136:36   'Good name'. Magnus. *Edward VII*. 91.
137:1   Wholesale slaughter. Windsor. *Album*. 43.
137:28   Practical jokes. Ponsonby, M. 5.
138:3   'Complete resignation'. Stamper. 31–2.
138:15   'La Plage'. Stamper. 47.
138:24   Prince's chaff. Williams. 215–16.
138:36   'Fulsome telegram'. St. Aubyn. 268.
139:1   Composing quarrels. Blunt. 446.
139:2   'Feminine desire'. Warwick. *Ebb*. 157.
139:5   'Conciliatory charm'. Redesdale. *Memories*. i. 171.
139:9   Naturally 'inquisitive'. Field. *Recollections*. 9.
139:13   Loyal friend. Raymond. 12.
139:18   'Great principle'. Lee. *Edward VII*. i. 172.
140:23   'Generosity'. Bennett, G. 315.
140:26   'Human kindness'. Grey, Visct. ii. 15.
140:31   'Pleasant word'. Waddington. 186.
140:34   'Easy grace'. Stamper. 43, 235.
141:7   '*Faithful* servants'. McClintock. 144–5.
141:20   'Much beloved'. McClintock. 167.
142:24   'Indian etiquette'. Ponsonby, A. 131.
142:33   Munshi shunned. Mallet. Intro. xxiii.
143:18   'Uneasy spirits'. Esher. *Journals*. i. 279.
145:32   'Tailoring'. Wolseley Papers. Royal United Service Institution. 25. ix. 82.
145:40   'Uncommon particular'. Benson. *Edward VII*. 68.
146:10   'Wrong buttons'. Fitzroy. i. 203.
146:13   'Old suit'. Wortham. *Profession*. 298.
146:18   'Judicious mixture'. Rose. *Cecils*. 46–7.
146:28   'Bishop Ponsonby'. Ponsonby, J. 170–1.
146:35   'Costume ball'. Arthur. *Reading*. 32.
147:3   Nicolson's 'bauble'. Nicolson. *Carnock*. 271.
147:12   Rossmore's solecism. Rossmore. 163.
147:40   King's appetite. Sewell. 39.
148:23   Social pleasures. Lee. *Edward VII*. i. 566.
149:1   Benson. *Edward VII*. 150.
149:17   'Lambeth Penitents'. Benson. *As We Were*. 101, 103.
149:34   'Little wickedness'. Blunt. 722.

CHAPTER FOUR

151:7   Avoiding scandal. Warwick. *Ebb.* 172.
154:25 'No letters'. Fielding. 191.
155:17 Susan's marriage. Fulford. *Dearest.* 249, 251.
155:31 'Touching letter'. Kennedy. *Duchess.* 101–3.
156:6   'Regularly mad'. Kennedy. *Duchess.* 153–4.
156:12 'Left penniless'. Fulford. *Mama.* 347–8.
157:36 'Disagreeable stories'. Bahlman. i. 355.
159:22 Harriet's confession. *The Times.* 19. ii. 70.
160:3   Two questions. Harrison. *Details.* 102.
161:15 'Such truth!'. Wyndham. 372.
161:17 'Great truthfulness'. Magnus. *Edward VII.* 7, 10.
161:25 'Old Mama'. Fulford. *Letter.* 89.
162:31 'Bertie's appearance'. Fulford. *Letter.* 262–3.
163:3   Unfit to rule. *Reynolds's Newspaper.* 20. ii. 70.
163:17 Unjust treatment. *The Law Journal.* 27. ii. 70.
164:1   'Spanish ships'. Churchill, R. i. 293.
164:17 Many enemies. Napier. 98.
164:28 'Too hot!'. Shore. 115.
165:7   'Disagreeable' charge. Shore. 31.
165:14 Emphatic denial. Shore. 32.
165:27 Solemn undertaking. Shore. Intro. iii.–iv.
166:2   Contract broken? Sewell. 22.
166:12 Loyal friend. Warwick. *Ebb.* 12.
166:23 Verdict wrong. Clarke. 297–8.
166:36 Inadequate evidence. *Truth.* 18. vi. 91.
167:6   Plaintiff 'victimized'. Magnus. *Edward VII.* 227.
167:17 Queen's Regulations. Shore. 21.
168:22 Lycett Green's evidence. Shore. 158–61.
169:3   Cheating expected. Shore. 231–2.
169:17 'Back him!'. Asquith. *Memories.* 84.
169:25 'Moral elephants'. Benson. *As We Were.* 212.
169:34 Prince rebuked. *The Times.* 10. vi. 91.
170:14 Kaiser's protest. Legge. *Colours.* 58.
170:28 Baccarat scandal. Stephenson. 181.
171:5   Royal counters. Benson. *As We Were.* 215.
171:13 Wilson played. Shore. 170.
171:29 Plaintiff watched? Shore. 157, 224–5.
176:5   Cool relations. Ponsonby. *Recollections.* 128.
177:4   'Grave matters'. Magnus. *Edward VII.* 145.
177:13 'Order carriage'. Battiscombe. *Alexandra.* 134.
177:22 'Unpardonable'. Churchill, R. Comp. i. i. 31.
182:38 'Not compromising'. Churchill, R. Comp. i. i. 37.
183:24 Randolph's claim. Churchill, R. Comp. i. i. 34.
183:27 Statements false. Churchill, R. Comp. i. i. 57.
187:36 'Sad news'. Leslie. *Jennie.* 176.
188:5   Letters found. Churchill, R. Comp. i. i. 44, 72.
188:38 'Trifle cracky'. *Q.V.L.* II. ii. 563.

189:1 Burlington Beadle. Benson. *Edward VII.* 106.
190:21 'Blameless' wife. Bennett, G. 165.
191:12 Open slight. Bennett, G. 169, 171.

CHAPTER FIVE

194:3 Early initiation. Magnus. *Edward VII.* 7.
194:18 Queen's logic. Victoria, Queen. *Further.* 146.
194:21 Royal employment. Maxwell. ii. 284.
195:5 Albert's 'wishes'. Drew. 94.
195:8 *'Firm resolve'. Q.V.L.* I. iii. 606.
195:11 Prince ignored. Benson. *As We Were.* 99–100.
195:21 Trinity House. Connell. 327–8.
195:37 'Father's place'. Fulford. *Letter.* 82.
195:39 Investiture. *Q.V.L.* II. ii. 140.
196:12 Incurable indiscretion. Lee. *D.N.B.* 584.
196:17 *'Private observation'*. Hough. *Grand-daughter.* 56.
196:23 King's discretion. Ponsonby. *Recollections.* 273.
196:37 Punchestown Races. *Q.V.L.* II. i. 514.
197:3 Bertie's unfitness. Fulford. *Dearest.* 174.
197:6 Later doubts. Bolitho. *Widow.* 71.
197:9 Unsound 'judgement'. Ramm. *Granville.* ii. 375.
197:12 'Much struck'. Bahlman. ii. 840, 853.
197:27 'Hospitality'. Dasent. ii. 54, 130.
197:41 'Pooh-poohed'. Ponsonby, A. 108.
198:9 Cabinet key. Wortham. *Profession.* 162.
198:16 'Magnanimity'. Alice, Princess. 25–6.
198:25 'Wasted' years. Cust. 258–9.
198:31 'Envy Fritz'. Ponsonby. *Empress.* 89.
198:39 Piled boxes. Dangerfield. 223.
199:4 'Same thing'. Nicolson. *George V.* 82.
199:9 'Amour propre'. Esher. *Towers.* 173–4.
200:14 'History repeats'. Nicolson. *George V.* 82.
200:20 Forbidden boxes. Windsor. *Story.* 211–12.
201:2 'Wholesome advice'. Villiers, G. 316–17.
201:9 See despatches. *Q.V.L.* II. i. 210.
201:16 Queen 'rejoices'. *Q.V.L.* II. i. 210–11.
201:27 'Exercise control'. Magnus. *Edward VII.* 81.
201:33 'Little inclined'. Ramm. ii. 316.
203:11 Prince's 'anxiety'. Gwynn. *Dilke.* i. 392, 427.
203:20 Cabinet decisions. Bahlman. ii. 860–1.
204:2 'Closer insight'. Bahlman. ii. 272.
204:3 'Communications'. Guedalla. 666.
204:22 Kept informed. Lee. *Edward VII.* i. 416.
204:24 'Good terms'. Bahlman. ii. 873.
205:13 'Melancholy' outlook. Ramm. i. 170–1.
206:10 'Treason vanished'. Battiscombe. *Alexandra.* 95–6.
206:22 'Priceless opportunity'. Guedalla. 381.

206:26   Irish Residence. *Q.V.L.* II. ii. 137–8.
208:8   'Young Knollys'. Guedalla. 347–8.
208:17   Prince willing. Ramm. ii. 293.
208:21   'Prince dislikes'. *Q.V.L.* II. ii. 201-2.
209:36   'Half ashamed'. Lee. *Edward VII.* i. 248.
209:37   Deep regrets. *Q.V.L.* II. i. 175.
210:9   'Popular idol'. *Q.V.L.* II. i. 175–6.
210:32   Prince's visit. Nevill. 209.
210:35   'Incredible folly'. Fulford. *Mama.* 324.
211:18   'Much shocked'. Magnus. *Edward VII.* 84.
212:1   Meeting 'hailed'. Magnus. *Edward VII.* 84.
212:27   Newcastle speech. Gwynn. *Dilke.* i. 139.
212:32   Academic Republicanism. Gwynn. *Dilke.* i. 145.
213:10   'Wrong way'. Gwynn. *Dilke.* i. 10.
213:24   'Earnest desire'. Bonner. i. 167.
213:29   'Democratic feeling'. Longford. 381.
214:11   Printed placard. Paget. i. 263.
214:19   'Dear Alix'. *Q.V.L.* II. ii. 171, 175.
214:36   'Most distressing'. *Q.V.L.* II. ii. 179.
215:2   Broken vows. Noel. 172.
215:7   'Touching' feeling. *Q.V.L.* II. ii. 176–7.
215:24   'Anxious forebodings'. *Q.V.L.* II. ii. 178–9.
215:36   'Kind heartedness'. Baillie. *Later Letters.* 149–50.
215:41   'Cheering news'. *Q.V.L.* II. ii. 179–80.
216:8   Simple worship. Guedalla. 352, 356, 361.
216:21   'Very lame'. *Q.V.L.* II. ii. 194.
216:34   'Wonderful enthusiasm'. *Q.V.L.* II. ii. 195–6.
217:18   'Simply ludicrous'. Green. 311.
218:17   'Political infancy'. Gwynn. *Dilke.* i. 490.
219:4   Meets Dilke. Gwynn. *Dilke.* i. 302.
219:11   'Social affinity'. Jenkins. *Dilke.* 143.
220:26   'Municipal politics'. Churchill. *Great.* 44, 49, 47.
221:14   Radical Mayor. Ponsonby, A. 267.
221:24   Tenniel cartoon. *Punch.* 14. xi. 74.
221:27   'Wild man'. Ponsonby. *Recollections.* 42.
221:37   Mr Mundella. MacDonagh. 172.
222:12   'Society grows'. Warwick. 145–6.
222:25   'Inconvenience'. Bahlman. ii. 878.
222:29   Queen 'ready'. *Q.V.L.* II. iii. 657–8.
222:38   Opinion required. Guedalla. 668–9.
223:12   'Accelerate return'. *Q.V.L.* II. iii. 659.
223:13   'Queen declines'. Bahlman. ii. 898.
224:5   'Return south'. *Q.V.L.* II. iii. 662–3.
224:27   'London twain?' Churchill. *Life.* 82.
224:29   Week's delay. Bahlman. ii. 881, 885.
225:1   Peerage offered. *Q.V.L.* II. iii. 666.
225:3   'Most generous'. Morley. *Gladstone.* iii. 200, 210.
225:28   Bertie's help. *Q.V.L.* II. iii. 679–80.
226:16   'Dangerous fanatic'. Ponsonby, A. 216.

226:28   'Revolutionary appeal'. *Q.V.L.* III. ii. 126.
226:32   Rosebery's radicalism. *Q.V.L.* III. ii. 119–20.
226:40   Queen 'insists'. Ponsonby, A. 217, 216.
227:28   Hamilton dined. James. *Rosebery.* 236–7.
228:1   Hamilton unsure. *Q.V.L.* III. ii. 131.
228:4   Prince suggested. *Q.V.L.* III. ii. 132.
228:7   'Personal friend'. Ponsonby, A. 217.
229:1   Prince's letter. *Q.V.L.* III. ii. 144 5.
229:32   'So be it'. James. *Rosebery.* 249.
231:8   'Warmest thanks'. Lee. *Edward VII.* i. 538.
231:30   'Only record'. West. *Diaries.* 289.
231:37   Queen 'wrong'. Asquith. *Memories.* 217.
232:11   'No royalty'. Gower. *Diaries.* 264.
232:29   'Overt slight'. Bahlman. i. 7.
233:6   'Magic voice'. Magnus. *Gladstone.* 263, 269–70.
233:23   'Violent invective'. *Q.V.L.* II. iii. 75.
233:25   Gladstone 'devoted'. Ponsonby, A. 188.
233:34   'Sooner abdicate'. Ponsonby, A. 184.
234:23   'Dearest Mama'. *Q.V.L.* II. iii. 79–80.
235:1   Prince 'sure'. Lee. *Edward VII.* i. 514.
235:6   'Strong opinion'. Lee. *Edward VII.* i. 514.
235:18   '*No* right'. Magnus. *Edward VII.* 166.
236:10   Heaven's 'mercy'. St. Aubyn. 268.
236:27   Alix's letter. Drew. 195–6.
237:4   'Bad leg'. Masterman. 438–9.
237:10   'Few lines'. *Q.V.L.* III. ii. 370.
237:22   'Daring act'. James. *Rosebery.* 328.
237:38   Rosebery's 'duty'. *Q.V.L.* III. ii. 429, 439.
238:11   Cypher telegram. *Q.V.L.* III. ii. 431–2.
238:39   'Strong Conservative'. Gwynn. *Dilke.* i. 500.
239:22   'Unwilling consent'. *Q.V.L.* II. ii. 397–8.
240:5   'Unresting progress'. Beresford. i. 158.
240:10   'Very wearing'. Fulford. *Darling.* 204.
240:21   Duke lost. Beresford. i. 164.
241:18   Supreme success. Beresford. i. 158.
242:23   'Painful duty'. Battiscombe. *Alexandra.* 131.
243:12   'Grandiose conceptions'. Lee. *Edward VII.* i. 403.
243:18   'Threatening tone'. *Q.V.L.* II. ii. 450.
243:21   'Party move'. Ponsonby, A. 139.
244:24   Knollys's protest. Magnus. *Edward VII.* 147.
247:34   Randolph's explanation. *Q.V.L.* III. i. 233.
248:3   'Strange' action. Ponsonby, A. 107.
248:16   Courageous act. Magnus. *Edward VII.* 197.
248:29   Randolph 'unfit'. Martin, R. 280.
248:38   Jubilee's 'success'. Holmes. ii. 280.
250:3   'Beloved husband'. *Q.V.L.* III. i. 324, 326, 341.
250:15   '*Perfect* success'. St. Aubyn. 232.
250:32   'New uniform'. St. Aubyn. 233.
252:10   'Sixty years'. Pope-Hennessy. *Mary.* 355.

252:16   Loyalty displayed. *Q.V.L.* III. iii. 180.
253:19   'Bad places'. Magnus. *Edward VII.* 179.
253:23   Prince's speech. Lee. *Edward VII.* i. 550.
253:36   'Good house'. Duff. *Louise.* 138.
254:18   'Unusual' devotion. Gwynn. *Dilke.* ii. 26.
255:3   Regular attendance. Stuart. 254.

CHAPTER SIX

257:3   'So cautious'. Bülow. i. 449.
257:38   'Best understanding'. Victoria, Queen. *Further.* 122.
258:7   'Poor things'. Fulford. *Letter.* 88.
258:12   'Beloved child'. Fulford. *Letter.* 287.
258:16   One mercy. Esher. *Journals.* ii. 292.
259:12   'Divided interests'. Fulford. *Letter.* 287–8.
259:41   Reciprocal interests. Lee. *Edward VII.* i. 360.
260:2   'Exaggerated' view. Bülow. iv. 462.
260:15   'General interests'. Lee. *Edward VII.* i. 360.
260:25   'Abject court'. Fulford. *Letter.* 299–300.
260:38   'Sodom'. Fulford. *Darling.* 16–17.
261:2   'Female notorieties'. Battiscombe. *Alexandra.* 85.
261:16   Bernstorff's despatch. Guedalla. 283–4.
261:20   Story 'untrue'. Fulford. *Letter.* 287–8, 307.
261:34   Prince's denial. Lee. *Edward VII.* i. 305.
261:41   'Great misfortune'. Guedalla. 282–3.
262:15   'Be of use'. Lee. *Edward VII.* i. 307.
262:29   'Powerful Germany'. Lee. *Edward VII.* i. 311.
262:38   Macleod's sermon. Arthur. *Alexandra.* 104.
262:41   'Immoral people'. Lee. *Edward VII.* i. 303–4.
263:15   Chiswick offered. Lee. *Edward VII.* i. 309.
263:28   'Just heard'. Fulford. *Darling.* 74.
264:5   '*Very* venturesome'. St. Aubyn. 101.
264:11   Mind changed. *Q.V.L.* II. iii. 36.
264:14   'Quite inexplicable'. St. Aubyn. 182.
264:17   'Incredible'. *Q.V.L.* II. iii. 33.
264:22   'Horrible death'. Lee. *Edward VII.* i. 341–2.
264:39   'Chapelle Ardente'. *Q.V.L.* II. iii. 30–1.
265:30   Gambetta's work. Paléologue. 25.
265:36   'Vulgar' manner. Paoli. 206.
266:28   Prince's 'skill'. Newton. *Lyons.* ii. 152.
266:32   Prince's 'dream'. Lee. *Edward VII.* i. 451.
266:36   'Great Statesman'. Gwynn. *Dilke.* ii. 507.
268:3   '*A bas*'. Warwick. *Ebb.* 137.
269:33   'Natural allies'. Eckardstein. 217.
270:36   'Kind face'. Lee. 202, 150.
271:1   'Uncle Fritz'. Nicolson. *George V.* 40.
271:39   'Devoted affection'. *Q.V.L.* III. i. 390.
272:3   'Stricken man'. Ponsonby. *Empress.* 287.

272:32   'Brave men'. Radziwill, Princess. 218.
272:39   'Ambitions' crushed. Battiscombe. *Alexandra*. 174.
273:5   'Family assembled'. *Q.V.L.* III. i. 418–19.
273:24   'So *like*'. Lee. 83.
275:23   'Greatest object'. Corti. 200.
275:28   'Abandon dreams'. Ponsonby. *Empress*. 215.
276:12   'Anglophils'. Waldersee. 120.
276:13   'Deplorable friends'. Ponsonby. *Empress*. 322–3.
277:9   'Volcano'. Churchill. *Great*. 23.
277:15   'Quicksilver'. Fulford. *Dearest*. 367, 209.
277:33   William's confirmation. *Ponsonby*. 134.
278:3   'Nicer boys'. Lee. *Edward VII*. i. 431.
278:19   'Matchmaker'. Rich. ii. 145.
278:25   'Extraordinary fruit'. Lee. *Edward VII*. i. 485.
279:8   'Complete cleavage'. Bülow. i. 338.
279:22   'Too infamous'. Nicolson. *George V*. 40.
279:27   'Inward' enemy. Bülow. iv. 665.
281:34   Outrageous behaviour. Hough. *Grand-daughter*. 97.
281:38   Bismarck's minute. *Q.V.L.* III. i. 438–9.
282:12   'Simply absurd'. *Q.V.L.* III. i. 440–1.
283:15   'No idea'. Ponsonby. *Empress*. 360–1.
283:28   'Historical friendship'. Lee. *Edward VII*. i. 667.
283:37   'Perpetual visits'. Eckardstein. 57.
284:16   Cowes regatta. Eckardstein. 55.
285:13   'Jameson Raid'. Bülow. i. 469.
285:22   'Sincere congratulations'. Lee. *Edward VII*. i. 722.
286:1   'Spontaneous outburst'. Bülow. iv. 665.
286:3   'Good snubbing'. Lee. *Edward VII*. i. 724.
286:5   'Emperor's message'. *Q.V.L.* III. iii. 7–8.
286:12   'Cutting answers'. *Q.V.L.* III. iii. 20.
288:26   William's reply. Eckardstein. 122.
289:9   'Tom-cat'. Bülow. i. 339.
290:4   'Perfectly natural'. *Q.V.L.* II. i. 369.
290:11   '*Entente cordiale*'. Lee. *Edward VII*. i. 269.
290:33   'Russian notions'. Longford. 393–4.
290:41   'The murder'. Fulford. *Darling*. 103.
291:2   'Reserved manner'. Fulford. *Darling*. 105.
291:12   'Slippery youth'. Fulford. *Mama*. 271.
291:16   'High opinion'. Fulford. *Darling*. 153–4.
291:30   'Frowning Tsars'. Baillie. *Later*. 201, 203.
291:40   Affie 'imprudent'. Fulford. *Darling*. 255–6.
292:31   'Bulgarian horrors'. Monypenny. vi. 60.
292:34   'Present agitation'. Lee. *Edward VII*. i. 420.
292:41   Gladstone's speeches. *Q.V.L.* II. ii. 481.
293:23   'Turkophil party'. Lee. *Edward VII*. i. 424–5.
293:30   'Good beating'. Lee. *Edward VII*. i. 434.
293:33   'Corrupt country'. Hough. *Grand-daughter*. 80, 53, 82.
294:15   'Old elephant'. Paget. i. 101.
295:1   'Monday last'. *Q.V.L.* III. i. 368–9.

295:13   Randolph's mission. *Q.V.L.* III. i. 373-4.
298:37   'In love'. Pope-Hennessy. *Mary.* 307.
300:12   Rosebery's congratulations. Lee. *Edward VII.* i. 691.
300:38   'Stormy morning'. Lutyens. 79.
301:4   'Cinematograph'. *Q.V.L.* III. iii. 87-8.
301:11   'Very jolly'. Lutyens. 80.
301:13   Nicky's complaints. Bing. 110.
301:21   Racing. Lutyens. 82.
301:33   Queen's warning. *Q.V.L.* III. iii. 343-4.
302:11   Kaiser's proposal. Lee. *Edward VII.* i. 762-3.
303:14   'Simply outrageous'. Lee. *Edward VII.* i. 779.
303:26   'Wonderful courage'. Redesdale. *Memories.* i. 186.

CHAPTER SEVEN

304:16   'Uncle Arthur'. Aston. 223.
304:18   Die 'peacefully'. Fulford. *Dearest.* 281.
304:21   'Very dreadful'. Longford. 561.
305:39   'Silent hour'. Lee. *Edward VII.* i. 802.
306:2   Queen's deathbed. Esher. *Journals.* i. 281.
306:17   'Beloved Mama'. Bennett, D. 331-2.
307:25   'Purple wreath'. St. Michael's Mount Archives.
308:18   'Right or wrong'. Ponsonby. *Recollections.* 89.
308:27   'Child's coffin'. Fitzroy. i. 44-5.
308:39   Guard relieved. St. Michael's Mount Archives.
309:10   'Too strong'. Bell. i. 357.
309:12   Last duty. St. Michael's Mount Archives.
309:34   'Laughing gas'. Leslie, S. *Film.* 163.
310:14   'Disturbed'. Villiers, G. 315.
310:24   'Heir-Apparent'. Fulford. *Letter.* 238.
311:9   King insists. Gwynn. *Spring Rice.* ii. 17.
311:11   'Gracious advocacy'. Monger. 102.
311:12   'Unerring judgement'. Esher. *Journals.* ii. 460.
311:23   No policy. Gooch and Temperley. ii. 88.
311:35   'Novel obligations'. Gooch and Temperley. ii. 194-5.
312:23   'Private property'. Warwick. *Afterthoughts.* 32.
313:6   'Fall short'. *Q.V.L.* III. iii. 615.
313:9   'Cynical acts'. *National Review.* December. 1900.
313:12   'Bad precedent'. *Daily Mail.* i. xi. 1900.
313:28   Chatsworth meeting. Eckardstein. 184-6.
314:15   'Kindness itself'. Magnus. *Edward VII.* 272.
314:23   'Cordial relations'. Eckardstein. 191.
314:28   'Two nations'. Lee. *Edward VII.* ii. 11.
315:7   Complete secret. Ponsonby. *Recollections.* 110.
315:13   'Own words'. Ponsonby. *Empress.* Intro. ix.
316:19   'Renewed abuse'. Eckardstein. 227-8, 230.
318:7   'Spoilt child'. Magnus. *Edward VII.* 303.
318:18   'Exceeded instructions'. Magnus. *Edward VII.* 304.

318:34 'Few trumps'. Magnus. *Edward VII*. 305.
320:10 'Excellent' letter. Lee. *Edward VII*. ii. 218.
320:14 Important journey. Brook-Shepherd. 153.
320:30 'King alone'. Maurois. 154.
320:33 'Own initiative'. Lee. *Edward VII*. ii. 242.
321:5 'Command arrived'. Lee. *Edward VII*. ii. 59.
321:13 'Political consideration'. Brook-Shepherd. 156.
321:32 'Unmistakable delight'. Brook-Shepherd. 160.
322:5 'Informal affair'. Lee. *Edward VII*. ii. 223.
322:11 Ministers 'averse'. Redesdale. *Memories*. ii. 758.
322:29 'Unusual' appointment. Hardinge. 85.
323:24 Incognito. Ponsonby. *Recollections*. 161.
323:34 'Third footman'. Hibbert. 241.
323:38 Hardinge's lecture. Magnus. *Edward VII*. 310.
324:21 Fisher rebuked. Fisher, J. 5.
324:30 Protestant petitions. Ponsonby. *Recollections*. 164.
325:18 Qualified enthusiasm. Hardinge. 35.
325:21 Ponsonby jeered. Ponsonby. *Recollections*. 170.
325:27 'Hardly necessary'. Lee. *Edward VII*. ii. 237.
326:5 Théâtre Français. Lee. *Edward VII*. ii. 238.
326:11 'At home'. Lee. *Edward VII*. ii. 239.
326:32 Kaiser 'mad'. Andrew. 209.
327:17 'Such ovations'. Documents Diplomatiques Français. iii. 502.
327:22 'Vast coalition'. Paléologue. 83–4.
327:36 Agreement signed. Paléologue. 56–7.
328:6 Balfour's letter. Newton. *Lansdowne*. 293.
328:35 '*Entente*'. Lee. *Edward VII*. i. 259.
329:1 'Decisive role'. Steiner. 202.
329:6 Reputation 'mythical'. Monger. 263.
329:7 Influence exaggerated. Ensor. 567.
329:17 'Any clerk'. Ponsonby. *Recollections*. 173.
329:23 Complete 'success'. Magnus. *Edward VII*. 313.
329:29 Favourable 'impression'. Lee. *Edward VII*. ii. 241.
329:37 Hardinge's verdict. Fortescue. 288.
330:3 'Almost impossible'. Hardinge. 96.
330:12 King's achievement. Young. 247.
331:2 'Platonic relations.' Nicolson. *Carnock*. 157.
331:10 'Official existence'. Nicolson. *Carnock*. 159–60.
331:37 'Gratuitous insult'. Hough. *Louis*. 188.
332:3 'Positively cheerful'. Paléologue. 216.
332:20 King's telegram. Maurois. 171.
332:24 'Unusual step'. Newton. *Lansdowne*. 342.
332:40 'Every assistance'. Paléologue. 250.
334:17 'Unseemly romping'. Lee. *Edward VII*. ii. 351–2.
334:39 'Astonishing' ignorance. Blunt. 723.
335:12 'Franco-German War'. Paléologue. 311–12.
335:23 'Royal confidences'. Paléologue. 313.
335:29 'Secret discussions'. Paléologue. 313–14.
336:5 Mutual 'understanding'. Grey, Visct. i. 133–4.

336:20 Unqualified 'support'. Lee. *Edward VII*. ii. 361.
336:23 'Morocco Conference'. Nicolson. *Carnock*. 175.
337:18 'Old friends'. Lee. *Edward VII*. ii. 525.
337:23 'Warm friendship'. Lee. *Edward VII*. ii. 525–6.
337:31 Dona's letter. Bülow. ii. 238.
338:11 'Foolish' Press. Bülow. ii. 287.
338:21 'Virulent' influenza. Lee. *Edward VII*. ii. 554.
339:8 Teasing speech. Lee. *Edward VII*. ii. 557.
339:15 'Bygone days'. Lee. *Edward VII*. ii. 558.
339:23 'Obstinate misconceptions'. Lee. *Edward VII*. ii. 561.
339:35 'Too German'. Blunt. 619.
339:39 'Annual cure'. Lee. *Edward VII*. ii. 614.
340:6 Naval reduction. Lee. *Edward VII*. ii. 616.
340:11 Briefing King. Hardinge. 158.
340:21 'All sunshine'. Lee. *Edward VII*. ii. 618.
340:28 Berlin 'mission'. Steed. i. 282.
343:3 Emperor's hatred. Lee. *Edward VII*. ii. 622.
343:17 'Pacifist elements'. Brook-Shepherd. 336.
343:36 'Wild language'. Churchill, R. ii. 511–12.
344:8 'Braggart call'. Morris. 144.
344:25 King's prejudice. Wilson. 499.
345:6 'Useful results'. Lee. *Edward VII*. ii. 673.
345:41 'Very seedy'. Bruce. 126.
347:29 Francis Joseph. Brook-Shepherd. 292.
348:25 First drive. Brook-Shepherd. 311.
349:2 Capital success. Lee. *Edward VII*. ii. 626.
349:7 Steed's warning. Steed. i. 283.
349:24 Terribly 'moved'. Redesdale. *Memories*. i. 178.
349:35 'European war'. Lee. *Edward VII*. ii. 664.
350:12 'Small society'. Wilson. 142.
350:20 'Tainted ladies'. Wilson. 143.
351:26 'Good company'. Ponsonby. *Recollections*. 234.
352:2 Law maker. Bruce. 106.
352:8 'Specially opportune'. Lee. *Edward VII*. ii. 551.
352:23 Not 'Trafalgar'. Steed. i. 283.
352:34 Parting words. Fortescue. 369.
353:3 Russia 'indispensible'. Paléologue. 83–4.
353:10 'Much impressed'. Lee. *Edward VII*. ii. 281.
353:13 'Similar arrangement'. Monger. 160.
354:2 '*Entente analogue*'. Lee. *Edward VII*. ii. 284.
354:32 'Damned fools'. Magnus. *Edward VII*. ii. 341.
354:36 'Innocent fishermen'. Lee. *Edward VII*. ii. 301.
355:4 'Untoward incident'. Lee. *Edward VII*. ii. 301–2.
356:9 'Level best'. Steiner. 95.
356:15 'Unwelcome change'. Trevelyan. 183.
356:22 Return visit. Trevelyan. 183.
356:35 'Considerable misgivings'. Nicolson. *Carnock*. 206–~
357:12 Visit delayed. Lee. *Edward VII*. ii. 565.
358:34 'Dubious' advantage. *The Times*. 11. vi. 07.

358:35 England 'trapped'. *Albany Review.* August, 1907.
359:6   Encircled. Nicolson. *Carnock.* 257.
359:8   King's 'triumph'. Hardinge. 146.
359:12 Nicolson praised. Hardinge. 146.
359:26 'An insult'. Morris. 176.
359:38 'Condoning atrocities'. Lee. *Edward VII.* ii. 588–9.
360:16 'Object lesson'. Grey, Visct. ii. 19–20.
360:39 '*Un homme d'état*'. Nicolson. *Carnock.* 275.
361:17 'Strong ties'. Lee. *Edward VII.* ii. 591.
362:4   Stolypin 'fascinated'. Nicolson. *Carnock.* 272.
362:27 'Changed atmosphere'. Fisher, J. 234.
362:29 Tsar's 'satisfaction'. Grey, Visct. ii. 27.

CHAPTER EIGHT

365:10 'Albert Edward'. *Q.V.L.* II. i. 152.
365:22 'Melancholy duty'. Lee. *Edward VII.* ii. 4–5.
366:18 'Happy duty'. Lee. *Edward VII.* ii. 26.
368:9   'Much surprised'. Lee. *Edward VII..* ii. 50.
370:1   'Bad news'. Sermoneta. 54–5.
370:8   Treves' 'conviction'. de Stoeckl. 98.
370:17 King convalesces. Esher. *Journals.* i. 343–4.
370:39 'Undue levity'. Adams. 13–14.
371:14 Copies retrieved. Mersey. 200.
371:33 'Crowned Queen'. Windsor. *Story.* 83.
372:15 Hansell's prayer. Windsor. *Crown.* 14.
372:27 Archbishop's homage. Holmes. ii. 516.
372:35 'Go away!' Fitzroy. i. 99.
373:22 Cust 'alone'. Cust. 11.
373:33 Palaces 'explored'. Cust. 12–13.
373:38 'Offer it up!'. Lee. *Edward VII.* ii. 69.
375:19 'Grand Vizier'. Esher. *Journals.* i. 328.
375:23 'Wonderful footing'. Magnus. *Edward VII.* 287.
375:37 'Éminence grise'. Fraser. 81.
376:17 'Mal vu'. Mersey. 220.
377:11 'Mysterious power'. Fraser. 242–3.
377:25 'Unusual hours'. Midleton. 149.
377:34 Strong point. Ponsonby. *Recollections.* 129.
377:36 Nation's 'benefit'. Cust. 145.
378:25 'Superhuman charity'. Battiscombe. *Alexandra.* 209–10.
379:17 Slum visit. Leslie. *Edwardians.* 233.
379:22 'Delicate matter'. Magnus. *Edward VII.* 260.
380:13 Cancer cure. Lee. *Edward VII.* ii. 404.
381:13 'Bad dog'. Stamper. 72–3.
381:30 'Horrible machines'. Portland. 316.
381:39 'Fine run'. Stamper. 8, 6.
382:6   King's character. Stamper. 3–4.
382:19 German accent. Stamper. 59.

382:24   King's vitality. Stamper. 317:158.
382:34   'Amazing simplicity'. Ormathwaite. 170.
383:13   Peppery temper. Askwith, B. 83.
383:18   Friends 'terrified'. Ponsonby. *Recollections*. 275.
383:22   'Angry bellow'. Westminster. 32.
383:30   'Royal acquisitiveness'. Wortham. *Profession*. 309.
383:41   Margot's opinion. Asquith. *Memories*. 223.
384:1   Knollys proposes. Asquith. *Memories*. 223.
384:7   King 'considerate'. Ponsonby. *Recollections*. 124.
384:12   'Kindest' Master. Fortescue. 199.
384:18   'Extraordinary kindness'. Churchill. *Life*. 170–1.
384:30   Practical compassion. Sewell. 75.
385:1   'Unfailing encouragement'. Lee. *Edward VII*. ii. 215.
385:10   Generosity. Ponsonby. *Recollections*. 274.
385:12   Paoli's 'souvenir'. Paoli. 228.
385:17   'Real discomfort'. Grey, Visct. ii. 15.
385:21   Beresford's 'devotion'. Bennett, G. 315.
385:28   Royal memory. Hunt. ii. 243–4.
386:39   Balfour's affability. Churchill. *Great*. 186.
387:39   'Wonderful news'. Jenkins. *Asquith*. 137.
388:16   'Royal commission?'. Lee. *Edward VII*. ii. 173–4.
388:26   'Serious loss'. Lee. *Edward VII*. ii. 176.
388:35   Resignations. Gollin. 283.
389:4   'Tax rich'. Askwith, Lord. 277–8.
389:16   'Frenzied enthusiasm'. Mackail and Wyndeam. ii. 459.
389:26   King's 'coolness'. Leslie. *Different*. 197.
389:33   'Quite understand'. Stamper. 272.
390:24   'Curzon right'. Churchill. *Great*. 216.
390:37   'We soldiers'. Lee. *Edward VII*. ii. 377.
391:22   Curzon's services. Young. 242.
393:11   'Plain test'. Lee. *Edward VII*. ii. 187.
393:29   'Once for all'. James. *Rosebery*. 454.

CHAPTER NINE

394:5   Knollys's letter. Wilson. 441.
394:20   'Most amiable'. Asquith. *Autobiography*. 71–3.
395:18   'Unworthy policy'. Lee. *Edward VII*. ii. 78.
396:3   Carrington's assurance. Wilson. 405.
396:10   'Wise' Sovereign. Münz. 130.
396:25   'Me and 'im'. Hirst. 263.
397:1   Surprising 'declaration'. Lee. *Edward VII*. ii. 448.
397:29   'Radical wave'. Magnus. *Edward VII*. 348.
397:36   'New era'. Lee. *Edward VII*. ii. 449.
398:3   'Old idea'. Magnus. *Edward VII*. 348.
398:39   'Meagre' information. Wilson. 506.
399:6   'Trivial' letters. Esher. *Journals*. ii. 160–1.
399:19   C.B. 'incurable'. Esher. *Journals*. ii. 265.

399:38 Like 'Bourbons'. Wilson. 497, 499.
400:35 'Bad business'. Bell. i. 523.
401:7 Concessionary 'spirit'. Lee. *Edward VII.* ii. 463.
401:26 'Unionist Party'. Jenkins. *Poodle.* 36, 39.
402:1 'Abolish House'. Wilson. 561.
402:8 'Exalted Chamber'. Lee. *Edward VII.* ii. 456–7.
402:22 Foremost issue. Lee. *Edward VII.* ii. 457.
402:25 'Sovereign's name'. Owen. 150.
403:4 Liberal resolution. Wilson. 563.
403:11 Balfour's 'treachery'. Wilson. 563.
403:19 'Rancorous speech'. Wilson. 565.
404:4 'No patience'. Wilson. 573–4.
405:1 'Sinister document'. Wilson. 577–8.
406:15 'Outrageous'. Lee. *Edward VII.* ii. 468.
406:23 'Dreadful women'. Wilson. 511.
406:34 '*Two* classes'. Nowell-Smith. 98.
407:5 Continental disease. Dugdale. i. 329.
407:19 C.B.'s successor. Petrie. *Chamberlain.* i. 213.
408:8 Asquith chosen. Wilson. 620–1.
408:29 King's visit. Wilson. 621.
409:7 'Earnest hope'. Wilson. 623.
409:16 'Kissing of hands'. Magnus. *Edward VII.* 403.
412:31 Resignation accepted. Spender. *Sir Henry.* ii. 389.
413:24 'Sound Asquith'. Ponsonby. *Recollections.* 251.
413:33 Asquith appointed. Jenkins. *Asquith.* 180.
414:6 Buckle incredulous. Jenkins. *Asquith.* 179.
414:15 'Precedent' broken. *The Times.* 8. iv. 08.
415:2 'No wonder'. Edwards. 220.
415:12 Doctors' statement. Lee. *Edward VII.* ii. 685–6.
416:2 'Good talk'. Jenkins. *Asquith.* 211.
417:17 'War Budget'. Owen. 171.
418:3 'Tyrannical' proposals. Jenkins. *Poodle.* 76.
418:13 'Foolish' speeches. Magnus. *Edward VII.* 431.
418:18 Limehouse speech. *The Times.* 31. vii. 09.
418:40 King 'annoyed'. Pope-Hennessy. *Crewe.* 72–3.
419:12 Crewe's reply. Pope-Hennessy. *Crewe.* 73–5.
419:30 Chancellor's 'regret'. Owen. 180–1.
420:3 Class 'passions'. Owen. 181–2.
420:20 'Teasing goldfish'. Churchill, R. ii. 326–7.
420:35 'Royal intervention'. Churchill, R. ii. 327.
421:4 Constitutional practice. Lee. *Edward VII.* ii. 666–7.
421:19 'Audacious attempt'. Lee. *Edward VII.* ii. 668.
421:22 King's opposition. Esher. *Journals.* ii. 411.
424:7 'Constitutional lines'. Spender. *Asquith.* i. 257–8.
424:19 Chancellor's questions. *The Times.* 11. vi. 09.
424:36 Balfour 'uncommunicative'. Magnus. *Edward VII.* 437.
426:14 Rosebery's objections. Rose. *Cecils.* 247.
426:36 Almost impossible. Jenkins. *Asquith.* 202.
427:3 'Got them!'. Owen. 183.

427:6   'Lords mad'. Fitzroy. i. 389.
427:7   Rights usurped. Lee. *Edward VII.*. ii. 669
428:1   Not 'justified'. Spender. *Asquith*. i. 261.
428:25 Necessary 'safeguards'. Lee. *Edward VII*. ii. 670.
429:14 Politicians' 'duty'. Hardie. *Monarchy*. 113.
429:23 'Disappointed cries'. Spender. *Asquith*. i. 273.
430:25 'Discreditable transaction'. Magnus. *Edward VII*. 451–2.
430:34 'Necessary steps'. Magnus. *Edward VII*. 452.
431:4   'Coup d'état'. Fraser. 213.
431:22 'Greatest outrage'. Magnus. *Edward VII*. 453.
433:28 Disgraceful behaviour. Young. 301.
434:1   Knollys's conversion. Nicolson. *George V*. 138–9.
434:39 King George's Minute. Nicolson. *George V*. 219–30.

CHAPTER TEN

437:6   'Pure madness'. Ponsonby. *Empress*. 147.
438:21 'Gone aloft'. Esher. *Journals*. iv. 262.
438:35 Churchill's delusion. Churchill, R. ii. 282.
441:2   'Only enemy'. Nicolson. *George V*. 95–6.
441:28 Fisher slandered. Fisher, J. 207, 191, 192.
441:36 'Enemies clamorous'. Esher. *Journals*. ii. 398.
442:13 'Backed up'. Marder. *Dread Nought*. ii. 141.
442:29 Queen's support. Battiscombe. *Alexandra*. 230–1.
442:41 'Pruning knife'. Churchill. *Crisis*. 73–4.
443:13 'Delicate instrument'. Esher. *Journals*. ii. 199.
444:24 Combative nature. Nowell-Smith. 504.
444:31 'Less friction'. Marder. *Dread Nought*. ii. 79.
445:5   'Strong regard'. Churchill. *Crisis*. 78–9.
445:11 'Pretty dull'. Bacon. ii. 66.
445:14 Beware sailors. Bacon. i. 94.
445:20 'Backed winner'. Fisher, J. 226.
445:29 'Great blank'. Fisher, J. 203.
445:38 'Immense combination'. Magnus. *Edward VII*. 367.
446:33 'Not a man'. *The Times*. 6, ii. 08.
447:2   'New departure'. Lee. *Edward VII*. ii. 606.
447:14 'Bicycle tour'. Esher. *Journals*. ii. 291.
447:32 'Patently potty'. Vansittart. 77.
447:34 'Unmitigated balderdash'. Balfour, M. 282–3.
448:19 'Very sad'. Magnus. *Edward VII*. 376.
449:17 Naval quarrels. Bennett, G. 281.
449:35 'Look pretty'. Bennett, G. 290–2.
450:39 Never forget. Bennett, G. 290.
451:2   'Deep impression'. Lee. *Edward VII*. ii. 600.
451:9   'Turned his back'. Mackay. 400.
451:12 'Full view'. Esher. *Journals*. ii. 312.
452:5   'Give trouble'. Marder. *Dread Nought*. i. 104.
452:21 Wilson's authority. Lee. *Edward VII*. ii. 601–2.

453:24   'Bosh'. Magnus. *Edward VII*. 372.
453:36   'Past belief'. Marder. *Dread Nought*. ii. 247, 267.
455:22   'Much disturbed'. Lee. *Edward VII*. ii. 680–1.
457:3   Final compromise. Churchill. *Crisis*. 37.
457:25   Beresford's toast. Bennett, G. 310.
457:29   'Unity shattered'. Nowell-Smith. 316.
458:8   'Swollen estimates'. Lee. *Edward VII*. ii. 332.
458:14   'Fisher right'. Churchill. *Crisis*. 74–5.
458:33   Kitchener 'hampered'. Lee. *Edward VII*. ii. 79–80.
459:12   'Military disaster'. Esher. *Journals*. ii. 51.
459:16   'Searching' enquiry. Lee. *Edward VII*. ii. 91, 93.
459:22   'Better prepared'. Fraser. 91.
459:24   'Mutual admiration'. Magnus. *Edward VII*. 324–5.
459:36   'Dirty linen'. Lee. *Edward VII*. ii. 91.
460:21   Frequent audiences. Midleton. 159–62.
461:3   'Taken aback'. Esher. *Journals*. ii. 14.
461:9   Esher's reluctance. Esher. *Journals*. ii. 16, 20.
461:37   'Martyr's spirit'. Fitzroy. i. 212.
462:5   Forster's '*manner*'. Magnus. *Edward VII*. 326.
462:18   'Naval Basis'. Fraser. 95.
462:40   'Natural head'. Fraser. 91.
463:5   'Great benefit'. Lee. *Edward VII*. ii. 197.
463:24   'Active service'. Lee. *Edward VII*. ii. 193.
463:40   'More invisible'. Lee. *Edward VII*. ii. 208–10.
465:7   'Consulting King'. Fraser. 132.
466:8   'Half measures'. Lee. *Edward VII*. ii. 205–6.
466:26   Roberts's warning. Morris. 72.
467:9   'Proud line'. Münz. 146.
467:18   Guest list. Haldane. 247.
467:25   'Constant support'. Nowell-Smith. 332.
468:23   Grateful letter. Lee. *Edward VII*. ii. 501.
469:18   Churchill's Memo. Morris. 91, 93.
470:18   'Much annoyed'. Lee. *Edward VII*. ii. 196–7.
470:41   'Criminal folly'. Raymond. 329.
471:6   Fortescue's tribute. Fortescue. xiii. 570.
471:8   'National army'. Steed. i. 287.
471:22   Haig's Dispatches. Spender. *Men*. 22.

CHAPTER ELEVEN

472:3   *Chantecler* 'childish'. Magnus. *Edward VII*. 150.
472:18   'Great sigh'. Redesdale. *Memories*. i. 182.
473:10   'Work to end'. Redesdale. *Edward VII*. 33.
473:24   Oxygen cylinder. de Stoeckl. 100.
473:30   Bulletin. Lee. *Edward VII*. ii. 716.
473:38   Cassel's visit. Lee. *Edward VII*. ii. 717.
474:11   'Touching' grief. Bell. i. 608.
474:28   'Catholic guests'. Leslie. *Film*. 312.

E.VII   S

475:13   'Took away'. Roosevelt. 115.
475:18   'Child asleep'. Esher. *Journals*. iii. 1–2.
475:39   Ponsonby's visit. Ponsonby. *Recollections*. 271.
476:29   'Impressive proceedings'. Bell. i. 610.
477:10   *'Where's Master?'*. Esher. *Journals*. iii. 5–6.
477:19   'Poor dog'. Asquith. *Memories*. 162–3.
478:10   'Minor canons'. Fitzroy. ii. 408.
478:24   'Transitory life'. Holmes. ii. 646.
478:30   'Sinister suggestion'. Arthur. *Alexandra*. 270.
480:8   Country's 'delirium'. Blunt. 721–2.
481:7   Duty 'first'. Asquith. *Memories*. 231.
481:23   'Most kingly'. Esher. *Journals*. ii. 461.

Index

Compiled by Mrs P. M. McDougall

The following abbreviations have been used in the index:

Alix *for* Queen Alexandra; Eddy *for* Prince Albert Victor; E. VII *for* Edward VII; PM *for* Prime Minister; QV *for* Queen Victoria; Wm. II *for* Emperor William II

Victoria, Queen [*contd.*]
Tsar and Tsarina to Balmoral, 300–1;
attempts on her life, 302; last illness
and death, 304–6; QV's funeral,
306–10; public grief, 307; suggests
Lansdowne for Foreign Office, 313;
and E. VII's title as Sovereign, 365;
threatened Memoir of John Brown,
373; shrines to Albert's memory, 373;
disapproval of motor cars, 381;
treatment of her Household, 384; and
Balfour, 387; *Highland Journal*, 85
Victoria, Princess ('Toria') (1868–1935),
103, 114, 360; and Alix, 473
Victoria, Princess of Hesse (1863–1950),
281; Wm. II forbids her marriage to
Prince Alexander of Battenberg, 278,
279
Vincent, Sir Edgar, *see* D' Abernon,
Viscount
Voisin, Dr, E. VII's French tutor, 34,
161

Waddington, Mme, on E. VII, 140
Waddington, William Henry (1826–94),
256
Wakefield, Rev. H. Russell (1854–1933),
possible Bishop of Chichester, 404
Waldegrave, Lady Frances Elizabeth
(1821–79), on E. VII, 121
Wallace, Sir Donald (1841–1919), on
Russia and the Duma, 357–8
Wantage, Robert Lindsay, Baron (1832–
1901), 39; on Gibbs, 31
War Office, 457; E. VII on, 459;
reorganization proposals, 462–3
Warwick, Frances Greville, Countess of
(1861–1938), 131, 196, 378; socialist
aristocrat, 89, 189, 222; on Knollys,
89; on E. VII, 123, 139; on Society
and morality, 150; and Baccarat Case,
166; liaison with Beresford, 189, 193;
accuses him of 'infidelity', 189–90;
appeals to E. VII, 190–1; in Paris,
267–8
Warwick, Francis Greville, fifth Earl of
(1853–1924), and his wife's infidelities,
189
Waterford, John Beresford, fifth Marquess
of (1844–95), and Lady Brooke's
letter to Beresford, 190
Watts, George Frederick (1817–1909),
OM, 369
Webb, Beatrice, *see* Passfield, Lady
Wellesley, Gerald Valerian (1809–82),
Dean of Windsor, 39, 76
Wellington, Arthur Wellesley, first Duke
of (1769–1852), 17, 24, 289; at birth
of E. VII, 15; and E. VII's wedding,
76; on reformed Commons, 398
Wells, H. G. (1866–1946), 467

West, Sir Algernon (1832–1921), 284
Westminster, Duchess of, 82
Westminster, Hugh Grosvenor, second
Duke of (1825–99), his wealth, 84;
entertains E. VII at Eaton Hall, 125;
Liberal peer, 226
Whatman, Mrs Harriet, go-between for
Susan Vane-Tempest and E. VII,
156–8
White, Arnold, and E. VII's social life,
148
Wilberforce, Samuel, Bishop of Oxford
(1805–73), 19, 26, 78, 169; and
E. VII's wedding, 78, 81
William IV, King (1765–1837), 55, 104,
105; drab Court, 124
William I, King of Prussia, first
Emperor of Germany (1797–1888),
visited by QV, 146; death and funeral,
120, 271, 272
William II, King of Prussia and third
German Emperor (Kaiser) (1859–
1942), 34, 113, 469; relationship with
E. VII, 34, 127, 129, 269, 277–8, 315,
333–5, 337–8, 353; and Baccarat
Case, 170; and Beresford, 192; and
Golden Jubilee, 249, 278; controller
and master of German policy, 257,
284; fear of QV, 257; 'drops the
Pilot', 269, 295; and his father's
death, 273, 279, 281; treatment of his
mother, 275, 278, 279; character,
275–7, 282, 288; challenges his
parents' ideas, 275–6, 278; attitude to
England, 276, 278, 283–4; fugitive in
Holland, 276, 315; marriage, 278;
forbids his sister's marriage, 279; and
Russia, 281, 293–4, 295; Vienna
affront to E. VII, 281–2; behaviour at
Cowes, 284–5; Kruger telegram,
285–6; influence on Anglo-German
relations, 285, 314; sides with the
Boers, 285; Senden dispute, 286–8;
State Visits to England, 288–9, 338–9;
and Anglo-Russian relations, 301, 302;
and attempt on E. VII's life, 303; and
QV's illness and death, 304, 305–6,
307, 312; foreign ambitions, 312;
honoured by E. VII, 314; exploits his
mother's funeral, 315; and an attack
on France, 330, 335, 336; Moroccan
venture, 331–2; visit of Crown
Prince, 333–4; and Algeciras
Conference, 336–7; and naval
expenditure, 340, 436–7; approves
Daily Telegraph article, 341–2;
interview with Hale, 342–3; and E.
VII's and Alix's visit, 1909, 345–7;
and Nicholas II, 355, 363; double
dealings with England, 355–6, 359;
complains of 'encirclement', 363; on